Principles of Insurance

Principles of Insurance

Robert I. Mehr
Professor of Finance
University of Illinois at Urbana-Champaign

Emerson Cammack
Professor of Finance and Associate Dean
University of Illinois at Urbana-Champaign

Terry Rose
Associate Professor
West Virginia University

Eighth Edition   1985

RICHARD D. IRWIN, INC.
Homewood, Illinois   60430

ISBN 0-256-03008-1

Library of Congress Catalog Card No. 84–62326

Printed in the United States of America

1 2 3 4 5 6 7 8 9 0 D 2 1 0 9 8 7 6 5

To my dear and true friend Heriberto Purcell, a highly respected San Juan insurance broker whose love for his fellow man and esteem for education motivate him to give unselfishly of himself in developing successful insurance education programs in Puerto Rico and throughout Latin America—a truly unique and remarkable person whose contributions to society will endure forever.

R. I. M.

To my friends and former students in the insurance business who continue to strive to do what is right for the insurance consumer and the insurance industry.

And to Ingeborg, Joy, and Brent, whose sacrifice for this work was exceeded only by their support.

T. L. R.

robert i. mehr

101 W. Windsor Road
Apartment 1102
Urbana, Illinois   61801

terry l. rose

430 Armstrong Hall
West Virginia University
Morgantown, West Virginia   26506

A Prefatory Letter

February 1985

Dear Reader:

Thirty-three years have elapsed since the first edition of this book was published. Despite the introduction of many new beginning texts during this period, this one has withstood the test of time as indicated by its strong survival through seven editions against generally good competition. Timely revisions have kept the book up-to-date, reflecting the many changes that have occurred in insurance principles and practices. Each revision has been a major one, and this eighth edition is no exception.

An important change has been the addition of a new coauthor, Professor Terry L. Rose of West Virginia University, a former student of the senior author. In 1972 Professor Rose returned to the University of Illinois to earn his Ph.D. after spending five years with a major insurance company. Upon completion of his Ph.D., he moved on in the academic world where he is known for his excellent teaching.

Aside from the addition of a new coauthor, a second chapter on life insurance, and the recognition of a new set of problems in the chapter on current issues in insurance, most of our concern with this revision has been in updating the book. About 29 years ago, when the first revision of this book was in process, Richard D. Irwin cautioned against operating on a well patient. That advice was pretty good then and is still good. So it has been followed in the preparation of this edition. We have rewritten the text only where necessary to bring the discussion up-to-date and to simplify statements that may appear complicated.

As in the seventh edition, an effort has been made to control the size of the book. If an idea or concept can be explained in 10 words, why use 20; if a 5-letter word is appropriate, why use a 10-letter word? Furthermore, if an explanation is clear, why belabor the point with excessive examples? Finally, one should be discriminating in the knowledge to be acquired given a necessity for establishing priorities in this era of information explosion. Therefore, a good textbook discussion of a topic is one in which the authors know when to terminate it. So we have made an effort to terminate discussions even though we wanted to tell you much more about many of the topics covered. We believe we have succeeded without eliminating any substantive material.

Because the book is written for students, we found student input rewarding. Paraphrasing from *Reflections on the Psalms* by C. S. Lewis, we learned that it often happens that two students can solve each other's learning problems better than the teacher. When students take a problem to the teacher, they may receive a great deal of unwanted information but might be told nothing about the problem puzzling them. Because fellow students know less, they can help more. We wanted students to explain to us the difficulties that they have recently faced in their insurance studies. Experts experienced these difficulties so long ago that they have forgotten them. Teachers see the whole subject in such a different light that they cannot conceive what is really troubling the students. Instead they see a dozen other difficulties which *ought* to be troubling the student but are not. The student input helped give us perspective for "it is difficult to see the picture when you are inside the frame."

A number of students were involved in this effort at student input. Questions and comments from Charles Bailey, a 1984 graduate of Auburn University, helped in a number of sections of the early chapters. Suggestions from other Auburn students also have been incorporated throughout this revision. John Knowles and Art Parker, Auburn insurance graduates, provided valuable factual information from their "real world" experiences. Charles is a successful field representative for Metropolitan Life. John is a regional vice president for brokerage operations for Life of Virginia Insurance Company. Art is Director of Ordinary Life Insurance for the firm of Osborn & Osborn, Inc. These former students, however, are not alone in their contributions, and the comments of many Auburn insurance alumni were considered during the revision process.

Two former University of Illinois students were helpful in the previous edition because of their varied interests and backgrounds: Stephen P. D'Arcy and Jeffrey L. Shade. Steve, a cum laude graduate in mathematics from Harvard University, a consulting casualty actuary, and a Ph.D. from the University of Illinois, is an Assistant Professor of Finance at the University of Illinois. Jeff, a cum laude graduate in economics from Dartmouth College, holds the M.S. degree in finance (insurance) from the University of Illinois. Jeff is now associated with the Bennett-Shade Insurance Agency in Decatur, Illinois. Steve was helpful on those chapters involving insurer practices, whereas Jeff was helpful on those chapters on insurance policies and coverage. Appreciation for the help of these two fine persons in preparing the seventh edition is reaffirmed. Finally, appreciation is reaffirmed to former coauthor, Professor Emerson Cammack, for his many contributions that still remain in this edition.

Not only have many changes occurred since the seventh edition was written, but they continue to flow at a pace that taxes the ability of anyone trying to keep abreast of the field. New developments will appear after the eighth edition is printed, for no "now" exists. Once we have written a word, our "now" becomes "then." While an up-to-the-minute textbook would be a unique accomplishment, we neither want nor expect needed industry changes to be postponed to accommodate us in our textbook-writing activities. However, even though a time lag in revisions is inevitable, not much is lost by it. The principles are generally the same, the differences are likely to be more annoying than sweeping, and you are not likely to be misled because you know that no bound volume can be a study of current events. To keep current in insurance, you must read one of the many weekly trade journals. Loose-leaf services such as the Fire, Casualty, and Surety bulletins (Cincinnati: The National Underwriters Co.) will keep you informed of changes in coverage under various types of insurance policies.

Thanks to Judy Thompson and Dr. Robert J. Myers, several sections of this edition contain accurate and up-to-date information not readily available from other sources. Ms. Thompson's field experience and association with the University Agency in Auburn, Alabama, were helpful in the discussions of commercial lines products. Dr. Myers read the chapter on social insurance and provided current information, some of which had not yet left the government's printing office. In addition, Auburn University, the University of North Florida, and West Virginia University provided the time and facilities that were needed to complete this revision. We are indebted to these institutions for their support.

An English philosopher once said, "When a new book comes out I read an old one." I suppose that this philosophy is based on the belief that "books, like proverbs, receive their chief value from the stamp and esteem of the ages through which they have passed." But adherence to this philosophy creates a problem for those seeking a fresh textbook for use in an up-to-date course, unless they are willing to settle for a new "old book." The eighth edition of the *Principles of Insurance* is precisely that: a new "old book."

Sincerely yours,

Robert I. Mehr

Terry L. Rose

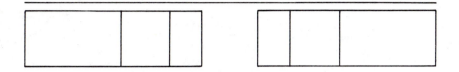

Contents

bonds. Contract bonds. License (or permit) bonds. Official bonds. Miscellaneous bonds. Miscellaneous Coverages: *Comprehensive glass insurance. Boiler and machinery insurance. Credit insurance. Accounts receivable insurance. Valuable papers and records insurance. Title insurance. Municipal Bond Insurance Association (MBIA). Mutual fund insurance. Aviation insurance.* Multiple Line Coverages. Historical Development: *Special Multi-Peril program. Businessowners program. Miscellaneous multiple line coverages.*

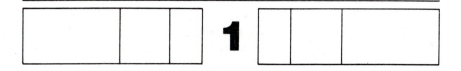

What insurance is all about

Insurance is a vital subject. It is an important field of study for those charged with the duties of financial management, whether for a family unit or a business firm. Insurance premiums exceed 7 percent of the U.S. gross national product. These premiums pay for insurance protection of individuals and business against financial losses arising from a host of causes.

In addition, insurance is a dramatically changing field, as shown by the number of current news stories relating to insurance issues. No-fault automobile insurance has been a perennial federal issue since the early 1970s, while 24 states have taken independent action in this area. Health insurance and health care costs have become an important political issue, splitting both parties and candidates within the parties. The economic health of the social security system is diagnosed periodically in the press. The problems of insurance availability at affordable prices continue to linger in medical malpractice and products liability insurance.

Further examples of significant newspaper items are kidnappings for ransom of American business executives (and locals) working for U.S. companies in foreign countries, alleged unfair discrimination in insurance pricing by the use of sex and age as rate classification factors,

1

concern for the health and safety of workers through numerous administrative rulings and actions relating to the federal Occupational Safety and Health Act of 1970 (OSHA), the federal Consumer Products Safety Act of 1972 (CPSA), problems in financial regulation of insurers in light of the aftermath of the Chapter 11 protective bankruptcy filing of the bereft Baldwin-United Corporation. Baldwin, originally a manufacturer of pianos, owned six financially ailing insurers which were taken over by state regulators for rehabilitation and fine tuning. These insurers had written nearly $4 million of single-premium deferred annuities. The movement of industrial corporations and insurers through subsidaries into a broadly based financial service business has caused a renewed study of the regulation of insurers and other financial institutions.

The people of the United States seem to be the most security minded in the world. Everyone is concerned with insurance. Many contend they are "insurance poor," meaning that too much of their income is spent for insurance. The insurance agent is everywhere, sometimes looking for potential insureds, but often searching for potential insurers.

Many articles have been written in recent months about the inability of insurers to write policies at "affordable rates." Liberal jury awards in liability cases have forced insurers to increase rates or withdraw from various markets. For example, many medical malpractice suits have resulted in judgments in excess of $1 million and some have produced judgments approaching $5 million or more. These "high" awards have caused medical malpractice insurance premiums to increase to the point where some medical specialists have been charged more than $100,000 a year for their medical malpractice insurance. These levels of insurance cost have encouraged many surgeons either (1) to "hang up their scalpels" and concentrate their efforts on hypochondriacs, limiting their treatment to such undramatic illnesses as the common cold and flu or (2) to charge more for their treatment and practice defensive medicine, using precautionary services that might be unnecessary to play it "doubly safe" against possible malpractice suits. Some experts fear that the effect of recent dramatic efforts to control medical care costs might cause physicians to become economy minded in the treatment recommended, further exposing themselves to medical malpractice suits.

Where to Start

What is insurance? Why is it so hard to obtain and sometimes even harder to keep? The task is to help unravel this mystery.

The difficulty with the subject of insurance is that the student needs to know everything at once. Similar to a circle, a clear starting point is lacking. In geometry, one can begin with a few axioms and postulates and proceed to build the whole apparatus. In history, one can start at the beginning, or at any intermediate point, and proceed through any desired period. But in insurance, what is needed is comprehensive knowledge of most facets of the subject in advance. Because that is impossible, the issue is where to jump into the subject. Should study of the theoretical background of insurance be the starting point? Should the subject be treated as a branch of mathematics, for instance? Should it be examined historically? Or should the first concern be the types of insurers engaged in the business or the kinds of insurance policies they offer? Should the study begin with risk management problems that insurance can help solve? No one has the answer.

This chapter is introductory rather than comprehensive. It is designed to give readers a rapid whirl around the insurance world but without stopping to gain a comprehensive knowledge of insurance.

The Burden of Financial Loss

When plans for the 1984 Olympic games were being completed by the American Broadcasting Company and the Los Angeles Olympic Committee, the two groups announced the purchase of multimillion dollar insurance packages. This insurance would protect against losses sustained by political disturbances (such as the 1972 terrorist attack on the Israeli team in Munich) on the withdrawal of a specified major national team, in addition to losses caused by customary exposures arising from events of this type. Relief from the burden of financial loss caused by the peril of terrorist activity or, more likely, one of the mundane perils such as fire, auto accidents, sickness, and "premature" death usually is the first thought one has when thinking of insurance. Other important aspects of insurance must be noted, but one place to begin is with an examination of the problem of the burden of financial loss.

Newspapers relate stories in every edition about financial losses. A father 25 years of age dies, leaving a wife and three small children. A ransom of $10 million is demanded for the release of a kidnapped American executive in South America. Someone embezzles over $10 million from a California bank. Fire burns a new house. A pedestrian is seriously injured when hit by an automobile.

Who bears the financial losses? Who must now support the widow and her three children? Who will pay the $10 million ransom? What is the source of recovery for the embezzled funds? How will the money be provided to rebuild the house? Where will the funds be obtained to offset the cost of medical expenses and loss of work time of the injured pedestrian? Usually, in the absence of legal remedies, contractual arrangements or cooperative efforts of friends and neighbors, these losses are allowed to remain where they fall; that is, with the widow and children, the kidnapped executive, the bank, the homeowner, and the pedestrian.

Shifting the burden by law

If the loss is caused by negligence of another, in the absence of no-fault statutes, it might be shifted by society through common law to the responsible person. If the young father dies as a result of alleged malpractice by the physician, the loss might be shifted to the doctor. If the house is burned by a spreading fire carelessly set by a neighbor, the loss might be shifted to that person. If the pedestrian is injured by a reckless driver or a defective automobile, the loss might be shifted to the motorist or the car manufacturer. *Might be shifted* is the language used in the foregoing illustrations for two reasons: (1) fault has to be proved to the court's satisfaction; and (2) if fault is proved, the guilty party must have the resources to pay the damages.

Where society believes that common-law allocation of loss is not in the public interest, it has passed statutes to redistribute the loss. For example, workers' compensation laws place losses from industrial accidents on employers, without regard to fault. In addition, the laws provide that employers must guarantee the availability of funds for these losses. If the death of the 25-year-old father resulted from an industrial accident, the loss would be shifted in part to the employer.

Financial responsibility laws also have been passed by the states to reduce the number of unpaid judgments resulting from automobile accidents. If the pedestrian is awarded a judgment against a motorist, financial responsibility laws increase the probability that the motorist will have the resources to meet the judgment. Some movement noted in the automobile reparations system today is toward requiring insurance coverage for the person on whom the loss falls rather than shifting it to the person responsible. Thus, in recent years many states and Puerto Rico have enacted some type of no-fault auto insurance law. These laws provide that part (if not all) of the costs to persons injured in an automobile accident will be compensated by their own insurance.

Social security laws have been passed to redistribute income losses resulting from unemployment, disability, old age, and death. If the 25-year-old father were employed in covered employment, the loss would be partly shifted to the social security fund. If the pedestrian were a worker in one of the six jurisdictions requiring compensation for nonoccupational disability, the loss would be shifted in part to that fund.

Insurance and the burden of loss

Whether the burden of the loss remains where it falls or is shifted by law, that loss may cause someone financial difficulty. The owner whose property is destroyed or damaged or the family whose income is interrupted by death, disability, or forced retirement of the breadwinner is likely to suffer a heavy financial loss. A person who becomes legally liable to someone else for bodily injury or property damage can suffer disastrous financial consequences.

Family and business units exposed to serious property, income, and liability losses seek methods to offset these losses. One effective solution is a private contractual arrangement allocating the burden of individual losses to members of a selected group who are exposed to similar losses. These loss-sharing arrangements are called insurance policies.

Insurance is vital to nearly every American family and business, who, in 1982 paid about $222 billion for private insurance and more than $200 billion under government-sponsored social insurance plans. The 1982 assets of private insurers reached $820 billion and government insurance funds amounted to nearly one half that amount.[1]

The Insurance Business

While the principle of insurance is simple, its application is complex, involving many skills.

The insurer

First, organizations known as "insurers," must be formed to administer insurance plans. They may be corporations, partnerships, or syndicates of individual underwriters. The safe operation of the insurance principle depends upon a large number of insureds who are acquired by most insurers through sales representatives. These representatives, known as the "field force," are either employees or independent agents. Recruiting, training, supervising, and compensating a field force require the services of sales management experts.

The contract

Insurers deal primarily in promises described in legal documents known as "contracts." Insurance contracts define circumstances under which the insurer will pay and the amount to be paid. Lawyers are involved in preparing contracts and handling disputes over their interpretation. The latter function also might require aid from the courts.

Developing an insurance contract is not solely a matter of drafting a legal instrument. It is preceded by an intensive analysis of economic and technical considerations to determine not only the kinds of insurance to be written but also the rates and restrictions to be applied. These "underwriting decisions" are made by specialists, such as engineers, statisticians, physicians, meteorologists, and economists.

Insurance contracts seem unnecessarily long and complicated. It has been said an insurance policy contains enough provisions to sustain a shipwrecked couple for a year on a desolate island. An analysis of insuring agreements, limitations, exclusions, and conditions is important in understanding insurance coverage.

---

[1] Data cited in this paragraph are found in the *Life Insurance Fact Book,* published by the American Council of Life Insurance, 1850 K Street, N.W., Washington, D.C. 20006, *Insurance Facts* published by the Insurance Information Institute, 110 Williams Street, New York, N.Y. 10038, and the U.S. Department of Commerce, Social and Economic Statistics Administration, Bureau of Economic Analysis. For relatively current data, see the latest editions of these sources.

Underwriting and rating

The success of a cooperative plan, such as insurance, requires as equitable a distribution of costs among participants as possible. Maintaining a semblance of equity among policyowners is the job of the underwriters who classify and rate each loss exposure. If a local merchant wants insurance against financial loss resulting from burglary, a rate comparable to the exposure will be charged. The more probable the loss and the more severe it is likely to be, the higher should be the premium. For example, loss statistics show that a sporting goods shop in Chicago should be charged more than a similar one in Champaign. A sporting goods shop in Champaign should be charged more than a dental supply firm in Champaign. Shops employing guards should pay less than those without them. Insureds with burglary alarm systems should pay less than those without them. The job of preparing equitable classification systems and rate schedules belongs to actuaries.

Although a large number of policyowners is essential to the operation of the insurance principle, insurers may be unable to insure all applicants. Safe operation requires skill in the selection of insureds. Underwriters must know when to refuse applications. They must restrict the amount of liability assumed on exposures in some areas and on some properties. Highly concentrated exposures run counter to sound underwriting principles. Refusal to accept an application also can be based on the physical nature of the property or the moral character of its owner.

Finance

The nature of insurance requires handling and investing large sums of money. Persons skilled in investment analysis must invest these funds prudently. Insurance as a major financial institution has a significant effect on the economy.

Public control

Because insurance has been held to be "affected with a public interest" it is subject to a greater degree of public control than most other businesses. Nearly all aspects of insurance are regulated, starting with the formation of insurers and ending with their liquidation. Criteria and standards for policy provisions, rates, expense limitations, valuation of assets and liabilities, investment of funds, and the qualifications of sales representatives are established by the individual states. Regulation is more complete and sometimes more complicated for some forms of insurance than others. Also, the extent of regulation varies from state to state.

Many bills are introduced into legislatures every year which, if passed, could be harmful to the insuring public or to the insurance business. Insurers and their agents have organized into several associations that have as a principal function lobbying activities to promote favorable legislation and to guard against what they consider unfavorable legislation. Corporate insurance buyers have organized into associations and these groups also engage in lobbying activities.

Fields of Insurance

Insurance may be divided into several branches. The broadest division is between private and government.

Private insurance

Traditionally, the private insurance business in the United States has been separated into three branches: life, fire and marine, and casualty and surety. Insurers in most states were chartered to write coverage only in one of these branches. Life insurers could write only life insurance, health insurance, and annuities. The following coverages are classified as fire and marine insurance: fire; extended coverage (windstorm, hail, explosion, riot and civil commotion, damage by aircraft or vehicle, and smoke); vandalism and malicious mischief; water damage; sprinkler leakage; earthquake; ocean marine (cargo, hull, and freight); inland marine (transportation, instrumentalities of transportation, all risk property floaters, and bailee coverages); and automobile and aircraft physical damage, including collision. Casualty and surety coverages include general liability, workers' compensation, automobile and aircraft liability, automobile and aircraft collision, burglary and theft, glass, boiler and machinery, fidelity, surety, credit, livestock, and health. Note the lack of logic in the classifications of casualty and surety coverages. Casualty insurance coverages include property as well as liability insurance. It includes coverages that are also classified as fire and marine insurance (auto collision) and as life insurance (health insurance).

The writing of fire and marine insurance and of casualty and surety coverages were not always restricted to separate insurers. The first underwriting limitation was confined to the writing of either life or nonlife as it is today. However, at one time in U.S. insurance history insurers were free to underwrite whatever coverage they wished. This freedom is allowed in many foreign countries.

Separation of the business into life and nonlife insurers originated with the New York General Insurance Act of 1849 which provided that any insurer chartered after that date could be empowered to write fire and marine insurance (either, or both) or life and health insurance (either, or both). In 1853 the Life and Health Insurance Companies Act further limited the underwriting powers of life insurers by giving them the right to issue either (1) life insurance and annuities or (2) health insurance on individuals and insurance on the lives of livestock. In the same year, the Fire Insurance Companies Act divided insurers into those writing fire and inland marine insurance (either, or both) and those writing ocean marine insurance. Thus there emerged four mutually exclusive classes of insurers: fire and inland marine, ocean marine, life insurance, and health insurance.

Subsequent legislation permitted property insurers to write fire and marine or casualty insurance (health insurance was included in casualty lines), whereas life insurers were permitted to write life insurance, annuities, and health insurance. New York law, then as now, was the most important single factor in the regulation of insurance and was widely followed by other states in formulating their insurance codes.

For a long time many insurance experts doubted the wisdom of such strict division of the business. They insisted only life insurance should be singled out as a separate type of operation. A classification that labeled some coverages fire lines and others, closely related, as casualty lines seemed ridiculous. Automobile insurance, as noted, was split between fire insurers (for physical damage) and casualty insurers (for liability), with either type of insurer allowed to write collision coverage. This classification system meant the theft of an automobile could be covered by a fire insurer but theft of other property had to be covered by a casualty insurer (except when included under all-risk marine coverage).

Agitation against this artificial classification resulted in a recommendation in 1947 by the National Association of Insurance Commissioners that states pass legislation providing for full multiple line underwriting powers for fire and casualty insurers that have a policyowner's surplus[2] of not less than $2 million. As a result, all states have passed multiple line legislation allowing an individual insurer to write both fire and casualty insurance. Capital and surplus requirements vary among the states. Multiple line underwriting powers, however, do not extend to life insurance except in 13 states which had never required separation of underwriting powers. A former classification of fire, marine, casualty, and surety is not dead, as some insurers still restrict operations to one field. Multiple line underwriting allows insurers to design special policy forms to cover the major property and liability losses of particular customers, such as homeowners and business owners. Thus by 1949, 100 years after legislation had outlawed multiple line underwriting, it was again legal.

With the advent of multiple line underwriting powers, private insurance can be classified into two major branches: life and property.

Life insurance. Life insurers write three types of coverages: life insurance, annuities, and health insurance. Life insurance provides money upon the death of the insured to be used to pay death expenses and to continue an income to survivors. Annuities are the reverse of life insurance, in that they liquidate an estate under an arrangement whereby the annuitant is guaranteed an income for life. Health insurance provides money for payment of medical expenses caused by accident or

---

[2] Sum of paid-in capital, if any, and net surplus, including voluntary contingency reserves.

illness and protects the insured against loss of income resulting from disability.

Property and liability insurance.   The two fields of private insurance—life insurance and property and liability insurance—are close to each other with respect to premium volume. Life insurance companies wrote approximately $118 billion in premiums in 1982, whereas property and liability insurers wrote $104 billion. However, with respect to assets, life insurance is considerably larger due to the nature of its contract. In 1982, life insurers had assets of $588 billion compared to $232 billion of assets held by property and liability insurers.[3]

Coverage written by property and liability insurers may be divided into five types: (1) Physical damage or loss; (2) loss of income and extra expenses resulting from physical damage to property; (3) liability; (4) health; and (5) surety. Physical damage or loss coverage protects the insured against loss of or damage to owned property. Examples are financial protection against direct loss from fire, windstorm, and theft. Loss of income and extra expense coverage protects insureds against income loss and extra expense incurred because of damage to their property or property of others. Liability coverage protects the insured against third-party claims for bodily injury or property damage caused by negligence or imposed by statute or contract. Automobile liability, workers' compensation, and contractual liability insurance are examples of this type of coverage. Health coverage protects the insured against medical care expenses and income loss resulting from accident or illness. Examples are accident, sickness, major medical, and hospital insurance. Suretyship coverage is a means whereby parties may offer others a financial guarantee of their honesty or of their performance under a contract or agreement. Fidelity, construction, and bail bonds are examples of this type of coverage.

Government insurance

Government insurance is written by federal and state agencies and may be voluntary or compulsory.

Voluntary government insurance.   Consumers may purchase voluntary government insurance plans written by the federal government that include crop insurance, military personnel life insurance, deposit insurance, savings and loan insurance, securities investor protection insurance (for cash and security balances held with participating brokers), crime insurance, mortgage and property improvement loan insurance, supplemental Medicare insurance for the aged written with basic social security Medicare, insurance against foreign expropriation of a limited class of U.S.-owned companies (those with new or substantially increased investments in developing countries), and backup programs

---

[3] See footnote 1 of this chapter.

written in cooperation with private insurers for coverage against perils of flood and riot in qualified areas, and for writing of surety bonds for small minority contractors. Voluntary insurance plans written by one or more state governments include hail, life (Wisconsin), title, auto (Maryland), medical malpractice, and workers' compensation.

Compulsory government insurance. When government insurance coverage is required of consumers, it generally is referred to as "social insurance" and is written both by federal and state governments. The federal social insurance program, popularly known as social security, offers income coverage for qualified survivors of deceased covered workers, disability and retirement income coverage for qualified workers and their dependents, and medical care coverage for qualified persons upon reaching age 65. Pension termination insurance is another form of compulsory federal coverage. New federal insurance plans continue to be proposed and discussed. For example, National Health Insurance has received close scrutiny in recent years.

Although workers' compensation insurance is required in most states, the coverage can be written by private insurers. In those states where automobile liability insurance is required of car owners, the insurance also is written by private insurers.

Social insurance plans administered by state governments include coverage for unemployment benefits. Compulsory nonoccupational health insurance is required in five states and in Puerto Rico, and six states operate monopolistic state funds (no private insurance allowed) for workers' compensation. Twelve states operate workers' compensation funds competing with private insurance.

The total spent for government insurance (both voluntary and compulsory) in the United States in 1983 was approximately $210 billion annually, with most of it for federal plans.[4]

Insurance and Society

The contributions of insurance to society are significant, although not without their costs. On balance, however, the gains outweigh the costs.

Social values of insurance

Insurance tends to bring about a closer approach to an optimum allocation of resources. The effect is the same as that attempted through legislation designed to restrict monopoly in that insurance eliminates one of the barriers to the establishment of a business. If an individual planning to invest in a grocery business found that fire insurance was

---

[4] Ibid.

unavailable, the person might change plans and invest in another business in which insurance is available. Other investors might do the same, for they, too, would be unwilling to risk a total loss of their investment in a fire. The resulting reluctance to invest in grocery stores would mean higher prices through higher sales margins for those few willing to enter the business. The rise of England as a great trading nation and, at the same time as a nation with exceptional insurance facilities, was no coincidence. A trader who dreamed of sending a shipload of finished goods to America to exchange for raw materials might have remained content with domestic trade had there been no ocean marine insurance available in the coffeehouses of London.

One of the influences that interferes with the smooth function of competition is imperfect knowledge. To the extent that insurance eliminates the uncertainty of financial losses resulting from a given set of causes, it increases knowledge, thus decreasing one of the obstacles to competition. For example, the tragic MGM Grand Hotel fire in Las Vegas prompted MGM to seek liability insurance after the fire. The uncertainty of the amount of awards arising from expected liability suits for loss of life and property was of such importance to MGM that the post loss purchase of insurance was deemed worthwhile even at the premium level that had to be charged.

Insurers through loss prevention activities also contribute to the economy by decreasing the chance of loss. Insurers not only maintain large engineering staffs to determine why accidents occur and how to prevent them, but also support safety research, medical research, and health education.

An important value of insurance is its indemnity function. Many family and business units are able to continue intact because a loss is offset in full or in part by insurance funds. Thus insurance contributes to social and business stability.

Insurance is of primary importance as the basis of the credit system. Becky may trust her friend Irma to repay the $200 she lent her last payday. Undoubtedly, she will pay her if she lives and continues to work. However, if she dies or becomes disabled, she can use life and disability income insurance to protect her creditor. The same principle applies to loans made on the security of property. What good is an ironclad mortgage to a banker if a fire occurs and the building is not covered by fire insurance? The mortgagee would be in no better position than if the money was loaned on the signature of the borrower.

Insurance not only alleviates some of the business fears of the insured, but also some of the worries at home. It is impossible to estimate the accomplishments of life insurance in relieving mental anguish. Parents have deep-seated fears that they may die before building financial security for the family. Life insurance banishes that worry by providing funds to keep the family together until the children are grown and to pay the surviving spouse a lifetime income. Annuities for the aged perform a similar service.

Insurance is a useful device to solve complex social problems. Compensating victims of industrial accidents is handled by compulsory workers' compensation insurance; and indemnifying innocent automobile accident victims is met to some extent by financial responsibility laws under which most people comply by furnishing evidence of ownership of automobile liability insurance. Social insurance is used to help solve the financial problems of unemployment, old age, disability, death, and medical care for the aged.

Insurers play an active role in finance, influencing the investment and financial markets of the world. Insurers fund the growth of basic industries and engage in financing government projects. Some insurers have decided not to restrict their activities exclusively to insurance. They argue that they are in the "financial planning" business, and this view has led them to activities that only can be described as extracurricular (or extra-insurance). Some have become part of conglomerate corporations or have created conglomerates themselves. They have organized mutual funds, real estate investment trusts, and financial consulting services. This book ignores these activities and limits itself to insurance only, as the field of insurance is sufficiently vast to command the entire attention of this text.

In 1967, nearly 175 life insurers pledged $1 billion for investment in urban ghetto areas that previously did not qualify for loans from most financial institutions. This program was known as I-CAP (Inner-City Capital Investment Program). Although retaining control over the distribution of these funds, the insurers were subject to guidelines. These guidelines made eligible for loans: (1) projects not ordinarily financed by life insurers because of the "risk" or location involved, (2) housing and residential projects providing improved living space for low- and moderate-income families now living in blighted urban areas, and (3) businesses offering new job opportunities or medical community services for people living in the inner city.

After investing most of the first $1 billion, in 1969 the life insurers pledged another $1 billion. These funds have been loaned to ghetto residents to finance many projects, including, among others, factories, apartments, hospitals, office buildings, job-creating enterprises, shopping centers, and single-family dwellings. One large insurer pledging approximately 35 percent of the total commitment reported a default rate of about 15 percent of the funds at the end of 1974. This rate, believed to be typical for the industry, is about double the average experience. Only a small percentage of the loans were government guaranteed, and these through the Federal Housing Authority (FHA).

One of the early problems faced by life insurers investing these funds was their inability to find property insurers willing to write coverage against physical damage to the structures pledged as security for mortgage loans. This problem was partially solved by an industry-government-sponsored facility known as the FAIR plan (fair access to insurance requirements) discussed later.

Social costs of insurance

The social costs of insurance should not be overlooked. Not all premiums paid by policyholders are used to pay losses. For example, during the decade of the 70s capital stock property insurers incurred annual losses (including loss adjustment expenses) ranging from 66 to 79 percent of annual premiums earned. About 78 percent of the annual income of life insurers is used to pay current or future claims of policyowners. Expenses of capital stock property insurers for the same decade ranged from 27 to 30 percent of annual premiums written. Life insurers' operating expenses have ranged from about 16 to 18 percent of annual income.[5] The seemingly greater efficiency of life insurers is misleading. Life insurers experience a lower percentage of operating expenses to income because of their higher investment income. Life insurers are more than insurance institutions. They function also as savings intermediaries.

The difference between premiums earned and losses paid is used to compensate those who either work in insurance or provide it with operating capital, supplies, and space. Some funds are used in loss prevention activity and for building surpluses for future use in expanding the operations or strengthening the company. Large numbers of people are required to operate the industry. The insurance business in 1982 employed nearly 2 million people.[6] The business also uses land and capital resources. The tying-up of these resources is part of the social cost of insurance. The net social cost of capital used in insurance, however, is reduced because the assets offsetting the large reserves insurers must maintain are invested in other industries and services.

Several other costs of insurance are noted. Insurance is the cause of many fraudulent losses. Insurers are the victims of arson, murder, and suicide claims. Willful destruction of lives and property to collect insurance proceeds is a cost of insurance to society. Insurance also may reduce the incentive to protect property against loss. The reduction of this incentive may be responsible for losses that otherwise would have been prevented. In addition, because payment for certain services generally is made by a third party, the insurer interferes with normal cost control mechanisms between consumer and provider. For example, increases in the cost of medical care have been caused, in part, because the consumer does not have to pay directly for much of the service but simply passes the bill on to the insurer.

Social responsibility

Technological changes that lead to the operation of jumbo jets and automobiles, manufacturing processes and consumption patterns that give rise to pollution, a set of twisted social values that produces criminal

---

[5] Ibid.

[6] Ibid.

attacks on persons and property, an unstable economic climate that permits inflation and recession, the growing consumerism movement, the need for an efficient health care delivery system, and many other realities of the time create a need for the insurance mechanism to be adapted to facilitate the operation of society. The placement director for the Graduate School of Business of the University of Chicago considers insurance to be "in the top 10 percent of socially appealing career opportunities" because it is "an enterprise with obvious relevance to the problems of society." Ralph Nader has commented that the insurance industry with its large pool of assets has the greatest opportunity to improve the quality of life in this country with its interest in highway safety, industrial safety, pollution control, housing, crime prevention, health care delivery services, and public health.

Even though the business is said to be "affected with the public interest," the exact meaning of this concept is not clear. Some observers believe that insurance should be regulated the same as railroads and public utilities. Others favor increased competition in the business. Although the exact role of insurers in solving social problems is in dispute, clearly these problems will not solve themselves. If the industry does not aid in the solution of those problems for which it has both the expertise and the opportunity, the federal government surely will, and not always in a manner attractive to the insurance business.

The objectives of the insurance industry conform closely with many social goals. Achieving a high degree of loss predictability by reducing social unrest, minimizing the chance of unexpected loss, lessening damage from catastrophes, and encouraging loss prevention all provide useful social functions in addition to stabilizing insurers' profitability.

Summary

1. Insurance contracts are agreements to reduce the financial burden of losses arising from specific kinds of risks. These agreements provide the mechanism for allocating individual losses to members of a group exposed to similar losses.
2. Insurers primarily are business organizations formed to administer the insurance mechanism for distributing losses. To function effectively, insurers need sales representatives to obtain large numbers of insureds to apply the law of large numbers in order to improve predictability and thus reduce risk to a manageable level.
3. Operation of the insurance business requires the use of many specialists to draft contracts, determine underwriting standards, establish premium rates which are adequate, not excessive, and not unfairly discriminatory, manage investments, develop and administer loss prevention programs, process claims, and handle other functions involved in the administration of a business.
4. Insurance is "affected with the public interest" and consequently subject to government regulation mostly by the states.

5. The two broad divisions of insurance are private and government. Private insurance is divided into life and property insurance. Government insurance is written by federal and state agencies and may be voluntary or compulsory.

6. The social values and social responsibility of insurance far outweigh its social costs. Insurance contributes to society by favorably affecting the allocation of resources, engaging in loss prevention, indemnifying losses, serving as a basis of the credit structure, eliminating worry, and providing a channel for investable funds. These contributions are not without cost. A large part of the premiums is used to pay expenses of operation. Insurance employs substantial amounts of labor, capital, and land. Insurance is the cause of a number of fraudulent losses. It is also responsible in some cases for losses induced by carelessness because insurance may eliminate one's incentive to protect property or control losses once they occur.

7. Societal changes have many implications for insurance and insurers. While it is not clear how far social responsibility of business should extend, the thought is that insurance should assume greater responsibility than most other businesses.

Questions for Review

1. A large number of insureds are necessary for a private insurance system to operate effectively. Why are many insureds needed? What channels of distribution are used by insurance companies to reach potential insureds?

2. Modern society considers some types of loss situations to be unfairly or inadequately handled under common law. Therefore, laws have been passed to redistribute loss in these cases. Cite two examples of types of losses in which the common-law solution has been changed by statute.

3. A number of specialists are needed by the private insurance industry to make underwriting decisions. Name the specialists and explain why each is needed?

4. A convenience store chain has three identical units located in three areas. One outlet is charged a higher premium for the same amount of crime coverage than another, and the third was denied crime insurance by the same insurer. What underwriting factors might account for the discrimination?

5. What is meant by the statement that insurance has many social values? Are the values of insurance to society different from those to specific individuals? Explain.

6. The assets of life insurers exceed $588 billion whereas those of property insurers are about $232 billion even though the life insurance premium volume is only about 13.5 percent higher. Why are the assets so much higher with only a small difference in premiums?

7. What are the social costs of insurance? On what grounds does the text conclude that the social values outweigh the social costs? Can you give examples of insurance in which the social costs outweigh the social benefits?

8. Define the concept of social responsibility as it relates to the insurance business. Specifically, what is required for a business to be considered socially responsible?

9. What historical developments led to the granting of multiple line underwriting powers to insurers? Do multiple line underwriting powers extend to life insurance and annuities? What kind of insurance can be written by either a life insurer or property liability insurer? Why?

10. Even before its announcement, the boycott of the 1984 Olympic Games by the Soviet Union and other communist nations was not completely unexpected. In view of the relatively high probability of a major nation's withdrawal from the 1984 Games (recall the U.S. withdrawal from the 1980 Olympic Games in Moscow), why would an insurer agree to cover this contingency?

Questions for Discussion

1. Should the factors affecting underwriting decisions in government insurance differ from those in private insurance? What criteria and standards have you used in developing your answer?

2. Do you believe the government "owes" the right to buy insurance to every homeowner? Every auto owner? Explain the criteria and standards used to reach your conclusion.

3. Explain how such companies as the Prudential Insurance Company of America and the Metropolitan Life Insurance Company have entered the property insurance business if life insurers are prohibited from writing property insurance. How was the State Farm Mutual Automobile Insurance Company able to enter the life insurance business?

4. Explain why the social costs of insurance are higher in an economic recession or depression than in periods of economic growth and prosperity.

5. To what extent do you believe the government is justified in intervening in the operations of private insurers? Explain in terms of criteria and standards you have developed for approaching this issue. To what extent do you believe the government is justified in competing with private insurers as in workers' compensation insurance, life insurance, and crop hail insurance? Again develop criteria and standards used to reach your conclusions.

2

Risk management and insurance

Insurance is purchased to offset the *risk* resulting from perils which expose a person or organization to loss. Note the use of the term "risk." What does it mean? Often "risk," "hazard," and "chance of loss" are used interchangeably. The assignment of precise meanings to these terms will help in the understanding of insurance.

Basic Definitions

Certain terms such as "chance of loss," "risk," "peril," "hazard," and "loss," not only have several connotations outside the business but also are subject to varying usage within the business. Such variations can be a source of misunderstanding to the beginning student. The definitions developed in this text have been designed to create distinctions among terms so as to explain them in a manner that best leads to a clear understanding of insurance.[1]

---

[1] Occasional lapses into the jargon of the insurance agent are found in later chapters where, for example, the word "risk" is used to mean the property or person covered by a policy.

Chance of loss

Chance of loss is the long-run relative frequency of loss. Chance of loss is best expressed as a fraction or a percentage. It indicates the probable number and severity of losses out of a given number of exposures. Expressed as a fraction, the probable number of losses is the numerator, and the given number of exposures is the denominator. If a person flips a coin for a cup of coffee, the chance of loss is ½, or 50 percent. If a prize is offered for drawing a white ball out of a box that contains nine black balls and one white, the chance of loss is ⁹⁄₁₀, or 90 percent. Thus:

$$\text{Chance of loss} = \frac{\text{Probable losses}}{\text{Total exposures to loss}}$$

In these cases chance of loss is easy to understand and measure. But what about exposure to loss by fire, windstorm, and other perils? Here one cannot rely solely on logic; instead, a mass of statistical data must be collected.

In measuring chance of loss for standard insurance loss exposures, empirical probability is computed by using statistical methods. (Statistics has been defined as using incomplete data and questionable methods to reach foregone conclusions.) Thus, if the interest is in the probability of loss or damage to a house by fire, all possible statistics must be collected concerning fires on comparable houses. One must know how many fires occurred during a given time and how many houses were exposed to fire losses during that period. If, out of 100,000 similar houses, 100 have burned, the chance of loss or damage to one of these houses by fire during any equivalent period will be 100/100,000, or 0.1 percent. This figure, however, gives the *loss frequency* only. For insurance purposes, *loss severity* figures are more important. Suppose the houses were worth $60,000 each, making a total value of $6 billion, and that the total value of the losses was $3 million (most losses were partial). The chance of loss, expressed in terms of severity, would be 3 million/6 billion, or 0.05 percent. The loss cost then would be 5 cents for each $100 of exposure, or $30 for each house.

The same principle is used in determining the chance of death at any given age. If, out of 1,000 persons alive at the age of 75, 65 die before reaching their 76th birthday, the chance of death during the 75th year can be expressed as the fraction 65/1,000, or 6.5 percent. Since death is permanent and total, loss frequency and loss severity statistics produce the same results.

Chance of loss is important in insurance, for it is a basis on which rates are established. A reasonable degree of accuracy in measuring loss probabilities is necessary if adequate, equitable, and nonexcessive insurance rates are to be developed. Furthermore, chance of loss affects the decision concerning how risk should be handled. If the chance of loss is "relatively high," risk avoidance or risk assumption coupled with a major loss prevention effort appears to be the most efficient method of dealing with risk. If the chance of loss is infinitesimal, the best approach may be simply to ignore the risk.

Definition of risk

Risk is a concept with several meanings depending on the context and the scientific discipline in which it is used. For people who use the term loosely, the concept of risk means exposure to adversity or danger. Mathematicians are interested in the behavior of phenomena and define risk as the degree of dispersion of values in a distribution around the central position occurring in random, chance patterns. The larger the degree of dispersion, the greater is the risk. Harald Cremér, a pioneer in risk theory, in his book *On the Mathematical Theory of Risk* (1930) explains: "The object of the theory of risk is to give a mathematical analysis of the random fluctuations in an insurance business, and to discuss the various means of protection against their inconvenient effects." Behavioral scientists are interested in behavior of people in reaction to the behavior of phenomena, and rarely define risk because they use it to reflect several different concepts that are not always clear. When they do define the term they are inconsistent in its use.

In this text, the focus is on an operational definition of risk for the study of insurance. The definition of risk that both facilitates communication and analysis of risk as it affects insurance is a simple one: *risk is uncertainty concerning loss.* This definition contains two concepts: uncertainty and loss. While both concepts are important to insurance, risk represents the uncertainty and not the loss, the cause of loss, or the chance of loss. The basic function of insurance is to handle risk, and this definition of risk considers effectively the question of how insurance deals with risk. It limits attention to pure risk rather than speculative risk, and therefore confines attention to risk from the viewpoint of the insured rather than the insurer. Pure risk can produce loss only, whereas speculative risk can result in either gain or loss. To illustrate: If lightning strikes and damages a house, the result is loss, but if the lightning bypasses the house, the homeowner does not gain; that is, his or her financial position is not improved. (An operational definition of risk for the insurer follows the completion of the present section.)

Assume that the chance of loss by fire to a store is 1 in 1,000. If a person owned one store the loss cannot be predicted. Either it will or will not burn. No basis exists for predicting the outcome, so the owner is faced with complete uncertainty even though the chance of loss is low. Suppose, however, a chain of 1,000 similar stores is owned. The risk is reduced, and now at least one store can be expected to burn as the probability of loss is 1 in 1,000. But even here one has no assurance that the actual losses will equal expected losses. Because the outcome still is uncertain, risk remains. If two stores burn, the actual loss exceeds expected loss by 100 percent. However, the loss of one more store represents only 0.1 percent of the exposure.

But suppose one owns 100,000 stores. Then 100 stores can be expected to burn. If as many as 10 more burn, the actual loss exceeds the expected loss by only 10 percent or 0.01 percent of the exposure. The large number of stores improves loss predictability; that is, it reduces the probable margin of error in predicted results. Thus, with 100,000 stores, the degree of risk is reduced; yet the chance of loss still remains 1 in 1,000. The risk is not entirely eliminated, however, because actual losses will rarely, if ever, equal expected losses. (Another way to put it is that expected losses are not really expected—apparently a strange adaptation of the word expected.)

TABLE 2–1
Residential fires in two groups of similar homes

Year	Group A	Group B
1	4	18
2	3	21
3	6	16
4	7	23
5	5	24
6	4	17
7	6	21
8	5	20
Total number of losses	40	160
Average losses per year	5	20

Table 2–1 shows the actual number of residential fires recorded during an eight-year period for each of two groups of similar homes. The number of exposures in group A is 100 homes while the group B exposure is 400 homes. Group A's average annual losses are 5 fires, and the chance of loss is 5 in 100, or 5 percent. Losses range from 3 to 7, a fluctuation of 2 from the average of 5. When the number of exposure units is increased to 400 in group B, the average increases to 20 with actual losses varying from 16 to 24. Thus, the chance of loss remains 5 percent (20 out of 400). However, the variation of 4, as a percentage of average losses, has declined from the percentage variation experienced in group A. Predictability of losses is better in group B than group A due to the larger number of exposures, and risk is reduced. Figure 2–1 is a graphical representation of the data in Table 2–1 and illustrates the risk effects of the increase in the number of exposure units.

Unlike the insured, the *insurer* is exposed to *speculative risk* in that the value of actual claims incurred may be higher or lower than that projected in the rate structure. If they are higher, the insurer loses; if they are lower, the insurer gains. Risk for the insurer, therefore, is defined as the exposure to fluctuations between actual claims incurred and those expected.

FIGURE 2-1
The risk effects of an increase in the number of exposure units using residential fire losses by year and group of similar homes

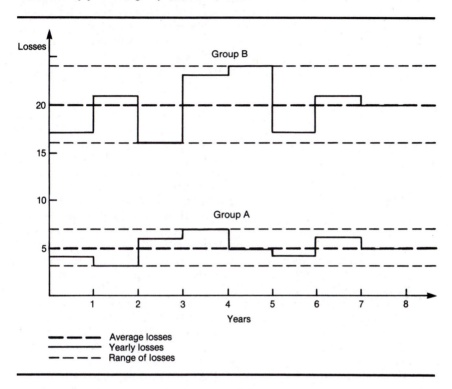

Average losses
Yearly losses
Range of losses

Degree of risk

The accuracy with which losses can be predicted is the measure of degree of risk. The degree of risk is measured by the probable variation of actual experience from expected experience.
Thus:

$$\text{Degree of risk} = \frac{\text{Actual number of losses—Probable number of losses}}{\text{Probable number of losses}}$$

The lower the probable percentage of variation, the smaller is the risk. This percentage variation decreases as the number of exposures increases. Mathematicians express this concept by stating that as the number of exposures increases, the probable variation of actual experience from expected experience increases, but only in proportion to the square root of the increased number of exposures. This observation means that as the number of exposures increases the number of cases that vary from the expected also increases but the percentage variation decreases.

In Figure 2–1, note that although the exposures in group B are 4 times greater than in group A, the variation between actual and expected losses is only twice as great (4 instead of 2). In fact the variations, as a percentage of expected losses, declined from 40 percent (2 divided by 5) to 20 percent (4 divided by 20). Thus, the expected losses increased in direct proportion to the increase in exposures (from 5 to 20), but variations increased (from 2 to 4) only in proportion to the square root of the fourfold increase in exposures. The degree of risk, as measured by the percentage variation, is thus reduced.

Assume that over time on the average 1 out of 100 trucks is damaged by collision each year. If 10,000 trucks are covered by insurance, the expected number of trucks damaged in any given year is 100. Assume that experience shows the actual figure has varied between 80 and 120, so the standard error of the estimate is 20. Thus, with 10,000 trucks, the area of uncertainty is 20/100, or 20 percent. Suppose now the number of covered trucks increases a hundredfold from 10,000 to 1 million. The expected damage now is 10,000 trucks. However, the sampling error of this estimate rises not one 100-fold, but only 10-fold, so that the standard error is 200 trucks. The expectation is that the actual number of trucks damaged will vary between 9,800 and 10,200. Thus the relative area of uncertainty is 200/10,000, or only 2 percent, rather than 20 percent as before.[2]

When the future course of events is perfectly predictable, no risk exists. If it is known that something will or will not occur, no uncertainty prevails and hence no risk. The inability to predict the course of future events is the essence of risk. And, as events become more predictable, risk is reduced.

Risk makes insurance both desirable and possible. If in a given case a loss were certain to occur, insurance could not be obtained. No insurer could write it at commercially feasible rates. If in a given case a loss were certain not to occur, insurance also would not be written. No one would buy it. Thus, the owners of a house located on a river bank where flood damage occurs three years out of four would be eager to buy flood insurance, if offered. The owners of houses on a nearby hill would not buy the insurance as no flood ever causes them damage. Insurance exists because people do not know what will happen to their property or to their personal earning power in the future. They prefer a small certain cost for which they can budget (the insurance premium) to an uncertain, but potentially large, loss for which they may be unable to budget (actual loss, up to the limit of the policy).

Chance of loss versus degree of risk. The distinction between chance of loss and degree of risk is clarified by a simple illustration. Assume that A and B represent two groups of exposures to loss. The chance of

---

[2] See any statistics textbook for further discussion of concepts relating to standard error in sampling.

loss in each group is 10 out of 1,000 (1 percent). In group A, over a period of years, annual losses varied from 3 to 18, whereas in group B losses varied from 8 to 12. The annual experience is more stable for group B. Therefore, losses are more predictable because of the low degree of variability. The more predictable the loss, the less is the degree of risk. So notwithstanding an equal chance of loss (1 percent), the degree of risk is less for group B. The degree of risk is in part a function of the probability distribution of losses over time.

Peril

Peril may be defined as the cause of a loss. People are subject to loss or damage from many perils. Typical perils are fire, windstorm, explosion, collision, premature death, accidents and sickness, negligence, and crime. Causes of loss often are loosely called risks. Correctly, risk is the uncertainty about the occurrence of the event that creates the loss, whereas the peril is the loss-producing agent. Perils to which property and income are exposed must be studied by prospective insureds and their agents and brokers so the appropriate insurance protection can be arranged when desirable.

Hazard

Behind the ostensible cause of loss (peril) is hazard. The fire breaking out in the garage is the peril; but the pile of oily rags in the garage is the cause of the fire and thus the basic cause of loss. Further investigation would reveal that poor housekeeping is the fundamental cause. Yet, for insurance purposes, fire is the cause of the loss; and it is the peril against which the fire policy is written.

Hazard is defined as a condition that may create or increase the chance of loss arising from a given peril. Carelessness, poor housekeeping, bad highways, unguarded machines, and dangerous employments are examples of hazards, for they increase chance of loss.

Some writers distinguish three types of hazards: physical, moral, and morale. *Physical hazard* is a material condition increasing chance of loss. The production of gunpowder in a building is a physical hazard increasing chance of loss by fire or explosion. *Moral hazard* is an individual characteristic of the insured that increases the probability of loss arising from the dishonesty of the insured. For example, dishonest insureds increase arson losses. *Morale hazard,* also an individual characteristic of the insured, is indifference to loss. This condition is observed in those insureds with the general attitude expressed in the thought: "What, me worry? I've got insurance!" For example, carelessness in the safekeeping of property increases the chance of loss by theft. Moral hazard arises when insureds induce or fake a loss to collect on their policies. Morale hazard exists when the insured fails to protect property from loss because it is covered by insurance or when the insured has a careless attitude about the loss. This subtle difference between moral and morale hazard is rarely made in insurance underwriting. The term moral hazard is considered by practicing underwriters to include morale hazard. However, the distinction between the two is useful in clarifying the issues involved.

Insurers must review hazards when applications for insurance are submitted. If the hazards exceed those contemplated in the rate schedule, the insurer generally rejects the application, restricts the coverage, or increases the premium. Insurers are interested in loss prevention activities, so they study hazards in order to discover methods of reducing or eliminating losses.

The insurance buyer must have knowledge of hazards to recognize those that can cause loss and to know which exposures to cover with insurance. Only through a systematic study of these exposures can they be handled intelligently. For example, if the insurance manager of a firm decides to purchase adequate coverage for the liability exposure (a wise decision) but overlooks the elevator and products hazards, a financial shock can be expected when a liability suit arises from one of these hazards.[3]

Loss

Loss is an unintentional decline in, or disappearance of, value arising from a contingency. The adjective "unintentional" is an essential part of the definition. If a college student gives his girlfriend a diamond ring, he has certainly parted with something of value; but he would not likely admit (at least at this stage of the game) he has suffered a loss. Medical and hospital care expenses may be considered losses, although their payment is not unintentional. The occurrence (accident or illness) generating them usually is unintentional.

Loss does not necessarily imply the loss of a physical article. The owner of common stock, for example, has a paper loss if its market price declines, yet the certificate remains intact. Technical obsolescence is another example of loss not resulting from physical damage to the article. Large desk calculating machines have most of their value because of the availability of more sophisticated and less expensive electronic pocket calculators. Losses brought about by changing conditions of the market are called speculative losses, and generally are not insurable because they do not meet some of the criteria for insurable exposures to be explained later.

Losses in which a physical article is damaged or destroyed are called pure losses and generally are insurable. Losses resulting from destruction of property may be of three types: loss of the article, loss of its income or use until the article can be replaced, and extra expenses incurred because of the loss. If a house is destroyed by fire the person not only has lost the house, but also must pay rent elsewhere until it is rebuilt. If a room were rented that income also is lost. If the family

---

[3] See Chapter 24 for an additional discussion of physical and moral hazards.

moves to a motel at considerably increased expenses or must spend several hundred dollars to remove the debris of the house from the street following the fire, substantial extra expense will be incurred. Insurance should be planned to cover these three types of losses.

A final type of loss involves liability to others. A fire caused by burning leaves may spread to a neighbor's house. The neighbor may bring suit against the leaf burner charging negligence. The defendant will incur the defense cost of the legal action, and if found guilty, will be obligated to pay the damages awarded by the court. These losses also require insurance protection.

Risk and Risk Bearing

Risk involves social as well as individual cost. Therefore, both society and individuals are interested in the ways in which it may be handled.

Social cost of risk

Because most persons are risk averters, risk creates a social cost by retarding economic progress. The cost of risk is apart from the cost of replacing destroyed or damaged property, and is usually unrecognizable except on close analysis.

Risk discourages investors and affects the allocation of resources. Many resources are used in industries where risk is slight, whereas fewer quantities are used in industries exposed to a high degree of risk. The result is that resource allocation is not maximized for society. If risk were eliminated, some resources eventually would move from industries formerly exposed to a lower degree of risk to those formerly subject to a higher degree of risk, thus maximizing resource allocation. The utility loss resulting from withdrawal of some resources from their former uses would be less than the gain in utility realized from employment of these resources in their new uses, thus increasing total utility to society. Economists explain this observation by applying the principle of diminishing marginal utility. Perfect competition and downward sloping demand curves are assumed.

The effect of risk on the economy is the same as that of socially undesirable monopolies. Both similarly affect production and prices by discouraging production, restricting supply and thus leading to high prices. The social cost of risk is its effect on the allocation of resources. It is the loss of economic goods and services whose production is discouraged by the existence of uncertainty. It is not the actual loss of capital which results from the occurrence of an uncertain event. That loss is *in addition* to the cost of risk itself.

Some areas of economic activity are deemed so important to society that the government intervenes in the risk process. When the risk is so great that it totally discourages needed capital investment, the government may, through legislation, reduce the amount of risk in order to encourage investment. For example, the Price-Anderson Act limits the aggregate liability resulting from a nuclear accident to a maximum of $560 million. By limiting the maximum loss, the amount of risk is reduced to an "acceptable" level. This limitation has resulted in increased investment in nuclear energy. Another example of government involvement to reduce the amount at risk is the Swine Flu Program of 1976. In order to encourage drug manufacturers to produce the vaccine, the government, by legislation, assumed the liability for settling and paying all claims resulting from the mass immunization, reserving the right to proceed against the drug manufacturers only in cases involving negligence or breach of contract with the government. This action removed the responsibility for the drug manufacturers of settling the many nuisance claims that recently tend to develop in any program of this type. Through these activities to reduce the amount of risk, the government encouraged additional investments in these endeavors.

Chance of loss also can exert an influence on economic activity. A high chance of severe loss discourages business activity more than that resulting from a relatively low chance of loss, irrespective of the degree of risk involved.

Methods of handling risk

Jawaharlal Nehru once wrote: "People avoid action often because they are afraid of the consequences, for action means risk and danger." He adds that while these results seem frightening from a distance, they are not so bad if one looks closely. And often risk "is a pleasant companion, adding to the zest and delight of life." Most people, however, do not regard risk so kindly and seek to cope with it efficiently. Risk is universal, present in all things, all lives, inherent in being. The concept of a person free from all risk is as theoretical as the concept of perfection. What can be done about risk? Methods of dealing with economic risks faced by families and businesses may be classified under six headings: (1) risk may be avoided, (2) risk may be retained, (3) hazard may be reduced, (4) loss may be reduced, (5) risk may be shifted, and (6) risk may be reduced.

1. Risk may be avoided. To quote an old "chestnut": "There is a way— but it's not much fun." The British humor magazine *Punch* once published "Advice to a Young Man Who Is about to Marry." The advice consisted of a single word: "DON'T!" A couple can avoid the risk of a fire loss to their house by selling the house or simply setting fire to it. The uncertainty of the date of death can be avoided instantly through judicious use of a knife or gun. Truly, it is not much fun.

Often alternative choices are available when the nature and extent of risk are determining factors in reaching a decision that cannot be avoided. For example, upon graduation from the university, Phyllis Klock is offered two jobs: one a salaried position in the home office of a property and liability insurer, the other a commission-paying connection with a local general insurance agency. Phyllis believes she would enjoy the work more in the agency, but does not know if the earnings would be adequately rewarding during the years required to become established. Although not so promising for the future nor so challenging, the salaried position in the home office does offer a regular income. Phyllis must make a choice. Her decision rests on how she balances the net utility of the commission-paying agency job (the utility of job satisfaction less the disutility of incurring the risk) against the net utility of the salaried job. Everyone does not measure equally the disutility of risk bearing. When the reluctance to accept risk is so great it cannot be counterbalanced by the utility gained from the risky action, the risk should be avoided. Avoidance is possible, however, only if that choice exists. If the risk cannot be avoided it must be handled some other way.

2. Risk may be retained.   The business firm, family, or individual bearing its own risks (as all must do to an important degree) must be prepared to withstand not only the risk but also the loss. The retention of risk often is the path of least resistance in meeting uncertainty. Risk may be retained out of ignorance. For example, owning a house involves risk of loss from many sources: fire, windstorm, explosion, and so on. The homeowner can insure against loss resulting from all these perils and yet not be fully insulated against risk. Financial loss may be suffered because of legal liability for persons injured on the premises. Failure to insure against this liability exposure may be a result of unawareness rather than a conscious decision to retain the risk.

Risks are also retained out of inertia. A couple may realize the family faces risk of loss of income should the breadwinner die prematurely, and that the family cannot assume this risk. Yet they delay buying life insurance until pressured by an agent.

Risks are retained also if there is no way to meet them. A person might wish to insure the risk of death, but if one's occupation is racing motorcycles, insurance may be unattainable. Risk retention, however, may be the result of positive action. Many instances may be found in which retention is the most economical solution to the risk problem. Operators of truck lines have frequent oral tilts with highway regulatory authorities. Tests indicate weights exceeding certain limits produce an extra-heavy strain on highways, so laws of most states prohibit trucks containing axle weight loads over stated maximums. Some truckers frequently carry weights far in excess of the maximums. They are aware of the law but are taking a calculated risk. Excessive loads are so much more profitable that truckers find it advantageous to haul illegal loads and to pay fines when they are caught by state authorities.

Risk also is retained if the loss exposure is too small to be of concern. For example, students are forever losing pens and pencils, but they are willing to retain this risk with little concern. These relatively inexpensive losses can be replaced without financial burden.

If the maximum loss is small and losses are frequent, the business may be able to handle them on a current basis without funding them.

If the losses are too irregular and too large to be absorbed as they occur, some funding might be required. The purpose of the fund is to spread the losses over time. The cost is borne by a steady series of small payments to the fund even though the loss occurs infrequently and for a large amount. Difficulties arise in using this method because losses may occur more often than expected or before the fund is sufficient to offset them; also it might be difficult to persuade management to keep the fund intact for its designated purpose.

Business executives sometimes accumulate sinking funds to meet uncertainty in the erroneous belief that they are operating scientifically. Assume the manager of a store that has escaped fire losses begins to cast covetous eyes at the firm's annual fire insurance bill. The manager is loss prevention conscious, conducts monthly fire drills, and is never out of arm's reach of a fire extinguisher. So the decision is made to "self-insure" the fire loss exposure. Instead of renewing the insurance, the premiums are placed in a new account, "Fire Self-Insurance Fund." (As is soon explained, the term "self-insurance" is used incorrectly here.) One evening when the manager has locked up the extinguisher for the night, a hungry rat, who is new in the building and has missed the fire drills, gnaws into the casing of an electric line causing a short circuit, which, before morning, starts a fire that cannot be extinguished. The loss is $500,000 to be offset by a fund of $3,500. What then is the effectiveness of the "self-insurance" fund?

This observation does not suggest that self-insurance is impossible in all instances. Suppose this store was one unit of a national chain which has hundreds of similar stores. Such an organization probably could predict its fire losses within reasonable limits and thus self-insure its risk. The principal objection to such a plan is that, even with its hundreds of units, the company will not have the broad basis for predicting losses available even to a medium-sized fire insurer. A particularly unfavorable year may exhaust the insurance fund before all losses have been replaced. See Chapter 22 for further discussion of self-insurance and the conditions under which it may be desirable.

Sometimes it is impossible to buy insurance because insurers are either unable or unwilling to write the coverage. In these instances, the accumulation of a sinking fund presents the best way to handle a difficult problem. Thus the motorcycle racer who cannot buy life insurance should set aside a relatively large portion of his or her winnings to create a "life insurance fund," which, if luck holds, may be sizable before the last race is lost.

3. The hazard may be reduced. Efforts may be made to reduce the hazard. The use of metal conduits in constructing the aforementioned store would have prevented the rat from causing the fire, or at least would have deterred it for many years. Well-defined safety precautions cut down accidents in industry. Progress in medical science has done much in recent years to eliminate or control diseases greatly feared a generation ago. It is significant that much loss prevention research is conducted by insurers or others financed by insurers. For example, Underwriters' Laboratories, Inc., originally was established by midwestern fire insurers to test materials, devices, and processes against fire hazards.[4] The cost of losses is an important factor and must be distinguished from the cost of risk. The cost of risk is the before-the-fact evaluation of the economic cost of the uncertainty about possible losses. For example, the cost of risk could be equated with loss control expenditures and with the necessary periodic contribution to a fund to be used to pay for losses. Budgeting for the before-the-fact cost of risk can reduce the cost of loss, as a prepared-for loss generally costs less than an unprepared-for loss. The cost of loss is the after-the-fact evaluation of the loss. Thus in the foregoing illustration, the building of a fund represents the cost of the risk. That cost primarily is the opportunity cost of holding the fund liquid. When the fund is spent to pay for a loss, that expenditure is the cost of loss. That cost is likely to be less because funds are immediately available to help offset it. The risk manager has important duties in connection with loss control. Loss control requires a variety of trained specialists, such as loss control engineers, accounting system analysts, attorneys, and others. The risk manager's most important loss control task is to motivate all management personnel to strive to control losses. In several insurance lines (e.g., boiler and machinery) the coverage provides important loss control services. General management must be made to realize that when some risks are retained rather than insured, loss control services must be provided by the business through its own personnel and/or outside consultants.

4. Losses may be reduced.   Action is possible to minimize a loss if one occurs. The chance of a loss occurring is not eliminated, but its severity is reduced. Fire extinguishers or automatic sprinklers throughout a factory do not change the likelihood that a fire will start, but do curtail the spread of the fire. Periodic medical examinations may not in themselves reduce the chance of heart disease; however, regular visits to a doctor can result in recommendations and treatment capable of diminishing or ceasing existing adverse physical conditions. Hazard reduction and minimizing loss often are coexistent aims and usually are found together. Thus, a physical checkup not only will reduce the loss from disease, but the doctor's recommendation in some respects also will reduce the hazard. An automatic traffic signal at an intersection of two heavily traveled highways will reduce the frequency rate of accidents. At the same time, it reduces the severity rate because the signal usually slows traffic. The result is that, although collisions still may occur, both the impact and resulting damage is lessened.

5. Risk may be shifted.   Hedging, subcontracting, the use of surety bonds, incorporation, and insurance are examples of methods of shifting risk to another party.

---

[4] Underwriters' Laboratories, Inc., is now an independently self-supporting organization.

Hedging is making commitments on both sides of a transaction so the risks offset each other. A simple illustration is a betting transaction: an overenthusiastic sophomore bets $5 that the home team will win its game Saturday. During the week preceding the game, the student's enthusiasm wanes in the light of cold, hard realism. One way to offset the risk is to shift it to someone else. So a naïve freshman full of school spirit is enticed to bet $5 on the home team with the sophomore taking the opponent, a perennial conference power. Now, with offsetting bets, whichever team wins, the sophomore will "break even."

In legitimate business, the operations of a country grain elevator present an example of hedging. The elevator operator buys grain from farmers in the area for shipment to a central market. Each farmer receives the price prevailing the day the grain is purchased although it will be some time before it is shipped. When the grain arrives at the central market, prices may have dropped so the elevator operator cannot sell the grain for a price high enough to cover the amount paid the farmer plus the cost of handling. However, prices may be up the day the grain arrives. In that case a speculative profit will be made. But at the time of purchase no one knows what the price of the grain will be on arrival at the central market.

As it is not the practice of the elevator operator to retain the unexpected gain or loss resulting from risk of price changes, the risk is shifted to the grain speculator, whose business is to buy and sell "futures"; that is, to make contracts to buy or sell grain at a given time in the future for a specified price.

Subcontracting is a second method of shifting risk. A general contractor is building a dormitory at an agreed-upon price. Subcontracts are let for various operations. A contract may be let for plumbing, one for electrical wiring, one for roofing, and so on, all at fixed prices. Although the general contractor still has residual liability for the entire job, portions of the risk of increasing costs have been shifted to the subcontractors. If the price of bathroom fixtures or electrical conduits rises, the subcontractors must bear their proportionate share.

Surety bonding, a third method of shifting risk, is a three-party agreement in which a bonding company (the surety) and the principal (the contractor, for example) promise an obligee (for whom the work is to be done) a specific performance. Thus, a surety bond is a contractual obligation whereby the surety must answer for the default of the principal. The general contractor must furnish a surety bond to the school guaranteeing that its dormitory will be built as specified and within the time agreed upon. Should the contractor be unable to finish by that time, the bonding company might be obligated to make daily payments of specified amounts to the school until the contractor has fulfilled the obligation. If the contractor cannot complete the building, the surety is obligated to pay the necessary additional costs to have another contractor finish it.

Incorporation is another method of shifting risk. The corporation has been defined as "an ingenious device for obtaining individual profit without individual responsibility." The stockholders, if their shares of stock are fully paid, have no liability. Their losses are limited to their investment in the stock. In unincorporated business the owners are the principal bearers of the risk that the business assets will be insufficient to pay all claims. In the corporation, because of limited liability, this risk is shifted to creditors.

Insurance is the most commonly used method for shifting risk. By purchasing insurance, the insured shifts the financial consequences of a loss to the insurer. If a loss occurs, the insured is reimbursed by the insurer for the loss incurred subject to the terms of the policy.

6. Risk may be reduced. In the previous examples, methods for retaining or shifting risk were explained. These methods attempt to cushion the loss or transfer it to someone else.

Even loss prevention activities do not reduce risk unless the chance of loss is reduced to zero—an unlikely event. In fact, loss prevention activities may increase risk; for example, if the chance of loss is reduced to an infinitesimal level, it might become impossible to accumulate enough exposures to the loss to give sufficient credibility to the meager loss statistics. The methods discussed in this section succeed in reducing the degree of risk.

Large-scale business is a method of reducing risk. A person who has erected a telephone pole for the sole purpose of supporting a television antenna will lose this entertainment source if lightning strikes the pole. The degree of risk is high. The chance of lightning striking is not great, but this small chance of loss does not decrease the uncertainty. AT&T (plus its seven recently weaned offsprings) with millions of poles, does not have this high degree of risk. Because of its large number of widely scattered poles it can predict within an acceptable range the number of poles that will be lost each year through lightning—as well as through termites, motorists, and those who "borrow" a pole to use as a base for a television antenna.

Many kinds of managerial controls tend to reduce risk. Materials control systems, audits and other accounting controls, and process and product inspection plans improve prediction and hence reduce risk.

From an individual's point of view, insurance can be viewed as a method of shifting risk. However, insurance also is a method for reducing risk. Insurers are willing to assume the risk because with a large number of exposures, the number of losses becomes more predictable. For instance, a couple owning a home knows that some houses will burn, but are uncertain as to whether their house will burn. They also are uncertain about the loss they will suffer if a fire does occur. They cannot set up an adequate sinking fund for these losses, because, as pointed out, that method is unsuitable when only one piece of property is involved. They could buy 9,999 other houses so their loss would be more predictable, but most homeowners would consider this solution neither sensible nor practical. They can achieve the same end by combining their risk with the risks of thousands of other homeowners through an insurer. When risks are combined, losses become more predictable, and risk is reduced. All members of the group then know the amount of their share of the loss. They can budget for this small fixed amount, knowing this charge is the most that a fire will cost.

Life insurance is comparable. "Nothing more certain than death; nothing more uncertain than the hour of death." The possibility that even the healthiest person may die this year always is present, but whether the possibility will become a reality is unknown. By combining the death risk of one person with that of many, the uncertainty of financial loss can be eliminated. Each individual's share of the cost can be determined and spread equitably among the members of the group.

Insurance as a Device for Handling Risk

The real nature of insurance is often confused. The word "insurance" sometimes is applied to a fund accumulated to meet uncertain losses. For example, a specialty shop dealing in seasonal goods must charge more early in the season to build up funds to cover the possibility of loss at the end of the season, when the price must be reduced below cost to sell the product. This method of meeting a risk is not insurance. An accumulation of funds for meeting uncertain losses is not sufficient to qualify as insurance.

A transfer of risk often is called insurance. A store selling television sets promises to service the set for one year without additional charge and to replace the picture tube should the glories of televised spring football prove too much for its delicate wiring. This agreement, loosely referred to as an "insurance policy," is simply one that transfers risk, and risk transfer in itself is insufficient for an economic or legal definition of insurance. If it were, then insurance regulation would extend to a host of commercial promises for which the insurance regulating system was not designed.

Definition of insurance

An adequate definition of insurance must include either the accumulation of a fund or the transference of risk, but not necessarily both. In addition, it must include a combination of a large number of separate, independent exposure units having the same common risk characteristics into an interrelated group.

Insurance may be defined as a device for reducing risk by combining a sufficient number of exposure units to make their individual losses collectively predictable. The predictable loss is then shared proportionately by all units in the combination.

These exposure units include both an entity (for example, one automobile, one house, or one business) and a time unit (for example, one year). Commonly, insurance involves spreading losses over more than one entity within one unit of time. However, insurance also can involve spreading losses of one entity over a long enough time period to increase the predictability of the losses. This technique of spreading losses for a single entity over a long time span is known as self-insurance. The question of whether that technique should be called insurance has caused considerable controversy within academic circles, the accounting profession, and in Internal Revenue Service rulings. That issue is tangential to the discussion at this point. The important characteristics of the concept of insurance as used in this text is that *uncertainty is reduced* and that *losses are shared or distributed* among the exposure units.

Insurance allows the individual insured to substitute a small, definite cost (the premium) for a large but uncertain loss (not to exceed the amount of the insurance) under an arrangement whereby the fortunate many who escape loss will help compensate the unfortunate few who suffer loss. Even if no loss materializes, insurance helps to eliminate any anxiety the insured might have about a potential loss. Insurance, therefore, provides the insured not only postloss but also preloss utility.

Indemnity

With some notable exceptions discussed in Chapter 10 the purpose of an insurance contract is to provide indemnity. Webster defines indemnity as "security against hurt, loss, or damage." Thus insurance policies limit payments for loss to the amount of that loss subject to policy limits. For example, if an insured has a $75,000 fire policy covering a $50,000 house and later sells it during the policy term, nothing will be paid if the house is destroyed by fire, for no loss is suffered by the insured. If the house is destroyed before it is sold, the insured can collect only $50,000, for that is the extent of the loss. Indemnity is the only legitimate use for insurance, for otherwise insurance would be a gambling instrument and therefore contrary to public policy.

Insurance may be distinguished from gambling. In gambling, the risk is created by the transaction; in insurance, the risk is reduced by the transaction. For example, no chance of loss exists at the racetrack until a bet has been placed; but the risk of loss of property by fire or windstorm is present until reduced or eliminated by insurance. Therefore, gambling and insurance are opposites: one creates risk, the other reduces it.

The law of large numbers

At first glance, it may seem strange that a combination of individual risks would result in the reduction of total risk. The principle that explains this phenomenon is called the "law of large numbers."[5] It is sometimes loosely termed the "law of averages," or the "law of probability." However, it is but one portion of the subject of probability. The latter is not a law but an entire branch of mathematics.

---

[5] Called the "law of great numbers" by our British cousins. Economist John Maynard Keynes suggests a more accurate term would be the "stability of statistical frequencies."

In the 17th century, European mathematicians were constructing crude mortality tables. From these investigations they discovered the percentage of male and female deaths among each year's births tended toward a constant if sufficient numbers of births were tabulated. In the 19th century, Simeon Denis Poisson named this principle the "law of large numbers." This law is based on the regularity of events. What seems random occurrence in the individual happening appears so because of insufficient or incomplete knowledge of what is expected. For practical purposes, the law of large numbers may be stated as follows: The greater the number of exposures, the more nearly will the actual results obtained approach the probable result expected with an infinite number of exposures. Thus if a coin is flipped a sufficiently large number of times, the results of the trials will approach half heads and half tails—the theoretical probability if the coin is flipped an infinite number of times.

Events that seem the result of chance occur with surprising regularity as the number of observations increase. A car races around a corner one July 4th. A tire blows, and the car crashes, killing the driver. If the car had been moving slowly and its tires were in good condition, the accident might not have happened. It seems impossible to have predicted this particular accident, yet the National Safety Council predicts within a small margin of error how many motorists will die in accidents over the July 4th holiday. Even more accurate is the Safety Council's estimates of yearly accidental deaths, as the greater the number of exposures to loss, the closer are the results to the underlying probability.

Similarly, insurers with statistics on millions of lives can make a close forecast of the number of deaths in a given period; the longer the period, the greater accuracy. The prediction of the number of persons in a college class who will die during the year probably would be far from accurate. The prediction on the basis of enrollment in a large university would show a moderate degree of accuracy; and the prediction of deaths in all U.S. colleges and universities would have a high degree of accuracy.

The law of large numbers is the basis of insurance. Under this law, the impossibility of predicting a happening in an individual case is replaced by the demonstrable ability to forecast collective losses when considering a large number of cases. Applying these conclusions to insurance, one observes that every year a given number of dwellings burn or a particular number of deaths occur. If a small group of cases were isolated, a wide variation between actual loss experienced and average loss expected might be found. Insurers within their financial limits use the benefits of the law of large numbers by insuring the greatest possible number of acceptable exposure units to facilitate loss forecasting. In addition, the insurers want the units spread widely to minimize deviation from underlying probabilities occurring when the units are concentrated in one location.

Insurance does not completely eliminate risk because achieving an infinite number of exposure units is impossible. Thus some deviation of actual from expected results can be anticipated. Furthermore, statistics on which predictions are based are not perfect. Even if they were, no reason exists to believe that tomorrow's losses will conform to yesterday's because so many dynamic elements are involved. The possibility of the presence of moral hazards also may interfere with loss prediction.

Criteria of an insurable exposure

Considering that insurance seems such a logical method of handling risk, why not combine all uncertainties in one big pool and rid the world of most risk? The limiting factor is that several broad criteria need to be considered before attempting to operate a successful insurance plan: (1) a large group of homogeneous exposure units must be involved, (2) the loss produced by the peril must be definite, (3) the occurrence of the loss in the individual cases must be accidental or fortuitous, (4) the potential loss must be large enough to cause hardship, (5) the cost of the insurance must be economically feasible, (6) the chance of loss must be calculable, and (7) the peril must be unlikely to produce loss to a great many insured units at one time.

Among these criteria, a few are essential whereas most are only requisite. The difference between essential and requisite is the importance of the characteristic to the concept under consideration. Essential is more strict. If a criterion of insurability is deemed essential, insurance is impossible without it. A requisite provides one means to an end, but there may be others. If a criterion of insurability is considered a requisite, insurance is possible without it by substituting some other characteristic. Which of the foregoing characteristics are considered essential and which are considered requisite is a function of the rigidity with which insurance is defined. It has been suggested that the rigidity of the definition be sufficiently relaxed so that none of the criteria is essential or requisite. The assertion is made that an insurable exposure is one for which insurance can be purchased, and that in turn is a function of the knowledge and persuasiveness of the broker and the knowledge, imagination and courage of the insurer rather than a list of criteria for insurability. However, to support precise thinking, a rigid definition of insurance is used in this text. Accordingly, not every contract written by an insurer is one of insurance even though it is called insurance. Essential criteria in the foregoing list, for the purpose of this text, are (1) and (7). The others are considered requisites. The rationale becomes apparent as the discussion develops.

1. A large group of homogeneous exposure units. To predict probable loss through use of the law of large numbers, it is essential that a large number of similar, though not necessarily identical, units be exposed to the same peril. Large numbers, in this context, means numbers large enough to make losses predictable within ranges compatible to insurers. A fire insurer cannot operate with only 25 or 50 houses to insure. With so few exposures, the difference between losses experienced from those expected likely will be excessive. Insurance is impractical when the probable deviation from the predicted loss is so large that a reasonable addition to the premium to offset the risk increases insurance rates to levels unattractive to buyers. In life insurance many persons are needed in each age, health, and occupational classification. To accommodate this essential criterion, classifications in insurance frequently are broad.

2. Definite loss. The loss must be difficult to counterfeit. Death, perhaps, comes closest to perfection in meeting this requisite. In sickness insurance, claims personnel sometimes find it difficult to determine if a loss has occurred. During the depression of the 1930s, sickness claims rose sharply. Persons unable to find jobs either worried themselves sick or faked illness in order to collect benefits. During this period, a common observation was that to collect under an accident policy, all one needed was a covered accidental injury, but to collect under *a sickness policy* all one needed was a sickness policy. Inability to recognize fraudulent claims was in part responsible for the receivership of several insurers writing disability insurance during the 1920s and 1930s. Disability income insurance contracts are subject to stricter underwriting standards today than they were 50 years ago because of that adverse experience. Coverage is more liberal for disability resulting from accident than that arising from sickness partly because accidental injury is more easily confirmed than illness.

3. Accidental loss. Although some losses are expected for the group, specific individual losses themselves must be unexpected; that is, fortuitous. Ideally, the loss should be beyond the control of the insured. Under mercantile theft insurance normal (anticipated) shoplifting losses are excluded. In credit insurance, bad debt losses which are normal for the trade are not covered. The risk of loss from death is not insurable because everyone is certain to die. Insurance, however, is written against losses arising from untimely death, as the hour of death is uncertain.

4. Large loss. The peril covered must be capable of producing a loss so large the insured could not bear it without economic distress. Insurance against breakage of shoestrings is unknown. The loss involved is so small that it is not worth the time, effort, and expense to enter into an insurance contract to indemnify the loss. (And insureds probably would be furious at the insurer because most shoestring breakage is due to wear and tear, which would not be covered by the policy.) This example is a *reductio ad absurdum;* but it illustrates the principle. Nevertheless insurance often is written to cover small losses. Insurance for losses that can be absorbed is uneconomical because the insurance premium includes not only the loss cost but also an expense margin.

5. Economically feasible cost. To be insurable, the chance of loss must be small. The cost of the policy consists of the pure premium (amount needed for claims) and the expense addition. If the chance of loss is much above 40 percent, the policy cost will exceed the amount the insurer must pay under the contract. For example, a life insurer could issue a $1,000 policy on a man aged 99. The pure premium alone, however, would be about $980, to which would be added an amount for expenses increasing the total premium to more than the policy amount. For insurance to be attractive for the consumer, the coverage must exceed the premium. The amount by which the coverage must exceed the premium depends on the degree of the individual's risk aversion. The chance of loss involving small damage to autos by collision is so high that collision policies usually are written to exclude the first $100 of loss.

6. Chance of loss must be calculable. Some probabilities of loss can be determined by logic alone, for example, the probabilities involved in a flip of a coin. Others must be determined empirically; that is, by a tabulation of experience with a projection of that experience into the future. Most types of insurance probabilities are determined empirically. Some chances of loss, however, cannot be determined either by logic or from experience. Unemployment is an example because it occurs with such irregularity that no one, as yet, has succeeded in determining its future incidence. If no statistics on the chance of loss are available, the degree of accuracy in loss prediction is low in spite of a large number of exposures.

The essential criterion of a large number of homogeneous exposure units and the requisite of a measurable chance of loss are violated by "insurance" on loss exposures, such as the fingers of a pianist or the pitching arm of a baseball player. These types of policies are not true insurance. They are transfers of risk from "the insured" to the "insurer" but do not combine exposures to reduce risk. Several factors make it possible for insurers to accept these risks. The "insured" has no knowledge of the chance of loss, and tends to overestimate it. Few competitive rates are available for comparison. As is usual in an insurance purchase, the insured assigns a far higher utility value to postloss dollars relative to preloss dollars, and consequently is willing to pay what might appear subjectively to be a high price for the coverage. Furthermore, mass underwriting often is used as a substitute for mass exposure. The potential loss is spread among a number of "insurers," each accepting a part small enough to manage financially. Each "insurer" or underwriter becomes a speculator because the chance of loss has been calculated subjectively rather than objectively. Frequently for new exposures (fiduciary liability insurance fostered by the Employee Retirement Income Security Act of 1974, for instance) and even for old ones (ocean marine insurance, for example) insurers rely heavily on subjective probabilities in estimating the chance of loss and in determining the premium.

7. Unlikely to produce loss to a great many at the same time. No insurer can afford to insure a type of loss likely to happen to a large percentage of those exposed to it. A large percentage as used in this context means one so high a single occurrence could force well-managed insurers and their reinsurers into (or close to the brink of) insolvency. Life insurers write coverage against death, even though all policyowners will die eventually. Its premium rates and asset accumulations are calculated to pay claims as they mature without causing the insurer financial hardship. If all policyowners of a life insurer should die prematurely, it would be insolvent just as a fire insurer would whose policyowners all lost their houses by fire.

Unemployment insurance written by private insurers violates this essential criterion. Individuals with secure jobs (Where are these jobs in this world of fast-changing technology?) would be poor prospects for unemployment insurance. Prospective customers would be only those feeling insecure in their employment. During a business recession many of them would lose their jobs at the same time. Through insurance the unfortunate few who lose are indemnified by the fortunate many who escape loss. If the many suffer the loss, the few will prove inadequate to indemnify them properly, except at an uneconomic premium. In order to guard against catastrophic losses, fire insurers for instance seek a wide distribution of exposures and apply underwriting standards prohibiting concentrations of business in small sections of a city. They also exclude from coverage losses caused by war, thus relieving them of this particular danger of catastrophic loss. Life insurers often insert war clauses in new policies when war seems imminent.

The foregoing criteria of insurability are not rigidly followed. Cases are on record in which coverage is written in violation of one or more of them (e.g., insurance covering the legs of an outstanding running back, or covering the obvious assets of a glamorous male or female screen personality). Insurers write policies for small amounts; they write insurance for which no adequate statistics are available for scientific rate-making; they write contracts when the chance of loss is high or the exposure is catastrophic; they write coverage where the loss is not accidental; and they cover losses that are not definite in time, amount, and place. These criteria must be viewed as the optimum to achieve rather than characteristics to be met in every instance.

The Function of Risk Management

In one sense, the history of risk management began with the dawn of civilization. Long before women's lib, when primitive man had his mate sleep nearer the mouth of their cave so that the noise of her being attacked by a saber-toothed tiger would give him time to grab a firebrand and make his escape, he was engaging in a rudimentary form of risk management. Today's liberated women rightfully no longer would cooperate in this male chauvinistic risk management behavior. Modern history of risk management originated with the organization in 1931 of the insurance section of the American Management Association. The insurance section holds many conferences and workshops each year, with attention devoted to all aspects of risk management and insurance.

In 1932 the Insurance Buyers of New York was organized by representatives of several big New York businesses concerned with problems involving insurance buying for their firms. They met regularly to exchange information and ideas in risk management. This organization was succeeded by the Risk Research Institute, which organized risk managers on a national basis. Its successor organization, the American Society of Insurance Management, changed its name in 1975 to the Risk and Insurance Management Society (RIMS). RIMS has local chapters throughout the country.

In the 30s the person in charge of business insurance usually was called "the insurance buyer," later titled "insurance manager." The term "risk manager" is of recent origin. The responsibilities of risk managers have grown, and as increasing attention is given to this function in business, insurance managers will have to become skilled and effective full-scale risk managers or be relegated to a subordinate role.

The nature of business risks

Earlier in this chapter, risk was defined as uncertainty about a loss. In business the future appears more cloudy than clear. Business progress usually is measured by profits. Conditions that make profit unpredictable are the source of risk in business. Sources of risk in business may be classified as speculative and pure.

What Galbraith has called "the economy of the central tradition" in American economic life assumes competitive conditions. The control this tradition "came to exercise on men's minds has often been remarked. There was no equally explicit appreciation of the fact that it committed men to a remarkable measure of uncertainty. The penalty for falling behind in the race for increased efficiency was bankruptcy. This result also could be the penalty of mere bad luck in the case of the producer whose product no longer was wanted."[6]

Mehr and Hedges in *Risk Management in the Business Enterprise* divide speculative sources of risk into three categories: management, political, and innovative.[7] Management risks may be further subdivided into market, financial, and production risks. Market risks arise from uncertainty whether production can be sold at a price high enough to yield a fair return on the firm's investment. The size and characteristics of the market for the firm's products always are changing. Consumers' tastes change. Competitors alter their tactics.

Financial risks are involved in obtaining and administering company funds. Decisions must be made on the relative use of long- and short-term financial instruments, and whether to use equity or debt financing. Dividend policy and many other details concerning use of earnings must

---

[6] John K. Galbraith, *The Affluent Society* (Boston: Houghton Mifflin, 1958), pp. 40–41.

[7] Robert I. Mehr and Bob A. Hedges, *Risk Management in the Business Enterprise* (Homewood, Ill.: Richard D. Irwin, 1963), p. 4.

be decided. Every uncertainty of the future adds to the problems of financial management.

Production risks relate to personnel, manufacturing techniques, and materials procurement. Should the firm use different raw materials or alter its labor capital mix in producing its products? Should a change be made in inventory policy? Negotiation of labor contracts poses many problems. Management of fringe benefits has become an important aspect of personnel management. Obsolescence of machinery and production techniques is a constant source of uncertainty. Two other types of speculative risks must be added: political and innovative. A change in national policy toward foreign investments may destroy an overseas expansion program. An innovative risk develops when a new product is introduced.

Speculative risk does not always result in loss. One company's loss may be another's gain, as when the crowd switches from cars to mopeds. Speculative risk offers both a chance of loss and of gain. If the business plans (or guesses) correctly, it may earn handsome profits.

Static sources of risk

A firm operating in a stable economy with loyal customers, good buying and selling judgment, dedicated employees, and a favorable political climate still would be subject to pure risk. That risk remains even though all dynamic factors are static. Pure risk offers no opportunity for gain; only an exposure to adversity. Pure risk falls into five categories: physical damage to assets; fraud and criminal violence; adverse judgments at law; damage to property of others on which the business depends for sales or raw materials; and death or disability of key employees or owners. These loss exposures are discussed in Chapters 3 and 4.

The risk manager's primary concern is pure risk, a function ignored by other personnel in most businesses. Speculative risk is of interest only to the extent that it can influence pure risk management decisions.[8] Three important observations may be noted in comparing pure risk with speculative risk: (1) both pure and speculative risks involve uncertainty but in pure risk the uncertainty relates only to the occurrence of a loss—no chance of profit exists; (2) although statistical analysis is useful in dealing with either type of risk, the characteristics of pure risk make it more adaptable to pooling and loss sharing; and (3) in speculative risks firms may suffer losses from events that result in social gain—in pure risks if a firm suffers loss, society usually also loses.

Objectives of Risk Management

Business management involves several specialists: production, personnel, finance, research, and marketing, for instance. What justifies

---

[8] See Robert I. Mehr and Bob A. Hedges, *Risk Management Concepts and Applications* (Homewood, Ill.: Richard D. Irwin, 1974), passim.

including the risk manager as a management specialist? Management is the adaptation of means to multiple ends. Its basic purpose is to maximize productive efficiency by achieving an optimum balance between benefits and costs. The distinguishing objective of risk management is to make the most efficient preloss arrangement for postloss balance between resources needed and resources available to preserve the effective operation of the business. Implied in this objective is control over the amount of needed postloss resources by the use of systematic programs of loss prevention and control. The risk manager's attention is focused primarily on the determinants of the nature and quantity of resources needed and the identity and characteristics of sources from which they may be obtained.

To accomplish this objective, the risk manager must understand not only the rules, but how to apply them. The basic rules of risk management are: The size of the potential loss must bear a reasonable relationship to resources of the loss bearer, and the benefits of taking the risk must bear a reasonable relationship to its cost. These two precepts advise against risking more than one can afford to lose, to consider the odds, and not to risk a lot for a little. These precepts are valuable whether one is playing poker, choosing one's elective courses, or planning an insurance program. To apply these rules, the risk manager must know: how to identify and measure the loss potential of exposures; how to measure the resources available to meet loss potential; and how to measure benefits and costs of alternative risk-bearing devices.

In addition, risk management decisions must be formulated and integrated with the basic objectives of the organization. Patently, risk managers must be fully aware of these objectives to accomplish their mission. Thus, for many risk management decisions, an open communication line between the risk manager and the organization's top decision makers is essential. Absence of clear and free communications among these parties can create serious difficulties. For example, the failure of one large firm to include a risk manager in decisions concerning the design of a new plant was found to be a major contributing factor to the severity of a fire that completely destroyed the new facility. A postloss investigation revealed that the production process was arranged in an open, single-level configuration. Raw materials were stored so as to make them readily accessible for each succeeding step in the manufacturing operation. Unfortunately, the combustibility of supplies progressed from the most combustible at one end of the factory to the least combustible at the other. The fire started in the highly combustible material and became hotter as it spread. By the time it reached the relatively fire resistant supplies, it was hot enough to ignite them also. In addition, the open layout of the plant meant that fireproof walls and doors were not available to contain the fire. Upon completion of the investigation, the firm established a risk management department whose head reported directly to the chief operating officer.

The postloss analysis convinced the company's management that its basic objective of growth would have led a risk manager to suggest various design alternatives. The alternatives likely would have reduced the loss, or at least allowed the firm to prepare itself better for a major loss. That is, even if the cost of loss control alternatives had been deemed too expensive to meet the firm's growth objective, other preloss arrangements could have minimized the effects of the loss.

As noted in the foregoing example, risk management decisions must be made with a clear understanding of the organization's goals. A hierarchy of a corporation's goals (listed in descending order of desirability) might be: (1) growth in assets, markets, and profits, (2) stable profits, (3) no losses, and (4) survival of the firm. Writers proclaim that the basic and only corporate goal is to maximize shareholders' wealth. An analysis of risk management decisions required to operate at the various levels following a loss reveals that the growth objective is much more expensive to meet than the survival goal. Thus when a risk management decision is affirmed by top-level policymakers, they not only have considered the corporation's preloss objectives, but also, due to the affirmation, are made aware of the potential postloss consequences. In this manner, top managers are protected from the one result they dislike most—an unpleasant surprise.

The Risk Management Process

The risk management process involves setting and achieving the risk management goal.

Achieving the risk management goal

The steps for achieving the risk management goal are: (1) to discover the risk problems, (2) to consider the different methods available to solve the problems and choose which methods are the most efficient, (3) to implement the decision, and (4) to evaluate the results.

These four steps can be expressed in terms of three basic responsibilities of the risk manager: (1) to identify and evaluate the firm's exposure to losses from pure risk, (2) to select the optimum methods of handling these exposures, and (3) to check and verify that the optimum methods are used efficiently.

Identifying and evaluating exposure to loss. Chapters 3 and 4 deal with loss exposures. The risk manager must determine the exposure to pure risk in three broad areas: life and health values, property values, and liability. The exposure to loss resulting from disability or death of a key person in a firm, along with employee benefit plans involving disability income, medical care, survivorship benefits, and retirement income all concern the risk manager.

The problem of measuring loss potential in property values includes a survey of loss possibilities caused by damage to or destruction of assets, loss of income resulting from their damage or damage to assets belonging to suppliers or customers, and loss of net profits arising from increased operating expenses incurred because of asset damage.

Identifying and measuring loss potential from liability exposures appear to be the most complicated. Professional risk managers are aware of the large liability loss exposure. But so many liability hazards exist that to uncover all of them is difficult. Even when one knows all the liability exposures, no accurate estimate of the maximum loss potential (short of complete demise of the business) can be made with any degree of confidence.

Selecting optimum methods of dealing with exposures.   Once the risk manager has identified and evaluated exposures to pure losses, the optimum method of dealing with them must be selected. The risk manager has to decide what must be done to reduce resources required (loss prevention and control) and determine the arrangements to be made to provide the residual amount needed. In making loss prevention and control decisions and choosing necessary resources to offset loss, the techniques selected must produce the most favorable balance between costs and benefits. In measuring costs and benefits of a risk management tool, the cost is determined by the amount of the outlay: the benefit is measured by the loss that would be averted if the outlays are made.

Identifying the costs and benefits is not always easy. For example, how much is lost if a $1 million building is destroyed by fire? If the business lacks the resources to rebuild the structure, then the loss could exceed $1 million if the building is essential to the efficient operation of the business. What would it cost to rely on the credit resources of the business to provide needed funds? How might a severe loss affect the credit rating of the business and the interest rate it must pay for a substantial loan if one could be arranged?

Resources available to a business for offsetting losses are of three types: (1) resources within the business including additional resources the owners are willing to provide, (2) credit resources, and (3) claims against others arising from the loss. In this last category are claims against those who because of statutory or common law are legally responsible to indemnify the business for its loss, and claims against those to whom the risk has been transferred through contractual agreement. Insurance contracts are in the latter class and in many instances prove to be the most efficient preloss arrangement for the postloss resources needed. The criteria for measuring the desirability of postloss resources are adequacy, reliability, and cost. The risk manager must measure the preloss arrangements for postloss resources against these criteria.

Using optimum methods efficiently.   After the risk manager has decided which loss exposures will be covered and how to cover them, the problem remains to assure that the arrangements are handled efficiently. It must be determined that loss prevention and control programs are conscientiously administered, risk transfer through leases and other contracts are executed according to the company risk management policy, no risks are assumed out of ignorance or carelessness, planned risk assumption is considered in view of any change in the company's financial position, and no risk is accepted that is not in accordance with company risk management policy.

To perform effectively, a risk manager must communicate intelligently with statisticians, lawyers, engineers, accountants, financial managers, personnel managers, and other management specialists. Many risk managers are preparing themselves to meet the challenge through the Insurance Institute of America's risk management diploma course and by attending seminars of the American Management Association and of the Risk and Insurance Management Society. Large insurance brokerage firms and various universities operate risk management seminars. Usually the risk management program is built around commercial insurance. The risk manager has many duties in implementing the insurance portion of the risk management program.

The risk manager's functions relative to insurance

Once risk managers have decided to use insurance as a tool their duties are to: (1) develop specifications for coverage and arrange contracts that meet them; (2) establish criteria and standards to use in qualifying insurers and their representatives, then select from among those eligible; (3) buy insurance at prices as low as possible, compatible with services desired; and (4) use insurers', brokers', and agents' services effectively during the policy period.[9]

Developing specifications for the coverage. In many policies the coverage is standardized by law, custom, or intercompany agreement, but even with the most rigid policy, leeway is given through the use of standard riders attached to the basic policy. Two important reasons for the risk manager to develop specifications are: to clarify the coverage needed in the policy and to cover gaps by a different policy or by some other risk management technique. In many specific types of policies coverage differs, and the trend seems to be away from standardization.[10] Special contracts often are tailored specifically to the desires of the risk manager.

Establishing criteria for insurers and agents. The risk manager, having established specifications for coverage must select the insurer and the agent best equipped to write the coverage. The insurer's claims philosophy and financial standing are important considerations. Often extra-insurance factors affect the decision, such as an insurance agent who is a relative of the president or an insurer who is an important customer. Also loss prevention and risk analysis service might be important factors.

---

[9] Chapter 21 includes suggestions on insurance buying.

[10] Today one hardly dares talk about *a* standard automobile policy let alone *the* standard automobile policy!

Buying insurance—at what price? The pricing of insurance is a complicated matter,[11] making a fair price difficult to determine. Often shopping among reliable agents and insurers is necessary to find the best buy. Complete understanding between the risk manager and the insurer regarding the specifications of the contract and the services is vital in bargaining. Many risk managers invite bids from insurers based on clearly stated specifications. Sometimes the cost of insurance can be cut by omitting some services. The risk manager must decide whether or not to accept this type of arrangement. In some circumstances, the risk manager may not want insurance coverage but only the nonindemnity services of an insurer. In this event, an administrative services only (ASO) contract with the insurer will be used under which only the special services sought are provided.

For a quiet night's sleep, some risk managers believe that good policy dictates staying with an old and trusted insurance relationship, even at higher cost, rather than shifting to a different and untried insurer or agent. Convenience, protection of markets for hard to place coverage, and a sound risk management program often are reasons for maintaining the status quo.

Summary

1. An understanding of the definitions of terms that have both analytical and communicative value in studying insurance is important.
   a. *Chance of loss.* The long-run relative frequency of a loss, best expressed as the probable number and severity of losses out of a given amount of exposures; when expressed as a fraction, using the probable number of losses times its average severity as the numerator and the total value exposed to loss as the denominator.
   b. *Risk.* Uncertainty concerning loss.
   c. *Degree of risk.* The range of accuracy within which a loss can be predicted, given the desired level of probability of a successful prediction.
   d. *Peril.* The cause of the loss.
   e. *Hazard.* A condition that may create or increase the chance of loss.
   f. *Loss.* An unintentional decline in value resulting from a contingency.
2. Economic fear, which causes an uneconomic allocation of resources, is the real cost of risk to society. Insurance eliminates or reduces this fear, thus helping to optimize resource allocation, thereby increasing the total utility produced and leading to a higher standard of living.
3. Six basic methods are available for the management of risk:
   a. The risk may be *avoided.*
   b. The risk may be *retained.*

---

[11] See Chapter 25.

    c. The *hazard* may be *reduced.*

    d. The *loss* may be *reduced.*

    e. The *risk* and consequently, the loss may be *transferred.*

    f. The *risk* may be *reduced.*

4. The foundation of insurance is based on loss prediction and loss sharing. It assumes a calculable chance of loss and a combination of loss exposures to permit a reasonably accurate prediction. The predicted loss is shared proportionately by all members of the group.

5. Indemnity (compensation for actual losses incurred) is the principal function of most property insurance contracts.

6. A number of criteria must be considered in determining the insurability of a loss exposure. Two of these criteria are essential whereas the others are only requisite. These criteria are:

    a. There must be a large number of homogeneous exposure units.

    b. The loss must be definite in amount, time, and place.

    c. The loss must be fortuitous (accidental in origin).

    d. The peril must be capable of producing a loss large enough to have serious adverse financial effects on the insured, otherwise the insurance would not be economically attractive.

    e. The chance of loss must be small enough so the insurance cost will not be prohibitive.

    f. The chance of loss must be calculable to permit the insurer to devise a premium scale sufficient to pay losses and expenses as they occur.

    g. The loss must not happen to a great many insureds at the same time, because a catastrophic loss may cause insolvency for an insurer. Criteria *(a)* and *(g)* are essential.

7. The foregoing criteria are not strictly followed at all times by all insurers. They are meant to be viewed as the optimum to be achieved rather than characteristics to be met in every instance.

8. The objective of risk management is to maximize the productive efficiency of the enterprise according to goals set by top management. The risk manager is concerned with an efficient preloss plan for effective postloss balance between resources needed and resources available. The risk manager must:

    a. Identify and evaluate the firm's exposures to losses from pure risk.

    b. Select the optimum methods of dealing with those exposures.

    c. Assure the optimum methods are used efficiently. In choosing among risk management tools, benefits must be weighed against their costs.

9. The risk manager's functions in many instances will be focused on insurance and will require:

    a. Developing specifications for the desired coverage.

    b. Creating a set of criteria and standards for qualifying insurers and their representatives for consideration, then selecting from among eligible suppliers.

    c. Purchasing insurance contracts at prices as low as possible, compatible with the coverage and services desired.

Questions for Review

1. The "cost of risk" and the "cost of loss" are concepts important to the study of risk and insurance. Define each and explain how they differ.

2. Two rural farm fire mutual insurance companies each provide fire insurance for farmers in their respective counties. The Bureau County company covers 100 farmsteads, while the Marshall County insurer covers 1,600. If the loss frequency is 4 percent and the degree of risk 50 percent for the Bureau County farms, what can you predict about the Marshall County company's loss experience? (Assume that the properties insured in the two companies are similar in all but their number.)

3. Moral hazard is a factor that must be considered in the underwriting (selection) process of fire insurance carriers. Discuss its existence in fire insurance. Does it exist in life insurance? Explain.

4. Aside from the moral hazard, what other types of hazards are important to insurers? Distinguish between the types of hazards and explain the relationship each type could have to a specific peril.

5. Distinguish among the six methods of dealing with risk by giving an example of each. Explain with examples how more than one method can be used simultaneously in handling the same risk.

6. The top management of the Dezined-to-Brake Toy Company has decided to expand the production of their best selling toy, the Figure 8 Racer. The expansion plans call for a new building to be erected to house new manufacturing facilities. Explain the role of the risk manager in the expansion decision and the subsequent building program.

7. For an insurer, is there a difference in the uncertainty involved in insuring a homeowner against the flood peril as opposed to the tornado peril in areas in which the homeowner is exposed to one of these perils? Explain.

8. The authors state: "In speculative risks, firms may suffer losses from events that result in social gain—in pure risks if a firm suffers loss society usually also loses." Give an example of a loss a firm may suffer that will be a gain to society. Give an example of a loss a firm may suffer that will also be a loss to society.

9. Insurance is only one of several risk-bearing devices. Explain how loss probability and loss severity should enter into a decision whether to insure a given exposure. What other considerations are important in reaching a decision on how a risk should be handled?

10. Explain the difference between an essential criterion and a requisite criterion of insurability. What criteria are essential? Why? Select two of the other criteria and explain why they are requisite rather than essential.

Questions for Discussion

1. What is self-insurance? How does it differ from risk retention? Is it possible to have a satisfactory plan of self-insurance? Is it possible that, even if the requisites for self-insurance were met, the risk manager might have good reasons to buy commercial insurance instead? Explain.

2. From the viewpoint of the insured, the risk has been shifted to an insurer. Is this conclusion true from the point of view of society? How do you account for any difference you may find?

3. In your answer to question 5 under "Questions for Review," you discussed six methods for dealing with risk. In your opinion, do these methods, taken together, completely solve the risk problem? Explain.

4. The text states that "the criteria of insurability are not rigidly followed." Yet some insurers offer insurance for the legs of a running back or the hands of a famous piano player. Is this practice consistent with the criteria of insurability? Why or why not? Do violations of these criteria make them meaningless for the study of insurance? Explain.

5. If you were the risk manager for the Procrastination Catering Service, Inc., how would you proceed to develop specifications for insurance coverage and criteria and standards for qualifying insurers and agents? Under what set of conditions would you dispense with the nonindemnity services of an insurer? Under what set of conditions would you seek an ASO contract from the insurer?

3

Risk analysis: Life and property exposures

Risk analysis is the process of locating loss exposures, measuring the amount of losses that can be produced from these exposures, estimating the probability that losses will occur, and evaluating the exposures to determine actions necessary to meet business or family risk management objectives. Risk analysis is not simple. The risk manager's success depends on awareness of the types of information needed, knowledge of how to acquire this information, and an understanding of how to use the information. The job of risk analysis is keyed to finding the answers to three basic questions: (1) What can cause loss? (2) What postloss resources will be needed to continue effective operation?, and (3) What methods are the most efficient in obtaining or reducing the amount of needed postloss resources? The risk manager must be prepared to answer these questions whether making decisions for a large corporation or a family.

Identifying and Evaluating Loss Exposures

In locating and measuring loss exposures, the risk manager must organize the search as well as the information itself.

Organizing the search

Discovery and evaluation of loss exposures require knowledge of pertinent facts about assets, income, and activities of the business or family. The risk manager has several available sources of information.

Financial information and supporting records are an important source of information for risk analysis within the business. The *balance sheet* will reveal what the business owns. A systematic study of each asset item will help locate loss exposures if appropriate questions are asked. Pertinent questions concerning assets involve their location, their replacement cost, their utility value, perils, and hazards to which they are exposed, and loss control devices available for their protection. The *income statement* will provide information relative to operating activities. Questions about sources of income and expense items help reveal and measure loss exposures not otherwise detected.

Another source of information is a *flowchart* showing the flow of raw materials through the plant to customers. The chart indicates where raw materials are bought, the processes performed, and auxiliary operations such as transportation, research, advertising, and storage. Special-risk situations may be revealed by these charts.

Risk analysis information can be developed from a systematic *physical inspection* of the premises plus a study of all *contracts* entered into by the company (e.g., leases, sales agreements, and warranties on products). Usually an exposure guide is used to direct attention to facts required for a thorough risk analysis. The American Management Association has published a *Risk Analysis Questionnaire* that serves as a checklist to be used "with the understanding that it will uncover many—but not all—of the facts" necessary for a complete risk analysis. The 43-page document covers questions relating to the nature of the business, financial information, personnel, buildings owned or rented, contents, automobiles owned or hired, glass exposure, elevators, boilers and machinery, crime exposures, business interruption exposures, extra-expense exposures, transportation exposures, boat and aircraft exposures, key person exposures, and exposures arising out of employee benefit programs. Over 200 questions are included with many having as much as six subparts. The questionnaire also has a section for recording losses incurred during the past five years. These data are helpful in measuring loss probabilities.

Risk managers in a business need help from other specialists in analyzing their risks. Important collaborators are engineers, accountants, attorneys, health experts, and statisticians. In addition, risk managers require the cooperation of department heads and operating personnel to help uncover unusual risk situations.

Organizing the information

How the information is to be used is the controlling factor in its organization. Risk analysis information is used in making risk management decisions. Because insurance is the most common method of handling pure risk, most risk managers organize their information to produce data needed for underwriting and rating loss exposures and for developing the most efficient insurance programs for these exposures. Information developed for insurance purposes also is helpful in the efficient use of noninsurance methods of handling risk.

Broadly conceived, the information must be organized to facilitate analysis of types of losses, potential amounts of losses, rates of loss, perils that can cause loss, and hazards that increase the chance of loss. The remainder of this chapter is concerned with life, health, and property loss exposures. Liability exposures are analyzed in Chapter 4. Some of the problems involved in buying insurance to deal with these loss exposures are discussed in Chapter 21. Although the following discussion treats loss exposures separately, they must be considered as a unit in making risk management decisions.

Life and Health Exposures for the Business Firm

Businesses are composed of people, most of whom occasionally become sick, and all of whom eventually die. The firm's possible loss exposures arising from disability and death of human resources are subject to analysis by the risk manager.

Loss of key employees

Potential net income losses may result from the disability or death of key personnel in the form of reduction of revenues (a top salesperson becomes disabled or dies) or increase in expenses (an exceptionally efficient department manager becomes disabled or dies). The replacement of key employees likely will involve extra expenses for training replacements and short-time losses in efficiency. Companies can lose key employees who may be lured away by higher salaries or better fringe benefits. Employee benefit plans, therefore, are important in protecting the life values of the business.

The sole proprietorship exposure

Over 90 percent of the business units in the United States are sole proprietorships. In estate planning, sole proprietorships can be hazardous. Seldom are sole proprietors aware of the pitfalls. They tend to think of their businesses apart from their personal estates—something their families can operate if disability, death, or old age occurs. No legal distinction is made in the sole proprietorship between the personal and the business estate. The debts of the business are the debts of the estate and vice versa. Many personal estates have been depleted either by the debts of sole proprietorships or by attempts to operate the business while the proprietors are disabled or after their death. Often the families would have fared better without the businesses. To look upon a business as the means of support for the family may be wishful thinking. Instead, the family might have to support the business.

In the event of death or disability of a sole proprietor, a decision must be made to continue the business, sell it, or liquidate it. In the vast majority of sole proprietorships, the owners also are the active managers. They function as employees, usually key employees. If they are absent because of disability or death, usually someone must be hired to replace them. Perhaps everyone advances and someone is hired at the lowest level; but whatever the arrangement, someone is added to the payroll, reducing the income for the family. In addition, revenues may decline because of the loss of the proprietor's skill. Much of the success of the business is attributable to the proprietors themselves; for example, the customers know them; they have a special knack for making the business a success.

When the proprietor dies, another problem might arise. Estates do not pass directly to heirs. Before the heirs receive any property the court must be satisfied that creditors have been paid. The first step in transferring estate property to heirs is the appointment of an executor or administrator. The former serves usually when the decedent has a will; the latter, when no will exists. Both are appointed by the court and are officers of the court, primarily responsible to it and not to the heirs. The executor (or administrator)[1] must dispose of the business unless the last will and testament of the owner contains express instructions "in direct, explicit, and unequivocable language" for continuing the business, or unless all heirs are adults and agree to assume the responsibilities of continuing the business. If neither of these conditions prevails, the executor must liquidate the business with reasonable dispatch. If the business is continued beyond the time necessary to sell or liquidate it, the executor may be held personally responsible to the heirs for any loss. For this reason, the executor may dispose of the business as soon as possible. "As soon as possible" often means a forced sale, which rarely produces a favorable price.

Thus, the risk manager of a sole proprietorship needs to make preloss arrangements to protect the proprietor's general estate against the debts of the business and, if possible, arrange for a buyer of the business in the event the owner dies or becomes permanently disabled. Sometimes a buyer can be found in advance through a binding buy-and-sell agreement with a key employee who is interested in owning the business after the proprietor's death or permanent disability. In this event, the key employee agrees to buy and the sole proprietor provides for the estate to sell at a price usually set by formula. A buyer is not necessary if the owner's disability is temporary, but an additional employee may be needed. During the disability period, earnings may drop because of

---

[1] The executor and administrator both are court appointed. However, the executor is named by the deceased in the will whereas the administrator is nominated by the courts.

the absence of the sole proprietor. Therefore, the risk manager must arrange to deal with these exposures.

The partnership exposure

The legal relationship between partners is a personal one. The partnership does not exist apart from them. Each is fully responsible for the business acts and debts of all others. If one partner withdraws from the firm, the partnership is terminated. It then must be either liquidated or reorganized. In either case the withdrawing partner or the heirs must receive compensation. The disability of an active partner may cause a severe drain on its resources. With one partner unable to work, the business loses a key employee. If the primary function of the partners is to acquire business, partnership income drops. Even though expenses are increasing and income is decreasing, the partners may feel compelled to continue the income to the disabled partner at the same level. If a partner is permanently disabled, it may be to the firm's advantage to buy the disabled partner's interest, but the partnership is not legally compelled to liquidate or reorganize. So long as all partners live, the partnership can continue legally even if one of the partners is inactive. But when a partner dies, the partnership is dissolved.[2] When it is either liquidated or reorganized, the heirs must be paid the value of the deceased partner's interest.

The heirs of the deceased might become partners in the new partnership, but that action would have to satisfy the heirs as well as the surviving partners. A partnership is voluntary in that the law does not force one partner to accept another.

The interest of the deceased may be paid by liquidating the assets of the business and dividing the proceeds proportionately among survivors and heirs. Rarely will this solution prove satisfactory. First, liquidation nearly always results in loss. Second, it means the survivors are out of jobs. In some cases, the business may be sold without a loss as a "going concern" with the survivors retained in an executive capacity, but the survivors might prefer the independence, satisfaction, job security, and profit potential of working for themselves.

Other ways of handling the problem are for the heirs to sell the deceased's interest to a third party, or to buy out the survivors. Usually neither alternative is workable. Finding a buyer acceptable to the surviving partners and willing to pay the purchase price is difficult. Also, rarely will the heirs be willing or able to buy out the survivors.

The most satisfactory solution usually is for the survivors to buy out the heirs. Two problems arise: (1) setting the price and (2) finding the money to finance the purchase. Heirs usually think of the deceased's income as an investment return from the business. They tend to ignore that much of the income was produced from the deceased's service as

---

[2] After dissolution, when a partner withdraws or dies, the firm continues as long as necessary to honor preexisting obligations. However, it may not incur new commitments.

an employee. They expect a price that reflects the return the deceased had been drawing from the partnership. The survivors, faced with replacing the deceased as an employee or with the loss of the business attributable to the deceased, will be thinking in terms of a much lower price.

The solution to the problem of price is a mutually binding buy-and-sell agreement effected among the partners while all are alive and in equal bargaining positions. The agreement either sets a specific price for the share of each partner or, more commonly, a formula for valuation at time of death of a partner.

At the death of a partner, if the price specified is paid to the heirs, the ownership of the deceased's interest is transferred to the survivors who can organize as a new partnership and continue the business.

The risk manager of a partnership should be aware of its legal problems in order to deal properly with its life and health exposures. If the partners have a buy-and-sell agreement, the risk manager also must arrange for the funding of that agreement.

The close corporation exposure

The close (or "closed") corporation is one in which the stock is closely held by a few individuals, in contrast to one whose stock is offered for public sale. Usually the stockholders are company employees, with the relationship among them similar to a partnership. In fact, the close corporation often is called an "incorporated partnership."

If an employee stockholder becomes disabled, the same problems arise as with a disabled partner. If the disability is permanent, either the other stockholders or the corporation itself (if legally permitted) may buy the disabled stockholder's shares. The risk manager must plan for funds to be available when needed to make the purchase.

When a shareholder dies, the corporation's existence is not affected. Whereas the law protects the partners from an unwanted partner, it does not grant similar protection to the surviving stockholders; that is, the heirs have legal ownership of the deceased's shares. Further, if they can find a buyer, they may sell the shares even to a competitor. For the heirs to retain the shares of the deceased may prove unsatisfactory to the survivors and to the heirs. Stock in a close corporation generally is considered a poor investment for minority stockholders, especially when they are not also employees. Because the surviving shareholders usually are employees, they believe that corporation profits are primarily the result of their efforts. They may resent sharing profits with nonproductive shareholders. They may use profits to expand the business or to increase their salaries. While minority stockholders have rights and can demand an accounting to determine if excessive salaries are paid or if profits are reinvested in the business unnecessarily, an investment which leads to bickering, personal recriminations, and even legal actions is not a sound one for the heirs.

A good solution to the problem of the disposition of a deceased stock-holder's shares is for the surviving stockholders (or the corporation if legally permitted) to buy them. The problems involved are the same as those faced in the disposition of the interest of a deceased partner: determining the price and finding the money to pay that price. The risk manager will have to be concerned with the various solutions and execute the most efficient ones.

Life and Health Exposures for the Family

Families, just as businesses, are exposed to income and expense losses due to the perils of death and disability. When a person dies, the estate—assets and debts of the deceased—is evaluated. Debts and taxes must be paid before the remaining estate resources become available to the heirs. Additionally, a family must be concerned with an effort to forecast income needs during the retirement of the breadwinners.

Final expenses

Dying is expensive. To put it bluntly, someone must be paid to dispose of the body. In the majority of cases, doctors' bills, hospital and nursing expenses, and other medical expenses will have accumulated. The spouse also will be left with other bills, such as charge accounts, bank loans, utility bills, accrued taxes, cost of estate administration, and death taxes. The death of any member of the family will cost money, but the major nonmedical expenses usually will be associated with the death of the husband or wife. When an estate includes large amounts of invest-ments, an estate-planning problem may exist. Death can result in a substantial loss to estate property because of federal and state death taxes (a tax on the right to transfer property at death), state inheritance taxes (a tax on the right to receive property after the death of the bene-factor), and other expenses of estate administration.

Because the estate settlement costs must be paid before any property passes to the heirs, the money must be provided from the estate.[3] These costs must be paid in cash. If there is insufficient cash, estate assets that might cause forced sales (which often mean losses) must be liqui-dated. The solution is a periodic review of the estate to estimate as closely as possible the cash needed for estate administration, taxes, and out-standing liabilities at death. Arrangements then should be made to have that amount of cash available.

---

[3] The cost of estate administration, debts, and final expenses has been estimated at 10.2 percent on estates of $500,000, 9.8 percent on estates of $750,000, and 9.5 percent on estates of $1 million. Where no other estate deductions are available (e.g., marital or charitable deductions), taxes can bring these costs to 13.5, 22.4 and 28.2 percent, respectively. These estimates provide rough approximations and wide variation can be found among individual estates.

Adjustment income

Even if the spouses are skillful money managers they may not be able to reduce expenditures immediately upon the death of the bread-winner. In the event of disability, the family will be even less able to cut expenses instantly. First, disabilities create many extra costs, such as special foods and household help, which cannot be covered by medical insurance. Second, disability rarely seems as final as death. The family may continue with its usual budget assuming that the breadwinner will be at work again. The idea may persist for months while savings are exhausted and debts are incurred to maintain the usual standard of living. In today's "easy payment," "consolidate your bills with one loan" economy, many people operate on credit without experiencing its effect until the debt has become crippling. Also, to cut costs over time rather than overnight is easier. An immediate budget cut will add to the psychological strain already suffered because of the tragedy. The family risk manager must recognize the problem of reducing the standard of living following the loss of the breadwinner's income. If possible, arrangements should be made to provide an adjustment income.

Mortgage or rent fund

If the income of the family is lost due to the breadwinner's disability or death, plans must be made for paying the costs of housing. These costs include mortgage or rent payments, property taxes, and home maintenance expenses.

A decision must be made whether or not to pay off the mortgage loan when the breadwinner dies. Even free of debt, the house might be too expensive; but with no mortgage payments to meet, the family may feel no pressure for an immediate sale and can wait for the "right price." However, some mortgage loan agreements may restrict the amount of prepayment, and, in some cases, a prepayment penalty is charged. Furthermore, the contract interest rate for the mortgage loan may be lower than the market rate for new loans, so the family might want to continue the mortgage payments and earn higher interest on the funds that would have been used to prepay the mortgage loan. Also, a low-interest rate mortgage loan will facilitate the sale of the house if the buyer is allowed to assume the existing loan. The family risk manager needs to be aware of the circumstances concerning the mortgage loan so that an efficient decision can be made in financial planning regarding future housing after the disability or death of the breadwinner.

Family period income

The years before the children are self-supporting usually are the financially critical ones. The expense of rearing the children often makes this period financially burdensome. Also, the children's need for parental care and guidance during these years inhibits the mother from entering the labor market, especially when the children are under six. Women's liberation notwithstanding, it may be undesirable for the mother to seek employment outside the home while the children are young. Therefore, if possible, family financial programs should provide enough income for the mother to stay home during the critical preschool period. The budgetary problem of planning a livable income for the family after the death of the breadwinner has been eased by social security, which provides much of the income needed during the child-raising period for moderate-income families.

Lifetime income for the surviving spouse

After the children are grown, the surviving spouse still will need income. Social security benefits are suspended for the years between the time the youngest child reaches age 16 until the widow reaches age 60. Income also will be needed for family support in case the breadwinner is disabled. A widow, for example, may be able to find employment; however, work for older women is not found easily—especially for those who have not worked for many years. If the breadwinner is disabled, the surviving spouse's full-time attention might be required at home. Although the children, now grown, can contribute to the support of the family, this burden on children should be avoided if possible. Also, the remaining parent probably would be unhappy accepting help from his or her children, so the family risk manager may want to plan for the spouse to have a minimum income for life after the children are grown.

Education fund

The importance the family risk manager will attach to financing college educations for children in the event of the death or disability of the breadwinner will vary among individuals. While a college degree has become increasingly important, some people who have been reevaluating educational goals recommend reconsideration of the college education myth (or sheepskin psychosis, as one writer has termed it). They suggest that more attention be given to short-term vocational training in skills for those enrolled in college without a real interest in a college education. Whether the interests and abilities of the children will lie in a college education is difficult to predict. Whether or not the parents expect their children to attend college will influence the family risk manager in the decision concerning an education fund. Often it is too early to know the answer when the planning must be initiated.

Emergency fund

No matter how well the risk manager has provided for the expenses of a family following a loss, unforeseeable events, or "emergencies" requiring the outlay of cash could occur. Thus, the risk manager should consider making provisions for such contingencies.

Expenses resulting from the death of the wife

The death of the wife just as with the demise of any other family member creates burial and other final expenses for which plans must be made. Furthermore, if the wife has an earned income, her death will decrease the family's total income. The loss exposures discussed in the previous sections apply equally to those arising from the premature death or disability of the wife if she is the family's primary breadwinner. However, even if she does not contribute significantly to the family's income, the death of a mother of young children can cause a financial loss for the family. First, the income tax bill will increase because the husband no longer can take advantage of the split-income feature of the tax law, and, at progressive tax rates, the result may be a drain on future income. Second, someone must care for the children. The cost of hiring such a person is deductible in part from taxable income (for federal income tax, but rarely for state or municipal income taxes); however, the deduction will offset only a small part of the cost (except for those in high tax brackets where the cost is of little consequence). Child-care expenses also must be considered if the mother becomes disabled.

Medical expenses

Many of the foregoing loss exposures deal with the income loss of the breadwinner resulting from disability or death. In addition, injury to and sickness of any family member can create medical expenses which represent a large loss potential. When a life is threatened, few people weigh the cost of medical loss in seeking treatment. High-paid specialists will be consulted, if necessary, and concern about payment for their services will be postponed. To perform the task adequately, the family risk manager should understand this psychology, and make suitable arrangements for the loss exposure.

Retirement income

Some people do not look forward to the day when they can "quit work and take it easy," because they find that after 40 years or so, their job has become not only a vocation but also an avocation. Even when employees do not want to quit work, business (if not their heatlh) forces them to retire. Even though compulsory retirement before age 70, subject to some exceptions, is now prohibited by federal law, one still must make plans for a retirement income.

Planning for income in old age is difficult. The increasing standard of living (luxuries steadily are transforming into necessities), the continued growth of superselling to cater to one's weaknesses, progressive income taxation, and lack of expertise in investment all tend to restrict funds that can be accumulated for old age. And although social security and employee retirement plans provide a large part of the retirement income for an increasing number of people, the typical person finds that some or all of accumulated capital must be liquidated to generate the level of retirement income desired. The capital must be withdrawn systematically, however, so that the retired person is not left without an income.

Four needs are important in retirement:

1. An income sufficient for the retired person to live comfortably.
2. An estate clearance fund whenever a person dies. (Arrangements made for this fund should be continued during retirement.)
3. Adequate provisions for medical expenses.
4. Sufficient income for the survivor when the retired husband or wife dies.

Property Exposures for the Business Firm

Three types of property value losses can be identified: loss of the property, loss of its use including loss of income, and extra expenses that may arise because of the destruction of the property. Losses also may occur to property of customers and suppliers. The risk manager must identify and consider a wide variety of perils in risk analysis.

Loss of the property

Risk managers must be aware of all property and its location. They need to consider when title passes on incoming or outgoing goods, whether any goods are stored or processed off premises, where money, securities, and other valuables are kept, how they are moved to and from the bank, whether delivery trucks and other vehicles are always stored in a central garage, or sometimes elsewhere. In listing properties, interests other than those of the tenant or owner should be considered. Among these interests are those of remaindermen, mortgagees, sellers of merchandise under installment purchase plans, and bailees.

Questions must be raised to determine the perils to which the property is exposed. Buildings may be subject to losses resulting from fire, windstorm, hail, explosion, smoke damage, glass breakage, water damage, sprinkler leakage, riot damage, malicious damage, damage by aircraft and other vehicles, earthquake damage, and other perils. Equipment, machinery, stock, and other personal property are exposed to the additional perils of burglary, theft, misplacement, disappearance, temperature changes, breakage, spotting, collision, and others. No perils that could cause a serious loss should be ignored.

Loss to the property may be either direct or indirect and may be on or off premises. The measurement of potential property losses from a single event requires the risk manager to consider all these possibilities. Direct loss or damage may occur on the premises to buildings and their contents. Direct loss also may occur to neighboring buildings, power lines, or equipment damaged by falling trees or walls on the premises. Indirect or consequential loss may result from temperature or humidity changes that damage property. Food stored in a freezer at a university dorm may be spoiled beyond use even to serve university students as a result of a power interruption caused, for example, by lightning. Consequential damage can occur because of the destruction of part of a pair or set. A fire destroys the pants, but the coat is not damaged. The value of the suit coat is significantly reduced.

Loss of use

When property is destroyed or damaged the use of that property is lost. This loss may be reflected in reduced revenues when the property is rented to others or when the owners are barred from using the property. In this category would be loss of profits when caps and gowns burn just prior to graduation. Direct losses would be the cost of the garments. The loss of the rental fees is in addition to the direct loss.

Late on the evening of January 16, 1967, exhibitors at a food equipment show were putting the finishing touches on their displays in the giant McCormick Place in Chicago built in 1960 at a cost of about $40 million. Fire gutted the building. The loss was estimated at about $31 million. However, the loss of income before the premises could be reopened (four years later) was at least as much as the direct loss. The November 1980 fire at the MGM Grand Hotel claimed the lives of 85 people and injured an additional 679. Of the estimated $110 million loss (excluding liability for injuries and deaths), about $60 million was paid by insurers to cover eight months of business interruption preceding the reopening of the hotel. These circumstances are not unusual; yet many risk managers consider direct damage fully without planning for loss of use. Losses caused by business interruption are a major consideration in risk analysis. Sometimes income losses can result from the destruction of property not owned or used by the firm. The study of loss exposures must give the data necessary for determining all potential sources of income losses, so that arrangements can be made to deal with them efficiently.

In measuring income exposures, expenses not continuing after a loss should be deducted from gross income. Noncontinuing expenses often are difficult to estimate. For example, if an apartment building becomes totally untenantable, many expenses can be eliminated; if only one unit is affected, little difference appears in maintenance outlays.

Incomes other than rent must be analyzed as to source. Income losses may be incurred as a result of damage away from the main business properties (e.g., warehouses). Risk managers must consider loss exposures resulting from damage to plants belonging to their subcontractors and to their suppliers of raw materials, parts, fuel, and power. Also of concern is damage to premises belonging to customers and to their customers' customers (and perhaps even to their customers' customers' customers and so on)!

Extra expense

Closely allied to the loss of use is extra expense arising from a peril. A major fire on a college campus may close the area for two months, and cause the school to be closed a full term. If the college decides to continue its operation, using more expensive facilities, the loss will be the increased cost of operations rather than a loss of gross revenues. Newspapers that experience fires often continue operation at increased expenses because they believe that a temporary closing would cause former readers to become interested permanently in a competing paper. Therefore, the publisher determines to remain in business regardless of the extra expenses. The risk manager must plan for this determination.

Property Exposures for the Family

Individuals planning their personal risk management programs will have problems similar to those of the professional risk manager, but generally on a smaller scale.

Loss of the property itself

Individuals must know the extent and location of their property. Householders may have property stored in the garage, at another person's home, at a summer cottage, or in a commercial warehouse. Direct damage to an individual's house, the family car, and other personal property can be caused by the numerous perils listed previously.

Loss of use and extra expense

The typical family exposure to loss of use is additional living expenses arising from the destruction of the family dwelling until it can be restored. The family may have to live at an expensive motel and experience higher food and transportation costs. If the owner rented a room to a student, the rental income would be lost during the same period. Other loss of use exposures may exist. Suppose that Tatiana and her husband are raising tomatoes in their yard to sell at a roadside stand. If the neighborhood children snatch the tomatoes to fling at passersby, the couple will have little or no produce to market, and hence, will suffer an income loss. People who perform services, such as laundry or catering for parties, in their own homes for others are exposed to loss of income if their homes become uninhabitable because of a fire or other peril.

Summary

1. Risk analysis is the process of locating loss exposures, measuring the amount of loss that these exposures can produce, estimating their loss probability, and evaluating the exposures to determine actions necessary to meet risk management objectives.
2. The risk analyst's job is keyed to answering three basic questions:
   a. What can cause loss?
   b. What postloss resources will be necessary to continue effective operation?
   c. What are the most efficient methods of obtaining or reducing the amount of needed postloss resources?
3. In this chapter, the focus is on identifying loss exposures, ignoring other risk analysis procedures.
4. In locating and measuring a business firm's loss exposures, the risk manager should conduct a physical inspection of the premises, study all company contracts, and examine all financial information and supporting records.
5. Businesses must protect themselves from the reduction in revenues or increases in expenses caused by the loss of a key employee as a result of disability, death, or resignation.
6. Sole proprietorships, partnerships, and closely held corporations must be concerned with arrangements to facilitate the transfer of ownership following the death or disability of a proprietor, partner, or shareholder.
7. The family risk manager must plan for handling various family needs following the death or disability of a family member. Some of the needs include: cash for final expenses, adjustment income, mortgage or rent fund, income during the family period, income for the widow after the children are grown, education fund, money for emergencies, cash for expenses attributable to the death of the wife, funds for medical expenses, and retirement income.
8. A business firm is exposed to three types of property value losses:
   a. Loss of the property.
   b. Loss of use.
   c. Extra expenses that arise as a result of the occurrence of a peril.
9. A family is exposed to the same types of property value losses, although loss of property and extra expenses are the predominant ones.

Questions for Review

1. Explain the purpose of risk analysis and its importance to the family and business enterprise. What questions should the analysis answer? How can it be determined whether a risk analysis has been successful?
2. What sources are available to the risk manager of a business to aid his analysis of risks faced by the firm? Are there any drawbacks to the use of the sources you have listed? If so, explain.

3. Describe the most important functions of a risk manager when dealing with a sole proprietorship.

4. Explain the importance of insurance in the task of organizing risk analysis information. If the method of organization which you have described is used, how could it be applied to noninsurance techniques of handling risk?

5. A partnership is a business relationship based on "choice." Explain the legal relationship of partners and the role that "choice" plays in the risk of life exposures faced by the firm.

6. How is the purchase price determined for a buy-and-sell agreement? Explain the use of this agreement in the three types of business organizations discussed in the text.

7. Explain what is meant by the term "final expenses." Discuss the types of expenses incurred when a mother-wife dies. Are these the same types of expenses incurred if she is also the breadwinner? Would the expenses be different if the father-husband died?

8. What is an indirect or consequential loss to property?

9. Explain the various types of loss of use exposure to property.

10. How do property exposures in a business differ from those in a family? How do life and health exposures in a business differ from those in a family? Explain.

Questions for Discussion

1. How is a "key" employee distinguished from an ordinary employee? Why is the distinction important?

2. What life and health exposures exist primarily because of children within a family unit?

3. When a sole proprietor dies, it may be wishful thinking to look upon the business as "insurance" for the surviving family members. Why?

4. When a partner dies, the partnership is dissolved. If a shareholder in a close corporation dies, the shares are passed on to the heirs and the corporation remains intact. Of what use, then, is a buy-and-sell agreement for the shareholders of a close corporation?

5. Do you believe legislation should be enacted prohibiting compulsory retirement on the grounds that such practice is unfairly discriminatory? What problems could such legislation create? Discuss.

6. The mortgage or rent fund has been criticized by one researcher for being inflexible and inadequate to properly provide housing needs during the family period and lifetime of the surviving spouse. In your opinion, what could account for the inadequacy and inflexibility of this fund? How can the problem be solved?

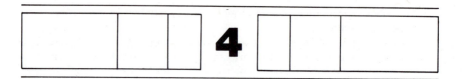

Risk analysis: Liability exposures

It had been a long hot summer in New York. The political atmosphere was tense, and tempers were short. The governor had ideological differences with the president of the United States. Thus it was not too surprising when rioting and looting began July 12. When the disturbance ended four days later, many had died and $2 million in property had been destroyed. Suits totaling $1.3 million were filed against governmental authorities. This incident was the New York "draft riot" of July 1863.

In Greece a widow preparing a funeral banquet made a mistake that has played a pivotal part of many old slapstick film comedies by accidentally adding the wrong ingredient to the cake. The mistake was not made with alum, but with insect poison. Instead of a humorous contraction of the mouth rendering speech impossible, the result was sudden death to nearly 50 mourners.

In a Chicago suburb a car suddenly goes out of control. A bevy of teenagers crossing the street is hit. Four are killed immediately; others suffer permanent injury.

These losses can be compensated in several ways. If the New York residents had riot insurance, they could collect from their insurers. If the Greek widow's victims had life insurance, those insurers would compensate for the deaths. Similarly in Chicago, life and health insurance would offset much of the losses. However, another route to compensation may be available. If New York officials, the widow, or the driver of the car had been *negligent* in their actions, then civil suits could be instituted for damages.

Large and Unexpected Sources of Loss

Liability exposures often result in large losses. In 1975 a Maryland court awarded damages amounting to $12.1 million in a case involving the brutal rape and murder of a young mother. The award included $11.1 million in punitive damages assessed because the defendant, a New York-based real estate conglomerate, had lulled the tenants of the building in which the rape occurred into a false sense of security concerning the safety of the building. Punitive damages are awards to plaintiffs in excess of full compensation for injuries sustained (called compensatory damages) and are made to punish the defendant and discourage others from engaging in conduct causing injuries.

Recently, defective products have produced some of the largest liability settlements. In 1978 a large arms manufacturer agreed to pay $6.8 million to a man who was rendered paraplegic when one of its rifles discharged as the safety was pushed to the "off" position. In 1983 a Georgia court awarded $6 million to a man whose mother died after taking the arthritis drug Oraflex. In addition, the manufacturer, Eli Lilly and Co., faces more than 100 other suits stemming from the use of this drug. A business or family may find itself subject to liability claims from a variety of sources, some of them surprising. A New Jersey resident lent his car to a friend who drove it to New York City and injured a New Yorker. The New Jerseyite was sued for damages. The U.S. Supreme Court ordered the judgment paid even though the New Jersey citizen had not been to New York and, under New Jersey law, would not have been liable for the accident. The Court imposed New York law on the out-of-state car owner.

The legal bases for liability exposures are torts and contracts. These bases are not mutually exclusive in that a person claiming to have been wronged may seek action either under tort or contract, or in some instances under both.

Torts

The word "tort" is derived from the past participle of the Latin verb *torquere*—to twist (from the same root as the word "torture"). A tort has been defined as "A wrongful act committed by one person against another person or his [or her] property. It is the breach of a legal duty imposed by law other than by contract." A tort is a wrong other than a breach of contract for which a civil action can be brought. Although most tort claims arise from negligence, three other grounds are intentional interference, absolute liability, and strict liability.

Intentional torts

If an intentional act committed with the objective of accomplishing a given result causes injury to another, that act may be deemed an intentional tort regardless of whether the intention is to benefit or harm. Unless the actor's conduct is "privileged," the consequences may be liability for intentional tort. (The question of privilege is discussed following the introduction of the types of intentional torts.)

Intentional interference with the person. Intentional torts may be classified as (1) intentional interference with the person and (2) intentional interference with property. Examples of the former are battery, assault, infliction of mental and emotional disturbance, defamation, and false imprisonment.

Battery. Battery is the intentional, unpermitted, and unprivileged contact with the person of others. This action includes contact with anything connected or associated with others, such as the clothes they are wearing, the cars they are driving, or the packages they are carrying. No harm need be done nor any hostility intended. Only the absence of expressed or implied consent of the violated person is necessary to constitute battery. Although any unpermitted intentional contact with another technically is battery, some personal contact is inevitable. A person is assumed to consent to contact customary in everyday life. Thus a friendly grasp of the arm would not be considered battery.

Assault. Assault is an attempt at or a physical threat of violence to another. It differs from battery in that assault involves apprehension over threatened contact, whereas battery requires actual physical contact. An intent to carry out a threat is not a factor in an assault; a belief by the threatened person that the threat may materialize is sufficient cause for action. If one aims a pistol at a person, such action would constitute assault if it causes apprehension. If the person is unaware of the aimed pistol, no assault is committed because no apprehension is involved. Neither verbal threats nor insults are assaults unless accompanied by threatening gestures. Assault and battery frequently accompany one another. A threat of violence followed by violence would subject the actor to liability for assault and battery.

Mental distress. Liability may arise from intentional acts that cause someone mental or emotional distress which is proven to be both severe and extreme. Insults or abuses merely causing simple anxiety do not offer grounds for liability. Serious physical illness arising from the mental distress often is necessary to qualify for damages. A creditor, for example, who repeatedly threatens and harasses a debtor, causing the debtor to suffer a nervous breakdown can be held liable for infliction of emotional distress.

Defamation. Defamation involves actions which injure another's reputation. Defamatory acts may be either libel or slander. Historically, libel was a written defamation whereas slander was oral. New forms of communication have blurred the distinction between libel and slander. The trend is to base the distinction on the permanence of the form of defamation or on its potential harm with the more permanent or harmful forms considered libelous. To be actionable, defamatory statements must be intentionally or negligently communicated to *someone other than the defamed party.* Where a basis for tort action exists, the defamed party need establish only that (1) the action was intentional or negligent and (2) the defamatory meaning is reasonably understood by others. The treatment of libel and slander differs substantially among jurisdictions, with the present state of the law characterized by inconsistency and confusion.[1]

False imprisonment. The intentional restraint of another's freedom of movement may impose liability for false imprisonment. While the restraint may be brief, it must be total for liability to occur. The restraint must be intended but does not have to be malicious. Thus, even if the actor believes the restraint is necessary for the good of the person restrained, the actor may be liable for false imprisonment. Furthermore, the restraint need not be physical, but may consist of threats of force which intimidate another into compliance with the actor's wishes. For example, Hofflander and Hammond are in a room. Hammond threatens bodily harm to Hofflander if he leaves the room. In submission, Hofflander remains. Hammond could be held liable for false imprisonment. False imprisonment must not be confused with malicious prosecution: the malicious institution of groundless criminal proceedings against another person.

Intentional interference with property. Trespass to real or personal property and conversion are examples of actionable intentional interference with property.

Trespass. Trespass to real property arises from the wrongful entry on the land of another or failure to remove property from another's land when an obligation exists to do so. Trespass includes invasion of the area above and below the land as well as the surface of the land. Intentional invasion requires no proof of damage to establish liability, whereas intrusion without the knowledge of the intruder requires proof of damage before liability can be imposed. Trespass to personal property arises from intentional interference with its possession or physical con-

---

[1] See Chapter 5 for an explanation of how to use a law library to find the law for a particular jurisdiction.

dition, without legal justification. Proof of damage usually is required to establish a cause of action. As in trespass to real property, an innocent mistake is no defense against liability.

Conversion. Conversion is the intentional interference with the personal property of others which deprives the owner of its use and possession to such a degree that a forced sale of the property to the converter is justified. Conversion is accomplished by: (1) taking possession of goods to exercise control adverse to the owner; (2) depriving the owner of control through an unauthorized transfer of goods, as in the misdelivery of goods by a bailee; (3) refusing to surrender goods to one who has a right to them; (4) misusing the goods in defiance of the owners, such as driving a car left at the garage to be washed; and (5) intentional damage to, destruction of, or alteration of the property, such as changing the appearance of a stolen coat. The main purpose of tort law dealing with conversion is to give wronged persons a cause of action in a civil court to recover the property value for which they were wrongfully deprived.

Privilege. An individual will not be held liable for an intentional tort if the conduct is privileged. The purpose of privilege is to allow a person freedom to act in a manner which serves the public interest. Whether or not the conduct of an individual will be deemed privileged will depend on the circumstances involved and the attitude of the court. Persons have no advance assurance their conduct is privileged and not subject to tort liability. Common types of privilege are mistakes, consent, and protective acts.

Mistakes. Mistakes are privileged under limited conditions. An act may be privileged if the actor moves quickly to protect a right believed to be endangered, even if the party is mistaken. Thus, a person may be privileged to use force as a defense regardless of whether the defense was necessary.

Consent. Certain acts are privileged if the actor reasonably infers the consent of the party upon whom the act is committed. For example, a person is privileged to kiss the lips offered, and consequently could not be held liable for battery even if the offerer is displeased with the results.

Protective acts. A person is privileged to use reasonable force to prevent interference with one's property or person. One may also use reasonable force to defend others if they are privileged to defend themselves. The jury decides what is reasonable force. Shooting a child in the act of stealing a bicycle would not be considered reasonable, whereas shooting a rapist while the rape is in progress would probably be deemed reasonable force by the jury and thus privileged. Suppose Linda Smith noticing someone stealing her excellent *Principles of Insurance* textbook (this one), grabs the thief and threatens a thrashing unless the classic is returned. She would not be liable for false imprisonment, assault, or battery because of the protective acts privilege.

Absolute liability

Absolute liability, also known as *liability without fault,* is imposed when public policy demands a person be held liable for injury to others although the injury may be neither intentionally nor negligently inflicted. Examples of this type of liability include: damage arising out of vibrations of the earth set in motion by blasting operations, operation of aircraft, storage of explosives and keeping domestic animals known to have dangerous tendencies (a sign saying DANGER—BAD DOG, is a dead giveaway!). Maintaining wild animals imposes absolute liability on their keepers even if the animals are domesticated. The foregoing rules are subject to local modification and interpretation. Keepers of elephants would have absolute liability imposed on them if they live in Cairo, Illinois, but not if they live in Rangoon, Burma. The rationale of absolute liability is that in ultradangerous activity in which losses are almost inevitable, the loss is shifted to those best able to control it.

Strict liability

Strict liability, as compared to absolute liability, most commonly is applied to products liability. Under the concept of strict liability, manufacturers and merchandisers of goods are held liable for injuries caused by defective products sold by them, regardless of the manufacturers' fault or negligence. Strict liability is distinguished from absolute liability in that the claimant must prove the product defective and that the defect made the product unreasonably dangerous. Furthermore, manufacturers may not be held liable for experimental products that prove to be defective, or for those that are unavoidably unsafe. The claimant also must prove the defect in the product existed at the time of sale, that such defect was the proximate cause of the injury, and that the product was being used for its intended purpose in order to recover. If the injured party proves these facts, the defendant is held "strictly" liable (without regard to fault or negligence). Thus strict liability is not absolute.

Drastic changes in the operation of strict liability would result, however, if a new bill pending in Congress is enacted. The Senate Commerce Committee has approved a measure that would require the claimant to prove negligence on the part of the manufacturer in addition to the aforementioned facts concerning the defect and injury. Further, punitive damages would be limited to the first claimant to bring such a suit, thus protecting a firm against punitive awards to victims filing subsequent actions. It is not surprising that the bill has the support of attorneys representing manufacturing and drug companies, and the opposition of those who represent consumers in products liability cases. Advocates for both sides agree that, if the measure becomes law, awards are likely to decrease in number and amount.

Although risk managers for business must be aware of and plan for the adverse effects of intentional torts and absolute liability, they should be most concerned with strict liability and liability arising from negligence. Family risk managers also should be concerned with all tort exposures but their primary emphasis is liability resulting from negligence. The interest of risk managers in the tort exposure is twofold: (1) the exposure to loss caused by a tort action against them and (2) the opportunity to be indemnified for loss through tort actions against those causing the loss. Tort actions, therefore, not only are important sources of losses but also provide major postloss resources.

Negligence

Everyone is exposed to loss from damage claims arising out of allegations of negligence. The law imposes an obligation on all persons to use care in their actions. People must use prudence in conducting their affairs so they do not cause others to suffer bodily injury or property damage. If one fails to perform as a reasonable and prudent person (either by doing what a prudent person ordinarily would not do or by not doing what a prudent person ordinarily would do) under similar circumstances a negligent act may have been committed if someone is injured. "Injury" means either bodily injury or property damage. Whenever a person is injured through failure of another to exercise the standard of care required by law, that person has a right of action against the wrongdoer (called the *tort-feasor*). Damage claims may be made and, if substantiated, damages may be awarded the injured party by the court.

Negligence is the act of an unreasonable and imprudent person. Often it results from carelessness or thoughtlessness, but it may be due to forgetfulness, bad temper, ignorance, bad judgment, or stupidity. Negligence never involves intent. A husband who deliberately runs over his wife and her boyfriend as they leave a tavern is guilty of battery, not negligence (although leaving his wife with time on her hands and the opportunity to meet other men may be negligence). The husband, however, who, in his haste to reach the tavern before the departure of the couple, runs a red light and hits a stranger, is guilty of negligence. The negligent person has no desire to cause harm but behaves in a manner that creates unreasonable danger to others. The standard by which "reasonableness" is measured is based on what society expects of the individual rather than what the individual considers reasonable. The conduct must be reasonable in view of the risk involved. Chief Justice Learned Hand once expressed it algebraically as the probability of an occurrence called P, the injury L, and the burden of adequate precautions B. "Liability depends upon whether B is less than L multiplied by P; that is, whether B is less than PL."[2]

---

[2] *U.S.* v. *Carroll Towing Co.*, 2 Cir., 1947, 159 F.2d 169.

The standard of care that an owner or tenant owes trespassers is less than ordinary, except when attractive nuisances are involved. An attractive nuisance is any novel device particularly enticing to children, such as an unusual piece of machinery or a swimming pool. Owners and tenants are required to give sufficient warning or protection to children who may be attracted to these potentially dangerous devices. Defenses available are that the child was old enough to perceive the danger or that the device was common to the locality and therefore not novel. A study of court decisions, however, demonstrates the difficulty of avoiding liability through use of the defenses.

In many states the doctrine of attractive nuisance has been replaced by Section 339 of the *Restatement of Torts (Second)*. Under this statute the owners or tenants are held liable for injuries to trespassing children under the following conditions: (1) They may maintain on their property a condition which may be reasonably expected to attract children incapable of perceiving the hazards, and (2) the condition provides the owner or tenant small utility compared to the risk involved for young children. The defenses available to landlords and tenants are that the owner or tenant could not be reasonably expected to know the condition would attract children and that the condition was unreasonably hazardous to children. A third defense is that the utility of the condition to the owner or tenant was far greater than the disutility of the hazards involved.

With the adult trespasser, the owner or tenant need only avoid deliberate injury. Recently, a burglar tried to break into a vacant Iowa farmhouse and was greeted with a blast from a shotgun set to hit anyone opening the door. The Iowa court awarded over $50,000 damages to this trespasser. The judgment was sustained by the higher court. The standard of care required for licensees (those on the premises with permission but for their own benefit, such as to use the phone) is less than ordinary but greater than that owed a trespasser. The standard of care required for invitees (persons on the premises for the benefit of the owner or tenant) is greater than that owed trespassers and licensees. If the invitees are social guests they must prove more than ordinary carelessness to substantiate a tort claim. If, however, the invitee is on the premises for the exclusive benefit of the owner or tenant (for example, a friend repairing the TV set gratis), the standard of care required is greater than ordinary. What constitutes ordinary care and the gradations of care required are decided by the courts, and the courts seem to believe the "prudent man" of today is more careful than his grandparents. The result is that an increasing standard of care is expected.

Three states have eliminated the distinctions among trespasser, licensee, and invitee as a method of differentiating the standard of care required. The California Supreme Court in *Rowland* v. *Christian* stated:

> A man's life or limb does not become less worthy of protection by the law nor a loss less worthy of compensation under the law because he has come upon the land of another without permission or with permission without a business purpose. Reasonable people do not ordinarily vary their conduct depending upon such matters, and to focus upon the status of the injured party as a trespasser, licensee, or invitee in order to determine the question

of whether the landowner has a duty of care, is contrary to our modern social mores and humanitarian values. The common law rules obscure rather than illuminate the proper considerations which should govern determination of the question of duty.[3]

The Supreme Court of Hawaii in *Packard* v. *City and County of Honolulu* and the Supreme Court of Rhode Island in *Mariorengi* v. *Joseph DiPonte, Inc.* expressed similar sentiments.[4] Aside from these states, no broadly based move has yet developed to dispose of the classifications of trespasser, invitee, and licensee in evaluating the standard of care required. The majority opinion at present is that reasonableness and fairness require a lesser degree of care toward trespassers than toward licensees and invitees. However courts change their views to reflect current attitudes. Therefore, the present position cannot be relied upon to continue, creating a juridical risk in this area of law.

The reasonable man

In negligence cases the judge may decide that the judgment of reasonable men could not differ in deciding if the tort-feasor has conformed to the particular standard required. Or, the judge may rule that reasonable men might differ in the determination of the standard of conduct required. In that event the jury will decide the issue. Much hinges on the definition of the "reasonable man."

A. P. Herbert, British humorist, poet, and long-time independent member of Parliament for Oxford discusses the reasonable man.

> The Common Law of England has been laboriously built about a mythical figure—the figure of "The Reasonable Man." In the field of jurisprudence this legendary individual occupies the place which in another science is held by the Economic Man, and in social and political discussions by the Average or Plain Man. He is an ideal, a standard, the embodiment of all those qualities which we demand of the good citizen. No matter what may be the particular department of human life which fails to be considered in these Courts, sooner or later we have to face the question: Was this or was it not the conduct of a reasonable man? Did the plaintiff take such precautions to inform himself of the circumstances as any reasonable man would expect of an ordinary person having the ordinary knowledge of an ordinary person of the habits of wild bulls when goaded with gardenforks and the persistent agitation of red flags?
>
> * * * * *
>
> He is one who invariably looks where he is going, and is careful to examine the immediate foreground before he executes a leap or a bound; who neither star-gazes nor is lost in meditation when approaching trapdoors or the margin of a dock; who never mounts a moving omnibus and does not alight from any car while the train is in motion; who investigates exhaustively the bona fides of every mendicant before distributing alms,

---

[3] 70 Cal. Rptr., 97, 443 P.2d 561 (Calif. 1968).

[4] 452 P.2d 446 (Hawaii 1969) and 333 Atl. 2d 127 (Rhode Island 1975).

and will inform himself of the history and habits of a day before administering a caress; who believes no gossip, nor repeats it, without firm basis for believing it to be true; who never drives his ball till those in front of him have definitely vacated the putting-green which is his own objective; who never from one year's end to another makes an excessive demand upon his wife, his neighbours, his servants, his ox, or his ass; who in the way of business looks only for the narrow margin of profit which twelve men such as himself would reckon to be "fair," and contemplates his fellow merchants, their agents, and their goods, with that degree of suspicion and distrust which the law deems admirable; who never swears, gambles, or loses his temper, who uses nothing except in moderation, and even while he flogs his child is meditating only on the golden mean. Devoid, in short, of any human weakness, with not one single saving vice, sans prejudice, procrastination, ill-nature, avarice, and absence of mind, as careful for his own safety as he is for that of others, this excellent but odious creature stands like a monument in our Courts of Justice, vainly appealing to his fellow citizens to order their lives after his own example.[5]

Herbert goes on to point out "that in all that mass of authorities which bears upon this branch of the law there is no single mention of a reasonable woman." The assumption is made that the term "man" encompasses the whole human race, and thus includes women.

The reasonable man is assumed to have the minimum perception, memory, experience, and information common to the community and to have normal intelligence and mental capacity. The legally insane, children, and those who are senile have a lesser standard applied to them. Persons engaged in practicing a trade or profession are expected to have the minimum knowledge necessary to practice that trade or profession.

Presumed negligence

When Charles Edmonds was taken for his postoperative X rays following his appendectomy, a piece of metal shaped like a barbless fishhook could be seen where his appendix had resided just three days earlier. Although murmurings were heard among his friends about how he probably choked on one of his preposterous fish stories and accidentally swallowed his own line (one wag even commented that maybe Charlie really had finally hooked a big one), the subsequent invasion of his abdomen produced a surgical sewing needle and not the anticipated fishhook. If Edmonds brings suit against the surgeon, the court will likely relieve him of the burden of proving negligence, and apply instead the common-law doctrine of *res ipsa loquitor* ("the thing speaks for itself"). *Res ipsa loquitor* is used to establish presumed negligence when the court believes the facts alone constitute a legally sufficient case of negligence. The doctrine is applied where it may be difficult or impossible to prove negligence (e.g., doctors are reluctant to testify against one another in a negligence case), or where the conditions and circumstances surround-

---

[5] A. P. Herbert, *Misleading Cases in Common Law* (London, 1930), pp. 12 ff.

ing an accident clearly suggest that a finding other than negligence would be unreasonable.

Presumed negligence exists when (1) the thing (meaning either the action or the object) which caused the injury was defective, (2) the injury could not reasonably have occurred without the defendant's negligence, and (3) the thing causing injury was in the control of the defendant.

Types of cases in which presumed negligence is applied include accidents where no witnesses are available, transportation disasters, professional malpractice claims (especially medical malpractice), and products liability cases. The last of these would appear to present substantial problems for the claimant because he or she (and not the defendant) is usually in control of the product when the injury occurs. Yet the courts have held that, due to the manufacturer's control over product design and quality, and the consumer's ignorance of all but the proper use of the product, the doctrine of *res ipsa loquitor* may be applied only if the product had not been altered since its manufacture. Thus, a finding was handed down for the claimant when a woman suffered a frozen hand (frost bite—not icy applause) and was knocked unconscious after receiving a severe electrical shock from a defective refrigerator.

However, a number of circumstances can preclude the application of presumed negligence. The doctrine will not be applied if the plaintiff is guilty of contributory negligence. If any other means, including physical conditions, could have caused the injury, presumed negligence cannot be relied upon by the plaintiff. For example, if the electrical shock from the refrigerator occurred when the claimant was barefoot and standing in 12 inches of flood water that had inundated her kitchen (presumably the refrigerator also would be in 12 inches of water), the manufacturer might have avoided liability. Avoidance could have been based on contributory negligence (one should never go wading with a refrigerator that is still plugged in) or on the presence of a physical condition that could have contributed to the cause of the loss (most refrigerators are not designed to operate in a foot of water). Similarly, if the thing causing the loss is beyond the control of the defendant, an action based on the presumed negligence doctrine will not be allowed. Finally, any contribution to the loss from a third party or from physical or mechanical actions will negate presumed negligence. Had the injury from the defective refrigerator occurred during a violent electrical storm, defense attorneys might have successfully argued that the injury could have been the result of a power surge. Power surges are frequently generated when lightning strikes power lines or transformers during electrical storms. Thus, the doctrine is applied when the defendant's behavior is the only cause of the accident.

Imputed negligence

The negligence of one party may be held to be the responsibility of another under the doctrine of imputed negligence (vicarious liability).

An employer whose employee commits a negligent act, may be held liable. (The employee may be held liable in addition to the employer.) An employer who hires an independent contractor can be made responsible for the contractor's actions if the employer was negligent in selecting the contractor provided faulty tools or improper directions. If auto owners lend their vehicles to someone else, they may be held liable for losses caused by the driver. Thus, while presumed negligence cannot be applied where a third party is involved in an accident, imputed negligence can hold a third party liable even though that party is only indirectly connected to the tort-feasors actions.

Liability Arising from Negligence

Allegations of negligence present major problems in tort liability. Art Buchwald has said that the American Dream is to be hit accidentally by a Greyhound bus or a Coca-Cola truck. Although the folklore is that to collect, one need only be injured in this manner, it is not that simple.

Essential elements of a negligent act

Four elements of a negligent act are essential for a court to award damages: (1) the existence of a legal duty to protect the injured party, (2) a breach of that duty, (3) an injury to the person, property, legal rights, or reputation must be suffered by the claimant, and (4) a reasonably close causal relationship between the breach of duty and the claimant's injury.

Existence of a duty to protect the injured party. A station wagon slowly sinks into the Wabash River. The driver, with great difficulty, crawls from inside the vehicle to its roof. People on the bank listen to the motorist's pleas for help indicating an inability to swim! The onlookers stand mute as the victim drowns. Have the relatives a cause of action against these watchers? Suppose that the Indiana swimming team is on the bank; would the victim's survivors have a valid case against them? The law is clear. For a successful suit a duty must exist to exercise a particular standard of care toward the victim.

The law does not impose on anyone the obligation to aid another in distress and even may penalize a good samaritan. Because Doug Shroyer, a poor swimmer, jumped into the water to aid a drowning child, Marcia Morey, an excellent swimmer, refrained. Had Doug not made the unsuccessful attempt, Marcia would have made the rescue. If Doug failed in his rescue attempt he might be sued by the family of the decedent. If the child were drowning in a swimming pool, the owner, the operator, as well as the lifeguard who had been ogling a scantily clad swimmer all might be liable for the drowning.

To whom duty is owed is a vast and complicated question. The answer varies with changing social conditions, the ability of the litigants to bear the losses, the encouragement of greater care in the future, ease of administration, and many other factors. Whether a duty was owed a litigant and whether that duty was breached is decided by the courts. The judge decides questions of law and the jury questions of fact. Unfortunately, negligence cases usually are not divisible into two such neat compartments, and juries are not experts. The prevalence of unwarranted verdicts and awards has led some members of the bar to call for the abolition of jury trials in negligence cases. A character in a popular novel puts the matter nicely:

> Did Levine have a lawyer? A specialist in accident cases? If not, he recommended Coniff, on Court Street. Coniff the *Goniff.* Out of a cracked sidewalk, a rusty nail, a cigarette burn, a piece of bad wiring, he mounted claims for thousands. Let two A&P shopping carts collide and a son went through medical school.[6]

Often awards allegedly are made on the basis of ability to pay (i.e., the size of the insurance policy available) or other extralegal grounds. Some members of the bar question whether abolition of jury trials would solve the problem and argue that serious reform of the judiciary also is necessary.

Breach of that duty. The plaintiff must show that the alleged tort-feasor not only had a duty to the injured person but that the duty was breached. A trial judge may conclude that the defendant performed that duty and thus dismiss the case. However, most often, the facts are nebulous, causing the judge to turn them over to the jury. So questions concerning breach of duty nearly always are decided by jurors.

Injury must be suffered by the claimant. For the plaintiff's suit to be successful, the injury must have resulted from a breach of duty. The injury may be property damage, bodily injury, loss of income, and such harm as humiliation, pain, and suffering.

The general rule is that mental disturbance is not considered an injury unless physical harm also is involved. Cases concerning alleged injury because of the plaintiff's reaction to harm caused another generally have not been successful. Thus, a person who suffers a heart attack from seeing a child hit by a train would have no cause of action against the railroad. In a Louisiana case, suit was brought by a bystander who, observing a truck crash into a gasoline pump, "suddenly became overwhelmed by fear and realized for the first time in his life that he was not the omnipotent, fearless man his psyche had envisioned him to be." He alleged that this realization "precipitated great emotional and psychic tensions manifesting themselves as psychosomatic headaches, pains in legs and such, a loss of general interest, a disposition to withdraw from social and family contacts and the like." The court denied the claim and hinted that the man should be grateful for his return to

---

[6] Wallace Markfield, *To an Early Grave* (New York: Simon & Schuster, 1964).

reality by being forced "to leave Mount Olympus to rejoin the other mortals in Baton Rouge." However, had the plaintiff suffered the same symptoms after physical involvement in the accident, the court decision likely would have been different.

The rule denying recovery for emotional distress suffered by bystanders recently has been modified in several negligence cases. A California court awarded a mother damages for emotional illness resulting from viewing her son shortly after he was injured by a negligently caused explosion.[7] Recovery of bystanders for negligently caused emotional illness, however, is still limited, usually requiring (1) the plaintiff to be near the scene of the occurrence, (2) the event to cause a direct emotional impact, and (3) the existence of a close relationship between the plaintiff and victim. Recovery by bystanders in negligence cases is expected to increase during the next few years.

Reasonably close causal relationship.   The final essential is a reasonably close causal relationship between the breach of duty and the claimant's injury. The breach of duty must be a *proximate cause* of the injury. In a sense, any act may be said to have its origin in the beginning of time and that the consequences of an act go forward to the day of doom. Courts often must decide whether a result was a direct consequence of a particular act, and although these events neither originate with the dawn of civilization nor go forward to the day of doom, they do cause much litigation. A homeowner is burning leaves in the yard. A strong wind begins and the fire spreads, destroying a neighbor's house. Is the leaf burner liable for the loss of the house next door? Suppose that the fire spreads to destroy the entire block?

A bank teller negligently sets off a burglar alarm. In the rush to reach the bank, a law officer runs a red light and causes a multiple-car collision. Is the bank teller liable?[8]

During World War I, the powder magazine on Black Tom Island in New York Harbor exploded. Concussion damage was suffered in a 25–30 mile radius. Was the federal government liable for these losses? New York courts said no, in the Black Tom case. New York courts, alone, hold that the consequences must be quite close in time and space for liability to exist. The leaf burner is responsible for burning the adjacent house, but is absolved from liability if additional houses are destroyed. (In Kansas, liability is limited to within four miles of the negligently set fire.) In all other courts remoteness in time and space will be important but not decisive factors in determining liability.

In many cases the problem of causation can be handled by the *sine qua non* (without which not) rule. Under this rule, a person's conduct is not held to be the cause of the loss if the loss would have occurred anyway. For example, the Supreme Court of Minnesota found that the failure of a train to give required bell and whistle signals upon approach-

---

[7] *Archibald* v. *Braverman,* 79 Cal. Rptr. 723 (4 Dist. 1969).
[8] See *Gasset* v. *Burnett* 164 SE 2d 578 (S.C. 1967).

ing a crossing was not the proximate cause of a collision between the train and an approaching auto because the auto struck the 68th car of the train. The court stated

> Where so long a train has gotten so much of its length over a crossing only to have an automobile driven into its rear by a grossly negligent chauffeur, who admits to a speed of 35 miles per hour at the moment, it is futile to argue that the failure to make use of the signals, assuming, contrary to convincing evidence, that there was such a failure, was a proximate cause.[9]

When the rule of *sine qua non* is not applicable, other factors must be considered. Furthermore, the *sine qua non* rule does not mean that liability always will be automatic if the injury would not have occurred without the action of the defendant. Other factors will still be considered before an action is held to be the proximate cause of the loss.

If an act has unforeseeable consequences, no liability will exist. Usually however, a person will be held liable for all direct consequences stemming from a breach of duty even though no reasonable person would have expected such results. Sometimes an intervening cause is present, and if it is unforeseen, courts usually will find the defendant not liable. As for the leaf-burning homeowner, if there had been no wind when the fire was set, a sudden violent windstorm, scattering leaves and thus setting fire to other houses probably would not create liability for the losses. An ordinary wind sufficient to spread the fire to the neighbor's house would not permit the leaf burner to escape liability.

In *Palsgraf* v. *Long Island Railroad,* the N.Y. Court of Appeals was asked to decide a case in which proximate cause played a key role. A New Yorker with a ticket for Rockaway Beach was standing on the platform when a train pulled in headed for another destination. Two men ran to catch this train. One reached it safely, although the train was moving. The other carrying a package jumped aboard the car but teetered on the edge of the steps as if he were about to fall. A guard on the train, who had held the door open for him, reached forward to pull him in, while a platform guard pushed him in from behind. During this effort, the package which contained fireworks fell to the rails and exploded. The shock of the explosion upset some scales at the other end of the platform many feet away and struck the plaintiff, still waiting for the Rockaway Beach train. She brought suit against the railroad.

Justice Cardoza, speaking for the majority, denied the claim. He said,

> The conduct of the defendant's guard, if a wrong in its relation to the holder of the package, was not a wrong in its relation to the plaintiff standing far away. Relative to her it was not negligence at all. Nothing in the situation gave notice that the falling package had in it the potency of peril to persons thus removed. Negligence is not actionable unless it involves the invasion of a legally protected interest, the violation of a right.

And later;

---

[9] *Sullivan* v. *Boone,* 1935, 205 Minn. 437.

One who jostles one's neighbor in a crowd does not invade the rights of others standing at the outer fringe when the unintended contact casts a bomb upon the ground. The wrongdoer as to them is the man who carries the bomb, not the one who explodes it without suspicion of the danger. Life will have to be made over, and human nature transformed, before prevision so extravagant can be accepted as the norm of conduct, the customary standard to which behavior must conform. [248 NY 309, 225 NY Supp. 412, 162 NE 99 (1928).]

This decision has been accepted in section 430 of the *Restatement of Torts (Second),* but many courts in similar situations have awarded damages on grounds that the causal connection was sufficient. Understanding the difficulty in making substantive statements about whether or not an act will be deemed the proximate cause of an injury is important. In most cases, the decision will be the function of numerous variables rather than based on clear-cut rules.

Defenses in negligence actions

An injured person may prove all four of the foregoing points and yet not be awarded damages. Several defenses are available to the defendant to defeat the plaintiff's suit. The two principal ones in negligence actions are the allegation of contributory negligence and the assumption of risk, both having first appeared at the beginning of the 19th century.

A few courts hold that an essential part of the plaintiff's case is to show freedom from assumption of risk and contributory negligence. In these jurisdictions, the burden of proof is on the plaintiff. In the vast majority of courts, however, the defendant must prove either of these conditions if used as a defense.

Assumption of risk. Assumption of risk as a defense argues that the plaintiff consented expressly or by implication to relieve the defendant of the duty to protect, and accepted the chance of injury from the particular risk causing the injury. The risk may be assumed by written agreement, as in leases signed by apartment renters. The lease may waive the tenant's right of action against the landlord as well as require the tenant to assume liability to others that normally would lie with the landlord. Thus Ms. Ferber may agree that if an invitee trips over a broom left in the hall by the janitor, she, rather than the landlord, will be liable for any injuries.

The more interesting and troublesome cases arise in the absence of a written agreement. Jeff Shade and Molly Sills are wrestling. Molly slams Jeff to the mat breaking Jeff's nose. Does Jeff have a cause of action against Molly? No, the presumption is assumption of risk. Suppose that Jeff picks up Molly and throws her off the mat onto the lap of a spectator. Does the spectator have a cause of action against Jeff? Once again the answer is no. Justice Cardoza, in rejecting such a claim for damages, once wrote: "The timorous may stay at home."

Contributory negligence. The defendant in a negligence action may use as a defense the allegation of contributory negligence. If the plaintiff's conduct failed to meet the standard required for his or her own protection, and that failure contributed as a legal cause of the loss, he or she may be denied recovery. The existence of contributory negligence does not relieve the defendant of any duty toward the plaintiff, but rather denies the plaintiff recovery if both parties are at fault.

The first case *(Butterfield* v. *Forrester)* involving contributory negligence was tried in 1809.[10] Forrester was repairing his house and in the process had blocked part of the public highway with a pole. However, he had left a passageway on the far side of the road. Butterfield left a pub at dusk and, riding fast into the twilight, hit the pole and was thrown to the road, with severe injury. The judge directed the jury that "if a person riding with reasonable and ordinary care could have seen and avoided the obstruction; and if they were satisfied that the plaintiff was riding along the street extremely hard, and without ordinary care, they should find a verdict for the defendant." The jury so found and held for the defendant. Lord Ellenborough, the chief justice, commented:

> A party is not to cast himself upon an obstruction which has been made by the fault of another and avail himself of it, if he does not himself use common and ordinary caution to be in the right. In cases of persons riding upon what is considered to be the wrong side of the road, that would not authorize another purposely to ride up against them. One person being in fault will not dispense with another's using ordinary care for himself.

In using the words "he" and "himself" the judge did not mean to exclude women for they also can be guilty of contributory negligence.

Two variations of the contributory negligence rule have been widely used: the doctrines of *comparative negligence* and of *last clear chance.* The contributory negligence rule, in most courts, places on the plaintiff the entire burden of a loss for which both the plaintiff and defendant are responsible. The defendant may be grossly negligent, the plaintiff slightly negligent, yet the operation of the doctrine relieves the grossly negligent from any responsibility. This result has led to the development in a few jurisdictions of the doctrine of comparative negligence in which the court (often the jury) attempts to scale the verdict according to the comparative degrees of negligence of the two parties. Some states have statutes providing for such apportionment of damages. A few courts and legislatures also have tried to grade the degrees of negligence to provide that certain combinations of gross and ordinary negligence shall be treated in a particular way. Thus a plaintiff guilty of ordinary negligence would be allowed to collect from a grossly negligent defendant. The apportionment of damages between two parties involved in an accident may be relatively simple, but what about the case of a 22-car superhighway accident?

The most widespread modification of the doctrine of contributory

---

[10] 103 Eng. Rep. 926 (KB 1809).

negligence is the doctrine of last clear chance. A large number of courts accept this doctrine in some form. It originated in *Davies* v. *Mann,* tried in England in 1842. The plaintiff had fettered his ass on the public highway, where it was hit by the defendant. The jury found for the plaintiff and returned a verdict for 40 shillings or £2 (the good old days—$9.50 for an ass at current exchange rates). The judge asked the jury to ignore that the animal was on the highway illegally, and that if they

> were of the opinion that it was caused by the fault of the defendant's servant in driving too fast, or, which is the same thing, at a smartish pace, the mere fact of putting the ass upon the road would not bar the plaintiff of his action. . . . Were this not so, a man might justify the driving over goods left on the public highway, or even over a man lying asleep there, or the purposely running against a carriage going on the wrong side of the road.

The most acceptable form of the last clear chance doctrine to the courts is where the plaintiff is unable to avoid the peril because of prior negligence, and the defendant, by proper care, could discover that peril in time. Where both plaintiff and defendant were inattentive, the doctrine does not apply.

Role of the jury.   The jury often plays a crucial role in negligence cases as illustrated by *Rush* v. *Commercial Realty Company.* The Commercial Realty Company owned the house in which Mrs. Rush lived and also the adjacent house. The landlord provided a detached privy for the use of both houses. Mrs. Rush, while using this privy, fell nine feet through the floor, or a trapdoor, into the accumulation at the bottom, and had to be extricated by use of a ladder. The defendant denied the existence of a pit and claimed the floor was only nine inches above ground. This alleged fact, like several other features of the case, presented a disputed question for the jury. The judge noted that the jury had found the facts to be favorable for Mrs. Rush, as follows:

> . . . the situation was that of a building under the control of the landlord for the use of tenants generally, and maintained by the landlord; a consequent duty of care in maintenance; a defective condition in the floor which the jury might say was due to negligent maintenance by the defendant; and an accident resulting therefrom. In such a situation, it would seem that the argument for a nonsuit or for a direction must be restricted to the questions of contributory negligence and assumption of risk. In dealing with these, it should be observed that Mrs. Rush had no choice, when impelled by the calls of nature, but to use the facilities placed at her disposal by the landlord, to wit, a privy with a trapdoor in the floor, poorly maintained. We hardly think this was the assumption of a risk; she was not required to leave the premises and go elsewhere. Whether it was contributory negligence to step on a floor, which she testified was in bad order, was a question for the jury to solve according to its finding of the conditions and her knowledge of them, or what she should have known of them; it does not seem to be a court question.

Statutory modifications of the common law of negligence

The common law of negligence has been modified by statute. The courts with some important recent exceptions (the doctrine of charitable immunity, the defense of "open and obvious," and the abolition in some states of the doctrine of assumed risk, for some examples) appear reluctant to make substantial changes in common law, holding that such changes usually should be reserved for the legislature. The doctrines of the last clear chance or of comparative negligence have been embodied in the statutes of several states. The liability of employers for injuries to their employees has been modified as discussed in Chapter 13. Other statutory modifications include doctrines relating to automobile liability and survival and wrongful death.

Automobile liability. The law has moved in two directions in the United States concerning treatment of liability toward others involving the use of automobiles. It has become more strict as to the operator's liability to those hit by the automobile. However, for injuries suffered by guests in the car, the law has moved toward relaxing the liability of the operator.

Seven major European countries (France, Germany, Great Britain, Sweden, Switzerland, Italy, and the Netherlands) have partially extended the liability of the auto operator to certain losses without regard to fault. All seven countries provide payment of medical expenses and wage losses to victims of automobile accidents on a prompt no-fault basis, while maintaining the driver's responsibility for damages negligently inflicted on vehicles and other property.[11] This type of legislation has its advocates in the United States, and in recent years the question of the uncompensated or poorly compensated accident victim has received much attention. Some concerned persons advocate the extension of the "no-fault" principle to property damage as well as to bodily injury. Florida, Massachusetts, and Michigan included property damage in their original no-fault statutes, but only the Michigan plan has retained this coverage. In 1968 Puerto Rico adopted a plan that insures the full medical expenses and partial replacement of wages lost for every accident victim. In 1970 Massachusetts adopted a modified no-fault insurance plan that provides coverage for medical expenses and lost wages, together with an elimination of most liability claims under $2,000. Many state legislatures now are debating similar proposals and a large number have passed some type of no-fault legislation. As of mid-1983, 15 states have no-fault laws that restrict lawsuits. In addition, nine states have compulsory add-on no-fault coverage to supplement (not replace) tort liability law, usually in the form of compulsory personal injury protection. These states place no restrictions on tort liability.

The Michigan Supreme Court on June 8, 1978 in a 4–3 decision ruled its no-fault auto insurance law unconstitutional. It found that the law

---

[11] Weiner Pfennigstorf, *Compensation of Auto Accidents Victims in Europe* (Chicago: American Insurance Mutual Alliance, 1972).

violated the due process clause of the 14th Amendment requiring formal notice and adversary hearings. However, the court delayed for 18 months (until December 8, 1979) the effective data for its unconstitutionality finding to allow the state legislature and insurance commissioner to "seek to remedy the constitutional deficiencies" and assure that "rates shall not be inadequate and unfairly discriminatory."

In spite of strong efforts of a large segment of the insurance industry and the Michigan state authorities, the U.S. Supreme Court declined to review the Michigan court's ruling. In urging the U.S. Supreme Court to review the ruling, one large auto insurer contended that the requirements necessary to offset the Michigan Supreme Court's objections would subject insurers to "the overwhelming burden of providing formal notice and adversary hearings at every stage of their routine business transactions." Following extensive debate resulting in trade-offs involving rating methods and selection (underwriting) standards, legislation was passed in 1979 which enabled the Michigan Supreme Court to rule that the law is now constitutional. Although 39 percent of the U.S. population lived in states with no-fault benefits, the U.S. Congress still was debating federal no-fault auto legislation. The various approaches to the problem of compensating victims of auto accidents are discussed in Chapter 14.

As to the liability of the operator to guests injured in the car, some states have laws that modify the common-law rule that the operator of an automobile has the duty to use reasonable care for the protection of a guest. Under common law, the driver is required to tell the guest of any defects in the car that the driver knows about. (Strict enforcement of this principle would result in a lost evening before the recital of the car's defects could be concluded!) These "guest statutes" provide a rare example of restriction rather than expansion of circumstances in which one person is liable for injury to another. A "guest"—one who neither pays for the ride nor serves the host in any fashion—is due a lesser standard of care than the common law would require. The driver is not liable unless guilty of "gross negligence," "willful," "wanton," and/or "reckless" action. The purpose of these statutes primarily is to protect insurers from suits arising from collusion between the operator and the guest and to protect the operator from ingratitude on the part of the guest.

At the beginning of 1970, 28 states had "guest statutes." But by the end of 1982, that number was reduced to five (Alabama, Arkansas, Delaware, Indiana, and Utah). Beginning with the case of *Brown* v. *Merlo,* in which the California Supreme Court found the California guest statute unconstitutional under the Equal Protection Clause of the U.S. Constitution, a move toward abolishing the automobile guest statutes was under way.[12] As of early 1980, supreme courts in Idaho, Michigan, Ne-

---

[12] *Brown* v. *Merlo* 506 P2d 212, 1973. This ruling applied only to the nonowner-passenger portion of the guest statute. The owner-passenger portion was declared unconstitutional in 1975 (534 P2d 73), held constitutional in 1976 (16 Cal. 3d 514), but again held unconstitutional in 1978 (582 P2d 604). (Better to bend than break!)

vada, New Mexico, North Dakota, Ohio, and Wyoming have followed the California ruling. Guest statutes appear destined to become a matter of history, leaving no effective method of preventing collusion between driver and passenger, at the expense of the automobile liability premium-paying public.

About one fourth of the states have modified the common-law rule of negligence to hold the owner of a vehicle liable for the negligent use of it by another person, provided that use was within the scope of the permission granted. Dan Anderson lends Norma Larsen his new Mercedes to rush her overdue book to the library. En route Norma hits a motor scooter operated by Don Cho, who breaks his arm. These statutes make Dan, the owner of the car, liable for Don's injury. This approach is one of absolute liability. Had Norma deviated in her route to eat a pizza and injured Don there, Dan would not be liable because the car was not being used within the scope of the permission granted.

Survival and wrongful death. A basic principle of the common law of negligence was that only the injured person had a right of action against the wrongdoer and that this right died with the injured person. The death of the wrongdoer also terminated any action. This law leads to several amusing tales: Pullman beds are made up so that passengers must sleep with their heads in the direction the train is moving; thus a wreck is more likely to be fatal. Glass-enclosed axes on trains are for employees to use on injured but surviving passengers. And the advice that when one hits a pedestrian who is still wiggling, then back up for another try! These are legends only!

Today all states have statutes that provide a remedy for wrongful death. Most provide that in the event of a "wrongful death" the survivors have a new right of action against the wrongdoer. Many states limited the amount of recovery to $5,000 for a single wrongful death. As time passed and inflation continued this amount was raised. Today, only seven states limit the recovery (generally from $35,000 to $75,000). In those states where a limit is stated, this amount is for the wrongful death only. The survivors are entitled also to awards for loss of income, loss of consortium (the services of the spouse), and other losses.

Liability Imposed by Contract

A business or individual may be subject to liability imposed by contract. This liability may be either assumed explicitly under contract or arise from a breach of an implied warranty.

Class action suits

The current age is one of consumerism. For the first time in history consumers have banded together to force manufacturers and retailers to meet higher standards of product quality and safety and to demand ethical and competent performance standards from security dealers, financial reporters, and professional personnel generally. Frequently newspapers report class actions against various organizations. Under these proceedings, one person can sue on behalf of everyone injured by a defective article or incompetent service. The consequences of such legal actions may be shattering.

Class action is a legal device allowing a group of individuals with a claim against a company or individual to join together as plaintiffs in a single suit. Its purpose is to allow a number of persons with small claims to accumulate an amount large enough to attract a lawyer and justify the expense of litigation. Thus suits are filed which otherwise would never see action. The number of class action suits has greatly increased in the early 1970s. The U.S. Supreme Court in the case of *Eisen* v. *Carlisle & Jacquelin* took the first step toward imposing potentially substantial cost burdens on plaintiffs.[13] Individual notices must be sent all class members who can be identified with reasonable effort, and the plaintiff must pay for the cost of notices. But the *Eisen* case did not answer the question of whether plaintiffs had to bear the cost of preparing and mailing the notices. In the *Sanders* case (1978), the U.S. Supreme Court decided that the district court should consider which party should be responsible for performing the particular tasks necessary to the sending of notices.[14] If the defendant is held responsible, the district court "must exercise its discretion in deciding whether to leave the cost of complying with its order where it falls, on the defendant, or place it on the party that benefits, the representative plaintiff." The U.S. Supreme Court in the *Coopers and Lybrand* case (1978) severely limited appeals by plaintiffs.[15] Thus, the recent trend is to scrutinize carefully the qualifications of the named plaintiff before permitting him or her to represent a class action. In the past, unless the interests of the named plaintiff were not inconsistent with those of the whole class, the class action litigation could proceed regardless of improper motivation, the capability or willingness of bearing the cost of litigation, and the knowledge about the underlying transactions. Although the effect of these court decisions appears to limit some class action litigation, a number of these suits continue to be pressed. In March of 1984, owners of the X-cars, a 1980 model General Motors product, filed a class action suit based on allegations that GM knowingly sold cars with defective brakes. This filing was instigated while GM was defending itself against a much publicized federal suit based on the same alleged defective brakes brought by the National Highway Traffic Safety Administration. Owners claimed that their automobiles were worth about $1,000 less than if the brake systems had been adequate. Thus, with 1.1 million owners, if the suit is successful, it could cost GM in excess of $1 billion excluding any punitive damages that might be awarded.

---

[13] *Eisen* v. *Carlisle & Jacquelin,* 417 U.S. 156 (1974).

[14] Fed. Sec. L. Rep. (CCH) 96,470 (1978), *reversing Sanders* v. *Levy,* 558 F.2d 646 (2d Cir, 1977).

[15] Fed. Sec. L. Rep. (CCH) 96,475 (1978).

Liability assumed under contract

An individual or a business may contract to assume in whole or in part the liability of another. When students sign leases for apartments, they may be agreeing to assume the liability the common law imposes on the landlords. The use of these clauses in a lease is standard. A business firm may also assume liability of others in connection with railroad switch track agreements, contracts to supply goods or services to others, or permits obtained from municipal authorities.

Products liability

A person injured through use of a defective product may bring suit for breach of contract. Actions for breach of contract arise from the breach of an implied warranty. Such action does not require proof of negligence, as it is a contract action. Unless it is clear they have been disclaimed, two warranties are implied: merchantability and fitness for a particular purpose. Both are for the protection of the buyer and exist even if the seller is ignorant of the defect. The Uniform Commercial Code (Sec. 2–314 and 315) provides, among other requirements, that, to be merchantable, goods: "pass without objection in the trade under contract"; "are fit for the ordinary purposes for which such goods are used"; "are adequately contained, packaged, and labeled as the agreement may require"; and "conform to the promises or affirmations of fact made on the container or label if any."

The warranty of fitness is in effect if the seller has reason to know the particular purpose for which the product is being bought and that the customer is relying on the expertise of the seller in furnishing suitable goods.

A screwdriver (the real thing, not a mixed drink) provides a good example of the two implied warranties. When Tom Tole bought a screwdriver from Deuce Hardware, both he and the seller understood that the tool was intended to be used to tighten and untighten screws. Tom told the salesperson that he intended to use the tool to install the electrical wiring in his new barn. The salesperson said that this product had an insulated handle, the type used by electricians on such jobs. If a defect caused injury to Tom when the screwdriver broke while he was tightening a screw, he likely would bring suit based on a breach of the implied warranty of merchantability. However, if the injury is sustained as a result of an electrical shock transmitted through the screwdriver handle, then Tom's suit would be based on a breach of the implied warranty of fitness, as the product did not meet the standards for use for this particular purpose.

Historically, the principle of privity of contract prevented direct action by a consumer against a manufacturer of a defective product. The principle of privity allowed only one who was a party to the contract to bring action for a breach of contract. Because many manufacturers sell to consumers through wholesalers and retailers, the privity requirement left the consumer recourse only against the retailer. The privity requirement, however, has undergone a gradual erosion with the result that consumers in most states can sue directly a manufacturer of a defective product for breach of implied warranty.

In addition to a suit for breach of contract, a person injured by a defective product has two causes of action in tort: negligence and strict liability. An injured party suing on grounds of negligence must prove that the seller or manufacturer failed to exercise the standard of care required in producing or handling the product. The concept of strict products liability eliminates the necessity for the plaintiff to prove negligence of the defendant. The extension of strict liability to products liability has significantly increased the products liability exposure of manufacturers and sellers. Under strict liability, the person injured need only prove that: (1) a defect in the product existed making the product unreasonably dangerous, (2) the defect existed when leaving the defendant's possession, (3) the defect was the proximate cause of the injury suffered, and (4) the use of the product was reasonable.

Typically, a person injured by a defective product will bring suit for breach of implied warranty, for negligence, and under strict liability, hoping to recover on at least one of these three causes of action. With the advent of strict liability, actions for breach of contract and negligence are becoming less important. As in other liability cases, court decisions establishing the requisites for a successful products liability action vary among jurisdictions.

Professional liability

Liability for breach of contract involving physicians, attorneys, accountants, beauticians, and other professional persons or skilled tradepersons, also has as its basis the violation of an implied warranty to render the service for which the professional has been hired.

The plaintiff also may bring suit alleging negligence. The number of suits alleging negligence of professionals has increased dramatically during the past years. Professionals are being held liable with much greater frequency and for increasing amounts of damages for failure to exercise the required (sometimes more stringent) standard of care.[16] This development has drastically increased the cost of liability insurance for professionals, especially physicians, and still insurers are suffering losses on these exposures. How to solve the problem of the increasing frequency and severity of professional liability claims and the maintenance of adequate markets for professional liability insurance at affordable prices continues to be a controversy in the 1980s.

Accountants' liability. Historically the courts have been lenient in protecting accountants from negligence actions brought against them by

---

[16] Physicians and others are being held for conduct standards above what is normal for the profession, leaving the professionals in a quandary as to what is expected.

third parties. However, inspired by consumerism, the courts have been extending responsibility for losses to those best able to prevent them and most able to afford them. Accountants' liability has not been isolated from the change.

Traditionally, accountants have not been held liable to third parties for negligently made errors in the preparation of financial statements. As long as accountants adhered to generally accepted accounting principles, they could not be found negligent. In a leading case *(U.S.* v. *Simon)* two partners and an associate of an accounting firm were found guilty of approving a financial statement which was materially false and misleading.[17] Although eight expert witnesses testified that the statement was in accordance with generally accepted accounting principles, the defendants still were found guilty of violating the full disclosure rules of the Securities Exchange Act of 1934. In the charge to the jury, the judge stated that adherence to generally accepted accounting principles was not the crucial question, but instead whether or not the accountants displayed good faith in preparing a statement which fairly represented the company's financial position. In *Escott* v. *Bar Chris Construction Corporation* the liability of accountants was extended to those who rely on negligently prepared financial statements when purchasing a registered security.[18]

Thus, the courts have held that the purpose of financial statements is to inform laypersons fully, and that willful or negligent misrepresentations in these statements can impose liability on accountants to third parties who must rely on such financial information. The adherence to generally accepted accounting principles in the preparation of financial statements will not provide a complete defense. To avoid liability an accountant must use good faith in the preparation of statements which provide an accurate representation of a company's financial position. These decisions and others have resulted in substantial and continued increases in litigation involving accountants' liability.

Medical malpractice liability. Growing dissatisfaction with physicians' services has resulted in a phenomenal increase in medical malpractice suits.

The period from 1974 to 1975 produced a medical malpractice insurance "crisis" as the number of suits based on breach of contract by negligence of physicians escalated. In addition, large increases in defense costs and plaintiffs' awards compounded the problem. For example, in Cook County (Chicago) in 1974 the number of suits increased by 56 percent. In 1974 and 1975 more medical malpractice claims were filed in Cook County than throughout its entire previous history. At that time, many doctors could not buy adequate malpractice liability insurance at any price, and those who could had to pay soaring premiums as insurers attempted to increase rates to prevent anticipated massive

---

[17] 519 P.2d891 (Wash 1974).

[18] 283 F. Supp. 643 (S.D.N.Y. 1968).

underwriting losses. For example, a Chicago hospital's malpractice insurance premiums were increased from $500,000 to $3 million, causing the hospital to raise its room rates by $12 a day. By 1980 the crisis seemed to have abated as medical malpractice insurance had become more available and more affordable than during the 1974–75 period—but not for long. Malpractice suits filed in 1982 were up 50 percent, after an increase of only 9 percent in 1981. A large number of states have done little more than alleviate the symptoms of the medical malpractice problem.

Some observers believed the malpractice problem of the mid-1970s was the result of an overreaction by insurers to a rapid increase in the frequency and severity of malpractice losses. When the dust settled, insurers introduced a more rational pricing system influenced in part by newly developed competition from physician-owned cooperative medical malpractice plans. Physicians were forced to practice defensive medicine—ordering extensive precautionary tests—thus reducing the chance of malpractice claims, but increasing the cost of medical care. Despite these efforts to establish loss-control procedures which appeared to slow the rate of increase of malpractice litigation, physicians once again are faced with a steeply increasing number of malpractice claims.

The causes of the increase of medical malpractice liability claims are numerous. The filing of a malpractice suit by a patient represents the ultimate breakdown of the physician-patient relationship. Unlike the "make believe" activities of TV heroes, Drs. Gonzo Gates and Trapper John, the short supply of doctors limits the time they are able to spend; therefore patients (particularly those that view TV medical shows) now sue because they blame adverse medical consequences on the lack of time and attention of doctors. However, lawyers fearing countersuits by doctors for harassment arising from cases that have no obvious merit has reduced the number of frivolous cases.

Suits are also multiplying because of the changing standards applied by the courts. The standard of care required of doctors has been extended. Juries are increasingly awarding damages to plaintiffs suffering unfortunate consequences of standard medical treatment, rather than to true victims of a doctor's negligence. Some observers believe the public holds an illusory view of the level of expertise in medical practice by considering it an exact science rather than an art, its true status. Individuals thus tend to sue over unfortunate ramifications of treatment regardless of whether a physician's conduct was negligent. Also many suits are "nuisance suits," filed hoping the insurer will pay to avoid a trial. Of course, *many* legitimate claims are filed, and the victims should be adequately compensated.

The increase of suits and liability judgments against physicians is also having adverse effects on the practice of medicine. Fearful of malpractice suits, doctors often prescribe unnecessary tests and consultations that, although not required for adequate medical care, are essential for protection in case of malpractice suits. Defensive medicine, and the passing of its costs along with that of malpractice coverage to patients are increasing medical care costs. Strikes and slowdowns in increasing numbers have occurred among doctors and in hospitals, causing some hospitals to face the possibility of bankruptcy.

Many solutions have been proposed (some enacted) for the malpractice problem with most observers agreeing that a limitation on doctors' and hospitals' tort liability is essential. Other solutions are: (1) the hearing and adjudication of claims by a patient's compensation board composed of panels including doctors, lawyers, and laypersons, (2) requiring joint underwriting associations (JUAs) under which insurers writing designated types of insurance in the state would share malpractice claims on a specified basis, (3) creation of state insurance funds, (4) organization of physicians' mutual insurers to underwrite the malpractice exposure, (5) regulation of lawyers' contingent fees to reduce them to "reasonable" levels, (6) improvements in the quality of health care through suspension or revocation of licenses for any of a list of damaging causes such as patient abandonment, filing false reports, deterioration through aging, incompetence, and so on, (7) elimination of specific dollar requests in malpractice litigation, (8) consideration of plaintiff's receipts from other insurance and benefits in fixing awards, (9) shortening the statute of limitations for filing malpractice claims, (10) forbidding use of the *res ipsa loquitur* doctrine (the thing speaks for itself) as proof of malpractice, thus forcing the burden of proof on the plaintiff, (11) establishing pretrial screening or arbitration panels, and (12) limiting the amount recoverable for malpractice claims. Some of the solutions enacted into law in various states have been held unconstitutional in those states. The allegation has been made that medical malpractice suits are higher in those states with no-fault auto insurance laws, insinuating that lawyers have revised their ambulance chasing habits to extend all the way to the operating rooms.

Actuaries' professional liability. ERISA (the Pension Reform Act of 1974) exposes actuaries to a liability for negligent acts and errors or omissions resulting from performance in a professional capacity. The complexity of the law and the heavy involvement of actuaries in decision making suggest a liability exposure that actuaries cannot ignore.

Federal tort claims act. The Federal Tort Claims Act of 1966 allows suit against the U.S. government, with certain exceptions and for limited amounts. In the case of *Dalehite et al.* v. *United States,* the U.S. Supreme Court commented: "The Federal Tort Claims Act is a waiver of sovereign immunity from suit for certain specified torts of federal employees, but it does not assure injured persons damages for all injuries caused by such employees." However, the exceptions and exclusions of the act limits its value to injured parties. Some examples of these exceptions and limitations are that settlements for more than $25,000 require the written approval of the attorney general or his or her designee; that a claim must be filed within two years after it arises; and that the tort action must be brought within six months after final denial of the administrative claim.

Examples of Tort Liability Hazards

Liability hazards (factors which increase the chance of loss from tort liability) are many. This section provides some examples of hazards resulting in a possible tort liability loss.

Business liability exposures

Any property or premises owned or rented by the business or for which the business has responsibility can be the source of liability claims; for instance, if an individual including an employee is injured on the premises. Liability also may result from injuries caused by business operations. If an injury occurs because of an employee's negligence, the employer may be held liable to the injured person. Employers and professionals also are exposed to liability claims due to the actions of individuals operating as their agents. In a California case, a salesperson involved in an accident while driving to a company meeting was held to be acting as an employee, and the employer was held liable for the $10,000 judgment even though the car was owned by the employee.

Employers also are exposed to liability under workers' compensation laws for injuries to employees. They also may be exposed to liability for injuries to independent contractors and their employees while engaged by that business and for losses to others caused by activities of the independent contractors and their employees while performing their operations.

Businesses such as laundries, dry cleaners, warehouses, and repair establishments which handle customers' goods are considered bailees. Although bailees have a legal liability for goods deposited with them, the liability is not absolute. Losses for which bailees are not responsible are those caused by "acts of God" rather than the negligence of the business. However, many businesses dealing with consumers rather than other firms realize that sound business practice dictates reimbursing customers for losses regardless of legal responsibility if the business seeks to retain customer goodwill and thus remain in business. Consumers, unlike businesses, generally are unaware that the bailee is not liable for every loss of customers' property regardless of its cause.

Fiduciary liability is another hazard which businesses, especially those with pension funds, must consider. Investment managers of pension funds are exposed to suits for "mistakes" made in managing the fund. Historically, fiduciaries needed only to conform to a "prudent man" standard of conduct, in which investment decisions were analyzed in accordance with what was expected of a prudent man in similar circumstances. The rules established for pension fund managers under the

Employee Retirement Income Security Act of 1974 are expected by some observers to require a pension fund manager to conform to a "prudent expert" standard of care, in which investment decisions will be analyzed in comparison to how a prudent expert would have performed in similar circumstances. The expectation is that the application of the "prudent expert rule" will increase the number of fiduciary liability claims.

Owners and operators of taverns are exposed to the "dramshop" hazard. Many states have enacted dramshop laws making the seller of alcoholic beverages liable for bodily injury and property damage committed by persons under the influence of alcohol consumed in the seller's establishment. Furthermore, owners and operators of liquor establishments may be held liable for the wrongful death or injury of the intoxicated person and in some jurisdictions may be held liable for loss of consortium damages to the decedent's spouse. Owners and operators of taverns should become familiar with the dramshop act as interpreted by the courts in their jurisdiction so as to identify the nature of this exposure.

A business should be aware of its exposure to large losses from the products recall hazard. Once a product liability claim has arisen from the use of a defective product and often before such a claim occurs, a manufacturer is required to recall all products which probably contain defects in order to prevent any (or additional) injury to the public.

Personal liability exposures

Individuals also must be aware of hazards which may increase the chance of liability losses. Sidewalks, stairways, freshly waxed floors, defective doors, unsecured rugs, falling ceilings, and unprotected pipes and radiators increase the chance of loss from liability exposures. For example, an icy sidewalk may or may not present a liability hazard to owners or tenants. The general rule is that owners or tenants are not obligated to remove ice from a sidewalk on their property resulting from natural causes, but may be held liable for injuries if a fall on a slippery sidewalk is the result of accumulated ice caused by a condition of the owners' or tenants' property, such as leakage from a gutter attached to an owner's house.

As noted, the same standard of care is not owed by the owner or tenant to trespassers, invitees, or licensees except in a few states. However, the individual does not know before an accident whether the court will interpret that the proper standard of care toward a particular individual has been exercised. Thus, the classification of trespasser, invitee, and licensee is of little use in evaluating liability hazards except in some cases involving obvious attractive nuisances.

One who rents a house must be aware of the same liability hazards as a homeowner, because tenants have the same duty as owners to protect others from injury. Optimists may believe that bonds of friendship would prevent close companions from filing suits against them for injury sustained on their property. However, in the words of one expert on liability hazards, "When injury results, friendship is strained; when an attorney is retained, it wanes; and when those who are involved go to court, it ceases to exist."[19]

Owners of dogs that chew on mail carriers may find themselves in court. Uninitiated drivers of snowmobiles may accidentally cause damage to a passerby who decides it is better to sue than forgive. The ownership of boats similarly will constitute a liability hazard. Finally, the golf game presents a liability hazard to those whose misplaced tee shots injure other golfers unless ample warning is given by shouting "fore" loudly and clearly before hitting the ball. However, if the ball strikes another golfer after ricocheting off a tree, the errant golfer would not have been duty-bound to give warning. The injured golfer is assumed to have accepted the risk of injury.

This brief survey of liability hazards is by no means complete and is intended solely to provide a few examples of exposures that may increase the chance of liability loss. A comprehensive discussion of liability hazards would require its own textbook.

Erosion of the Tort System

The tort system, the jury system, and the adversary system have been eroded. Common examples are the federal and state commissions which judge complaints and whose findings are conclusive when supported by substantial evidence. Some of the administrative acts in this category are the National Labor Relations Act, the Railway Labor Act, the Longshoremen and Harbor Workers Act, the Occupational Safety and Health Act, and the Equal Employment Opportunity Act.

Summary

1. Liability exposures, often resulting in large and unexpected losses, may be classified as:
   a. Intentional torts.
   b. Absolute liability.
   c. Strict liability.
   d. Liability arising out of negligence.
   e. Liability imposed by contract.
2. Intentional torts may be classified as intentional interference with the person (battery, assault, false imprisonment, infliction of mental distress, and defamation) or intentional interference with property (trespass, conversion). Imposition of liability depends on whether or not the actor's conduct is privileged.
3. Absolute liability imposes liability on those who engage in ultradan-

---

[19] Reginald W. Spell, *Public Liability Hazards* (Indianapolis, Ind.: Rough Notes Co., Inc., 1941), p. 228.

gerous acts causing injuries to others and is imposed without regard to fault or negligence. To prove absolute liability the plaintiff need only show a loss was suffered as a result of an ultradangerous activity.

4. Strict liability is similar to absolute liability in that it imposes liability without regard to fault or negligence. However, they differ in that strict liability demands a greater burden of proof for the plaintiff who must prove more than mere injury. For example, in products liability (the prime example of strict liability), the plaintiff must prove the defect existed at the time of sale and the defect made the product unreasonably dangerous. Once the plaintiff has proven these factors, liability is imposed without regard to fault or negligence.

5. Negligence arises from the failure of an individual to exercise the required standard of care for the protection of others.

6. To prove negligence, a plaintiff must establish that
   a. The defendant had a duty to protect the plaintiff,
   b. The defendant failed to perform that duty,
   c. The failure to perform was the proximate cause of the plaintiff's injury, and
   d. The plaintiff in fact did suffer an injury.

7. Defenses in negligence actions consist of contributory negligence and assumption of risk by the plaintiff. The common-law defense of contributory negligence has been modified by the doctrines of last clear chance and comparative negligence, the latter in an increasing number of jurisdictions.

8. Statutory modifications of the common-law doctrine of negligence have occurred in automobile liability and survival and wrongful death. These modifications have increased the liability of an operator of a vehicle with respect to individuals injured outside the vehicle, decreased the liability of the operator for injuries suffered by passengers in the vehicle, and have extended the liability for actions resulting in wrongful death. "No-fault" automobile insurance laws have been passed in a number of states to reduce litigation and to eliminate tort liability in the event of economic losses below specified amounts.

9. Liability may be either assumed under contract as in the case of a tenant of an apartment, or may be imposed by breach of implied warranty as in the cases of products and professional liability. (Products and professional liability may also arise out of negligence and strict liability.)

10. The areas of products and professional liability have undergone significant expansion in recent years, resulting from the consumer movement and the changing attitudes of the judicial system. This expansion is expected to continue in the future. However, the medical malpractice problem has been met by a more rational pricing system on the part of the insurers, competition from physician-owned cooperative medical malpractice plans, and effective loss control procedures.

Questions for Review

1. Explain the difference between negligence and intentional torts. Give an example of each intentional tort.

2. "Guest statutes" have been repealed in all but five states. What effect do you expect their repeal will have. Why?

3. The doctrines of strict and absolute liability allow claimants to collect from defendant without proving negligence. Do you believe this is fair? Why, or why not?

4. What is the logic behind the modifications of the doctrine of contributory negligence? Give an example of the use of each of these modifications. Can you cite a situation where you believe the doctrine of the last clear chance is subject to misuse?

5. How might the existence of privilege preclude intentional tort liability? Explain, using examples of various kinds of privileged actions.

6. Distinguish between the standard of care owed trespassers, licensees, and invitees. What is the justification for different standards of care?

7. What role does the jury play in negligence actions?

8. Explain the types of liability hazards to which you are exposed. How may these hazards be classified?

9. Explain the types of liability hazards to which the local department store is exposed. How would you classify these hazards?

10. What kinds of limitations are imposed on class action suits? How are these limitations imposed and what effect have they had?

11. What are the problems that produced the medical malpractice insurance crisis during the years 1974, 1975, and 1982? How did the insurers react to these problems? What is your expectation about the future availability of medical malpractice insurance at affordable prices?

Questions for Discussion

1. Three states have eliminated the distinctions between trespassers, licensees, and invitees. Develop arguments for and against the distinctions. Comment on the usefulness and equity of these distinctions.

2. The areas of products and professional liability have undergone tremendous expansion in recent years. What are some of the reasons for this expansion? What possible problems may result if further expansion occurs?

3. Over one third of all Americans live in states which have some form of no-fault auto insurance. What are the possible advantages and disadvantages of no-fault auto insurance? Are you in favor of the abolition of tort liability for automobile accidents?

4. Liability awards have been skyrocketing during recent years. What is your opinion of multimillion dollar awards in personal injury or wrongful death cases? What role does the jury play in these "jumbo awards"? Should the role of the jury be deemphasized? Why?

5. The medical malpractice problem has reached crisis proportions. Do you feel insurers should be forced to provide medical malpractice coverage, even if rates are inadequate? What are some other possible solutions to the problem? What is the present status of the medical malpractice exposure in your state?

Insurance and the law

A revolt by traveling salesmen may be given credit for the origin of the first insurance contracts. The story begins about 5,000 years ago in the Euphrates Valley. The Babylonians had increased industry to the extent that they needed a wider market for their goods and a wider source of raw materials than was provided by nearby areas. The local industrialists at first sent their slaves, brothers-in-law, or other representatives into the surrounding countryside on short trading excursions. These representatives, acting only as servants, did not share in the profits or losses of these trips. Soon the slaves and brothers-in-law no longer were adequate, so traveling salesmen were required. The businessman made arrangements with a *darmatha* (which is Babylonian for "drummer") to engage in buying and selling trips extending throughout the known world. No more than a Chicago businessperson would a Babylonian businessman trust goods and money to a traveling salesman without assurance of his fidelity. As fidelity bonds were not yet available, the businessman required the salesman, as security for the transaction, to pledge his property, wife, and children.

In return for the "loan" of the money and goods, the salesman paid the businessman half the profits of the trip. This arrangement proved satisfactory. An occasional salesman, preferring life abroad with the goods and money to life in Babylon and his wife, would abscond with the loan and leave his wife to the mercy of the businessman. But such incidents were rare. The trouble arose from the nature of the ethical codes of people in the foreign lands where both brigandage and piracy were considered more honorable ways of making a living than trading. Thus, many an honest *darmatha* lost his merchandise and was forced to forfeit his security through no fault of his own. As trade extended into less civilized areas, the problem increased and eventually became intolerable to the salesman.

The salesmen then revolted. As the businessmen and salesmen needed each other, they negotiated and reached a compromise. The former system was retained with the additional provision that in the event the caravan should be pillaged, through no connivance or negligence on the part of the salesman, he would be freed from debt by swearing to those facts upon return from the trip. This arrangement became widespread throughout the area, and the practice spread to Phoenicia, where the principle was applied to all kinds of shipping, and from there, throughout the ancient world. The Code of Hammurabi, compiled about 2250 B.C. in Babylon, made provisions to govern the foregoing arrangement and included others that today would be considered in the province of insurance. For example, Section 23 of that code stated: "If the brigand has not been caught, the man who has been despoiled shall recount . . . what he has lost, and the City and Governor in whose land . . . the brigandage took place shall render back to him whatsoever of his that was lost."

Since that time, every compilation of law has included rules that are of significance to buyers of insurance. In fact, by early 1982, 33 states had enacted legislation to compensate victims of violent crimes through compensation laws that partially cover loss of earnings and medical expenses resulting from physical injury. The maximum benefits range from $5,000 to $45,000. In some states, benefits are based on need whereas in others they are paid as a right regardless of need. Dependents are paid a survivor's benefit if the crime results in the victim's death.

As in most areas of law, the concern here primarily is with Anglo-American common law and its subsequent modification by statute and judicial interpretation. Some knowledge of insurance law is of more than academic interest to the insurance buyer, for in this area lie many traps for unwary policyowners.

The Nature of Law

"The law is sort of a hocus-pocus science that smiles in your face while it picks your pocket; and the glorious uncertainty of it is of more use to the professors than the justice of it."

The law, with all of its hocus-pocus and glorious uncertainty may be defined as the principles and regulations established by a government in the form of legislation or recognized custom enforced by judicial decision. Thus two of the important sources of law affecting insurance are statutes and court decisions.

Statutory law

Statutory law is written law established by the legislative body and incorporated in a formal document. A compilation of these formal documents, systematically organized, brought up to date, indexed and enacted in its revised form, is called a code. Thus, an insurance code is a collection of existing laws governing insurance. Each state has its own insurance code. These codes primarily are regulatory, including provisions relating to the formation of insurers, the licensing of insurers and their agents, insurer financial and accounting practices, insurance marketing activity, and insurance contract provisions.

In addition to imposing regulations upon insurers, statutory law affects agency law—the body of law dealing with the principal-agent relationship, and insurance contract law—the body of law dealing with the rights and obligations of the contracting parties. The effects of statutory law on insurance agency relationships and insurance contract performance are discussed in this and the following chapter.

Court decisions

A body of law known as common law has been established by court decisions. Common law evolved from 12th-century England and reflects what the judges over these hundreds of years considered to be just. In its nascent form, the term "common law" was used to mean those principles of law that were common to all England as distinguished from those applying only in certain localities. It also applied to everyone alike, including noblemen as well as commoners. In the United States today, the common law as used in most jurisdictions is composed of (1) the body of rules evidenced by appellate court decisions and (2) that part of English law not contrary to the public policy of the jurisdiction where applied. In any dispute involving a contest at law, the court will apply the written law (constitutional or statutory), if any; otherwise in most jurisdictions the common law will be applied.

Doctrine of "stare decisis." Common law is based on the principle that previous court decisions provide precedent to be followed in subsequent cases involving essentially the same facts and the same question of law. Because a court under the doctrine of "stare decisis" is reluctant to depart from established precedents, common law provides stability. However, as "common law is not a brooding omnipresence in the sky," the court will reject "stare decisis" when it believes that justice is better served by creating rather than following precedents. Many forces can contribute to reversing a precedent such as a change in court personnel, a change in public attitudes, or the belief that such precedent was in error.

Cases of first impression.　Questions of law arise when neither an applicable statute nor previous court decisions govern. The court then must render a decision based on an unwritten system of law composed of a heritage of general rules, judicial assertions called dicta, and principles based on the English law so long as the decision is consistent with public policy and basic concepts of justice for the jurisdiction applied. Decisions in these cases then may be used as precedents.

The law of agency and the law of contracts primarily are embodied in common law and have been shaped principally by court decisions rather than by legislative enactments.

Application of the law

The law establishes precise definitions of acceptable procedures and details strict consequences that apply to deviations from these procedures. In insurance law the duties of the insured regarding warranties, representations, and concealment are presented in detail. Violation of these duties technically enables the insurer to avoid the contract. Apparently the courts do not consider a strict interpretation of the law to be in the public interest when in their judgment the results would unfairly harm the insured. Unfortunately for insurers, insureds, and the student, variation from strict legal terminology is annoyingly inconsistent. Depending upon individual circumstances, courts will arrive at different conclusions. Thus, so as not to be lulled into a false sense of security when reading cases that seemingly violate strict legal definitions, concerned parties should be aware that they can rely only on a legal decision that meets the strict standards defined in this text. A more lenient verdict might be rendered in some cases, but to rely on a prior favorable verdict would be unwise. The realities of the legal world are accepted with the realization that variations from strict legal terminology, and thus inconsistency, is a fact of life.

Locating the applicable law

References are made to *the law* throughout this text. However, laws vary among jurisdictions and over time. As George Herbert wrote, "the law is not the same at morning and at night." That the law is not necessarily the same in one state as another can be added to Herbert's observation. Variations in the law complicate its study and require a nonlegal text to focus on such terms as *generally, usually, majority consensus,* and so on.

Laws of an individual state can be found in law libraries. Statutes are consolidated in a series of volumes for the 50 states and the federal government. Statutory law for each jurisdiction is divided by volumes into subtopics (e.g., insurance, criminal law, commercial law). Considering the voluminous nature of the statutory provisions of every jurisdiction (the *Smith-Hurd Illinois Annotated Statutes* have 71 bound volumes), indexes are requisite. These indexes are similar to any other index except for their detail. A general multivolume index is compiled for each jurisdiction. Supplemental indexes are included for each subtopic. The references are classified by descriptive work titles, popular statute names, and general topics, all in convenient alphabetical order. Locating the statute is routine. The index is checked for the statutory description. References to the separate subtopic index also are required. The index refers the researcher to explicit statutory provisions.

Shephard's Citations is a compilation of references to the published texts of the jurisdiction's constitution, legislation, judicial and administrative decisions and rules, city and county ordinances, and topical law articles referring to the particular citation. It provides the legal researcher with the current status of the law.

Shepard's (the lawyer's word for it) indexes each citation and lists all legal action and pertinent discussion in the literature following a legal pronouncement relative to the merits of the original action; that is, if the statement of law has been set aside (reversed, repealed, or overruled), distinguished (points out the dissimilarities among cases which on the surface appear identical), or affirmed. Conscientious readers are encouraged to check the applicable law of their jurisdiction by consulting these indexes for a useful learning experience.

Insurable Interest

The principle of insurable interest is basic to the structure of insurance. The requirement of an insurable interest marks the legal distinction between the operation of an insurer and the operation of a bookmaker on a horse race. In studying insurable interest, property and life insurance should be considered separately as several sharp distinctions exist in the application of the principle in the two fields.

What is an insurable interest?

In property insurance, an insurable interest is any financial interest based on some legal right in the preservation of the property. An exposure to a financial loss must exist for there to be an insurable interest in the occurrence of some event. In life insurance, an insurable interest is any reasonable expectation of financial loss arising from the death of the person whose life is insured.

Why is an insurable interest required?

A basic legal principle is that no contract contrary to public policy is enforceable. What conforms to public policy and hence is lawful has varied over time and place. (Lawful, in this respect, may be defined as "compatible with the will and judgment of a court having jurisdiction.")

In property insurance, the law requires an insurable interest so that insurance policies are neither gambling devices nor tools in the hands of those who would seek to profit by deliberately destroying the property of others. If Bob Bray, who has no insurable interest in Jeff Morton's house were allowed to collect on a fire policy covering Jeff's house, the contract would be a wagering contract rather than an insurance contract: Bob would be betting the cost of the insurance that Jeff's house will burn before the policy expires. Furthermore, if Bob should suddenly realize that premiums paid in terms of fire damage probabilities have produced a bad gamble for him (e.g., his insurance professor had just explained to him that to cover its expenses, an insurer must charge a premium in excess of the chance of loss multiplied by the average size of loss), he might be tempted to set fire to Jeff's house to salvage his bet. Thus property insurance policies lacking an insurable interest are held to be against public policy, and hence unenforceable.

In life insurance, if one buys a policy on another's life, the buyer is required by law to have an insurable interest in that life. In 17th-century England, insurance was bought as a wagering contract. Sometimes they were bought without the consent of the subject of the insurance. If such a policy were purchased by a leading London cutthroat (Mack the Knife), the person whose death determined the maturity date of the policy, no doubt, would have seriously considered emigrating to the New World fearing the possibility that the policyowner would tire of waiting for the law of averages to work. Therefore, England passed a statute in the 18th century declaring life insurance contracts to be against public policy unless the buyer had an insurable interest in the subject of the insurance, and this rule has become law in the United States.

If a person without an insurable interest buys a policy on the life of another, can the insurer lawfully refuse to pay the face amount of the insurance to the beneficiary on the grounds that the policy is a wagering contract and, therefore, void from its inception? The answer is subject to conflicting theories. Under the *public policy theory,* the insurer is allowed to use the defense of illegality of the contract to avoid payment. Whether the insurer is at fault in issuing a policy without the required insurable interest is not an issue. The insurer cannot waive the insurable interest requirement. If the insurer's agent led the applicant to believe that an insurable interest existed, that applicant would be entitled to a refund of premiums. Otherwise, premium refunds would be considered by the courts only in those states in which the law requires that premiums be refunded to applicants who believed that they had an insurable interest when they bought the policy. Under the *insurer protection theory,* the insurer is estopped from using the lack of insurable interest as a defense against paying a claim. The view is that as the insurable interest requirement is for the insurer's protection, the insurer can waive the requirement. This interpretation appears to be the majority opinion.

That the insurable interest requirement in life insurance is not solely for protection of the insurer was made clear the hard way to three life insurers. They had issued policies totaling $6,500 to an aunt-in-law on the life of her deceased husband's minor niece. In order to indicate that an insurable interest was present, the aunt-in-law misrepresented the relationship between herself and the niece. The aunt-in-law put arsenic in the child's soft drink and was later convicted of murder. The aggrieved (and grieved) father sued the life insurers on the ground that the wrongful and negligent act of the insurers in issuing policies when no insurable interest existed provided the motive for the murder. The jury's award of $75,000 damages to the father was upheld by the Alabama Supreme Court, which reasoned that the purpose of the insurable interest requirement also was to protect human life.

Under New York law, the estate of the insured may sue to recover benefits paid under life and health insurance contracts that violate the insurable interest requirement. However, only the insurer can object to the lack of an insurable interest.[1] Only a few cases develop where the question of the lack of insurable interest is at issue as the majority of policies are purchased by the person whose life is insured, and insurers closely investigate persons who buy insurance on the lives of others.

Who has an insurable interest?

Property insurance. Anyone owning a house, furniture, or an auto has an insurable interest in that property. Less obvious are insurable interests based on other relationships. An expectation of benefit from the continued existence of property is sufficient to support an insurable interest if the expectation is based on a legal right. A mortgagee has an insurable interest in the property pledged as security for a debt. A TV mechanic holding a lien on a television set while awaiting payment for charges has an insurable interest in that instrument. Possession may give the holder of goods an insurable interest. Thus, a bailee (one holding property for another) has an insurable interest (called a representative interest) in goods left in its care and custody. The buyer in good faith of stolen goods has an insurable interest in those articles. A business has an insurable interest in the profits it could lose if another person's property; for example, the plant of a principal supplier or of a customer is damaged. The insurable interest is in its own profits and not in its customer's or supplier's plant.

An insurable interest may be based on a legal liability arising from an event that could impose an obligation to pay damages to another person. The liability could arise from a tort or a contract, and the insurable interest is the economic return expected from the preservation of assets.

Several separate and distinct insurable interests can be held in relation to the same property. Assume that Steve Haroldson owns a building which he rented a few years ago to Irwin Cochrun under a 30-year lease. Irwin invested several thousand dollars in improvements to adapt the building for use as an office for his firm of business management

---

[1] See *Insurance Law of New York*, vol. 27, sec. 146. Also see *Moran v. Moran*, 1973, 74 Misc. 2d 384, 346 N.Y.S. 2d 424.

consultants. The rent under the lease is less than the building could command now at present rental rates for comparable property. Under the lease agreement, the contract may be cancelled if the building is severely damaged by fire or other peril. Some of the insurable interests developed from this arrangement are:

1. Both Steve and Irwin, have an insurable interest in the improvements in the building. Steve's interest is an ownership interest, whereas Irwin's interest is a use interest (known as a usufruct interest).

2. Steve has an insurable interest not only in the property but also in the rents he collects.

3. Irwin has an insurable interest in his lease as he is able to acquire the use of the property for a rental payment less than current rental value (known as a leasehold interest).

4. If, under the rental agreement, Irwin agrees to return the property in the same condition as received, then Irwin also has an insurable interest in the building.

5. If someone is injured on the premises, either Irwin or Steve or both may be held liable. Therefore, both Irwin and Steve have an insurable interest in their legal liability arising from the property. Steve's interest results from his ownership and Irwin's interest is based on his operation of the building.

Steve and Irwin must insure the correct interest. Thus, Steve may insure his property interest in the building, his interest in the improvements and betterments, his interest in the rental income, and his interest in the legal liability for bodily injury and property damage. Irwin may insure his use interest in the improvements and betterments, the value of his leasehold interest, his contractual obligation to return the property in its original condition, and his interest in the legal liability for bodily injury and property damage. The insurance coverages available for these interests are discussed in Chapters 11 and 13.

Life insurance. A person has an insurable interest in the life of another whenever a financial benefit is expected from the continuation of that life. This expectation need not have a legal basis, as in property insurance. Thus a *general* creditor has an insurable interest in the life of the debtor but not in any specific property of the debtor.

The doctrine of insurable interest does not apply when a person buys a policy on one's own life. Although others may suffer a pecuniary loss as a result of the death of the insured subject, the deceased is in no position to incur a financial loss, or, indeed, a loss of any kind. In the first place, legal tender is not negotiable in the deceased's new locale, and no researcher (dead or alive) has reported evidence to the contrary. In the second place, even if a system could be devised for the deceased to take along one's wealth, no insurer would be able to employ a messenger (except one who happens to be going that way) to deliver the proceeds of the policy. Many writers dismiss the matter by stating that "anyone is held to have an unlimited insurable interest in one's own life." Although this concept may be easy to understand, it is difficult to reconcile with the definition of insurable interest. For this reason, the law decrees that insurable interest is not material when a person buys life insurance on one's own life. Furthermore, persons are permitted to name anyone as the beneficiary of policies which they buy on their own life.

To understand insurable interest in life insurance, three terms are useful: subject, owner, and beneficiary. The subject is the person whose death causes the proceeds of the policy to be payable. The owner is the one who has the authority to exercise all rights in the policy, such as dividend options, assignment privileges, surrender options, change of beneficiary, and policy loans. The owner is usually, although not always, the purchaser of the policy. The beneficiary is the person entitled to the proceeds of the policy upon the death of the subject. All three parties, or any two parties, can be the same person. For example, when James Parker insures his own life and names himself (i.e., his estate) as beneficiary, he is the subject, owner, and beneficiary. When he insures the life of his debtor, Willard Phillips, and names himself as beneficiary, he is both owner and beneficiary. When James insures his life, retaining all incidents of ownership but naming Morgan Lynge his creditor, as beneficiary, he is both owner and subject. When he insures the life of Alice Long, his employee, naming Alice's estate as beneficiary but retaining the incidents of ownership for himself, Alice is the subject and the beneficiary of the insurance. And when James insures the life of his father and names his mother as beneficiary, but retains the incidents of ownership, the subject, the owner, and the beneficiary are three different people. *The rule of insurable interest is that either the owner or the beneficiary must have an insurable interest in (or actually be) the subject of the insurance.* Thus, James may insure the life of anyone and name a third person as beneficiary if either James or the beneficiary has an insurable interest in the insured subject. The rule is called the subject-owner-beneficiary rule, or the SOB rule.

Older court decisions have held that insurable interest in life insurance existed only when the buyer of the policy could prove a monetary interest in the continued life of another. The widely accepted principle now is that closeness of blood or legal relationship creates a sufficient presumption of insurable interest without requiring proof of financial ties. As the New York statute puts it: "The term insurable interest . . . shall mean in the case of persons related closely by blood or by law, a substantial interest engendered by love and affection. . . ." This rule means that relationships between husband and wife, parent and child, grandparent and grandchild, and siblings usually are sufficient to meet the insurable interest requirement. This principle usually does not extend to more remote family relationships, such as uncles, aunts, nephews, nieces, or cousins. What constitutes a family relationship close enough to establish an insurable interest is a matter for the courts. A blood relationship may be held sufficiently close to support an insurable interest in one jurisdiction but not in another.

Insurable interest based on close family relationships is one in which natural ties of love and affection are sufficient to assure that the continued life of the subject is in the interest of the beneficiaries. What about love and affection without a close blood relationship—two gay men or women, for example, or a close blood relationship without love and affection such as Cain and Abel, for instance? Are these relationships sufficient to support an insurable interest? The courts have not answered this question, but logic suggests (1) love and affection between nonrelated persons would be insufficient and (2) a close blood relationship without love and affection also would be insufficient. An actual or factual expectation of an economic benefit from the continuation of the life of the insured would appear to be necessary in these relationships.

In business relationships, a number of circumstances produce an insurable interest. An employer has an insurable interest in the lives of key employees; a partner has an insurable interest in the lives of co-partners; a stockholder in a close corporation has an insurable interest in the lives of the other stockholders; a close corporation has an insurable interest in the lives of its stockholders; a surety (one who has guaranteed the performance of another under a contract) has an insurable interest in the life of the principal (one whose performance has been guaranteed). The insurable interest in business relationships, as in some personal relationships, is based on a reasonable expectation of financial benefits from the continuation of the life of the insured or a reasonable expectation of expenses upon the death of the insured.

Even though one person has an insurable interest in the life of another, as a precautionary measure against foul play, the prospective buyer is not allowed to insure that person's life without the subject's consent. Exceptions are made in some jurisdictions that allow a wife to insure the life of her husband without his consent, and a parent to insure the lives of minor children without their consent.

When must the insurable interest exist?

In *property insurance* the insurable interest need exist only at the time of the loss. Still, an insurer will not write a fire policy on the Brooklyn Bridge for anyone who may ask for it, not even if the prospect assures the agent of intentions to acquire ownership of the bridge. The insurer has underwriting rules that prohibit the writing of policies if an insurable interest does not exist or if it is apparent that no interest will exist in the near future. In those cases where insurance is bought before ownership of the property has been acquired, the insurer will indemnify the named insured if an insurable interest exists at the time of the loss. For example, a homeowner may buy fire insurance to cover the contents of a new home before the furniture has been purchased. If the fire occurs after the furniture is purchased and moved into the house, the owner will be indemnified for the actual cash value of the lost furniture.

In *life insurance,* insurable interest is required only at the inception of the policy; it is not required at the time the policy matures. However, this rule has not always been the law. An 1807 court decision held that an insurer's obligation under a life insurance policy terminated when the insurable interest expired. That decision was overruled in 1854 when the court reasoned that (1) insurers, considering it good business practice, customarily paid claims even though the incipient insurable interest no longer existed, (2) technically, life insurance contracts are not promises to indemnify for losses (the concept of indemnity is discussed in Chapter 6), and (3) termination of coverage following expiration of the insurable interest would be unfair to policyowners who had paid their premiums. (At that time policyowners were not entitled to cash surrender values as they are today.)

One argument is that equitable treatment would be for the insurer to pay only the amount of cash value of the policy at the time the insurable interest terminates plus premiums paid thereafter, augmented by interest. But given that a life insurance policy is not a contract of indemnity, would this approach be fair? Suppose that the Moag Macaroon Manufacturing Corporation has an especially valuable macaroon maker who produces twice as many macaroons as the next most efficient worker. The corporation buys a $200,000 whole life policy on the life of this person to reimburse itself for the financial loss likely to be caused by this worker's death. The policy has a cash value of $10,000 after five years. Would it be fair to force the corporation to take this cash value if the macaroon maker leaves its employment or should the firm be allowed to continue the policy? The policy easily might be worth more than its guaranteed cash value to the Moag Macaroon Corporation if the former macaroon maker had meanwhile become uninsurable as a result of exceptional performance in the consumption as in the production of the product. The impaired health of the former macaroon maker has increased the probability of death and, thus, the expected value of the policy. To force the surrender of the policy for its cash value would be unfair, because the policyowner would be required to exchange the policy for an amount less than its expected value.

Insurable interest as a measure of recovery

In *property insurance,* the amount of the insurable interest generally is measurable and usually sets a maximum limit which the insured can collect following a loss. A $95,000 policy covering the insured's $75,000 house is valid because ownership satisfies the insurable interest requirement. But, the insured is limited to $75,000 as the maximum amount that can be recovered following a loss.

In *life insurance,* insurable interest generally is impossible to measure. Furthermore, life insurance policies are not contracts of indemnity. So the law holds that the amount of interest is unimportant and has no relationship to the amount payable under the policy. As long as an insurable interest exists at the policy's inception, the contract will be honored for its face amount. The one exception is life insurance purchased by a creditor on the life of a debtor. In most jurisdictions, the face amount of the insurance must bear a reasonable relationship to the size of the debt when the policy is written. The determination of what is reasonable is a matter for the courts in disputed cases. The courts have been liberal in allowing amounts significantly in excess of the debt as reasonable so that the creditor would have adequate insurance to offset the unpaid principal, the premiums paid, and the interest on the debt and the premiums.

Agents and Brokers

Customarily, insurance is written by corporations which are intangible legal creations acting through real people operating under either a principal-agent relationship or a master-servant relationship. Where general or specified authority to make contracts for the corporation is granted, the relationship is one of principal-agent; otherwise it is one of master-servant.

For the most part, the marketing of insurance is conducted through representatives of insurers known as "agents." An insurance agent is anyone authorized by an insurer to solicit, create, modify, or terminate contracts of insurance between the insurer and the insuring public. Also involved in the marketing process are insurance brokers. An insurance broker is a person who, for a consideration, solicits and negotiates contracts of insurance for an insured and is the agent of the insured and not of the insurer. This relationship is not a "distinction without a difference," as soon will become apparent.

Creation of an agency relationship

An agency relationship may be established between principals and agents by mutual assent. This assent usually is given in an express agreement known as an agency contract. Most insurance agency relationships are based on expressed agreements. Mutual assent, however, can be reached after a transaction has occurred by one party sanctioning the actions of another as those of one's own, creating an *agency by ratification*. For example, if Gary Eldred appears to David Klock to be acting as an agent for the Antique Car Insurance Company and writes a policy for David covering his Maxwell, the Antique Car Insurance Company, if it has full knowledge of the facts, may ratify Gary's act either expressly or by conduct that implies ratification. The result is a legal contract to which all parties are bound.

While an agency relationship between principal and agent usually may be created only with the consent of the principal by agreement or ratification, special circumstances are construed to deny the principal the right to claim that no agency relationship existed. These circumstances establish an agency by estoppel or a *presumptive agency*. Thus, if the insurer's behavior causes a reasonable person to believe that a particular individual is an agent of the company, a court is likely to hold that a presumption of agency exists. In Oklahoma City, an employee of an insurance agent had been sent by the agent to a sales school conducted by an insurer for which the office acted as agent. The employee did not have an agent's license but seemed a likely lad with a promising future in the insurance business. At the school the employee was given a kit of sample forms. He used one of them (a binder) to bind the insurer on a $100,000 liability policy to cover oil-drilling equipment. He signed John Doe, on the binder. When the oil operator had an accident with the equipment and was involved in lawsuits for over $100,000, the insurer denied liability. The court held that the agent

> . . . was given the implied authority to act as soliciting agent for the company. . . . The company specifically instructed him in the technique of soliciting; instructed him in the use of binders and furnished to him and for his use the actual binder forms. His authority or lack of it was never defined or explained to him and as a result he issued a binder, was permitted to sign the name of the general agent and to collect a premium. The very act that the company had trained him to do and furnished him the tools with which to do, he did.

Thus, although the insurer did not consent to any agency relationship either by agreement or ratification, and did not intend that an agency relationship be created, nevertheless insofar as the insured's rights were concerned, an agency relationship was presumed to exist. Therefore, the insurer was estopped (prevented) from relying on the defense that no such relationship was present.

The power and authority of the agent

The power of an agent rests primarily on the authority granted in the agency contract. However, the power to bind the principal extends beyond the contractual authority specifically granted.

Insurance agents have three kinds of authority. First, the agent has the *stipulated* or *expressed* authority bestowed by the terms of the contract with the insurer. The insurer specifies what types of insureds, what types of coverage, and how much insurance may be written.

Second, the agent has *implied* authority. The law gives agents that power which the public reasonably may believe them to have. The legal rule is that the public cannot be expected to know or to inquire into the terms of each agency agreement. If the public is reasonable in believing that an agent has the power to perform some particular act, then the law gives the agent such power. The assumption is reasonable that a life insurance agent has the right to accept the initial premium with the application. Therefore, if a life insurer, for inexplicable reasons, should not specifically empower an agent to accept the first premium, the agent would be granted that right through the doctrine of implied authority. Even if the insurer stated specifically in the agency contract that the agent was not empowered to collect the first premium, if this restriction was not communicated to every applicant, the courts would hold that applicants could pay their initial premium to the agent. In disputed issues, what is reasonable for the public to believe is decided by the court, and not by the policyowner or the insurer. The question of reasonableness is resolved on the basis of what actions are necessary and customary for the agent.

Third, the agent has *apparent* authority—that authority which the agent has exercised and in which the insurer has acquiesced by failure to protest. Assume that Agent Pinzur's company told him not to write auto insurance on drivers under 25. Yet, he writes one for an 18-year-old sophomore. The insurer accepts the premium and by this act acquiesces, thus bestowing on the agent the power to sell such policies.

Responsibility of principals

The acts of the insurance agent operating within the scope of expressed or apparent authority are viewed as acts of the insurer. The law considers the agent and the insurer as one and the same. Thus, the insurer is legally responsible for the actions of its agents while performing their prescribed duties, even if such agents make fraudulent assertions unknown to or unauthorized by the insurer.

While the insurer may limit the agent's authority and such limitations are binding on the agent, they are not always binding on third parties. Third parties may rely on a "normal" agency relationship. Therefore, "unreasonable" limitations on the agent's authority are not binding on insureds unless effectively communicated to them. The court will determine what is "unreasonable and normal" in disputed cases. Knowledge of the agent is presumed to be knowledge of the insurer. Any factor pertaining to the risk to be insured known by the agent is presumed to be known by the insurer. Thus, if the insurer's agent knows that the applicant's health has been (and continues to be) seriously impaired by the excessive use of dangerous drugs, such knowledge is imputable to the insurer, regardless of whether this information has been communicated to the insurer by its agent. If the insurer issues the policy, it is estopped from asserting drug addiction as grounds for challenging the validity of the contract. Insurers have attempted to neutralize this rule of agency law by providing that only statements made in the policy application or declarations are to be considered as knowledge of the insurer, but courts have been in conflict in rulings on the validity of such disclaimers.

Brokers as agents

A difference exists when insurance is bought through a broker in that an agent customarily has the power to bind a property liability insurer to a contract with the insured. The broker is an agent of the insured and thus has no power to bind the insurer. While acting within the scope of their authority, brokers may bind only the insured. Furthermore, because the brokers are the insured's agent rather than the insurer's agent knowledge, actions, and assertions of brokers acting within the scope of their authority remain with them and their clients and are not presumed to extend to the insurer.

Payment of premiums to the broker, unlike payment to the agent, is not payment to the insurer in absence of a statute to the contrary. In some states the broker is made an agent of the insurer for collecting premiums. Also, some states make anyone who, through solicitation, generates the issuance of a policy, the agent of the insurer. Insurance buyers, insurers, and brokers need to be informed of state law to determine the circumstances which create a statutory agency for the insurer.

Remedies

Remedies have been developed by statutes and legal precedent to be applied when disputes arise among parties to insurance contracts regarding their rights and obligations. These remedies may be broadly classified as *legal* and *equitable*. The doctrines of waiver and estoppel are important common-law (legal) remedies. Reformation and rescission are important equitable remedies.

Waiver and estoppel

The terms "waiver" and "estoppel" define methods by which an insured may gain a decision more favorable than the contractual language would indicate. Simplified definitions of these terms to assist in the understanding of these concepts are as follows:

> Waiver is the giving up of a contractual right. Estoppel is the prevention of the reliance by one party on a right it has previously waived. Waiver can be either direct or indirect, intentional or unintentional.

An insurer normally requires payment of the next policy premium prior to renewal. If an insurer sends an insured a revised declarations page for a new policy period, the insurer by this action (mistaken or otherwise) waives the right to deny renewal. If the insurer refuses to pay a claim under the renewed policy, legal action could be brought against the insurer to enforce payment. The doctrine of estoppel would prevent the insurer from using as a defense the assertion that because the premium had not been paid prior to renewal, the policy had not been renewed.

The term "waiver" has been defined by the New York Court of Appeals as "the voluntary abandonment or extinguishment by a party of some right or advantage." This definition means that if the insurer consents to some action of the insured, it must be bound by that consent. This same court has defined the term "estoppel" as the doctrine ". . . that a party may be precluded by his [or her] acts or conduct from asserting a right to the detriment or prejudice of another party who, entitled to rely on such conduct, has acted upon it." This concept means that if an insurer has led the insured to believe that certain contract provisions may be ignored, the insurer cannot use the resulting behavior of the insured as grounds for avoiding the contract.

Questions of waiver and estoppel arise largely in matters involving the relationship of agent and policyowners. Sometimes an applicant for a policy will inform the agent of some condition which would seem to be a breach of the policy at its inception. For example, a prospect for auto insurance may indicate that she regularly drives co-employees to work and charges them each a fare and thus profits from this arrangement. The agent explains that the practice is permissible; or perhaps the agent says nothing, issues the policy, and collects the premium.

A loss occurs while the insured is driving to work. When the adjuster learns about the small-scale taxi service and files a report with the home office, the insurer likely will deny liability based on the exclusion "to any automobile while used as a public or livery conveyance." The insured hires a lawyer. The insurer is not without its lawyer. The insurer's attorney points out the following clause in the contract: "No provision affecting this insurance shall exist, or waiver of any provision be valid, unless granted herein or expressed in writing added hereto." The insured's attorney is not impressed. The matter goes to court, and in most jurisdictions the insurer will be forced to pay the claim. These courts rule that the action of the agent constituted a waiver of the livery conveyance exclusion, and the insurer cannot disclaim liability. A dwindling minority of courts do not recognize in full these propositions concerning waiver and estoppel. They have held that an insurer is entitled to full use of the defense offered by the wording of the policy because of the policy's nonwaiver clause which these courts have held to be nonwaivable by the agent.

The insurer, by actions taken after a loss has occurred, may waive some breach of the contract by the insured. Thus, if the insurer, while investigating the loss, requires some action of the insured, a court might hold that the insurer has waived its right to invalidate the contract. For example, in a case where the insured was required to help the adjuster obtain figures from the burned account books, the court held that previous breaches of provisions of the insurance policy were waived by the insurer. In a frustrating Arkansas case (frustrating to the insurer but not to the insured), the court upheld the contention of an insured that silence or inaction on the part of an insurer following receipt of notice of loss from the policyowner constituted a waiver by the insurer of certain of its rights. Although the Arkansas Supreme Court affirmed this decision, one justice dissented and commented as follows:

> We have held that a denial of liability (within the time for filing proof of loss) is a waiver; we have held that sending blanks to the insured is a waiver of the time requirement; we have held that retaining the proof of loss is a waiver of its defects; we have held that questioning any attempted proof of loss is a waiver of its defects; now we are holding that the failure to do anything is a waiver of proof of loss. Thus the insurance company is really "between a rock and a hard place"; heretofore if the insurance company answered the letter and did anything at all, such was a waiver;

> and now if the insurance company does not do anything, it is a waiver. In short, the proof of loss requirement in an insurance contract is just about entirely eliminated by judicial *destruction!*

The opinion of the dissenting justice notwithstanding, the ruling is a sound one. A waiver could have been avoided in the foregoing instance if the insurer had notified the insured immediately of its decision to disclaim responsibility under the contract. In the absence of such notification it was reasonable for the insured to have assumed that the insurer had intended to perform under the contract.

Insureds, however, must not place too much reliance on the leniency of the courts in circumstances involving alleged waivers by insurers or their agents. In judging whether a particular action or inaction constitutes a waiver, the courts usually consider a number of questions. Was the insurer or its agent expressing an informal opinion or making a formal statement of fact? Did the agent have the authority to create the alleged waiver? Would the conduct of the insured have been different had there been no reliance on the agent's or the insurer's behavior? How important is the default giving rise to the waiver defense? The answers are not always black and white, and when they are gray different courts will render conflicting decisions on similar facts.

Parol evidence rule. The parol (oral) evidence rule places important limitations on the operation of waiver and estoppel by disallowing any evidence to be introduced to prove that the terms of the policy are other than those written in the contract. The U.S. Supreme Court in *Northern Assurance Company* v. *Grand View Building Association* stated:

> The contracts in writing, if in unambiguous terms, must be permitted to speak for themselves, and cannot by the courts, at the instance of one of the parties, be altered or contradicted by parol evidence, unless in case of fraud or mutual mistake of facts; that this principle is applicable to cases of insurance contracts as fully as to contracts on other subjects; . . . that it is competent and reasonable for insurance companies to make it a matter of condition in their policies that their agents shall not be deemed to have authority to alter or contradict the express terms of the policies as executed and delivered; . . .

The parol evidence rule applies only to the terms of the contract, and then only to statements made *previous* to the creation of the formal contract. For example, a multiple location reporting form was issued by a fire insurer to cover farm equipment and automobiles at three locations. The face amount of the policy was written for $76,000 with a limit of coverage of $35,000 at the first location, $1,000 at the second, and $40,000 at the third. A monthly report was required to show the values at each location. *After* the policy was issued, the agent informed the insured that irrespective of the location limits shown in the policy, any loss would be settled on the basis of the values shown at each location in the monthly report upon which the premium was based and paid. The insured had a $60,000 loss at the first location. The values shown on the monthly report at that location just before the fire were $60,000. The insured asked $60,000 indemnity. The insurer offered only $35,000, the policy limit at that location. The court said:

> It is well settled law that an oral agreement cannot vary the terms and provisions of a written contract. It is also well settled that a policy provision to the effect that an agent is not empowered to alter the terms of a policy contract is binding. However, neither of these rules applies here. As a general agent of the insurer, the agent had authority to issue oral binders. His statements to the president of the insured equipment company constituted an oral binder; hence, a new contract was brought into existence and the suit is under such new contract.

The insured was paid $60,000.[2]

Waiver provisions.   Many policies include "waiver" or "change" clauses. Insurers are represented by many agents eager to obtain business, who in order to sell, occasionally promise coverage not contemplated by the contract or waive conditions important to the insurer. As a result, the previously mentioned waiver clause is inserted in the policies for the protection of insurers. For example, the contract clause in a life insurance policy includes the words "only the president, a vice president, or the secretary of the company has authority to alter this contract or to waive any of its provisions." The legal interpretation of the waiver clause is unclear. Even though the Supreme Court years ago held the waiver clause valid and one that should be given full force and effect, conflicting court decisions are difficult to reconcile.

Oral (parol) waivers may be made prior to, or at the inception of, a contract or after the policy has been issued. Some courts applying the parol evidence rule hold that parol waivers made by agents before the contract is issued are not effective. Others hold them binding on the insurers, under the theory that the insured did not know that the agent's authority was limited and therefore had no reason to believe that the agent was acting beyond the authority granted.

Just as confusing are decisions relating to parol waivers after the policy has been issued. Most courts uphold the requirement that the waiver must be in writing and conform to the policy provision, although other courts have allowed oral waivers in spite of the contract provision to the contrary. These courts insist that, because agents have the authority to waive certain provisions, they can waive the waiver clause as that clause is for the insurer's benefit. The theory is that either party has the option to waive a provision made in its favor.

Some policies include a clause that reads as follows:

> Notice to any agent or knowledge possessed by any agent or by any other person shall not effect a waiver or a change in any part of this policy or estop the Company from asserting any right under the terms of this

---

[2] *Federated Mutual Implement and Hardware Company* v. *Fairfax Equipment Company,* 261 F.2d 207, U.S. App., 10th Cir., Okla.

policy, nor shall the terms of this policy be waived or changed except by endorsement issued to form a part of this policy.

One of the purposes of this provision is to protect the insurer against the assertion after a loss that additional agreements not incorporated in the contract are in effect. The clause also is designed to prohibit the law of estoppel from barring the insurer from using some right reserved under the policy. Another purpose is to allow the insurer to assert all its rights under the policy, regardless of the agent's actions. A final purpose is to require that all changes or waivers be made only by endorsements (written provisions) and that they form a part of the policy. The intention of the insurer is that the policy shall contain all the agreements between the parties and that it cannot be varied by parol evidence. As with the "waiver" clause, some confusion exists as to the legal interpretation of the "change" clause.

Because the restricted nature of the life insurance agent's powers is or is presumed to be better known to the public than that of the property agent, oral waivers in life insurance seldom create a problem.

Rescission

If evidence shows that one party by fraud or misrepresentation of a material fact causes another to enter into a contract, the wronged party may seek the equitable remedy of rescission—that is, to have the contract declared void from its inception. To take advantage of this remedy, the injured party must act as soon as knowledge of the wrong is apparent and must return whatever was received under the contract. The doctrines of warranty, representation, and concealment and how they might lead to rescission are discussed later.

Reformation

Waiver and estoppel provide remedies under common law against unfair consequences of strict adherence to terms of the contract. Liberal interpretation of documents by the courts also provides a legal remedy. If, in the opinion of the court, the language is either inconsistent or ambiguous, the court may construe contracts to reflect the court's interpretation of the intentions of the parties. The application of these legal remedies, however, is limited by the parol evidence rule.

When an adequate legal remedy is unavailable, an effort can be made to achieve justice by a suit in equity. Maxims (principles of conduct) rather than rules of law are used in determining equitable remedies. Decisions in equity are based on natural justice and moral rather than legal rights.

An important equitable remedy is a suit for reformation of the contract. In these suits, the parol evidence rule does not apply. Where proof is conclusive that a prior agreement between the insured and the insurer had been reached which—either by mistake on both sides or by a mistake on one and fraud on the other—does not appear in the written contract, the court will correct the mistake by reforming the contract to express the original intention of both parties. For example, the insured told the agent of the intended use of the auto while touring Europe. The agent agreed to endorse the insured's auto insurance policy to provide coverage while the insured explored Europe. Failure of the agent to endorse the policy either by mistake or fraud, is sufficient cause for reformation of the contract to include this coverage—assuming that the agent is acting within the apparent scope of authority.

Reformation also can be used by the insurer to rectify mistakes in the policy made in favor of the policyowner. Hunt and the insurer's agent clearly intended to insure a house known as the Byrd Hill dwelling. Instead, the policy incorrectly covered a second house owned by Hunt. The second house burned, and Hunt decided to take advantage of the mistake in the writing of the policy. The court, however, ordered the policy reformed to conform to the parties' intentions.

Cases involving legal remedies are decided by juries, whereas suits in equity usually are tried without jury. The belief is that juries generally are harsher on insurers than are judges, and furthermore, juries usually are more easily deceived by dishonest policyowners than are judges. Therefore, insurers are more comfortable in suits in equity than in suits involving legal remedies. Conversely insureds are more secure seeking legal rather than equitable remedies.

Doctrines of Warranty, Representation, and Concealment

Warranties, representations, and concealment have a special bearing on contracts of insurance. In most business arrangements, for example, transactions involving the purchase and sale of used cars, warranties and representations are designed to protect the buyer from the seller. In insurance, however, the use of warranties and representations is to protect the seller from the buyer. The basic principle arose under the common-law doctrine (discussed in Chapter 6) that insurance is a contract *uberrimae fidei* (utmost good faith). Insurers rely on information furnished by prospective buyers in deciding whether or not to write the insurance and in determining the premium. If the information is spurious or incomplete, the insurer may be able to avoid the contract on the grounds of warranty violation, misrepresentation, or concealment.

The common-law doctrine of warranty

A warranty in insurance is defined as a *stipulation in the policy* relating to the nature of the risk insured, which conditions the insurer's liability. Thus, in a theft insurance contract, if the insured agrees to keep the doors locked while the house is unattended, that promise is a warranty. If the insured states in the policy that a watchdog is used, that statement is also a warranty. Noncompliance with a warranty, or a falsely warranted statement, furnishes grounds for the insurer to avoid the contract. The materiality of a warranty is never questioned if the contract becomes the subject of litigation.[3] A warranty is presumed to be material. To avoid the contract, the insurer need prove only that a warranty has been violated. Breach of a warranty may void a policy even if the insured gave the information to the best of his or her knowledge.

Even if the fact is more favorable to the insurer than that warranted, breach of a warranty can be used by the insurer to abrogate the contract. This reasoning conforms with the English common-law rule that courts require strict compliance without considering the importance of the warranty to the risk. In a case tried years ago in the U.S. Supreme Court, the insured had warranted in buying life insurance that he was not married. Later it was revealed that the insured had been married for some time before buying the policy. As noted by actuaries, married men live longer than single men,[4] yet the insurer succeeded in rescinding the contract on grounds of a breach of a warranty, even though the fact was more favorable to the insurer than that warranted. Decisions such as this one led to modifications in the United States of the strict English common-law doctrine of warranty.

Warranties are of two types: *promissory* and *affirmative*. A promissory warranty states that a fact is presently true and will continue to be true. The affirmative warranty states that a fact is true but makes no statement about the future.

If an insured obtains a special rate for fire insurance because of the installation of an automatic sprinkler system, that system must be kept in good working order throughout the life of the contract. If a fire occurs and the sprinkler system was not in good order, the insurer can avoid the claim because the warranty would be held to be promissory.

In the absence of proof that a warranty is intended to be promissory, it will be construed by the courts as affirmative. In a case in which an applicant for insurance had warranted that no smoking was permitted on the premises, smoking was the cause of a fire that destroyed the property. The court ordered the insurer to pay for the loss, holding that the warranty was affirmative. The insurer could have insisted that the no smoking rule be a promissory warranty; but the policy would have had to declare that a promissory warranty was made by the insured.

Implied warranties. Generally, a warranty must be written and made a part of the contract either by attaching it to the policy or by a specific policy reference to it. An exception is in marine insurance where three warranties not written in the contract are implied: seaworthiness, no deviation, and legality. The shipowner, in buying a marine policy, warrants that the vessel is seaworthy. The implied warranty of no deviation

---

[3] A false statement is considered to be material if the insurer would have rejected the insurance or asked for better terms had the matter been stated correctly.

[4] Some cynics would say it just seems longer.

is a promise that the ship will move on the customary course between the ports named. Deviation is permitted only to avoid storms or for errands of mercy. The third implied warranty is a promise that the vessel will not be used in an illegal enterprise. As the shipper usually has no knowledge of the ship on which goods will be carried, these warranties generally are removed by the insurer from cargo policies.

The common-law doctrine of representation

Representations, as distinguished from warranties, are not a part of the contract but are statements made by the applicant to the insurer in the process of obtaining a policy. Representations may be oral or included in a written application. Oral representations, however, are difficult to prove.

Unlike the warranty, no presumption is made that a representation is material. If the contract becomes a subject of litigation, the insurer has the burden of proof of the materiality of a representation. The insurer must show that, if the truth had been known, it would not have issued the policy on the terms quoted. In an increasing number of jurisdictions, courts are considering customary underwriting practices within the industry and the practices of the contesting insurer, in ruling on the question of materiality.

A second difference is that, although warranties must be absolutely true, any representation dealing with the applicant's belief, intention, or opinion need only be substantially true. That is, these representations are regarded as statements of opinion, and, unless given fraudulently, cannot be used by the insurer as a basis for avoiding the contract regardless of their materiality. For example, if the applicant writes in an application for life insurance that no change in employment is contemplated, the insurer cannot claim a misrepresentation even though at the very time the applicant said "no" to this question, his venturesome wife was, without his knowledge, buying two tickets for the wilds of Africa where, she decided, they would go into the safari business.

Representations concerning past or present conditions for which knowledge is available must be given accurately by the applicant, or, under the common law, the insurer might be able to avoid the contract. For example, if an applicant for life insurance states in the application that no doctor had been consulted in the last five years, but three doctors had been consulted on 10 occasions within that time, the applicant is guilty of a misrepresentation. However, if these 10 consultations were for minor ailments such as a mild cold after a skinny dip, they likely would be considered immaterial to the risk, and therefore not sufficient grounds for avoiding the policy.

Representations need be only false and material to furnish grounds for policy rescission. The prevailing court opinion is that they need not be fraudulent. An innocent misrepresentation of a material fact is grounds for avoidance. Furthermore, a fraudulent misrepresentation of an immaterial fact is insufficient grounds for rescission. These rules express only the common-law doctrine of representation. The purpose of the doctrine is to protect insurers, not punish dishonest insureds.

When an insurer is allowed to rescind a contract on grounds of a misrepresentation, it must return the premium. Avoidance of a contract because of a breach of warranty, however, does not require a premium refund unless the breach occurs before the insurer assumes the risk.

Modification of the English common law

The English common-law doctrine of warranty in its pure form requires strict compliance. A breach in any form or degree is sufficient to avoid the policy. No consideration is given to the materiality of the breach. Except in marine insurance, the majority of American courts do not follow the strict English common law.

Doctrine of informal warranties. British courts hold that every statement in a policy is a warranty but American courts have recognized a difference between formal and informal warranties. Formal warranties are introduced by words such as "it is warranted that," or "provided that," whereas informal warranties are flat statements made without an introduction. For example, if, in her application, the insured names "Burt Reynolds, my husband" as beneficiary, such a statement would be a formal warranty only if it were specifically warranted. Some courts have held that a blanket provision that all statements in the application are warranted to be true is sufficient, but the trend is to ignore these clauses and to judge each individual statement separately. The statement becomes an informal warranty only if the fact in question seems to be material. If the "my husband" part of the foregoing beneficiary designation is only wishful thinking by the insured, no warranty has been violated if the court concludes that "my husband" was used to identify the beneficiary and not to evaluate the hazard. Descriptive words in a policy are considered warranties only when they relate to conditions affecting the risk. Thus, the common-law doctrine of warranty has been softened by the refusal of the courts to consider as warranties immaterial statements not specifically warranted.

Doctrine of beneficent interpretation. The decision as to whether or not a warranty has been violated is dependent on the courts' interpretation which may be literal, functional, or equitable. When the construction is literal, the exact meaning of the words used in the policy is applied in determining if a breach has occurred. A functional construction interprets the warranty in relation to its purpose. In an equitable interpretation, the literal or functional meaning may be badly warped by the court to accommodate standards of reasonableness or mercy. The following example illustrates the three standards of interpretation.

Scott Harrington had a burglary insurance policy in which he had promised to have two guards on duty while the premises were not regularly open for business who recorded hourly rounds on a clock. A loss occurred and it was found that Scott had changed his protection system to one guard signaling an outside central station every hour. If the warranty is interpreted literally, there would be a breach. But if the court determines that the protection under the new system is as effective as under the old, it might hold that there has been no breach. This interpretation would be functional and is applied by an increasing number of courts, although the number is still a minority.

Suppose that the system had not been changed, but at the time of the loss only one guard was present. The other guard, who until now had enjoyed an unimpeachable reputation for reliability, had temporarily left the premises in violation of company rules. The warranty would have been breached if it were interpreted either literally or functionally. But if the court determines that the insured had acted reasonably by employing what appeared to be a reliable guard, it may decide that there has been no breach. This view is an equitable interpretation of a warranty. Thus, the common-law doctrine of warranty has been softened by a more liberal interpretation of compliance. Most courts interpret warranties liberally where a literal construction shows only a superficial breach affecting the risk temporarily or insignificantly.

Doctrine of fraudulent misrepresentations. To the dismay of legal scholars, an increasing number of court decisions tend to blur the distinction between misrepresentation of opinion and misrepresentation of fact by ruling that the insured's duty is performed by making representations "to the best of his [or her] knowledge and belief." These decisions are especially prevalent in disputes involving life insurance. They are accomplished principally through the interpretation of representations as statements of opinion, rather than statement of fact in which the slightest doubt exists.

Statutory modification. In many states, a softening of the harsher aspects of the warranty and misrepresentation doctrines developed through judicial interpretation and by statute. In nearly every case, however, the doctrine of warranty in marine insurance remains in its pristine form. One type of statute—the entire contract statute—provides, or requires the policy to provide, that the policy and the application attached to it shall constitute the entire contract between the parties. These statutes are found in many states but usually are limited to life and health insurance. The effect of these statutes is to prevent the insurer from using misrepresentations made by the insured as grounds for avoiding the policy unless these representations are written in an application as a part of the policy. Statements written in an application and incorporated into the policy become warranties rather than representations.

To relieve the insured of the adverse effects of stricter interpretation of warranties over representations, statutes often provide, or require the policy to provide, that all statements made by the insured in the application shall, in the absence of fraud, be deemed representations and not warranties. Most of these statutes apply to life insurance only or are restricted to life and health insurance. Their effect is to require the insurer to prove the materiality, as well as the falsity, of statements when seeking to avoid a policy on the grounds of breach of warranty. If the statements are fraudulently made, however, it would seem that because of the modifying phrase "in the absence of fraud," to avoid the policy the insurer need prove only intent to deceive along with falsity, and not be concerned with the question of materiality. Courts logically have given little attention to the fraud exception, taking the position that unless the matter is material, no meaningful intention to deceive is possible because no deception could be accomplished. As a result, the fraud exception has been deleted from the statutes in most states.

In a few states, the common law has been modified by statute so that no breach of warranty or misrepresentation can be used to avoid a contract unless the violation caused or contributed to the loss. (Under common law, a breach of warranty does not have to be a cause of loss.) The effect is to rule out avoidance of a contract for breach of warranty or a misrepresentation, no matter how material the warranty or representation may be, if the breach did not contribute to the loss. Thus, if the applicant says her mother died at age 98 from overexertion on the dance floor, when her mother actually died of cancer at the age of 53, the insurer cannot use this falsely warranted statement to deny a claim if the insured's subsequent death resulted from a moped accident.

Standing between the "contribute to the loss" and the "warranties shall be deemed representation" statutes are the "increase in hazard" statutes. These statutes provide that unless a breached warranty or a misrepresentation increases the hazard, the insurer may not use the breach as grounds for denying a claim under the policy. The "increase in hazard" statutes seem similar to the "warranties shall be deemed representation" statutes. They differ only if the courts choose to interpret them differently. When a warranty is deemed to be a representation, the represented facts must be false and material for the insurer to have grounds for contract rescission. The test of materiality is if the statement in any manner induces the insurer to write the insurance which otherwise would have been declined or offered on different terms. To be material, the breached warranty (misrepresented fact) need not increase the hazard. That it influences the insurer's decision to underwrite the insurance is sufficient. But under the "increase in hazard" statutes the breached warranty (misrepresented fact) must increase the hazard. An increase in hazard exists if the deviation between the facts and the warranted or represented facts is sufficient to increase the frequency or severity of an insured loss. This test is stiffer than proving only that the warranty or representation is material. No assumption is made that the hazard is affected solely because the insured's statement influences the insurer to write the policy. The court must determine if a breach of warranty (misrepresented fact) causes an increase in hazard.

As noted, under common law fraudulent misrepresentations of immaterial facts are not grounds for the insurer to avoid the policy. However, some state statutes modifying the common law of warranty and representation include the phrase that "no such misrepresentation or false warranty shall defeat or avoid the policy unless it shall have been made with actual intent to deceive or materially affects either the acceptance of the risk or the hazard assumed. . . ." But the courts have found these statutes misleading and have followed the common law when the statement affects neither the acceptance of the risk nor the hazard assumed by the insurer.

The statutes modifying the common law of warranty and representation vary among the states. The "warranties shall be deemed representations" statutes and the "increase in hazard" statutes generally apply to all forms of insurance except marine. The largest variation is among the "contribute to loss" statutes. Some of these statutes apply to warranties only, whereas others apply to warranties and representations. A few statutes are restricted to life insurance and others to all insurance except life. One applies to all forms of insurance. The effect of these various statutes is conditioned by court interpretation which has varied so widely that several states have defined the terms in their statutes. In these states, when the effect of a breach of warranty or representation is covered by statute, the courts are better able to determine what the statute covers—and so are the parties to the contract.

The doctrine of concealment

Concealment is the failure to disclose known facts. Insurance is a contract of utmost good faith, thus compelling the contracting parties to reveal to each other every fact material to the contract. These common-law rules concerning full disclosure first were developed in marine insurance. In the early days the insurer generally had to rely on the insured's description of the exposure. Thus, the courts placed the burden of full disclosure on the contracting parties. Now, although the intelligence services of Lloyd's and others provide insurers vast amounts of information, the earlier doctrines still are operative.

The English rule is that every material fact the insurer should know must be revealed by the applicant. Failure to reveal, whether or not with intent to defraud, will give the insurer the right to avoid the contract. The applicant's lack of awareness of the fact is of no consequence. While this rule is applied by the English courts to all forms of insurance, the American courts generally apply it only to marine insurance. All other forms of insurance are subject to the American common law which adds several qualifying conditions to the English rule. The insured must be aware of the fact, know it is material, and understand that the insurer has no knowledge of it. Also, deception of the insurer must be the motive for silence. Thus, in the United States, a nonmarine insurer is not permitted to avoid the contract unless the fact concealed not only was obviously material but also was concealed by the insured with intent to defraud. Furthermore, courts place the burden of proof on the insurer.

The doctrine of concealment applied by the American courts offers the nonmarine insurer little protection. Courts tend to interpret the doctrine in favor of the insured. For instance, it is not enough that the concealed fact be material to the insurer, its materiality also must be so obvious that it does not escape notice of the insured. Thus, failure of an applicant for fire insurance to reveal that a neighbor's house was burning at the time the application was made likely would be held to constitute a concealment of a fact which the insured knew to be material, and thus fraudulent. On the other hand, failure to tell of a suspicion that an arsonist loose in the neighborhood had an eye on the property might be held to be an innocent concealment of a material fact, unless the applicant is an insurance professor who presumably would know that the fact is material to the acceptance of the risk.

Even if the insured knows a fact to be material, failure to disclose it does not always constitute fraud. The insured is under no obligation to disclose facts of common knowledge or facts that the insurer is expected to know. Thus, if a swinger's bar near a college campus is known as a "hangout" for undisciplined students, its insurer probably would not be successful in an attempt to avoid a claim for a fire loss on the grounds that the proprietor did not reveal that these students were the principal customers. Finally, the motive for silence may be solely that of protecting the applicant's reputation and not one of deceiving the insurer. Thus, a married applicant for life insurance who fails to tell the insurer of discreetly seeing another married person might not be guilty of concealment even though the applicant knows that fact to be material to the risk, especially because the spouses of both parties involved are insanely jealous. The purpose of the silence is not to deceive the insurer but to protect the reputations of the concerned persons. The courts in some cases have accepted that there are certain matters that gentlefolks should not be expected to talk about regardless of their materiality to the risk.

Statutory modification. The American common law of concealment is modified in California by a statute making concealment, whether intentional or unintentional, grounds for avoidance of the contract.[5]

Basis for an insurer avoiding a contract:

Doctrine	Action must be:
Warranty	False at time of loss, if promissory
	False at time of statement, if affirmative
Representation	False and material
Concealment	Material and intentional (fraudulent)

An item is material if the insurer would not have issued the coverage if the true facts had been known.

---

[5] Vol. 42, sec. 330, Annotated Calif. Codes.

Summary

1. Insurable interest is required in insurance contracts as a matter of public policy to discourage gambling and willful destruction of lives and property. One exception is the purchase of life insurance on one's own life.
2. For property insurance, an insurable interest is any financial interest based on a legal right in the preservation of the property. The insurable interest need exist only at the time of loss.
3. For life insurance, an insurable interest is any reasonable expectation of a financial gain from the continued life of the subject insured.
4. In life insurance, either the owner of the policy or the beneficiary must have an insurable interest in (or be) the subject of the insurance. The insurable interest need exist only at the policy inception.
5. Agents have the expressed powers granted by their agency contracts with the principal (insurer). Agents also have implied powers that may arise from business usage and custom or by the principal's (insurer's) failure to disclaim previous similar actions taken by the agent.
6. A broker is the agent of the insured and thus does not have the power to bind the insurer.
7. The courts consider knowledge of the agent to be knowledge of the insurer. However, knowledge of the broker is knowledge only of the broker and the insured.
8. Waiver is the giving up of a contractual right.
9. Estoppel is the prevention of the reliance by one party on a right it has previously waived.
10. Waiver and estoppel may prevent avoidance of a policy by an insurer or the refusal of the insurer to pay a claim even if the insured has breached the contract.
11. The parol evidence rule disallows the use of any evidence to prove that the terms of the insurance policy are other than those written in the contract.
12. Rescission is an equitable remedy which declares the contract void from its inception, thus restoring the parties to the position they would have held in the absence of a contract.
13. Reformation occurs when the court corrects a mistake made by both parties or a mistake made by one party coupled with fraud by the other. The court reforms the contract to express the original intention of the parties. The parol evidence rule does not apply in reformation cases where conclusive proof exists that a prior agreement between the insured and the insurer does not conform with the written contract.
14. Warranties are guarantees included in the policy. Representations are statements made by the insured in obtaining the coverage but are not part of the policy. Representations attached to the policy become warranties.

15. The doctrine of concealment applies to material facts known to the insured but intentionally not reported to the insurer.

Questions for Review

1. "The principle of insurable interest is basic to the structure of insurance," according to the text. Explain the rationale for this statement. How is insurable interest applied to property insurance? How does its application differ when applied to life insurance? Explain these differences.

2. Your professor offers to buy a policy on the life of the student who scores the highest grade on the midterm examination. Would such a purchase create a valid contract? Explain, keeping in mind the SOB principle of insurable interest in life insurance. If your professor offered to sell you a policy on his life which he already owned, would the contract's validity be affected?

3. Is it ever possible for a person to buy life insurance even though that person has no insurable interest in the life? Is it possible for a person to buy fire insurance on a dwelling even though that person does not have an insurable interest?

4. How does an insurance agent differ from an insurance broker and how are insurance buyers affected by the difference?

5. The authority granted to an agent is either expressed, implied, or apparent. State the source of each type of authority; that is, contracts, statutes, or court decisions. If based on court decisions, what is the rule of law supporting these decisions?

6. Define the concepts of waiver and estoppel and explain how the parol evidence rule limits their operation.

7. Give an example of each of the legal and each of the equitable remedies. When is each type of remedy used?

8. Define the doctrines of warranty, misrepresentation, and concealment. Does a representation made in an application and attached to the insurance contract remain a representation? Explain the importance of the answer to this question to the insurer and the insured.

9. What is the meaning of the term "materiality"? What effect does it have in cases involving a breach of warranty, a misrepresentation, and a concealment?

10. Even when an insured breaches a warranty, the insurer may still be required to pay the insured's claim. Explain the basis upon which a court might find for the insured despite the breach.

Questions for Discussion

1. Frank Gile owns a car which he sells to a new faculty member in physics. Frank is insured under his family's auto policy, covering three cars. He tenders a bill of sale to the new owner in return for the purchase price, but cannot deliver the certificate of title until next week when he can get it from his bank safety deposit box. If the bill of sale is dated on Saturday,

but the title certificate is not given the buyer until Wednesday, is the new buyer insured by Frank's policy during the weekend? Explain.

2. In the preceding question the property insurable interest will never exceed the value of the car. Is this limit fair? Explain, in view of your concept of the proper basis for measuring the value of the car. Would the value produced by your basis of measurement produce a figure acceptable to both the insured and the insurer? Explain.

3. The law makes no attempt to impose a limit or measure the insurable interest in a human life. Do you think this approach is fair in light of your answer to the preceding question? Would it be legal when a couple is separated for one spouse to buy life insurance on the other? If so, should some precautionary action be required? Explain.

4. To what extent (if any) may an agent legally waive a provision in a life insurance contract? In a property insurance contract?

5. Because of poor loss experience, insurers have been more restrictive in their writing of auto insurance. Agent Jahankhani has been told by his company to write no more auto insurance for those households that have a teenage driver. In spite of this restriction, Agent Jahankhani sells a policy to Ms. Reilly, who has an 18-year-old son, Jim. Later Jim wrecks the car. Outline the position of Ms. Reilly, Jim, Jahankhani, and the insurer.

6. Dave Whitford buys fire insurance through an insurance broker. He tells the broker that he soon will be storing some dynamite in his basement as an accommodation to a friend "in the movement." The broker tells Dave that this increase in the hazard is permissible. If a loss results from the dynamite storage, will the insurer pay the claim? If a loss results but is in no way connected with the increase in the hazard, will the insurer pay?

7. Suppose, in question (6) Dave had been dealing with an agent rather than a broker. Would your answer be different? Explain.

8. What is common law? Why does it change? How does it differ from statutory law?

9. Why do you think the majority of American courts do not abide consistently by the strict English common law?

10. What is the logic of permitting implied warranties in marine insurance?

6

Insurance contracts

The insurance policy is a contract and therefore subject to contract law. The nature of insurance contracts, their creation, and how they differ from other contracts are discussed in this chapter. Insurance contracts frequently are called policies. The terms "policy" and "contract" are used interchangeably in this text.

The Formation of the Contract

Two basic instruments used in connection with insurance transactions are (1) the application and (2) the binder.

The application

The function of the insurance agent technically is one of soliciting prospects to apply for insurance (and in some cases finding an insurer to write the coverage) rather than one of offering insurance for sale. In life, health, hail, livestock, and credit insurance, as well as surety bonding, the application must be in writing on forms supplied by insurers. Applications for property and liability insurance, with a few exceptions, are oral and informal. One exception is that insurers mass marketing personal lines policies provide potential applicants with application forms.

Legal status of an application.   An application usually is an offer, although under some conditions it is only an invitation to the insurer to make an offer. An application cannot be an acceptance of an offer, because the agent, in inviting the application, has not made an offer.

A written application states the kind and amount of insurance desired, the premium to be paid, and detailed information about the exposure. Some applications include a notice that the agent does not have the authority to modify the terms either of the application or of the policy. The information in the application is used chiefly for underwriting and identification. Although applications for insurance, in some cases, may have no legal consequences in creating the contract, they do contain a number of representations that affect the contract after it is made. In life and health insurance, the application is made a part of the contract because most states prohibit insurers from using statements of the insured in defense of a claim unless these statements are part of the written contract. Because oral misrepresentations are difficult to prove, the custom is to include written policy declarations in nonlife insurance even though oral representations are allowed.

Declarations.   Declarations are statements providing information about the risk to be insured and usually form the basis for a decision regarding the issuance and rating of the insurance. In some types of insurance, the declarations are included in the written application and attached to the policy, but where a written application is not required, a schedule of declarations is included in the policy and becomes part of the contract when accepted.

The information in the declarations is supplied by the insured or the broker. Declarations include the name of the insured, location of the exposure, type of business, and other pertinent facts. In mercantile open-stock burglary insurance, for example, the declarations indicate if a burglary alarm system is used, its type and whether it will be properly maintained. The declarations also specify if private guards will be on duty within the premises. The insured must state in the declarations if a burglary loss has occurred during the preceding five years, and if any burglary insurance has been cancelled or denied by other insurers. The existence of similar insurance on the same insurable interest also is a subject of the declarations. Information in the declarations is used not only for rating and underwriting but also for identification.

The binder

A binder is a temporary contract, pending the issuance of the policy. Binders may be either written or oral. The disadvantage of an oral contract is the difficulty of proving its existence. Nevertheless, oral binders in insurance often precede their written confirmation. In many types of coverage, insurance attaches when the agent convinces the prospect of the need for insurance. If the prospect says the insurance is wanted and the agent says, "You have it!" then a legal oral binder has been executed—subject to the other legal contract requirements, such as consideration, legal purpose, meeting of the minds, and so on. Immediately upon creating an oral binder, the agent should record the time the binder is made, the terms of the coverage, and the parties involved. The oral binder should be followed by a written binder whenever a delay occurs in issuing the policy, in order to reduce the possibility of disputes. A written binder is especially important in those lines in which policies are not standardized. Only through a written binder can there be clear-cut evidence of an understanding by both parties of what the insurance covers, the amount of insurance, the premium charged, and the insurer(s) writing the insurance. When policies are standardized, the courts assume that the binder conforms to standard policy provisions.

Analysis of the binder. A fire insurance binder contains a number of provisions as follows:

1. The binder includes the name of the particular insurer(s) in which the risk is bound because fire insurance agents usually represent more than one insurer.

2. The binder states the amount of insurance to be used in limiting loss and payments and in determining the premium. One reason for issuing a binder instead of a policy is that the rate may not yet have been established. The binder provides immediate coverage. When the rate is determined, it will apply retroactively to the period covered by the binder.

3. The binder applies only until the policy is issued.

4. The binder names the insured and describes the types of losses, perils, and property insured. This information is to identify the risk.

5. The time of coverage is stated by indicating the date of inception and the date of termination. The time period covered by the binder usually is short, often limited to 30 days or less.

6. The binder cites clauses such as coinsurance, pro rata, and deductibles that apply and are to be included in the policy.

7. The binder states that the insurance is subject to the terms of the policy regularly issued by the insurer where the property is located.

8. The binder specifies that in the event of loss before the binder expires, the full annual premium is due. If no loss occurs, the premium will be based on the time the coverage existed.

9. Finally, a binder might include a clause allowing the insurer to cancel the bound insurance on a few days' notice.

Even though a formal written binder is not required, the agent should maintain a written record of the insurance consisting of the information included in a written binder. Most buyers do not demand a formal binder, although it is good practice for the insured to request some type of evidence that the insurance has been effected.

Uses of binders. Generally, property insurance agents have the power to bind the insurer to a risk. Preparation and issuance of the policy may be time consuming; meanwhile, the risk is covered by the binder.

For certain lines of coverage, insurers prefer that their agents use binders before they write the policies. The insurers then have the opportunity to inspect the risk to see if it meets underwriting standards. Workers' compensation and steam boiler exposures are examples of lines in which a delay may occur in issuing the policy. Some exposures require investigation of the moral character and financial status of the applicant. When other underwriting factors are favorable, insurers generally are willing to be bound temporarily while the investigation is conducted. Until they are certain that they want to accept the risk for the term of the contract, insurers are not willing to issue the policy because of the expense involved if it is cancelled a few days later.

Binders generally are not used by life insurers because life insurance sales representatives are soliciting agents and not contract-writing agents. As life insurance policies are noncancellable, insurers want to approve the application in the home office before writing the policy. Most insurers do not want to be bound even temporarily by an agent. Nevertheless, to a small degree an increasing number of insurers issue binding receipts which give the applicant immediate and continuing coverage until the application has been acted upon at the home office or until a stated period of four to six weeks has elapsed. The true binding receipt used by these insurers is different from the "conditional receipt" used by nearly all other life insurers.

Conditional receipts are given by insurers only when the first premium is tendered by the applicant with the application. The most common conditional receipt provides that the face amount of the policy will be paid to the beneficiary of an applicant who dies before the policy is issued if, at the date of the application (or medical examination, if one is required), the applicant met the insurer's requirements for acceptability at the premium rate and for the policy plan specified in the application. To illustrate: Ross applies for a $10,000 policy which requires no medical examination. He pays the premium for the first year and leaves the agent's office. Absentmindedly he steps into the elevator shaft thinking the elevator has arrived and tumbles 32 stories to his death. If the insurer, upon receipt of his application, would have approved Ross for life insurance (except for the technicality that he is now dead), the insurer would issue a check for the face amount of the policy.

A second type of conditional receipt provides that protection begins as soon as the application and other accompanying documents have been approved at the home office. This latter type of conditional receipt is more restrictive because it offers no protection for the period between the filing of the application and its approval. Had Ross been given this form of conditional receipt, his 32-story fall would have produced no insurance benefits even though Ross was in the best of health before being shafted.

When the first premium does not accompany the application, no conditional receipt can be issued. Therefore, the policy cannot become effective until (1) it is delivered to the applicant while in good health, and (2) the premium is paid. For example, if the applicant does not tender the first premium with the application, the applicant will not be entitled to a conditional receipt. Then if the applicant becomes seriously ill after the application is approved but before the policy is delivered, the contract cannot be completed. Therefore the insurance will not become effective. However, if the applicant soon recovers, the contract may be completed.

Abuses of binders. Binders may offer unscrupulous people a means to have free insurance. An agent may bind an insurance contract, and then, when the policy is issued, the buyer may refuse it if no losses have occurred. Legally, the client is obligated to pay the premium for the period of coverage; but in practice, agents seldom insist on payment. Instead, they cancel the policy "flat"—that is, back to its inception date— and assume that no coverage ever attached. By acquiring a series of binders, one after the other, a scheming person can have free insurance continuously until the operation is uncovered.

Agents also may be guilty of abuse of binders. Sometimes they issue oral binders when they have no binding authority, or they mislead the applicant into thinking that coverage begins before the effective date.[1] The insurance buyer, therefore, must be sure that the agent has the authority to execute an immediate binder.

The Insurance Contract Defined

Included among insurance arrangements are so many dissimilar contracts that no short, precise definition would be adequate to distinguish insurance completely from similar devices.[2] It would be useful if insurance could be defined simply, as:

> Insurance is a financial arrangement in which one party agrees to compensate another upon the occurrence of a specified contingent event.

Unfortunately, this overly broad definition would classify gambling as insurance. Therefore, the definition must be restricted to:

> Insurance is a financial arrangement in which one party agrees to compensate another for a loss if the loss results from the occurrence of a specified contingent event.

The addition of "for a loss" excludes life insurance from definition as the payment made upon the death of the subject does not compensate

---

[1] See Chapter 5.

[2] For a comprehensive discussion of the definition of insurance, see Herbert S. Denenberg, "The Legal Definition of Insurance," *The Journal of Insurance* 30, no. 3 (September 1963), pp. 319–43.

for the loss, but only mitigates some of the financial impact of the death for the beneficiaries.

However, even with this restricted definition, noninsurance activities would be mistakenly classified as insurance. In the case of a guarantee, the seller agrees to repair or replace the item if a mechanical breakdown occurs within a specified time. This type of agreement, in effect, provides for compensating another party for a loss subject to the occurrence of a specified contingent event. However, nonrenewable service contracts under which manufacturers or dealers agree to maintain merchandise and replace parts for a specified period are *not* insurance contracts if the agreements exclude loss by external causes, such as fire and theft. These types of contracts may be written on a renewal basis by the manufacturer, dealer, or any service organization, and escape the classification as insurance only if the promise is restricted to the labor involved in making normal repairs and does not include the replacement of parts.

At this point one may question the importance of precisely defining insurance. The need to differentiate between insurance and noninsurance arrangements arises because if an activity is classified as insurance, it becomes subject to insurance regulation. In addition, the rights of the parties involved in a contract held to be insurance are determined by common law and statutes peculiar to insurance. Finally, as corporations operate under charters which set limits on their activities, a concern found to be writing insurance without the necessary charter and licenses will be committing an ultra vires (beyond the authority) act.

A Philadelphia newspaper fell afoul of the legal distinction between permitted and prohibited acts of corporations by advertising that if anyone were killed while possessing a copy of that newspaper, the heirs would be paid a certain amount of money by the publisher. In a test case, the court decided that this promise was a contract of insurance and that the newspaper publisher was committing an ultra vires act. Rather than trying to obtain a charter as a life insurer, the newspaper publisher discontinued the offer.

Some years ago, a group of southern young men formed an association of bachelors. Each paid an entry fee and promised not to marry for two years. At the end of two years, the member was free to marry and as a wedding gift was to be given $1,000. A suit was brought (perhaps instigated by an association to protect southern womanhood). The court decided that this agreement was not insurance, but a gambling contract in restraint of marriage, and hence illegal.[3]

The question often arises as to whether fidelity and surety bonding are insurance. Although persons in the business will argue that surety bonding is not insurance (note their reasons given in Chapter 15), legally, corporate suretyship is considered insurance. An individual who acts as a personal surety for another is not deemed to have engaged in the insurance business. However, a corporation engaging regularly in the surety business for a premium is considered to be in the insurance busi-

---

[3] *White* v. *Equitable Nuptial Benevolent Union,* 76 Ala. 251 (1884).

ness. Thus, state laws tend to treat some transactions as insurance which on their face appear to be some other form of risk management device.

Contingent service contracts frequently are confused with insurance contracts. The folklore is that in ancient China the doctor was paid a regular fee so long as the patients remained well, but received no payment if one fell sick. These transactions are not contracts of insurance. Also a lawyer's retainer is not payment for insurance. Agreements between a veterinarian and a group of dog and cat owners to provide their pets with all necessary medical, dental, and psychiatric treatment during the term of the contract in exchange for a fixed fee were ruled to be insurance contracts and thus subject to state insurance law.

The U.S. Supreme Court reversed the lower courts and held that variable annuities are primarily securities and thus subject to regulation by the Securities and Exchange Commission. The insurance aspect of the variable annuity, the Court said, "is apparent, not real; superficial, not substantial." According to the Court, "a company must bear a substantial part of the investment risk associated with the contract, as well as the mortality and expense risks, in order to qualify its products as 'insurance.'" The variable annuity shifts the investment risk entirely to the policyholder. In a 1965 court case involving the variable annuity in which the insurer guaranteed the principal only, the Securities and Exchange Commission (SEC) argued that "a contract is not 'insurance' unless interest as well as principal is guaranteed." The Supreme Court in 1967 ruled in favor of the SEC, holding the contract to be a security.

Life insurance proceeds payable by reason of death are not subject to federal income tax, but in 1964 the Commissioner of Internal Revenue was successful in a court battle with Atlantic Oil Company in his effort to tax the death proceeds from a policy taken out by the company on an employee truckdriver. The commissioner contended that as Atlantic had no insurable interest in the truckdriver, the proceeds in excess of premiums paid were taxable income from a wagering contract rather than nontaxable income from an insurance contract.

The difficulty in developing a short but accurate definition of insurance was recognized by the court in the following statement:

> "Necessarily, in defining insurance in a single sentence, only the most general terms can be used, and any general definition must be extended to cover the ever-changing phases in which the subject is presented to the public."[4]

A study of court decisions involving definitions of insurance contracts leaves the student with a lack of direction. But for the student to expect anything else is to fall victim to the "fallacy of legal certainty—that sure, certain, and consistent results can be projected when a legal problem arises. . . ."[5]

With the understanding that no short definition can be completely

[4] *State* v. *Hogan,* 1899, 8 N.D. 301, 78 N.W. 1051, 45 L.R.A. 166, 73 Am. St. Rep. 759.
[5] Denenberg, "Legal Definition of Insurance," p. 325.

accurate, an acceptable definition of insurance is, as developed in Chapter 2:

> Insurance may be defined as a device for reducing risk by combining a sufficient number of exposure units to make their individual losses collectively predictable. The predictable loss is then shared proportionately by all units in combination.

FIGURE 6–1
Illustrative court rulings on definition of insurance

Insurance	Not insurance
Life insurance for holders of a specific newspaper at time of death	Payments in event of refraining from marriage for a specified time
Corporate surety bonding	Personal insurance bonding
Life insurance where a required insurable interest exists	Life insurance where a required insurable interest does not exist
Prepaid veterinarian medical fees	Retainers paid to lawyers
	Contingent service contracts
	Variable annuities

Essential Elements of an Insurance Contract

Knowledge of the legal form and conditions for valid contracts, and its application to insurance are useful in understanding insurance.

Agreement—Offer and acceptance

Agreement consists of an offer made by one party and accepted by another. In insurance the principal type of offer is that made by the prospect when an application is submitted. Rarely does the insurer make the offer. A noted exception is in life insurance when the first premium does not accompany the application.

In many forms of insurance the application is oral. A couple deciding to insure against loss arising from destruction of their house by fire may apply by telephone, and the only other contact with the agent will be the receipt of the policy and a bill for the premium. When the homeowners requested the insurance, the policy was effective immediately upon affirmation by the agent. Offer and acceptance had taken place because the agent had the power to bind the insurer.

In contrast, the life insurance application always is in writing. The life agent usually does not have binding power, so the insurance cannot become effective upon submission of the application. For the application to be considered an offer, it must be accompanied by the first premium. In return, the agent gives the customer a conditional receipt usually providing that if underwriting standards of the insurer are met as of the date of the completed application, the contract is effective as of the date the premium is paid.

In 1965 a New Jersey court ruled that if the premium accompanies the application for life insurance, the policy is in effect from that moment until the applicant is rejected and so notified. This ruling means that upon payment of a premium with a life insurance application, the subject has life insurance immediately without regard to the underwriting standards of the insurer, thus placing greater underwriting responsibility on the agent. The ruling expresses what appears to be an increasing, though still small, minority view and is based on what the court considers just and equitable.

> It . . . would fulfill the applicant's reasonable expectations while avoiding the serious impracticalities which would result from acceptance of the company's position that liability should turn on its good faith determination of insurability; these impracticalities are particularly evident where . . . no industrywide standards of insurability appear, and the company places its reliance on a judgment determination of uninsurability first made by its own medical director after he had knowledge of the applicant's death.

The majority view is that the court will not rewrite the contract if the customary language of the conditional receipt is definite and clear, and that nothing in it misleads the applicant to believe that the coverage is other than conditional.

If the premium does not accompany the application, the insurer has only an invitation to make an offer by issuing the policy. The offer is accepted when the policy is delivered to the applicant while in good health. Even if the premium payment accompanies the application, the insurer may reject the offer. When an application is unacceptable to the underwriter, the insurer might make a counterproposal of a different policy. The original offer then is rejected and a counteroffer made. The prospect may accept or reject this offer.

As under the general law of contracts, silence on the part of the offeree after receiving an offer ordinarily does not constitute an acceptance. In most jurisdictions, silence is rejection, but in a number of jurisdictions an insurer may be held guilty of negligence and subject to damages for failure to act upon an application within a reasonable time. (However, the majority opinion holds that if the insured fails to cancel within a reasonable time upon receipt of a renewal policy the delay is interpreted as acceptance, and the insured is liable for the premium for the period covered.) When buying life insurance, the applicant should pay the first premium to take advantage of the protection given by the conditional receipt.

Competent parties

Insurance contracts to be valid must be made by competent parties. Two problems arise: minors and the mentally incompetent. Once there was a third problem—married women. This aspect of the woman problem has been resolved (along with others) by statutes.

Minors. The general rule is that minors are legally incapable of binding themselves to a contract. A minor may disaffirm a contract. The right to disaffirm may be exercised even at majority, if accomplished within a reasonable time and before committing some act that would constitute ratification of the contract. No reason need be given for repudiation. Although the right to void a contract is personal to minors, their heirs may invoke it after the minor's death. Also, a guardian acting on the minor's behalf, may avoid a disadvantageous contract. A minor may escape performance even though mistaken for an adult.

An exception to the general rule applies to contracts made for necessaries. These obligations may not be disaffirmed because the law holds minors (or "infants" as referred to by law) responsible for *the reasonable value* of necessaries furnished them. As insurance generally has not been considered a necessity for minors, contracts of insurance can be disaffirmed by a minor. Most courts hold that, upon disaffirming the contract, the minor is entitled to a return of all premiums paid without deduction for the value of the insurance protection received during the time the policy was in force.

A minor, though legally incapable of being bound, has the legal capacity to bind an insurer to a contract. In many states, statutes have been enacted reducing the age at which adult status is acquired in contracting for life and health insurance. These statutes usually apply only to minors contracting for insurance on their own lives for the benefit of their father, mother, husband, wife, child, brother, or sister. The reduced legal age ranges from 14½ to 16, with 14½ the most common.

Mentally incompetent. A person officially declared insane is not a legally competent party and may not make a valid contract of insurance—or of anything else. If an insane person is not yet officially declared insane, the contract is not void but is voidable at the option of the insane person. The test of insanity has been stated to be the ability of the person to understand the nature of the transaction. The rigid application of this test to purchasers of insurance, however, might expand the numbers eligible for admission to mental institutions.

Insurers. The insurer also must have the legal capacity to contract. For the corporate insurer, its capacity is expressed in its charter or articles of incorporation. In some states agreements made with legally incompetent insurers are void by statute. In these jurisdictions the insurer will be held liable only for a return of premiums, and the corporate officers responsible for the ultra vires act are subject to personal liability under the contract. In most jurisdictions, courts will uphold the insured's agreement with a legally incompetent insurer if the agreement was made in good faith and without the insured's knowledge of the incompetency. The insured cannot be expected to know whether the insurer has complied with the regulations necessary for legal competency. If an insurer operates in a state without complying with that state's requirements, the contracts nevertheless are binding on the insurer. The responsible officers of these insurers would be subject to penalties.

Legal purpose

Not only do courts refuse to enforce a contract if the purpose is illegal, they also refuse to enforce any insurance contract that promotes results contrary to the public interest. Thus, crop insurance written to cover a field of marijuana would be illegal and unenforceable. No valid contract can be made to insure goods illegally held. The illegality of an enterprise does not prohibit insuring articles that do not enter directly into the illegal aspect of the business. Valid fire insurance may be bought on furniture in an illegal gambling house, although insurance covering the croupier's equipment might be questionable. After much legal wrangling, the courts held that furniture in a house of prostitution could be insured against fire.

An insurance contract usually is held to be against public policy if the insured has no insurable interest in the subject of the insurance because the transaction then would be a gambling contract. Also insurance contracts made with enemy aliens would be considered against public policy.

Consideration

No contract is valid unless each party has given value or assumed some obligation toward the other. Insurance contracts often state that the consideration of the insured is "the provisions and stipulations herein and of the premium specified." This statement does not mean that the premiums must be paid in cash before the policy is effective. Most property and liability insurance policies are in force before premium payments are received. The promise to pay is the consideration. The insurer, too, gives consideration in the form of promises to make payments upon the occurrence of stipulated events.

Characteristics of the Insurance Contract

Certain characteristics are peculiar to insurance contracts or are found in few contracts other than insurance.

Aleatory contract

Contracts may be either *commutative* or *aleatory*. Most contracts are commutative: each party gives up goods or services presumed to be of equal value. The insurance contract, however, is aleatory: the contracting parties realize that the dollar amount to be exchanged will not be equal. If a loss is suffered a much larger amount may be received from the insurer than was paid in premiums, and if no loss is suffered (the more likely outcome), nothing will be paid. The distinguishing feature of an aleatory contract is the presence of chance. This characteristic does not mean that the buyer pays more or less than the insurance is worth or that the insurer collects more or less than the anticipated amount needed to conduct its business. The insurer expects to collect enough in premiums to pay its claims and expenses. Although specializing in aleatory contracts, the insurance business is no more aleatory than most other businesses.

All gambling contracts are aleatory, but not all aleatory contracts are gambling contracts. Unlike a gambling contract insurance is not designed to offer insureds a chance for profit but the opportunity to offset possible losses by providing a method of reducing risks. In addition, the gambling transaction creates risk, whereas insurance is a method of handling existing risk.

Contract of adhesion

In contradistinction to a bargaining contract, the insurance contract usually is a contract of adhesion. The agreement generally is prepared by lawyers and other representatives of the insurer, or perhaps by representatives of the state regulatory bodies and offered to the prospective insured on a "take it or leave it" basis. The typical applicant can make no counterproposal or suggest that the insurer directly alter a provision or change a word in line 75. However, insureds may have their coverage altered, within limits, through the use of standard endorsements or riders; but they must select their coverage from standard policies and other forms provided by the insurer. This characteristic of the contract, however, works to the benefit of the insured if the contract becomes a subject of litigation. Courts rule that, as the insurer drew up the contract, any ambiguity in it must be construed in favor of the insured.

This principle has resulted in the development of long, seemingly repetitious lists of exclusions in many policies. For example, the insurer wants to exclude war from coverage under the fire policy. In the early days of fire insurance a phrase "enemy attack by armed forces, including action taken by military, naval, or air forces in resisting an actual or an immediately impending enemy attack" was inserted. Along came an insured with a loss and argued that it was not caused by "enemy attack, etc." but by invasion. The insurer had to pay, but it then inserted a further exclusion, "invasion." Furthermore, the list was extended to include "insurrection," "rebellion," "revolution," "civil war," and "usurped power." Most of these terms are distinctions without differences to the reader of the policy today, but they once meant the difference between whether or not the insurer would have to pay for a loss.

A hunter using his automobile for a gun rest takes aim and pulls the trigger. The bullet ricochets from a rock, hitting his companion and causing serious injury. The companion sues the hunter, alleging negligence. The hunter's automobile liability insurer soon learns from a Colorado court that it has to defend the suit and be prepared to pay damages because the injury was construed to be one arising out of the use of the automobile. Under the ambiguity-construed-in-favor-of-the-insured theory, the hunter might well have had protection also under his comprehensive personal liability coverage, which excludes the automobile hazard. The court probably would hold that, in the ordinary sense, the foregoing loss is not one resulting from the use of an automobile. Considering that ambiguity is construed for the insured, the courts would be consistent in holding that for coverage under the auto liability policy, the insured was using the car, but for coverage under the comprehensive liability policy, he was not using the car.

Manuscript policies, as distinguished from printed policies, are prepared by large brokerage firms to fit coverage to their clients' specific needs. Large corporate risk management departments familiar with the insurance market will prepare policies that meet their individual needs. In these cases, the common-law doctrine relating to contracts of adhesion is modified by the courts in interpreting disputed provisions.

Unilateral contract

Contracts may be bilateral or unilateral. An exchange of a promise for a promise is bilateral, whereas an exchange of an act for a promise is unilateral. In general, the insurance contract is unilateral in that after the insured has paid the premium, only the insurer is exposed to a further legally enforceable promise. The insurer has promised performance. Except in assessment policies, the insured has made no legally enforceable promises and cannot be held for breach of contract.

Conditional contract

The insurance contract is conditional. The nonassessable contract becomes completely executed by the insured with the payment of the premium and only the insurer is obligated to keep a promise. However, the insured does have further conditions to meet in order to collect for losses. The difference between promises and conditions is that only promises, not conditions, are legally enforceable. A breached condition by the insured makes the insurance uncollectible. Under the fire insurance contract, the insurer promises to indemnify the insured for losses caused by fire. The insured is subject to several conditions concerning filing proofs of loss but is under no legal obligation to do so. However, they must be filed in order for the insured to collect. On the other hand, the fire insurer can be forced by law to keep its promise to pay indemnity if the insured has met all the contract conditions. Insureds are under no obligation to continue premium payments if they discontinue the policy. Premium payments must be made only for the protection before the date of cancellation.

Utmost good faith

Most ordinary contracts are *bona fide* or good faith contracts. Insurance contracts, however, are contracts *uberrimae fidei*, or contracts of utmost good faith. The greatest degree of good faith is needed in the negotiations preceding the issuance of the contract. In underwriting decisions, the insurer must be able to rely on information furnished by the applicant. In the earliest days of marine insurance, contracts were formed in places remote from the ships and cargoes to be covered. The insurer and insured had to bargain on a higher level of good faith than usually required in commercial intercourse of that time. This requirement is the foundation upon which the doctrines of warranty, misrepresentation, and concealment are based.

Personal contract

The *property* insurance contract is as personal as a wedding contract. Both the insured and the insurer dealing in utmost good faith take notice not only of the contract to be negotiated but also of the character, conduct, and credit of each other. Although in common parlance, a certain piece of property is spoken of as being "insured," the insured is the property owner, not the property. The insurance is not attached to the property and does not pass with it to a new purchaser. The assent of the insurer is necessary to assign an insurance contract before a loss except for life and some health insurance policies. The life insurance contract is not personal, so it may be assigned without the permission of the insurer. Once a loss has occurred, an insurance contract of any type becomes solely a money claim and therefore freely assignable.

Principle of indemnity

Property and liability insurance contracts, in general, are contracts of indemnity; that is, they provide for compensation of the insured only for the amount of the loss or damage, assuming that an adequate amount of insurance is bought. One problem in applying the indemnity principle is measuring the exact amount of compensation which will avoid profit or loss from the event insured against.

Life insurance policies are not contracts of indemnity, but contracts to pay the face amount of the policy upon the death of the insured. While health insurance may be written as indemnity contracts, particularly for medical care, the lack of coordination of benefits among nongroup policies leads to the violation of the indemnity principle if a person has more than one policy covering the same loss. The insurer may agree to pay the costs of medical and hospital care, and certain surgical procedures up to a maximum limit; but if the charges are less than the maximum limit, the insurer will pay only the expenses incurred. However, under individual health policies, the insured may be allowed to collect from more than one insurer for the same loss. Furthermore, when one person is injured by the negligent act of another, the injured person may collect twice for the same loss: (1) from the health insurer and (2) from the person causing the injury (assuming a successful tort action). Either of these events would violate the indemnity principle if the insured were overcompensated for the loss. For accidental death, dismemberment, and loss of time benefits, health and life insurance contracts are similar: they are agreements to pay a stated amount upon the occurrence of the insured contingency.

In property insurance, the indemnity principle may be defeated by the use of valued policies which provide that a specific amount will be paid in the event of a total loss. Many policies covering objects of art against all perils are written on a valued policy basis. While valued policies in fire insurance are illegal in most states, some states have valued policy laws requiring an insurer to pay the face amount of the policy for a *total loss of real property* regardless of its actual cash value at the time of the loss. The indemnity principle has been further liberalized by the writing of replacement cost insurance.

Three important doctrines arise from the principle of indemnity: insurable interest, limitations on the amount of recovery under an insurance policy, and subrogation. Insurable interest is discussed in Chapter 5. Limitations on the amount of recovery are discussed in Chapter 9. The remainder of this chapter is concerned with subrogation.

Subrogation. An important principle arising from the doctrine of indemnity is the right of the insurer to subrogation of the insured's claim against those responsible for the loss. To permit the insured to collect the proceeds of a policy from the insurer and then to collect again from the person responsible for the loss would be contrary to the principle of indemnity. Suppose that Mark Chen crashes into Linda Fletcher's parked automobile one morning when he is rushing his daughter to a Little League game. If Mark pays Linda's loss in full, she may not collect from her insurer. On the other hand, if Linda applies to her insurer for indemnity under her collision policy, she will not be permitted to retain Mark's payment except for that amount unindemnified by the insurer, the amount of the deductible, for example. However, Linda's insurer will be entitled to payment from Mark for the amount it paid under Linda's policy.

Under most insurance policies, the insurer can require the insured to assign all rights of recovery against a third party who caused the loss, but only for the amount of the payment by the insurer to the insured. This process, called subrogation, is applied only against third parties. If a loss results from the insured's own negligence, there can be no subrogation. The right of subrogation gives the insurer only that right of action held by the insured, and even the bar association president would find it difficult to convince one to bring suit against oneself.

Insurers protect themselves against loss of the right of recovery against third parties by including in their policies a subrogation clause discussed later in this chapter. However, in special situations, insurers will waive their rights under subrogation.

Insurers for years failed to take advantage of their rights of subrogation in fire insurance. For this reason, insurance agents and buyers tended to ignore fire legal liability insurance. The *General Mills* case, however, changed this attitude.[6] Early in 1948 a building leased by General Mills burned. The owner of the building, a Mr. Goldman, believing that the fire was caused by the negligence of a General Mills employee, sued General Mills for $342,500 to recover the loss of the building, its rents, and the cost of removing the debris. Goldman's insurer joined as an intervener.[7] The lower court awarded Goldman and his insurer $142,500. General Mills had no insurance to pay this judgment. Luckily for General Mills and its stockholders, the Court of Appeals reversed this decision in a divided opinion. The basis of the reversal was a lease provision requiring the tenant to return the premises to the lessor at the expiration of the lease in the same condition as when leased, *loss by fire and ordinary wear excepted.* The implications of this decision disturbed many risk managers and generated extensive (and, to a much lesser extent, intensive) discussion of the fire legal liability hazard. This unsettling experience was reinforced by another decision three months after the *General Mills* ruling. In the case of *Standard Brands Inc.* v. *Bateman et al.,*[8] a tenant was held liable for a fire caused by operations of an independent contractor engaged by him. Court decisions involving fire legal liability have increased in number, making more apparent the need for insurance against this exposure.

Other circumstances that could involve subrogation are: fire spreads to a house after a neighbor carelessly burns leaves, sparks escape from the smokestack of a neighboring plant, faulty electrical equipment is installed in a house, and deliverers put gasoline into the oil burner by mistake—in each case causing fire damage to another person's property. That person's fire insurer will pay its insured for the fire loss and, if it seems advisable, will proceed against the wrongdoer (tort-feasor) for reimbursement in a tort action.

Reasons for right of subrogation.   If the insurer was not allowed subrogation rights, either (1) the insured could collect twice for the same loss, or (2) the tort-feasor could escape liability although responsible for a loss. Neither alternative is in the public interest. A reasonable solution is to allow the insurer to collect from the wrongdoer under the right of subrogation.

Effect of the subrogation clause.   The right of subrogation exists in equity independent of the contract. A basic legal principle (other than in life and health insurance), is that the insurer, upon payment of a claim to an insured, is entitled to all the insured's legal and equitable rights of action against responsible third parties. However, where applicable, insurers include a subrogation clause in their insurance contracts stating that the insurer can require from the insured an assignment

---

[6] *Goldman* v. *General Mills,* 18, C.C.H. (Negligence) 644.

[7] A person or organization voluntarily becoming a party to a legal proceeding to protect an alleged interest is called an "intervener"; that is, one not an original party who intervenes in a suit.

[8] CCH (Negligence) 866.

of all rights of recovery against any party for loss to the extent that payment is made by the insurer. The purpose of the clause is to discourage the insured from signing away an important right which would accrue to the insurer by subrogation, because subrogation cannot give the insurer any right that the insured does not possess. According to the subrogation clause, if the insured waives the right after the insurance contract becomes effective, the right to receive indemnity from the insurer also is waived.

Operation of subrogation. The claim first must be paid before the insurer can exercise the subrogation right. If the insured collects indemnity from the tort-feasor rather than from the insurer, the insurance claim is reduced accordingly. If the policyowner receives a settlement from the wrongdoer after collecting from the insurer, the insurer is entitled to a refund up to its claim payment. The insurer has no right of subrogation, however, until the insured has been fully indemnified for the loss, including costs of collecting the claim from the responsible third party. For example, Colonel Sanders' chicken house is burned by sparks from a steam locomotive making a reminiscent run. If the insurer pays the fire claim, it may be entitled to collect damages from the railroad. If the damages collected exceed the amount of insurance paid plus costs of collection, the excess must be given to Colonel Sanders. If the colonel had collected in full from the railroad, no legitimate claim could be made against the insurer. If the insurer pays the full loss and later restitution is made by the railroad to the insured, the insurer is entitled to reimbursement for any net[9] payments received from the railroad up to the amount of the insurance claim.

If the insured has a deductible policy or insufficient insurance, how are funds collected from the negligent third party distributed between the insured and the insurer? For example, assume that Colonel Sanders' chicken house is insured for $90,000, but the loss is $150,000. The insurer pays the $90,000 claim. Although the railroad is liable for the full $150,000 loss, it was willing to settle out of court for $95,000 (or is able to pay only $95,000 of the $150,000 judgment). Who gets what? The usual rule is that the insured is entitled to full indemnity before the insurer is entitled to recovery. Thus, Colonel Sanders receives $90,000 from the insurer and $60,000 from the railroad. The insurer receives the remaining $35,000 paid by the railroad.

Benefit of insurance. The subrogation clause gives the insurer only those rights of action held by the insured. If Dorothy Halverson has insurance on goods which are destroyed in transit and the transportation company is liable, the insurer will pay the claim and then sue the transportation carrier. Transportation carriers became tired of paying claims to insurers, so they looked for a way out. They finally decided on the ingenious device of including a clause in the bill of lading giving them-

---

[9] That is, net of costs of collection.

selves the benefit of any insurance held by the shippers. In effect, they said that if the shipper had insurance, the transportation carrier would not be liable for the loss. This clause defeated the insurer's right of subrogation. Insurers were not as stupid as the transit people thought. They devised a clause to offset the ingenuity of the transportation companies. This clause is common in marine insurance and other policies involving transportation. It states:

> It is agreed by the Assured that this insurance shall not inure directly or indirectly to the benefit of any carrier, bailee, or other party, by stipulation in the bill of lading or otherwise, and any breach of this agreement shall render this policy of insurance null and void.

So long as a "benefit of insurance" clause is included in the bill of lading, insurers must include the aforementioned clause in their policies, or they will have no right of subrogation. When both of these clauses are used, the insurer lends the money to the shipper instead of paying the claim. The insurer then helps the shipper press the claim against the carrier. The shipper is obligated to pay off the loan after collecting from the carrier. If collection from the transportation company is not possible, the debt to the insurer is cancelled and the loan becomes an insurance benefit instead. By this procedure, the insurers deny the benefit of the insurance to the transportation companies without denying protection to the policyholder—in effect, retaining the benefit of subrogation although the bill of lading attempts to take it away.

Extent of subrogation clauses. Many policies contain subrogation clauses. Subrogation claims are not so frequent in liability as in property coverages. In liability insurance the opportunity for subrogation arises when the insured is held liable for the negligence of another. For example, if an employer is held liable for an accident involving an employee who is using the family automobile, the employer's nonownership automobile liability insurer will pay the loss and then proceed against the employee's insurer for reimbursement. A workers' compensation insurer can proceed against a third party who negligently causes injury to a covered employee.

Life and most health insurance contracts do not include subrogation clauses as these policies are not strictly contracts of indemnity. A widow can collect the life insurance proceeds from her husband's policy and still retain the benefits from a judgment against the culprit who caused his death based on the court's belief that it is impossible to set dollar limits on the value of a human life. Subrogation does not apply in disability income insurance for a similar reason. No accurate method has been developed to determine the monetary value of pain and suffering or the loss of personal services of an individual to other family members. The insured, therefore, is allowed to retain whatever can be collected through legal processes. Furthermore, courts usually hold that large policy limits do not cause insureds to bring about losses deliberately through suicide or intentional inflicted disability. Underwriters disagree, especially with regard to disability income insurance. Many well-documented cases of malingering and fake illnesses are on record, not to mention self-inflicted injuries among insureds. Therefore, underwriters try to limit a policyowner's insurance collections to provable economic income by not writing excessive amounts of insurance to anyone, and, by including other insurance clauses in their policies to limit double recovery.

Although no logical basis appears for omitting subrogation clauses from medical expenses policies, some of these policies do not include them. However, recognizing that medical expense insurance should be written on an indemnity basis as a cost control measure, an increasing number of insurers are including subrogation clauses in medical expense coverage.

Summary

1. Four documents are important in the creation of an insurance contract:
   a. The application.
   b. The binder.
   c. The policy.
   d. Riders and endorsements.
2. Written applications are necessary in some forms of insurance (e.g., life, health, and bonding). Oral applications are acceptable in other forms of insurance.
3. When oral applications are accepted, declarations often form a part of the policy and contain much of the information usually found in written applications.
4. The information contained in applications is used chiefly for rating and underwriting. Generally, these statements are treated as representations rather than warranties.
5. The binder is a temporary insurance contract which exists pending issuance of the policy. Binders give the insurance buyer immediate protection while the insurer considers the risk and determines whether to accept it and at what premium. If the risk is acceptable, the insurer then prepares the policy.
6. Binders seldom are used in life insurance because the agent rarely has the power to bind the insurer even for a short period. Instead, the agent issues a receipt for the first premium, if offered with the application, which gives conditional coverage to the applicant; that is, provides coverage if the applicant was acceptable at the time of the application or medical examination if required. These receipts are called conditional receipts and the more limited ones grant coverage only after the insurer has determined that the applicant is insurable.
7. Insurance is a device for reducing risk by combining a sufficient

number of exposure units to make individual losses collectively predictable. The predictable loss is then shared proportionately by all units in the combination.

8. The insurance policy must conform to the requirements that apply to all contracts:
   a. Agreement (offer and acceptance).
   b. Competent parties.
   c. Legal purpose.
   d. Consideration.
9. Insurance contracts have some unique characteristics:
   a. *Aleatory contracts.* An unequal exchange of dollar values.
   b. *Contracts of adhesion.* Unalterable provisions established by the insurer.
   c. *Unilateral.* Only the insurer makes legally enforceable promises.
   d. *Conditional.* Although the insured cannot be forced by law to perform certain duties, one must meet the conditions necessary to collect benefits under the contract.
   e. *Utmost good faith.* The greatest degree of good faith is required prior to the issuance of the contract.
   f. *Personal* (for property and liability coverages). The rights and obligations do not pass with the property when transferred.
   g. *Contracts of indemnity.* The insured should not be permitted to profit from a loss. Life and many health insurance contracts are not indemnity contracts.
10. The doctrine of insurable interest, limits of recovery, and subrogation arise from the principle of indemnity. Subrogation grants to the insurer the insured's rights of action against a third party for any losses sustained.

Questions for Review

1. What is the purpose of the application in insurance? When is it possible to buy an insurance policy without a written application?
2. What is the function of the insurance binder? Must the binder be in writing?
3. The text discusses several definitions of insurance. Is a precise definition of insurance important? Explain.
4. Distinguish between the types of conditional receipts used in life insurance transactions, showing how one type is more restrictive than the other.
5. When does a life insurance policy become effective if no conditional receipt is issued?
6. Define each of the four essential elements of an insurance contract. Do these elements differ from those required in the formation of any other contract? Explain.
7. Define the seven characteristics that are generally unique to insurance contracts. Cite an example for each characteristic.

Questions for Discussion

1. Explain how a dishonest insured can make a profit through the use of binders. Can a dishonest agent also make a profit from the use of binders? Explain.

2. Is a contingent service contract a type of insurance? Explain.

3. "Silence gives consent." To what extent is this statement applicable in determining an offer and acceptance of an insurance contract?

4. Typically, the insurance buyer is presented with an insurance contract that must be accepted without the right to bargain over terms. Does this arrangement give any advantages to the buyer?

5. Do valued contracts represent a violation of the principle of indemnity? Are your views different about a valued property insurance policy and a valued life insurance policy? Explain.

6. Is life insurance a personal contract? Why is the answer to this question important?

7. The standard fire insurance policy, the Homeowners policies, and some others exclude fire or other loss caused by enemy attack by armed forces, invasion, insurrection, rebellion, revolution, civil war, and usurped power. Are there subtle distinctions between these terms?

8. What is the significance of the *General Mills* case for the college student?

9. Pedro was driving his car down Beach Street when Angela backed out of a driveway and damaged Pedro's car. Since Angela is the proprietor of a body shop, she repaired the car. Pedro meanwhile applies to his insurer to collect on his collision coverage. Angela did not charge Pedro for the repair work; and Pedro, as he drove out of the shop, thought of the insurance check soon to be received and invited Angela to run into him anytime. Is Pedro's attitude a sound one? Explain.

7

Policy analysis: General considerations and the Homeowners series*

A rich American who spent many years traveling abroad insisted that for successful travel in a foreign country one's knowledge of the language need consist only of "How much?" and "Too much!" The insurance buyer's vocabulary also contains these two phrases, plus a third, "What will the policy cover?" The insurance policy is a conditional contract in that the insurer's promise to pay depends upon the occurrence of certain events. The insurance buyer wants to know: "What events are covered?" "How much am I going to get?" and "How do I get it?"

---

* Note: It would be helpful to refer to specimen policy forms in the study and discussion of this and the next three chapters. The student should have the complete document rather than bits and pieces for discussion of a particular clause. A separate copy of the policy creates a feel for the contract that cannot be obtained from an isolated clause or two or by the awkward procedure of referring to policies reproduced in an appendix. Policy kits are distributed by the Alliance of American Insurers, 1501 Woodfield Road, Schaumburg, Ill. 60195; the Insurance Information Institute, 110 William Street, New York, N.Y. 10038; American Council of Life Insurance, 1850 K Street, N.W., Washington, D.C. 2000.

The main source of answers to these questions is the policy. Even so, owners seldom read their insurance contracts until a loss occurs, and often not then. Since losses are few compared with the number of policies written, insurance contracts may be the nation's greatest "unread" best sellers. As a result, the first realization by a policyowner that insurance does not cover "everything" comes with notification that a claim has been denied. At this point the policyowner might be advised by "friends" that "what insurance companies give you in big print, they take away in small print."[1] It would be more helpful to all (insurer, agent, buyer, and insurance commissioners) if the disappointed policyowner had been warned by friends to read the contract. With the possible exception of the marriage agreement, an insurance contract is the only one people generally enter without carefully examining its contents. Many insurance buyers seemingly believe that the exclusions and conditions included in modern contracts of insurance are so negligible and unimportant that they are not worth reading. The following clause reminds clients humorously that the policy has exclusions.[2]

SYMPATHY CLAUSE

Attached to and forming part of Policy No _____ of the

_____ [NAME OF INSURANCE COMPANY] _____ is-

sued at its _____ [CITY OR TOWN] _____ Illinois Agency

Date _____   _____ Agent

In consideration of the premium for which this policy is written, and subject to the terms and conditions in the policy to which this clause is attached, it is hereby expressly stipulated and agreed that, in the event of occurrence of loss and/or damage to the property insured hereunder as a result of perils not covered under this policy, or in the event of occurrence of loss and/or damage to other property of the insured not insured hereunder, the Company does hereby extend its deepest sympathy and regret in respect to all such losses and/or damages.

_____ Agent

All coverage under insurance contracts is subject to limitations. If insureds knew of these limitations *in advance of a loss,* they could respond by buying appropriate combinations of policies to achieve their risk management objectives efficiently.

---

[1] The saying is literally untrue, as most states have laws providing that "conditions" and "exclusions" must be in type at least as large and clear as the statements of coverage or, in certain cases, in larger type or in boldface type.

[2] The clause has been used by a few playful agents and attached to policies issued by their agencies.

The Insurance Policy

An insurance policy is the document containing the contract between the insured and the insurer. It may be a short, uncomplicated agreement such as the limited coverage accident policy written with a newspaper subscription or a long, complex document with agreements insuring properties of diverse interests scattered throughout the world against many perils. Regardless of length and complexity, the policy defines the rights and duties of the contracting parties.

The policy layout

Insurance policies all have the same components: declarations, insuring agreements, exclusions, and conditions.

The personal auto policy (PAP) begins with declarations, followed by four parts detailing the coverage (each part has its own insuring agreements and exclusions), and ends with general provisions (conditions).

The Homeowners (HO) policy consists of declaration, followed by coverage provided in two sections. Each section has its own insuring agreements, exclusions, and conditions. The policy ends with a set of conditions applying to both sections of coverage (i.e., the entire policy). Seven different Homeowners policies varying as to the scope of protection are available. The following discussion is concerned with HO–3, the special form, as this is the form most widely sold. Section I of the HO–3 describes the four property coverages, the additional coverages, the perils insured against, exclusions, and conditions. Section II describes the personal liability and medical payments coverages, additional coverages, exclusions, and conditions.

Declarations.   Declarations include descriptive material relating to subjects covered, persons insured, premium to be paid, period of coverage, policy limits, and warranties or promises made by the insured regarding the nature and control of the hazard. Declarations are discussed in Chapter 6.

Insuring agreements.   The coverages in an insurance policy are defined broadly in the insuring agreements. The insuring agreements in Section II of HO–3 provide coverage for liability claims arising from the insured's negligent actions. They promise to defend any suit to which the coverage applies brought against the insured alleging liability, and to provide medical expense coverage for persons accidentally injured by the insured or on the insured's premises.

The definitions of important policy terms also may be found in the insuring agreements. (In the new readable HO and PAP policies, an entire section is devoted to such definitions.) The following terms are defined in the HO–3: "bodily injury," "business," "insured," "insured location," "residence premises," "motor vehicle," "property damage," and "residence employee." In the PAP, terms such as "your covered auto," "trailer," "family member," "occupying," "covered person," "uninsured motor vehicle," and "collision" are defined. In both policies (and all the new readable policies) defined terms are printed in boldface type when used throughout the policy.

Exclusions. Exclusions eliminate coverages otherwise provided by the insuring agreements. Insurers modify insuring agreements to: (1) facilitate management of physical and moral hazard, (2) eliminate duplicate coverage in other policies the insured may have, (3) eliminate coverage not needed by the typical insured even though important to some insureds, (4) eliminate uninsurable perils, and (5) eliminate specialized coverage that the insurer is not qualified to offer or that requires special underwriting and rating, more conveniently insured under other contracts. Exclusions help keep the price of the coverage within reasonable levels. Typical exclusions in the liability section of the HO–3 are: business and professional liability; automobile, watercraft, and aircraft liability; intentionally caused injuries and claims eligible to be paid under workers' compensation laws.

Conditions. The ground rules of the transaction are stated in the conditions that control the insurer's liability for covered losses by imposing obligations on the insured and insurer. Typical conditions are those relating to postloss duties and obligations of the insured, time limit for paying claims, time limit for bringing suit against the insurer, other insurance, subrogation, alteration of the policy, assignment, cancellation, concealment, fraud, and optional settlements. Each of these conditions and others are discussed later.

Endorsements and riders. Standard or printed policies often do not suit a particular need. Modification of standard policies is made by adding special provisions to the basic contract. In life insurance, these provisions generally are called *riders,* whereas in property and liability insurance, they usually are known as *endorsements.*

Endorsements and riders are used to complete a contract, alter coverages to satisfy particular needs, and to change policies in effect. The standard fire policy is not complete until an endorsement describing the property covered is attached. To satisfy particular needs, endorsements and riders may alter the coverage to include additional perils, property, losses, places, hazards, and people, or may be used to eliminate coverages in the standard form. Subsequent to the issuance of the policy, endorsements or riders may be added to revise the amount of insurance, correct errors in the contract, adjust a rate, or include coverage of newly acquired property. Endorsements and riders supersede the standard policy provisions and may be altered by later endorsements or riders.

The Homeowners series

In 1958, a series of policies was developed to provide property damage and liability insurance to homeowners. These package policies (so-called because they included more than one type of coverage in the same contract) were named the Homeowners series. Since its introduction, the series has been revised and expanded to meet the changing protection needs of tenants and condominium owners as well as those of homeowners. In addition, revisions have been made to restrict and delete some basic coverages to eliminate juridical risks associated with these coverages. The Homeowners 76 program of the Insurance Services Office (a rating bureau discussed in Chapter 25) was introduced in December 1975. The "readable" policies of the program were designed to make the policies more comprehensible to the insurance-buying (and selling!) public. Readability was improved through many techniques. As compared to the policies of the previous Homeowners program, the number of words has been reduced by 40 percent, and the type size used is 25 percent larger. Key words are specifically defined on the first page of the policy and are always printed in boldface type when used elsewhere in the contract. The Insurance Services Office also eliminated much of the traditional language in favor of more direct wording. For example, the clause in the nonsimplified form granting the insured permission to make reasonable repairs on the property reads:

> Permission granted for Insured, in the event of loss hereunder, to make reasonable repairs, temporary or permanent, provided such repairs are confined solely to the protection of the property from further damage and provided further that the Insured shall keep an accurate record of such repair expenditures. The cost of any such repairs directly attributable to damage by any peril insured against shall be included in determining the amount of loss hereunder. Nothing herein contained is intended to modify the policy requirements applicable in case loss occurs, and in particular the requirement that in case loss occurs the Insured shall protect the property from further damage.

The simplified version of this clause reads:

> We will pay the reasonable cost incurred by you for necessary repairs made solely to protect covered property from further damage provided coverage is afforded for the peril causing the loss. This coverage does not increase the limit of liability applying to the property being repaired.

A more orderly sequence of policy provisions is found in the new policies. As the New York 1943 165-line Standard Fire Policy (SFP) is not included in the HO, its applicable provisions are found in the appropriate parts of the policy.[3] Previously, the SFP might have restricted coverage in certain areas, while provisions found later in the same policy relaxed those restrictions. This approach had a tendency to be confusing in many instances, due to the use of exclusions to exclusions.

The Homeowners 76 series consists of the seven forms (called, with some originality, Form No. 1, No. 2, No. 3, No. 4, No. 5, No. 6, and No. 8) described in this section. The detailed analysis of the Homeowners policy in this chapter is restricted to Form No. 3. The question of selection

---

[3] Most of the provisions of the SFP are included in the HO, although they may appear in modified form. The SFP is discussed in Chapter 11.

of forms is deferred to Chapter 21, dealing with the principles of insurance buying.

Form No. 1: The basic form (HO–1).   Section I of Form No. 1 (HO–1) lists four coverages: coverage A, the dwelling; coverage B, other structures; coverage C, personal property; and coverage D, loss of use. The basic form further lists five additional coverages, including coverage for debris removal; fire department service charges; trees, shrubs, and other plants; theft of a credit card; and property removal.

HO–1 insures against direct loss to the property and interests covered if caused by any of 10 groups of listed perils. Covered perils include fire and lightning, windstorm or hail, explosion, riot or civil commotion, vehicles, aircraft, smoke, vandalism or malicious mischief, breakage of glass, and theft. The form then lists the exclusions and conditions applying to Section I.

Section II of HO–1 consists of coverage E, personal liability; coverage F, medical payments to others; exclusions that apply only to Section II; and three supplementary coverages including damage to property of others and first-aid expenses.

Form No. 2: The broad form (HO–2).   The basic coverages, supplementary coverages, additional exclusions, and conditions in Section I of HO–2 are identical to those found in Section I of HO–1. HO–2, however, insures against loss resulting from 17 listed perils. The first 10 correspond to the basic form. The additional seven insured perils include falling objects; weight of ice, snow or sleet; collapse of buildings; damage resulting from a steam or hot-water heating system; accidental discharge or overflow of water or steam; freezing of plumbing, heating and air-conditioning systems, and domestic appliances; and accidental damage from artificially generated electrical currents.

Section II of HO–2 corresponds exactly to that in HO–1.

Form No. 3: The special form (HO–3).   HO–3 is identical to HO–2 except that coverages A and B are insured against all risks or perils. Coverage C (personal property) is insured against the 17 perils listed in HO–2, excluding breakage of glass.

HO–3 differs from HO–2 with respect to coverages A and B in that to recover under HO–2 the insured must prove that the loss was the result of a listed peril, whereas under HO–3, the insurer must prove that a certain peril is specifically excluded to deny payment. HO–3 also provides the insured with coverage against a wider variety of perils than HO–2. Damage caused by paint, for example, would not be covered under HO–2 because it is not a listed peril. However, it is not specifically excluded under HO–3, and is, therefore, covered. If an insured, for example, while painting the ceiling, spills a bucket of paint on the hardwood floor, the loss is covered by HO–3, but not by HO–2.

Form No. 4: The contents broad form (HO–4).   HO–4 is also known as the "tenant's form." It applies only to the contents of the residence and is identical to HO–2 except that coverages A (dwelling) and B (other structures) are excluded.

Form No. 5: The comprehensive form (HO–5). HO–5 is identical to HO–3 except that all risk protection is extended to coverage C, personal property. It provides broader coverage than HO–3, but at a higher price.

Form No. 6: The condominium unit owners' form (HO–6). HO–6 was introduced in 1974 to satisfy the unique needs of condominium unit owners who, like apartment tenants, are exposed to losses to unscheduled personal property and losses resulting from liability exposures. HO–6 is a reproduction of HO–4 except for two changes necessary to make the policy appropriate for condominium unit owners. One change provides $1,000 of coverage for damage to additions and alterations made by the unit owners within the inside walls of the unit. The other change provides that the additions and alterations coverage will be excess insurance over any insurance the condominium association (the owners of the building) has protecting the same property.

Condominium unit owners are exposed to additional losses that may be covered by endorsement to the HO–6. Under the bylaws of most condominium associations, uninsured property losses, and liability claims against the association are offset by assessing unit owners. Under a Loss Assessment Coverage Endorsement, the insurer agrees to pay assessments if the unit owner's policy would have covered the loss had the event directly involved the unit owner.

Form No. 8: The modified coverage form (HO–8). HO–8 is virtually identical to HO–1 except that all losses are settled on an actual cash value basis in contrast to a replacement cost basis.[4] The HO–8 is recommended for homeowners whose dwellings have a replacement cost greatly exceeding what the owner might spend to replace the structure using modern materials and construction techniques.

Homeowners series endorsements

Various endorsements are available for an additional premium to extend the coverage of the Homeowners policies to satisfy policyowners' needs. The *inflation guard endorsement* increases quarterly the limits of liability of Section I of HO–1, HO–2, HO–3, HO–5, and HO–8 by 1, 1.5, or 2 percent or some other fixed amount. The endorsement allows policyowners to cover their property for increasing amounts to offset inflation. The *scheduled personal property endorsement* allows the insured to cover on an "all-risk" basis valuable personal property for higher amounts than provided for in the basic policy. An endorsement may be used to increase limits of recovery for *money and securities.* A *watercraft endorsement* is available for Section II to extend personal liability and medical payments coverage to bodily injury and property

---

[4] Actual cash value and replacement costs are discussed in Chapter 9.

damage arising from the ownership, maintenance, use, loading, or unloading of watercraft powered by outboard motors. The *theft extension endorsement* provides theft coverage for personal property left in an unlocked automobile (it deletes the requirement that the policyowner must show signs of forcible entry to recover for a theft loss).

Numerous other endorsements are available for the special needs of policyowners. These endorsements give flexibility to the Homeowners forms.

New Homeowners programs

In July 1982 the Insurance Services Office (ISO) introduced a new Homeowners series. The 1982 Homeowners program, plus revisions made in September 1983, includes substantial changes from the Homeowners 76 package. The HO–5 form is eliminated. The HO–5 is dropped in favor of the HO–3 with a new endorsement (the special personal property coverage) that extends all-risk protection to coverage C. Form HO–8 is deleted without replacement (but was reinstated in the 1984 Homeowners program). The basic deductible used in Section I is $250, raised from $100. The latter amount is available for an additional premium. Policy limits on certain items in coverage C also are increased (e.g., coverage on guns is $2,000 instead of $1,000; the jewelry limit is $1,000, up from $500; and theft of silverware, goldware, and pewterware is covered for $2,500 instead of $1,000). Theft of personal property from an unlocked vehicle is covered, whereas the Homeowners 76 program requires evidence of forced entry before coverage applies.

Section II provisions also are revised. The limit in the basic policy for coverage E, personal liability, is increased to $100,000 from $25,000. Basic limits for coverage F and supplementary coverages are raised as well. A number of definitions in both policy sections are revised from those contained in the Homeowners 76 series. Changes were made to expand the restrictions on property, perils, and losses covered as well as to include more additional coverages.

The ISO followed their 1982 program with the addition of the 1984 Homeowners series in April of that year. Sixteen changes from the 1982 package were emphasized by the ISO. The 1984 edition is based on the 1982 revision and, in addition to the numerous policy limit increases, the new program provides coverages which are not part of either of the earlier forms. For example, business property that is excluded under the 1976 and 1982 versions is covered, and volcanic eruption, windstorm, and hail loss coverage are extended to protect insureds in all states instead of offering these coverages only to those living outside the western and southeastern states, respectively.

California was the first state to approve and adopt the 1982 program. Although Colorado, Georgia, Massachusetts, Oregon, and Wisconsin followed California's lead, most of the nation continues to use the earlier series. When the 1984 edition was announced, the ISO expressed its intention to file this latest form in about 25 percent of the states during

1984, then throughout the remainder of the country in 1985. However, the process of obtaining nationwide regulatory approval (not to mention industrywide acceptance) of the new program is time consuming. Even in the unlikely event that all state insurance authorities respond quickly, the process will probably take at least two or three years.

Therefore, unless otherwise noted, discussion in these pages of the HO–3 policy will be limited to the Homeowners 76 form. (Students interested in the details of these later forms can refer to sample copies of them. They are obtainable from agents who write these forms.) Because HO policies (and others) vary among insurers, the coverage offered by any one insurer should be studied individually. The purpose of the discussion here is to provide a format for making this study.

The personal auto policy (PAP)

In a move to make the Family Combination Automobile Policy (FAP) more readable, the ISO introduced the PAP in January 1977. The format of the PAP is similar to the policies in the HO series.

Part A of the PAP consists of liability coverage for bodily injury and property damage. Under this coverage, the insurer agrees to pay damages for bodily injury or property damage for which any covered person becomes legally responsible because of an auto accident.

Under Part B, the insurer agrees to pay reasonable expenses incurred for necessary medical and funeral services because of bodily injury caused by accident and sustained by a covered person.

Part C pays damages that a covered person is legally entitled to recover from the owner or operator of an uninsured motor vehicle because of bodily injury sustained by a covered person.

Part D provides protection against loss resulting from physical damage to a covered automobile.

Each part of the PAP contains its own recovery limitations, insuring agreements, and exclusions. Parts E and F consist of provisions applying to the various sections.

Personal auto coverage varies among insurers not using the standard ISO bureau form. Also, a number of limited policies are available at lower cost. The PAP analyzed in this and the next three chapters is the ISO form. Automobile insurance is discussed in detail in Chapter 14.

A sample no-fault auto policy

No-fault auto policies are used in 15 states, with the statutes varying widely among the states. No-fault auto insurance is discussed in Chapter 14. The immediate objective is to describe one no-fault policy to give readers a basis for studying no-fault coverage in their own states. The illustration used is the no-fault policy written in Michigan by a major national insurer.

Section I consists of liability protection, personal insurance protection

(PIP) benefits, and property protection coverage. The bodily injury and property damage liability coverages are similar to those in the FAP. Under the PIP coverage, the insurer agrees to pay each eligible injured person (or dependent survivors) benefits consisting of allowable medical expenses, work loss, and survivors' income loss because of bodily injury resulting from the ownership, maintenance, or use of a motor vehicle. The purpose of this section is to provide prompt payment to the insured, up to stated statutory maximums, without regard to fault, thus eliminating tort liability suits of "small amounts."

Under the property protection coverage of Section I, the insurer agrees to pay for damage to properly parked vehicles and fixed location physical property (up to $1 million) caused by accidents arising out of ownership, maintenance, or use of the covered auto as a motor vehicle. The purpose of this coverage is to eliminate the necessity for the owner of damaged property to sue the insured in order to recover, thus assuring prompt payment for loss and consequently reducing tort liability litigation.

Section II of the no-fault policy provides protection against bodily injury loss caused by an uninsured motorist and is similar to Part IV of the FAP.

Section III provides protection against loss to the automobile and is similar to Part III of the FAP except that the insurer must pay, under the limited collision coverage, for loss to the automobile owned by the insured, which the insured otherwise would be legally entitled to recover through tort liability against an at-fault driver. (Excluded from this no-fault coverage are uninsured drivers, drivers of stolen vehicles, and those who intentionally cause injury or damage with a motor vehicle.)

The basic modifications in the no-fault policy, therefore, are designed to allow insureds to recover for either bodily injury or collision loss, up to stated maximums, directly from their own insurer without resorting to tort liability. In addition, property damage caused by the insured will be paid by the insurer without requiring the owner of the damaged property to sue for damages. The Michigan no-fault law thus restricts tort liability actions unless (1) economic losses exceed no-fault benefits; (2) injuries result in death, serious impairment of bodily function or serious permanent disfigurement, in which case suits for pain and suffering are allowed, or (3) injuries are caused by intentional action. Many no-fault laws apply only to bodily injury claims. Whether they should apply to property damage claims is discussed in Chapter 14.

Forms used for illustrating policy analysis

The HO–3 and the PAP provide a rather complete nonbusiness property insurance portfolio for the typical homeowning insured. The principles involved in these policies are similar to those in business insurance contracts, so the reader who masters the procedure developed in Chapters 7 through 10 should have little difficulty with policies designed for business. Business coverages are discussed in Chapters 11 through 15 and also in Chapter 19. If some point fundamental to understanding policy analysis cannot be illustrated with the two personal contracts, reference is made to other forms. In each case, the illustrations are based on Midwest forms. That forms used elsewhere may vary slightly does no harm to the chapters' objective of providing a format for analyzing insurance policies. The illustrations are based on standard forms; some variation occurs among nonstandard policies.[5]

How to Read a Policy

The main purpose of this chapter and the two following ones is to give the reader a procedure to use in analyzing the coverage under any insurance policy. The *procedure* is the important consideration, rather than the specific details. Two policies are analyzed in depth, the HO–3 in this chapter and the PAP in Chapter 8, because these two policies are usually the most relevant to college students. Every student belongs to a household and drives a car (or so it seems when the professor tries to cross the street).

In the past 27 years, the Homeowners policies (HO–1 to HO–8) have proved popular with insurance buyers. As stated earlier, the Homeowners series provides coverage in two sections: Section I may cover the real and personal property of the insured, while Section II provides comprehensive personal liability coverage.

The PAP provides broad coverage on automobiles owned by the family and also protects the family members against liability claims that may arise through their use of automobiles. In no-fault states, the PAP is modified to include required benefits such as personal injury protection (PIP).

To determine the protection offered by an insurance policy, a systematic approach is useful. Eight questions must be answered to ascertain if a given event is covered and, if so, for what amount.

1. Is the peril covered?
2. Is the property covered?
3. Is the type of loss covered?
4. Is the person covered?
5. Is the location covered?
6. Is the time period covered?
7. Are there hazards that exclude or suspend coverage?
8. What is the amount of coverage?

If the answer is "no" to any of the first seven questions, no coverage exists. To determine these answers, the policy must be read thoroughly. In some policies, coverage may first appear to be present only to be suspended by a subsequent exclusion. However, one should not stop at this point because the coverage may be reinstated by a supplementary

---

[5] Because policy forms vary from territory to territory and from insurer to insurer, the reader must be careful to examine the policy that will be applicable in his or her case.

coverage clause, an endorsement or rider, or by an exclusion to an exclusion found later in the policy. If coverage applies, then a list of additional questions discussed in Chapter 9 must be answered to find the amount payable under the policy.

For the remainder of this chapter, the HO–3 will be analyzed with respect to the first seven of the foregoing questions. Question eight is deferred until Chapter 9.

Defining the Perils Covered

To determine if a peril is covered, the policy must be examined to see whether it is a specified peril or an all-risk contract. When the perils are named, their meaning must be defined. Furthermore, coverage limitations on the perils need examination. Also, whether the peril is the proximate cause of the loss must be ascertained.

Specified perils and all-risk contracts

Peril is defined as the cause of loss. Typical insurable perils are fire, windstorm, explosion, burglary, negligence, collision, accident, sickness, and death. A policy may cover one or more perils. Policies that name the perils covered are called "specified perils contracts." All coverage in the HO–2 is provided on a specified perils basis, as is coverage C (personal property) in the HO–3. When the coverage is written on a specified perils basis, no payment will be made by the insurer unless one of the specified perils is the proximate cause of the loss. (See page 152 for a list of the perils included in these different coverages.)

Section II, coverage E, of the HO–3 covers personal liability and is essentially equivalent to the comprehensive personal liability policy available as a separate contract. The comprehensive personal liability policy, in spite of its name, is a specified perils contract. The term "comprehensive" here refers to hazards, not to perils.[6] The contract could be called an "all-hazards" contract to indicate that it covers all hazards relating to the covered peril except those otherwise excluded. The peril covered is the negligence or alleged negligence of the insured (and under certain conditions the landlord's negligence, if the lease requires the insured to assume this liability). Coverage F of Section II covers reasonable and necessary medical expenses of others arising from accidents.

The second basic type of perils clause in a policy is one that provides coverage for all perils except those specifically excluded. When written in this manner, the coverage is called "all-risk." Coverages A, B, C, and D of the HO–5 along with coverages A and B of the HO–3 (note that coverage C is on a specified perils basis) insure for all risks of physical loss to the property described in the applicable coverage except for those

---

[6] Remember that "hazard" is defined as anything that increases the chance of loss from a given peril. For example, the ownership or use of a motorboat is a liability hazard, as it increases the chance of loss from suits alleging negligence.

types of losses excluded elsewhere in the policy. Thus, the exclusions of the policy should be of great interest to the policyowner.

As the policy is a readable form, nothing is lost by simply reproducing the peril exclusions as they are stated in the policy. The exclusions in the HO–3 applying to coverages A and B are:

1. Losses excluded under Section I, "Exclusions":
    a. *Ordinance of law,* meaning enforcement of any ordinance or law regulating the construction, repair, or demolition of a building or other structure, unless specifically provided under this policy.
    b. *Earth movement.* Direct loss by fire, explosion, theft, or breakage of glass or safety glazing materials resulting from earth movement is covered.
    c. *Water damage,* meaning:
        (1) Flood, surface water, waves, tidal water, overflow of a body of water, or spray from any of these, whether or not driven by wind;
        (2) Water which backs up through sewers or drains; or
        (3) Water below the surface of the ground, including water which exerts pressure on, or seeps or leaks through a building, sidewalk, driveway, foundation, swimming pool, or other structure. Direct loss by fire, explosion, or theft resulting from water damage is covered.
    d. *Power interruption,* meaning the interruption of power or other utility service if the interruption takes place away from the *residence premises.* If a peril insured against ensues on the *residence premises,* we will pay only for loss caused by the ensuing peril.
    e. *Neglect,* meaning neglect of the *insured* to use all reasonable means to save and preserve property at and after the time of a loss, or when property is endangered by a peril insured against.
    f. *War,* including undeclared war, civil war, insurrection, rebellion, revolution, warlike act by a military force or military personnel, destruction, or seizure or use for a military purpose, and including any consequence of any of these. Discharge of a nuclear weapon shall be deemed a warlike act even if accidental.
    g. *Nuclear hazard,* to the extent set forth in the Nuclear Hazard Clause of Section I—Conditions.[7]
2. Freezing of a plumbing, heating, or air-conditioning system or of a household appliance, or by discharge, leakage, or overflow from within the system or appliance caused by freezing, while the dwelling is vacant, unoccupied, or being constructed unless you have used reasonable care to:
    a. Maintain heat in the building; or
    b. Shut off the water supply and drain the system and appliances of water.
3. Freezing, thawing, pressure or weight of water or ice, whether driven by wind or not, to a fence, pavement, patio, swimming pool, foundation, retaining wall, bulkhead, pier, wharf, or dock.
4. Theft in or to a dwelling under construction, or of materials and supplies for use in the construction until the dwelling is completed and occupied.
5. Vandalism and malicious mischief or breakage of glass and safety glaz-

---

[7] The Section I exclusions also apply to coverages C and D.

ing materials if the dwelling has been vacant for more than 30 consecutive days immediately before the loss. A dwelling being constructed is not considered vacant.

6. Continuous or repeated seepage or leakage of water or steam over a period of time from within a plumbing, heating, or air-conditioning system or from within a household appliance.

7. Wear and tear; marring; deterioration; inherent vice;[8] latent defect; mechanical breakdown; rust; mold; wet or dry rot; contamination; smog; smoke from agricultural smudging or industrial operations; settling, cracking, shrinking, bulging, or expansion of pavements, patios, foundations, walls, floors, roofs, or ceilings; birds, vermin, rodents, insects, or domestic animals. If any of these cause water to escape from a plumbing, heating, or air-conditioning system or household appliance, we cover loss caused by the water. We also cover the cost of tearing out and replacing any part of a building necessary to repair the system or appliance. We do not cover loss to the system or appliance from which this water escaped.

Interpreting the peril

In addition to knowing by name the covered perils, the insured must know what the perils mean. What are the meanings of the words "fire," "collision," "riot," "accident," and "smoke"? The insurance meaning may differ from everyday usage.

The principal source of information is the policy itself. As noted, definitions are given for key terms used in the HOs and the PAP. By contrast, the fire policy contains no definition of terms used in the policy—not even a definition of what constitutes "fire." For the meaning of terms not defined in the policy, students must either look to statutory provisions or court decisions.

Consider the story of the person who bought a box of expensive cigars, insured them against fire, smoked them, and then filed a claim with the fire insurer. The insurer denied the claim, and the case was taken to court. Legend has it that the judge sided with the insured and ordered the insurer to pay the claim, as the cigars were destroyed by fire. The insurer paid the claim and had the insured jailed for arson. Of course, no judge versed in the law would have ordered the payment, because the force that destroyed the cigars was not "fire" as the term is used in insurance. Long ago, the courts decided that the policy meaning of "fire" is restricted to one that is hostile or unfriendly; that is, one that has left its intended receptacle. A friendly fire is one located where it should be—a fireplace, stove, or at the end of a cigar. But if a friendly fire leaps from the fireplace onto a table nearby where the box of cigars is located, the fire becomes unfriendly at that point and any fire damage is covered by the fire policy.

To be a fire—either friendly or unfriendly—sufficiently rapid combustion must occur to cause ignition. The combustion of a fallen tree in

---

[8] Inherent vice is a latent defect in the property that may cause loss or damage to it. The policy does not guarantee the soundness ("merchantability") of articles bought!

the forest (decay) and the combustion of an iron stake in the ground (rust) are not sufficiently rapid to cause ignition and consequently are not perils covered by the fire policy. A flame or glow is required. For example, a student is pressing a pair of jeans (don't ask why) when the phone rings. The student answers the phone. The hot iron is left on the pants. Upon returning from the disappointing call, the student finds the jeans scorched. Although fire insurance applied to the jeans, the loss is not covered, as the combustion was not rapid enough to produce ignition. Damage by heat is not sufficient for recovery. Note, however, that if an unfriendly fire happens, all damage resulting directly from it (such as water damage, explosion, blistering, heat, charring, smoke, and so on) is covered. If the clothing had been set on fire by the hot iron, coverage would apply.[9]

What is the peril under the riot and civil commotion coverage? The contract does not define a riot. Instead, the coverage depends upon the state law. The Illinois law defines a riot as follows:

> If two or more persons actually do an unlawful act with force or violence against the person or property of another with or without a common cause of quarrel, or even do a lawful act in a violent or tumultuous manner, the persons so offending shall be deemed guilty of a riot.[10]

Most states have similar laws, except that many require that at least three persons be involved. Even with a legal definition, it is not always clear if a riot has occurred. When cases are decided in court, the burden of proof of a riot is on the insured.

Limitations on the peril

When covered perils and their meanings are ascertained, the next step is to determine the extent to which the policy protects against these perils. Often, the coverage for a peril is limited to specific circumstances. All fire losses are not covered under a fire policy, nor is all smoke damage under smoke damage coverage. Neither is all negligence covered under a liability policy. For example, the HO–3 excludes losses resulting from neglect of the insured to use all reasonable means to protect property, at and after a loss, or when endangered by a peril insured against. Consider the case of Homero Antonio Lopez, who was airing out his wife's $10,000 full-length fur coat on the clothesline next to his house. While watching the coat air, Homero noticed that the tortilla parlor next door was on fire. Since Homero was fascinated by fires, he went into the house to get a camera. When he came out, he found the coat destroyed

---

[9] Some insurers pay claims for cigarette burns even though difficulty exists in proving an unfriendly flame. Insurers also have been liberal in other borderline cases.

[10] Note that "riot" requires the unlawful act to be with force or violence. Courts have held that the damage caused by a group of people does not constitute a riot unless accompanied by force or violence. An unruly crowd of college students who cause damage while protesting the presence of army recruiters in the student union building may be construed to be a riot.

by the fire. Homero's HO insurer denied coverage due to Homero's failure to protect property endangered by a peril that was insured against.

The policy must be read carefully in order to determine those circumstances under which perils otherwise covered are excluded.

The doctrine of proximate cause

Which came first—the chicken or the egg? This question may seem to be of no more practical interest than the preoccupation of the medieval scholar with the number of angels that could stand on the head of a pin. In insurance, a close inspection of seemingly equivalent cases will reveal significant differences. A $200,000 building is destroyed by fire and explosion. If the policy insures against fire only, considerable difference exists depending on whether fire caused the explosion or the explosion caused the fire. (So much dispute arose that insurers threw in the towel and added the "inherent explosion clause" making the fire policy insure this loss no matter which came first.)

For the particular policy to cover a loss, that loss must result from a designated peril. The efficient cause of the loss is called the "proximate cause" and has been defined as follows:

> In the event of the concurrence of several causes, the loss will be deemed to have been caused by the dominating peril so long as an unbroken chain of cause and effect exists between the peril and the loss, whether or not the peril is active at the consummation of the loss. Proximate cause means the immediate, efficient cause *without which* the results could not or would not have happened.

For the policy to cover, the loss must have an insured peril either as the proximate cause or in the chain of causation that links the proximate cause with the loss. The proximate cause is not necessarily the cause that was nearest to the destruction either in time or place, but the cause that through an unbroken chain of causation was responsible for the loss.

Proximate cause in property insurance. Problems involving the doctrine of proximate cause arise most often in the field of property insurance. Most of the discussion has centered around the interpretation of the fire policy. Fire fighters are summoned to put out a fire in a neighbor's house. Through error, the fire fighters smash their way into your house. Will your fire policy cover this damage? Yes, say the courts. The hostile fire next door was the proximate cause of the loss. Suppose that on the way to put out the fire in your neighbor's house, the fire truck sideswiped your car parked down the street. Is the hostile fire the proximate cause of loss to your car? No, say the courts. Where is the line to be drawn? The courts draw it somewhere between the smashed house next door and the car down the street. Exactly where is up to the courts. How remote the fire can be and yet be covered by the fire policy is shown by the leading case of *Lynn Gas and Electric Company* v. *Meriden Fire Insurance Company.* A fire in a wire tower in a remote part of the building caused a short in electrical wiring, making a machine run too fast, which in turn broke a belt, leaving a flywheel spinning freely. The flywheel flew off its moorings, extensively damaging the machinery and building. The court held the small fire in the distant tower to be the proximate cause of the loss, and the insurer had to pay.

Formerly, proximate cause questions involving explosion often arose but now have been resolved by the "inherent explosion" clause, the extended coverage endorsement, and the HO forms. The result is that both fire and explosions are covered. Formerly, if the explosion caused the fire, the fire policy would pay only for the actual cash value of the property when the fire began—that is, the value of a post- rather than a pre-exploded building.

Insureds can collect for some portion of a loss if they have a policy covering *any* of the "causes" of loss, from the proximate to the immediate cause. Assume a pile of oily rags catch on fire in a building covered only by a fire policy. While the damage done by the fire is minimal, the smoke and water damage resulting from the fire severely damages the structure. Due to the fact that the fire was the proximate cause of the loss, the insured can collect under his or her fire policy for the smoke and water damage, even though those perils were not listed in the policy.

Proximate cause in life and health insurance. In life insurance, the doctrine of proximate cause has little significance. With the exception of suicide within the policy's first year or two (and the occasional war and aviation restrictions), life insurance covers any cause of death. Whether the cause was proximate or otherwise is of no concern.

In health insurance, the doctrine of proximate cause has more significance. A problem arises when the policy contains a requirement that the loss must be "independent of all other causes" or "not contributed to by any other cause." Suppose that an 80-year-old person with severe rheumatism owns an accident policy. One day, while crossing a street, the octogenarian is unable to outrun a motorcycle and, as a result, suffers a broken leg. If the insured had been 20 and healthy, the accident might not have happened. Yet the courts invariably rule the accident to be the proximate cause of the injury and ignore age and health factors. In an opinion involving this question the judge stated: "A policy of insurance is not accepted with the thought that the coverage is to be restricted to an Apollo or a Hercules." Many accident policies require that the accident be the *sole* cause of loss for benefit payments.

Defining the Property Covered

Insurance contracts do not cover all the insured's property. They usually define the property protected. Property covered, like perils, may be defined comprehensively or on a specified property basis.

The HO–3 provides examples both of specified and comprehensive property coverages. Coverages A and B (dwelling and other structures) are specified coverages, for they state specifically the property covered. Coverage C (personal property) is comprehensive coverage, for it states that all household and personal property incidental or usual to the occupancy of the dwelling and owned or used by any insured is covered with certain exceptions.

The property covered under coverages A and B includes: (1) the dwelling described, including structures attached to it, occupied principally as a private residence; (2) materials and supplies located on or adjacent to the residence premises for use in the construction, alteration or repair of the dwelling or other structures located on the premises; (3) other structures on the residence premises, separated from the dwelling by clear space including such items as TV satellite dish receivers that are permanently affixed to the ground. The insuring agreements exclude structures on the premises used for business purposes and structures (except those used exclusively for a private garage) rented to or leased to other than a tenant of the dwelling. Coverage is also provided for trees, shrubs, plants, or lawns on the residence premises for loss caused by fire, lightning, explosion, riot, civil commotion, vandalism, malicious mischief, theft, aircraft, or vehicles not owned or operated by a resident of the premises. The limit of liability is 5 percent of the dwelling limit, and no more than $500 will be paid for any one tree, shrub, or plant. (Plants grown for business purposes are also excluded.)

The exceptions to personal property covered under coverage C include animals; birds; fish; motorized land vehicles licensed for road use; aircraft; property of roomers, boarders, and other tenants not related to any insured; property contained in an apartment rented to others; business property held as a sample or for sale or delivery after sale; business property pertaining to a business conducted on the residence premises; and business property away from the residence premises. Any property separately described and covered specifically in the HO contract or any other insurance contract is excluded, as is any device used for the transmitting, recording, receiving, or reproduction of sound that is operated by power from the electrical system of a motor vehicle.

Coverage E, personal liability, does not apply to damage to property owned by the insured; property damage to property rented to, occupied or used by or in the care of the insured is also excluded unless the property damage is caused by fire, smoke, or explosion. Thus, if the family rents a motel room and negligently causes a fire that destroys an upholstered chair, its liability to the motel is covered under Section II of HO–3. However, if the chair is damaged by beer stains and cigarette burns during a party given by the 18-year-old offspring while the parents were out on the town, the policy will not cover the liability to the motel owner, as the loss is not the result of a peril named in this exclusion.

Property exclusions are inappropriate in life insurance and also in health insurance, except for false teeth, artificial limbs, and so on.

Defining the Losses Covered

Losses can be classified as follows: (1) direct: the physical loss of the object; (2) indirect: *(a)* loss of net income resulting from inability to use the services of damaged property, *(b)* loss arising from perils such as temperature and humidity changes and loss of a part of a set or pair (these losses often are referred to as *consequential* losses); (3) extra-expense losses, such as the cost of defending a liability suit and the expenses incurred in obtaining the use of temporary facilities until damaged property is restored. Many policies cover direct losses only; others cover some forms of indirect losses and extra expenses.

The standard fire insurance policy covers property for direct loss or damage only. It does not provide indemnity for rebuilding expenses required by an ordinance or law regulating construction or repair. (The HO–3 has a similar exclusion.) For example, some zoning laws require that a frame building more than 50 percent destroyed by fire must be replaced with a fireproof structure. Fire policies do not pay the additional replacement cost resulting from these codes unless the policy is endorsed to cover this loss. Nor is loss of use covered while the property is being replaced. If a building is destroyed by fire, the fire policy will pay the cost of repairing the building, but will not pay for loss of business that may occur until repairs are completed. Other types of indirect losses, such as those resulting from temperature changes also are not covered by the standard fire policy unless specifically endorsed to provide the protection.

Because the Homeowners 76 series incorporates (in easy-to-read language) most of the provisions of the standard fire policy, the HO policies would not cover such indirect and extra-expense losses unless the coverage was not otherwise provided. The HO–3 adds coverage for debris removal, fire department service charge (up to $250), loss of use, and certain other indirect and extra expense losses. If, following a tornado, a house covered by an HO must be removed from the middle of the street, that removal cost will be paid under the policy. The insurer's limit of liability for this coverage and the coverage on the damaged property is the limit of liability applying to the damaged property. If the sum of these losses exceeds the limit applying to the covered property, an additional 5 percent of that limit of liability will be available to cover debris removal expense. Coverage D, loss of use, covers the necessary increase in living expenses resulting from a property loss caused by an insured peril. The expenses covered are those incurred by the insured to continue as nearly as practicable the normal standard of living of the household for the shortest time required to repair or replace the premises, or for the household to settle permanently elsewhere. In addition, coverage is provided for the fair rental value of any part of the residence premises rented to others or held for rental that is made uninhabitable by an insured peril. This coverage is provided for the shortest time required to repair or replace the part of the premises rented or held for rent.

Under HO–3 the insurer also pays consequential loss to unscheduled personal property caused by temperature changes resulting from physical damage to the described buildings and equipment on the premises. If lightning strikes electric wires on the premises, the insured will be reimbursed by the insurer for food spoilage in the freezer. If lightning knocks out a power line off the premises, the food spoilage loss is not covered by the typical HO–3. (Losses stemming from off-premises interruption of power, however, may be eventually covered. As of mid-1984, at least, several insurers were providing coverage for this type of loss at no additional premium. Whether other insurers will follow is uncertain.) The consequential loss exclusion for off-premises power failures has created confusion. Assume that lightning strikes a power line across the street from the insured dwelling, damaging its heating system, causing the plumbing to freeze. Does the HO–3 cover repair of the plumbing? Yes, because the freezing of plumbing is not an excluded peril in the HO–3; but confusion could arise because an off-premises power failure led to the loss. To eliminate confusion, many territories are adopting a mandatory endorsement (HO–245) to clarify that the power failure exclusion never was intended to exclude direct damage from a specified peril. The HO policy also provides for $250 maximum to pay fire department charges if the covered property is located outside the fire protection district that provides the insured service.

Coverage for up to $500 is included in the HO–3 for

1. The legal obligation of *any insured* to pay because of the theft or unauthorized use of any credit card issued to or registered in *any insured's* name. We do not cover use by a resident of your household, a person who has been entrusted with the credit card, or any person if *any insured* has not complied with all terms and conditions under which the credit card is issued.
2. Loss to *any insured* caused by forgery or alteration of any check or negotiable instrument.
3. Loss to *any insured* through acceptance in good faith of counterfeit United States or Canadian paper currency.

Coverage E of Section II covers bodily injury and property damage claims to which the coverage applies and for which the insured is legally liable. Coverage F pays medical expenses arising out of bodily injury caused by a covered accident. Additional coverages of Section II include expenses incurred by the insurer and taxed against any insured in a suit defended by the insurer: premiums on bonds required in a suit defended by the insurer; reasonable expenses incurred by any insured at the insurer's request, including actual loss of earnings (but not loss of other income) up to $50 per day for assisting the insurer in the investigation or defense of any claim or suit; and interest on the entire judgment that accrues after entry of the judgment and before the judgment is paid.

In life insurance, defining losses covered is simple. The insurer pays the face amount upon the death of the subject. In health insurance, contracts may be written to cover medical, surgical, and hospital expenses or loss of time benefits (monthly income benefit for an insured who is disabled and cannot work) or both types of losses.

In studying the coverage provided by a contract, the insured must not overlook the importance of coverage for indirect and extra-expense losses if coverage is needed and available, because these losses can damage the financial position of an individual or a business. Business interruption losses (discussed in Chapter 3) often are more severe than direct losses causing the interruption.

Defining the Persons Covered

Some policies (e.g., the standard fire policy) cover only named insureds and their representatives, whereas others cover additional persons. Representatives include the insured's executors or heirs and receivers in bankruptcy. In addition to providing coverage for the named insureds and their legal representatives, the HO provides coverage for the following residents of the household: (1) the spouse; (2) relatives; (3) any other person under the age of 21 who is in the care of any person named above. With respect to Section II (liability) of the HO–3, the policy covers (in addition to the above) persons or organizations legally responsible for animals and watercraft owned by an insured.

The HO–3 extends coverage at the named insured's request to personal property of others while the property is on that part of the residence premises occupied by any insured or while the property is in any residence occupied by any insured.

The medical payments section of the HO–3 (coverage F) provides coverage for medical expenses incurred (or ascertained) within three years from the date of the accident for each person accidentally injured while on the insured location (with permission of any insured), or elsewhere (under specified circumstances). The coverage is available only if the bodily injury (1) arises out of a condition on the insured location or the ways immediately adjoining; (2) is caused by activities of an insured or by a residence employee in the course of employment; (3) is caused by an animal owned by or in care of an insured; or (4) is sustained by any residence employee and arises out of and in the course of employment by an insured. Coverage does not extend to the named insured or regular residents of the household, other than residence employees; nor does coverage apply to a residence employee if the bodily injury occurs off the insured location and does not arise out of or in the course of the residence employee's employment by any insured. Any person covered under a workers' compensation law is also denied coverage under this section.

Insurers under life insurance contracts pay on the death of the named insured only. The persons protected are the beneficiaries. Any number of persons may be beneficiaries of a life policy. Health insurance policies providing disability income have only one named insured. Health policies covering medical expenses may be written with one named insured, but most frequently are written to cover all immediate family members including the named insured, spouse, and all dependent children. Dependency usually is limited to a maximum age, although some policies modify this limit for students or the mentally or physically incompetent.

The mortgagee

The mortgagee of a house or automobile has an insurable interest in the mortgaged property and can buy insurance to protect that interest. Special policy provisions give mortgagees special treatment in policies bought by mortgagors.

A mortgagee is a holder of a mortgage on a piece of property as security for a loan. The property owner who has borrowed the money and given the mortgage to the mortgagee is the mortgagor. The modern mortgagee is not a villain with a whip, a high silk hat, and a handlebar mustache, as portrayed throughout a whole generation of theatrical entertainment. Instead, the typical mortgagee is a financial institution. The modern mortgagor, though still a possible victim of foreclosure in which the old farm is lost, has it easier because of amortized mortgages and mortgage protection life insurance.

Suppose that Sarah Devlin wants to borrow money to buy a house. She can have the bank grant her a long-term loan and accept a mortgage on the house as security. If the house subsequently should burn completely, Sarah will lose the amount she has invested and still owe the mortgage debt. The bank will lose the security required when it lent Sarah the money. Thus both mortgagor and mortgagee have an insurable interest that needs coverage. Most mortgages contain provisions that dictate how the insurance is to be arranged. If these provisions are omitted, the mortgagor and/or the mortgagee may buy insurance on the house.

Three ways are available to protect these interests: (1) the mortgagor and mortgagee can insure their own interests, (2) the mortgagor may buy insurance and assign it to the mortgagee or have a "loss payable" clause inserted in the policy, or (3) the mortgagor may buy a policy containing the mortgage clause.

If the mortgagor and mortgagee insure their own interests, two policies must be bought, and a double premium charged. If the mortgagor buys a policy and assigns it to the mortgagee, only one premium is charged, but if the mortgagor commits an act that voids the policy (such as increasing the hazard), no insurance will be available for either party. A similar objection applies to the loss payable clause. Some courts hold that in the latter event the mortgagee is not denied insurance if the mortgagor is involved in prohibited acts, but many courts treat the loss payable clause as a policy assignment.

The mortgage clause. The mortgage clause is incorporated in the fire insurance and HO policies without additional charge and is the most common way to protect the mortgagee's interest. In virtually all situations, it offers the only acceptable method. (The PAP allows a similar arrangement to protect the interest of a finance company.) The mortgage clause in the HO provides that loss shall be paid to the mortgagee up to the amount of its interest. The mortgagee's right to payment shall not be denied if the mortgagee (1) notifies the insurer of any change in ownership, occupancy, or substantial change in risk of which it is aware; (2) pays any premium due under the policy on demand if the insured neglected to do so, and (3) submits a signed, sworn statement of loss within 60 days after receiving notice from the insurer of insured's failure to do so. In addition, the mortgagee (as well as the mortgagor) must be given at least 10 days' notice before cancellation of the policy. The mortgagee is also granted the right to sue under the policy. If the insurer pays the mortgagee for any loss, and at the same time denies payment to the named insured, the insurer is subrogated to all the rights of the mortgagee. The insurer instead may pay the principal plus accrued interest to the mortgagee and receive a full assignment and transfer of the mortgage and all securities held as collateral for the mortgage debt. However, mortgagees have the right to recover fully their claim regardless of the insurer's right of subrogation.

The mortgagee's agreement to pay the premiums is not an unconditional legal promise, as no covenant in the mortgage clause requires the mortgagee to pay the premium if the mortgagor does not pay it. The mortgagee must pay the premium only if coverage is to continue beyond the expiration of the cancellation notice, and then the premium is only the amount due from that date.

How would a mortgage clause apply in the insurance on Sarah's house? Assume that Sarah has borrowed $80,000 to buy a $100,000 house. If the bank is protected by a mortgage clause and Sarah is operating a dry-cleaning plant in the basement without the bank's knowledge, a fire loss will be paid in full to the bank (up to the amount of the mortgage). Because Sarah violated her contract with the insurer and has no valid insurance, the insurer would subrogate against the bank to obtain the mortgage on Sarah's house for the amount paid the bank. In the event of an $80,000 loss, the insurer would pay the bank $80,000 and would acquire the $80,000 mortgage on Sarah's house. If the mortgage were for more than $80,000, the insurer can either acquire an amount of the mortgage equal to the loss or can retire the full debt on Sarah's house and acquire the whole mortgage. In any event, Sarah still owes the mortgaged debt, but now to the insurer, not the bank. If the bank knew of the dry-cleaning plant but had not notified the insurer, the policy would cover neither Sarah nor the bank, because the hazard was increased with the knowledge of both.

The inclusion of the mortgage clause in the HO policy does not produce a panacea for mortgagors because it exposes them to the interest rate risk. Assume that Janet Forbes borrows $50,000 to buy a house in 1974, agreeing to pay 8 percent interest. In 1984, the house burns, resulting in $40,000 damage. Janet's insurer pays the bank $40,000, decreasing the mortgage by that amount. If Janet wants to rebuild her house, a new mortgage loan must be negotiated at a time when interest rates on long-term home mortgage loans have risen to 13 percent, requiring Janet to pay a substantially higher rate for the new mortgage. Thus, the mortgage clause will not fully protect the mortgagor during rising interest rates. An increase from 8 to 13 percent over a 20-year period for a $40,000 mortgage loan amounts to about $32,200 in additional interest payments, amortized monthly. To be protected from this interest rate risk, Janet could attempt to arrange an agreement with the mortgagee specifying that if a loss resulted causing the payment of the proceeds to the lender and retiring the debt, the loan would be renewed without an increase in the interest rate. In the absence of such an agreement, apparently nothing prohibits the insurer from developing a coverage to be added to the mortgage clause to insure this significant loss exposure. This coverage, though rare, can now be found in the insurance market, usually only after an extensive search. Where variable interest rate mortgage loans are used, this loss exposure no longer exists. As of 1984, however, with the exception of variable rate mortgages, none of these solutions was used, leaving the mortgagor subject to the interest rate risk under the mortgage clause in event of a major loss.

For small losses, the mortgagee usually continues the loan in force at its original interest rate if the mortgagor uses the policy proceeds to repair the property to preserve the mortgagee's security.

Defining the Locations Covered

Insurers limit coverage as to location. Some policies cover one location only, others include several. In some policies protection is restricted to the United States and Canada, in others coverage is limited to the Western Hemisphere. Some provide worldwide protection. The New York 1943 standard fire contract covers the insured property only while located on described premises, except for pro rata coverage for five days at each proper place to which the property shall necessarily be removed for preservation against insured perils. The HO–3 extends the applicable limit of liability for removal coverage to a period of not more than 30 days while such covered property is removed from premises endangered by a peril insured against. This coverage does not change the overall limit of liability applicable to the covered property. The off-premises coverage for personal property in the HO–3 is worldwide, and the insured may recover for off-premises losses to insured property up to the full limit of liability applying to personal property. However, the limit of liability for personal property usually situated at any insured's residence other than the residence premises is 10 percent of the limit of liability of coverage C, or $1,000, whichever is greater. Thus, the personal property of students living away from home is affected by this limitation.

The comprehensive personal liability coverage of the HO has no territorial exclusions. If a policy does not specifically restrict the area of coverage, then coverage is worldwide.

As noted above, medical payments coverage is available to a person on the insured location with the permission of any insured, or to a person off the insured premises if the bodily injury arises from a covered exposure. The insured location is defined as:

a. The residence premises.

b. The part of any other premises, other structures, and grounds, used by you as a residence and which is shown in the Declarations or which is acquired by you during the policy period for your use as a residence.

c. Any premises used by you in connection with the premises included in *a* or *b.*

d. Any part of a premises not owned by any insured but where any insured is temporarily residing.

e. Vacant land owned by or rented to any insured other than farmland.

f. Land owned by or rented to any insured on which a one- or two-family dwelling is being constructed as a residence for any insured.

g. Individual or family cemetery plots or burial vaults of any insured.

h. Any part of a premises occasionally rented to any insured for other than business purposes.

Protection under a life insurance policy usually is worldwide, although some policies exclude travel in various areas for an initial period. Thus, the beneficiary usually may collect, no matter where the insured might die. Health insurance policies usually are also worldwide.

Defining the Time of Coverage

Although many insurance policies are written for one year, some policies are written for longer or shorter periods. Other policies—life insurance, for example—may be written for indefinite duration.

Term of the policy

One-year policies are called "annual policies" and sell for the basic rate. In property and liability insurance, policies written for more than a year, called "term policies," often are written at a discount. Policy rules and rate manuals indicate which policies may be written for periods longer than a year. Various available budget plans allow policyowners to take advantage of term premiums without making large initial outlays.

Policies written for less than one year, called "short-rate" or "short-term" policies, often are written at higher rates. Auto insurance is an exception. Many insurers write six-month policies and quote semiannual rates. In their quest for adequate rates, insurers issue six-month policies to maintain flexibility to raise premiums for the next policy period if statistics justify a state-approved rate increase.

When an insured cancels a policy during its term, the premium refund is based on a short-rate table, often printed in the policy. These rates apply on the expired portion. Under a typical fire or HO policy, three months' coverage would cost 35 percent of the annual premium, six months' coverage costs 60 percent, and nine months' coverage costs 80 percent of the annual premium. In many motorcycle policies, the rates are "shorter" and no refund is paid if the policy has been in force at least six months.

Two reasons account for the higher premium on short-term policies. (1) If the high acquisition cost will be spread over less than a year, the premium must be larger for each day of insurance. (2) Policies for short periods are likely to coincide with the time during which the loss exposure is greatest and, therefore, a higher daily rate should be charged for protection. If the policy were in force for the year, good experience periods might offset bad ones. Averaging experience under short-term policies might be impossible.

Life insurance is written for an indefinite duration, paying death benefits when the subject reaches age 100 (called whole life policies), or for specified terms; for example, 1 year, 10 years, or to the subject's age 65 (called term insurance policies). Health insurance policies usually are written on an annual basis.

Hour of inception

The HO policies run from 12:01 A.M. standard time at the residence premises on the date of expiration. It is important to note that the governing time zone is the one associated with the residence premises. For example, Cindy Kyse loses her clothing in a Los Angeles fire that commenced at 11:00 P.M. Pacific Standard Time on the day before her policy expired. Her residence premise is in Illinois, where she bought the policy, and there the time that the fire started was 1:00 A.M. As the contract had expired in Illinois at 12:01 A.M. (it had expired in Los Angeles at 10:01 P.M.), no coverage was provided under her policy.

Effect of policy period

Most policies require only that the *onset* of the insured damage must take place during the policy period. Thus, if Betty Johnson's pet shop catches fire at 11:55 P.M. on the day her policy expires, all damage from that fire is covered regardless of the fire's duration. If the shop catches fire at 11:55 P.M., however, on the day before her policy is effective, no damage from that fire is covered even though the fire fighters finally extinguish the blaze at 6:30 A.M. on the day the policy is effective.

The policy expiration date does not limit the insured's right to collect in full under loss of use coverages. The additional living expense coverage in the HO provides for any necessary increase in living expenses due to a covered loss making the residence premises uninhabitable for the shortest time to repair, replace, or relocate the premises, not limited by the expiration of the policy. Under a disability income policy, if the insured's accident occurred or illness began while the policy was in force, the policy need not continue in force for the insured to collect the full policy limits for a continuing disability.

All life and most health policies written on a continuing basis include a grace period to pay renewal premiums. Protection continues for 31 days after the end of the policy period. Any loss during the grace period is a valid claim.

Defining the Hazards that Exclude or Suspend Coverage

Insurance policies may have provisions designed to suspend coverage when the hazard is increased beyond that contemplated by the insurer. These provisions, which help the insurer control risk, usually are "while" clauses; that is, suspending coverage *while* the hazard is increased. When the hazard is reduced, coverage is restored. Occasionally, "if" clauses are found, voiding the policy *if* certain conditions are present. A new policy is then necessary to restore coverage. Finally, policies may specify particular hazards that are excluded from coverage.

The standard fire policy includes several conditions that suspend or restrict the insurance. Some of them may be eliminated by endorsements, many requiring no premium increase. Typical of an "if" clause is the fraud and concealment clause in the standard fire policy, which states that the policy will be void *if*, whether before or after a loss, the insured has willfully concealed or misrepresented any material fact or circumstance. Concealment and misrepresentation are the only "if" conditions of voidance in the standard fire policy. Examples of "while" clauses in the fire contract deal with increases in the hazard or with vacancy and unoccupancy. The standard fire policy states that the insurer is not liable for loss occurring *while* the hazard is increased within the insured's control or knowledge or *while* the building is vacant or unoccupied more than 60 consecutive days.

If the insured experimented with a small hydrogen bomb plant in the cellar and a fire resulted, the loss would not be covered by the fire policy, as the activity increases the hazard. In most jurisdictions the insurance would not cover, even if no connection existed between the fire and the bomb plant. If the insured lit firecrackers in the basement, the policy would cover, even though the hazard was temporarily increased. The increase in hazard condition is interpreted by the courts to mean a substantial and permanent change in the premises or in their use. Customary and minor hazard increases are not within the meaning of the condition. The policy may be endorsed to allow certain hazard increases.

An unoccupied or vacant building may be more hazardous than one in use. A vacant building is one with no furnishings. A furnished but untenanted building is classified as unoccupied. The HO forms automatically grant permission for the described premises to be vacant or unoccupied without time limit. However, some of the coverages provided by the forms (e.g., freezing of plumbing and vandalism in the HO–3) may be taken away after a stated time period. For coverage of commercial property, the policy may need specific endorsements to grant permission

174

to leave it vacant or unoccupied for periods longer than those granted in the policy.

The HO forms, as do most—if not all—property insurance contracts, specify the following excluded hazards: "war, including undeclared war, civil war, insurrection, rebellion, revolution, warlike act by a military force or military personnel, destruction or seizure or use for a military purpose, and including any consequence of any of these. Discharge of a nuclear weapon shall be deemed a warlike act even if accidental." The nuclear hazard (any nuclear reaction, radiation, or radioactive contamination, all whether controlled or uncontrolled) is also excluded from coverage. However, direct loss by fire resulting from the nuclear hazard is covered.

The comprehensive personal liability coverage, Section II of the HO forms, excludes the business and professional liability hazard. The liability hazard from premises owned, rented, or controlled by the insured (other than those premises defined in the contract as insured locations) also is excluded, except for limited coverage for property in the insured's control. Personal liability resulting from the ownership, maintenance, use, loading or unloading of an aircraft, motor vehicle, or watercraft is excluded except for bodily injury to any residence employee arising out of and in the course of that employee's employment by any insured. The watercraft exclusion does not apply to boats with inboard motors of less than 50 horsepower and sailing vessels under 26 feet in overall length and powered by less than 25 total horsepower. The watercraft exclusion also does not apply while the watercraft is stored, or to the use of watercraft not owned or rented (e.g., borrowed) by any insured. An insured should check each policy to determine the nature of the hazard exclusions.

Most life insurance policies contain no suspending conditions. During periods of war or impending war, insurers usually include in their contracts a "war clause," excluding coverage of certain war deaths. In the past, some policies have excluded death resulting from aviation. Hazard exclusions will be found in health insurance policies. They vary among insurers but often include war, aviation, and industrial accidents.

Mechanics of the HO Policy

In most states, an HO policy can be written only on a one- or two-family owner-occupied dwelling. In addition, HO forms must be written for at least minimum coverage amounts. The minimums vary by HO forms and among insurers.

For example, an insurer might require a minimum of $15,000 for coverage A of an HO–3. The minimum could be as high as $40,000, depending on the insurer. The amounts of coverage available for coverages B, C, and D are based on the amount of coverage A, as the following table shows:

A. Dwelling	$15,000 minimum
B. Other structures	10 percent coverage A
C. Personal property	50 percent coverage A
D. Loss of use	20 percent coverage A
E. Personal liability	$25,000 per occurrence
F. Medical payments	$500 per person; $25,000 per accident[11]

The basic limits of liability for coverages B, C, D, E, or F may be increased for an additional premium, and the basic limits of coverage C may be reduced to 40 percent of the amount on the dwelling for a small premium reduction. This reduction option is not allowed in Form No. 5. As of mid-1984, some insurers had increased the basic limit for coverage C to 55 percent. In addition, at least one major insurer also had increased its HO–5 contract to a 75 percent basic limit on personal property.

In Form No. 4, the minimum amount for coverage C might be $4,000. Loss of use coverage is 20 percent of the limit on coverage C.

Form No. 6, for condominium owners, also requires a minimum for coverage C of $4,000. Loss of use coverage is 40 percent of the limit on coverage C. The form provides up to $1,000 of additional coverage for loss to additions, alterations, or other betterments within the inside walls of the individual unit. This limit is frequently increased by endorsement. A loss assessment endorsement is available to cover the insured's share of otherwise uninsured losses that occur within the commonly owned areas of the condominium. A $250 deductible applies to the coverage.

The HO–6 is expected to become increasingly important, since some federal authorities predict that 50 percent of the population will live in some form of condominium within 20 years. The condominium association needs insurance for the common areas—that is, those owned by all members, such as a swimming pool. The association's directors and officers are responsible for obtaining adequate coverage. If they do not perform their duties prudently, they may be held liable. Some insurers include directors' and officers' liability (D&O) coverage (Chapter 13) in their package policies covering the condominium's common areas. As yet, this protection is not sold separately. The loss exposure is one that should not be overlooked.

Summary

1. Insurance policies all have the same components: declarations, insuring agreements, exclusions, and conditions.
2. The Homeowners series consists of seven forms varying as to the

---

[11] Note that coverage E (personal liability) is written on an "occurrence" basis, while coverage F (medical payments) is written on an "accident" basis. The difference between these two bases is discussed in Chapter 8.

perils and property covered. The coverages that may be included in the forms are for *(a)* the dwelling, *(b)* other structures, *(c)* personal property, and *(d)* loss of use. All the forms provide coverage for personal liability and medical payments.

3. Eight questions must be answered to ascertain if a given event is covered and, if so, for what amount. A simple method for remembering the eight points of coverage is to note that five of them can begin with a P. Thus, the points can be listed as follows:

   a. Perils.
   b. Property.
   c. Persons.
   d. Places.
   e. Period.
   f. Losses.
   g. Hazards.
   h. Amount.

4. Policies are written on either a specified peril (to be covered, the loss must be caused by a named peril) or "all-risk" (to be covered, the loss must be caused by a peril that is not excluded from coverage) basis.

5. Losses may be classified as direct, indirect, consequential, and extra expenses. *Direct loss* is defined as physical loss or damage to the object concerned. *Indirect loss* results from the loss of use of the physically damaged property such as business interruption losses, rent and rental value losses, and losses of profits and commissions on finished goods. *Consequential loss* is a function of direct damage to such equipment as a refrigerator (food spoilage) or one item in a pair or set (damage to one shoe results in a loss to the undamaged one). Extra-expense losses are those created by an accident or occurrence such as the cost of defense and any damages assessed in a liability suit, additional living expenses because of fire damage to the dwelling, and medical costs arising from accidents or sickness. To determine coverage, a policy must be analyzed as to types of losses covered.

6. Policies vary as to the persons covered. Some policies cover only the insureds and their legal representatives (the standard fire policy); others cover additional persons (the HO series and the PAP). Policies must be examined to define who is covered and under what conditions.

7. The use of mortgage clauses provides an efficient method of protecting the interests of both the mortgagee and the mortgagor in property pledged as security for a loan. Mortgage clauses, however, may expose mortgagors to an interest rate risk by forcing them to negotiate a new mortgage loan after a major loss, at a time when market interest rates may be higher than the contract interest rate paid for the original loan.

8. Provisions in some policies may exclude or suspend coverage when certain hazards are increased. These provisions may be "while"

clauses, which suspend coverage only while the hazard is increased, or "if" clauses which void the policy if a certain hazard is increased. These clauses are designed to allow the insurer to control the risk so that the insurance is affordable.

Questions for Review

1. When the owner's home burns, it must be rebuilt with brick instead of wood. This construction change will cost $90,000 instead of $60,000. Will the owner's $90,000 HO–3 policy pay the full $90,000? Explain.
2. Define short-rate tables. How may they be justified?
3. Why are exclusions used in insurance contracts? Who benefits from exclusions, the insurer or the insured? Explain.
4. Describe a procedure that could be used effectively to determine if a policy covers a particular event.
5. Would it be sufficient to consult a dictionary to determine the meaning of a term used in an insurance contract? Explain.
6. Ken Kennedy rents a cabin for a weekend fishing trip. While smoking in bed, he falls asleep. A fire ensues, causing $1,000 damage to the cabin. The cabin owner sues Ken. Will Ken's HO–3 policy cover the loss? Explain.
7. Under what circumstances might a mortgagor be exposed to loss through the operation of a mortgage clause? Could this possible loss exposure in the mortgage clause ever work to the advantage of the mortgagor?
8. Two students, Tom and Jerry, are wrestling. Tom gets a crossbody ride on Jerry, and as a result Jerry's back is injured. Will Tom's father's HO–3 policy offer protection for Tom if Jerry brings suit against him?
9. Betty Coleman has an HO–3 policy on her dwelling. Because of her negligence fire breaks out in her basement, burns her house to the ground, and spreads to the Dunns' house next door. Dunn sues Betty. Is Betty covered for her liability? If not, how could she have been covered? Is Betty covered for the damage to her own house? If not, how could she have been covered?

Questions for Discussion

1. Insurance policies have been criticized as unreadable. Do you agree with this criticism? Do you believe more insureds would read their policies if they were simplified? What possible problem could be created by a complete revision of policies to make them "readable"?
2. Although a number of insurance policies carry the name "all-risk" or "comprehensive," no truly all-risk or comprehensive policies exist. Why not? Then why are they called "all-risk"? What should they be called?
3. The HO–3 excludes coverage of personal liability resulting from bodily injury or property damage that is either expected or intended from the standpoint of the insured. The PAP has a similar exclusion. What is the purpose of these exclusions? Is the type of loss to which these exclusions are meant to apply insurable? Discuss.
4. Consider the HO–3 and explain why each exclusion is included in the contract.

8

Policy analysis: The personal auto policy and policy standardization

The personal auto policy (PAP) is used to insure owners of private passenger autos and certain types of nonbusiness trucks (business coverage exists for these vehicles if they are not customarily used in the insured's occupation or business) owned or rented under a long-term lease by an individual or married couple. The PAP is composed of four coverages: Part A, liability; Part B, medical payments; Part C, uninsured motorists coverage; and Part D, coverage for damage to the insured's auto. The insured is not obligated to buy all of the coverages available under the policy. Usually, the most frequent coverage deleted is that for damage to the insured's auto. This coverage may not be bought by persons owning older cars and cars in poor condition because of their low value. Also a number of insurers refuse to write this coverage for old cars. Each of the coverages has a wide range of amount limits to meet the needs of the insured. For example, liability coverage can be written for as little as $25,000 per accident up to (depending on the insurer) $500,000 or more per accident. The limits for medical payments coverage may range from a low of $1,000 to a high of $100,000 or more. An analysis of the PAP organized according to the eight questions posed in Chapter 7 comprises the rest of this chapter.

Defining the Perils Covered

Part A (liability coverage) of the PAP covers damages for bodily injury or property damage for which any covered person becomes legally responsible because of an auto accident.

In Part B (medical payments), the insurer agrees to pay reasonable expenses incurred for necessary medical and funeral services because of bodily injury caused by accident and sustained by a covered driver or passenger.

Under Part C (uninsured motorists coverage), if a covered person suffers bodily injury in an accident caused by a hit-and-run or financially irresponsible driver, the insurer will pay up to a specified amount as compensation for the insured's inability to collect damages from the wrongdoer.

Coverage for damage to the insured's auto is handled in Part D of the policy. The insurer agrees to pay for direct and accidental loss to a covered auto. However, the insurer will pay for loss caused by collision only if the declarations of the policy indicate that collision coverage is provided. (What is called "comprehensive coverage" in the family auto policy is called "other than collision" coverage in the PAP. The scope of the coverage—to pay for damage to the covered auto by perils other than those excluded—has not been changed.)

Many unusual losses have been paid under the other than collision coverage, including damage to the car's finish by Halloween pranksters, damages to the auto resulting from transporting a leaking battery, and loss from oil spilled on upholstery by mechanics. These losses were covered because the policy does not contain Halloween prankster, battery acid spill, or careless mechanic exclusions. The excluded perils are: collision or upset; war losses; damage due and confined to wear and tear, road damage to tires, freezing, and mechanical or electrical breakdown, unless that damage is the result of other losses covered by the policy; and loss caused by radioactive contamination.

Interpreting the peril

What is collision? Doug Cogswell had other than collision (OTC) coverage with no deductible and $100 deductible collision coverage on his new sports car.[1] In a windstorm a telephone pole fell on his car, causing $1,500 damage. Is this loss collision, or is it payable under the OTC coverage? The answer is important to Doug because, if the loss is collision, he must bear the first $100. If the loss is not collision, then he has full coverage, as no deductible clause is included in his OTC coverage. No doubt exists that the pole collided with the car, but the OTC coverage states that breakage of glass and loss caused by missiles, falling objects, fire, theft, explosion, earthquake, windstorm, hail, water, flood,

---

[1] The $100 deductible provision means that Doug will have to bear the first $100 of each loss. Deductible clauses are discussed in Chapter 9.

vandalism, riot or civil commotion, or collision with a bird or animal shall not be deemed loss caused by collision or upset for purposes of this coverage. Thus, on two counts, the loss would not be considered collision. The loss was caused both by a windstorm and by a falling object. Therefore, Doug can collect the full $1,500 under his OTC coverage. If, however, Doug had had only collision coverage, the loss would be paid as a collision loss subject to the $100 deductible.

Many insurance policies use the word "accident." Thus its definition is important. One judge defined *accident* as "an undesigned, sudden and unexpected event, usually of an afflictive or unfortunate character, and often accompanied by a manifestation of force." Another definition is from *Couch on Insurance* and is often quoted by judges:

> . . . anything that begins to be, that happens, or that is a result which is not anticipated and is unforeseen and unexpected by the person injured or affected thereby—that is, takes place without the insured's foresight or expectation and without design or intentional causation on his part. In other words, an accident is an undesigned contingency, a casualty, a happening by chance, something out of the usual course of things, unusual, fortuitous, not anticipated, and not naturally to be expected.

Under Part D of the PAP (damage to the insured's auto), the insurer pays only for direct and accidental loss. (Coverages A, B, and C also are written on an accident basis.) *How can the foregoing definitions be applied?* If a burglar breaks the left front window of the car in an attempted theft, the glass loss is accidental to the car owner. Even though the culprit intended both the action and the result, neither was intended by the owner. On the other hand, if the owner breaks the window to recover the keys that were absentmindedly locked inside, the glass damage is not accidental and the OTC coverage provides no protection; both the action and the results were intended. A motorist, stuck in the mud, spins the wheels at varying rates of speed to rock and roll as a means of escape. The friction causes the tire to burn, and the resulting heat damages the car's finish. That damage is accidental. Even though the action was intended, the results were unintended; that is, accidental. A student drives the car to a beach cottage and leaves it there for several weeks while acquiring the tan necessary to last through the summer. While the sun and salt are tanning the motorist, they are also tanning the powder blue Subaru. The loss, however, is *not* accidental in this case, even though the results were not intended. The term "accident" has been interpreted by the courts to mean a sudden, unexpected event, identifiable in time and place. Damage occurring gradually over time is construed as resulting from an occurrence rather than an accident. *Occurrence* is defined strictly as an accident, but including continuous or repeated exposure to conditions, that results in bodily injury or property damage neither expected nor intended by the insured. As noted, the personal liability coverage of the HO is written on an occurrence basis.

Examples indicating the necessity for a precise definition of perils abound. They show that it may not be possible always to depend on the everyday meaning of words and that it may be necessary to look to courts, in contracts, or even at state statutes for an interpretation. It is also important to recognize that court decisions vary, and contracts and statutes undergo changes.

As discussed in Chapter 6, the wording of insurance policies also is important to the insurer. For example, readability requirements, mandated by law in some states, have caused insurers to simplify the language used. The "named insured" and "the spouse if a resident of the same household" are definitions used to allow the policy to refer to the insured as "you" and to the insured auto as "your covered auto." Because insurance policies are contracts of adhesion, any ambiguous terms in the policy will be construed in the insured's favor if the case should reach court. Ambiguity of policy wording thus exposes insurers to "juridical risk," the risk that the courts may deem a word to be ambiguous and thus have a meaning different from that which the company intended. In the PAP, for example, the word "occupying" is defined as, "in, upon, getting in, on, out, or off." The word "upon" is not defined. Various court decisions have held that persons injured while in any actual physical contact with the automobile were in fact *upon* the automobile. In one decision, an insured was held to be upon the automobile when injured while placing a tire in the trunk of the auto, although not in actual contact with the automobile at the time of injury.[2]

Defining the Property Covered

As defined in the definition section of the PAP, "your covered auto" means:

1. Any vehicle shown in the declarations.
2. Any of the following types of vehicles on the date you become the owner:
   a. A private passenger auto.
   b. A pickup, panel truck, or van.
This provision applies only if:
   a. You acquire the vehicle during the policy period.
   b. You ask us to insure it within 30 days after you become the owner.
   c. With respect to a pickup, panel truck, or van, no other insurance policy provides coverage for that vehicle.
If the vehicle you acquire replaces one shown in the declarations, it will have the same coverage as the vehicle it replaced. You must ask us to insure a replacement vehicle within 30 days only if:
   a. You wish to add or continue coverage for damage to your auto.
   b. It is a pickup, panel truck, or van used in any business or occupation, other than farming or ranching.
If the vehicle you acquire is in addition to any shown in the declarations,

---

[2] *Madden* v. *Farm Bureau Mutual Automobile Ins. Co.,* 79 N.C. (2d) S86.

it will have the broadest coverage we now provide for any vehicle shown in the declarations.

3. Any *trailer* you own.
4. Any auto or *trailer* you do not own while used as a temporary substitute for any other vehicle described in this definition which is out of normal use because of its:
   a. Breakdown.
   b. Repair.
   c. Servicing.
   d. Loss.
   e. Destruction.

Part D (coverage for damage to the insured's auto) provides coverage for loss to any of the foregoing vehicles except loss to a temporary substitute vehicle. Physical damage coverage for temporary substitute automobiles is found under the liability portion of the policy.

Liability coverage is provided in Part A for damage to the following types of vehicles not owned by or furnished or available for the regular use of the named insured or any family member but which have been rented to, used by, or in the care of these people: *(a)* private passenger autos; *(b)* trailers; or *(c)* pickups, panel trucks, or vans.

Only the named insured is provided liability coverage for the ownership, maintenance, or use of any vehicle, other than the covered auto, that is owned by or furnished to or available for the regular use of any family member. No liability coverage is provided for the ownership, maintenance, or use of a motorcycle or any other self-propelled vehicle having less than four wheels, or for any vehicle, other than the covered auto, which is owned by or furnished or available for the named insured's regular use. Any insurance provided for a vehicle not owned by the named insured shall be excess over any other collectible insurance.

The PAP does not extend coverage to any personal effects while such items are in or upon the covered auto. Coverage is provided for sound reproduction equipment permanently installed in the covered auto. Coverage is not extended to loss of tapes, records, or other devices for use with the sound reproduction equipment. Also, citizens' band radios, two-way mobile radios, telephones and their accessories, or antennas are excluded from coverage.

The PAP does not provide liability coverage to any person for damage to property owned or being transported by that person, or for damage to property other than a residence or private garage rented to, used by, or in the care of that person. (The "care, custody, or control" exclusion is common to most liability policies.[3] Other policies, usually fire, marine,

---

[3] The question of what constitutes care, custody, or control has brought about many interesting cases. In one decision, an Arkansas court held that a trespasser, with no right to possession of an airplane that ran wild while he was at its controls, did not have care, custody, or control of the airplane. Insurers then changed the wording of the exclusion to exclude damage to "property occupied or used by the insured," in addition to property in the insured's care, custody, and control.

and fire legal liability contracts, are written to cover this property. See Chapters 4, 11, 12, and 14 for a discussion of these policies.) For example, if Gary Zebrowski forgets to open the door to his rented garage and backs his car out through the closed door, liability coverage would be provided for the damage done to the door (and to the car under Part D). If he also ran over his bicycle while making this graceful exit, no coverage would apply to it because that damage is to property owned by the operator of the auto. If he ran over the bicycle belonging to the owner of the garage, Gary would have coverage for his liability for damage to the bicycle under Part A of the PAP.

Defining the Types of Losses Covered

The physical damage section of the PAP provides principally direct loss coverage. Only for theft is coverage available for loss of use. The insurer promises under Part D to reimburse the insured for actual expense incurred for rental of a substitute automobile, including taxicabs, not to exceed $10 a day, or totaling more than $300. Reimbursement is limited to covered expense incurred during the period commencing 48 hours after the theft has been reported to the insurer and the police, and terminating the day the auto is recovered *and* returned to the insured or when the insurer pays for the theft loss. The loss of use protection allows the insurer ample time to locate the stolen car without seriously inconveniencing the insured. The insurer pays the cost of returning the recovered automobile to the named insured or, at the insurer's option, to the address shown in the policy declarations. For insured losses caused by perils other than theft, no rental reimbursement coverage is included in the PAP. Rental reimbursement coverage can be endorsed on the PAP for $6 per car per year. The coverage applies whenever the covered automobile is "withdrawn from normal use for a period in excess of 24 hours." The maximum reimbursement is $10 per day and not more than $300 for the period.

In addition to paying bodily injury and property damage liability claims, the insurer agrees to make supplementary payments (as described in Chapter 7) including up to $250 for the cost of bail bonds required because of an accident resulting in bodily injury or property damage covered under the policy.

Defining the Persons Covered

The liability section (Part A) of the PAP covers the following persons:

1. You or any *family member* for the ownership, maintenance or use of any auto or *trailer.*
2. Any person using *your covered auto.*
3. For *your covered auto,* any person or organization but only with

respect to legal responsibility for acts or omissions of a person for whom coverage is afforded under this part.

4. For any auto or *trailer,* other than *your covered auto,* any person or organization but only with respect to legal responsibility for acts or omissions of you or any *family member* for whom coverage is afforded under this part. This provision applies only if the person or organization does not own or hire the auto or *trailer.*

As an example of (3), assume that Charytyna is running an errand in her capacity as a United Way volunteer. While on the errand, she is involved in an accident. Her PAP would cover any liability imputed to her as well as any liability imputed to the United Way arising out of her acts or omissions.

The automobile liability coverage applies separately and individually to each insured. For example, if Mario has $50,000 of liability coverage on his car and lends it to Myung to drive to Chicago, both are "insureds" within the meaning of the contract. Myung hits Madhu, who is injured. She sues Myung for $50,000, alleging negligence, and sues Mario for $50,000 for not properly preparing the car for the trip. The total liability of the insurer will be only $50,000. That the term "the insured" can be stretched to include additional persons does not increase the limits of the insurer's liability. A similar clause is in the liability section of HO–3 and most other liability coverages.

The PAP provides medical payments (Part B) to the named insured and any family member while occupying, or as a pedestrian when struck by, a motor vehicle designed for use mainly on public roads or by a trailer of any type.

The uninsured motorists coverage protects:

1. The named insured or any family member.
2. Any other person occupying the insured's covered auto.
3. Any person for damages that person is entitled to recover because of bodily injury sustained by a person described in (1) or (2) and to which coverage applies.

Coverage for collision and OTC is provided for covered autos (except temporary substitute vehicles) and generally is not affected by the identity of the person who may be operating the vehicle at the time of the loss. A limitation to these coverages is that the insurance shall not directly or indirectly benefit any carrier or other bailee. Thus, if Mike Jacobs's car is damaged by a negligent mechanic while on a test drive, the mechanic (a bailee) would not be able to benefit under Mike's PAP.

Assignment

Most contracts have assignment provisions. Some policies require written consent of the insurer, others notice to the insurer; some prohibit assignment. In a few policies, assignment is freely permitted.

Consent of insurer.   The HO policies and the PAP require written consent of the insurer to validate an assignment. This requirement conforms to the law that would apply in the absence of contract agreement. These policies insure the property owner against loss, not the property. If the property is sold, the insurance is still held by the former owner unless the insurer agrees to an assignment. Insurers may select policyowners and cannot be forced by assignment to insure anyone who acquires an insurable interest in the property.

An assignment without the insurer's consent seldom voids the policy. The assignment is simply not recognized. Thus, if Dorothy Morey sells her auto and assigns the insurance to the buyer, the policy is not void. The insurer merely will not pay in case of loss because the insured no longer has an insurable interest in the destroyed auto. If Dorothy repurchases the car, the policy covers, for then the insured regains her insurable interest.

Consent of the insurer is necessary for a valid assignment of most property and liability policies, and may be given by the local agent of the insurer. A clause similar to the following is found in nearly all the contracts:

> If, however, the insured shall die, or be adjudged bankrupt, or insolvent within the policy period, this policy, unless cancelled, shall, if written notice be given to the company within sixty days after the date of such death or adjudication, cover the insured's legal representative of the insured.

Some policies set 30 days as the time within which notice must be given. This clause is not in fire policies, as the legal representatives of the insured are specifically covered in the insuring agreement.

Types of assignments.   An assignment of a policy may or may not result in a new contract. If the insured disposes of the covered property and transfers the insurance also, no interest is retained in either the property or insurance. If the insurer agrees to the assignment, the majority opinion is that a new contract, subject to the old terms, has been created between the insurer and the assignee and that any prior actions of the assignor cannot affect it. If the insurer agrees to an assignment while the assignor still owes premiums for the policy, the assignee is not responsible for these premiums.

If the policy is assigned as security for a debt, the insured retains an interest in both the property and insurance. The insured is in possession and control of the property and in case of loss may collect insurance proceeds in excess of the amount due the creditor. This type of assignment does not create a new contract. The rights of the assignee are the same as those of the assignor. Both prior and subsequent actions of the assignor may invalidate the policy.

Assignment after a loss.   Assignment clauses apply only to assignments before a loss. After a loss the policy represents a right of action and may be assigned by the insured without the consent of the insurer. This type of assignment cannot increase moral or morale hazard. The loss has occurred, and the claim is due. The assignment changes only the payee. In the case of a partial loss, only that part of the policy covering the loss may be assigned without consent.

Notice to company. Insurance policies assignable without the insurer's consent usually require that notice of assignment be given. This rule is applied in life and health insurance. A typical assignment clause in life insurance reads:

> No assignment of this policy shall be binding upon the company unless and until the original or a duplicate thereof is filed at its Home Office. The company does not assume any responsibility for the validity of an assignment.

Under these conditions, if an assignment is made without notifying the insurer, and upon death of the insured the insurer pays the proceeds to the beneficiary or to the insured's estate, the assignee has no claim against the insurer for failure to recognize the assignment. However, in most jurisdictions, an insurer may recognize an assignment even though no notice has been given. The purpose of the assignment clause in life and health insurance is to free the insurer from determining the validity or effect of an assignment. If a question arises concerning who is entitled to the proceeds, the insurer can pay the proceeds to a court for disposition under an interpleader action. An assignment in life and health insurance can be made without the consent of the insurer because of the presumption that the assignment cannot affect the hazard.

Prohibited and free assignments. Some policies are not assignable, whereas others are freely assignable. An example of the former is credit insurance. However, by agreement proceeds may be made payable to a bank, a trust company, or some other payee for the insured's account.

By custom, some ocean marine insurance contracts covering cargo are freely assignable because the cargo usually is outside the custody of the insured. Moral or morale hazard probably is not increased by allowing free assignment of cargo policies.

Determining the Locations Covered

The PAP restricts coverage to the United States, its territories or possessions, Puerto Rico, and Canada, or in transit between their ports. If Vic Hallman plans to drive his car to Mexico, he needs his auto insurance endorsed to extend coverage to include that country. Many insurance experts recommend purchasing a liability policy from a Mexican insurer rather than adding an endorsement to an American policy, because Mexican officials are more likely to accept their own policies in meeting their law.

Defining the Period of Coverage

The PAP runs from 12:01 A.M. standard time on the date of expiration. Standard time at the address of the named insured governs whether the coverage is in effect.

Cancellation

Most property and liability contracts give the insurer and insured the right to cancel the policy before its expiration date.

The standard fire insurance policy states:

> This policy shall be cancelled at any time at the request of the insured, in which case this Company shall, upon demand and surrender of this policy, refund the excess paid premium above the customary short rates for the expired time. This policy may be cancelled at any time by this Company by giving to the insured a five days' written notice of cancellation with or without tender of the excess of paid premium above the pro rata premium for the expired time, which excess, if not tendered, shall be refunded on demand. Notice of cancellation shall state that said excess premium (if not tendered) will be refunded on demand.

Note that the insured may cancel immediately, but the insurer must give five days' written notice. The five-day requirement is to allow the insured time to negotiate for other insurance to take effect at date of cancellation. Another reason is to prevent an unscrupulous insurer from cancelling during a conflagration near the insured's property.

Variations among cancellation clauses.   The cancellation clause in the HO forms is much more restrictive than that of the SFP as to when and why the insurer may cancel the policy. The insurer (or agent) may cancel the policy at any time by notifying the named insured at least 10 days before the date cancellation takes place. When the policy has been in effect for less than 60 days and is not a renewal, the insurer may cancel for any reason by notifying the insured at least 10 days before the cancellation takes place.

The insurer may also cancel if (1) a fact is discovered that would have altered the insurer's original acceptance of the risk, or (2) if the risk has changed substantially since the policy was issued.

In recent years a controversy has centered around the frequent difficulty drivers have in obtaining and retaining automobile insurance. As of mid-1984, 46 states had statutes limiting in some measure the cancellation of automobile insurance policies. Two additional states and the District of Columbia had established guidelines and regulations concerning cancellations. The statutory restriction and administrative regulations of the insurer's right to cancel generally are restricted to policies written to cover private passenger automobiles. The states' cancellation provisions vary as to the coverages to which they apply. A few states have statutes that do not refer to particular coverage; others have provisions that apply to various combinations of bodily injury and property damage liability, medical payments, uninsured motorists, and physical damage insurance.

Nearly all states allow insurers freedom to cancel new insureds only within a certain period after the inception of the policy, the period ranging from 30 to 90 days. After this period has elapsed, the insurers may cancel only for specified reasons varying significantly among states. Examples of permissible reasons for cancellation found in most states include nonpayment of premium and suspension or revocation of the insured's driver's license. Other permissible reasons found in statutes of various states are:[4]

1. Insurance obtained through fraudulent misrepresentation.
2. The named insured or other customary operator of the vehicle:
   a. Is or becomes subject to epilepsy or heart attacks without presenting a physician's statement testifying as to the person's ability to operate a motor vehicle.
   b. Is convicted of driving while intoxicated or is a habitual drinker of alcohol.
   c. Has within a three-year period prior to cancellation been addicted to narcotics or other drugs.
3. The named insured or other customary operator of the vehicle who has forfeited bail or is or has been convicted within a three-year period prior to cancellation, for:
   a. Felony.
   b. Leaving the scene of an accident.
   c. Reckless driving.
   d. Theft of a motor vehicle.
   e. Conviction or forfeiture of bail for a third speeding violation during the 18 months prior to cancellation. (The 55-mile-per-hour speed limit makes this requirement a tough one, especially for those driving on interstate highways, in those rare instances where the law is strictly enforced.)

Nearly all state laws include provisions specifying the number of days' notice that must be given (from 10 to 60 days) and requiring that a reason for cancellation be given by the insurer upon the request of the insured or with the notice. Provisions relating to nonrenewal of policies deal mostly with the time required to issue notices of nonrenewal before policy expiration (ranging from 10 to 60 days). Most states require that a written explanation of the reason for nonrenewal accompany the notice or that one be supplied on demand.

In the past, insurers were not required to give a reason for cancellation. To require the insurer to give a reason would be inhibiting, especially if the reason for cancellation was the suspicion of a moral hazard. Allegations of moral hazard could produce legal action by the insured

---

[4] A complete and up-to-date listing of permissible cancellation reasons for the particular states may be found in the *FC&S Bulletins,* Casualty and Surety Section, Auto, Cra-7 (Cincinnati: National Underwriter Co., monthly).

against the insurer for slander or libel. To avoid such actions, most state statutes requiring explanation of cancellation or nonrenewal by the insurer also provide the insurer immunity from any tort action that might result. However, in six states, insurers are not granted immunity.

Because of the diverse state laws concerning automobile insurance cancellation, cancellation provisions of the PAP vary among states.

Time limits for notice vary among inland marine policies from 5 to 60 days. Fifteen- and 30-day notice provisions are common. In addition to the standard cancellation clause, some inland marine forms include a "cancellation by nonpayment of premium" clause, making it a condition of the policy that if the premium is not paid within 60 days from the contract's inception, it shall be null and void while the premium is past due and unpaid. The policy is reinstated upon payment of the premium. Under this automatic cancellation clause the policy is voidable at the election of the insurer. The insurer, through its actions, can waive the clause. Thus, if after the expiration of the 60-day period the insurer acted as if the policy was still in force by insisting on payment or threatening to cancel, the automatic cancellation clause would be waived.

Cancellation clauses in workers' compensation insurance present significant differences from the usual clause. Because workers' compensation insurance is a form of social insurance and is compulsory for many employers, the states require that notice of cancellation be given to a board, commission, or other state agency for control purposes. The policy requires a minimum of 10 days' notice before cancellation that applies both to the insurer and the insured. Another difference is that if the policy is cancelled by the insured, the minimum premium must be paid regardless of how little protection had been received.[5] If the business is discontinued, however, the employer may cancel pro rata.

The cancellation clause in health insurance is optional but is included in many policies. Some health policies do not include cancellation clauses, but if the policies are not automatically renewable at the end of each policy year, the effect is nearly the same as cancellation. The difference is that the insurer cannot terminate the contract until the end of the premium period. The policy also has a clause relating to cancellation by the insured. If the insured changes occupations to one less hazardous, the policy may be cancelled and the unearned premium returned. Under no other conditions may the insured cancel the policy and collect the unearned premium.

The method of giving notice is another variation among cancellation clauses. The majority of policies states that mailing a notice of cancellation to the insured at the address shown in the policy, or the last known address, satisfies the notice requirement. This clause is found in most inland marine and liability forms and in auto policies. Effective cancel-

---

[5] The initial cost of writing workers' compensation insurance often is higher than the initial cost of writing other forms of insurance, as this line requires a considerable amount of engineering and inspection service.

lation in this clause requires proof that notice was mailed. The use of first-class mail with a postmaster's receipt is ample proof in most cases, but in some jurisdictions the use of certified or registered mail is required.

Other cancellation clauses (e.g., the one in the standard fire policy) provide that notice be given, but ignore the method. Any procedure is permissible, *but the insurer must be able to prove that the insured received notice.*

Sometimes proving that notice was given to the insured is difficult. Delivering a written notice in person and obtaining a signed receipt is the safest but also the most expensive method. Registered mail has produced litigation. If registered mail is used, an affirmative action—the signing of the receipt card—is required on the part of the addressee to prove delivery. Several cases indicate that first-class mail with a postmaster's receipt is adequate proof that the notice was received (in the absence of a statutory requirement to the contrary).[6] The presumption is that a letter properly mailed will be delivered. The insured has burden of proof that the letter was not received.

Legal interpretations. If insureds or insurers want to cancel a contract, they must cancel the entire policy. Exceptions are made for policies with scheduled optional coverages as in the 3-D crime policy discussed in Chapter 15.

In determining the time limit, the day the notice is received is ignored. Under the HO policy, the contract is terminated in most states at midnight on the 10th day, not counting the day the insured receives the notice. If this 10th day is Sunday, the policy is terminated Monday at midnight. The insured may cancel the policy specifying the date the contract is to be cancelled. Otherwise, the policy terminates when the insurer receives notice. So, if a covered building burns while the owner is mailing the cancellation notice, the policy covers.

Is notice to the broker notice to the insured? Generally it is not, as the broker usually is the agent of the insured only for buying insurance. Once the policy is delivered, the agency terminates.

Premium refunds in cancellation. If the insurer cancels the policy, the insured receives a pro rata return of premium. Under most insurance contracts a uniform exposure to loss is assumed during the policy term. If the annual premium is $480 and the policy is cancelled by the insurer after two months, the insured is refunded $400. If the policyowner cancels the contract, the refund will be less, because the short rate is used. If, in the foregoing example, the insured cancelled the policy, the insurer's retention for two months' protection would be 27 percent under most policies, and the refund would be $350.40.

---

[6] *Harding* v. *American Insurance Co.,* 142 Fed. 2d 257; *Dias* v. *Farm Bureau Mutual Fire Insurance Co.,* 155 Fed. 2d 788; *Hawes* v. *American Central Insurance Co.,* 7 S.W. 2d 479.

Some policies require a return of the unearned premium as a condition precedent to cancellation, but commonly the premium is refundable on demand. Thus the insurer may cancel first and adjust the premium later. Insurers generally do not consider refunding premiums with notice of cancellation good practice, as the agent may have financed the insured's premium. Premium adjustments, therefore, are best made through the agent.

Reasons for cancellation.   Cancellation clauses are included in insurance for several reasons. First, these clauses are necessary to give insurers some control over the risk after the contract is written. Circumstances may change, or conditions may be discovered that may make a risk no longer desirable. The ability to postselect is important to insurers, allowing them to select "out" as well as "in." The cancellation clause is particularly valuable when an insurer wants to discontinue writing a particular kind of insurance, withdraw from a geographic area, or retire from the business. The cancellation clause also is useful when an agent wishes the insurer to terminate a policy for nonpayment of premium. Generally, the insurer does not have to give a reason for cancelling a policy, just as no reason must be given for rejecting an application. However, as discussed earlier, statutes and administrative rulings in many states require that insurers give reasons for cancellation (and nonrenewal), particularly of personal auto insurance.

Insureds also find cancellation clauses useful. If Walter Primeaux sells his auto, he no longer needs auto insurance. He can terminate his policy and collect a premium refund. The insured also does not need to give a reason for cancellation.

As a person cannot ordinarily enter and break an agreement at will, cancellation clauses are important; they give a legal procedure for discontinuing a contract when either party finds it no longer advantageous. Without a cancellation clause both parties must perform, unless the contract is terminated by mutual agreement.

Not all policies are cancellable.   The cancellation privilege is not included in some policies because the time factor is important. Rain insurance would be nearly worthless if the insurer could cancel when rain was predicted. If the forecast is for clear weather, to allow the insured to cancel and collect a refund also would be inequitable. Similarly, neither the insured nor the insurer has a cancellation right in life insurance. The insured, however, may terminate the policy at the end of any premium period by ignoring the next premium within the 31-day grace period. In absence of fraud the insurer may never terminate a life insurance policy. A life insurance policy might be worthless if the insurer could cancel the policy when the insured's health became seriously impaired. Some health policies are both noncancellable and guaranteed renewable (see Chapter 18).

Defining the Hazards that Exclude or Suspend Coverage

The PAP excludes coverage for certain hazardous exposures. Coverage does not apply to any person or auto while it is being used to transport persons or property for a fee. This exclusion does not apply to a share the expense car pool. For example, if Stu Arnold takes a friend with him on vacation and they share the expenses, the policy will cover. If he hires out his auto for a profit, however, coverage for any resulting loss will be denied. Automobiles used as taxicabs, buses, and rental cars are typically exposed to greater hazards and thus are more likely to suffer losses than are autos driven for private passenger purposes only. Therefore, a higher premium is needed for this coverage.

No coverage is provided to any person using a vehicle without reasonable belief that the person is entitled to do so. Liability and medical payments coverages do not apply to the use of motorcycles or to the business use of *other than* private passenger autos, pickups, panel trucks, or vans owned by the named insured. The PAP does not cover liability while the insured auto is used in an automobile business by persons *other than* a named insured, a resident of the named insured's household, a partnership involving one of the above, or any partner, agent, or employee of such resident or partnership. (Automobile business is defined as a business or occupation of selling, repairing, servicing, storing, or parking of vehicles designed for use mainly on public highways, including road testing and delivery. The intention of this exclusion is to eliminate coverage for a garage or parking-lot attendant who may drive the car with permission of an insured. Persons engaged in the automobile business are expected to buy their own automobile liability and physical damage protection.) In addition, liability coverage does not apply for any intentional acts or for bodily injury to an employee of any person during the course of employment. Coverage would apply for bodily injury to a domestic employee if the employee is not eligible for workers' compensation benefits.

Medical payments and physical damage coverage exclude losses arising out of war hazards, the discharge of a nuclear weapon, or from nuclear radiation.

Policy Standardization

In early days the insurer and the insured had complete freedom in designing the policy. As insurance became highly technical, this freedom was a disadvantage to policyowners and insurers. An insured with several insurance policies often discovered, on close inspection, that overlapping and conflicting coverage existed. The insured might own two policies, yet each policy might contain a provision denying coverage if other insurance was maintained on the property. In insurance language, the policies were nonconcurrent, unnecessarily increasing insurance costs or voiding one or more of the coverages. More often than not, these distressing facts became known only after a loss had occurred. Furthermore, policy competition hurt insurers by making it difficult for those with straightforward contracts to match the rates of insurers issuing deceptive policies. The need for standardization was patent. The HO–3 and the PAP are examples of standardized policies.

Policies are standardized in three ways: custom, statute, and intercompany agreement. Not all policies are standardized, and when they are, risk managers for large businesses do not have to purchase the standard form. Instead, they might develop forms of their own to meet particular needs and then seek insurers to write the tailored coverage. A standard policy may be defined as one that is substantially like the majority of policies written by insurers in a particular field.

Custom

As early as 1764, the underwriters at Lloyd's coffeehouse realized that it was to their advantage as well as that of their insureds to adopt a standard policy. In 1779, they agreed to use a standard marine form developed by fellow underwriters, known as "Lloyd's standard policy." Through the years a body of insurance law developed from many court decisions concerning the policy. Almost every word of the Lloyd's policy has been subject to court interpretation, so that, in spite of its archaic wording, any insurer writing the policy is confident of the meaning.

The Marine Insurance Bill of 1899 and the Marine Insurance Act of 1906 recognized the Lloyd's policy as the standard policy for England, but it has never become the required form in America. Policy forms used in the United States by marine underwriters vary considerably from the Lloyd's policy, but stem directly from it. In the United States the Lloyd's policy had been standardized by custom and varied by competition. The Lloyd's policy, therefore, provides an illustration of the types of standardization found among policies, first standardized by intercompany agreement, then by law in England and finally by custom in the United States.

Standardization by state law

Standardization by state statute is accomplished either by prescribing a particular contract or minimum standard provisions.

Standard contract

The only example of a policy in which the exact wording of the contract is prescribed by law is the standard fire insurance policy. Historically, each fire insurer wrote its own policy. These forms varied widely, not only among insurers but even among policies written by the same insurer.

At first, business originated only with the home offices. With the introduction of the agency system, it became apparent to home office underwriters that insurance contracts would have to be tightly drawn to protect the insurer. Some insurers granted liberal terms on the face of the contract but then buried many unwarranted exclusions and unfair conditions throughout the policy.

Chief Justice Doe, of the New Hampshire Supreme Court, in 1873 summed up the issue in a classic decision in insurance jurisprudence, if not in American humor. Said the justice:

> Forms of applications and policies (like those used in this case), of a most complicated and elaborate structure, were prepared, and filled with covenants, exceptions, stipulations, provisos, rules, regulations, and conditions, rendering the policy void in a great number of contingencies. These provisions were of such bulk and character that they would not be understood by men in general, even if subjected to a careful and laborious study; by men in general, they were sure not to be studied at all. The study of them was rendered particularly unattractive by a profuse intermixture of discourses on subjects in which a premium payer would have no interest. The compound, if read by him, would, unless he were an extraordinary man, be an inexplicable riddle, a mere flood of darkness and confusion. Some of the most material stipulations were concealed in a mass of rubbish, on the back side of the policy, and the following page, where few would expect to find anything more than a dull appendix, and where scarcely anyone would think of looking for information so important as that the company claimed a special exemption from the operation of the general law of the land relating to the only business in which the company professed to be engaged. As if it were feared that, notwithstanding these discouraging circumstances, some extremely eccentric person might attempt to examine and understand the meaning of the involved and intricate net in which he was to be entangled, it was printed in such small type, and in lines so long and so crowded, that the perusal of it was made physically difficult, painful, and injurious. Seldom has the art of typography been so successfully diverted from the diffusion of knowledge to the suppression of it.

> * * * * *

> When the premium payer complained that he had been defrauded, it was not, in the opinion of the legislature, a sufficient answer to say that, if he had been wise enough, taken time enough, had good eyes enough, and been reckless enough in the use of them to read the mass of fine print, and had been scholar, business man, and lawyer enough to understand its full force and effect, he would have been alarmed, and would not have been decoyed into the trap that was set for him.[7]

The National Board of Fire Underwriters, founded in 1866, soon sought uniformity in fire policies. In 1873 Massachusetts enacted a bill providing the form in which fire policies sold in the state had to be written, beginning in 1880. Impetus for passage of the bill that created a standard New York fire policy came from a legislator who was also on the Buffalo YMCA board of trustees. This unsung hero had, in his capacity as a member of the committee on insurance, wrestled hard and long with the YMCA's fire policies. In the words of Chief Justice

---

[7] *Delancey* v. *Rockingham Farmers' Mutual Fire Insurance Company,* 52 N.H.

Doe, he found the task "physically difficult, painful, and injurious." He solicited enough supporters with similar difficulties to get a bill through the 1886 legislature asking the New York Board of Fire Underwriters to draft a standard form to be obligatory the following year. The 1886 New York standard fire policy was revised in 1918 and again in 1943. The 1943 version, or a reasonable facsimile, is required in virtually every state. The fire insurance contract is unique as the only insurance contract whose exact wording is prescribed by statute.

A standard automobile insurance policy was proposed by the West Virginia legislature in 1934. Insurers were invited to help in preparing the policy. The West Virginia supervising authorities hoped that their standard policy would be used nationwide. Although this was not accomplished, the proposed introduction of a standard policy into West Virginia had a salutary effect upon insurers which feared that more states would follow West Virginia and standardize automobile policies. To prevent statutory standardization insurers agreed to include many voluntary standard provisions in automobile policies.

Standardization through standard provisions. Rather than require a standard policy for some coverages, the states prescribe minimum standard provisions. Some are mandatory; others are optional. The use of certain additional provisions is expressly forbidden. Life and health policies are standardized through standard provisions. The life insurance forms written by the more than 1,800 U.S. life insurers are not identical, but they must contain certain provisions concerning grace periods for premium payments, nonforfeiture options, reinstatement, and incontestability. Life insurers cannot exclude or restrict coverage except for war, suicide, aviation, and hazardous occupations.[8]

Health policies achieve a measure of standardization through required "uniform provisions." These provisions deal with such items as change of the insured's occupation, changes in the policy, policy reinstatement, cancellation by the insured, rights of beneficiaries, and claim-settlement procedure. The uniform provisions do not deal with benefit clauses, so benefits vary widely among policies.[9]

In workers' compensation insurance, the policy must incorporate the provisions of the state workers' compensation law. The basic policy, however, is standardized by intercompany agreements, not by state law. In some surety bonds applying to public officials, statutory provisions must be included. These statutes, though not printed in the contracts, are assumed to be in the policies.

Standardization by intercompany agreement

Recognizing the advantages of standard policies, insurers often develop uniform contracts through intercompany agreement. Standard

---

[8] For a discussion of standard provisions in life insurance, see Chapter 17.

[9] For a discussion of uniform provisions and coverage in health insurance, see Chapter 18.

policies eliminate undesirable "fine print" competition among insurers and simplify interpretation of policies. Standardization by intercompany agreement also eliminates need for standard policy laws. Insurers prefer voluntary intercompany action to legislative compulsion.

Automobile insurance provides the best known example of standardization through intercompany agreement, which began in 1936. The original standard automobile policy (called the basic policy), as developed by a joint committee of mutual and stock companies working with the insurance committee of the American Bar Association, covered liability only. Through many revisions, coverage has been extended to include physical damage and to some extent personal accidents. In 1956, a standard family automobile policy appeared offering broader coverage for individuals with private passenger automobiles. In 1977 the family auto policy was revised to provide a more readable contract, resulting in the PAP.

Automobile insurance is not the only field in which policies are voluntarily standardized. Although no standard policy is required for inland marine insurance, much inland marine business is written on policies standardized by rating bureaus. In casualty insurance, policies such as the comprehensive personal liability, comprehensive general liability, glass, and many crime coverages also are standardized by rating bureaus. These standard forms are known as "bureau forms." Some insurers do not use bureau forms. Some policies, therefore, vary from the "typical contract," making it necessary to read bastard policies carefully (the term "bastard" is technical and not necessarily uncomplimentary). In fact, some "nonstandard" policies offer more protection than standard policies.

An advantage of standardization can be obtained from the long-term usage of standard contracts. With the passage of time, contract language is tested in the courts and precedent is established. The juridical risk insurance companies face is reduced as questions of vagueness concerning the meanings of words and phrases are answered. Recall that insurance contracts are contracts of adhesion and are strongly construed in favor of the insured when judged ambiguous. The greater degree of certainty about which losses are and which are not covered enables insurers to better assess their potential liabilities. Patently, this increased knowledge can have a beneficial effect on rates and competition.

Disadvantages of standardization

It is possible for standardization to impede progress by delaying the liberalization of contracts. Statutory standardization may eliminate experimentation by individual insurers and thus retard innovation. Although cooperative action is more time consuming than individual action, standardization by intercompany agreement or custom does not necessarily impede progress. As long as some insurers refuse to join cooperative organizations, believing that their innovative efforts would be restricted, innovation is possible. If the efforts of these insurers are successful, competitive pressure will cause the rest of the industry to adopt the change. If unsuccessful, the industry and the public will have been little affected by the individual experimentation. Prospective insureds, however, should be aware that some insurers not using standard forms may be offering inferior coverage.

Summary

1. The PAP is used to insure private passenger autos and nonbusiness light trucks owned or leased by individuals or married couples.
2. The PAP provides four coverages: *(a)* liability, *(b)* medical expenses, *(c)* uninsured motorists coverage, and *(d)* coverage for damage to the insured's auto.
3. Policies are written either on an accident (sudden or unexpected event) or occurrence (an accident, including continuous or repeated exposure to conditions) basis.
4. Some insurance contracts require the insurer's consent for an assignment to be valid (the HO series and the PAP); others require only that the insurer be notified of the assignment (life insurance). Still other policies are freely assignable (ocean marine cargo) and some prohibit assignment under any circumstances (credit insurance). Restrictions are applied only to preloss assignments.
5. Most property and liability insurance contracts give both the insurer and the insured the right to cancel the policy before its expiration date. Life insurance, however, cannot be cancelled by either party, although the insured may terminate premium payments and let the policy lapse. In recent years many states have enacted statutes that limit the cancellation of automobile insurance after the policy has been in force for a specified period.
6. Policies differ as to location and time period of coverage. Some policies (e.g., the PAP) limit coverage to a specified geographical area; others offer worldwide coverage (e.g., Section II, HO–3). Although most property and liability contracts are written on an annual basis, many are written for shorter periods (short-rate policies) and longer periods (term policies).
7. Policy standardization is accomplished by custom, statute, and intercompany agreement. Nonstandard policies often left insureds with noncurrent coverages and caused insurers to face price competition on dissimilar policies. Policy standardization alleviates these two problems, but it may also impede policy innovation and liberalization.

Questions for Review

1. Why are HO policies not freely assigned by their owners to anyone who buys the covered dwelling?

2. Sister Marie parks her car by the church. A playful student throws a missal to another student who misses, and the volume hits and breaks Sister Marie's windshield. Will her auto collision coverage protect her for the loss? Is there any other way she might collect?

3. Why are some policies noncancellable while others may be cancelled either by the insurer or the insured?

4. Construct a situation where an occurrence-basis policy would pay but an accident-basis policy would not pay.

5. When covered by a PAP, is an insured granted full coverage for any vehicle that he or she may choose to drive? If not, what are the exceptions?

6. Often one sees in auto repair shops a sign saying, "We are not responsible for damage to your car." If your auto is damaged while out on a test drive by a mechanic from a garage displaying this sign, will your PAP pay for the damage? Do you believe that the disclaimer carries any weight?

Questions for Discussion

1. The automobile policy is often cited as an example of a policy standardized through intercompany agreement. Yet some people state that there is no such thing as a standard automobile policy. Can these statements both be correct? Is there a standard life policy? If not, should there be?

2. Many states require insurers to supply a reason for cancellation along with the notification of cancellation to the insured. What are a few possible reasons why six of these states provide no immunity to the insurer for liability that might arise from compliance with these statutes?

3. "The dangers of the standardization of insurance policies outweigh the advantages." Explain why you agree or disagree with this statement.

4. The ability to practice postselection is critical to insurers, yet many states have severely limited automobile insurers' right to cancel. What possible justification could these states have for their action? Should an insurer have the right to cancel a policy solely because the insured has had a bad loss experience? Explain.

Limitations on amount of recovery

Insurers do not issue blank checks when they write policies. Limitations which determine the amount of their liability include the (1) extent of insurable interest; (2) actual cash value of the loss; (3) policy limits; (4) other insurance; (5) coinsurance, contribution, and average clauses; and (6) deductibles.

A *limitation* establishes the maximum amount the insurer will pay for a loss. The smallest limit applies in every instance, for if a "limitation" *other* than the smallest is applied, the smallest would be no limitation at all! Although the *actual cash value of the loss* and the *policy limits* are those most often governing, any of the limits may be the lowest and therefore determine the amount to be paid. The purpose of this chapter is to define these limits and explain their operation in typical insurance contracts.

Extent of Insurable Interest

The maximum reimbursement for property losses is limited to the insured's interest. Thus the 1943 New York standard fire policy (SFP) limits the insurer's liability to no more than the insured's interest. Suppose that Fred Dugle, half owner of an $800,000 building, insures the building for $800,000 in his own name. In the event of total loss, he can collect only $400,000, the amount of his loss, even though both the policy face and the value of the destroyed property are $800,000. The insurable interest limitation denies recovery in excess of the amount of indemnity in an effort to prevent gambling and reduce moral hazard. Reimbursement in excess of the loss sustained would violate the indemnity principle.

Representative insurable interest

In some instances, the insurer is liable for losses even though the policyowner does not have a *direct* insurable interest in the damaged property. An example is a bailee policy covering the interest of a bailor. A bailor is one who places property in trust with another for a special purpose, such as storage, transportation, or servicing. A bailee is the one who receives the property.

Bob Strain acts as a bailee when he accepts John Long's (the bailor's) suit for cleaning. Pan Am is a bailee when accepting David Shpilberg's package to be delivered to Patrick Doyle in Venezuela. If property in the hands of a bailee is damaged, the bailee may or may not be legally liable to the bailor. Regardless of legal liability, however. the bailee has a representative insurable interest in the bailor's goods. If John's suit is stolen from the Strain Cleaners, the bailee's insurer will pay for the loss. The bailee may not keep the proceeds but must pay them to the bailor (John). The bailee acts as the bailor's agent in paying for the damaged goods. Thus the principle of indemnity is upheld as the person suffering the loss receives the insurance proceeds. In the HO policies, coverage may be extended at the option of the insured to include property of members of the insured's family, guests, and servants, another example of a representative interest.

Insurable interest in life insurance

In life insurance the *amount* of the insurable interest does not limit recovery. If an interest exists, generally it is held to be for the full face amount of the policy. Most states hold that the life insurance contract is not an indemnity contract. The beneficiary does not have to establish the amount of loss. The one exception is insurance bought by creditors upon the life of a debtor. The courts require a reasonable relationship between the insurance amount and the indebtedness at the inception of the policy. Although the courts vary they are liberal in determining what is reasonable. Courts have allowed a $5,000 policy on a debt of $2,823[1] and a $6,500 policy on a debt of $1,000.[2] The courts will allow

---

[1] *Wright* v. *Mutual Benefit Life Association,* 118 N.Y. 237 (1890).
[2] *Rittler* v. *Smith,* 70 Md. 261 (1884).

an amount sufficient to offset premiums and other costs as well as the debt, plus accrued interest on both.

Actual Cash Value

Property insurance contracts usually limit recovery to the actual cash value (ACV) of the loss. For instance, the SFP states that it insures "to the extent of the actual cash value of the property at the time of the loss." Coverage C of the HO–3 also is written on an ACV basis. Regardless of the ACV, the insurer will not pay an amount exceeding the "cost to repair or replace the property with materials of like kind and quality within a reasonable time after such loss." Like kind and quality does not mean the *exact* kind and quality, because often it is impractical or impossible to reproduce property (buildings and equipment) with the same materials and construction methods. Therefore, insureds and insurers use the concept of replacement rather than reproduction cost. Replacement cost is limited to the style, quality, and function of the destroyed or damaged property. No allowances are made for increased costs of repair, or reconstruction caused by ordinances or laws regulating construction or repair.

What is actual cash value?

Sufficient cases have been adjudicated to support the rule that actual cash value is replacement cost new less observed depreciation. (In a few isolated cases, ACV has been equated with market value. In these cases, settlement on an ACV basis would have resulted in an unjust enrichment of the insured.) The application of this rule requires that replacement cost be determined and depreciation measured. These tasks are not simple.

Replacement cost.   Replacement cost is a function of the type of property, the owner's position in the trade channel, and the data available to the appraiser. The replacement cost of raw materials quoted on commodity exchanges is measured by those prices less the cost of transporting the commodities to market. Market value should not be confused with selling price. Selling price includes owners' profits, and these profits are not part of replacement cost. Profits insurance might be available if the insured wants to extend protection to selling price. The replacement cost of processed commodities depends on the insured's position in the trade channel. Thus the replacement cost of a commodity will be more for the retailer than the wholesaler, and even more for the ultimate consumer. If an automobile burns as it rolls off the assembly line in Detroit, the manufacturer's replacement cost is the cost of reproducing the automobile. If the car burned in the dealer's showroom, the replacement cost for the dealer would be the wholesale price. If the car burned immediately after it was sold to the consumer, the owner's replacement cost would be the retail price.

The cost approach is most often used to determine replacement cost of a building and its equipment because it uses available valuation data and emphasizes the appropriate factors. The valuation procedure is similar to a contractor's preparation of a bid. Estimated prices for labor and material are added to an amount for overhead. These estimates vary among appraisers, producing figures that contain subjective elements.

Depreciation. As an accounting concept, depreciation attempts to distribute the cost of capital assets, less any salvage, over their estimated useful life. The process is one of cost allocation in the profit and loss statement, not of valuation. Depreciation, however, determining the measure of actual cash value is a valuation concept reflecting total loss of value from all causes by deducting physical deterioration, obsolescence, and location deterioration from replacement cost. The deductions are not related directly to the age of the building but to economic and physical factors that place old property at a competitive disadvantage with new property. For example, the penalty for physical deterioration is based on the life span of each item in the building that wears out and is replaceable, such as the roof, mechanical equipment, paint, and plaster. The cost of replacement is measured with reasonable accuracy. If the life of a roof is estimated to be 10 years and the replacement cost is $10,000, the physical deterioration penalty (assuming linear depreciation) would be $6,000 for a 6-year-old roof, even though the building is 30 years old.

The penalty for obsolescence reflects technological and social changes. If obsolescence can be eliminated by remodeling or new equipment, the penalty is their cost. If the obsolescence results from poor functional design, unattractive architecture, poor relation of the building to the site, or some other hopeless cause, the penalty is based on the difference between the productivity, operation costs, and maintenance costs for an ideal building at that location and the damaged building. If the building is improperly located compared to the ideal location for the ideal building in performing its functions, a penalty for location deterioration is assessed.

Measuring depreciation is a major problem in calculating actual cash value. Competent appraisers are relied on; but disagreements between the insured and the insurer may still end in court. However, the policy has provisions (discussed in Chapter 10) designed to keep court action to a minimum.

Actual cash value and liability insurance

In liability insurance, measurement of the actual cash value of a loss is settled by negotiation between claimant and insurer, not between insurer and insured. If a litigated claim reaches a verdict, the verdict usually includes the actual cash value of the economic loss and compensation for general damages (pain and suffering) incurred by the claimant. The verdict also may include the claimant's attorney's fees and other claim costs. In bodily injury cases, the economic damages usually consist of medical expenses incurred by the claimant plus an amount the jury believes sufficient to cover future medical outlays expected for the claimant's injuries. Defense costs including court costs, premiums on bonds, and cost of investigation also are considered. The court often instructs the jury to determine the actual cash value of damaged property by subtracting depreciation from replacement cost then adding reasonable compensation for loss of use of the damaged property and loss of profits.

The question of whether insurers are liable for punitive damages is undecided in most states. Punitive damages are damages awarded in excess of normal compensation to the plaintiff to punish a defendant for a serious wrong as a means of deterring similar conduct by others. (Somewhat parallel is the tale about Billy's parent who urged the teacher to smack Jimmy if Billy misbehaves because such action will so frighten Billy that he will become angelic.) For punitive damages to be awarded, the defendant must be guilty of more than ordinary negligence (i.e., gross negligence or willful and wanton misconduct). The personal liability coverage (Section II) of the HO–3 states, "we will pay up to our limit of liability for the damages for which the insured is legally liable. . . ." The PAP has a similar provision. Thus it would appear that punitive damages should be paid by the insurer, if the total amount of liability does not exceed the policy limit. The use of insurance proceeds to pay punitive damages, however, would eliminate any punitive or deterrent effect that they might otherwise have. If punitive damages do deter antisocial behavior, then public policy should preclude insurers from paying these damages. This dichotomy has led some courts to require liability insurers to pay punitive damages, whereas others have prohibited insurers from paying them. Although a few states avoid the problem by denying the courts the right to assess punitive damages, most states have taken no statutory initiative, leaving the courts with the sticky problem of deciding in individual cases whether insurers must pay punitive damages on behalf of their insureds. Professor John Long notes that the status of liability insurance for punitive damages is unsettled:

> A few states disallow punitive damages altogether or restrict them to relatively rare application. . . . Among the states allowing punitive damages the conduct sufficiently culpable to justify such awards varies markedly from one state to another. . . . At the other extreme, several states by common law have established relatively loose punitive damages criteria.[3]

Thus little evidence indicates the abolition of punitive damages among states in the near future.

---

[3] John D. Long, "Should Punitive Damages Be Insured?" *The Journal of Risk and Insurance,* 44, no. 1 (March 1977), pp. 1–20.

Actual cash value in life and health insurance

In life insurance the policy face is held to be the amount of the loss involved. No attempt is made to restrict payment to the actual cash value of a deceased person. A wife collects the full face amount of her husband's policy even though two days before his death she called him a worthless bum.

In health insurance often no face amount of the policy exists in the narrow sense. In disability income insurance, an amount payable per period if the insured is disabled is stated, and a time limit named for the benefit period, possibly to age 65, or for a stated number of years. In medical expense coverage, the limit may be expressed in dollars or service. The policy might provide $100 daily for hospital room and board for a maximum period of 180 days. Or it might promise to provide 180 days' hospital room and board in semiprivate accommodations. The major medical policy does not schedule benefits, but names a blanket amount that may be spent to cover medical and hospital bills. (Many major medical policies, however, do limit the amount or type of service per day for hospital room and board.)

Exceptions to the actual cash value limitation

Under several circumstances the insured may collect more than the actual cash value of the loss.

Valued policies. Chapter 6 mentioned valued policies, under which the face amount is paid *in case of total loss of real property* without regard to its actual cash value at the time of loss. As of early 1984, 19 states had valued policy laws requiring the insurer to pay the face of the policy for a total loss of real property. In these states all insured real property would have to be appraised before the insurance is written to avoid the possibility of overinsurance. However, because only few real property losses are total, insurers find it less expensive to pay an occasional excessive claim than to appraise the property in advance. These practices violate the principle of indemnity and increase moral hazard.

Valued policies also are used to cover special types of property difficult or impossible to replace or for which the value at time of loss is difficult to establish. When an item is irreplaceable (paintings, historical documents), actual cash value does not qualify as a useful indemnity measure. Property difficult to value at time of loss, for example, would be a ship and cargo lost at sea. The values of these items are agreed on in advance by the insurer and insured and are used as the basis for loss payments.

In health insurance, an insured also can collect more than the actual cash value of the loss. Professor Neumann who is disabled can collect the $2,000 a month provided under a disability income policy, even if the university continues to pay the professor's $4,000 monthly salary. In life insurance, the widow can collect the $100,000 proceeds of her husband's policy, even though his death was an economic gain for her in every respect.

Bankruptcy and insolvency.   Another exception to the actual cash value limitation arises from the "bankruptcy or insolvency" provision in liability policies. Ordinary liability claims are part of the general claims against a bankrupt's estate. Therefore, if the claims of all general creditors are scaled down to a percentage of their original value, either under a compromise of debts or by order of a bankruptcy court, the actual cash outlay necessary to satisfy any ordinary[4] civil liability judgments against the bankrupt also will be reduced to a percentage of their original value. But, by the terms of the liability policy, the bankrupt's liability insurer remains liable for 100 percent of each liability claim—more than the "actual cash value" of the loss to the insured. Liability insurance policies contain the "bankruptcy or insolvency" clause as a matter of public policy. Society is interested in protecting injured persons for humanitarian reasons and to keep them from becoming public wards. Underwriters do not object to violating the principle of indemnity here because the operation of the clause does not create a moral or morale hazard.

Replacement cost insurance

Some insurance authorities believe that to pay replacement cost without a deduction for depreciation would violate the principle of indemnity and create a moral hazard. Even so, insurance is written to pay the actual cost of repairing or replacing damaged property without deduction for depreciation. Replacement cost insurance offers additional protection for the difference between the actual cash value of the loss and the restoration cost.

Replacement cost insurance is usually written as an endorsement to the ACV fire forms. In the HO policies (except HO–8) replacement cost insurance for coverages A and B is included as one of the insuring agreements. The replacement cost provision of the HOs limits the extent of recovery to the ratio the amount of insurance owned bears to 80 percent of the full replacement cost of the insured dwelling immediately prior to the loss:[5]

$$\frac{\text{Amount carried}}{80\% \times \text{Replacement cost}} \times \text{Loss} = \text{Maximum amount of recovery}$$

For example, if the full replacement cost of the dwelling is \$100,000 and the insured has at least \$80,000 of insurance on the dwelling, the

---

[4] Liabilities for the following claims are not released by a discharge in bankruptcy: willful and malicious injuries to the person or property of others; obtaining property by false pretenses or false representations; alimony due or to become due; maintenance or support of wife or child; seduction of an unmarried male or female; or criminal conduct.

[5] In determining full replacement cost, the value of excavation, underground flues and pipes, underground wiring and drains, and brick, stone, or concrete foundations, piers, and other supports below the ground, and land values may be disregarded.

full replacement cost of the loss will be paid (up to the face amount of the policy).

If the above formula yields less than the ACV of the loss, the ACV will be paid. Thus, if, in the foregoing example, the insured is carrying only $40,000 of dwelling coverage and experiences a loss of $30,000 on a replacement cost basis, or $25,000 on an ACV basis, the insured will receive $25,000 from the insurer.[6]

As is usual with replacement cost coverage, the HO–3 provides that, unless the loss is small (less than $1,000 or less than 5 percent of the amount of insurance), the insurer will pay no more than the ACV of that loss until the repair of replacement is finished. Also, the measure of replacement cost is the cost of replacing the building or any part of it with a similar structure on the same premises intended for the same occupancy and use. Furthermore, the recovery under replacement cost insurance can never be more than the amount actually and necessarily expended in repairing or replacing the building.

The reimbursement of an insured on a replacement cost basis eliminates an otherwise uncovered exposure. Although the insured may be given a new garage to replace the old one, moral hazard probably is not increased if the old one was adequate. However, financing the amount deducted for depreciation (it is impossible to build a depreciated garage), may create a hardship, especially if the new garage yields no more utility than the old one. Replacement cost insurance, however, forces the insurer to inspect the property and take precautions if it seeks to prevent the coverage from creating moral hazard.

Demolition cost

Assume that José Vetosa owns a tenement house of frame construction which was three fourths destroyed by fire. The actual cash value of the damage is $90,000. If a local ordinance prohibits him from reconstructing the same type of building on that site, he will have to pay part of the loss. If José rebuilds, he must meet new and more expensive standards of construction. He finds that the cost to replace the building is $125,000. His policy will not pay for any increased cost of repair or reconstruction by reason of an ordinance or law regulating construction or repair. He must pay from his own funds both for the increased cost of repair and demolition of the part of the old building still standing. Coverage called "demolition insurance," or insurance against *contingent liability from the operation of building or zoning laws,* is available to protect against part of this loss.

Two types of protection are available: (1) In most states a property insurance contract may be endorsed (or a separate policy written) to extend coverage to losses from demolition up to the actual cash value of the building; and (2) in some territories, policies may cover the demoli-

---

[6] $$\$25,000 > \frac{\$40,000}{\$80,000} \times \$30,000$$

tion cost and the additional cost of constructing a building that will conform to building- or zoning-law requirements.

Policy Face or Limits

Unless otherwise provided, an insurer will not pay under a property insurance contract more than the policy face amount or in excess of its policy limits.[7] The SFP states that the insurer will pay up to an amount not exceeding that specified in the policy. Although the face amount of the policy serves as a maximum limit of recovery, it is not paid unconditionally for every total loss, unless the contract is a valued policy for the covered loss.

Types of policy limits

Most, but not all, policies have face amount limits. Automobile physical damage policies, for example, generally are written on an *actual cash value* basis under which the insurer promises to pay the actual cash value of the loss. In addition to an overall policy limit, a contract may contain limits applying to different types of property, losses, locations, perils, or hazards.

Divided coverage.   Policy limits may be of several types, the most common being *divided coverage* in which the face amount is spread among two or more parts of the policy. In the usual fire policy (an example of divided coverage), a specific amount of insurance is applied to the building covered under the policy, another sum applied to contents of the building, and other amounts for rental value and other items. The total of these amounts equals the policy face. None of the insurance on the building may be applied to contents loss, and none of the contents insurance may be applied to rental value loss and so on. Each section of the divided coverage is independent, as though each item has been insured in a separate policy, written together principally for convenience and economy. The HO policies are other examples of divided coverage.

Blanket coverage.   When a single face amount of the policy applies to either two or more locations, two or more types of property, or a combination of locations and types of property, the contract is called blanket. For example, blanket policies frequently are written to cover goods stored at several locations when the total values involved are nearly constant although the value at individual locations may fluctuate widely.

---

[7] In liability insurance, cost of defense, premiums on bonds, cost of investigation, and so on generally are not included under the policy limits. The limits usually apply only to judgments awarded by the court. Also, indemnities under the "sue and labor clause" in the marine contract may be in addition to the face of the policy. The sue and labor clause is discussed in Chapter 10.

Priority coverage.   When a single face amount of the policy applies to all the coverages it contains, it may provide for loss settlement on a priority basis. Sometimes a policy will have several insuring clauses and coverages under one policy limit, with the priority of coverage listed in the contract. For example, the boiler and machinery policy covers direct damage, expediting permanent and temporary repairs, property damage liability, and bodily injury liability. The first priority is direct loss of the insured's property resulting from an accident to the covered boiler or machine. If the indemnity for this loss is less than the full amount of insurance, then the cost of making temporary repairs or of expediting permanent repairs is paid, subject to a designated maximum. Next is payment of claims arising from liability for property damage. Finally, any insurance remaining is available for bodily injury liability claims from the accident. The first priority is given to losses not otherwise covered. The last priority, bodily injury liability, is covered under general liability insurance which probably will be owned by most buyers of boiler and machinery policies.

Sublimits.   Sublimits, another type of policy limit, are placed principally on property whose nature or location might make it more subject to loss. The premium for these policies is insufficient to provide full coverage of these hazardous exposures. Full coverage may be bought at a higher premium. For example, the HO–3 may have a $30,000 limit under coverage C, unscheduled personal property, but sublimits apply as follows:

1. $100 on money, bank notes, bullion, gold other than goldware, silver other than silverware, platinum, coins, and medals.
2. $500 on securities, accounts, deeds, evidences of debt, letters of credit, notes other than bank notes, manuscripts, passports, tickets, and stamps.
3. $500 on watercraft, including their trailers, furnishings, equipment, and outboard motors.
4. $500 on trailers not used with watercraft.
5. $500 on grave markers.
6. $500 for loss by theft of jewelry, watches, furs, precious, and semiprecious stones.
7. $1,000 for loss by theft of silverware, silver-plated ware, goldware, gold-plated ware, and pewterware.
8. $1,000 for loss by theft of guns.

Remember that sublimits do not add to the overall face amount of the policy.

Additional amounts.   Another type of policy limit offers coverage in addition to basic policy limits. For example, the HO–3 grants an additional 5 percent of the applicable limit of liability (of either coverage A, B, or C) to cover debris removal expenses when the amount payable for the property loss plus the expense for debris removal exceeds the limit of liability for the damaged property. Under the PAP theft coverage, the insurer promises to pay up to $10 a day, subject to a total limit of $300, to offset expenses incurred for necessary substitute transportation services. The $300 limit is *in addition* to the face of the policy. Thus, if the stolen car is not recovered, the insured could also collect the full cash value of the car.

Insurers under some policies promise to pay double the face amount under a given set of conditions. For example, life insurance policies may contain a clause offering double the face amount if death results from accidental means. Health policies may also offer double indemnity if injuries are sustained under special conditions involving, for example, public conveyances, elevators, steam boiler explosions, lightning, tornadoes, collapse of the outer walls of a building, or fires. Double indemnity provisions, however, seem to be sales frills offering perverse speculative appeal.

Limits in liability insurance. Limits in liability insurance are usually handled in one of three ways, depending on the policy in question. The traditional manner is to have two policy limits for bodily injury (one relating to the maximum amount payable per injured person, and the other relating to the maximum amount payable for all the persons injured in a single accident or occurrence) and one policy limit applying per accident or occurrence for property damage.

For example, Bill Scheel has an auto policy with bodily injury limits of $10,000 per person and $20,000 per accident (commonly written as $10,000/$20,000). Suppose that Bill negligently crashes into an oncoming vehicle occupied by five people. Four people survive the accident and sue Bill for $50,000 each. The widow of the fifth person sues for $100,000. The court awards the claimants the requested amounts. Bill's policy will only pay $20,000 with not more than $10,000 to one person. Bill, therefore would be faced with uninsured claims totaling $280,000. Higher limits (in this case, $100,000/$300,000) would be necessary to relieve Bill of all loss for bodily injury claims.

Currently, an increasing number of liability policies are written with only one limit of liability. This limit applies per accident or occurrence to both bodily injury and property damage coverages. The liability coverage of the PAP and the personal liability coverage of the HO are written with a single, undivided limit. The basic limit of the PAP and HO is $25,000.

Policy limits can be increased beyond the basic limits for a modest premium increase, and the buyer should insist on high limits (remember the fate of Bill Scheel in the foregoing example!). With courts becoming more liberal in awards, it is foolish economy for a buyer to purchase low limits.

Business liability policies typically are written with a single limit of liability applying per occurrence to bodily injury and a single limit applying per occurrence to property damage. In addition, a policy may have an aggregate limit of liability applying to bodily injury and/or property damage. For example, a firm might have a liability policy with a property damage limit of $50,000 per occurrence and an aggregate limit of $100,000 applying to all property damage losses occurring during the policy term.

The cost of defense provided for by nearly all liability policies is not made a part of the basic limits and is covered without limit. The PAP provides for payment on behalf of a covered person up to $250 for the cost of bail bonds required because of an accident resulting in bodily injury or property damage covered by the policy. Premiums on appeal bonds and bonds to release attachments in any suit defended by the insurer also are covered.

In summary, a policy may have several limits, depending on the peril, property, location, loss, or hazard. Therefore, in analyzing a contract, the insured must check the policy thoroughly for all individual and special amount limits.

Restoration and nonreduction of amounts of insurance

What happens to the face amount of insurance when a loss occurs? Does it remain the same, or is it reduced by the amount of the loss? The answers to these questions vary among policies.

Liability insurance. In most liability insurance contracts the payment of claims does not reduce the face amount of insurance. The insurer promises to pay up to the limits of the policy for each loss and for as many different losses as may occur during the policy period. Assume that Ken Perry has three automobile accidents in one year, each resulting in two individual judgments against him for $50,000. If he has a $100,000 per accident limit, his auto liability policy will pay all six judgments. He is not required to pay additional premiums after each accident to restore the amount of the policy.[8] Aggregate limits (an annual limit on claims), found in some liability policies, are the exception to the rule. Products liability offers an example of aggregate limits.

The products liability policy contains four liability limits. The bodily injury liability coverage has as basic limits $25,000 per occurrence and a $50,000 annual aggregate limit. The property damage liability coverage has basic limits of $5,000 per occurrence and a $25,000 annual aggregate limit. A question of the definition of an occurrence often arises. Assume that a carryout pizza parlor owning a products liability policy with basic limits accidentally poisons 27 customers in one night. Does the preparation of the tainted pizzas constitute one occurrence and thus limit the insurer's obligation to $25,000, or does the sale of each contaminated pizza institute an occurrence increasing the insurer's obligation to the

---

[8] Upon paying the second or third loss, however, the insurer might like to give serious consideration to the advisability of cancelling the policy. If successful, Ken would be entitled to a pro rata return of premium. In many policies, the right of the insurer to cancel is limited to certain specified conditions. About 46 states now require some limitation on the insurer's right to cancel automobile insurance. (See Chapter 8.)

aggregate limit of $50,000? In a similar case, a court held that the insured's liability was created by the sale of a poisoned product and that each sale constituted a separate occurrence. The insurer was required to pay the aggregate limit.[9]

Property insurance.   In property insurance, unless the policy states otherwise, each loss reduces the amount of insurance by the amount of the claim paid. Although this rule is not specifically included in the policy, courts have upheld the principle that an insurer is not obligated to pay in excess of the policy face. However, virtually every property insurance form provides for automatic restoration of the face amount following a loss without payment of an additional premium. The initial premium considers the possibility of multiple losses. Some Homeowners policies contain the following clause: "Losses hereunder shall not reduce the applicable limit of liability under this policy." For some reason unknown and mystifying to the author (a thorough effort was made to find one), this clause is not included in any of the present ISO's readable Homeowners series. Perhaps its omission was an oversight. However, the ISO did not omit this type of clause from its readable Businessowners policies. These policies state that "Any loss hereunder shall not reduce the amount of this insurance." One can only speculate that insurers writing the ISO's Homeowners readable forms intend to restore or reinstate the amount of property coverage following a loss. As yet, the issue has not been presented to the courts. Automatic reinstatement eliminates costs of handling reinstatement endorsements involving small premiums.

Life and health insurance.   Because the subject matter is irreplaceable, no questions involving restoration arise in life insurance. Most health insurance policies do not reduce coverage after a loss, although some medical expense policies contain aggregate lifetime limits.

Other Insurance

What happens if more than one policy covers the same loss? This issue is handled by "other insurance" clauses.

Types of other insurance clauses

An other insurance clause may prohibit other insurance to be written on the same interest or provide that losses are to be shared with all other applicable insurance. Clauses providing for sharing of claims are either contributing, primary, or excess.

---

[9] The insured would be safer with higher limits per occurrence (if available) as a juridical risk exists. The courts everywhere and over time might not rule alike.

Other insurance prohibited.   In some instances, an insurance policy may prohibit any other insurance on the property. The SFP states that "other insurance may be prohibited or the amount of insurance may be limited by endorsement attached hereto." Thus, it is possible for a form attached to the SFP to prohibit other insurance on the insured property.

Contributing insurance.   Under contributing insurance two methods of handling losses when two or more policies cover the same loss and interest are pro rata and limit of liability.

Pro rata liability.   The pro rata liability clause printed in the SFP states: "This company shall not be liable for a greater proportion of any loss than the amount hereby insured shall bear to the whole insurance covering the property against the peril involved, whether collectible or not." Similar clauses are found in other contracts. In some policies (Section I of the HO) only valid and collectible insurance is made contributing.

The pro rata other insurance clause works as follows: Michael Smith has a mother-in-law and a son-in-law in the insurance business. To keep peace in the family, he insures his $200,000 building, $100,000 with his mother-in-law in insurer A, and $100,000 with his son-in-law in insurer B. Lightning causes $60,000 damage to the building; so as each insurer writes half the insurance, each pays half the loss, $30,000. If insurer A had written $40,000 and insurer B, $160,000, A would pay one fifth of the loss and B would pay four fifths, or $12,000 and $48,000, respectively.[10]

Limit of liability.   Some policies provide that the basis for allocating losses among insurers shall be the limit of liability rather than pro rata liability. Thus rather than apportioning the loss over the total face amounts of the existing insurance, the apportionment is over the sum of the amounts for which each insurer would have been liable had there been no other policy.

Assume that two policies cover the same interest. Policy A is written for $20,000 and policy B for $80,000. Assume a $50,000 loss. Policy A would pay $20,000 if it were the only policy covering. Policy B would pay $50,000. Under the limit of liability rule insurer A will pay 20/70 of the loss, or $14,286, and B will pay 50/70 of the loss, or $35,714. This type of loss apportionment is found in the boiler and machinery policy, among others.[11]

Excess coverage.   Sometimes a policy provides that the insurer will pay nothing until all other valid insurance has been exhausted in paying

---

[10] Insurer A's or B's liability $= \dfrac{\text{Insurance with insurer A } or \text{ B}}{\text{Insurance with insurers A } and \text{ B}} \times$ Amount of loss.

[11] Insurer A's or B's liability $= \dfrac{\substack{\text{Liability of insurer A } or \text{ B, if}\\ \text{each wrote the only policy}}}{\substack{\text{Liability of insurers A } and \text{ B, if}\\ \text{each wrote the only policy}}} \times$ Amount of loss.

the loss. Mercantile open-stock policies, for example, state that if there is any other valid and collectible insurance that would apply to loss, the mercantile open-stock policy shall apply only as excess insurance. Thus, if Carol Carrillo has a $30,000 open-stock burglary policy and suffers a $45,000 loss for which $21,000 coverage is available from other applicable insurance, the open-stock insurer will pay $24,000. If a loss occurs involving several policies, each of which provides that its insurance shall be excess, the insurers will contribute pro rata in the absence of an agreement on how losses are to be distributed.

Primary coverage.   In ocean marine insurance if more than one policy covers the same interest, the policy bearing the earliest date offers primary coverage, and policies bought later are void for the amount of the prior policy. On April 1, a shipper buys a $900 cargo policy. On April 2, the consignee buys a second $900 policy. The ship sinks, and the cargo valued at $1,500 is lost. The first policy covers $900 of the loss, and the second, nothing, as its face amount did not exceed that of the first policy. If the face amount of the second policy had been $1,500, it would have covered $600 of the loss. The subsequent insurer agrees to return the premium on the inapplicable insurance. In the foregoing example, the second insurer must return the full premium. This principle was developed to prevent recovery by both shipper and consignee both of whom might have bought the insurance. In this case, the policy bought first is the only valid coverage *up to its face amount.*

Policy provisions and practice

The practice among insurers in distributing losses among various policies may not conform strictly to contract provisions. Most insurers adhere to the *Guiding Principles for Overlapping Insurance Coverages,* effective in 1963. One of the agreements in the *Guiding Principles* states that:

> As among insurance companies, the "other insurance" clause(s) which is (are) contained in a policy(ies) of insurance and which may include an excess provision, shall be set aside and be inoperative to the extent that it is (they are) in conflict with the purpose of these Principles.

These intercompany agreements do not affect the owner's right of recovery.

Reasons for other insurance limits

If insureds were allowed to collect the full amount of loss from several insurers, they would gain substantially from a loss, violating public policy, the principle of indemnity, and creating moral hazard. Insurance would then be a gambling transaction. The courts would not allow double recovery except in life and health insurance even though contracts did not contain other insurance clauses. Before these clauses were used, the insured could select one insurer to pay the full loss. The insurer chosen then could seek equitable contribution from other insurers liable for the loss. Other insurance clauses eliminate the need for roundabout action, clearly fixing the liability of each insurer.

Other insurance clauses in various policies

When insurance contracts are analyzed, the analyst will have no trouble in determining the applicable other insurance arrangement.

Automobile. In automobile liability insurance other insurance is contributing insurance except for temporary substitute and nonowned automobiles, in which case the coverage is excess over any other valid and collectible insurance. For example, if Albert Auxier while driving Jerry Caswell's car with permission, injures Dawn Parker, Jerry's liability insurer will pay any claim assessed on Al up to the policy limits. If the claim exceeds Jerry's policy limits, Al's insurer will pay. Insurance on the car is primary, that on the driver is excess. The same rule applies to automobile medical payments coverage.

Life. In life insurance, the insurer will pay the face amount of the policy regardless of the number of policies involved. Life insurers presumably refrain from accepting applications when overinsurance is apparent. Life insurance applications require a statement of the amount of insurance owned and the amount of insurance applied for and pending, if any. If additional insurance increases coverage beyond amounts considered sound by underwriters, the application is rejected. Sensible underwriting alleviates the need for other insurance clauses in life insurance.

Health. Health insurance policies can include other-insurance clauses as part of the permissible uniform provisions (see Chapter 18), although most forms omit them except for disability income coverage.

Two types of other insurance clauses may be included in health policies: one considers insurance with *other* insurers; the other, insurance with the *same* insurer. The first states that if the insured has insurance with other insurers covering the same loss without written notification to the insurer, the insurer shall be liable only for such portion of the indemnity promised as the indemnity bears to the total amount of indemnity in all policies covering the loss. The insurer will return the premium paid for the excess uncollectible pro rata portion of the insurance. Thus, if the insured had $800 monthly disability protection with insurer A and later added $800 with insurer B without notifying A, then A would be liable only for $400 a month. The purpose of the provision is to simplify administration of underwriting rules. The clause is different from other insurance clauses in property insurance as the contribution is required only if the insured fails to give written notice concerning other insurance.

The second type of other insurance clauses states that:

If policies previously issued by the insurer to the insured are in force concurrently with this policy, making the aggregate indemnity in excess of
[the particular maximum], the excess insurance shall be void and all premiums paid for such excess shall be returned to the insured or the estate.

A variation states that insurance effective at any time under like policies
of this insurer is limited to the policy elected by the insured (beneficiary
or estate), and the insurer will return premiums paid for other policies.
These clauses enable the insurer to control the amount of insurance it
writes on an applicant.

A provision similar to other insurance clauses is the "relation of earning to insurance" provision found occasionally in disability income policies. This clause applies only if insurance benefits payable from all
policies exceed $200 monthly, stating that if the monthly income prom-
ised from all insurance exceeds either the monthly earnings of the insured at the time of disability or the average earnings for the two years
preceding disability, the insurer is liable only for its proportionate share
of the insurance necessary to reduce benefits to the higher of the two
limits. Assume that average earnings of the insured over the past two
years were $900 a month, but were $800 a month just prior to disability.
The insured has disability income insurance from three insurers totaling
$1,200 a month, of which $400 was with Robust Health Insurance Company. Robust would be liable for $300 a month, because $900 a month
is the maximum payable. Robust has one third of the insurance and
is liable for one third of the loss. This clause allows the insurer to manage
moral hazard by keeping indemnity in line with earnings.

Apportionment clause

The apportionment clause used with the extended coverage endorsement is an important limitation on the amount of recovery. This clause
restricts liability of the insurer to the proportion of the loss that the
amount of insurance bears to the whole amount of *fire insurance* covering the property, whether collectible or not and whether or not such
other fire insurance applies to these additional perils. Thus, if George
Potter protects his $200,000 building with four $50,000 fire insurance
policies and endorses only one for extended coverage, he can collect
only one fourth of each extended coverage loss, subject to the maximum
of $50,000. If a windstorm destroys half the building (a $100,000 loss),
George can collect only $25,000. If the building is destroyed completely
by windstorm, he can collect the face amount of the policy, $50,000,
because this amount does not exceed one fourth of the loss. The purpose
of the apportionment clause is to produce an adequate premium for
the insurer by discouraging underinsurance of extended coverage perils.

Coinsurance

Some contracts contain coinsurance clauses, restricting recovery on
partial losses if the insured does not insure the property for a given

percentage of its actual cash value at the time of loss.[12] Coinsurance is optional in some policies, required in others. A typical coinsurance clause is:

> In consideration of the produced rate and/or form . . . , it is expressly stipulated . . . that in the event of loss this company shall be liable for no greater proportion . . . than the amount hereby insured bears to __ percent of the actual cash value of the property . . . at the time [of] loss nor for more than the proportion which this policy bears to the total insurance thereon.[13]

Note that the foregoing clause gives the insured a reduced rate. For example, an 80 percent clause with a fire insurance policy on a fire-resistant building in a large central Illinois town reduces the rate by 70 percent; a 50 percent coinsurance clause reduces it 56 percent. The theory behind the reduction is explained later.

How coinsurance works

For a rate reduction the insured agrees to protect the property for an amount equal to at least the stated percentage of the actual cash value of the covered property at the time of the loss with the provision that if the percentage is not met, the insured becomes a coinsurer to the extent of the difference between the amount of insurance required and the amount of insurance owned, and, on that basis, will contribute pro rata to incurred losses. Assume that a building with an "actual cash value" of $300,000 *at the time of the loss* is insured under an 80 percent coinsurance clause. The property is covered for $180,000. Compliance with the coinsurance provision requires $240,000 of insurance (80 percent of $300,000), so the insurance deficiency is $60,000 ($240,000 − $180,000). The insured becomes a coinsurer of this deficiency and on that basis contributes to all losses. Thus, if the building burns and damages are $32,000, the insurer pays three fourths ($180,000/$240,000) of the loss ($24,000), and the insured must bear one fourth of the loss. The insurer has written three fourths of the required insurance. The insured is a coinsurer for $60,000 and thus has assumed one fourth of the insurance burden ($60,000/$240,000). Based on the amount of insurance required, the insured has a 25 percent deficiency in coverage ($60,000 is 25 percent of $240,000) and must bear 25 percent of any losses which occur ($8,000 is 25 percent of $32,000).

The following formulas are useful in figuring the amount payable for a partial loss under a policy written with a coinsurance clause.

1. Determine the amount of insurance required:

Actual cash value of property at time of loss × Coinsurance percentage = Amount of insurance required.

2. Determine the amount of recovery:

---

[12] In replacement cost coverage the percentage is applied to the cost of replacement.

[13] The clause quoted is frequently called a "reduced rate average clause."

$$\frac{\text{Amount of insurance owned}}{\text{Amount of insurance required}} \times \text{Loss} = \text{Maximum amount of recovery.}$$

In the foregoing example, these formulas work as follows:

1. $300,000 × 80 percent = $240,000, amount of insurance required.

2. $\dfrac{\$180,000}{\$240,000} \times \$32,000 = \$24,000$, amount of recovery.

If the building increases in value and the insurance is not increased correspondingly, the coinsurance deficiency becomes greater. Suppose that, because of inflation, the value of the building increased from $300,000 to $450,000. If the insurance is not increased proportionately, the deficiency would increase from $60,000 to $180,000 because $360,000 of insurance (80 percent of $450,000) would now be required ($360,000 − $180,000 = $180,000). If a loss of $32,000 were to occur under the new value, the insurer and the insured both would bear half, for each is responsible for $180,000 of insurance. The insured now has a 50 percent deficiency in coverage and must bear 50 percent of the loss. Applying the formulas:

1. $450,000 × 80 percent = $360,000, amount of insurance required.

2. $\dfrac{\$180,000}{\$360,000} \times \$32,000 = \$16,000$, amount of recovery.

Coinsurance would have no effect on the liability of the insurer if the loss equals or exceeds the required amount of insurance. Thus, if the loss in the foregoing example were $380,000, the insurer could not be responsible for half the loss, because that would produce a figure in excess of the face amount of the policy. In this case, the policy limit of $180,000 would govern.

If the required amount of insurance is bought, full coverage is available for losses up to the face amount of the policy. If a building valued at $200,000 is covered for $180,000 under a 90 percent coinsurance clause, the insurer will pay in full all losses up to $180,000 because the insured has no coinsurance deficiency. If the value of the building increases and the amount of insurance remains level, a coinsurance deficiency develops, and the insured must bear a part of every loss. Thus, if the value of the building increases to $220,000 and the insurance remains at $180,000, the coinsurance deficiency would be $18,000, and the insured would have to bear one eleventh of all losses.[14]

In some coverages, 100 percent coinsurance is required. Under these conditions, the insured must watch values even more closely to avoid deficiencies.

The mercantile open-stock burglary policy has an unusual coinsur-

---

[14] The required amount of insurance is 90 percent of $220,000, or $198,000. The insured has purchased $180,000 or only ten elevenths of the required amount, hence must bear one eleventh of all losses.

ance arrangement in that two coinsurance limits are used: one a "coinsurance percentage" and the other a "coinsurance amount." The coinsurance percentage is a function of the geographical territory in which the property is located. The coinsurance amount generally depends solely on the business classification, because values likely to be taken by burglars in one haul vary among businesses. For instance, the coinsurance amount for a liquor store is $7,500, whereas it is $15,000 for a photographic supply store. The coinsurance percentage is 80 percent in Chicago and 50 percent in the remainder of Illinois. Assume that a policy is written in a territory requiring a coinsurance percentage of 50 percent for a retail liquor store with a coinsurance amount limit of $7,500. The limit that produces the smaller amount of required insurance applies. If the value of the stock is $20,000, then the coinsurance amount limit of $7,500 applies because it is less than the $10,000 required by the percentage limit. If the value of the stock was $6,000 then the 50 percent limit would apply because $3,000 is less than the amount limit of $7,500.

These illustrations of coinsurance indicate the importance of determining the amount of insurance to be bought when coinsurance applies and revising insurance amounts during the policy term to keep them in line with property values. The valuation to be used is that at the time of the loss.

Theory behind coinsurance

Although the principles are applicable to any type of coverage, fire insurance provides a clear example of how coinsurance helps achieve rate equity and adequacy. Most fire losses are partial losses with less than 2 percent of fires resulting in total loss and more than 80 percent producing damage of less than 10 percent of the total property value involved. A person buying insurance for only 10 percent of the property value will have full protection for most losses.

Suppose, however, that property owners believe that full insurance of their property value is essential, recognizing the possibility that they can be among the 2 percent having total losses. Without a coinsurance rate credit, they would pay 10 times as much for protection as persons insuring for only 10 percent of their property values. But expected losses of fully insured persons are not 10 times as great. Thus, with equal rates per $100 of insurance, persons buying full coverage for their losses would pay an inequitable premium.

Furthermore, those who realize most losses are partial and are willing to assume losses, for example, in excess of 30 percent of their property value may select against the insurer by buying $30,000 of insurance to cover a $100,000 building. Without a coinsurance clause this type of behavior leads to rate inadequacy.

One solution to these problems is to have a sliding rate scale—a quantity discount, with the rate for the first $5,000 of insurance much higher than that for the 10th $5,000. Burglars tend to concentrate on highly salable, easily portable materials; with one truckload representing the model burglary loss. Therefore, in crime insurance the rates are scaled so that the rate charged for the first few thousand dollars of insurance is higher than that charged for additional thousands. And the high rate is applied to the value approximating what ratemakers estimate to be the usual quantity taken in a single looting.[15]

In fire and windstorm insurance, a "small" loss does not refer to the absolute loss size, but to its relationship to the exposed value. Total losses are uncommon in fire or windstorm exposures because certain parts of the structures are strongly resistant to fire or wind damage. Masonry and steelwork are damageable, but not by ordinary fires or windstorms. Woodwork, wallpaper, shades and blinds, decorative trim, floors, and interior fixtures, however, are readily subject to fire and water damage. Roofs, exterior trim, and glass are commonly damaged by fires and windstorms. The total amount of readily damageable property in a building is not limited to any particular amount but will depend primarily on the size of the building and its type of construction. In a $1 million building $100,000 nearly always is readily destructible; but in a $100,000 building, some of that value will be relatively indestructible. A rate scale for fire, windstorm, and certain other types of insurance must consider these factors. Coinsurance clauses force the insured to buy protection in an amount at least equal to a given percentage of the value of their property thus eliminating the need for sliding rate scales, and simplifying ratemaking. Everyone whose policy has the clause is charged a flat rate for each $100 of insurance. Persons who insure for less than the coinsurance percentage are required to pay part of partial losses, meaning they effectively pay a higher rate for insurance than persons insuring their property for its full value.

Assume 10,000 small businesses, each with an identical building valued at $60,000. The total value of the property is $600 million. In a given year, two buildings are completely destroyed ($120,000 in losses), and 30 buildings have partial losses averaging $6,000 each ($180,000 in losses). Losses, therefore, total $300,000 representing a loss rate of 5 cents for each $100 of property ($300,000 $\div \dfrac{600,000,000}{100}$ = $0.05). If each building is covered for its full value, the basic insurance rate (ignoring expenses) would be 5 cents for each $100 of insurance, producing a premium of $30 a year from each business.

Now assume that each owner knows that most losses are partial and decides to insure the building only for half its value ($30,000). The payment for the total destruction now will be $30,000 each amounting to $60,000. The 30 partial losses totaling $180,000 still will be paid in full for a grand total of $240,000 spread over a base of $300 million as each building is covered for only $30,000. The loss of $240,000 over an exposure of $300 million yields an average loss of 8 cents per $100, producing a

---

[15] When total insured values are below these quantities, coinsurance clauses are inserted in burglary policies.

premium of $24 a year for each business (not including the insurer's expenses).

Suppose that the insurer charges a premium of 8 cents per $100, realizing that businesses are insuring their properties only for half their true worth. A business covering its property for its full value will be penalized, having to pay $48 a year for protection that was calculated as worth only $30. An equitable solution is to use a sliding rate scale and charge $24 a year for those with $30,000 of insurance while charging $30 a year for those buying the full $60,000 of insurance or, better yet, to use a coinsurance clause and charge the 5 cent rate to all persons agreeing to insure their property for full value, and requiring those that do not to share partial losses as coinsurers.

Deductible Clauses

Deductible clauses serve an important purpose in insurance. In some contracts they are mandatory whereas in others they are optional. Whether required or optional, the insured frequently has a choice of deductible amounts.

Types of deductibles

Some insurers use a deductible clause to eliminate coverage for small losses. Several different deductible clauses are used.

Straight deductible. A common type of deductible is the straight deductible, often found in automobile physical damage and Homeowners Section I coverages. The deductible usually is expressed as a given amount (e.g., $100, $250, or more). The straight deductible works as follows. Bob Witt has $100 deductible collision coverage on his automobile. If he runs into a telephone pole and has $500 damages to his car, his insurer will pay $400 and he will absorb $100 of the loss. The deductible means that Bob must bear the first $100 of damage in *every* loss, and the insurer will pay the rest.

Deductibles, often $250, but sometimes $500 or more, are used in major medical and hospital insurance. Most of these policies include deductibles from $200 to $500. Deductibles are not used in liability policies written for individuals except for umbrella forms (see Chapter 13) but are found occasionally in property damage liability insurance written for business.

Some straight deductibles are a percentage of value rather than a fixed dollar amount. In aviation hull insurance, a deductible of 2.5 to 10 percent of the insured value of the plane, applying to all losses except those caused by fire and theft, is common. Earthquake insurance often has a deductible of 2 percent of the actual cash value of the property.

Cumulative and participating deductible. Occasionally, an insurer writes a 50–50 or cumulative and participating deductible under which the insured pays 50 percent of the standard premium, then assumes losses until these losses equal an additional 50 percent of the standard premium. Then full coverage is available for all future losses during the policy period. This plan is not strictly a deductible, as losses are paid in full after the insured has accumulated losses equal to the premium paid. The arrangement differs from the convertible in that all losses apply toward the additional 50 percent of the premium. In no case is the insured required to pay an additional premium. This plan is used occasionally in glass insurance.

Franchise deductibles. Ocean marine insurance has still another type of deductible, the franchise, which differs from the straight deductible in that, if the loss exceeds the franchise, the insurer pays the entire loss, not just the excess. Assume that a shipment valued at $3,000 is covered subject to a 3 percent franchise. If a loss amounts to less than $90, the insurer is free of liability, but if the loss exceeds $90 (e.g., $500) the insurer is liable for the full amount. Were this a straight deductible rather than a franchise, the insurers would be liable for only $410 with the first $90 (3 percent of $3,000) deducted from the loss. Marine policies are written with either franchise or straight deductibles, although the franchise is the more common. The franchise percentage varies among commodities and policies.

Disappearing deductible. The disappearing deductible combines the franchise and straight deductibles. The typical version provides that no portion of a loss less than a minimum amount will be paid. Alternatively, the deductible does not apply at all if the loss exceeds a higher stated dollar limit. For losses falling between the minimum and the stated dollar limit, the insured receives a percentage—111 percent or 125 percent, depending on the contract—of the amount by which the loss exceeds the minimum amount.

For example, assume a minimum amount of $500 and a rate of 111 percent applying to losses over the minimum. If the insured has a loss totaling less than $500, the insurer has no liability under the contract. If a $3,000 loss occurred, the insurer would be liable for $2,775.[16] For losses exceeding $5,000, the insurer would be liable for the whole amount.

Disappearing deductibles are not widely used and many states make no provision for their use.[17] When used, they can be written only in conjunction with coverage for direct property damage by fire and allied perils.

Waiting periods. In health insurance, deductibles are called waiting periods. For example, in some disability income policies, no benefits are paid until after the first 14 days of illness. Others have waiting periods of 7, 30, 60, 90, or 120 days. Waiting periods are more common

---

[16] ($3,000 − $500) × 1.11 = $2,775.

[17] It is living up to its name!

in sickness than accident policies. Disability riders in life insurance usually require a six-month waiting period. In some states a waiting period is required following an injury to establish eligibility for workers' compensation benefits. In some of these states compensation benefits become retroactive if the worker's disability continues beyond a stated period. New York law provides a seven-day waiting period, with benefits becoming retroactive after two weeks. Benefits payable retroactively after a given period also are found in some disability income policies.

Reasons for deductibles

Deductible clauses excluding small frequent losses are based on sound insurance theory. Deductibles reduce the price of insurance by eliminating numerous small claims that are relatively expensive to handle. Deductibles also decrease moral hazard. An insured forced to pay a part of each loss may be more careful, thus encouraging loss prevention. Better loss experience is reflected in the rate. Some deductible arrangements, however, may increase moral hazard. The franchise, for example, may lead the insured to exaggerate the claim in an effort to collect the entire loss. In the foregoing example, the marine shipper collects nothing unless the damage to the $3,000 cargo exceeds $90. If loss exceeds $90, the full amount is paid. A dishonest insured might exaggerate cargo damage a bit in order to have a small loss paid. Similar temptations to aggravate losses are associated with disappearing deductibles.

Many insurance agents oppose deductibles, believing that, because they cause disgruntled claimants, poor public relations result.[18] Agents are convinced the payment of claims is their best advertisement. They also suspect insurers of using deductibles without reducing rates. And, finally, if rates are reduced, they oppose deductibles even more because lower rates mean lower commissions. However, sophisticated agents interested in their clients understand and appreciate the value of deductible clauses.

Summary

1. In contracts of indemnity, recovery for losses may not exceed the insured's insurable interest. The amount of insurable interest does not limit recovery in life insurance policies because they are not contracts of indemnity. Recovery in life insurance requires only that the owner of the policy have an insurable interest in the subject at the inception of the policy.
2. Property insurance contracts usually limit recovery to the actual cash value of the damaged or destroyed property. Actual cash value

---

[18] If deductible clauses lead to disgruntled claimants, the trouble is with agents who are unable or unwilling to explain deductible clauses to policyowners when the contracts are written.

equals the cost of replacing the property (new) less observed depreciation.

3. Actual cash value insurance requires the insured to bear the cost of depreciation on damaged or destroyed property, often resulting in hardship. Replacement cost insurance is designed to alleviate the problem by paying the insured full replacement cost for a loss. To be eligible for full replacement cost coverage, an insured commonly must cover property for at least a stated percentage of its full value.

4. Unless otherwise stated, property insurance contracts will not provide indemnity in excess of the policy face amount. In addition, most property insurance contracts, the HO–3 for example, contain internal limits applying to specified losses ($250 for fire department services charges), property ($100 for money), hazards ($250 for damage to property of others caused intentionally by persons under age 13), places (10 percent of the contents coverage for personal property usually situated at any insured's residence, other than the residence premises, but no less than $1,000), and perils (damage to trees, shrubs, and plants caused by several perils, limited to 5 percent of coverage A but not more than $500 for any one tree, shrub, or plant).

5. Liability insurance policies traditionally have contained three limitations on recovery per occurrence. Bodily injury liability coverage has one limit applying to the maximum amount payable to a single person, and a second limit setting the maximum amount payable to all persons injured during the occurrence. Property damage liability usually has a separate limit. Liability policies also are written with one limit applying per bodily injury occurrence and one limit applying per property damage occurrence *or* with one limit applying to both bodily injury and property damage per occurrence. In addition, the insurer agrees to bear certain costs not included in the policy limits, such as necessary costs in the defense of an insured involved in a liability suit.

6. When more than one insurance policy covers a loss, "other insurance" clauses determine how much each insurer will pay. An other insurance clause in a particular policy may provide that its coverage is shared with other insurance, will be excess over other insurance, will be primary, or that other insurance on the same property is prohibited.

7. Some contracts contain coinsurance clauses which restrict the amount of recovery on partial losses if the damaged property is not insured for at least a stated percentage of its actual cash value at the time of the loss. The purpose of coinsurance clauses is to help achieve rate equity and adequacy.

8. Deductible clauses are included in insurance contracts to eliminate coverage for small losses and to reduce morale hazard. Elimination of small loss payments allows the insurer to charge substantially lower premiums. Requiring the insured to pay part of a loss is likely to stimulate the policyowner to exercise more care and to practice loss prevention.

Questions for Review

1. Give an example (other than the one in the text) of how coinsurance helps to achieve equity and adequacy in rates. Explain.

2. How might the use of a disappearing deductible negate the purpose of a deductible?

3. Jeff Castles' HO–3 policy provides $40,000 coverage for his dwelling. A fire causes $4,000 damage to the roof, and while it is being repaired the house is untenantable. The fair rental value of the house is established at $450 per month. How much is Castles entitled to collect under his policy?

4. If the full replacement cost of the dwelling in question 3 were $60,000, how much would Castles recover for a replacement cost loss of $25,000 if the actual cash value of the loss were $20,000? Show your computations.

5. Under what situation is the use of blanket coverage warranted?

6. Shirley Kari owns two fire insurance policies on her $300,000 office building, one with insurer A for $200,000, the other with insurer B for $100,000. If the insurers share the loss on a pro rata basis, how much will each insurer pay in case of a $120,000 fire loss?

7. If the insurers in question 6 contribute on a limit of liability basis, how much will each pay for the $120,000 loss?

8. Compare the insurable interest requirement in property insurance as a measure of loss recovery with the insurable interest requirement in life insurance. If a difference exists, explain why.

9. Explain why sublimits are used in property insurance contracts.

10. Do valued policies violate the principle of indemnity? Do replacement–cost policies violate this principle? Explain.

Questions for Discussion

1. What problems might actual cash value insurance impose on an insurer? An insured? What problems might replacement cost coverage present an insurer? An insured?

2. Why do you think waiting periods are more common for disability income insurance if the peril is sickness rather than accident?

3. "Punitive damages deter antisocial behavior and should not be paid by liability insurers." Criticize (both pro and con) the above statement. Do you agree with it? Why or why not?

4. Edwin W. Patterson, once a professor of jurisprudence and a former Deputy Superintendent of Insurance of New York stated, "Valued policy laws represent a moribund experiment in legislative control of the insurance agents."[19] What factors may have led to this statement?

5. How may the use of deductibles help insurers adhere to several of the criteria for an insurable exposure explained in Chapter 2? Why are not all property insurance policies written on a deductible basis?

---

[19] Edwin W. Patterson, *Essentials of Insurance Law* (New York: McGraw-Hill, 1957), p. 146.

6. What would be advantages and disadvantages of including deductible clauses in liability insurance policies? Explain the logic of why deductibles are not used in most liability policies.

7. Explain why disagreement can arise as to the actual cash value of the property at the time of the loss. What, if anything, can the insured do to prevent or minimize such disagreement?

8. Why do you believe the ISO's readable Homeowners policies do not include an automatic reinstatement (restoration) value clause whereas their readable Businessowners forms do contain such a clause? If you were a claims manager, would you authorize payment of two $100,000 losses to a dwelling structure within a year (separated by two months) under an ISO readable HO–3 written for $100,000 on real property?

10

Loss-adjustment provisions

An insurance policy is most valuable after a loss. A large part of the policy describes procedures for loss adjustment. For example, of the 165 lines in the 1943 New York standard fire policy (SFP), 71 deal with settlement of claims.

Provisions pertaining to loss adjustment are: (1) notice of loss, (2) protection of property, (3) inventory, (4) evidence, (5) proof of loss, (6) assistance and cooperation, (7) appraisal, (8) abandonment and salvage, (9) settlement options, (10) time limit for paying claims, (11) time limit for bringing suits, and (12) miscellaneous clauses. Not every insurance contract includes each provision. Life insurance policies, for example, have just two—proof of loss and settlement options. This chapter examines and interprets loss adjustment provisions. Chapter 23 deals with insurer claim administration.

Notice of Loss

Many insurance policies (e.g., the SFP and the HO series) require the insured to give immediate written notice to the insurer of any loss. Others require notice "as soon as practicable." Notice of loss clauses also differ as to time limits for notice and the method of notification.

Immediate notice

The purpose of an "immediate notice" clause is to allow the insurer to investigate a loss while it is still recent. Delays can make investigation more difficult by increasing the opportunity for the insured to hide or eliminate evidence pointing to fraud. Immediate notice also allows the insurer to suggest measures to protect property from further loss. A delay in notification can adversely affect the insurer's position. Therefore, an insured's failure to comply relieves the insurer of liability if the failure materially affects the insurer's position.

The meaning of "immediate notice" is not literal. Courts have interpreted "immediate" to be as soon as reasonably possible. Thus, if a catastrophe wiped out an entire town and the insured unavoidably took a month or more to file notice, the contract condition would not be violated. In some cases, however, a delay of one or two days could be held unreasonable, voiding the policy. What constitutes reasonable notice depends on the facts of the case and how the court views them.

The liberal interpretation of the notice of loss clause has a sound legal basis. The courts consider the insured to have a vested right to recover which should not be forfeited by failure to comply with a condition that should be met.

Notice as soon as practicable

Many policies require notice "as soon as practicable" rather than immediate notice; for example, the workers' compensation policy. The PAP modified the "as soon as practicable" notice requirement of the family auto policy by requiring loss notification "promptly." Courts will have to interpret the meaning of the term "promptly." Courts have interpreted "as soon as practicable" even more liberally than "immediate notice." As soon as practicable means whatever is practical relative to all facts involved. A Florida court once interpreted the clause to mean as soon as an insured reasonably believes a claim will be made. In this case a man hit by the insured's automobile said, "Forget it, I'm OK." Nine months later he sued for loss of a leg. The insurer refused liability under the policy because the insured did not report the accident at once. The court ruled that the insured acted in a reasonably prudent manner. He was told to forget the accident, and he did. The court concluded that, by reporting the accident when sued, he had reported it as soon as "practicable."

The foregoing decision does not adhere to the insurer's intentions because in addition to a notice of loss, notice of claim also is required. Insurers want notice at both times. An insured, therefore, would be unwise to rely on the Florida court's decision. To be safe, an insured should give notice as soon as reasonably possible. Good faith requires this interpretation. Nearly all policies require notice of loss either immediately or as soon as practicable.

Variations among time limits for notice

Notice clauses also vary as to time limits. For example, the standard windstorm policy requires that the insurer be notified within 10 days after a loss. The hail policy requires notice within 48 hours. In health insurance a "uniform provision" requires written notice of claim to the insurer within 20 days after the occurrence of any loss covered by the policy, or as soon as reasonably possible. Because time limits for filing notice of loss vary, the insured must read the policy to determine its limit. The safest procedure is to give notice the day the loss occurs or as soon as possible.

Method of notice

Some policies require written notice, but this requirement may be waived by the insurer or its agents. If an oral notice of loss is given to an agent, and the agent accepts it without objection and provides for investigating the loss, the written notice requirement is held to have been waived. Furthermore, when the insurer acts upon a loss, it is estopped from claiming lack of notice to avoid liability.

Notice may be mailed rather than delivered in person. Notice also may be given to the insurer at its home office or to a duly authorized agent. In the workers' compensation policy, notice given to the employer by the injured employee is considered notice to the insurer. Telegraphic notice is required in some contracts. Crime insurers want notice of loss as quickly as possible. The sooner the insurers can begin their crime detection activities, the greater are their chances of apprehending the criminals and recovering the stolen property. The mercantile robbery and safe-burglary policy and the mercantile open-stock burglary policy (discussed in Chapter 15) have the following notice of loss clause:

> The assured upon knowledge of any loss shall give notice thereof as soon as practicable by telegraph at the company's expense, to the company at its home offices, or to a duly authorized agent of the company and shall also give immediate notice thereof to the public police or other peace authorities having jurisdiction.

Note that the insurer pays for the telegram and the contract requires the police to be notified.

Notice to a particular department of the insurer by registered mail may be required if immediate action in loss adjustment is essential. The hail policy contains a clause requiring the insured to notify the hail department of the insurer by registered mail, providing proof the notice was sent within the required time limit and assuring the insurer of prompt and safe delivery of the notice.

Notice provisions in liability policies

Liability policies generally contain two notice clauses. One deals with notice of accident (or occurrence), the other with notice of claim or suit.

The general liability policy has the following typical provisions:

1. In the event of an occurrence, written notice containing particulars sufficient to identify the Insured and also reasonably obtainable information with respect to the time, place, and circumstances thereof, and the names and addresses of the injured and of available witnesses, shall be given by or for the Insured to the Company or any of its authorized agents as soon as practicable.

2. If claim is made or suit is brought against the Insured, the Insured shall immediately forward to the Company every demand, notice, summons, or other process received by him [her] or his [her] representative.

Thus insureds are expected to give their insurer the knowledge they have or can reasonably obtain. The insurer needs the information in assembling the facts to handle the case. Note also that *immediate* notice is required for claims or suits. As soon as the insured is told that "this whole mess is your fault and you'll pay," the insurer must be notified of the claim. Failure to comply with notice clauses is interpreted by the insurer that the insured has elected to assume liability for the defense cost and the judgments for third-party claims arising from the accident.

Liability insurance is defense insurance, and the insurer needs the opportunity to investigate an accident to gather evidence to defend suits. Undue delay may make it difficult to find the necessary witnesses who remember (or care to remember) the accident details. Also, the notice clause reduces the moral hazard involved in cases of collusion between the insured and third parties. Immediate notice also may allow the insurer to avoid suit by offering prompt settlement to the injured person.

The foregoing discussion refers to the insurer's legal rights under the contract. In the absence of suspicious circumstances or flagrant violations, insurers will perform despite delays in notice or other failures of the insured to comply strictly with policy provisions. However, a wise insured complies with the policy terms rather than rely on the goodwill of the insurer.

Protection of Property

Another group of provisions concerns protection of property after a loss. The HO requires the insured to make the reasonable and necessary repairs required to protect the property from further damage. The SFP requires in addition that damaged and undamaged personal property be separated and put in the best possible order.

Although it may not be explicitly stated, most property insurance policies provide that the insurer bear the reasonable expenses incurred in protecting the property from further damage. For example, under the HO, the insured is indemnified for the cost of removing property from a burning dwelling, even though no such statement is made in the policy. To refuse payment for these expenses would weaken the value of the insurance, and could create a moral hazard.

Indemnifying the insured for expenses incurred in saving property from loss in effect is no different than indemnifying the insured for property that otherwise would have been damaged. The preservation expenses most likely will be less than the amount of the direct damage avoided.

Interpretation of the clause

The purpose of the protection provision is to minimize losses. If the insured fails to comply with this condition, the insurer is not relieved of all liability but only liability for losses resulting from the insured's failure to comply. However, the amount of loss caused by noncompliance with the protection clause often is not clear. The effort an insured must make to protect property from further damage also is a difficult question, usually decided by the courts. The adjuster, who frequently is better equipped to handle the job, may take over the insured's task of preventing further loss to avoid controversy.

Courts have relieved the insurer of all liability when the insured willfully neglects to protect property from further loss. To be safe, the insured should care for property after a loss as if it were uninsured. When the insured takes reasonable steps to protect covered property, the insurer will pay up to the policy limits for all reasonable expenses incurred.

The requirement in the SFP that damaged personal property be separated from undamaged property need not always be strictly obeyed. The condition is adequately met if the insurer is able to measure the extent of the loss. If, however, the insured leaves property in a disorderly state in order to exaggerate loss, the insurer can insist on compliance with the condition. The cost of separating damaged and undamaged personal property is paid by the insured, not the insurer.

Protection clauses in other insurance contracts

Many other property insurance contracts have similar provisions requiring property protection after a loss. The PAP requires a person seeking physical damage coverage to:

> Take reasonable steps after loss, at our expense, to protect your covered auto and its equipment from further loss.

Business interruption insurance forms[1] have two provisions designed to prevent further loss: The *expense to reduce loss* clause covers expenses necessarily incurred to reduce a loss. The expense must not exceed the amount by which loss under the policy is reduced. The *resumption of operations clause* provides that if the insured, by resumption of complete or partial operation of the business, could reduce the business interrup-

---

[1] Business interruption insurance is described in Chapter 11. This form protects the business against losses resulting from interruption by fire or other insured peril.

tion loss, such reduction will influence the amount of loss payable under the policy. Thus, if the loss would be less by operating the business than by remaining closed, the insured must operate it or bear a portion of the loss.

Marine insurance contracts[2] contain what are known as *sue and labor clauses,* typically worded as follows:

> In the case of any loss or damage, it shall be lawful and necessary for the insured, his [or her] or their factors, servants and assigns, to sue, labor and travel for, in and about the defense, safeguard and recovery of the property insured hereunder, or any part thereof, without prejudice to this insurance, nor shall the acts of the insured or this company in recovering, saving and preserving the property insured, in case of loss or damage be considered a waiver, or an acceptance of an abandonment; to the charge whereof this company will contribute according to the rate and quantity of the sum herein insured.

The clause mandates that the insured take steps to eliminate or reduce a covered loss. The insurer agrees to pay reasonable costs of attempts to reduce loss if the expenditures are in connection with covered property, perils, and losses and if the expenditures are made by the insured or agents of the insured. Reimbursement for these costs is in addition to the policy face amount. Also, deductible clauses do not apply to indemnities under the sue and labor clause. If attempts to reduce loss are unsuccessful, the insurer still is liable for the expenses. Thus, in case of total loss, a marine insurer may be liable for more than the face amount of the policy. Protection clauses are included to minimize losses. Policyowners should read their policies to ascertain their obligations in this regard.

Inventory

The HO provides that the insured prepare an inventory of damaged personal property showing in detail the quantity, description, actual cash value, and amount of loss. The insured must attach to the inventory all bills, receipts, and related documents that substantiate the figures in the inventory. The insured may not be able to comply with the detailed inventory requirements prescribed in the HO, especially when the evidence required to complete the inventory has been damaged. Therefore, only reasonable compliance with the inventory provisions is necessary.

The inventory clause of the SFP requires, in addition, that the insured furnish a complete inventory of the destroyed, damaged, and undamaged property. An inventory of undamaged goods is required, as a rule, only if the policy contains a coinsurance clause to enable the adjuster to determine the value of the property relative to the amount of insurance. In fire insurance a waiver clause often is used with the coinsurance clause, relieving the insured of the obligation to provide a physical in-

---

[2] Marine insurance is discussed in Chapter 12.

ventory of undamaged property if the loss is small—usually 5 percent of the amount of insurance or losses under $10,000. Thus a loss of $5,000 on a $500,000 exposure would not obligate the insured to prepare an inventory of the $495,000 of undamaged property. The coinsurance clause is not waived, but the insurer cannot insist on an inventory to determine whether the insured has maintained the coinsurance percentage.

Regardless of the existence of an inventory clause, an insured should maintain a complete inventory of property for insurance purposes. Some insurance agents furnish inventory forms for use by homeowners. An insured with adequate inventory records will be in a favorable position to deal with loss adjusters. These records should be kept in a fireproof safe.

Evidence

Insurance contracts have provisions concerning evidence designed to help the insurer determine the validity of a claim. For example, the HO provides that the insured:

> exhibit the damaged property as often as we reasonably require and submit to examination under oath.

The insured must receive ample notice of an examination, indicating the time, place, and names of the examiners. The examination is in addition to the sworn proof of loss statement, discussed next. If the insured, during the examination, answers material questions falsely, and fraud is involved, the policy may be voided. If the insured is asked to produce books of account, bills, and so on, and these items are unavailable, the insured is excused, for the insured cannot be expected to comply with impossible provisions. If the insured purposely destroys evidence, the contract may be voided. The insurer is required to be reasonable in the use of these conditions.

Evidence clauses in other contracts

A clause similar to the one in the HO is found in most property insurance contracts. In policies involving claimants other than the insured, all claimants shall submit to examination upon the insurer's request, except third-party claimants under liability suits. Evidence clauses in *liability policies* are restricted to indemnity under the *medical payments* coverage. The injured person, or a representative, is required to furnish reasonably obtainable information pertaining to the accident and injury and to authorize the insurer to obtain medical reports and records as soon as practicable after the insurer's request. The injured person must submit to physical examination by physicians selected by the insurer when and as often as the insurer may reasonably require. These provisions provide the insurer an opportunity to protect itself against fake claims. No evidence clause is needed in liability claims. The awarding of a judgment by the court is sufficient proof.

The *health policy* gives the insurer the right to examine the claimant when and as often as it may reasonably require. These rights are necessary, for some claimants could easily fake disability in order to enjoy a paid vacation. Moral hazard in disability income insurance is large, and insurers need protective devices to manage the hazard. Where not forbidden by law, the insurer may, but seldom does, request an autopsy. Evidence clauses are advantageous to an honest insured by helping control insurance costs and facilitating a speedy and fair claims settlement.

Proof of Loss

Insurers require proof of loss in various ways often expressed in the policy. The conditions applying to Section I of the HO obligate the insured to furnish a signed and sworn statement to the insurer within 60 days after the insurer requests such statement.[3] The statement provides the insurer with facts necessary to reach an equitable loss adjustment. The statement must include the following items designed to determine the insurer's liability:

1. The time and cause of loss.   This information ascertains if the loss occurred during the policy period and if coverage is provided for the particular type of loss that has occurred. If the insured does not know the origin, then a statement that the origin is unknown is sufficient. Information relating to the time of the loss is interpreted as that which is to the best of the insured's knowledge or belief.

2. The interest of the insured and all others in the property involved and all encumbrances on the property.   This information establishes the insurable interest of the insured and the extent of third-party interests in the loss. This information also serves as a factor limiting the insurer's liability.

3. Other insurance which may cover the loss.   This information is necessary, as the liability of the insurer is reduced proportionately if other insurance covers the loss.

4. Changes in title or occupancy of the property during the term of the policy.   This information enables the adjuster to determine who has an insurable interest and if any conditions of the policy have been violated.

5. Specifications of any damaged building and detailed estimates for repair of the damage.   This information is necessary in order to deter-

---

[3] For the purposes of the layperson, "sworn statements" can be read to mean "notarized affidavits" that are sworn to, and not at.

mine the replacement cost of the damaged building. (If the property is covered by an HO–8, the information will be used to obtain the ACV of the damaged building.)

6. An inventory of damaged personal property. This information is used to determine the ACV of the damaged personal property.

7. Receipts for additional living expenses incurred and records supporting the fair rental value loss. This information enables the insurer to determine its liability under coverage D (Loss of Use).

8. Evidence of affidavit supporting a claim under the credit card, forgery, and counterfeit money coverage, stating the amount and cause of loss.

Interpreting the clause

A proof of loss statement must be submitted by the insured to the insurer within 60 days following the insurer's request for such statement. If the policy is endorsed with a mortgage clause and the mortgagor fails to file proof of loss, the mortgagee has 60 days in which to do so after learning of the mortgagor's failure. The proof of loss must be given under oath and signed by the named insured (or the mortgagee, if necessary). If the insured fraudulently makes a false and material statement, the policy may be voided. Thus, if an insured reports a loss of $20,000 and it proves to be $5,000, the policy may be voided if the insurers can prove intent to deceive. If the courts find the discrepancy to be an honest mistake, the insured is excused and the policy covers. The insurer, however, need not be harmed by a fraudulent misstatement of a material fact to void the policy.

The insurer, by its actions, can waive the proof of loss requirement. If the insurer denies liability or handles a claim as if it intends to settle, it may be estopped from using the absence of proof of loss as a defense, should litigation arise. If a faulty proof of loss statement is filed and the insurer fails to return it within a reasonable time with suggestions for corrections, the statement is deemed to have satisfied the proof of loss requirement. If an insured swears to a proof of loss statement and later proves the loss was greater than that in the original statement, the courts will recognize the new evidence.

Other proof of loss clauses

Proof of loss clauses in most insurance contracts usually are not as elaborate as that in the HO and the SFP. The PAP requires a proof of loss only when required by the insurer. The policy does not describe the information that must be included in such proof of loss.

The proof of loss clause in most *inland marine forms* is simple, giving the insured 90 days to file; and, rather than prescribing exactly the contents of the proof of loss asks only for a detailed statement. In a dispute, what constitutes a detailed statement is up to the courts. The information included in the statement must enable the insurer to ascertain the cause and extent of the loss and allow the insurer to determine its subrogation rights. Insurers generally provide insureds with proof of loss blanks.

The *health policy* contains two mandatory proof of loss provisions. The first deals with claim forms stating:

> The Company, upon receipt of a notice of claim, will furnish to the claimant such forms as are usually furnished by it for filing proofs of loss. If such forms are not furnished within fifteen days after the giving of such notice the claimant shall be deemed to have complied within the requirements of this Policy as to proof of loss upon submitting, within the time fixed in the Policy for filing proofs of loss, written proof covering the occurrence, the character and the extent of the loss for which claim is made.

The second clause is the proof of loss clause and requires:

> Written proof of loss must be furnished to the Company at its said office in case of claim for loss for which this Policy provides any periodic payment contingent upon continuing loss within ninety days after the termination of the period for which the Company is liable and in case of claim for any other loss within ninety days after the date of such loss. Failure to furnish such proof within the time required shall not invalidate nor reduce any claim if it was not reasonably possible to give proof within such time, provided such proof is furnished as soon as reasonably possible and in no event, except in the absence of legal capacity, later than one year from the time proof is otherwise required.

For all other than continuing benefits the time limit for filing claims begins with the loss. The time limit for periodic payments begins with the termination of any other periodic payments by the insurer. For example, the policy may provide $200 a month for two years following an accident to Peter Kensicki provided he is unable to do any part of his own job. After two years, the payments continue for his lifetime provided he is unable to do any part of any job. The time limit for filing the second claim (for lifetime income) is 90 days from the end of the first two years of payments.

In *liability insurance* proof of loss is required for claims made under the supplementary and medical payments coverages. The typical clause requires that sworn written proof of the claim be given the insurer as soon as practicable after the cost of medical services rendered equals or exceeds the policy limits, or one year from the accident date, whichever is first. Because medical payments are restricted to medical expenses incurred during the year following the accident, or to the policy face amount, whichever is less, the filing of proof of loss is deferred until the extent of the insurer's liability can be determined. The proof of loss must include the name and address of each person and organization rendering services; the nature, extent, and dates of the services; itemized charges; and the amounts paid. Proof of loss is not necessary under liability coverage because the extent of loss is determined by a court judgment or a negotiated settlement signed by a representative of the insurer.

Life policies simply provide that the insurer will pay the face amount of the policy to the beneficiary immediately upon receipt of written proof of death occurring while the policy is in force.

In summary, proof of loss clauses vary as to time limit for filing notice and information required. Insurers generally furnish insureds proof of loss blanks, showing the information required.

Assistance and Cooperation

Provisions in insurance contracts calling for cooperation between the insurer and insured in dealing with other parties after a loss are found most often in crime and liability policies. Section II of the HO requires the insured, at the insurer's request, to assist in: (1) making settlement; (2) the enforcement of any right of contribution or indemnity against any person or organization who may be liable to any insured; (3) the conduct of suits and attend hearings and trials; and (4) securing and giving evidence and obtaining the attendance of witnesses.

In liability coverages the insurer needs the insured's cooperation in defending suits. The insured usually is an essential witness. The insurer is unwilling to defend an uncooperative insured. The insured, when dealing with third parties, is expected to act as though no insurance applied. The insured usually is required to contribute time and services without compensation. No reimbursement generally is made for loss of earnings from these activities but the insurer pays out-of-pocket expenses incurred at its request. Under the HO forms, the insurer reimburses the insured for expenses incurred at the insurer's request, including actual loss of earnings up to $50 per day for assisting the insurer in the investigation or defense of any claim or suit.

The HO states that:

> the insured shall not, except at the insured's own cost, voluntarily make any payments, assume any obligation or incur any expense other than for first aid to others at the time of the bodily injury.

Any other payments made by an insured might not be reimbursed. The insurer has the right to deny reimbursement for unauthorized expenses of investigation. Because the insurer has the obligation to investigate and defend all claims, it has the final decision as to necessary expenses. First-aid expenses are exempted from the voluntary payments clause because first aid might reduce the amount of the loss. Thus the insurer encourages the insured to arrange first aid for injured parties. If the insured voluntarily makes payments for damages claimed by the injured party the insured might forfeit all rights to payment under the contract. Voluntary payments might be construed as admission of liability and interfere with the insurer's defense of the insured. Clauses similar to those found in Section II of the HO policies are found in all liability policies.

A typical clause in *crime insurance* requires that an insured making a claim must take legal action at the insurer's request and expense to secure recovery of the property and arrest and prosecution of the offenders.

Appraisal

The HO includes the following appraisal clause:

> If you and we fail to agree on the amount of loss, either one can demand that the amount of the loss be set by appraisal. If either makes a written demand for appraisal, each shall select a competent, independent appraiser and notify the other of the appraiser's identity within 20 days of receipt of the written demand. The two appraisers shall then select a competent, impartial umpire. If the two appraisers are unable to agree upon an umpire within 15 days, you or we can ask a judge of a court of record in the state where the residence premises is located to select an umpire. The appraisers shall then set the amount of the loss. If the appraisers submit a written report of an agreement to us, the amount agreed upon shall be the amount of the loss. If the appraisers fail to agree within a reasonable time, they shall submit their differences to the umpire. Written agreement signed by any two of these three shall set the amount of the loss. Each appraiser shall be paid by the party selecting that appraiser. Other expenses of the appraisal and the compensation of the umpire shall be paid equally by you and us.

Similar clauses are found in other property insurance contracts. This clause does not apply to disagreement as to whether there is liability, but applies when disagreement exists over the *amount* of liability. If the insurer denies liability, the insured is free to sue immediately. If the amount of loss is disputed, the insured may sue immediately only if the insurer refuses to arbitrate the differences; otherwise the insured must fulfill the appraisal clause provisions. If the insured or the insurer is not satisfied with the appraiser's decision, either may sue. But it must be shown either that the appraisal involved fraud or that a mistake resulted in an inequitable award. During the appraisal the insured has the right to a hearing before both the umpire and the appraisers. If the appraisers refuse, grounds are established for court action to set aside the award. The courts, however, give strong weight to the appraisers' values. The burden of proof in setting aside the appraisal rests with the dissatisfied party.

Appraisal clauses are used to reduce the amount of litigation. Because the claimant might overestimate and the insurer underestimate the amount of loss, differences of opinion are likely. The appraisal clause helps keep differences out of court and facilitates faster loss adjustment.

Abandonment and Salvage

The terms "abandonment" and "salvage" have been defined as follows: *abandonment* is relinquishing of ownership of lost or damaged property by the insured to the insurer so that a total loss may be claimed; *salvage* is property taken over by an insurer to reduce its loss. The SFP and the HO forbid abandonment to the insurer of property. No matter how serious the damage, the insured may not force salvage upon the insurer. Abandonment clauses are found in several other property insurance policies. If no abandonment clause is in the policy, the clause is read into it by the courts as expressing the parties intention.

When a total loss is paid, the insurer has the salvage right. Thus, although the insured may not abandon property to the insurer and claim total loss, the insurer may pay a total loss and demand salvage.

Abandonment in marine insurance

The property covered in some forms of marine insurance makes salvage operations by the insured difficult. Therefore, the insured is given abandonment rights under specified conditions. In marine insurance a total loss may be *actual* or *constructive*. An *actual total loss* exists if the wreckage cannot be repaired or the property is not recoverable by the insured. Examples are mysterious disappearance, sinking, and complete destruction by perils of the sea or by fire. A *constructive total loss* occurs when the ship or cargo is so damaged or situated that the cost to save the property would be more than its worth when restored. If a total financial loss is inevitable, a constructive total loss exists. For example, a ship is partly destroyed by collision and the cost to restore the vessel exceeds the value of the ship after it is repaired. Also, if fire damages the cargo and the cost to renovate and deliver the cargo to its destination is more than its value, a constructive total loss of both ship and cargo prevails.

To claim a constructive total loss, the insured must abandon the property to the insurer unconditionally. Rules for constructive total loss in the United States and England differ. In the United States an insured can abandon the property if the cost of repair exceeds 50 percent of the property value after repairs. In England no constructive total loss can be claimed unless the cost of repair equals at least 100 percent of the property value after repairs. The English rule, although less liberal for the insured, is more equitable and has been incorporated in many American marine contracts by the following provision:

> No recovery for a Constructive Total Loss shall be had hereunder unless the property insured is reasonably abandoned on account of its actual total loss appearing to be unavoidable, or because it cannot be preserved from actual total loss without an expenditure which would exceed its value when the expenditure had been incurred.

A typical policy covering the ship may read as follows:

No recovery for a constructive total loss shall be had hereunder unless the expense of recovering and repairing the vessel shall exceed the insured value.

When the insured wishes to abandon, notice must be given to the insurer as soon as possible so that the insurer may take steps to prevent further loss. If the insurer rejects the notice, the insured must preserve the property as required under the sue and labor clause until the question of constructive total loss is settled. Once abandonment is offered and accepted, the action becomes binding on both parties, regardless of the eventual disposition of the property.

Settlement Options

Insurance policies may be settled in various ways. In some contracts the insurer has the settlement option, in others, the option is the insured's. Under the HO and SFP, an insurer may repair or replace damaged property rather than pay the actual cash value of the loss. If the insurer elects this option, notice of intention is required within 30 days after receipt of proof of loss. The insurer then must repair, rebuild, or replace the property with material of like kind and quality within a reasonable time. Insurers seldom exercise this option, because payment of cash is simpler than entering the construction business. Also, the insurer would be exposed to the insured's rejection of the repairs or replacement. The option is used to protect the insurer from unfair appraisals. The option is for 30 days after proof of loss is filed, during which time the insured must not engage in actions that may defeat the insurer's right to repair. For example, if the insured sells damaged property without the insurer's permission, the insurance is forfeited.

The repair or replace option is in many property insurance contracts. In some contracts insurers use the option more often than in others. In glass insurance, the insurer usually replaces the broken glass. Insurers work closely with the glass companies and obtain quick service and favorable prices.

Settlement options in health insurance

The health policy might provide an elective indemnity for certain scheduled injuries involving fractures and dislocations. The election is the insured's and in some policies must be exercised within 20 days after the accident. The following is typical of specific indemnity clauses:

> If weekly indemnity is provided under this policy, the Insured, if he [or she] so elects in writing, before accepting payment of weekly indemnity . . . may take, in lieu thereof, indemnity in one sum according to the following schedule if the injury is one set forth in said schedule, but not more than one specific indemnity, the largest, shall be paid for injuries resulting from one accident.

> If the weekly indemnity for total disability payable under this policy

is $50, the amounts named below shall be payable; if such weekly indemnity is greater or less than $50, the amounts to be paid shall be increased or decreased proportionately.

A schedule is then set up indicating specific indemnities such as $650 for complete fracture of the skull, $300 for complete dislocation of ankle joints, and $400 for removal of one or more toes. Sometimes the schedule is in terms of amounts equal to a given number of weeks of total disability indemnity.

If the specific benefit is elected, the insured is not entitled to additional benefits under the policy except medical benefits. Under some policies election is not required; the insurer pays the insured the highest amount of indemnity available with the specific indemnity schedule the minimum. If payments under the weekly loss of time benefits prove greater, they automatically will be paid. Specific indemnity clauses provide indemnity for certain accidents usually involving no serious loss of time but nevertheless causing injuries. Insurers believe that payments for these injuries are good for public relations.

Settlement options in life insurance

The proceeds or cash values of a life policy may be paid as a lump sum, as periodic payments over a limited period, or for life. These options may be selected by the insured or the beneficiary. The most common settlement options offered are (1) interest only, (2) installments for a fixed period, (3) installments of fixed amounts, and (4) life income. These options are discussed in detail in Chapter 17.

Time Limit for Paying Claims

Insurance policies specify time limits for paying claims and these limits vary among policies. The HO provides that payment of the loss for which the insurer is liable shall be made within 30 days after (a) agreement is reached, (b) a final judgment is entered, or (c) an appraisal award has been filed. The clause gives the insurer time to investigate the loss and arrange for payment. Generally, insurers do not defer payment for 30 days. Unless a waiting period is *required* by statute, the insurers pay approved claims promptly. The insurer is obligated to pay interest on the amount due if payment is delayed beyond the 30-day limit.

Time limits in other contracts

Several other contracts set time limits for paying claims. The limit is 15 days in the registered mail policy, and 7 days in the camera floater. The accounts receivable policy requires the insurer, within three months from date of loss, to pay shortages in collections resulting from damage or destruction caused by an insured peril. The health policy requires all indemnities other than payments for loss of time be paid immediately on receipt of proof. Upon request of the insured, and subject to proof of loss, all accrued indemnity for time loss caused by disability is paid at the end of each month during the period for which the insurer is liable; and any unpaid balance remaining at the end of the period is paid immediately upon receipt of proof. Payment of benefits in life insurance becomes due immediately upon receipt of proof of death. Insurers vary as to whether they pay interest following death until the payment of proceeds, the rate of interest paid, and the time period for which interest accumulates.

Time Limit for Bringing Suits

Insurance contracts set a time limit within which a suit may be brought against the insurer. These limits may be minimums, maximums, or both, and supersede the general statute of limitations otherwise applicable.

Time limit in the HO policy

Section I of the HO provides that no action shall be brought against the insurer unless the insured has complied with the policy provisions and the action is started within 12 months after the occurrence causing the loss or damage. The 12-month provision does not apply if the insurer takes the full 12-month period for negotiations or is not accessible to process serving. The insurer may waive the 12-month limit by actions that lead the insured reasonably to believe the limitation will not be enforced. Once the insurer agrees to a loss settlement the 12-month time limit no longer applies. The maximum time limit for bringing suits enables the insurer to terminate liability under its policies within a reasonable time, so that reserves for losses reported but not settled can be managed more easily and so that suits are filed before the facts grow old.

Time limits in other policies

The PAP permits no legal action against the insurer until there has been full compliance by the insured with all the terms of the contract. No actual time limit exists for bringing suits. Thus, if the insured does not appear in court at the insurer's request and give testimony, no action can be maintained against the insurer. If the insured does not comply with contract provisions, the insurer is not obligated to third parties seeking damages. The clause, therefore, establishes that failure of the insured to comply with policy conditions will operate as a forfeiture. Before these noncompliance clauses were added to contracts, the courts had held that compliance with policy provisions was not a condition precedent to contract enforcement.

The *health policy* includes a mandatory provision fixing both a minimum and a maximum time limit for bringing suit. A typical clause reads:

> No action at law or in equity shall be brought to recover on this policy prior to the expiration of sixty days after proof of loss has been filed in accordance with the requirements of this policy, nor shall such action be brought at all unless brought within three years from the expiration of the time at which proof of loss is required by the policy.

This 60-day limit gives the insurer time to process the claim. The three-year limit prevents the insurer from accumulating liability exposure for an indefinite time period.

Liability policies (e.g., Section II of HO and Part A of PAP) forbid action against the insurer until the amount of the insured's liability is finally determined, either by court decision or written agreement of the insured. Thus no suit against the insurer is allowed while litigation between the insured and the third-party claimant is in process, or an appeal is pending. This requirement is important, for if the insurer denies liability on the grounds that the policy does not cover, the insured first must defend the case in court in order to recover from the insurer. The insured must not allow the plaintiff to win by default and must not be indifferent to the suit or collusive with the plaintiff. Once a judgment is reached by trial, the policyowner may proceed against the insurer. If the insurer is found liable, it must pay the judgment and the defense cost. After a judgment is obtained or an agreement reached, third-party claimants are on a level with the insured in dealing with the insurer under the policy terms.

Thus provisions pertaining to time limits for bringing suits vary among contracts. If the maximum time limit in the policy is shorter than that required by state law for such policies, the longer time limit governs.

Miscellaneous Clauses

Many other clauses relating to loss adjustment may be discussed under the heading of miscellaneous clauses. The use of the heading miscellaneous, however, does not make them less important.

Relations with third parties

Some insurance contracts clarify the relations of the insurer to third parties involved in claims. A few contracts permit the insurer to deal directly with third parties, whereas others deny the insurer this right.

The bailees' customers' floater and the furriers' customers' custody policies provide that loss may be adjusted and paid to the insured or adjusted and paid directly to the insured's customers, at the insurer's option. Also, if legal proceedings are brought against the insured by third parties to recover loss of property owned by them but held by the insured, the insurer may defend against such action at no expense to the insured. In these coverages the simpler procedure may be for the insurer to settle with the property owner rather than the insured, eliminating an intermediary thus reaching an agreement with less delay.

On the other hand, the accounts receivable policy forbids the insurer to approach customers of the insured for collections or any other purpose in connection with the insurance, so the insured can protect customer relationships. The physicians', surgeons', and dentists' liability policy states that the insurer will not settle or compromise a claim or suit covered by the policy except with the insured's written consent regardless of anything to the contrary in the basic policy. A major purpose of the physicians', surgeons', and dentists' liability policy is to uphold the good name of the insured. If insurers could settle claims out of court, the effect would be to admit guilt which hurts the reputation of the insured. A decision for the plaintiff in a malpractice case is much more harmful to the defendant than the amount to be paid to the plaintiff. This provision, however, means that nearly all claims will be litigated, increasing expenses and insurance costs.

Pair or set

The HO series as well as many inland marine and burglary policies contain a pair or set clause providing that the insurer can either:

    a. Repair or replace any part to restore the pair or set to its value before the loss; or

    b. Pay the difference between the actual cash value of the property before and after the loss.

This clause informs the insured that a loss of one cuff link is not a total loss of the set. The insurer makes an effort under this clause to reach an equitable settlement. This effort could result in a payment exceeding 50 percent of the value of the pair.

Other provisions

Policies covering jewelry and silverware often specify that any antiquarian or historical value shall be excluded from the loss estimate. This clause eliminates a source of friction. Antiquarian and historical values ordinarily are protected by fine arts policies.

The medical payments coverage of liability policies provides that "payment [medical payments] under this policy does not constitute admission of liability of the insured or, except as to this policy, of the insurer." Because medical payments coverage is accident and not liability insurance, payments are made on behalf of the insured irrespective of liability. Insurers want to clarify that payment under medical coverage is not admission of liability under the bodily injury and property damage liability coverage.

Some forms of hail insurance provide that if the insured notifies the insurer of a loss less than 5 percent of the crop value, the insured must pay the investigation expense. Hail-loss investigation is expensive, and this provision reduces irresponsible loss reporting. This clause is in addition to the provision that if the loss is less than 5 percent of the crop value at the date of loss, the insurer is not liable.

Summary

1. Insurance policy provisions vary as to the rights and duties of the insured and the insurer after a loss. Insureds should examine their policies so they are not mistakenly guilty of actions or inactions that forfeit their right of recovery.
2. Nearly all property contracts require written notice of loss either "immediately" or "as soon as practicable" after a loss. Both requirements have been interpreted by the courts to mean as soon as is reasonably possible.
3. Liability policies generally contain two notice clauses; the first is written notice as soon as practicable after an accident, and the second obligates the insured to forward immediately every demand, notice, summons, or other process received concerning claims or suits brought against the insured.
4. To minimize losses, insureds are required to protect property from further damage after a loss. If the insured fails to comply with this provision, the insurer is not relieved of all liability, but only for losses resulting from the insured's failure to comply.
5. Some property contracts stipulate that the insured must furnish a complete inventory of damaged and undamaged property after a partial loss. The inventory of undamaged goods generally is required only if a coinsurance clause is used, so the insured's compliance with the coinsurance clause can be calculated.
6. Proof of loss statements provide insurers with the facts necessary to determine the existence and extent of their liability. Property policies call for a proof of loss statement to be submitted by the insured within a given time period after a loss. Liability policies require proof of loss statements only under the supplementary payments and medical payments coverage, because the insurer's liability is determined by court decision or negotiated settlement. Proof of loss clauses vary among policies as to time limit for filing and information necessary in the statement.
7. Assistance and cooperation clauses are most often found in crime and liability policies, requiring the insured to attend trials and hearings, assist in effecting settlements, securing evidence, and conducting suits upon request of the insurer. These clauses also forbid insureds to make voluntary payments, except for immediate medical relief to others at the time of an accident. Assistance and coopera-

tion clauses *(a)* facilitate the insurer's defense of the insured, *(b)* help the insurer control expenses, and *(c)* uphold the insurer's right of subrogation.

8. Appraisal clauses are designed to reduce litigation concerning the *amount* of the insurer's liability, by providing a system for arbitrating disputes between the insured and insurer. The clause stipulates that the insured may not file suit against the insurer until the terms of the appraisal clause have been fulfilled.

9. Settlement options vary among insurance contracts. Some policies give the insured the choice of options, others the insurer. For example, the SFP gives the insurer the option to settle in cash or repair or replace the damaged property. Alternatively, life insurance policies allow the insured or beneficiary to choose among a variety of settlement options, commonly including interest only on the proceeds, installment payments for a fixed time, or for a fixed amount or a lifetime income.

10. Insurance policies also set time limits for insurers to pay claims and time limits in which insureds may bring suit against insurers. These provisions assure the insured prompt payment and allow insurers to terminate their liability within a reasonable period of time.

Questions for Review

1. Under what circumstance would you expect an insurer to repair or replace damaged property rather than pay the actual cash value of the loss?

2. What is the theory behind the use of an appraisal clause in an insurance contract?

3. You own a $40,000 fire policy covering your dwelling, estimated to be worth $60,000. During the afternoon, fire breaks out causing a $2,000 loss. Later that night a second and separate fire destroys the rest of the house. How much can you collect on your policy?

4. What purpose is served by each of the eight items required in the proof of loss statement prescribed by the HO?

5. What is the function of evidence clauses? Why are evidence clauses restricted to certain supplementary payments and medical payments coverage in liability policies?

6. How does the operation of the sue and labor clause differ from that in the HO policies requiring protection of property from further damage?

7. When and why would an insured be required to furnish an inventory of undamaged property?

8. An HO policyowner has one earring stolen from a pair, valued at $500. What would be the minimum amount of recovery? The maximum? Explain.

9. The book value of your car is $2,500. You have a collision and the lowest repair estimate is $2,300, with the salvage value of your car estimated at $600. How would your insurer settle in order to minimize its loss? Explain.

10. Of what importance is salvage in life insurance?

Questions for Discussion

1. Which of the loss provisions in the HO-3 policy are designed to protect the insurer? Which are for protection of the insured?

2. For what possible reasons is the information required in the proof of loss for the HO more extensive than that required by other property contracts?

3. Given the correct answer in question 9 from the Questions for Review, comment on the equity of the procedure described. Would this type of loss adjustment necessarily indemnify the insured? If this method of adjustment were eliminated could there be any adverse consequences to the insured?

4. Under what circumstances would the operation of a pair or set clause fail to indemnify the insured? Design a coverage which would indemnify the insured who loses one member of a pair or set, and still uphold the indemnity principle.

5. Most HO insurers require proof of purchase and notification of police concerning stolen property before paying for a loss. To what extent might these requirements reduce moral hazard? What additional measures could reduce the moral hazard further?

Fire and associated lines

On Friday, September 2, 1666, an event important in the history of fire insurance occurred. An oven in the king's bakeshop became overheated resulting in a fire that nearly destroyed the city of London. The blaze raged for five days, causing extensive destruction of lives and property and forcing people to think about a solution to the problem of fire losses. Dr. Nicholas Barbon, only a moderately successful doctor, turned his attention to fire insurance. In 1667, he opened an office to offer fire insurance against loss to dwellings and business buildings. The doctor was much more successful at insurance than at doctoring, and his business prospered. (Nick's father, Praise-God Barbon [or Barebones], had two sons. Their baptismal names were Christ-came-into-the-world-to-save Barbon, and If-Christ-had-not-died-thou-hadst-been-damned Barbon. The record is not clear which of these was Nick, but it is clear that Nick's dad, a leather merchant and Baptist lay preacher, was deeply interested in religion.)

Development of Fire Insurance in America

The prevention of fire was a serious problem in early American life. Following a major Boston fire in 1630, the governor of Massachusetts proclaimed that wooden chimneys and thatched roofs would be banned in Boston. After another big fire in 1653, Boston decided to purchase and maintain municipal fire-fighting equipment. A costly fire in Philadelphia in 1730 resulted in the formation of the Union Fire Company, a volunteer fire-fighting company of which Benjamin Franklin was a founder. This company was the first of many volunteer fire-fighting companies, and in 1752 the energetic Franklin was instrumental in the formation of the Philadelphia Contributionship for the Insurance of Houses from Loss by Fire, discussed in Chapter 22.

In 1794, after three months of study, the board of the Insurance Company of North America (INA) decided to write fire insurance covering contents as well as buildings, thus becoming the first in America to insure contents. In 1795, INA offered fire insurance on "brick and stone houses within ten miles of the city," a departure from previous practice restricting fire coverage to areas served by volunteer fire-fighting companies. The following year INA made fire insurance available on properties anywhere in the United States.

Discrimination against out-of-state insurers

In the early part of the 19th century a large number of fire insurers were formed. Many small, local insurers began operation when a number of states passed discriminatory laws fostering in-state business. Massachusetts started the ball rolling in 1827 by passing a 10 percent premium tax on non-Massachusetts insurers operating in that state and limiting the amount of insurance a company could write to 10 percent of its capitalization. Also, no out-of-state insurer with less than $200,000 of capital was allowed to operate in the state. These regulations were the first attempt by states to protect policyowners' interests, as well as to promote the development of local insurers.

Pennsylvania retaliated with a similar law charging a 20 percent tax on out-of-state insurers, and soon seven more states had added taxes ranging from 4 to 10 percent of premiums. The discriminatory taxes meant that small, home-grown insurers could, by cutting rates—or, indeed, by charging fair rates—compete favorably with insurers from other states. Most out-of-state insurers met the challenge by raising their rates to include the premium tax, but some confined their business to their home states.

In 1835 New York City was swept by a great fire, with a brisk northeast wind spreading the flames which nearly destroyed the entire business district. The fire-fighting forces were unprepared for such a holocaust and, to make matters worse, water froze in the hoses as the fire began during bitter winter weather. The total loss has been estimated at about $18 million. Much of the insurance was with local insurers, as discriminatory taxes had allowed them to cut rates. This practice proved disastrous when all but 3 of the 26 local insurers went bankrupt. Subsequently New York reduced its premium tax on out-of-state insurers to 2 percent and the smaller insurers began to fade from the scene. The period following 1835 witnessed the growth of insurers writing business on a national scale, and competition became keen among these young giants. Viewing the New York experience, these insurers wanted to spread exposures, accumulate adequate reserves, and expand sales. In 1849 a fire on the St. Louis waterfront burned 27 steamboats and engulfed the business district. Insurers had learned their lesson well. With the exception of a few western insurers, the industry weathered this storm.

The influence of these disasters on fire insurance sales was pronounced. Following each of the major fires, huge increases in the purchase of fire insurance, particularly in those sections most affected by the blazes, were recorded. These fires also caused the fire insurers to draw together. In 1866 the fire insurers formed the National Board of Fire Underwriters. This organization, now part of the American Insurance Association, dealt with such matters as the compensation of agents, fire prevention, discovery and prevention of arson, ratemaking, and other problems faced by large stock insurers.

The great fires

On Sunday evening, October 8, 1871, Mrs. Jeremiah O'Leary left as usual to milk the cow in the O'Leary barn on the west side of Chicago, the present site of the University of Illinois Chicago Circle campus. It never has been determined whether the lamp was kicked over by cow O'Leary or by Mrs. O'Leary, but it is known that the blaze leveled 2,214 acres (two thirds of the buildings in the city), with a resulting loss of $190,526,500,[1] of which $100,225,780 was covered by 202 fire insurers. Of these 202 insurers 68 went bankrupt, 83 settled in part, and only 51 paid their claims in full. The result of the fire, besides the usual spurt in insurance sales, was a strengthening of state laws regarding the solvency of fire insurers.

Early in the morning of April 18, 1906, the San Francisco earthquake occurred. Fire was as great a destructive force as the earthquake. As the charters granted by most states did not permit fire insurers to write earthquake insurance, most of the fire policies contained a provision that fire affecting property damaged by earthquake would not be covered. This provision complicated loss adjustment. Many buildings clearly undamaged by the earthquake were destroyed by the fire that followed. In other cases, it was impossible to tell whether the damage was a fire or an earthquake loss.

Professor Whitney of the University of California estimates that of 108 insurers involved, 27 paid their claims in full, and only 18 paid less than 75 percent of their total claims. Five insurers went into receiv-

---

[1] On the occasion of the 80th anniversary of the fire, a former neighbor of the O'Learys said that the cow kicked over the lamp in anger at being milked twice in one night because of a late-evening desire of the O'Learys to have oyster stew. By the 100th anniversary, the Chicago Historical Society had firmly decided that a drunken neighbor and not the cow was responsible for starting the fire. No doubt the cow story will persist, however, for as a Chicago teacher commented, "the children find it so interesting."

ership, but made some settlement with policyowners; and four European companies paid nothing, as the fire was caused by earthquake and such fires were excluded by their policies. By paying more than $225 million in insurance benefits, the fire insurance business met its test well.

In 1909 Kansas enacted a law which gave the insurance commissioner power over rates charged by fire insurers. Until that time, state legislatures had been content to pass anticompact laws designed to prevent collusion by insurers in setting rates, and valued policy laws requiring the insurer to pay the face amount of the policy in cases of total loss to buildings, thus ignoring the principle of indemnity. Impetus to passage of such bills was the widespread belief that fire insurers were earning excess profits. Following the San Francisco fire, fire insurance rates were boosted considerably throughout the country, thus giving rise to further speculation as to the profits and practices of fire insurers.

The Merritt Committee

In 1910 a joint committee of the New York Senate and Assembly chaired by Senator Merritt was appointed to "investigate corrupt practices in connection with legislation, and the affairs of insurance companies, other than those doing life insurance business." After two and a half months of public hearings, the committee reported its findings covering 14 points. The principal recommendations were elimination of valued policy forms, prevention of rebates, licensing of agents, permission to use coinsurance in rate structures, emphasis on fire prevention by creating a state fire marshal and enacting a comprehensive building code, disclosure of the conflagration hazard to which an insurer is exposed, and improved statistics for nationwide classification of loss experience to enhance the degree of rate equity. An important recommendation dealt with rating. The report stated that

> Your committee believes that it would be most unfortunate for the public if a condition of open competition in rates were forced by the State. The safe policy to follow in treating this subject is to recognize the good which flows from combinations well regulated; to permit the companies to use rating associations and bureaus to develop the principle of schedule rating and to spread the cost of determining proper rates among the companies and to permit them to agree to maintain those rates.

The law enacted as a result of the work of the Merritt Committee served as models for the legislatures of other states. While rates are regulated by the states (see Chapters 27 and 28), the current trend is away from the Merritt Committee recommendation and toward open competition in rating, subject to the basic regulatory rules that rates be adequate, not excessive, and not unfairly discriminatory. Prior to the Merritt Committee's deliberations, states had begun to prescribe the exact wording of fire insurance contracts. The committee considered the then existing New York standard fire insurance policy and recommended no change.

The Standard Fire Insurance Policy

In 1873 Massachusetts prescribed the first standard fire policy, which became known as the New England standard form. In 1887 the legislature of New York required the use of the first New York standard fire policy, which underwent modification in 1918. Today, the 1943 New York standard fire policy (SFP) is used verbatim in 35 states and with minor variations in the rest. As noted in Chapter 7, the SFP is not included in the readable HO policies, although many of its provisions are included. The SFP is still widely used in insuring buildings and contents that do not qualify for the HO program (e.g., commercial exposures). However, readable commercial policies have been developed which include many of the provisions of the SFP but not the actual form. (The Business owners program is an example; see chapter 15.)

The 1943 New York standard policy consists of a document on the front of which is the insuring agreement along with space for listing the name of the insured and mortgagee (if any), the perils covered, the amount of insurance, rate and premium for each coverage, applicable coinsurance percentages, and a description and location of the property covered. Stipulations and conditions are on page 2, and, as these occupy 165 lines, this policy is called the "165-line form." Included are lists of uninsurable property and of property insured only if specifically named in the policy, perils not included in the coverage, conditions that suspend coverage or restrict recovery in the event of loss, provisions for policy cancellation, and the procedure to be followed if a loss occurs. Page 3 is left blank for attaching one or more additional forms. Although the standard fire policy is the starting point in all fire insurance coverages, the document is not complete. *At least one additional form must be attached to have a valid policy.* In the following discussion, primary emphasis is given to forms for business property, as personal coverages were emphasized in Chapters 8 through 11.

Forms used with the standard fire policy are classified into three groups: (1) forms that describe the property and locations covered, (2) forms that cover additional perils, and (3) forms that cover additional losses. Fire insurers also offer a variety of coverages known as "allied lines" which are sold as separate policies.

Analysis of the standard fire policy

Even though the SFP is not a complete contract by itself, its insuring agreement and 165 lines of stipulations and conditions can be analyzed according to the methods discussed in Chapters 7 through 10.

Perils.   The SFP provides coverage for the perils of fire and lightning. Removal coverage is included which protects property that has been removed from premises endangered by the perils insured against. Removal coverage generally is considered all risk (with no exclusions) and is granted for five days following the removal. Coverage is not provided for loss by theft, or loss occurring as a result of explosion or riot, unless fire ensues, and in that event for loss by fire only.

Property. The SFP does not define the property covered under the contract. At least one additional form defining the covered property must be added to the SFP in order to complete the contract. The SFP does list items that are not covered: accounts, bills, currency, deeds, evidences of debt, and money or securities. Bullion and manuscripts can be covered if they are specifically named in the policy declarations.

Losses. The SFP provides coverage for direct losses only. Specifically excluded are losses caused by "any increased cost of repair or reconstruction by reason of any ordinance or law regulating construction or repair, and without compensation for loss resulting from interruption of business or manufacture." As shown later, forms can be added to the SFP providing coverage for these and other excluded losses.

Persons. The SFP covers named insureds and their legal representatives. An example of a legal representative would be the executor of a deceased named insured.

Location. The SFP covers property only while located or contained as described in the declarations. Therefore, an accurate description of the insured property is essential. Inland marine forms are available to cover mobile property (see Chapter 12).

Time. Coverage begins under the SFP at 12:01 A.M. standard time at the location of the property involved on the inception date and ends at 12:01 A.M. standard time at the location of the property involved on the expiration date.

Hazards. The SFP does not cover losses caused, directly or indirectly by:

> (a) enemy attack by armed forces, including action taken by military, naval or air forces in resisting an actual or an immediately impending enemy attack; (b) invasion; (c) insurrection; (d) rebellion; (e) revolution; (f) civil war; (g) usurped power; (h) order of any civil authority except acts of destruction at the time of and for the purpose of preventing the spread of fire, provided that such fire did not originate from any of the perils excluded by this policy; (i) neglect of the insured to use all reasonable means to save and preserve the property at and after a loss, or when the property is endangered by fire in neighboring premises.

The SFP does not provide coverage for loss occurring:

> (a) while the hazard is increased by any means within the control or knowledge of the insured; or (b) while a described building, whether intended for occupancy by owner or tenant, is vacant or unoccupied beyond a period of 60 consecutive days.

The balance of the SFP deals with the conditions of the contract. As the HO forms include many of the provisions of the SFP, the analysis of the HO in Chapters 7 through 10 provides a comprehensive discussion of most of the conditions found in the SFP. The reader is referred to these chapters for a discussion of contract conditions dealing with cancellation, mortgage clause, pro rata liability, requirements in case of loss, appraisal, settlement options, abandonment, suit against insurer, and subrogation.

Forms Describing the Nature and Location of Property

Forms that describe the physical nature of the property vary with the type of property insured.

General property form

The general property form (GPF) is a standard form for insuring commercial buildings and contents.[2] The form is widely used because of its versatility. The standard fire policy with this form attached can be analyzed according to the methods discussed in Chapters 7 through 10.

Perils.   The perils covered are those listed in the standard fire policy: fire, lightning, and property removal from premises endangered by those perils. (Note that the coverage for removal is generally considered to include all risks of physical loss.) Use of the extended coverage endorsement and the vandalism or malicious mischief endorsement,[3] both of which are incorporated in the form, add other perils.

Property.   Section I of the GPF describes the covered property; Section II describes property not covered by the form. This form may be used to cover buildings, personal property of the insured, and personal property of others. The building coverage includes not only the building and attached additions and extensions but also machinery and equipment that are permanent parts of the building and are used in its service. In addition, nonpermanent personal property used for the maintenance or service of the building (e.g., fire extinguishing apparatus, outdoor furniture, floor coverings, refrigeration, and ventilating equipment) is covered.

Specifically excluded are: property covered by other insurance, wind and hail damage to radio or television equipment on the outside of the building, outdoor signs unless described on the first page of the policy

---

[2] The general property form was developed to replace the building and contents form in an effort to achieve territorial uniformity.

[3] Both of these endorsements are discussed later in this chapter.

or by endorsement and, if co-insurance is used, such items as excavations, foundations, and architect's fees.

The insurance for personal property of the insured covers business personal property owned by the named insured and usual to the occupancy of the named insured. Included as personal property of the insured are manuscripts, furniture, fixtures, equipment, and supplies not otherwise covered under the policy. Coverage also is provided in (or within 100 feet of) the described building for the named insured's interest in personal property owned by others to the extent of the value of labor, materials, and charges furnished, performed, or incurred by the named insured. Tenants' improvements and betterments—"the named insured's use interest in fixtures, alterations, installations or additions comprising a part of the buildings occupied but not owned by the named insured and made or acquired at the expense of the named insured exclusive of rent paid by the named insured, but which are not legally subject to removal by the named insured"—are also covered under this form. An example would be a new lighting fixture installed by the lessee of a pizza parlor.[4] Motor vehicles and trailers licensed for use on public highways (unless specifically described in the policy), aircraft, and lawns are not covered under this form.

The insurance for personal property of the insured is extended to cover personal property belonging to others in the care, custody, or control of the named insured while in or within 100 feet of the described premises. The named insured may apply at each location up to 2 percent, but not exceeding $2,000, of the amount applicable for personal property of the insured as an additional amount. The policy provides elective coverage for higher amounts.

Other extensions cover property temporarily removed from the premises for purposes of cleaning, repairing, reconstruction, or restoration; newly acquired property up to 30 days; personal effects belonging to the named insured, officers, partners, or employees; valuable papers and records; and outdoor trees, shrubs, and plants. Each of these extensions of coverage is subject to limitations and exclusions found immediately in the section that describes coverage extensions as well as any exclusions described elsewhere. Note that these extensions (with the exception of personal property of others) do not provide for additional amounts of insurance. In addition, the extensions of coverage apply only when coinsurance is issued.

The insured must be aware of the property covered, not only to ascertain if gaps and overlaps are present in the insurance but also to determine if an adequate amount of insurance is bought to escape a coinsurance deficiency.

Losses. The basic firm policy with the general property form covers primarily direct loss. However, one type of extra-expense coverage is

---

[4] Although tenants no longer own fixtures attached to a rental building, they do retain an interest in them, and this interest, called usufruct interest, is insurable. If the landlord has agreed to assume the responsibility for replacing fixtures in the event they are damaged, the landlord is exposed to the loss and is the one to purchase the insurance.

provided. At no additional charge the general property form includes debris removal coverage to pay the cost of hauling away the debris of covered property damaged by fire or any other insured peril. The total liability for both loss to property and debris removal expense shall not exceed the amount of insurance applicable to the covered property.

Persons. The GPF covers the named insured, legal representatives and the mortgagee, if any. Limited coverage is available for property of others in the insured's care, custody, or control and for personal effects belonging to the named insured, officers, partners, or employees thereof. Assignment of the policy is not valid, except with written consent of the insurer.

Locations. In general, coverage applies only to property at the building specified in the policy, or while located within 100 feet of the building in the open or in vehicles. If the premises are threatened by any insured peril, contents are covered for five days while temporarily moved for safekeeping.

Time. Coverage runs from 12:01 A.M. standard time on the day coverage becomes effective until 12:01 A.M. standard time on the day the policy expires. Standard time is the time at the location of the property. The insurer can cancel the policy upon 5 days' written notice to the insured and 10 days' written notice to the mortgagee. The insured can cancel the policy immediately upon notice to the insurer.

Hazards. No special conditions suspending coverage are added by the GPF, so only the basic clauses of the standard fire policy apply. Unless permission is granted by the insurer, coverage is suspended while the hazard is increased by any means within the control or knowledge of the insured or while the building is vacant or unoccupied beyond a period of 60 consecutive days. The insured is automatically granted permission to use the premises in any way required by the business, even though it increases the hazard. Thus, a manufacturer may try a new process that might be more hazardous without the suspension of the policy. Consent also is given automatically for alterations, repairs, and additions to the building. Specific authorization is needed for alterations and repairs if the building is protected by automatic sprinklers.

Amount. The standard fire policy with the GPF is subject to the usual amount limitations: actual cash value, insurable interest, policy face, coinsurance, other insurance, special limits on particular property, and the extended coverage apportionment clause. Liability for loss to books of account, drawings, card index systems, and other records is limited to the cost of the blank material and the actual cost of copying the records. However, the insured may apply up to $500 toward the cost of research involved in reproducing, restoring, or replacing the damaged records.

The liability for loss under the improvement and betterments coverage depends on whether or not the damaged improvements and better-ments are replaced and who replaces them. If the insured replaces them within a reasonable time after the loss, the liability is the actual cash value of these damaged items. If the landlord replaces them, the insurer has no liability. If they are not replaced, the insured may collect the value of the unused investment in them. This value is measured by the proportion of the original cost that the unexpired term of the lease bears to the remaining period of the lease when the improvements were made. For example, assume the original investment in the damaged improvements was $1,000 and this investment was made when 20 years remained under the lease. If the damage occurred when the lease had an unexpired term of 15 years, the liability of the insurer would be 15/20 or $750. Under the GPF, losses incurred shall not reduce the amount of the insurance.

Multiple-location and reporting forms

The standard fire policy with the GPF is used to cover specified goods in specified locations. Under this form, a chain store, for example, want-ing full coverage for its many retail outlets through the use of specific insurance, would be forced to buy for each store unit an amount of insurance equal to the maximum value of goods expected in any one store. This approach would require a greater amount of total insurance than the average amount of exposure would justify. Multiple-location policies were developed for these insureds.

Fire insurers began handling multiple-location properties by writing separate policies on each location then combining the coverage in one master policy. These policies were called general cover contracts. The procedure was complicated because the locations often were in several states, each having its own rules and rates. The difficulty was removed by the formation of the Interstate Underwriters Board to compute rates on interstate business and facilitate the writing of blanket coverage that sets no fixed limits per location. The board was superseded by the Fire Insurance Research and Actuarial Association. This organization did not publish a rate manual. Instead, it operated a clearinghouse for rating information relating to multiple-location insurance. The association's functions were eventually merged with those of the Insurance Services Office (ISO) thus combining the clearinghouse operation with the rating functions of the ISO.

With the multiple-location forms came the development of reporting forms, a system of varying the premium collected with the amounts at risk during a given period (usually monthly). Under monthly reporting forms, the insured submits a report stating the values that have been at risk.

Provided the insured reports the values correctly and promptly and maintains a limit of insurance sufficient to cover the highest value possi-ble at any time, the insured will be fully protected at all times and will pay a premium based on the values actually at risk. As several different multiple-location and reporting forms exist, one is probably available which closely corresponds to the needs of the insured. The forms may vary in terms of eligible property, reporting procedures, and minimum premiums.

Multiple-location reporting forms.   When covered under a multiple-location reporting form, the insured estimates the largest amount of insurance required at each specific location. The sum of these limits is the maximum liability of the insurer. The limit of insurance established at each location is the maximum the insurer will pay under the policy for losses at any one location. At the policy's inception, the insured pays a deposit premium based on the estimated exposure. The deposit premium is adjusted when the policy expires to reflect the values actually at risk as shown by the monthly report.

If the insured underreports the value at risk at a location, and a loss occurs at that location, the insured will be penalized through the "honesty clause" which limits payment of any loss to no more than the percentage the reported value bears to the actual value.

Multiple-location nonreporting form.   A multiple-location nonreporting form is useful when the values at the various locations do not fluctuate to the point where the task of making monthly reports seems either necessary or worthwhile. As an average rate (and possibly rate credits) is used in calculating the premium, a multiple-location nonreporting form may be more advantageous than specific or blanket coverage. This form is used when the amount of the property varies among the various locations owned by the insured, but the total value of the property remains reasonably constant. A firm operating a chain of clothing stores at New Jersey and Florida resort areas might be a customer for this form. The owner may be able to calculate accurately the value of the stock the stores will have throughout the year, but the location of this stock would vary. During the summer, the principal value will be in the New Jersey stores; during the winter, the principal value will be in Florida. The value of the stock, however, will remain nearly constant.

Single-location reporting form.   A reporting form is available for a business with one location but whose stock values fluctuate considerably over the year. A customer for this coverage is a department store that will have higher than average inventories before Christmas and Easter, and lower than average inventories after these peak seasons.

The dwelling buildings and contents form

The problem of selecting the policy to be used in insuring a dwelling or personal property once was simple: only one form was available, the dwellings buildings and contents (DB&C) form. But now the buyer is confronted with a host of broad forms and multiple line contracts. In Chapters 7 through 10 Homeowners policies are discussed in detail.

In many states a modified DB&C form is available for use in insuring farm properties. The farm form differs from the urban form in that space is provided to specify coverage on items usually found only on farms: farm machinery, family provisions in the smokehouse, farm animals, and grain, hay, and silage stored on the premises. That form also contains a number of terms and conditions pertinent to the nature of the rural risk.

The basic DB&C form can be analyzed according to the method discussed earlier in this text. In studying this section the readers should refer to the form used in their locale as some variation is found in the exact wording of the form among territories.

Perils. The perils covered are those of the SFP: fire, lightning, and removal of property from premises endangered by those perils, plus inherent explosion. The addition of the extended coverage endorsement and the vandalism or malicious mischief endorsement add other perils.

Property. Under the dwelling section the following property is covered: (1) the described dwelling; (2) if owned by the insured, building equipment and fixtures, and outdoor equipment pertaining to the service of the premises; (3) materials and supplies on premises or adjacent thereto, used to make alterations, additions, or repairs to the building, and (4) private structures for use with the dwelling and located on the premises. Excluded are: (1) trees, shrubs, plants, and lawns; (2) structures on the premises used for mercantile, manufacturing, or farming purposes; and (3) structures (except those used principally for private garage purposes) rented or leased to other than a tenant of the dwelling.

To define the contents covered, property exclusions in both the standard policy and the DB&C form must be studied. Excluded on lines 7 through 10 of the standard policy are accounts, bills, currency, deeds, evidences of debt, money or securities and, unless specifically insured, bullion or manuscripts. In the DB&C form, excluded are aircraft, motor vehicles other than motorized equipment used for maintenance of the premises, boats (other than rowboats and canoes), animals, birds, and fish. Improvements, alterations, or additions to the described building and to private structures appertaining to the dwelling are covered if the insured is a tenant, paid for the alterations, and has an insurable interest in them.

Losses. The standard fire policy covers property only for direct loss or damage. It does not provide indemnity for any additional cost of rebuilding arising from an ordinance or law regulating construction or repair. The DB&C form adds, as additional coverage, protection for loss of rental value while the building is untenantable. Thus, if a fire destroys the residence, the insured may collect for the loss of its use until the dwelling is rebuilt. The form also covers expenses incurred in the removal of debris of property covered following loss caused by an insured peril, without an increase in policy limits.

Persons.   The DB&C form covers the household and personal property of the named insured and family members of the same household as well as property for which the insured may be liable. Also covered, at the option of the insured, is personal property of guests and servants while such property is on the described premises.

Locations.   The standard fire policy covers the insured *real* property only while located as described in the policy. The DB&C form, however, grants limited off-premises coverage, allowing the insured to apply up to 10 percent of the contents insurance to cover personal property away from the premises. This coverage protects property belonging to the insured or any family member living with the insured while that property is away from the premises but in the United States or Canada. This off-premises extension does not apply to rowboats or canoes.

Time.   The standard fire policy provides that the coverage extends until 12:01 A.M. standard time on the day of expiration at the location of the property.

Conditions suspending coverage.   Although the standard fire policy contains those conditions previously discussed, the DB&C form has a "permission granted clause" that effectively eliminates three of the conditions suspending coverage. Permission is given for use of the premises as is usual to the operation of the house as a dwelling; for the insured to make alterations, additions, and repairs; and for the premises to be vacant or unoccupied without a time limit.

Forms Extending the Standard Form to Cover Additional Perils

The standard fire policy covers "direct loss by fire, lightning and by removal from premises endangered by the perils insured against." Fire insurers, however, offer protection against a number of perils. For protection against these additional perils, one or more forms must be attached to the standard fire policy.

Extended coverage endorsement

The extended coverage endorsement (EC) provides coverage against each of the following perils: windstorm, hail, explosion, riot and civil commotion, damage by aircraft or by vehicle, and smoke damage. When written on policies covering dwellings, a $100 deductible is used in most states. In some of these states the deductible is mandatory; in others it is optional.

The insured pays a lower rate for coverage against these perils if they are included in a single form than if the protection against each of them is bought separately. In many places the cost of the extended coverage package is only slightly more than the cost of windstorm insurance alone, as less expense is involved in writing coverage against several perils in one policy than in separate policies. Loss by certain of the perils (smoke damage, for example, as defined in the endorsement) often is remote and the apportionment clause discussed in Chapter 9 requires higher amounts of insurance to value than many insureds would buy otherwise.

The EC form has the advantage of removing many points where disagreement could arise following a loss. Suppose that a building is covered by fire insurance only. If an explosion occurs first, followed by fire, the difficulty is determining the damage caused by explosion (which is not covered) and that caused by fire (which is covered). Suppose that both fire and explosion are covered, but the explosion occurs during a riot. Disagreement might arise concerning which damage was caused by riot and which by explosion. By insuring these seven perils under one form, points of disagreement are minimized. EC is bought so often by insureds that it is printed as part of the usual GPF and the DB&C form. The protection is not extended unless a specific premium is paid. Extended coverage perils are as follows.

Windstorm. Coverage against windstorm including cyclones and tornadoes insures against direct damage caused by these perils but does not cover loss caused by snow, frost, dust, or rain, unless these elements enter through an opening made in the building by hail or windstorm. In some states, a deductible of $50, $100, or a prearranged percentage is applied against all windstorm losses, and in many states outside television and radio antennas are excluded unless specifically listed. Variations exist among the forms used in the various states and center principally on the property excluded.

Hail. Hail coverage contains restrictions similar to those in windstorm protection. Damage by water, snow, and other elements is not covered unless it results directly from entry by hail into the building. Damage to the building or contents resulting from hail breaking through the roof or through a window is covered. In some states, the windstorm deductible applies to covered hail damage.

Explosion. Explosion coverage insures against damage from explosions occurring either away from or on the premises. It includes direct loss resulting from the explosion of accumulated gases or unconsumed fuel within the firebox of any fired vessel or within the flues or passages conducting the gases. Damage caused by explosion in steam pipes, steam turbines, or flywheels, if they are owned, leased, or operated under the control of the insured is excluded. Thus, if a neighbor's steam boiler explodes and damages the insured's property, the loss is covered. Even if a steam boiler located in the same building explodes, the insured is covered if it is owned or operated by someone else. Concussion *not* caused by explosion is not covered, thus eliminating coverage for window breakage by thunder or "sonic boom."

Riot and civil commotion.   Riot and civil commotion coverage provides for payment for direct physical damage to property resulting from pillage and looting occurring at the scene of a riot, or riot attending a strike. In the absence of riot, damage caused by sit-down strikers (but not by other strikers) is covered. The protection may be broadened, by the vandalism and malicious mischief endorsement, to include damage by stealth (theft) or by a number of persons insufficient to qualify as a riot.

Aircraft damage.   Aircraft damage protects against direct physical loss caused by the actual contact of any kind of aircraft, or by objects falling from aircraft.

Vehicle damage.   The endorsement covers damage by any vehicle other than aircraft. Not covered is damage by a vehicle owned or operated by the insured or by a tenant occupying the premises. Generally, the coverage is restricted to damage caused by actual physical contact of the vehicle with the insured property or with the building containing the insured property. Damage to fences, driveways, walks, trees, shrubs, plants, and lawns is excluded.

Smoke damage.   The smoke damage coverage is limited to losses caused by "sudden and accidental damage from smoke, other than smoke from agricultural smudging or industrial operations." (Note that the basic DB&C form limits smoke damage coverage to "smoke due to a sudden, unusual and faulty operation of any heating or cooking unit, only when such unit is connected to a chimney by a smoke pipe or vent pipe but not smoke from fireplaces.") The word "sudden" excludes damage done over a long period of time; for example, by oil burners that may deposit a film of smudge throughout the premises.

General exclusions.   The endorsement contains three general exclusions: war and related hazards, nuclear hazards, and water losses. The *war risk exclusion clause* provides that the insurer is not liable for loss caused directly or indirectly by hostile or warlike action by any government; or by military, naval, or air forces or by an agent of such government. In addition, the insurer shall not be liable for loss caused directly or indirectly by insurrection, rebellion, revolution, civil war, or action taken by governmental authority in hindering, combating, or defending against these occurrences. The clause states that "any discharge, explosion, or use of any weapon of war employing atomic fission or radioactive force shall be conclusively presumed to be such a hostile or warlike action." Under this clause insurers intend that sneak attacks, such as that at Pearl Harbor in 1941, will be regarded as "war" whether declared or not, and that damage from acts committed by agents of foreign powers is not covered.

The *nuclear clause* excludes loss by nuclear reaction, radiation, or radioactive contamination, whether the loss is direct or indirect, proximate, or remote, caused in whole or in part or contributed to or aggravated by the extended coverage perils.

The *water exclusion clause* excludes losses caused by, resulting from, contributed to, or aggravated by overflow of bodies of water, flood, surface water, tidal water or tidal waves, water which backs up through sewers or drains, and water below the ground surface which seeps through insured property.

The purpose of these general exclusions is to relieve the insurers from liability unintended under extended coverage that was thrust on them by the courts' liberal interpretation of such terms as explosion and windstorm.

Vandalism or malicious mischief endorsement

The vandalism or malicious mischief endorsement (VMM) provides coverage against direct loss caused by willful and malicious damage to or destruction of the covered property. Specifically excluded is damage to glass (other than glass building blocks) constituting part of a building or an outdoor sign. Coverage is suspended if the property had been vacant or unoccupied beyond a period of 30 consecutive days immediately preceding the loss. This coverage is written only in conjunction with extended coverage.

Radioactive contamination assumption endorsement

Two endorsements are available to add coverage against radioactive contamination. Form A, the limited form, covers sudden and accidental radioactive contamination directly resulting from an insured peril. Form B adds radioactive contamination as an additional insured peril. Both forms cover only contamination caused by materials used or stored on the described premises. The nuclear exclusion clause commonly attached to all fire policies does not exclude fires caused by radioactivity.

Optional perils policy

A business may obtain coverage against selected additional perils through the optional perils policy. Four optional coverages are included: (1) explosion, (2) explosion and riot and civil commotion, (3) explosion, riot and civil commotion, and vandalism or malicious mischief, and (4) damage by motor vehicle or aircraft. Motor vehicle damage coverage may be written separately or with any of the other coverages; but riot coverage cannot be purchased unless combined with explosion coverage, and vandalism coverage is not available unless both explosion and riot coverage is purchased.

The optional perils contract appeals to those who want to buy less explosion insurance than fire insurance or do not care to pay the premium for the extended coverage package. By use of the optional perils policy, building owners can buy as much or as little coverage against these optional perils as they choose unrestricted by the apportionment clause discussed earlier.

The optional perils policy also may be used by those who do not buy fire insurance. Some modern buildings are so constructed that their owners believe (or hope) fire insurance is unnecessary. However, they may consider explosion insurance or insurance against damage by aircraft essential.

Additional perils coverage for dwellings

Three principal forms are used to extend the standard fire policy to cover additional perils: (1) the EC and VMM endorsements; (2) the dwelling buildings and contents, broad form; and (3) the dwelling buildings and contents, special form.

Dwelling buildings and contents, broad form. In essence, the broad form adds a number of perils to the extended coverage endorsement. The perils added include water damage from plumbing and heating systems, rupture or bursting of steam or hot-water systems, damage by vehicles owned or operated by the insured or by any tenant, damage by aircraft (actual physical contact is not required), snow and freezing, vandalism or malicious mischief, glass breakage, damage caused by objects falling from the weight of ice, damage caused by falling trees, damage to electrical appliances or wiring (except television picture tubes) caused by manufactured electricity, and structural collapse. Earthquake, the backing-up of sewers or drains, and damage by flood are excluded. The coverage may be purchased for dwelling, contents, or both. The protection for building structures is written on a replacement cost basis. Ten percent of the policy's face amount may be used as rental-value insurance, additional living-expense insurance, or a combination of the two. This extension is an addition to the face amount of insurance. Five percent of the face amount may be applied to damage to trees, shrubs, plants, or lawns subject to a $250 limit on each item.

Dwelling buildings and contents, special form. The dwelling buildings and contents special form covers against "all risks" of physical loss to the dwelling and appurtenant structures subject to exclusions or limitations. The form provides for named peril coverage on contents (the perils are the same as those found in the broad form). Ten percent of the face of the policy is added for rental value and additional living expense coverage.

The policy excludes damage to television antennas caused by wind, ice, or snow, damage to plumbing by freezing if the building is vacant—unless the insured has used "due diligence" to prevent such damage—insect damage, smoke from industrial operations, rust, rot, mechanical breakdown, earthquake, volcanic eruption, landslide, flood, tidal wave, backing-up of sewers, and war.

The policy is extended to cover property away from premises; improvements, alterations, and additions (if the insured is a tenant); and trees, shrubs, plants, and lawns. Each of these extensions is subject to its own special exclusions and limitations.

The insurance on the dwelling is written on a replacement cost basis with an 80 percent coinsurance clause, but if the insured does not rebuild, the limit is the actual cash value of the loss.

Forms Covering Additional Losses

Under the standard fire policy, fire, lightning, or another covered peril must be the proximate cause of physical damage to property for the insured to collect. Indirect loss, such as interruption of income because of fire, must be covered by a separate form attached to the standard fire policy.

Business interruption insurance

Business interruption insurance against fire and other perils covers loss of profits and those fixed charges that continue regardless of whether or not the business is operating.

Perils covered. Business interruption forms are designed to be attached to the standard fire policy with or without extended coverage. In addition to interruption losses caused by fire and other covered perils, the forms provide limited coverage for losses arising from the interruption of business when access to the premises is prohibited by civil authority as a result of an insured peril. Thus, if, as a result of a fire in the neighborhood, the fire department blocks the entrance to the insured's property, the business interruption policy will indemnify for a period up to 14 days.

Length of interruption covered. The insuring agreement states that the insurer shall be liable for the

> actual loss sustained, for not exceeding such length of time as would be required with the exercise of due diligence and dispatch, to rebuild, repair, or replace such part of the property described as covered by this policy as has been destroyed or damaged.

The insured is not forced to replace speedily nor even required to repair; but the amount of indemnity collectible is based on the length of time that would be required to do so with diligence and dispatch. The indemnity period extends for the time required to replace the stock of merchandise on its shelves. For manufacturers, time is given also to restock raw materials and goods in process.

The face amount of insurance places the upper limit on the period during which the insured can be indemnified for a shutdown. In determining the amount of business interruption coverage necessary, a business with seasonal fluctuations will require more insurance than if the business is stable throughout the year. A gasoline service station near a resort town might find most of its business limited to the few months of the peak tourist season. A loss by fire or other insured peril occurring at the beginning of the season, would eliminate the station from the market during the period of highest earning loss. An urban grocer's loss, however, would vary little regardless of when the damage occurs. The grocer, therefore, could buy a smaller proportion of insurance to the amount of yearly fixed charges and profits than could the owner of the resort gas station.

Forms. Two forms of business interruption insurance are sold: the gross earnings form and the earnings form. In *manufacturing* gross earnings are defined as the *sum* of *(a)* total net sales value of production, *(b)* total net sales of merchandise, and *(c)* other earnings derived from the operation of the business, *less* the cost of *(d)* the raw stock from which such production value is derived, *(e)* supplies consisting of materials consumed directly in the conversion of such raw stock into finished stock or in supplying the services sold by the insured, *(f)* merchandise sold, including packaging material, and *(g)* services, purchased from outsiders for resale, which do not continue under contract.

Gross earnings in *mercantile* coverage are less elaborately defined as the *sum* of *(a)* total net sales and *(b)* other earnings derived from the operation of the business, *less* the cost of *(c)* merchandise sold, including packaging materials, *(d)* materials and supplies consumed directly in services sold, and *(e)* services, purchased from outsiders for resale, which do not continue under contract.

The *gross earnings form* covers the actual loss of business earnings. The measure of loss is the reduction of gross earnings *less* charges and expenses that do not necessarily continue during the business interruption. Heat, light, and power are examples of noncontinuing expenses and therefore may be ignored in measuring the loss. Consideration is given to the continuation of normal charges and expenses (including payroll) if such continuance is necessary for the business to resume without lowering the quality of service.

A department store using the gross earnings form would insure its annual net sales less the cost of goods sold, plus charges under noncancellable contracts for advertising, legal, or other professional services. Coverage of payroll expenses is optional. When the full payroll is covered, its amount is included in the base for computing values to meet the required coinsurance percentage which ranges from 50 to 80 percent. When ordinary payroll (defined as all payroll except for officers, executives, department managers, employees under contract, and other key employees) is not covered, the amount of the annual ordinary payroll is excluded in computing the amount of insurance required under the coinsurance clause. Under these circumstances 80 percent coinsurance is required. As in other forms of insurance, the higher the required coinsurance percentage, the lower the rate will be. Typically, business interruption insurance rates are based on the 80 percent coinsurance rate for fire insurance on the building in which the business is located. (In New York, the fire insurance contents rate is the base.)

An *earnings form* of business interruption insurance is available to the operator of a small business. It is a simplified edition of the mercantile gross earnings form and usually is available only to mercantile and other nonmanufacturing businesses. Instead of a coinsurance clause it has a stipulation that no more than a stated percentage of the face amount of the policy can be used in any 30 consecutive calendar days. This percentage is chosen by the insured and can be 33⅓, 25, or 16⅔ percent. Thus, a store owner with a $40,000 earnings form and a 25 percent limit could collect no more than $10,000 over a 30-day period for loss of gross earnings. The cost of coverage under the earnings form, although usually related to the fire insurance rates for the building, is considerably higher than under other forms of business interruption coverage. The earnings form is available as an endorsement to the Special Multi-Peril policy program discussed in Chapter 15.

Selection of forms. The earnings form is used only by insureds whose operations are small. The higher rate on the earnings form does not deter its use if the amount of insurance is small, especially because the coverage is written without a coinsurance clause.

A major decision in buying business interruption insurance is whether or not to cover the payroll. For example, if the operation is large and the payroll small, it may prove cheaper to cover ordinary payroll and take advantage of the option of insuring only 50 percent rather than 80 percent of gross earnings.

If enough insurance is purchased to satisfy the 50 percent coinsurance requirement, the insurance will provide in full for cessation of operations for at least six months. If a partial shutdown can be substituted for a total cessation of operations, the insurance proceeds can be spread over a longer period of time. Generally, 50 percent coverage is sufficient for even severe business interruption losses, so the success of the gross earnings form with 50 percent coinsurance is understandable. If a long delay is expected, under the gross earnings plan the insured can reduce the payroll and use the insurance to protect profits beyond the six-month period. Assume that a business has current annual gross earnings of $600,000, of which $300,000 represents payroll. Under the 50 percent coinsurance form, the insured must buy at least $300,000 of insurance. This amount is sufficient to reimburse the insured in full for a total loss of gross earnings if the business is closed for six months. If the insured can eliminate the payroll, the insurance will protect against loss of the nonpayroll portion of gross earnings for a year.

For measuring compliance with the coinsurance clause, the policy states that in determining gross earnings, consideration shall be given to the experience of the business before the date of damage and the probable experience thereafter had no loss occurred. To assure meeting the coinsurance requirement, the insured should estimate gross earnings liberally, thus increasing the insurance bought. A premium adjustment endorsement is available under which the insured who has purchased more insurance than needed to satisfy the coinsurance requirement is refunded the excess premium subject to a minimum premium (usually $50 per policy).

Miscellaneous business interruption forms

Contingent business interruption insurance provides protection against the interruption of the insured's business through physical damage to the plant or store of another. For example, this coverage may be important to an automobile distributor whose business may suffer if the manufacturer's plant is closed as a result of damage by fire. A concern making parts for the automobile manufacturer would suffer a loss of earnings if the customer's plant burned.

A tuition form of business interruption insurance has been developed. If a school building is damaged by fire, the loss cannot be measured by the length of time required to restore the premises, because at least a semester's tuition will be lost. This form reimburses the school for loss of tuition plus board and room rents minus noncontinuing expenses. Similar forms are available for other operations, such as summer camps.

Profits and commissions form

Business interruption insurance indemnifies the insured for losses arising from the inability to conduct business because of damage by fire or other insured perils. It does not insure the manufacturer for damage to finished goods. For example, a fire occurs in Roy Anderson's factory where he manufactures Santa Claus suits. Although a guard's quick action prevents serious damage to the building or machinery, the stock of Santa Claus costumes is destroyed. It is too late for Roy to replace the stock, so he will be unable to sell any this Christmas. His standard fire policy will indemnify him for the cost of the suits, but not for the profit lost. His business interruption insurance will protect him for loss of production time he suffers until he can resume operation, but to protect prospective profit on finished goods, profits and commissions coverage is required. A manufacturer of products for a seasonal demand has a particular need for this coverage, as fire may destroy much, if not all, of the year's profits even though the factory is able to continue operations.

Often fire insurance for manufacturers includes a clause under which losses may be settled on the basis of market value instead of the usual basis of manufacturing costs. If a *market value clause* is used no need exists for profits and commissions insurance. A market value clause is of no use to the salesperson who does not own the goods. Only the profits and commissions form provides protection by insuring the commissions that will be lost if the items are destroyed by fire before they are sold.

Extra-expense form

To retain their goodwill, certain types of businesses must continue operations even though their plants are severely damaged by fire. A newspaper may have taken years to build its circulation. If fire destroys its plant, every effort will be made to continue publication, even at increased cost. To discontinue the paper with the hope of restoring circulation months later would be a dismal prospect for a newspaper owner. Extra-expense insurance will indemnify the newspaper for the added cost of continuing operations following the occurrence of an insured peril. It does not cover loss of income, profits, fixed charges, or the usual expenses of a business. Protection for these exposures is provided under the business interruption form.

Extra-expense insurance also appeals to banks, bakeries, and public utilities, all of which must continue operations, even if the cost is considerably increased. Since these types of concerns will operate regardless of extra expenses, they have no need for business interruption insurance unless some of their operations would be suspended during the period.

The extra-expense insurance rate is based on the fire insurance rate for the building and the percentage of the face amount that can be used during the first month of loss.

A form combining business interruption and extra-expense protection has been developed by the Fire Insurance Research and Actuarial Association and is available in some territories. The form is basically the gross earnings form for business interruption with extra-expense coverage as an extension. However, when this form is used, ordinary payroll expense cannot be excluded in determining the amount of the business interruption insurance necessary to satisfy the coinsurance requirement.

Additional living expense form

If a house is damaged by fire or other insured peril, the owner may have to move the family elsewhere until the house is restored. During this period, living costs probably will be much greater than normal: the family may have to live at a motel for a few weeks, children may need transportation to school, and meals in restaurants will cost more than eating at home. Additional living expense insurance provides reimbursement for necessary additional expenses. The coverage is available as a separate policy, as a form to be attached to a dwelling policy, and as a basic coverage in a Homeowners form.

Rent insurance forms

When a building is damaged by fire, someone loses the use of the premises until the building is restored. Rent insurance is available to protect the landlord if the property was rented to tenants. Rental value insurance is available to protect the owner from loss of use of owner-occupied property or to protect a tenant whose lease requires rent payments even during a period in which the property is untenable.

If loss occurs, the amount of recovery may be the value of the rent that would have been received from the entire building if it were 100 percent rented, or it may be limited to income from such portions of the property as are being used or rented at the time of the loss.

The policy may be written without a limit on the proportion of the face amount that may be paid in any one month. However, if the insured is willing to accept limitations on the proportion to be paid per month (for example, no more than one twelfth of the total face amount to be paid in any one month), the rate may be reduced. The rate charged generally is the same as that for the building because the rental value burns along with the structure.

Leasehold interest policy

If a business has a long-term lease on a property, and if the present rental value is greater than the rent agreed upon in the lease, the business has a bargain. The value of this bargain, known as a leasehold interest, is measured by the excess value between the market rate and the rate actually paid. If the lease provides for cancellation by the landlord in the event of substantial damage by fire, not only will the tenant's property be burned but also the tenant will be deprived of the profits generated by the favorable lease. The tenant can be protected against loss of the favored position through a leasehold interest policy. If Fred Wright is renting a building to operate a milk bar on a long-term lease at $1,200 a month, and if the same building would rent today for $2,400 a month, Wright will lose $1,200 a month if the building is damaged by fire and the landlord cancels the lease. If this lease has 10 years until expiration the present value of the lease is the discounted value of $1,200 a month for 9 years and 9 months (insurers pay only for losses greater than 3 months). The value of this cost advantage, using 6 percent interest as provided by underwriting rules, shows that the present value of this leasehold interest to Wright is $104,524. Leasehold interest insurance will protect Wright for this value. Rates are based both on the building fire rate and on the nature of the lease. Assuming that the difference between the market rental value of the property and its contract rent does not change (an unrealistic assumption in these days of price instability) the value of the leasehold interest will decrease monthly. The premium charged will be based on the average value for the year.

Demolition insurance

Present-day construction in urban areas is regulated by building codes established by communities. Buildings built before these codes became effective are not required to be torn down; but the laws often provide that if a fire or other peril destroys a certain proportion of their value the entire structure must be demolished. Zoning laws of cities create similar situations. When zoning laws change, many buildings will not meet the new zoning requirements. If these buildings are damaged by fire or other peril, they may have to be razed. Demolition insurance, sometimes called "insurance against contingent liability from operation of building or zoning codes," is of two broad types. Under one form the insurer will reimburse the insured for the cost of tearing down the building. Under the other, the insured will be paid the increased cost of reconstructing the building in conformity with the requirements of the building laws if the physical damage is written on a replacement cost basis and adequate amounts of insurance are bought. The coverage includes reimbursement for the undamaged portion of the building which must be destroyed. Both forms are needed to cover the exposure fully.

Consequential loss or damage

Under consequential loss or damage coverage, the insurer assumes liability for losses sustained indirectly from fire or other insured perils. Losses payable under this form are of two types: (1) damage to goods by temperature changes or changes in other physical conditions, and (2) damage to an integral part of a set, which reduces the value of the remaining part. Examples of these types of losses were given in Chapter 3. Protection against them may be provided by attaching a consequential loss form to the standard fire policy. In some policies, consequential damage coverage is included without an additional premium. For example, limited pair or set coverage is offered in the DB&C forms.

Replacement cost insurance

Replacement cost insurance provides that loss settlement in the event of damage by an insured peril will be on the basis of the cost of replacing damaged property without deduction for depreciation. Usually, the insured must rebuild or replace in order to collect an amount in excess of the actual cash value. Replacement cost insurance is included in several of the multiple line coverages discussed in Chapter 15. When replacement cost insurance is written, the coinsurance percentage is applied to the replacement cost of the property.

Allied Lines

Allied lines are types of insurance provided by separate policies rather than by forms attached to the standard fire policy. Many of these coverages are of minor importance and will be given only brief attention.

Several of them are included in the multi-peril policies discussed in Chapter 15.

Earthquake insurance

Earthquake insurance in the Far West usually is written as an endorsement on a fire contract. Elsewhere it is written as a separate earthquake and volcanic eruption policy. It is purchased extensively only on the Pacific coast, but buyers in other areas may find the coverage useful; earthquakes causing considerable property damage have been experienced in New England, New York, and parts of the Midwest. A deductible of at least 5 percent of the value of the property usually is required on the Pacific Coast form along with a minimum 70 percent coinsurance clause. Lower coinsurance percentages (50 percent) are usually required elsewhere. The Pacific Coast form has the apportionment clause used in the extended coverage endorsement, but no such clause is included in the separate policies written elsewhere. As often defined in the policy, all earthquake shocks occurring within a 72-hour period shall be deemed to be a single earthquake.

Rain insurance

Two standard forms are used for rain insurance: the basic form, written on an actual loss sustained basis, and the optional form, written on a valued basis. They may be written for periods of one or more days and for three or more consecutive hours each day. Insurance written for baseball games is an example of rain insurance. Such insurance must attach no later than three hours before the beginning of the game and terminates at the end of the fifth inning. The limit for which this policy can be written is 100 percent of the insured's share of the income from similar games in the past.

Sprinkler leakage

Sprinkler leakage insurance provides protection for direct damage caused by the discharge of fluid from (or collapse of a tank which is part of) an automatic sprinkler system. Specifically excluded are sprinkler leakage losses resulting from fire, lightning, windstorm, earthquake, blasting, explosion, rupture of steam boiler or fly wheel, and riot and civil commotion, as these losses are covered by other policies. Also excluded are sprinkler leakage losses caused by water from any source other than an automatic sprinkler system as well as losses caused by order of civil authority. Damage to the sprinkler system itself is excluded but may be covered by endorsement. Various endorsements are available which may be attached to this form to provide business interruption, extra-expense, consequential damage, and profits and commissions coverage.

Water damage

Water damage insurance covers losses arising from the accidental discharge, leakage, or overflow of water or steam from such sources as plumbing, heating, refrigerating, and air-conditioning systems. The insurance also covers losses from rain or snow which enters a building through open or defective doors, windows, ventilators, skylights, transoms, and roofs. Any damage from floods or sprinkler systems is excluded. Water damage coverage is now included in many dwellings, multi-peril, and Homeowners forms; thus, the water damage policy itself is rarely used today.

Crop hail insurance

Insurance against physical damage to growing crops caused by hail, fire, or lightning becomes effective from planting to harvest, or for most crops until some specified autumn date. The liability of the insurer usually is limited to a particular sum per acre. Various types of deductibles are used. A multi-peril crop-hail insurance policy is written by some insurers which, in addition to protection against hail, covers the perils of drought, excessive heat, flood, excessive moisture, insect infestation, livestock, plant disease, wildlife, wind, tornado, sleet, hurricane, frost, freeze, and snow. The Federal Crop Insurance Corporation writes an all-risk crop policy. Private insurers attempting to write all-risk crop insurance suffered disastrous losses, some as high as 800 percent of earned premiums. They found they could not compete with the government in the $300 million crop insurance premium market because the government's losses are subsidized by taxpayers. In an attempt to counter the government's advantage, private insurers have recommended that the following changes be implemented: (a) eliminate hail and fire insurance from FCIC coverages as these coverages are adequately provided by private companies; (b) a catastrophe reinsurance facility provided by the government through which private insurers could extend the availability of all-risk crop insurance. The recommendations were included in part in the Crop Insurance Act of 1980. While the act did establish the FCIC as the reinsurance facility sought by private insurers, it did not eliminate hail and fire coverages from the FCIC policy. These coverages are part of the multi-peril crop insurance now written by both the government and private industry. Private insurers reinsure their multi-peril coverages with the FCIC.

Differences in Conditions Insurance

Differences in conditions insurance (DIC) usually is written to supplement existing property insurance and thus reduce the chance of an uninsured loss. DIC contracts are written on an all-risk basis with an underlying layer of basic property insurance. For losses not covered by the underlying forms, a substantial deductible is charged. Although there is little similarity among available DIC policies, many of them exclude the fire and extended coverage perils, as well as vandalism, malicious mischief, and sprinkler leakage.

A DIC policy offers several advantages. A firm obtains protection against unknown perils and against perils not readily insurable separately. The contract may allow the insured to reduce insurance costs by eliminating duplicate coverages, and it can provide a multinational firm with consistent coverages worldwide by insuring the gaps which sometimes occur in contracts issued in foreign countries. Finally, the insured needing catastrophic limits for certain perils can layer a number of DIC policies to provide this protection.

Tailored Forms

In viewing the many specific forms available, the reader might think any loss exposure can be covered by a standard printed form. Yet the standard forms will not meet the needs of all insureds. Therefore, risk managers of large corporations may design their own forms to fit their needs arising from the specific nature of their exposures or the sheer size of the enterprise.

Availability of Insurance at Affordable Prices

Notwithstanding the hundreds of property insurance forms available to cover losses arising from a multitude of perils, coverage for some types of losses is largely unavailable from private insurers in the United States. Potential insureds can obtain these coverages only (if at all) from surplus lines insurers such as Lloyd's of London. The U.S. congressional view is that social justice demands that people be able to buy insurance against some perils considered uninsurable by private insurers, and that these people be offered the coverage at lower prices than offered by surplus lines insurers. Examples include floods, riots, and hurricanes in those areas particularly susceptible to loss from these perils.

Flood insurance

The owner of property safe from floods will not buy flood insurance. Those whose properties have been flooded or are so located that flooding is a certainty at some time will be greatly interested in buying the coverage. Such adverse selection hardly provides a proper underwriting basis. The attitude of insurers toward flood insurance is reflected in the statement made by the underwriting department of a large fire insurer that "while we have and will write this cover, nevertheless it is almost safe to say that ninety-nine of a hundred applications will be declined." The flood peril is covered only under some forms of inland marine policies covering all perils except those specifically excluded. Because of the unavailability of this protection, thousands of families have been left homeless, and many small businesses have been financially ruined. Periodically, following great regional disasters, efforts are made by Congress to "do something about floods." The Federal Flood Insurance Act was passed in 1956, but the funds necessary to put it into operation were not appropriated. A plan for providing flood insurance coverage finally became a reality with the passage of the National Flood Act in 1968. Basically, the plan provides flood insurance coverage to certain communities at subsidized rates for contents and structures of one- to four-family residential units and businesses. Mud slide coverage has been added to the plan, an extension of particular value to many Californians. The original legislation provides that this subsidized insurance will be made available only "if the community involved exhibits a willingness to set up and enforce standards for future control of those areas subject to flood." But at the present time, a community may participate in the program only after flood controls are actually in force. Thus, the significance of the act lies not only in its coverage of losses, but also in its contribution to loss prevention. Prior to January 1, 1978, the insurance itself was a cooperative effort between the U.S. Department of Housing and Urban Development (HUD) and the National Flood Insurers Association, a pool of private insurance companies pledging over $40 million for the first layer of flood insurance protection. The association supervised the sale of policies, premium collections, and claim payments. HUD had the responsibility for establishing rates, determining eligible areas, and approving the terms of the policy. In 1978 the partnership ended and national flood insurance is now written with the Federal Insurance Administration as the insurer. Marketing of flood insurance still is performed by licensed property insurance agents in communities enrolled in the program.

By 1983 more than 17,000 communities had become eligible for flood insurance. Two contracts are available—regular and emergency. Eligibility for the regular contract is based on the implementation of a federally approved watershed program. Businesses and homeowners in a flood-prone community can purchase temporary coverage under the emergency program while the community works toward the acceptance of its flood control plan. The current rate (1984) under the emergency program is 45 cents per $100 of insurance on dwellings and personal property and 55 cents per $100 on commercial buildings and contents. The program limits the amount of coverage to $35,000 for residential property and $10,000 for personal property. Coverage for commercial property is limited to $100,000 for buildings and a like amount on contents. These emergency plan rates reflect a federal subsidy of as much as 90 percent.

After a community has gained federal approval of its flood control program, homeowners and businesses insured under the emergency program are switched to the regular coverage. Annual rates for the regular plan vary widely depending on location, elevation, and use and occupancy. Residential rates range from 30 cents per $100 of value for the first $35,000 of insurance and 11 cents per $100 on amounts over $35,000, to $1.00 per $100 on all coverage. Premiums for business property start at 45 cents per $100 on the first $100,000 and 11 cents per $100 on the excess, and go as high as $1.50 per $100 on all coverage. Protection is limited to $185,000 per dwelling and $60,000 on personal property, and $250,000 on commercial buildings and $300,000 on business contents.

FAIR plan

For the five-year period following the Watts riot of 1965, riots and civil disorders resulted in property losses of more than $300 million. Until 1965, insurance coverage for riot losses was easily obtainable and premiums were low. Thereafter the riot insurance scene changed. Insurers began to reevaluate their practice and questioned the commercial insurability of losses arising from riots. In many instances, riots are neither predictable nor fortuitous and are catastrophic in nature. Also the problem of adverse selection is present. The persons primarily interested in the purchase of the coverage are those living in the inner cities. In fact, inner-city property owners had difficulty obtaining adequate property insurance before the Watts riots, and as riots became a way of life, the problem was amplified. Acting upon the recommendations of the Kerner Commission, President Johnson appointed the National Advisory Panel on Insurance in Riot-Affected Areas to investigate property insurance costs and availability. The panel, chaired by former Governor Hughes of New Jersey, also was asked to formulate possible solutions to property insurance availability problems. Three recommendations of the panel have been implemented. They are: (1) call upon the insurance industry to establish volunteer plans in all states to assure all property owners access to property insurance, (2) look to the states to cooperate with the industry in establishing these plans and in facilitating the insurability of urban core properties by supplementing these plans, and (3) urge the federal government to enact legislation creating a National Insurance Development Corporation (NIDC) to assist in achieving the goal of providing adequate insurance for inner cities. Through the NIDC, the state and federal governments can provide backup insurance for the contingency of large riot losses. The passage of Title II of the HUD Act of 1968 provided for recommendation 3 and also gave impetus to the implementation of the first two recommendations.

Title II, better known as the "federal riot reinsurance program," provided that insurers could buy federal riot reinsurance only in those states that had an acceptable pooling plan, as outlined in the first two recommendations. These pooling plans are known as "FAIR" (fair access to insurance requirements) plans. By 1982, FAIR plans were in operation in 26 states, the District of Columbia, and Puerto Rico. This number is lower than that attained in earlier years. The decrease is a result primarily of the increased availability of insurance in the voluntary market. The various states have different programs, but some similarities do exist. To be approved by HUD, all plans must include coverage for direct loss by fire and extended coverage (including riot). Although not required, vandalism and crime are covered in some plans. The FAIR plan in Georgia provides windstorm insurance on hurricane-exposed property along the coastline.

HUD allowed the states to determine the rates, as Congress did not wish to usurp the powers traditionally held by the states. Under HUD's provisions, a government organization was established to collect and correlate property insurance statistics on a national scale. The FAIR plans neither intended to replace normal distribution channels nor guarantee the insurability of any parcel of property. Their function is to give all property owners fair access to insurance based solely on the structural soundness of their property. Before FAIR, entire sections of a city (known as "blackout areas" or "red-line areas") were considered substandard by most, if not all, insurers and little insurance was available in these areas regardless of the condition of the specific property.

The FAIR plans provide for a method of inspecting property. A property owner, after a diligent but unsuccessful effort to obtain property insurance, may apply for insurance under the FAIR plan. A free inspection is then made and if the property is found to be structurally sound and insurable under normal underwriting standards, FAIR then provides a means for obtaining coverage. If the property is not insurable at standard rates but is insurable with a premium surcharge, coverage will be written, but these surcharges apply to all property in similar condition, regardless of neighborhood. When the property is not insurable even with the premium surcharge, an inspection report is given to the owner stating the conditions causing denial of the insurance. The property owner is given an opportunity to make improvements, and on their completion another inspection is made and the insurance granted if improvements follow the recommendations.

The overall results of the FAIR plans do not appear promising. In New York, the plan has become a dumping ground for all marginal or undesirable hazards. High-risk classifications such as bars, bowling alleys, and restaurants are forced into the plan because insurers refuse to cover them outside the plan. The losses that these properties suffer and losses resulting from properties with environmental hazards cost the pool millions of dollars in underwriting losses. This development is unfortunate and does not appear to be in the best long-run interest of insurers nor of persons for whom the FAIR plans were designed. Under the current plan in New York, rates are based on the loss experience of the group. Some rate increases have been granted and others have been requested. If the trend continues, many of those for whom the plan was designed will be unable to pay the high premiums. At least one FAIR administrator has admitted that the FAIR plan is a stop-gap and not a solution. Underwriting losses nationwide for 1982 were $62 million.

Summary

1. The fire and allied lines insurance industry in the United States has evolved in less than 200 years from a few insurers offering limited protection from fire to nearly 3,000 highly regulated companies offering protection against a number of perils in addition to fire.
2. The standard fire policy providing protection against direct loss from fire and lightning, is the starting point for much of the coverage sold by property insurers. Certain forms must be added to the standard policy to make it a complete document.
3. Among the types of forms that can be attached to the standard fire policy are those describing the nature and the location of the property. The general property form, the dwelling buildings and contents forms, and numerous multiple-location and reporting forms are among those commonly used.
4. Forms extending the standard policy to cover additional perils also can be attached to the standard fire policy. The most common of these forms is the extended coverage endorsement which provides the insured with protection from windstorm, hail, explosion, riot, and civil commotion, aircraft damage, vehicle damage, and smoke damage, in addition to the perils named in the standard fire policy. The vandalism or malicious mischief endorsement is also commonly added to the SFP. Some insureds choose the optional perils policy instead of the extended coverage endorsement. This policy allows the insured to select among four optional coverages: *(a)* explosion; *(b)* explosion and riot and civil commotion; *(c)* explosion, riot and civil commotion, and vandalism; and *(d)* damage by motor vehicle or aircraft.
5. Forms covering additional losses from fire or other perils available for attachment to the standard fire policy include business interruption, profits and commissions, rental income, leasehold interest, extra expenses, additional living expenses, and other consequential-type losses.
6. Insurance can be provided by separate policies rather than by forms attached to the standard fire policy. Coverage against earthquake, rain, sprinkler leakage, and water damage is written separately.
7. Differences in conditions insurance is written to supplement property insurance and to provide multinational firms with consistent coverages.
8. Large corporations, through their risk managers, often insure their properties by developing their own forms.
9. When private insurers cannot or will not provide certain needed insurance protection at an affordable rate, Congress has passed legislation to make such insurance available under prescribed conditions. The Department of Housing and Urban Development subsidizes flood insurance. Another approach was taken with respect to the FAIR plans which seek to provide equal access to insurance as opposed to guaranteeing the insurability of property.

Questions for Review

1. For what type of loss does the standard fire policy provide insurance? Describe two other types of losses that can result from fire.

2. Describe the property that can be covered under the general property form attached to the standard fire policy.

3. Explain the concept of the reporting form.

4. Which perils are insured against under the extended coverage endorsement? Describe the circumstances under which an insured would choose the optional perils policy rather than the extended coverage endorsement.

5. Indicate the decisions that must be made when considering the purchase of business interruption insurance. What factors are important in making each of these decisions?

6. Which types of businesses would be interested in purchasing extra-expense insurance? Why?

7. Define a leasehold interest. How is it valued for insurance purposes?

8. Why is damage from floods to property in fixed locations considered uninsurable in the absence of government subsidies?

9. Explain the nature of FAIR plans. Why were they established? What problems limit their effectiveness? Why are the number of plans declining?

10. What are improvements and betterments? Who might be interested in purchasing insurance covering them—the owner or the tenant? How are improvements and betterments valued for insurance purposes?

Questions for Discussion

1. What lessons were learned from the early practice of charging high premium taxes on out-of-state insurers? How could this problem have been solved without changing the tax structure?

2. The extended coverage endorsement includes three general exclusions: war and related hazards, nuclear hazards, and water losses. Explain the rationale behind these exclusions.

3. The sprinkler leakage policy excludes losses resulting from fire. As fire is likely to be the peril that causes water to be discharged from the sprinkler system, is the sprinkler leakage policy a poor buy?

4. What interest similar to a leasehold interest is insurable, but for which no printed form currently is available? Hint: consider the standard mortgage clause written with fire insurance policies.

5. The smoke damage coverage provided in the extended coverage endorsement does not cover smoke damage caused by an unfriendly fire in the residence. How can this omission be explained?

Ocean and inland marine insurance

A variety of coverages is written by marine insurers, and at first glance they seem to have no common factor. But virtually every marine policy embodies an element of transportation.

Two distinct branches of marine insurance are ocean and inland marine. Neither name expresses accurately the scope of its designated coverages. Ocean marine policies cover ships and cargoes on inland waters, whereas nothing in most inland marine coverages justifies the term "marine." The two branches often are referred to as "wet" and "dry" marine, respectively. These terms, although not entirely accurate either, provide a better indication of the coverages written by each branch. Ocean or wet marine is concerned primarily with waterborne commerce, whereas inland or dry marine includes land transportation and other land exposures.

Historical Development

The oldest branch of the insurance business is marine, its history linked closely with that of navigation and trade. Without marine insurance, progress in commerce and trade would have been seriously hampered.

Ocean marine insurance

If Greek shipowners wanted to send a ship to a foreign land to bring back cargo, they would finance the trip with borrowed money using the ship as collateral. The loan contract specified that if the vessel failed to return safely, the lenders would forfeit their claim. This type of agreement, known as a *bottomry* contract or bond, became common throughout the maritime countries. If the cargo was pledged as collateral, the contract was called a *respondentia* bond. In addition to the interest normally charged for a loan, the contract included a sum to compensate the lender for insuring the safety of the voyage. This amount logically was called a premium, and to this day the consideration paid for a contract of insurance is still referred to as a premium. While the additional interest rate was high, it seemed justified in view of the high chance of loss involved. To facilitate the activities of lenders and borrowers, an exchange was established in Athens. Not only were the purchase and sale of bottomry contracts made more easily, but also much information was gathered and available to interested parties.

Ocean marine insurance, as it is known today, was written as early as the 14th century. Rules governing the business evolved, and by the 15th century highly developed codes of rules were in force. In 1435 the magistrates of Barcelona promulgated rules governing marine insurance underwriting and the procedure to use in case of loss. In 1468 the Grand Council of Venice established a code of rules for conducting the business of marine insurance, which is strikingly similar to modern underwriting procedures.

Early marine policies were not written by insurance companies but by merchants who wrote marine insurance as a side line. The merchants of Lombardy, an Italian province, wrote much of the business, and the earliest policies written on English ships were in Italian. These merchants conducted their business through agents. In England, the chief location of these agents came to be known as "Lombard Street" because of the large number of Lombard merchants who had marine insurance offices there. But soon it was clear that insurance was a time-consuming business and the merchants were supplanted by full-time insurance underwriters who very early organized themselves into groups for writing insurance, spreading pertinent information and providing for mutual protection and assistance. The London coffeehouses (see Chapter 22) provided a logical meeting place where these insurers could spend a pleasant morning while conducting their business.

Developments in America. The first insurance policies sold in America were marine contracts issued through local agents of English underwriters until 1721, when a Philadelphian advertised in a local journal the opening of an "Office of Publick Insurance on Vessels, Goods and Merchandizes." Soon others followed, and by 1760 a substantial volume of marine insurance was transacted in the London Coffeehouse in Philadelphia, the American equivalent of Lloyd's, where the same type of marine information available to English underwriters abroad was found.

To meet the American challenge, English underwriters cut their rates. The Philadelphia underwriters then claimed Americans had a patriotic duty to keep their money at home and argued that claims against English insurers might not be settled for months while time-consuming negotiations took place by sea mail. One advantage American underwriters could not overcome was the English group's advantage of greater capital which permitted them to offer more insurance. This disadvantage was overcome in 1792, when the Insurance Company of North America was chartered with enough permanent capital and surplus to accept the largest risks with ease. This corporation, one of the strongest insurers today, had some of the most experienced Philadelphia underwriters among its officers and directors.

Following the establishment of marine insurers in the United States, industry changes were influenced principally by major wars. The Civil War ended the 19th-century growth of American shipping. The British shipbuilders and marine insurers at that time expanded their activities throughout the Western Hemisphere. The American merchant marine and the American marine insurance business declined with many insurers disbanding their marine departments. A period of great prosperity followed the depression of 1893. Business boomed, and the shipping industry benefited. Congress limited U.S. coastwide trade to U.S. ships. This action was a boon to domestic shipowners, shipbuilders, and American marine underwriters. Several new marine insurers were formed during this period.

This development appeared to be the beginning of a new era in American marine insurance but not to the extent anticipated. When World War I began, commerce, including the business of marine insurance, was thrown into panic. Although a few Allied ships sailed according to posted schedules, German and Austrian ships did not. Freighters of all registries stayed in port because they were unable to buy insurance. As no plan for action had been formulated, the marine insurance market was haphazard for the first few weeks. Rates varied widely among underwriters and countries. The divergence had little significance, however, as even the lowest rate was too high for most shippers. Soon business asked for government aid for those needing insurance. The result was the creation of the Bureau of War Risk Insurance. Marine coverage was available from the government when unavailable from private sources at affordable rates. The government action gave courage to private underwriters. Stability and normality of rates were restored by the end of the month before the bureau became operative. Knowledge that the German fleet was securely held in its home ports aided in restoring confidence.

With the increase in shipping, soaring values of both vessels and cargoes, and increased freight charges, the demand for insurance strained the capacity of the world market. During the war the number of insurers actively engaged in marine underwriting in New York City increased more than threefold. This increase in marine underwriting facilities proved embarrassing to the industry following the war when the industry was too large, tempting many to reduce rates below a safe minimum. The capacity remained too large until World War II when the volume of business again increased.

Inland marine insurance

Inland marine insurance is devoted to protecting objects moving, capable of being moved, or aiding in the movement of objects. These items were included under marine insurance because they were much more closely related to that branch than to fire or casualty insurance. Marine underwriters for centuries had been specialists in transportation insurance. Fire and casualty insurers were closely limited by their charters as to types of coverages they could write.

Aside from early policies on steamboat transportation, the earliest inland marine policies covered samples and personal effects of traveling salesmen. At the turn of the 20th century, the tourist baggage policy was introduced. In 1912 the Post Office Department began parcel post service, and inland marine policies were written for this transit exposure. By the 1920s the insurance of "instrumentalities of transportation" had been stretched to include the insurance of bridges and tunnels. The fire and casualty insurers began to view with alarm the rapid growth of inland marine insurance. The marine insurers, free from control by rate bureaus, could cut rates at will. The 1929 economic crash aggravated the issue. After discussions among underwriters and regulatory officials, inland marine underwriters initiated reforms.

The problem was to define inland marine insurance to clarify satisfactorily the types of coverage to be written by each branch of the property insurance business. The fire, marine, and casualty insurers through appropriate representatives formed the Joint Committee On Interpretation and Complaint to develop a definition of marine insurance, first published in 1933 and known as the "Nation-Wide Definition and Interpretation of the Insuring Powers of Marine and Transportation Underwriters." The definition was adopted into the codes of most states. Even in the few states where the definition was not adopted, nearly all insurers accepted it. Interpretation of the general statements of the definition was a function of the Joint Committee which issued interpretative bulletins from time to time. As years went by, various states decided to permit certain policies to be written by marine insurers in spite of direct prohibition by the definition. An outstanding example is the personal property floater (to be discussed later). Although specifically prohibited, this policy was permitted in each of the states adopting the definition. In 1953 the National Association of Insurance Commissioners recommended to the states a revised and broader version, now called the "Nation-Wide Marine Definition." This new version has been adopted by most states, although in some states minor exceptions are permitted. In all states where the definition has been adopted, modifications occasionally are made to reflect changes in the industry and its environment. The definition does not recognize a difference between ocean and inland marine insurance. It includes three subjects: domestic shipments, instrumentalities of transportation and communication, and property floaters covering movable property.

Ocean Marine Insurance

Although ocean marine insurance is the oldest branch of the industry, the business is not substantially different now from many years ago.

Classification of policies

Ocean marine forms may be classified as to nature of interest covered, valuation of interest, term of policy, treatment of insurable interest, and property insured.

Nature of interest covered. Ocean navigation involves four important interests: cargo, freight, hull, and liability. Often, these interests are held by different parties. Should the ship sink, the owner of the cargo will suffer loss of the shipment, and the shipowner will lose the value of the ship (hull). The insurable interest in the freight is not so obvious. The term "freight" means payment received for transportation of goods. It is equivalent to the use of the word "fare" to describe payments for transportation of people. The freight interest belongs to the person operating the vessel, who may be the owner or charterer of the ship. In addition is the ever-present liability interest. The ship may damage other ships, piers, and wharves. Passengers or crew may be injured with the owner or operator held liable. Suppose that Captain Jinks chartered a vessel from a New Orleans shipowner and contracted to move a load of cotton from New Orleans to Liverpool. The freight is payable upon delivery. The captain hires a crew, stocks the ship with supplies, loads the cotton and sails for Liverpool. The ship hits an iceberg, springs a leak and sinks. The value of the cotton is the cargo interest and is protected by a cargo policy. The vessel is protected by a hull policy. But what about the freight? The captain will lose the freight which was payable in Liverpool, as well as the store of supplies and the wages paid the crew. Freight is an insurable interest to be covered by ocean marine insurance. In arranging transportation of goods, the freight may be prepaid. Thus no separate freight interest need be insured, as freight will be included in the cargo value and will be protected by the cargo policy.

Valuation of interest. Ocean marine policies may be written on a *valued* or an *unvalued* basis. In a *valued* policy the insurer agrees in advance to pay the full face amount in the event of a total loss. In an *unvalued* policy the insurer agrees to pay only the actual cash value of the loss, with the policy limits setting the maximum. The fluctuation in the value of cargoes makes it simpler to issue cargo policies on a valued basis. The shipper expects the value of the goods to increase with location changes. Furthermore, their value during the trip will fluctuate with market values. Coverage on hulls is written on either form, whereas freight policies are written on an unvalued basis. Typically, policies bought by carriers to cover their liability for goods damaged while in their care are written on an unvalued basis.

Term of the policy. Ocean marine policies written for specified periods are called *time policies.* Policies covering one trip are called *voyage policies.* Policies without a terminating date are called *open contracts* and are effective until cancelled. The majority of cargo policies are written on open contracts. A large insurer reports that 95 percent of its cargo policies are on an open form. Some of its contracts have been in force for over 50 years. Noncargo interests usually are written as time policies.

Treatment of insurable interest. All cargo and much hull and freight insurance are written on an "interest" basis. The insured must prove the extent of the insurable interest to collect and recovery is limited by the insured's interest at the time of the loss. Conditions surrounding the underwriting of some freight and hull risks have led to the introduction of the *policy proof of interest form* (PPI) and the *full-interest admitted form* (FIA). These forms, two names for basically similar forms, often are used to insure anticipated freight. Suppose that after Captain Jinks hires the ship and supplies the crew, the ship sinks in the Mississippi while en route to pick up the cargo. Captain Jinks's loss is the cost of supplies and wages for the crew, because the contract with the cargo owner cannot be fulfilled, preventing collection of the freight. The PPI or FIA form permits the captain to be indemnified for the loss, even though unable to substantiate it by producing a contract of affreightment. Under these forms, losses are payable upon submission of proof of loss without requiring submission of proof of interest. These contracts are called "honor contracts," because the holder does not have a claim which would stand up in court. Payment depends on the insurer's honor.

Property insured. Cargo, freight, and hull may be insured on the same marine form. However, some distinct problems arise in insuring cargo and hulls that require separate discussion.

Cargo policies. Cargo policies may be written as voyage, open, or time policies. A *voyage policy* covers a single shipment. If a U.S. resident wishes to send a gift to an Irish girl, he should buy insurance for that shipment only. The *open-cargo policy* covers all shipments made over an indefinite period. The insured reports shipments to the insurer as they are made, and pays premiums monthly on the basis of actual shipments. This form, also known as a reporting form, is used for the bulk of the cargo insurance business. The policy may be cancelled either by the insurer or insured.

The floating or blanket form is written as a *time policy,* usually for one year. This coverage is similar to that of the open-cargo form, but different in the premium payment method. Under the floating form, the value of future shipments is estimated, and a premium deposit made. The insured reports shipments when made, and coverage is automatic. At the end of the period, actual shipments are compared with the estimate, and the premium deposit adjusted. Marine insurers complicate terminology by naming all reporting forms open forms. Thus, the open (floating) form must not be confused with the open (no expiration date) policy. The floating policy is an open, time policy as distinguished from an open, open policy.

Hull policies.   Hull insurance may be written either on an individual vessel or a fleet form insuring all ships of the same owner under one policy. If a shipowner has some defective ships, insurance may be bought for them more easily and less expensively under a fleet policy covering both adequate and defective ships.

Port risk only policies may be written to cover ships only while docked. If a ship is in dry dock or in port for extensive repairs, the shipowner buys this coverage as it is much cheaper than ordinary hull insurance. The insured must warrant that the vessel will be kept in port.

Total loss only forms provide indemnity only if the ship is a total loss. As most losses are partial, this coverage costs much less than regular hull insurance. This type of policy often is used by those who have difficulty buying full coverage for their vessels, because of the age of the ships or because of their high value when compared with the marine insurance market capacity.

The builder's risk policy offers protection for a ship under construction, often until delivery is made. Nearly all physical damage perils are covered except losses resulting from strikes, riots, civil commotions, and wars.

The ocean marine policy

To understand ocean marine insurance coverage, a discussion of the clauses often used in the policy is necessary.

Insuring clause.   Although many types of ocean marine insurance policies are in use, each is closely related in wording and phraseology to the policy agreed upon by Lloyd's underwriters in 1779. So carefully was the original wording adhered to that for years (perhaps centuries) marine contracts had the letters "S G" in the upper left-hand corner. No one knew what the letters meant, who put them there, or why they were there, but the practice continued until recently.[1] The Lloyd's insuring agreement, the basis for wording of U.S. contracts, reads:

> TOUCHING The adventures and perils which we the assurers are contented to bear and do take upon us in this Voyage, they are, of the Seas, Men-of-War, Fire, Enemies, Pirates, Rovers, Thieves, Jettisons, Letters of Mart and Countermart, Surprisals, Takings at Sea, Arrests, Restraints and Detainments of all Kings, Princes and People, of what Nation, Condition or Quality soever, Barratry of the Master and Mariners, and of all other like Perils, Losses and Misfortunes that have or shall come to the Hurt, Detriment or Damage of the said Goods and Merchandises and Ship, etc., or any Part thereof.

Perils of the sea include: stranding, sinking, collision, lightning, and tempestuous action of wind and waves. Fifty years ago, rats were considered perils of the sea; by statute in England and interpretation elsewhere, rats have been removed from this category. To jettison cargo is to throw it overboard to lighten the ship when it might otherwise sink. Letters of mart and countermart refer to authorizations given to people to engage in acts of war against other nations without the existence of a formal declaration of war. Barratry is the marine equivalent of embezzlement.

Clauses modifying coverage.   Clauses available to modify the basic coverage of the policy can be classified as to: peril, hazard, property, losses, or location.

Clauses affecting perils and hazards.   Two clauses cancel liability for losses caused by perils otherwise included in most current contracts. These clauses, called the *free of capture and seizure clause* (FC&S) and the *strike riots and civil commotion clause* (SR&CC) remove the underwriters' liability for claims resulting from war, strikes, riots, and civil commotion. The term "free" means that the coverage excludes these causes of loss.

A *sister ship clause* in hull policies gives the owner of many ships protection under the liability coverage if two of these ships collide. The *running-down clause* (or *collision clause*) provides liability protection for the shipowner if the vessel collides with another. This clause is necessary because the basic hull policy provides indemnity for damage only to the insured's ship. Liability is limited to claims for loss to the other ship, including loss of use, cargo, freight, and legal expenses for determining liability. The clause offers additional insurance for an amount equal to the face of the hull policy.

The *Inchmaree clause,* named for a vessel involved in court action testing basic marine policy coverage, may be attached to any policy insuring hull, cargo, or freight. It includes negligence of the captain or crew as a covered peril when it is the proximate cause of a loss.

The *free of particular average clause* relieves the insurer of liability

---

[1] Some say the letters stood for the Latin equivalent of "good luck." Perhaps the best guess is that it indicated that the form could be used to insure ship and/or goods.

for partial cargo losses. Two forms are available: American and English conditions. Under the American form, the insurer pays partial losses *caused* by the stranding, sinking, burning, or collision of the vessel with another. The English clause, due to a court decision years ago, is more favorable to the insured, providing payment for partial losses *if* the transporting vessel has been stranded, sunk, burned, or in collision during the voyage. Payment will be made even though no cause-and-effect connection exists between the damage to the ship and the damage to the cargo.

Suppose that Captain Jinks on the way to Liverpool hits shallow water while preparing to clear the harbor at New Orleans. The vessel must stay on the mud bank until high tide, when it proceeds on its way. If the cargo is covered by a policy containing an American conditions clause, the stay on the mud bank will have no effect unless the cargo is damaged. But, if the policy contains the English conditions clause, any partial losses occurring on the subsequent voyage will be borne by the insurer, as the ship has been stranded. Worldwide industry competition often forces inclusion of the English conditions.

The *explosion clause* extends coverage to include the explosion peril unless excluded by the FC&S or the SR&CC warranties. The *fumigation clause* obligates the insurer to pay for direct loss to cargo resulting from fumigation of the vessel. Marine policies also exclude *illicit or contraband* trade.

Clauses modifying property covered. Since 1748, the liability of marine underwriters for particular average losses to cargo has been modified by using the *memorandum clause* that lists many goods for which the insured must bear the loss unless damage exceeds a stated percentage of the total value. It also relieves the underwriters of liability for any loss to specified goods. A typical memorandum clause may provide no protection for loss to musical instruments or other easily damaged items. Another group such as special fibers (hemp, mats or matting material, and tobacco stems) will not be protected unless damaged by 20 percent of their value; coffee, pepper, or rice must be damaged by 10 percent to be protected. This clause prevents payments for small losses expected in the transportation of these products by ship. Uniform cargo rates, once popular, made the memorandum clause necessary to reflect different degrees of loss susceptibility. As uniform cargo rates are no longer the rule, this clause is not often used.

The *labels clause* provides that in case of damage to labels, capsules, or wrappers, the insurer is not liable for more than the cost of new labels, capsules, or wrappers and the cost of reconditioning the goods. The *machinery clause* states that if a machine is carried as cargo, the insurer is liable either for the insured value of any damaged part or, at its option, the cost (including labor and forwarding charges) of repairing or replacing the part.

Clauses affecting losses. The *protection and indemnity clause* (P&I) provides liability protection to the shipowner for damage caused by the ship to wharves, piers, and other harbor installations, damage to its cargo, and injury or illness of passengers or crew. It does not cover liability to other ships. Often this coverage is written separately.

The *delay clause* exempts the insurer from liability for loss of market, or loss, damage, or deterioration arising from delay unless assumed in writing as a part of the contract.

When the ship is clearly in danger, the captain is authorized to jettison cargo, incur extra expenses, and take other steps to save the ship. Under the doctrine of general average, all costs incurred are apportioned among the interests exposed to loss. The *general average clause* provides that these costs and any salvage charges incurred are payable by the insurer.

The *sue and labor clause* obligates the insured or the insured's representatives to take all reasonable and necessary steps to limit or reduce losses when they are imminent. The insured will be indemnified by the insurer for expenses incurred in complying with this clause.

Under the *constructive total loss clause* the insurer states the conditions under which it will be liable when the damage to or location of the ship or cargo is such that the cost to save the property would exceed its value when restored. An insured, in claiming a constructive total loss, must unconditionally abandon the insured property to the insurer. In the United States, abandonment is allowed if the estimated cost of repair exceeds 50 percent of the value of the property after repaired. Under the English rule, which has been incorporated in many American marine policies, the estimated repair cost must exceed 100 percent.

Clauses affecting locations covered. Originally, cargo coverage was limited to cargoes only while on board. Gradually, marine insurers extended coverage to insure the cargo until the shipment reached its destination. The clause extending this coverage is the *warehouse-to-warehouse clause*. The *craft clause* extends coverage to include transit by craft and lighter to and from the vessel. (A lighter is a barge used in loading and unloading ships.)

Inland Marine Insurance

The definition of marine insurance adopted by most states and discussed earlier includes three subjects eligible for coverage under inland marine forms: domestic shipments, instrumentalities of transportation and communications, and movable property covered under floater policies. With the adoption of multiple line underwriting (see Chapter 15) this latter class of property may be covered under other than inland marine forms.

Domestic shipments

Policies insuring goods in transit represent the oldest coverage sold by inland marine insurers. Such policies provide protection for nearly every type of domestic shipment. The available forms may be classified according to the mode of shipping. The annual transit form is used principally for shipments by truck, railroad, railway express, and coastwise steamers; the parcel post form, the registered mail form, and the first-class mail form are for postal shipments.

Annual transit policy.   The annual transit policy provides insurance for manufacturers and retailers on their shipments for one year. Transit policies benefit the policyowner in three ways: (1) the insured is indemnified immediately for the loss even though the transit carrier eventually may be held liable, (2) the insured is indemnified for losses in excess of the carrier's liability, and (3) the insured is protected against losses for which the carrier is not liable (e.g., acts of God). A basic transportation policy is used as a backer for this coverage. In each case, at least one of the many available endorsements must be attached to complete the policy. But unlike the standard fire policy, the transportation policy contains no insuring clause stating the perils covered. It states the face amount, name of the insured, nature of shipments to be made, duration of the coverage, and the general conditions. The endorsement must state the perils insured and the exclusions.

Perils covered by a typical endorsement to the annual transit policy are, *while on land:* fire, lightning, windstorm, rising waters, and perils of transportation such as collision, upset, and derailment. Policies covering express shipments only usually include additional perils: earthquake, landslide, and breakage, for example. Perils covered *while the shipment is waterborne* are fire and perils of the sea. The policy may be written to include theft of an entire shipping package, but pilferage (theft of part of the contents) is not covered. Certain perils are excluded: strike, riot, and civil commotion, unless endorsed; war, marring, scratching; dampening; or becoming spotted, discolored, moldy, rusted, or rotted. Leakage or breakage is not covered unless caused by one of the perils insured.

Property covered are "goods and merchandise including packages," as stated in the endorsement. Specifically excluded are accounts, bills, currency, deeds, evidences of debt, money, notes, and securities.

Persons covered are the named insureds only. When the goods are no longer at the named insured's risk, coverage ceases.

Losses covered are direct losses plus general average, salvage, and sue and labor charges. Partial loss to a package is covered only if the loss amounts to 3 percent of the value of the package. Loss due to shipping delay is not covered.

Where the policy covers is determined by the backer and the endorsement. The basic form limits the territory to the continental United States and Canada. One endorsement may limit coverage to land transit only, while another may permit Atlantic coast shipping but not river transit. Coverage attaches from shipping point to point of delivery but only while the goods are in custody of a common carrier. Exports are not covered after arrival at seaboard, and imports are not covered until the ocean marine policy ceases to cover. Mail and aircraft shipments are not covered unless otherwise provided.

The *time* of coverage is from noon standard time at the place of issuance until exactly one year later. The policy can be cancelled at any time by the insured and upon 15 days' written notice by the insurer.

The only *hazard restriction* in the backer is the "misrepresentation and fraud" clause. Hazards of illicit trade are excluded, and goods refused or returned by the receiver are not covered unless otherwise endorsed.

As for *amount* limits, the policy sets a maximum liability for any one casualty, and a maximum limit is sometimes set for losses in one location.

Most shipments are sent on a released value bill of lading, which releases the carrier from claims in excess of the value stated in the bill of lading and allows the railroad to charge less for the shipment. It is usually cheaper to ship via a released value bill of lading and buy insurance protection through a transit policy than to ship via a full-value bill of lading. Transit insurance coverage is also broader than that provided by common carriers, as common carriers ordinarily are not liable for damage caused by "acts of God" which include such perils as flood, windstorm, and lightning.

Trip transit policy. When only occasional shipments are made, a form known as the trip transit policy is used. This form is attached to the basic transportation policy to insure specified shipments made via common carriers. The covered perils and exclusions are similar to those in the annual transit policy. The trip transit form is used mostly as a personal coverage; for example, in moving household goods from one location to another by any means of public transportation. This form covers marring and scratching only if caused by fire, windstorm, or the collision or upset of the transporting vehicle, or the collapse of a bridge. Coastwise shipping is included in the coverage.

Parcel post forms. When the post office is used extensively for parcel shipments, parcel post policies may be used to cover the merchandise against all risks from the time the post office receives the parcel until delivery. Excluded from coverage are: accounts, bills, currency, deeds, evidences of debt, manuscripts, and securities; perishable merchandise except against fire, theft, pilferage, or nonarrival; war; shipments made to transients at hotels; packages bearing labels describing their contents; and packages not stating "return postage guaranteed."

Two forms of parcel post insurance are available: coupon and open. The coupon form is used by shippers who make relatively few shipments. A policy is issued, and the insured is given a book of coupons. A designated number of coupons is enclosed in each shipment to be insured. For those shipping many goods each year, the open form is more suitable. Under this form, the shipper pays the insurer a deposit premium at the beginning of the policy year then reports the value of shipments monthly or quarterly for use in premium adjustments. The open form usually has no definite term and continues until cancelled. Rates depend on the merchandise shipped and the loss experience of the shipper. These forms offer an absolute saving in cost and are more convenient to use than the government-provided parcel post insurance. No waiting in line is involved, and packages may be sent insured after regular post-office hours.

Registered mail and express forms. The registered mail and express forms are issued only to persons or firms of a fiduciary nature (banks, insurers, trustees, investment brokers, and so on). Two general types of coverage are available: trip shipment and reporting forms. Trip shipment forms cover a single shipment whereas reporting forms are available for frequent users of registered mail. The shipper may choose daily or monthly reporting, or annual premium adjustment forms. The annual value of insured registered mail shipments determines the appropriate forms: the higher the value, the more frequent the reporting.

Insureds having annual shipments under $2 million usually buy the annual premium adjustment form. All forms are sold on an open basis—good until cancelled. Broad coverage is provided. Only perils of war, weapons of war using atomic fission or radioactive force, contraband and illicit transportation, and trade are excluded. The only stipulation is that shipment be by registered mail or express. No limit is set on the value of a piece of registered mail, although the insurer requires prior notice if more than a designated number of shipments are sent to one address on a single day. The policy also limits the amount of currency to be shipped in a single package.

First-class mail floater. The first-class mail floater is written for financial and fiduciary organizations to cover shipments of negotiable and nonnegotiable securities, coupons, and other valuable papers. The broadest coverage is provided by Form A, covering all risks to incoming and outgoing shipments. Coverage is limited to $250,000 per package and $1.1 million per addressee per day. Form B, a more limited form, covers all risks to outgoing shipments only, and coverage is limited to $500 per package. The transfer agents' mail policy is a special form for trustees under bond indenture, transfer agents, registrars, and for corporations acting in these capacities for their own securities.

Instrumentalities of transportation and communication

The nationwide inland marine definition states that the following transportation and communication instrumentalities may be insured under inland marine forms:

> Bridges, tunnels and other instrumentalities of transportation and communication (excluding buildings, their furniture and furnishings, fixed contents and supplies held in storage) unless fire, tornado, sprinkler leakage, hail, explosion, earthquake, riot, and/or civil commotion are the only

hazards to be covered. Piers, wharves, docks and slips, excluding the risks of fire, tornado, sprinkler leakage, hail, explosion, earthquake, riot, and/ or civil commotion [sic]. Other aids to navigation and transportation, including dry docks and marine railways, against all risks [sic].

Official interpretation of this definition has included pipelines, radio towers, and airport floodlights, but baseball floodlights have been held ineligible for coverage.

Dry docks and marine railways are covered for all perils. Piers, wharves, and docks are insured under an inland marine form only if the perils commonly covered by fire insurers are excluded. Bridges and tunnels are covered by inland marine forms if the policy covers a peril in addition to the usual coverages written by fire insurers. So, if a bridge is insured against flood damage or collapse, it is eligible for inland marine coverage, and it may be insured against *any* peril desired. Borderline cases often arise concerning the eligibility of a risk for inland marine coverage. Questions are handled by interpretative bulletins which carry the same official weight as the original definition. Business interruption forms also are available to protect against income loss due to physical damage to the property.

Property floater policies

Property floaters often are written as forms attached to the scheduled property floater, which is similar to the basic transportation form and contains most provisions of the policy except the insuring agreements and exclusions. These latter provisions are included in the attached individual property floater forms. A few floater policies are written with the transportation policy as backer, and some are written as separate contracts. Property floater forms may be divided into two broad classes: policies for business use and policies for personal use.

Business property floaters. Floater policies which protect business interests are classified on the basis of property covered. The *salesperson's floater* protects against loss of samples carried by salespersons. Two forms are available: a limited and a broad form. The limited form provides insurance against specified perils: fire, lightning, windstorm, flood, perils of transportation, and theft while with a common carrier or in a public checkroom. The broad form provides all-risk coverage, with the following exceptions: infidelity of employees, breakage and marring (unless caused by fire or perils of transportation), war, strike, wear and tear, and unexplained shortages. Theft from an unattended automobile is excluded unless a higher premium is paid. Theft is covered only if an entire package is stolen and if it occurs while the goods are in custody of a common carrier, hotel, or motel. Because of prohibitions in the marine definition, this policy cannot provide coverage while the goods are on the premises of the insured.

The *contractors' equipment floater* is written as an endorsement to the scheduled property floater or the transportation policy to protect machinery and other equipment used by contractors against perils of fire, lightning, explosion, earthquake, flood, windstorm, theft, and perils of transportation. The coverage may be (and often is) written on an all-risk basis. A variety of forms is available, including one scheduled, one blanket, and one requiring a premium deposit adjusted monthly as the values fluctuate. Neither the policy form nor the policy rating is standardized, and each risk is individually written and rated. The *mining equipment floater* and the *oil well drilling equipment floater* are two similar coverages written to meet the specific needs of operators in these fields.

The *conditional or installment sales floater* protects firms which sell goods on the installment plan, lend or rent merchandise, or send it on approval. The goods are protected in transit or while in the custody of "business customers." The policy may be written to protect only the dealer's interest, or it may be extended, in the case of installment sales, to protect the customer's interest also.

One of the broadest commercial coverages is the *jewelers' block policy,* a forerunner of multiple line coverages. The policy protects against loss of stocks of jewelry, precious stones and metals, and dies and patterns, as well as loss to customers' jewelry if damaged while in the insured's custody. Losses occurring to stock out on approval with customers, on consignment from other jewelers, or in possession of traveling salespersons of the insured also are covered. Merchandise shipped by sealed express or registered mail is protected, and shipments by motor carrier are covered if shipment is by armored car, customer parcel delivery service, or the parcel transportation of a passenger bus.

Exclusions include war, breakage of brittle or fragile articles shipped by express or registered mail, unless caused by an unusual peril; goods sold on the installment plan; and jewelry worn by the jewelers, their families or employees. Unexplained shortages are not covered.

Coverage extends throughout the United States and Canada. Rates are determined individually: the nature of the jeweler's business, anti-burglar devices employed, type of safes used, number and type of window displays, how records are kept, the rating system used, inventory policy, loss record, number of salespersons and the territory they cover all are factors considered. Similar block policies are written for furriers and dealers in musical instruments, cameras, office machinery, household appliances, sporting goods, marine supplies, heating and air-conditioning equipment, scientific and professional instruments, and industrial machinery and tools.

The *livestock floater* provides protection against named perils that cause death or necessitate destruction of cattle, sheep, hogs, mules, or horses not used primarily for racing, show, or delivery. Perils covered include fire, lightning, windstorm, hail, explosion, earthquake, riot, collapse of bridges, flood, aircraft, and smoke. Limited transportation coverage is provided for losses caused by collision with vehicles (other than those owned or operated by the insured or a tenant) and stranding, sinking, burning, or collision of transporting vessels. The policy covers theft of livestock but not straying or mysterious disappearance. Infidelity of employees, war, and nuclear losses also are excluded.

The *physicians' and surgeons' equipment floater* covers all loss to commonly used instruments and apparatus. It may be extended to cover furniture and improvements or limited to portable equipment. The broader form covers building and equipment damage caused by attempted theft, if the insured owns the building or is legally liable for damage. Excluded are wear and tear, inherent vice, insects, vermin, damage to electrical apparatus by electricity (except by fire), war, nuclear reaction, or damage caused by remodeling or repairing the property insured (unless caused by fire or explosion). Glass breakage other than scientific instrument lenses is excluded, as is breakage, chipping, or scratching of brittle articles unless caused by actual or attempted theft, vandalism, riot, fire, lightning, windstorm, earthquake, flood, explosion, or accident to a transporting conveyance.

The *radium floater* is an all-risk policy which insures radium capsules against all damage except war and deterioration. Coinsurance of 100 percent is required. Coverage is limited to the United States and Canada. The radioactive contamination peril is excluded in marine contracts. A *radioactive contamination policy* (or form issued with the scheduled property floater) covers damage by sudden and accidental radioactive contamination from materials used or stored on the premises. Property in transit is covered under the shippers' radioactive contamination policy. Truck operators can protect their legal liability with the motor truck cargo radioactive contamination policy.

Personal floater policies. Forms are available for protecting nearly all personal property and are usually endorsements added to the *scheduled property floater.*

Unless otherwise noted, all the covers described below contain, in addition to the usual war and nuclear exclusions, clauses excluding losses caused by wear and tear, gradual deterioration, inherent vice, insects, and vermin. All are worldwide in coverage and often are available as separate policies.

The *personal articles floater* is the principal policy used to insure scheduled, valuable personal property on an all-risk basis. It incorporates the terms of the scheduled property floater.

The *bicycle floater,* attached to the scheduled property floater, provides all-risk coverage with the usual exceptions. The policy contains a $5 franchise clause, meaning that losses under $5 are not paid, but those exceeding $5 are paid in full.

One of the most interesting personal floater policies is the *wedding presents floater,* providing all-risk coverage from the time the gifts are sent until 90 days after the wedding. Presents not covered are: realty, animals, automobiles, motorcycles, aircraft, bicycles, boats, accounts, bills, deeds, evidences of debt, letters of credit, passports, documents, money, notes, securities, stamps, and tickets. The usual perils excluded are augmented by breaking, marring or scratching of fragile articles and furniture unless caused by theft, acts of nature, or conveyance upset.

The *personal effects floater* is a blanket policy covering any object usually carried by travelers. The all-risk protection is worldwide except that it does not cover at the insured's residence. Need for this policy has greatly diminished with the widespread use of Homeowners policies.

The *personal property floater* is an all-risk policy on virtually all personal property individuals have in and about their homes. The coverage on unscheduled jewelry, watches, and furs on an all-risk basis may be increased from the specified $250 limit per loss to $1,000. The $250-per-piece limit, however, remains. The basic policy provides 10 percent of the face amount as coverage on property ordinarily at secondary locations. This percentage can be increased by endorsement. Boats can be covered by endorsement against limited named perils. This floater is deluxe and expensive coverage. Many people who formerly bought this coverage are now buying one of the multiple line homeowners forms (discussed in Chapters 7 through 11).

Bailee forms

A bailee is one who has possession or custody of personal property of others. Bailees' customers' insurance is written mainly for laundries, dry cleaners, tailors, cold-storage locker operators, and fur storers to provide multi-peril protection for goods left for servicing. The customer has incomplete tort law protection, as a bailee's legal liability is limited to requiring reasonable care in handling customers' goods. Bailees are responsible only for their own negligence or that of employees. But a bailee who pays for damage to customers' goods only when legally liable is not likely to retain the public's goodwill or patronage. A bailees' customers' policy is available to reimburse the customers for loss without regard to liability.

Motor truck cargo policy. The motor truck cargo policy insures the *liability* of truck lines for damage to customers' property. A variation of the policy can be used by a shipper who uses its own trucks to carry its goods. In such cases, the policy provides property insurance coverage and not liability insurance coverage. Named perils include: fire, lightning, perils of the sea, collision, overturn, collapse of bridges, flood, explosion, and windstorm. Theft may be included, but underwriters are reluctant to write it. Exclusions are: loss of accounts, bills, currency, deeds, evidences of debt, money, notes, and securities; damage caused by the insured's failure to use all reasonable means to save the property after an insured disaster; loss from delay, wetness, dampness, or spoilage, except as a direct result of an insured peril; loss of trucks; loss caused by war, strikes, or riots; and loss of livestock, except in an accident causing death or rendering death necessary as a result of an insured peril. Insurance to a stated percentage of value is required. The policy can be endorsed to satisfy the financial responsibility requirement of the Interstate Commerce Commission (ICC). The endorsement states the insurance will cover any loss for which the insured is liable, but the trucker must reimburse the insurer for losses not otherwise covered by the policy.

Bailees' customers' form.   The bailees' customers' form provides insurance against loss of clothing in custody of the bailee. No protection exists for articles belonging to the bailee. This policy typically covers: fire, lightning, explosion, collision, theft, burglary, windstorm, hail, flood, sprinkler leakage, earthquake, strikes, and riot. Inability to identify the owner of goods as a result of any of these perils also is covered. Exclusions include damage to goods while in custody of other laundries or dry cleaners, loss to goods stored for pay, misdelivery, and unaccountable shortages. These policies are open with no termination date. Gross receipts of the business is the rate base, although little uniformity exists in rates or forms.

Furriers' customers' insurance policy.   The furriers' customers' policy protects the fur dealer from customers' claims for loss to property left for alteration, cleaning, repair, or storage. It also covers accrued storage and labor charges on lost or damaged property. The policy covers all risks except: insects, vermin, gradual deterioration, inherent vice (physical imperfection), or damage resulting from work upon the goods, war, or risks of contraband, or illegal transportation or trade. Excess insurance is available to cover liability for values over the amount declared on the customer's receipt.

Cold storage locker bailees' form.   Using the cold storage locker bailees' form, owners and operators of lockers can insure produce and meats in their care against most perils, including mechanical breakdown of the refrigerating system. This coverage requires careful underwriting, particularly regarding the possibility of breakdown of the cooling system. Two forms are available: monthly reporting forms and blanket forms. Rates are not standardized, but will depend on the type and condition of the locker to be covered, among other factors.

Yacht and motorboat insurance

At first glance, it seems that insurance on yachts and motorboats should be handled by ocean marine insurers. However, coverage is divided between ocean and inland marine insurers, with fire insurers participating in writing certain coverages. Underwriters divide private pleasure craft into two classes: yacht insurance, written on an ocean marine form, and outboard motorboat insurance, written on an inland marine form.

Yacht insurance.   Inboard boats, including sailboats with inboard auxiliary power, are insured under the yacht form, which consists of four principal divisions. *Hull insurance,* written on a valued basis, is discussed earlier in this chapter. *Protection and indemnity* insures the shipowner's legal liability for personal injury for those not making claim under the U.S. Longshorers' and Harbor Workers' Compensation Act, and also covers liability for property damage to wharves, piers, docks, and other permanent, immobile harbor installations. *Longshorers' and harbor workers' compensation* insures the liability under the federal statute. *Medical payments* coverage is similar to that in automobile insurance. Speedboats are insured similarly to yachts, but the policy excludes all loss resulting from an accident during an official race. Two speedboat operators may engage in a friendly race between themselves; the restriction applies only to officially scheduled contests. Also excluded is loss to the rudder, propeller, shaft, or machinery, unless caused by burning, stranding, sinking, or collision with another vessel.

Outboard boats and motors.   Outboard boats and motors are insured under inland marine forms. Coverage is written on one of three nonstandard forms: all-risk, broad-named perils, or limited-named perils. The all-risk form is the most popular, and exclusions are similar to those generally found in inland marine contracts. The limited form covers fire, lightning, theft of the entire motor, or boat, windstorm damage while the property is on land, and perils of transportation. Additionally the broad form insures against collision with another vessel and against perils of the sea, including loss of the motor overboard. Coverage does not apply when the property is used to carry passengers for hire, is rented, or is engaged in an official race.

Summary

1. Marine insurance is the oldest branch of insurance and has a history linked closely with navigation and trade. Greek bottomry and respondentia contracts (or bonds) were forerunners to modern ocean marine policies.
2. The development of ocean marine insurance paralleled the changes in shipping activity which took place due to various wars.
3. Inland marine insurance, a product of the 20th century, was not subject to the same rate and other regulations as fire and casualty insurers; thus, this line grew rapidly until checked by the adoption of the Nation-Wide definition of marine insurance which placed inland marine coverage into a particular scope.
4. Ocean marine insurance can be classified in many ways: nature of the interest covered (cargo, freight, hull or liability); valuation of interest (valued or unvalued); term of the contract (voyage, time, or open); treatment of insurable interest (proof of interest required or various "honor contracts"); and property insured (cargo or hull).
5. The insuring clause of most ocean marine policies is worded similarly to those written at Lloyd's many years ago. Clauses are usually added to exclude losses due to wars, strikes, riots, and civil commo-

tion, to add negligence to the list of insured perils and to modify perils, hazards, covered property, insured losses, and covered locations.

6. The three main categories of inland marine insurance are domestic shipments, instrumentalities of transportation and communication, and property floater policies.

7. Domestic shipment policies are available to fit the needs of a variety of insureds: annual transit, trip transit, motor truck cargo, and various kinds of mail shipments.

8. Instrumentalities of transportation and communication such as bridges, tunnels, piers, and wharves may be insured for direct physical damage loss as well as indirect loss of income due to physical damage.

9. Property floaters are available to cover business and personal property, but their importance is decreasing with the increase in the popularity of various multiple line packages.

10. Inland marine contracts are written to protect customers of laundries, dry cleaners, and so on against most damage to goods left in the care of the bailee.

11. Yachts are insured under ocean marine policies, while outboard boats and motors are covered by inland marine contracts.

Questions for Review

1. What is a bottomry contract? A contract of respondentia? What effect have they had on current insurance terminology?

2. How have wars influenced ocean marine insurance in the United States?

3. What is the scope of inland marine insurance?

4. Under what circumstances is it more appropriate to use a valued ocean marine contract than an unvalued one?

5. Explain the nature of the freight interest in marine insurance.

6. Distinguish an open, time policy from an open, open policy.

7. Identify: barratry, letters of mart and countermart, perils of the sea, and jettison.

8. Distinguish the free-of-particular-average, American conditions clause from the free-of-particular-average, English conditions clause in ocean marine insurance. What does the term "free" mean in ocean marine contracts? What does the term "average" mean?

9. Explain the doctrine of general average.

10. What is the function of the basic transportation policy in inland marine insurance?

11. What kinds of registered mail forms are available and when is the use of each form appropriate?

12. What is the conditional or installment sales floater?

13. Explain the purpose of the motor truck cargo policy.

14. Are pleasure boats insured under ocean marine or inland marine forms? Explain.

Questions for Discussion

1. The two branches of marine insurance are sometimes referred to as "wet" and "dry." What other terms may be more appropriate? Explain.

2. Why were the developments of trade, navigation, and ocean marine insurance so closely interrelated?

3. Is it really necessary today to have a standard definition of inland marine insurance?

4. Why do marine insurers make payments under "honor contracts" while other insurers deny claims of questionable legality made by insureds?

5. As premiums for bailees' customers' insurance are assumed to be passed on to the consumers, should not some bailees buy insurance to protect themselves only when legally liable and then charge lower prices for their services?

6. Is there any justification for insuring outboard motor boats under an inland marine policy? Explain.

7. A newly married couple sets sail from Miami on a honeymoon cruise aboard their yacht. Unobserved by anyone, however, a jealous rival bores holes in the hull. When the yacht is outside the three-mile limit it slowly sinks. The couple survives. Can they recover the value of the yacht from their marine insurer?

8. Review the list of excluded property under the wedding presents floater. Why do you believe these exclusions exist? Why is coverage provided for only 90 days following the wedding?

13

Liability insurance

The nature of the liability exposure was discussed in Chapter 4, where it was explained that the legal bases for the exposure are tort law and contractual relationships. Possible losses are cost of defense against lawsuits alleging liability and damages paid when the defense fails.

Liability Insurance Policies

As the contract between the insurer and the insured benefits a third party, liability coverages are referred to as third-party forms. (In most liability policies, rather than indemnifying the insured, the insurer pays the injured third party.) If an injury is caused intentionally or results from other criminal action, the responsible party may be subject to criminal proceedings as well as suit under civil law.[1] Criminal action settle-

---

[1] The difference between civil and criminal offenses is the difference between offenses committed against an individual and offenses committed against the state. In civil offenses the offender is not prosecuted unless prosecution is undertaken by the offended party. In criminal offenses, the offender is prosecuted by society to discourage similar conduct by other members of society. A given offense may result in both criminal and civil actions. For example, an intoxicated person driving an automobile may be guilty of a criminal offense punishable by the state. The driver also is subject to civil action by anyone suffering bodily injury, property damage, or personal injury (severe fright, for example) as a result of the drunken driving.

ment is not a liability insurer's obligation; it will not serve a jail sentence or pay a fine. The insurer's obligations are restricted to the insured's obligations under civil law. But except for bodily injuries committed intentionally by or at the direction of the insured, civil liability resulting from criminal law violation usually will be covered in liability policies. In addition to paying court awarded damages and all expenses of investigating and negotiating claims and defending suits, the insurer agrees to pay premiums on appeal bonds and bonds to release attachments, all reasonable expenses incurred by the insured at the insurer's request, and immediate medical and surgical expenses of others imperative at the time of the accident.

The liability exposures a firm faces can be grouped into three broad categories: *(a)* automobile exposure, *(b)* general liability exposure, and *(c)* employers' liability exposure. The automobile exposure is analyzed in Chapters 8 and 14. This chapter discusses both the general liability exposure and the employers' liability exposure.

General Liability Program

The general liability insurance program is similar to many fire and inland marine programs in that appropriate forms are inserted into a standard policy jacket. The policy jacket contains the common provisions, conditions, and definitions applying to all policies of the program.

The forms added to the policy jacket to complete the contract determine the general liability exposures covered by the policy. The available forms divide the general liability exposure into three broad areas:

1. Business liability.
2. Professional liability.
3. Personal liability.

Within each of these areas, various forms are available to tailor the policy further to the needs of the insured. For example, within the business liability area, available forms include owners', landlords', and tenants' (OL&T), manufacturers' and contractors' (M&C), and the comprehensive general liability (CGL). In addition, endorsements are available to cover specific hazards excluded by the foregoing forms, provide coverage beyond conventional liability limits, and to fill gaps in coverage.

The jacket of the general liability policy includes definitions and clarifications of the insurer's intent. For instance, it is specified that making or reserving the right to make inspections of the premises and operations neither constitutes a warranty as to the safety of the premises nor binds the insurer to make inspections. Territorial limits include international waters and airspace, provided the bodily injury or property damage does not occur during movement of people or goods to or from another country.

The definition of *insured* in business policies may include the corporation itself and also its directors, officers, and stockholders when performing their corporate duties.

Occurrence is currently defined as an accident, including continuous or repeated exposure to conditions, which results in bodily injury or property damage neither expected nor intended by the insured. When policies covered damage *caused by accident* rather than by occurrence, the wording produced a juridical risk. The term "accident" had different meanings for different courts, and even when the same definition was applied the courts did not always reach identical results. The use of *occurrence* was adopted to reduce the chance of disputes, but it later became necessary to broaden the original occurrence definition to avoid claim litigation involving injuries from repeated exposures to a condition. Thus, previously disputed claims, such as those involving loss due to continuous exposure to cement dust, are now paid routinely.

A number of exclusions found in the typical liability policy are similar to those discussed in Chapter 7 in connection with Part II (liability) of the Homeowners forms. The conditions of the typical liability policy contain the usual requirements concerning notice to the insurer of accidents, claims and suits, statements concerning other insurance, and rules regarding cancellation, subrogation, and assignment.

Business liability forms

One of the three forms (OL&T, M&C, CGL) is added to the general liability jacket to form the foundation of a business liability policy. Several other coverages then can be added to the basic contract to meet special needs of the insured. Some of these additional coverages would include contractual liability, owners' and contractors' protective, products, and completed operations, and personal injury liability coverage. (Some of these additional coverages are included in the CGL without the need for endorsements.)

The CGL policy provides the broadest coverage of the three business liability forms, making it the best form to use for covering the business liability exposure. While the importance of the OL&T and M&C has diminished, an analysis of these policies is instructive because of the many similarities they share with the CGL form; that is, many of the same excluded hazards. The CGL provides coverage for all hazards covered by an OL&T and an M&C, plus some hazards excluded from both these forms.

Owners', landlords', and tenants' form. The OL&T form covers the liability exposure arising from the ownership, maintenance, or use of the insured premises. It covers liability for damages to those sustaining bodily injury or property damage in and about the insured buildings and premises, and for damage sustained off the premises when arising from the insured's business operation. An example of a storeowner's off-premises liability would be a customer's injury caused by a delivery person who stumbles and drops a package on the customer's toe.

As mentioned, the OL&T, M&C, and CGL share many common exclusions to liability coverage. Although the following exclusions are discussed in relation to the OL&T form, this discussion also applies to the M&C and CGL.

Exclusions to the OL&T, M&C, and CGL.   Only limited coverage is provided for liability assumed under contract. Coverage is provided for liability assumed (1) under any easement agreement, except in connection with a railroad grade crossing, (2) under any agreement required by municipal ordinance, except in connection with work for the municipality, (3) under any lease of premises agreement, (4) under a sidetrack agreement, and (5) under an elevator maintenance agreement.

The coverage under these forms does not apply to (1) automobile or aircraft liability (although coverage does apply to the parking of an automobile on the insured's premises if the auto is not owned by or rented or loaned to any insured), (2) liability arising out of the transportation of mobile equipment or out of its use in any sort of contest, (3) off-premises watercraft liability, (4) pollution, unless its cause is sudden and accidental, (5) liability for war, (6) liability under any liquor control law, (7) bodily injury to an employee of the insured arising out of and in the cause of employment, (8) liability for property owned, occupied, or used by, or rented to, or in the care, custody, or control of the insured, (9) property damage to premises alienated (sold) by the insured, (10) loss of use of property which has not been damaged resulting from a delay in or lack of performance by the insured or from defective workmanship, (11) property damage to the insured's products arising out of a condition of the product, and (12) property damage to work performed by the insured arising out of defective materials, parts, or workmanship.

The elevator hazard which includes elevators, escalators, and hoists is included in the OL&T as well as the M&C and CGL. The coverage applies to injuries involving not only the elevator but also persons entering or leaving the elevator. Contrary to the general rule in liability policies, the elevator coverage also insures against property damage (other than to the elevator) arising from the use of the elevator at the insured premises. Otherwise the elevator's property damage liability coverage would be useless because any property in the elevator is in the insured's care, custody, or control.

Coverage for damage to elevators is property insurance and hence is not included in these three forms. But coverage for elevator collision damage is not written without property damage liability insurance. The collision insurance covers loss to the elevator and other property owned, rented, occupied, or used by the insured, resulting from collision of the elevator (or anything carried by it) with another object. Liability for damage to the elevator, elevator shaft, or loading platforms is covered. The insurer provides an inspection service designed to prevent elevator accidents. The right to inspect elevators at any time is reserved, and coverage on defective elevators may be suspended until defects are corrected.

Additional exclusions applying to OL&T. In addition to the foregoing exclusions, the OL&T further limits coverage in that it does not provide insurance for bodily injury or property damage: (1) arising out of operations on or from unspecified premises owned, rented, or controlled by the insured, (2) arising out of structural alterations which involve changing the size of or moving buildings or other structures, new construction, or demolition operations, and (3) included within the completed operations hazard or the products hazard (both to be discussed later).

As an example of (3), a department store installed wall-to-wall carpeting in a home, but the work was faulty. The rug was not securely fastened, causing a guest to trip and break a leg. The homeowner sued the store for negligence in installing the carpeting. The OL&T policy would not protect the store against the suit if the work was completed. If the guest had tripped over a roll of carpeting negligently left by the store the insurer would respond and pay the damages awarded.

Because coverage under the OL&T applies only to the insured premises (although coverage is granted for incidental operations away from the insured premises), the definition of the insured premises is important. The OL&T provides coverage at the insured's premises designated in the declarations, including the ways immediately adjoining and at alienated premises. Newly acquired premises automatically are covered if the insurer is notified within 30 days after acquisition.

Basic limits of the form are $25,000 per occurrence with a $5,000 limit for the property damage liability coverage. As with most liability policies, defense costs and immediate medical and surgical expenses at the time of the accident are paid in addition to the policy limits.

The OL&T is purchased mainly by mercantile establishments, service firms, and owners and operators of movie and other entertainment houses, hotels, office buildings, and apartments. Factors considered in rating OL&T contracts are territories and occupancies. Accidents are more frequent in some territories, and courts in some areas award higher damages than do courts elsewhere. As to occupancies, some types of businesses produce more liability claims than others and therefore are rated higher. The basis for premium calculations varies among insured classifications, but the rating factor often used is 100 square feet of area. Other bases are: admissions, frontage, receipts, and units (such as "per pupil," or "per pump"). When admissions are the exposure unit, the rate is based on each 100 persons admitted. Some classifications are based on frontage, which is the number of linear feet of the property line abutting a street or highway. Vacant land, excluding real estate development property, is an example of an exposure rated on frontage. When the base is receipts, the measure is each $100 of annual gross receipts. For some policies the rate base is the unit insured. For example, bulk gasoline operators renting pumps to service stations pay a rate based on the number of pumps rented.

The manufacturers' and contractors' form.   The OL&T form cannot be used to insure a risk whose activities embrace more than those arising out of designated premises. For example, a building contractor's liability exposure exists wherever the job site may be located, not just at the office of the contractor. Such coverage is provided by the manufacturers' and contractors' liability policy (M&C).

The M&C form is similar to the OL&T in that it shares the exclusions described above. The M&C (and OL&T) also excludes the completed operations hazard and the products hazard. The independent contractors' exclusion is unique to the M&C. Coverage is denied for:

> bodily injury or property damage arising out of operations performed for the named insured by independent contractors or acts or omissions of the named insured in connection with his general supervision of such operations, *other than* bodily injury or property damage which occurs in the course of (1) maintenance and repairs at premises owned by or rented to the named insured, or (2) structural alterations at such premises which do not involve changing the size of or moving buildings or other structures.

The independent contractors' hazard can be covered by endorsing an M&C with owners' and contractors' protective liability insurance (discussed later).

The M&C form includes coverage of new construction or demolition operations if performed by the insured's own employees. Additional exclusions unnecessary under the OL&T are property damage for blasting or explosion, collapse or structural injury to a building due to grading or excavation, and property damage to underground pipes, wires, and the like, from use of certain mechanical equipment.

Basic limits for the M&C are the same as the OL&T, except that property damage liability usually is subject to an annual aggregate limit. The rate basis for the M&C generally is payroll, but a few classifications use gross receipts. Rates vary widely.

The comprehensive general liability form.   The OL&T and M&C are inappropriate for businesses whose liability exposures demand an "all risk" treatment providing automatic coverage for all general liability exposures. The comprehensive general liability (CGL) form provides such protection in that it covers any newly acquired exposure eligible for coverage under the contract arising after the policy's inception. It is this feature—providing coverage for the "unknown hazard"—that distinguishes the CGL from the OL&T and M&C, making it the most complete business liability policy available.

In addition to encompassing all the coverage provided under the OL&T and M&C, the CGL adds coverage for the products and completed-operations liability exposure and the independent contractors' exposure. (The OL&T and M&C forms can be amended to include broader coverage for the independent contractors' exposure.) The exclusion peculiar to the CGL relates to the products recall exposure. (All three of these exposures are discussed below.)

Coverage can be added to all three forms for contractual liability and personal injury. A broad form liability endorsement extending the scope of coverage can be added to the CGL. (These forms also are discussed below.)

As noted, the CGL is uniquely different from the OL&T and M&C in that the insured is protected from unknown hazards—hazards that develop after the policy is written, and hazards unknown to the insured at the time the policy is bought. This protection offered by the CGL makes it the most important of the general liability forms.

Consider the case of a cellulose insulation manufacturer. Because of increased operating costs, the manufacturer determined it would be more profitable to discontinue the manufacture of insulation if the following operating changes were implemented:

1. Purchase insulation from another source and enter the insulation installation business.
2. Use the plant's equipment to produce worm food.

These changes were implemented but without any forewarning given the manufacturer's insurance agent. Luckily, its general liability exposure was covered by a CGL. Because the CGL covers unknown hazards that develop after the policy's inception, the insulation manufacturer turned insulation installer and worm food manufacturer had no lapse in coverage resulting from the change in exposure.

The CGL provides metered protection in that the premium is estimated in advance and determined by audit at the end of the policy year to reflect actual exposures. An additional premium is charged for coverage of the "unknown hazard." Just as in OL&T and M&C, policy limits are specified on a per occurrence basis with no breakdown in amounts applicable to any one injured person, as in auto liability insurance.

Contractual liability form. While the OL&T, M&C, and CGL cover liability assumed under certain types of incidental contracts, liability assumed under other types requires special contractual liability coverage. Every person signing a lease for equipment must read the contract to determine the liability assumed under hold harmless agreements. Contracts in which one party agrees to work for another frequently require assumption of all liability for accidents on the premises or arising from the work. Even contracts for supplying goods may contain a provision for liability assumption by the supplier. The rate basis is usually the individual agreement. With the great variety of contracts that may create a liability insurance need, the underwriter frequently must examine the contractual obligations before establishing a rate.

Owners' and contractors' protective liability insurance. Becker Brothers Better Biscuit Bakery needs to expand, so the brothers engage their brother-in-law, a contractor, to build a plant addition. The roofers accidentally spill tar and ruin the paint on a new Fiat. The Fiat owner sues the brothers who then find they are not protected under their M&C coverage. Owners' and contractors' liability coverage is needed. With this coverage the insured is protected against liability for actions of independent contractors, including liability due to the insured's failure in supervising independent contractors' work. No matter how carefully the insured selects a contractor and how ironclad the contract, the insured easily could be a party to a lawsuit arising from the contractor's actions. Some obligations, such as the owner's obligation to protect the public, cannot be transferred or delegated to the contractor. The owner may be sued even though the contractor uses great care as well as when the contractor fails to provide appropriate safety measures. Thus, the owner may be held responsible for the contractor's failure to provide proper protection of sidewalks during demolition of nearby buildings or for lack of safeguards in using dynamite. The owners' and contractors' liability form added to the M&C provides the answer to the resulting insurance problem. If alterations did not increase the building's size, the Becker Brothers would be covered for normal maintenance and repairs under their M&C policy, even though an independent contractor performed the work.

The contractor who sublets work faces problems similar to those of the owner. Owners' and contractors' coverage is needed, as certain obligations to the public cannot be delegated or signed away by contract.

The basis of the premium varies among jobs, but is based either on total cost of all work let or sublet or on the area of the building involved.

Products and completed operations liability form. Consumerism has affected the insurance market in many ways with consumers increasingly turning to courts for reparation because of injury from goods or services. In any product some characteristic may be present that subsequently will lead to lawsuits. A host of court decisions have held manufacturers and their agents liable for damages suffered by consumers, even when no contract or direct relationship exists between consumer and manufacturer and no negligence is shown. These decisions form the basis for a substantially different law from that providing the former basis for decisions in products liability cases. According to the California Supreme Court, a manufacturer who markets an article and knows it will be used without inspection for defects is liable if the product is defective and causes injury to persons or property. Under recent rulings the manufacturer may be held liable for a product causing damage even if the product has no defects. For example, some manufacturers have been held liable for damages caused by their products even though the products were not being used for their intended purpose, if such use was foreseeable.

The primary social problem is not that insurance rates and availability are adversely affected, but that thousands of avoidable injuries occur each year. Insurers can exercise social responsibility by becoming a force in product safety as powerful as they are in fire safety. A National Commission on Product Safety, after studying the problem for two years, reported in 1970 that the existing laws were deficient and more legislation was required if all unsafe products were to be removed from the market. The study led to the passage of the Consumer Products Safety Act (CPSA) designed to protect the public from the unreasonable injury risk resulting from consumer products. The act created the Consumer Products Safety Commission (CPSC) not only as a research, investigative, and information disseminating agency, but as an enforcement authority to file actions in federal district courts for product recall. Company executives may be held personally liable for heavy fines and are subject to imprisonment for CPSA violations. The CPSA led to increased loss prevention services offered by insurers. Compliance with the CPSA does not relieve a business of its common-law or statutory obligations. Action or lack of it by CPSC is inadmissible as evidence in products liability cases.

The first products liability contract was written in 1910. Insurers had been writing various kinds of liability policies for over 20 years when this coverage was introduced. Products liability insurance is written separately or as part of the CGL. The coverage protects against liability for damage claims from consumption or use of articles manufactured, sold, handled, or distributed by the insured, if the accident occurs away from the premises after possession has been relinquished to others. The on-premises products hazard usually is covered by the OL&T and M&C forms, but some exceptions are found. For example, the OL&T coverage for restaurants, hotels, and drugstores excludes the full products hazard on as well as off the premises. These insureds must purchase products liability coverage for the entire hazard and pay a premium for on-premises consumption and carryouts.

Grocers often have been held liable for selling defective products purchased from a manufacturer.[2] The grocer then may sue the manufacturer. Much expense and trouble result both for the grocer and manufacturer. In the majority of cases, the injured party will sue the manufacturer directly and the grocer may be named as codefendant, as it costs no more to sue a dozen parties than one.

A disturbing fact about products liability cases is that the manufacturer is never present when the mouse is found in a soft drink bottle or when the worm is discovered in a breakfast roll. Thus, the defense is in a difficult position when the case is tried. Another difficulty is that suits often are based solely on shattered nerves and mental strain.

An important chapter in products liability history—mouse in soft drink bottle division—was written years ago in Oklahoma City. Whenever an irate soft drink customer arrived in court to denounce bottlers for adding mice to their product, the defense showed the impossibility of mice finding their way into such predicaments. Of course, it can be

---

[2] Sometimes retailers enter into hold harmless agreements with the manufacturer under which the manufacturer agrees to assume liability and the defense in these types of situations.

understood how mice might wish to find such a blissful end, but it could be conclusively shown that the steps taken by the bottlers precluded mice from successful entry. Faced with such a stalemate—irate drinker and the near impossibility of a mouse sneaking into the bottle—the claims usually were settled out of court. However, in Oklahoma City the bottler permitted the case to go to court. The victim testified nausea had been caused by drinking the mouse-contaminated beverage and that the stomach condition was painful and enduring. The bottler, however, had an ace up his sleeve. A professor from the University of Oklahoma Medical School, testifying as an expert witness, announced that after analyzing the contents of the mouse-bottle, he found the acetic content of the drink was sufficient to have neutralized any bacteria introduced by the mouse. At this point the drinker's attorney flourished exhibit A, the bottle that still contained drink and mouse. "Would you be willing to drink it?" thundered the attorney. "I don't mind if I do," said the professor draining the contents, leaving only the mouse in the bottle. "A little musty," the professor said, smacking his lips, "but not really bad." The judge, who had watched the proceedings with mixed emotions, recovered his equilibrium and dismissed the case.

Under completed operations coverage, liability insurance is provided for injury caused by accident due to operations at a place away from premises owned, rented, or controlled by the insured, if it happens after such operation has been completed or abandoned. (Liability resulting from accidents involving pickup, delivery, and the existence of tools, uninstalled equipment, and abandonment of unused materials is not part of the completed operations hazard and is covered under the OL&T and M&C forms.)

Bodily injury and property damage liability insurance is provided under the products completed operations coverage. The property damage protection is restricted to other than the products involved. Basic policy limits for bodily injury are $25,000 per occurrence, subject to an overall aggregate limit of $50,000. Basic policy limits for property damage liability are $5,000 for one occurrence, with an overall limit of $25,000 for claims arising during the policy period. Medical payments coverage is not available.

The exposure unit for product liability insurance is sales, receipts, or units. In the case of sales and receipts (the most common), the unit is each $1,000 of annual gross sales or receipts. Where units are used as the rate base, the rate manual defines the unit; for example, 100 tons of flour for flour manufacturers.

Products recall insurance. Frequently one hears of the recall of automobiles, TV sets, electronic ovens, candy bars, or canned foods. Who bears the cost of this recall? The "sister ship exclusion" of the CGL form excludes damages claimed for the withdrawal, inspection, repair, replacement, or loss of use of the named insured's products or work completed by or for the named insured or of any property of which such products or work form a part, if such products, work, or property are withdrawn from the market or from use because of any known or suspected defect or deficiency therein.

In addition, coverage may be denied for subsequent products liability claims if the insured fails to recall the product following a damage claim. A product recall (product recapture or product withdrawal expense) policy is available to cover the recall exposure.

The policy always is written with at least a $1,000 deductible and requires the insured to share all losses above the deductible to an amount of 10 or 20 percent of the loss. Expenses covered include telephone, radio, or television announcements, and newspaper advertising; stationery and postage; necessary overtime wages for regular employees; additional employees hired; and disposal of the product if normal methods cannot be used without further harm. Loss of the product itself is not covered.

Personal injury liability policy. Personal injury liability coverage protects against liability claims for other than physical harm and property damage allegations. It covers claims alleging intentional torts such as false arrest, detention, malicious prosecution, libel, slander, wrongful entry, eviction, or invasion of privacy. This coverage, available for many years as a specialty line, is now available as an endorsement to general liability policies. Two limits of liability are used: an aggregate limit per person and a general aggregate limit. The first limit is the maximum the insurer will pay to one person during the policy period, and the second is the maximum paid for all claimants during the period. The policy always is written with a percentage participation in all losses (typically 15 percent), and some policies require the insured to participate in the defense costs. Other insurers follow the usual role of paying the full cost of defense.

Broad form CGL endorsement. This endorsement adds coverage for a broad range of liability exposures often faced by firms but nevertheless overlooked. The 12 coverages provided by the endorsement in package form are offered at a cost lower than would be charged if each of these coverages were purchased by separate endorsement. The disadvantage to the package concept is that the insured may not need all the coverages provided by the endorsement.

The coverages automatically included in the broad form CGL endorsement are: (1) contractual liability, (2) personal injury and advertising injury liability, (3) premises medical payments, (4) host liquor liability, (5) fire legal liability, (6) broad form property damage liability, (7) incidental medical malpractice liability, (8) nonowned watercraft liability, (9) limited worldwide liability, (10) additional persons insured [employees], (11) extended bodily injury, and (12) automatic coverage—newly acquired organizations. A description of all these coverages is beyond the scope of this text. Interested readers are referred to the *Casualty/Surety* volume of the FC&S *Bulletins,* page Bf-1 of *Public Liability.*

The storekeepers' liability policy. The storekeepers' liability form is a comprehensive liability policy tailored to meet the needs of owners and operators of eligible small shops. Written as a form attached to the standard general liability jacket, it is unique in using a single insuring clause with a single liability limit covering both bodily injury and property damage liability. The insurer will pay all sums that the insured will be legally obligated to pay as damages because of bodily injury or destruction of property arising from ownership, maintenance, or use of the premises or from operations necessary or incidental to the use of the premises. The policy provides limited contractual and products liability protection and full elevator liability coverage, and contains most of the usual exclusions in general liability policies. The coverage under the basic limits is subject to a $25,000 maximum for any occurrence, and medical payments coverage is included in the basic policy. The rate base is the store's area.

Dramshop[3] liability policy. A bleary-eyed citizen charged with smashing windows in 12 shops before being arrested is hauled before a magistrate. "Why did you get drunk in the first place?" asks the judge. "Your honor," replied the culprit, "I didn't—it was the third place." Under the dramshop or liquor control laws found in a number of states and discussed in Chapter 4, the first, second, and third places can be held liable for the window smashing. Any individual injured by an intoxicated person has a right of action against the tavern operator (and in some states against the owners of the premises where liquor is sold) who by selling liquor has caused the intoxication in whole, in part, first, or last. Tavern owners have a special liability to injured members of the general public and to the intoxicated person's family for loss of support. The OL&T form excludes liability arising from liquor control laws, so taverns faced with this exposure must purchase separate coverage. In states with no dramshop law, tavern owners have been held liable under common law for damage resulting from sale of liquor to minors or intoxicated persons. Tavern owners in these states also need liquor liability insurance.

Businesses not engaged in manufacture or distribution of alcoholic beverages are covered under the OL&T or M&C forms for any common-law liability arising from serving liquor to a drunken customer if the claim was caused by accident. Insurers write liquor liability coverage with understandable reluctance. Lloyd's of London was among the first to write this protection, and many insurers are happy to let Lloyd's have all this business.

Excess liability forms. Interest has developed in three closely related forms of excess coverage pioneered by Lloyd's. Many domestic insurers

---

[3] "Dramshop" is a euphemism for "bar" or "saloon." A commentary on the ways of legislators is that the Illinois statute which forbids the use of "saloon" and "bar" in any sign or advertisement is located next to a provision forbidding the sale of unmixed whiskey, gin, or rum in a container having a minimum capacity of less than one fluid ounce and requiring containers to have "at the time of sale at least one fluid ounce of the beverage being sold."

now also serve the market for excess liability insurance, excess aggregate coverage, and umbrella liability.

Excess liability insurance adds additional coverage above a specific amount up to a specified limit. For instance, a student with a bad driving record might be able to obtain minimum auto liability coverage only. Lloyd's might offer higher limits by writing an excess policy over the basic coverage up to some maximum level but at a higher cost than the same protection if offered by the insurer writing the basic coverage. The excess liability policy is needed because the primary insurer will not write the higher limits.

Excess aggregate insurance, designed for self-insurers, provides liability coverage up to an aggregate for all losses over a stated amount for the policy year. The insured must pay all liability claims (including loss adjustment expense) until the specified amount is reached. Then the excess aggregate policy assumes payment. This policy applies the principle of insuring catastrophic loss only rather than first-dollar coverage for all claims. Self-insurance is seldom used for the liability exposure, but the availability of excess aggregate coverage increases the attractiveness (or decreases the unattractiveness) of such risk management treatment.

The *umbrella liability insurance* policy, in spite of its name, does not refer to claims arising from a negligent umbrella wielder at the homecoming game (covered by the comprehensive personal liability policy). It is a contract that fills the gaps in liability protection associated with basic coverages or self-insured retentions. Lloyd's introduced this coverage in the United States in 1947. Typically, the insured must buy the following contracts to be eligible for the umbrella: comprehensive general liability insurance with limits of at least $100,000/$300,000, $100,000 property damage liability insurance, automobile liability insurance, and bailee liability insurance, and at least $100,000 of employers' liability insurance. Most insurers require the insured to absorb $25,000 of the loss on uninsured or self-insured exposures. For smaller enterprises, some insurers reduce this requirement to $10,000. Wide variation in rates is found among insurers.

The umbrella policy is excess in three respects: (1) it provides higher limits than the other coverages owned, (2) it covers exposures not otherwise covered, and (3) it provides automatic replacement for existing coverages exhausted or reduced by loss. A separate umbrella policy for individuals usually is written for business executives, professional people, and entertainers. The individual must first buy basic personal, auto, and aviation liability policies (if applicable) before buying an umbrella contract.

Other liability forms. Several special liability policies are available to cover exclusions in OL&T, M&C, and comprehensive policies such as the hazards of nuclear energy, fire legal liability, water damage, sprinkler leakage, employer's liability, aircraft liability, and automobile liability. Special bailee forms are available to cover liability for property in the insured's care, custody, or control.

Professional liability forms

Professional people need liability protection against malpractice suits arising from either faulty services rendered or failure to perform services expected of them under the circumstances. Coverage is sought by doctors, druggists, beauty parlor operators, architects, engineers, lawyers, employee benefit plan managers, fiduciaries, insurance agents, actuaries, and other professionals and has become increasingly important in this claim-conscious era.

Liability policies are written on either a *claims-made* basis or an *occurrence* basis. Liability insurance was first written on an occurrence basis but the trend is toward the claims-made approach for many types of professional liability coverages and for products liability coverage. An occurrence policy covers events that occur during the policy period. The insurer is obligated to defend and pay for any claims that arise from these occurrences at any time in the future. The problem with policies written on an occurrence basis is that many years often elapse between the issuance of a policy and the filing of a claim. This "long tail" can make it difficult for insurers to establish adequate rates and proper loss reserves. Because of the short time that usually elapses between the occurrence of the event and the filing of the claim, automobile liability and general liability policies are written on an occurrence basis.

Products liability and professional liability coverages do not lend themselves to occurrence coverage. The occurrence of the error, its discovery through bodily injury or property damage, and the resulting claims made against the insured may take place over a considerable period of time. To eliminate the problems arising from the "long tail," these types of coverages are written on a claims-made basis. A claims-made policy obligates an insurer for the defense and payment only for those claims made against the insured while the policy is in force. As a result, the insurer is aware at the policy's expiration of all claims in which it will be involved under the policy. The advantage of the claims-made approach is that the insurer will not be concerned with unknown claims that might be made in future years at inflated costs. Thus, the insurer can report more realistic loss reserves. (Loss reserves are discussed in Chapter 26.) The distinction between liability insurance policies written on an occurrence basis and those written on a claims-made basis should not be confused with the distinction made earlier in this chapter between liability insurance policies written on an occurrence basis and those written on an accident basis.

The physicians', surgeons', and dentists' form. The physicians', surgeons', and dentists' form is written to protect members of these professions from claims alleging malpractice. Physicians are said to bury their mistakes. But unless physicians can bury or otherwise dispose of their mistake's next of kin, a professional liability policy is needed. Dr. Jackson sews up a patient, leaving a sponge inside. If the patient discovers the error, the doctor may be sued. Under professional liability insurance the insurer pays the defense costs and any damages awarded up to the policy limits. Many doctors have found that by owning a professional liability policy they will be defended by some of the most competent malpractice defense lawyers available. As an out-of-court settlement made by the insurer might be interpreted as an admission of guilt, the professional can decide whether a settlement should be made or whether the case should be decided by the court.

Druggists' liability policy. The druggists' policy protects against claims arising from mistakes in filling prescriptions or from sale or misdelivery of drugs, medicines, or other merchandise generally sold in drugstores. Recalling what few items are not available in drugstores, the reader can appreciate the broadness of this coverage.

Accountants' professional liability policy. Accountants' professional liability insurance covers all sums the insured must legally pay as damages because of acts or omissions of the insured, any business predecessor of the insured, or any other person for whose acts or omissions the insured is legally responsible. The act or omission must result from performing professional services for others in the insured's capacity as an accountant. The policy does not cover bodily injury, death, or damage to tangible property. Dishonest, fraudulent, criminal, or malicious acts or omissions of the insured are not covered unless these acts are committed *for* the insured by an employee without the insured's knowledge. In states requiring accountants to post a bond, ownership of this policy often can be used to satisfy the bonding requirement.

Insurance agents' and brokers' liability policy. The insurance agents' and brokers' liability policy protects agents and brokers against claims caused by errors, omissions, or negligence in business conduct. In addition to covering liability to buyers, the policy may be extended to cover the agent's liability to insurers for losses caused them through failure to follow instructions. The policy generally is written with a single limit per policy year and is subject to a per loss deductible.

Lawyers' professional liability policy. Attorneys can purchase insurance to cover their liability because of any act or omission attributable directly to them or to any person for whose acts or omissions the insured is legally responsible, arising from the performance of professional services for others in the "insured's capacity as a lawyer." The insuring agreement provides broad coverage, but because attorneys perform many different services, borderline cases concerning whether or not a service was rendered in the insured's "capacity as a lawyer" arise because the meaning of this phrase has yet to be clarified.

Directors' and officers' liability insurance. Directors' and officers' liability insurance is designed to protect a director or officer of a firm for liability due to breaches of duty resulting from negligence, error, or omission. This field of insurance is highly specialized, as few insurers write the coverage and the potential exposure has not yet been clarified. Stockholders may sue and demand reimbursement from the firm for damages resulting from an action or inaction by an officer or director. Suits may also be brought by third parties such as creditors, competitors, the government, and the SEC. Insurers will not pay damages for libel or slander, personal profits illegally received by director or officer, salaries voted by directors, claims under the Federal Securities Act of 1934, and related state law or common law, dishonesty or fraud, and loss from contamination or pollution unless sudden and accidental. The policy usually is written with a $20,000 deductible and the insurer will pay 95 percent of all losses exceeding this amount. Underwriters consider the number of officers and directors, gross sales, total assets, type of industry, the corporation's reputation, and its financial and litigation history in determining premiums.

Trustees' and fiduciaries' liability insurance. The Pension Reform Act of 1974 imposes certain responsibilities on trustees, officers, employers, and others acting as fiduciaries for employee benefit plans. The law holds these people personally liable for damages resulting from a breach of their fiduciary duty. Appropriate liability insurance protection is available to cover this exposure, but it is not standardized among insurers. Limits of liability ranging from $250,000 to $15 million are available, but most contracts require a minimum $1,000 deductible. The deductible may or may not apply to defense costs, which are sometimes paid in addition to the stated aggregate limit. After cancellation of the policy, usually a period from six months to a year is given to discover errors which occurred during the policy period.

Employee benefits managers' liability policy. The employee benefits managers' liability policy protects against suits alleging negligence for improperly advising employees, and for incompetent bargaining with insurers for benefits for which employees must pay part of the cost.

Actuaries' professional liability policy. The actuaries and professional liability policy protects actuaries against liability arising under the terms of the Pension Reform Act of 1974. It covers actuaries for negligent acts, errors, or omissions performed in a professional capacity relative to their duties as employee benefit plan consultants. Limits are written up to $5 million plus court costs and legal fees.

Personal liability forms

Personal liability forms provide coverage for liability arising from conditions at the insured premises and from nonbusiness activities of an insured. A business liability policy should be purchased to cover the business activities of an insured. Personal liability forms are designed for two broad categories: nonfarmers and farmers.

The comprehensive personal liability policy. The comprehensive personal liability policy, the popular method for covering the personal liability exposure, is written separately or as part of the Homeowners policy. The coverage has only one insuring agreement, which protects the insured against claims arising from bodily injury or property damage liability. The basic policy limit is $25,000, but it can be increased for an additional premium. The personal liability coverage included in the HO series is discussed in Chapter 7.

The farmers' personal liability policy. The farmer needs liability protection, which is offered by the farmers' comprehensive personal liability policy, an adaption of the comprehensive personal liability policy to fit farmers' needs. This coverage also is included in the farm owners policy. The farm form includes some business liability coverage, for it insures the farmer while engaged in farming, but the comprehensive personal policy covers no business pursuits. The farm form also provides limited livestock mortality insurance. For a small additional premium, the insurer pays for the death of any cattle, horse, mule, hog, sheep, or goat owned by an insured when caused by collision between an animal and a motor vehicle neither owned nor operated by an insured or employee while the animal is on a public highway but not being transported. A single limit of $25,000 is provided, but the livestock mortality coverage is limited to the animal's market value at time of loss, not to exceed $300 each. Rates are higher than those for comprehensive personal liability because of the extra coverage. The form includes limited contractual coverage and products liability coverage. Liability for injuries to employees is excluded.

Recent developments in liability insurance

Injuries from exposure to asbestos products, particularly insulation, plaster, and brake linings, has produced product liability claims that may cost asbestos manufacturers billions of dollars. The extent of the problem may be observed by noting claims from a single group—plasterers. By early 1984 plaster workers filed over 60 suits based on exposure to plasterboard made with asbestos. Insurance industry representatives estimate that another 250,000 building workers may have been similarly exposed to asbestos fibers. Patently the estimate does not include members of the general public or any other group (insulation workers, for example) who may also file for asbestos-related injuries. Claims against one producer, the Manville Corporation, are so numerous and large that the company filed for protection from creditors under Chapter 11 of the federal Bankruptcy Code despite the fact that it was financially solvent at the time of filing in August 1982.

Manville's original plan was to split the firm into two entities, one to continue business operations and the other to settle asbestos claims. Difficulties in setting up the claims-paying group caused Manville to consider following the lead of six other major asbestos makers and their liability insurers. The insurers and asbestos producers formed the Asbestos Claims Facility to settle asbestos-related claims without the necessity of going to court. Some claims will still go through the litigation process, but legal costs are expected to be substantially reduced.

Professional liability, as well as products liability protection, cause major problems for insurers when written on an occurrence basis. The ill effects of a physician's mistake or breathing asbestos fibers may not show up until years after the occurrence. Liability insurance written to cover occurrences that took place during the policy term can bind a carrier to the insured exposure for a limitless time after the policy has expired. The insurer is expected to have anticipated potential claims and established premiums accordingly.

Problems in the product liability area have led the Insurance Services Office (ISO) to include, as part of a new CGL proposal, a product liability coverage written on a claims-made basis. This approach would cause an insurer to be responsible for occurrences that took place before the policy was issued while relieving the carrier from the long tail of slowly developing manifestations of loss. Insurers could set premiums based on the current loss situation rather than on future potential claims. (They would no longer be required to predict the unpredictable.) In addition, if a new federal products liability law, under current consideration, is passed, pricing this coverage could be made still easier by the imposition of restrictions on product liability claims. A detailed discussion of the proposed legislation can be found in Chapter 29.

Workers' Compensation and Employers' Liability

Every state has a system of workers' compensation requiring employers to compensate workers injured on the job or incurring job-connected diseases. Employers usually buy insurance to pay the sums for which they are liable. In a few states, the insurance must be bought from a state insurer called a workers' compensation fund. In a larger number of states, protection may be purchased only from private insurers. In the remaining states the employer has a choice between state and private insurance. In most states, qualified employers may self-insure the exposure.

Historical development

To understand workers' compensation legislation, the evolution of the degree of care required of employers toward workers needs to be considered.

Employers' liability. Legal liability is based on negligence law. A person has a duty to use care in dealing with others, and failure to do so is negligence. To sustain a negligence action, the injured person must show a direct, uninterrupted connection between the injury and the other party's failure to use care. Traditionally, the claimant must also be absolutely free of any contributory negligence. This requirement often has been modified. At one time, damages were collectible only if the injured person survived, as a claim was held to die with the injured person. Negligence law is discussed in Chapter 4.

About 1837 an accident occurred in England that would change the law of negligence. A butcher named Fowler hired Priestly to accompany a wagon driver in making deliveries to Fowler's customers. Priestly was injured and brought suit against Fowler for damages not as an employee, but as one member of the public suing another. Priestly won his case but later the decision was reversed on appeal. In the decision, the defenses available to an employer sued under similar conditions were enunciated.

Before the *Priestly* v. *Fowler* decision, an injured worker was assumed, as a member of the public, to have rights of action even as an employee against an employer. The rule that the principal was liable for acts of an agent had been applied to cases involving injured workers. So if one worker injured another, the injured worker could sue the employer. With the *Priestly* v. *Fowler* decision, this doctrine of *respondeat superior* (let the principal answer for the acts of the agent), was held inapplicable to employees' injuries. With respect to indemnification rights, employees became second-class citizens.

The doctrines of *assumption of risk* and *common employment* were developed in subsequent cases. The assumption of risk rule is that a worker, in accepting employment, voluntarily accepts the risks of the job. The assumption was that the employee was paid for such risks, therefore, no additional compensation should be paid for injuries. The common employment doctrine states that one's fellow workers are better judges of one's competence and fitness of fellow employees than the employer. Fellow workers discovering lapses of a fellow employee should notify the employer. Should the employer not remedy the condition, these workers should resign and seek an employer who will heed their reports. In any case, the employer hardly can be held responsible for accidents caused by fellow workers.

The common law considered minimum requirements which employers must meet. The employer is to provide: a safe working place, proper tools and machinery for the job, suitable safety rules, reasonably competent fellow workers, and warnings of dangers of which the employer is aware but of which the worker may be assumed ignorant. An injured worker could bring suit against an employer who failed to satisfy any of these requirements. The employer was entitled to three defenses: *assumption of risk, common employment,* and *contributory negligence.* This latter defense held that if a worker was in any way negligent in causing the accident the worker could not collect from the employer, even though the employer was grossly negligent.

These harsh doctrines soon were modified by court decisions and statutes. In 1851 *Little Miami Railroad Company* v. *Stevens* modified the common employment doctrine by setting forth the *vice principal rule.* This rule stated the employer was responsible for injuries caused by any employee's failure to perform a fundamental obligation assigned by the employer. Should one of the employer's important duties be entrusted to an employee, any injury to another employee resulting from the "vice principal's" failure to act cannot be excused on the basis of the doctrine of common employment. Other courts achieved similar results through the *conassociation rule* and the *superior servant rule,* both of which limit an employer's right to claim liability exemption on the grounds of the common-employment doctrine. These judicial modifications rapidly were included in many state statutes. Meanwhile an act was passed in England permitting families of deceased workers to sue employers for accidents resulting in death. A similar law was passed in nearly all states following passage of the English law.

Beginning with the Industrial Revolution until 1900, the philosophy was that every industrial accident was someone's fault. Justice was achieved by assessing the guilty person for damages. The usual decision was that the worker was to blame. The transition to the philosophy that accidents may be due simply to the "system" was gradual. The United States lagged behind much of the world in recognizing changing conditions.

Early attempts at workers' compensation.   Accidents are inherent in large-scale production, yet workers injured in industry have difficulty in winning awards from employers. Even if workers could obtain awards, years might pass before amounts are determined and paid. Also, as payments could be avoided for most injuries, employers have little incentive to improve their safety record.

The Prussian Employers' Liability Law of 1838 often is considered the birth of workers' compensation legislation. It provided that railroads were liable for injuries to both employees and passengers. No system of compensation was established, and responsibility for each accident still had to be fixed. The law served only to make it easier to prove the railroad's negligence. Prussia passed its sickness insurance law in 1883 and later added a law covering accident insurance. These laws constituted the first real workers' compensation plan the world had known. German workers were required to be insured. The cost was shared by the worker, but the employer had to bear the main financial burden.

In 1902 Maryland enacted a workers' compensation law which was declared unconstitutional within a year by the Baltimore Court of Common Pleas. In the next few years, Massachusetts and Illinois appointed commissions to investigate the possibility of enacting workers' compensation laws, but no decision was reached. In 1908 largely through the prodding of Samuel Gompers and the American Federation of Labor, a federal bill was passed providing compensation for civilian government employees. Previously federal workers could be compensated for work-connected injuries only by a special act of Congress. New York passed a workers' compensation act in 1910, but it was immediately declared unconstitutional. In 1913 New York amended its constitution to permit a compensation act which could withstand a court test. Other states also were active and with the passage of a Mississippi workers' compensation act in 1948, compensation laws were in operation in all states.

Occupational Safety and Health Act of 1970 (OSHA). During the 1960s employee job safety again became an issue culminating in the passage of the Occupational Safety and Health Act by Congress in 1970. Under OSHA, stringent work safety regulations have been promulgated and administrative machinery developed to enforce the rules by levying fines for violations and closing unsafe firms. Cooperation between insurers and insureds in helping businesses to improve work environment and to implement safe and legal work practices can result in reduced workers' compensation claims, reduced premiums, and an improved quality of life for workers.

Organization of the U.S. workers' compensation program

Although each state has its own system of compensation, enough similarities exist to permit discussion as a unit.

Coverage. Workers covered are specified by law. Agriculture workers usually are excluded, as are domestic servants and casual laborers in many states. The reasons for these exclusions are largely administrative; but in agriculture, the political influence of farmer organizations has been a factor in excluding farm workers in spite of the appalling frequency and severity of farm accidents. All states not only provide coverage for accidental injuries arising out of and in the course of employment, but also include coverage for various work-related diseases. In 1969 West Virginia coal miners struck for three weeks and marched to the state capitol to influence the legislature to include black lung disease under its workers' compensation law. The coal miners were successful, and this development prompted several other states to enact similar legislation.

Compensation laws may be compulsory or elective. Compulsory laws require all employers, with certain exceptions, to join the system and pay for industrial injuries as prescribed by the compensation law. Under the elective law, employers and employees decide whether to accept the compensation system. However, should the employer elect not to comply, the right to use the common-law defenses is denied. This restriction is a strong deterrent to employers who otherwise might elect not to participate, but a few prefer to take their chances under common law, even if deprived of defenses. Some compulsory laws exempt certain employers; for example, public employers, nonprofit organizations, and employers with few employees (three to five is typical). However, many jurisdictions make no exemptions based on number of employees.

Benefits. After a specified waiting period (usually seven days) an injured worker covered by workers' compensation is eligible for cash and medical benefits. However, if the disability continues beyond a certain period, such as four weeks, benefits often are paid retroactively for the first seven days. In recent years, rehabilitation and medical benefits have increased in importance.

The cash benefit is a percentage of the worker's wage. Most states provide minimum and maximum weekly payments as well as maximum total benefits available to a disabled employee. As of the beginning of 1983, weekly payments for temporary disability ranged from a low of $112 in Mississippi to a high of $996 in Alaska. (The maximum payable under the Federal Employees Compensation Act was $942.22.) Also, the amount paid for dismemberment or death is limited, usually to a multiple of the weekly benefit.

Finance. Because work accidents are a production cost, the burden of financing the compensation system is on the employer. In 47 states, employers are permitted to self-insure if they can meet prescribed standards. In six states, employers must buy insurance from a monopolistic state fund, a type of state-operated insurer. In 12 jurisdictions, state funds compete with private insurers. In these competitive states, private insurers are predominant, paying about two thirds of all compensation benefits.

Administration. The judicial system of many states formerly was as bogged down with industrial accident cases as they now are with auto accident cases. In only three states do the courts now exclusively administer the compensation system. Elsewhere the administrative work is performed by special commissions. Their fact findings are presumed correct in the absence of fraud or collusion, but their interpretations of law usually are subject to judicial review.

Workers' compensation insurance policies

Insurers have developed a universal standard workers' compensation and employers' liability policy to protect employers under compensation acts. This policy combines protection against any obligations the employer may have under the state compensation law with the protection needed should a worker bring suit under negligence law instead of (or in addition to) applying for compensation. Under coverage A of the policy the protection is not subject to a face amount limit. The insurer promises to make all payments required by the state's compensation law. This section may be endorsed to cover employees injured in other states and provide workers' compensation coverage for employees excluded by the law. Coverage B insures the liability of the employer to employees for a basic limit (usually $100,000) per accident or disease. The limit can be increased by paying an additional premium. The usual arrangement for supplementary payments for defense of suits, bond premiums, and so on is included. Even though the state has a workers' compensation law, the employer is exposed to suits arising from illegal employment of minors, losses claimed by the injured worker's spouse and, in some states, gross negligence. In Illinois, violation of the Scaffold Act requiring employers to provide employees with safe equipment (ladders, for example) provides grounds for employer liability action. Premiums are based on the dollar amount of payrolls and are subject to change, following a payroll audit at the end of the policy period.

Second-injury funds

Second-injury funds have been established to facilitate employment of physically handicapped workers. Under compensation laws, employers are liable for disability resulting from injuries incurred in employment, but not for preexisting handicaps. Additional compensation due because of the combination of two injuries is paid from the second-injury fund. For example, if a worker is blind in one eye when employed and later loses the other eye in a work accident, the employer will be responsible for only the scale of compensation paid for loss of one eye. The additional compensation for total disability (loss of sight in both eyes is considered total disability) is paid from the second-injury fund. The financing method of the fund varies among states. Usually insurers contribute on the basis of the total compensation paid during the year, or on premiums collected. Some states support the second-injury fund through legislative appropriations.

Direction of workers' compensation laws

The frequent changes made in state compensation laws are usually focused on flexible maximum weekly benefits, increases in medical benefits, and improved occupational disease laws. The legislative trend continues to be one of broadening coverage and increasing benefits. An amendment to the Occupational Safety and Health Act of 1970 established a National Commission on State Workmen's Compensation Laws to examine and evaluate the state workers' compensation structure. The commission made 19 "essential recommendations" including:

1. Coverage by workers' compensation laws should be compulsory.
2. Employers should not be exempted from workers' compensation coverage because of the small number of their employees.
3. Farm workers should be covered on the same basis as all other employees.

4. Adequate weekly cash benefits should be paid for temporary total disability, permanent total disability, and to employees' survivors.
5. No statutory limits of time or dollar amount should exist for any work-related impairments.

The findings of the commission have pressured states either to upgrade their laws or face replacement by a federal statute. (There have been several unsuccessful legislative proposals introduced at the federal level aimed at upgrading workers' compensation benefits.) States have made many changes in their workers' compensation laws following the commission's report, and this impetus toward state reform is expected to continue primarily because of powerful lobbying interests that oppose any federal intervention.

Throughout much of the history of workers' compensation law, injured workers were denied the right to sue an employer, under the doctrine of *exclusive remedy,* if the worker had received workers' compensation benefits. However, this doctrine has been eroded by successful suits based on the dual capacity of an employer, an intentional tort, and on third-party-over cases.

If an employer produces a product which injures an employee (an injury which arises from and in the course of employment) the worker may collect workers' compensation benefits as an employee and then sue and collect as a member of the public using a product manufactured by the employer. The product must be in the general stream of commerce in order for the dual capacity suit to be viable. Not all jurisdictions have accepted the doctrine of dual capacity. In 1982 the California legislature passed a law prohibiting such suits unless they were the result of an intentional tort or fraud on the part of the employer.

Suits based on an employer's intentional tort have been successful on one or more of three grounds: (1) injuries from intentional torts have been ruled not to be in the course of employment; (2) public policy does not permit the use of exclusive remedy to shield an employer when the intention is to injure or harm; and (3) many states grant employees the right to bring tort action when the employer's acts are "willful," "deliberate," or "intentional."

A third-party-over suit may be best explained by example. While working on an air-conditioning duct, Jake is injured on the job for his employer, Summer Heating and Winter Air Conditioning, Inc. (SHWACI, suppliers of heating and cooling systems for colleges, universities, and business buildings over one story tall). The ducts were being installed in the new business building according to a contract SHWACI had with the University of Nome, Alaska (UNA). Jake gets workers' compensation benefits from SHWACI and then successfully sues UNA. UNA officials are miffed at being forced to contribute to Jake's wealth, and sue SHWACI in a third-party-over action based on a hold-harmless clause in SHWACI's contract or on SHWACI's negligence that caused Jake's injury.

Each of the three methods used to defeat the doctrine of exclusive remedy produce the same two problems for insurers. First, an employee receives a tort produced award as well as workers' compensation benefits, a violation of the principle of indemnity. Second, workers' compensation insurers believe the tort awards should be paid by the employer's CGL policy—the CGL carriers think otherwise.

State and federal courts have ruled both for and against the doctrine of exclusive remedy. Further court cases as well as legislation similar to that of California are likely to address these issues in the future.

The 45 state legislatures that convened in 1978 enacted about 160 laws covering nearly all phases of workers' compensation. Benefits were increased, waiting periods were reduced, limits were removed from medical care payments (they are now unlimited in all states), administration of laws was improved, coverage for occupational diseases was broadened, and now all but three states have compulsory rather than elective workers' compensation laws.[4]

Summary

1. The general liability insurance program operates similarly to many fire and inland marine insurance programs. Forms such as the OL&T and the M&C contain the insuring agreement and are inserted into a jacket containing provisions, conditions, and definitions common to all contracts in the program.

2. The OL&T form covers liability arising from the ownership, maintenance, or use of premises occupied by the insured. The M&C form provides similar coverage for manufacturers and contractors, although altered to meet their specific needs.

3. The CGL form, along with available endorsements, provides broad automatic coverage for all general liability exposures.

4. Products liability insurance protects the manufacturer or retailer from liability due to defective products. Insurance is also available to cover expenses of recalling defective products.

5. Special liability policies may be purchased to cover exposures due to false arrests, libel, slander, invasion of privacy, liability resulting from dramshop laws, and professional liability. Contracts specifically designed for needs of individuals, farmers, and small store owners also are available.

6. Excess liability insurance can be purchased to extend the limits of a basic policy. Self-insurers may purchase excess aggregate insurance to cover their exposure to catastrophic losses. Umbrella liability insurance can be purchased to provide higher limits than the basic

---

[4] For an up-to-date analysis of state workers' compensation laws, including U.S. territories and also Canadian provinces, see *Analysis of Workers' Compensation Laws,* the Chamber of Commerce of the United States, 1615 H St., N.W., Washington, D.C. 20062, annual. The 1982 edition includes 15 valuable detailed charts comparing specific provisions of the various workers' compensation laws. (A magnifying glass would be useful as an aid in reading its footnotes.)

policy, insure exposures otherwise not covered, and replace existing insurance reduced by loss.

7. Employees once could sue employers as members of the general public. But court decisions subsequently denied that right. Gradually, laws were passed recognizing that accidents are inevitable and that employees should be compensated.

8. Workers' compensation insurance pays medical and rehabilitative expenses for injured employees, as well as a percentage of their lost wages. The trend in legislation is toward broadened workers' compensation coverage and benefits.

Questions for Review

1. In the typical liability policy, what payments does the insurer promise to make on behalf of the insured?

2. What is the sister ship exclusion? Why is it so named?

3. Distinguish tort liability from contractual liability.

4. How do professional liability forms differ significantly from other liability policies?

5. Under what circumstances would it be appropriate to recommend the CGL form?

6. Compare the M&C form to owners' and contractors' protective liability insurance.

7. What are dramshop laws? What is their significance with respect to liquor liability insurance?

8. Explain excess aggregate liability insurance. Who would be interested in buying it?

9. Trace the development of the various doctrines of employers' liability.

10. What kinds of workers are typically excluded from workers' compensation? Why?

11. If a state has an elective workers' compensation law, what might encourage the employer to elect to participate in the compensation system?

12. Explain why fiduciary liability insurance is becoming increasingly important.

Questions for Discussion

1. Since OSHA became law, firms can be closed by administrative officials if safe working conditions for employees are not provided. Is this practice justifiable? Are there less drastic alternative solutions? Explain.

2. A recent revision of the comprehensive general liability policy removed all per person limits of liability. What could have prompted such a change?

3. Some people believe the manufacturer should pay for all damages that result from the use of the manufactured product, regardless of whether or not the product was defective. Do you agree? Why or why not?

4. Suppose that the accountant for the XYZ Company understates the firm's liabilities, and Ms. Greene purchases XYZ common stock on the basis of this information. When the mistake is corrected, the stock price falls. Should Ms. Greene be able to collect damages from the accountant?

5. Why is liability insurance called third-party insurance? Has it always been third-party insurance in the strict sense?

6. What changes would you recommend be made in your state's workers' compensation law? Explain.

7. Is the term "sister ship" exclusion discussed in question 2 under questions for review sexist? Explain.

14

Automobile insurance

Automobile insurance is one of the most widely held coverages commonly purchased by both individuals and businesses and, in many states, required of all drivers. The owner and operator of an auto or other motor vehicle needs liability protection and physical damage coverage. Auto policies are designed to cover these needs.

The first auto bodily injury liability policy written in the United States was issued to Dr. Truman J. Martin in 1898, just three years after an English company had written the first such policy. The policy was written by the Travelers on a form that formerly had been used to insure the liability arising from the use of teams of horses or mules. The first auto collision policy was written in 1899. In 1902, the first auto property damage liability policy was written. The first large auto insurance claim was $9,500, paid in 1904 by the Boston Insurance Company to William Wallace, a vice president of the company. Wallace was on his way to Worcester from Boston when his gasoline tank exploded. (Today, that claim might also be filed as one involving products liability.)

Personal Automobile Insurance

An individual driving for pleasure or to work will need protection against liability claims because of injury to persons or property of others

327

arising from ownership, maintenance, or use of the automobile. Insurance is also available to indemnify for physical damage to the car by fire, collision, theft, or other perils. The private passenger auto insurance business has become competitive; new forms and rating methods have been introduced. But according to a major study of consumer buying habits, the single most important reason given for choosing a particular insurer is "reputation." And the primary reason for switching insurers is "rates."

Personal auto policy

Private passenger autos and certain types of nonbusiness trucks can be covered by the personal auto policy (PAP) if such vehicles are owned or rented under a long-term lease by an individual or a married couple residing in the same household. A vehicle rented to others or used as a public or livery conveyance is not eligible for the coverage. Also not eligible is a vehicle owned by a partnership or corporation. The PAP was designed to replace both the family auto policy (FAP) and the special package auto policy (SAP) as the "standard" form for insuring the foregoing eligible vehicles.[1] The PAP is discussed in Chapters 7 through 10. Because many insurance companies use nonstandard forms, the PAP will not be universally adopted and these companies will continue to use the FAP and SAP (or variations thereof) to insure private passenger automobiles and certain kinds of light trucks.

A few of the variations that exist among PAP, FAP, and SAP are found in Figure 14–1.

Nonownership coverage

Individuals who own and insure a private passenger auto are protected to some degree by their policies (PAP, FAP, SAP) when using a nonowned auto. Not all people who drive own a car. *Named nonowner* coverage is available to protect nonowners against *liability* when driving. If the insured acquires ownership of a car during the policy period, the automobile is covered under the nonowner coverage for a maximum of 30 days. If the owner buys insurance on the car during this 30-day period, coverage under the nonowner form will no longer apply to the owned car. Separate policies are available for insureds who desire *comprehensive and collision coverages* for nonowned vehicles. After graduating from college, Skip Cummins finds a position in Chicago, but living expenses are so high he is unable to buy a car. However, he arranges to use the Ferrari owned by his friend, Shafiq. He has learned from an insurance course that he will be covered under Shafiq's policy if he uses the Ferrari regularly. Later Shafiq cancels his policy. Consequently, Skip buys nonownership coverage. Because he does not want

---

[1] Owners of vehicles not eligible for coverage under the PAP must be insured under one of the available commercial auto policies; for example, the business auto policy.

FIGURE 14–1 Variations among four types of auto policies

PAP	FAP	SAP	BAP*
1. Single limit of liability per accident for bodily injury and/or property damage.	1. Split limits of liability per person and per accident for bodily injury and property damage.	1. Single limit of liability per occurrence for bodily injury and/or property damage.	1. Single limit of liability per occurrence for bodily injury and/or property damage. Split limit available upon selection.
2. Liability coverage provided for property damage to nonowned private passenger autos, trailers and small trucks in the custody of the insured.	2. No liability coverage for property in the care, custody or control of insured.	2. No liability coverage for property in the care, custody or control of insured.	2. Physical damage coverage provided for property damage to nonowned vehicles if selected by insured.
3. Nonowned vehicles covered under liability coverage on an excess basis.	3. Nonowned vehicles covered under physical damage section of policy on an excess basis.	3. Named insured and relatives covered under physical damage coverage while using nonowned private passenger autos only if legally liable.	3. Coverage for nonowned vehicles in physical damage section on an excess basis, or primary if selected.
4. Medical expenses incurred within three years from date of accident covered under medical payments.	4. Medical expenses incurred within one year from date of accident covered under medical payments coverage.	4. Medical expenses incurred within one year from date of accident covered under medical payments coverage.	4. Medical expenses incurred within one year of date of accident covered under medical expenses endorsement.
5. Medical payments coverage made primary with respect to automobile accidents.	5. Medical payments coverage made primary with respect to automobile accidents.	5. Medical payments coverage excess over accident, disability or hospitalization insurance available to an insured.	5. Medical payments coverage primary on medical expenses endorsement.
6. First-aid coverage is not included as a supplementary payment.	6. First-aid coverage is included as a supplementary payment.	6. First-aid coverage is included as a supplementary payment.	6. First-aid coverage is not included as a supplementary payment.
7. Physical damage coverage provided under a single insuring agreement. However, collision coverage is optional.	7. Collision and comprehensive (OTC) coverages are written as separate insuring agreements.	7. Collision and comprehensive (OTC) coverages are written as separate insuring agreements.	7. Comprehensive, special perils and collision coverages written under separate insuring agreements.
8. No personal effects coverage under physical damage section.	8. Personal effects covered for loss by fire and lightning while in the owned automobile.	8. Personal effects covered for loss by fire, lightning, flood, falling objects, explosions, earthquake, theft of auto and collision.	8. No personal effects coverage under physical damage section.
9. No coverage for persons using a vehicle without reasonable belief that they are entitled to do so.	9. Persons (other than relatives) must have permission to use the vehicle of the named insured before coverage applies.	9. Persons (other than relatives) must have permission to use the vehicle of named insured before coverage applies.	9. Persons must have permission of the named insured to use the vehicle before coverage applies.
10. Vehicles acquired during the term of the policy must be reported within 30 days for coverage.	10. Vehicles acquired during the term of the policy may be reported at any time during the policy period.	10. Vehicles acquired during the term of the policy must be reported within 30 days for coverage.	10. Vehicles acquired during the term of the policy are covered depending on selection.

* The business auto policy (BAP) provides the insured with extensive flexibility in available coverages. The BAP is discussed later in this chapter.

to be exposed to a physical damage loss, he also buys nonownership comprehensive and collision coverage. Three months later Skip's financial position improves and he buys both a Volkswagen and a Ford station wagon. A day later he accidentally drives the Ford into the lake; the station wagon is a total loss. Skip is indemnified by his nonownership policy because the accident occurred within 30 days of the car's acquisition. Two weeks later Skip buys a policy specifically for his VW. His nonownership policy will still apply to the Ferrari and other nonowned cars, but no longer to the Volkswagen.

Related vehicles

Special policies have been developed to insure owners of motor homes, van conversions, travel trailers, snowmobiles, golf carts, trail bikes, all-terrain vehicles, dune buggies, and most other recreational vehicles. Many insurers use one policy to cover this diverse collection of vehicles. These nonstandard forms typically are called *recreational vehicle policies*. They are similar to an automobile policy in that they provide liability, medical payments coverage, uninsured motorists, comprehensive, and collision. Other policies have been developed to meet the needs of owners of motorcycles and boats.[2]

Rating

In the good old days of few cars, accidents, and lawsuits, automobile rating seemed almost a pleasure. Rates were applied to three categories: autos not driven by youthful drivers, autos driven by youthful drivers, and autos used in business. Through the years rating became complicated, and in 1965 a completely new rating system, based on the old one, was introduced with 52 basic categories reflecting the age, sex, and marital status of the *driver,* and further modified according to *car use:* pleasure; driven less than 10 miles one way to work; driven more than 10 miles one way to work; cars used for business; and cars used by farmers. The combination of the driver and use categories produced 260 primary classifications. The primary classifications are modified if more than one car is covered under the same policy. Often these rates are further modified by the driver's accident experience. The same classifications determine rates for medical payments, collision, comprehensive physical damage, and liability coverage.

In 1970, and again in 1976, the number of primary classifications was reduced in the majority of states to 217 (in 1970) and then to 161 (in 1976). Further changes in auto insurance rating systems are expected due to pressure to disallow sex and marital status as factors in auto insurance rate making.

---

[2] Owners of boats can be insured for physical damage with inland marine forms. See Chapter 12.

Automobile insurance plans

To espouse the philosophy that all persons with valid drivers' licenses should be able to purchase automobile insurance is politically and socially expedient. However, insurers will not write policies voluntarily to cover drivers with poor accident records. Also, very old and very young drivers often are unable to obtain coverage. (However, some insurers offer discounts for older drivers who are retired.) In response to the auto insurance availability problem, most states have set up automobile insurance plans (AIPs), formerly known as assigned-risk plans, to provide insurance for the residual market (persons to whom insurers would prefer not to sell insurance). In the typical AIP, each automobile insurer is assigned "extra-risk" insureds in proportion to the amount of auto premiums written by the insurer in the state. So if an insurer wants to write auto insurance in California, for example, it must agree to insure its proportional share of California's residual auto insurance market. A person with a record of involvement in gambling, narcotics, or other illegal enterprises can be refused coverage in some states; in others, no one with a valid driver's license can be excluded from the AIP.

Although the plans provide coverage at higher than standard rates, the increment usually does not offset the poor loss experience. One solution often suggested is a further increase in AIP rates, but a strong view is that states should improve their licensing standards to preclude poor drivers from obtaining licenses. Alternatives other than AIPs are now being tested in some states. Maryland set up its State Automobile Fund in 1973, a state-owned insurer to handle undesirable insureds. The Fund has experienced not only a high claims rate but also higher than expected administrative expenses. High lapse and cancellation rates account for the Fund's excessive administration costs. Four states deal with the problem by requiring that all drivers be insured at standard rates. The states provide reinsurance facilities to pay claims incurred by those in the residual market. These states also have experienced underwriting losses with their plans. Florida set up a Joint Underwriting Association (JUA) in 1974 to cover the residual market. The JUA is composed of all auto insurers operating in the state. It sets its own rates and writes the policies, but policyowner services are provided by the large insurers. Underwriting losses are shared by all participants in proportion to the auto insurance premiums they write in Florida. Missouri and Hawaii have similar JUAs.

By mid-1975, pressure to develop alternatives to AIPs eased while states waited to evaluate the experience of existing alternative plans. Many questions are yet to be answered. Do the alternatives enhance or inhibit competition for voluntary business? Do the alternatives differ in making coverage readily available? Are there differences in consumer services and cost effectiveness? Are certain groups required to subsidize other groups under some alternatives? As these questions are answered and the experiences of the new plans are evaluated, more effective methods of providing auto insurance for the residual market hopefully can be expected.

Business Automobile Insurance

Several types of autos are used in business. Various methods are available to insure their owners against the liability and physical damage exposures they present.

Private passenger coverage

Private passenger autos owned or leased by individuals (sole proprietors) may be covered under the PAP, while autos owned (or leased) by partnerships or corporations must be covered under the business auto policy (BAP). Automobiles owned by individuals and used for business purposes qualify for the PAP. Thus, Bill Shade's privately owned auto can be covered under a PAP even though he uses his car extensively for business purposes.

The BAP became effective in 1978 as a replacement for both the basic auto policy and the comprehensive auto liability policy.[3] The new BAP follows the approach of the PAP and the HO series in that it is written in simplified and readable language. The mechanics of the policy allow great flexibility, and the BAP can be made as restrictive as the basic auto policy or as broad as the comprehensive auto liability policy (depending upon the needs of the insured). Many insurers who have not yet adopted the BAP continue to use both the basic and comprehensive auto policies.

Analysis of coverage

An unendorsed BAP provides coverage for liability and physical damage exposures. The policy can be expanded to provide coverage for medical payments, uninsured motorists insurance, and any no-fault provisions required by law. The insured is able to create the desired scope of coverage (in terms of autos covered) by selecting from the following list those autos for which coverage is to be bought. Nine classifications of covered autos exist, each represented by a numerical symbol.

1. *Any auto.*
2. *Owned autos only.* Only those autos you own (and for liability coverage any trailers you do not own while attached to power units you own). This includes those autos whose ownership you acquire after the policy begins.

---

[3] Generally, the basic auto policy covers the insured's named automobiles, while the comprehensive auto liability policy covers any auto used by an insured. The comprehensive auto liability coverage can be written in conjunction with the comprehensive general liability policy (as a package policy), whereas the BAP is a totally self-contained policy.

3. *Owned private passenger autos only.* Only the private passenger autos you own. This includes those private passenger autos whose ownership you acquire after the policy begins.
4. *Owned autos other than private passenger autos only.* Only those autos you own that are not of the private passenger type (and for liability coverage any trailers you do not own while attached to power units you own). This includes those autos, not of the private passenger type, whose ownership you acquire after the policy begins.
5. *Owned autos subject to no-fault.* Only those autos you own that are required to have no-fault benefits in the state where they are licensed or principally garaged. This includes those autos whose ownership you acquire after the policy begins provided they are required to have no-fault benefits in the state where they are licensed or principally garaged.
6. *Owned autos subject to compulsory uninsured motorist law.* Only those autos you own that, because of the law in the state where they are licensed or principally garaged, are required to have and cannot reject uninsured motorists insurance. This includes those autos whose ownership you acquire after the policy begins provided they are subject to the same state uninsured motorists requirement.
7. *Specifically described autos.* Only those autos described in Item Four for which a premium charge is shown (and for liability coverage any trailers you do not own while attached to any power unit described in Item Four).
8. *Hired autos only.* Only those autos you lease, hire, rent or borrow. This does not include any auto you lease, hire, rent or borrow from any of your employees or members of their households.
9. *Nonowned autos only.* Only those autos you do not own, lease, hire or borrow that are used in connection with your business. This includes autos owned by your employees or members of their households but only while used in your business or your personal affairs.

If coverage is desired for a classification or classifications (more than one symbol can be used for any one coverage), the numerical symbol of that classification is designated opposite the desired coverage scheduled on the declarations page of the policy. The classifications also can (and sometimes must) vary among the different coverages provided by the policy. For example, if a firm desires that any auto be covered for liability insurance but only owned autos be provided with physical damage coverage, the symbol 1 would be designated opposite the liability insurance coverage, while the symbol 2 would apply to physical damage insurance. Similarly, if the firm selected symbols 7 and 9, it would have coverage for all its specifically described autos as well as coverage for any autos that it does not own but that are used in its behalf (see "Nonownership Coverage").

While all nine classifications apply to the liability coverage, only five of the categories—2, 3, 4, 7, and 8—apply to the physical damage coverage. With any of these symbols except 7, coverage is extended to any new autos acquired during the policy term. If symbol 7 is indicated, new cars are covered only if

1. The insurer already insures all autos owned for that coverage or it replaces an auto you previously owned that had that coverage.

2. The insured tell the insurer within 30 days after acquiring the auto that he or she wants it insured for that coverage.

In addition to permitting selection of the scope of covered autos, the BAP allows the insured to choose the perils covered under the physical damage section of the policy. Three categories exist:

1. *Comprehensive coverage.* This coverage provides protection for losses from any cause except the covered auto's collision with another object or its overturn.
2. *Special perils coverage.* This coverage provides protection for losses caused by fire; explosion; theft; windstorm; hail; earthquake; flood; malicious mischief or vandalism; and the sinking, burning, collision, or derailment of any conveyance transporting the covered auto.
3. *Collision coverage.* This coverage provides protection for the covered auto's collision with another object or its overturn.

Exclusions to the foregoing coverages include wear and tear, freezing, mechanical or electrical breakdown, war, explosion of nuclear weapons, and loss caused by radioactive contamination.

Commercial vehicle coverage

Trucks are eligible for coverage under a BAP and under a truckers' policy specifically designed for long-haul truckers. Liability, physical damage, and medical payments coverage is available. For rating purposes, commercial vehicles were once divided into seven classes based on vehicle usage. Within each class, trucks were further classified as to size and territory. A new simplified rating plan devised by the Insurance Services Office (ISO) became effective in October 1975. It is similar to the private passenger plan in that primary and secondary rating factors are utilized. The primary factors are vehicle size, intensity of usage, and radius of operation. The secondary factors deal with special vehicle categories. The old rating plan relied heavily on "vehicle usage" for rate determinations, but loss experience showed rates were often inaccurate for the insured exposure. Thus, "usage" was replaced by "intensity of usage." Three classifications apply. Service use, or the transportation of personnel, supplies, and equipment to job sites, is the least intense use. The next higher intensity classification is retail use, or the pickup and delivery of goods to households. Finally, vehicles used for all other business purposes are classified as commercially used, the most intense and highest rated group. Another major change in the new rating plan involves truck fleets, which received discounts under the old plan. Loss statistics showed fleets have more claims than nonfleet trucks, so under the new plan a fleet surcharge is added.

Public vehicle coverage

A public auto is an auto of *any* type used as a public or livery conveyance for passengers. It also can be a private passenger car rented to others without a driver. Policies for public autos cover the named insured and any other person or organization using the auto or legally responsible for its use if permission for its use is granted by the named insured. The rate depends on the vehicle type, its size, and the territory involved. Underwriting of many public livery exposures is time-consuming. Many insurers refuse insurance on taxicabs and rental autos. The larger operators often have self-insurance plans to supplement or replace commercial coverage. Many insurers do not insure owners of any public autos other than buses.

Nonownership coverage

Frequently, an employee's car is used in the service of the employer. If an accident occurs, the employer and employee may be sued for damages. If the court holds that the car was under the employer's direction and control, the employer may be held liable. While the insurance (e.g., a PAP) on the employee-owned automobile normally would cover the employer for his or her vicarious liability,[4] certain actions of the employee/insured may have voided coverage. Furthermore, the liability limits of the employee's policy may not be adequate to cover fully the amount of the judgment against the employer. The nonowner form of auto liability insurance protects the employer in such cases.

Garage insurance

Garage insurance is available for those regularly engaged in auto sales; auto repair; operation of public gasoline stations; auto storage; and the sale and repair of self-propelled land equipment, such as tractors.

Garage liability form. Garage liability insurance has three coverage divisions: premises and operations, product and completed operations, and auto liability. Both bodily injury and property damage coverage is written on an occurrence basis. The policy provides for automobile and premises medical payments and uninsured motorists coverage. Garage keepers' legal liability coverage (a type of bailee coverage) may be added.

Garage keepers' legal liability form. The owner of an automobile repair shop, storage garage, or parking lot who receives customer's automobiles for repair or storage for a charge is legally a bailee and can be held legally liable for loss or damage caused by ordinary negligence. Because the garage liability policy excludes coverage for damage to property

---

[4] Vicarious liability arises when the law imputes to one party the negligent conduct of another. Coverage for vicarious liability is provided in the PAP under the definition of a covered person (Part A): "For your covered auto, any person or organization but only with respect to legal responsibility for acts or omission of a person for whom coverage is afforded under this Part."

of others in the care, custody, or control of the insured, garage keepers' legal liability policy is available to cover this exposure. The policy covers the garage owner's liability for damage to autos of others in the garage's care caused by:

1. Specified perils (fire, explosion, theft, riot or civil commotion, vandalism, or malicious mischief).
2. Comprehensive.
3. Collision.

In addition to insuring on the basis of legal liability, the insured has the option to broaden the coverage to cover customers' cars on either an excess (35 percent increase in premium) or primary (50 percent increase in premium) basis *without regard to legal liability*.

Rates are based on the maximum number of autos that will be stored in the garage at any one time. This coverage may be written in conjunction with a garage liability policy or may be added to a special multiperil policy (discussed in Chapter 15).

Compensating Victims of Automobile Accidents

A basic problem of auto insurance is the provision of an effective and efficient system for compensating accident victims. An *effective* system is one that guarantees those injured the payments due them according to law. Until recently most legislation dealt with improving the effectiveness of the tort system of reparations. An *efficient* system is one that provides reparations at the lowest cost (insurance premiums, costs of litigation, and delays in claim settlements) consistent with social justice. The current legislative thrust is toward improving efficiency by making fundamental changes in the reparation system. Basic arguments center about what changes are consistent with social justice.

The methods by which states attempt to provide for both effective and efficient reparation of auto accident victims include financial responsibility laws, compulsory automobile insurance, unsatisfied judgment funds, uninsured motorists insurance, and no-fault insurance. A brief discussion of each method follows.

Financial responsibility laws

Every state has a law to protect the public from financial loss caused by careless and financially irresponsible motorists. These laws require drivers to furnish evidence of financial responsibility. Usually this evidence need not be shown until after an accident (unfortunately); however, in several states responsibility must be shown when the car is registered. Statutes deferring evidence until after an accident are called *financial responsibility laws*. In general, these laws provide that all drivers and owners involved in an accident causing a given amount of property damage or any bodily injury must immediately post security to guarantee payment of judgments that could arise.[5] Proof of financial security may consist of an insurer's certification that the party involved has liability limits of a stated amount (ranging from $5,000/$10,000 bodily injury and $5,000 property damage to $25,000/$50,000 bodily injury and $25,000 property damage, with the majority of states near the high end of the range), the posting of a bond, or a cash deposit. In 14 states, in addition to posting security, those involved in an accident must show financial responsibility for future accidents.

The diversity of required limits among the various states could create a problem for many insureds when traveling from state to state. Many insureds either (1) choose not to purchase higher limits than required by law or (2) are not able to obtain higher limits because of some constraining factor (an insured may be a member of an AIP that will not write more than the minimum limits). The PAP remedies this problem by automatically providing the higher limits required by the state in which the accident occurs. The PAP also will meet the required minimum limits of the state in which an accident occurs if that state has a compulsory insurance law (see below). These provisions are either included in, or can be added to, other types of automobile liability insurance policies.

In most states, persons in an accident are notified of the suspension of their driver's licenses and auto registrations. If financial security can be shown within a certain period, the suspension does not become effective. If security is not shown, the license and registration are suspended for one year. After a year, suspension is lifted if no suit has commenced. It is lifted earlier if evidence is presented showing the case is settled. Financial responsibility laws do not guarantee that every driver is financially responsible, principally because responsibility does not have to be shown until after an accident. Judgments may be more easily obtained than collected.

The Motor Carrier Act of 1980, which brought deregulation to the trucking industry, set up federal guidelines for the financial responsibility of motor carriers. By July 1983, evidence of financial responsibility for some carriers of hazardous cargo required either a surety bond or insurance (usually the latter) which provided limits of at least $5 million for liability losses.

Compulsory automobile insurance

Since 1927, Massachusetts has required that before a motor vehicle can be registered, the owner has to show financial responsibility for bodily injuries due to negligent operation of the vehicle. The responsibility may be demonstrated by depositing with the state $5,000 in securities or cash, or by producing a surety bond or a liability policy with specified

---

[5] The U.S. Supreme Court in *Bell* v. *Burson, Director, Georgia Department of Public Safety,* 1971 CCH (Automobile) 7009, held that the license of an uninsured motorist involved in an accident may not be revoked for failure to show financial responsibility until the motorist is shown to be at fault. State supreme courts later made similar rulings.

limits. In 1957, most motorists buying New York license plates were required to have liability insurance with at least $10,000/$20,000 bodily injury and $5,000 property damage limits. In 1958, North Carolina passed a similar law. As of early 1984, more than half the states had some form of compulsory automobile insurance.

The success of compulsory auto insurance laws has been hotly debated in insurance circles. Insurers protest that the maximum rate permitted by the state is inadequate. Other arguments against the laws are the enforcement difficulties, the interference with individual freedom, the tendency to cause excessive claims consciousness, and the threat to private enterprise. Those favoring compulsory auto insurance reject these arguments as not strong enough to counteract the advantage of forcing every licensed car owner to demonstrate financial responsibility *before* even one accident.

Unsatisfied-judgment funds

The unsatisfied-judgment plan was first developed in Manitoba and now is used in nine Canadian provinces and five states. (Manitoba currently has a state-owned auto facility.) Funds are available to accident victims who cannot collect judgments from negligent drivers with insufficient resources (usually because these drivers have no valid, collectible insurance). The funds are financed by a fee charged all motorists, a fee charged uninsured motorists, or an assessment on insurers based on auto liability premiums written in the state. Unsatisfied-judgment funds differ as to deductibles applied, minimum amounts of loss covered, court action requirements, and claims for property damage liability. When a victim is compensated by this fund, the negligent driver's license is revoked until the fund is reimbursed with interest.

Uninsured motorists insurance

Uninsured motorists insurance is a required coverage in several states on all auto policies and strongly encouraged in all others. It covers the policyowner and family members if struck by a hit-and-run driver or by one who is uninsured, has insurance below limits required by financial responsibility laws, or is insured by a financially irresponsible insurer. The coverage extends to passengers in an auto covered under the policy and to those riding in nonowned autos operated by the named insured or spouse. In a few states uninsured motorist coverage applies to property damage with deductibles of $100 or more. The coverage is liability insurance and not accident insurance. Payments are made only to insureds who would have been entitled to damages had there been liability insurance covering an at-fault driver. In most states, the question of liability and amount of damages are determined by negotiation between the insured and insurer, or by arbitration using the rules of the American Arbitration Association.

Underinsured motorists endorsement

In many states an underinsured motorists endorsement may be added to the PAP and other auto policies. The insuring agreement requires the insurer to pay the difference between bodily injury losses of its insured and the limit of bodily injury liability insurance carried by an at-fault driver who caused the insured's loss. For example, Fred Wright was out for a Sunday drive at his usual and very legal pace of 55 miles per hour when Janice Hotshoe, who was hurrying home after her Saturday night date, failed to see Fred's car and hit it from the rear. The ensuing crash resulted in a whiplash injury to Fred and a traffic ticket to Janice for causing the accident by following too closely. Fred incurred $30,000 in medical and other costs (a small loss compared to the loss he suffered when his doctor told him he couldn't go trout fishing for six months). Unfortunately, Janice's insurance coverage provided only the minimum amount of bodily injury liability required by the state, $20,000 per person and $40,000 per accident. As Fred had purchased $40,000 of underinsured motorists protection with his PAP contract, his coverage was sufficient to cover the difference between the limits of Janice's policy and the extent of his losses. This endorsement protects the insured in situations where an at-fault driver is insured (thereby preventing the insured from collecting under uninsured motorists insurance), but for an amount less than the extent of the innocent victim's losses.

No-fault insurance

The logic of combining tort liability with insurance has been questioned and discussed from many viewpoints. The purpose of tort law is to place the accident cost on the one at fault. The purpose of insurance is to relieve the wrongdoer from the consequences of an act by paying defense costs and assessed damages. Is an insurance system in conflict with a tort system? Many argue that the two are in such conflict that together they lead to resource misallocation, whimsical behavior, and unfair results. Increasing pressures for changes to separate insurance from tort law when applied to bodily injuries suffered by auto accident victims are evident. One change is a "no-fault" system financed by compulsory insurance. The basic philosophy of no-fault plans is that one should be compensated for medical expenses and income losses by one's own insurer, regardless of fault. This idea is based on the assumption that auto accidents are similar to on-the-job accidents—they are inevitable, and assessing blame serves no useful purpose. Analogies to workers' compensation programs are used by no-fault advocates.

Pros and cons. Proponents of a no-fault system argue that the present tort system of compensating and administering claims (1) is cumbersome and slow (more than half the auto accident cases take in excess of two years to complete, and in several major cities even seriously injured victims must wait five or more years); (2) often overcompensates those with small losses and undercompensates those with large losses (insurers usually settle small nuisance claims involving income losses and medical expenses under $500 at more than quadruple that amount, but when these losses total more than $25,000, the claimants recover only about one third of their loss); (3) is costly to administer (auto cases consume much of the time of state and federal courts; lawyers' fees amount to about 12½ percent of premiums; and injured victims receive only about 44 percent of the premiums for claim payments); (4) is inadequate (many injured persons receive nothing because of financially irresponsible drivers; the fault system, as discussed in Chapter 4, except in comparative negligence states requires the injured party to be free from fault, thus causing many victims to settle out of court for inadequate amounts rather than take their chances in court); and (5) leads to corruption (those involved in tort action are likely to overstate the facts, magnify the issues, and sometimes blatantly lie).

Proponents of a no-fault system express concern for persons injured in auto accidents who receive no compensation if the injuries are not traceable to a third party's carelessness. The tort system has produced claim payments in less than half the accidents in which persons have been seriously injured or killed. Many proposed no-fault plans would remove most auto cases from the courts, restrict recovery for pain and suffering, and distribute limited reparations to all who experience losses. Advocates contend these changes will result in cost savings and premium reductions. Because fault will not be a factor in paying most claims, a more nearly equitable disbursement would be anticipated. Proponents of a no-fault system also claim that many tort-feasors (persons at fault for accidents) escape responsibility for their wrongs because liability insurance has eroded the concept of individual responsibility and retribution.

Critics of no-fault plans retort that the basic principle of the tort-fault system is that one causing loss to another should fairly and adequately provide compensation for those losses. They state that as the true purpose is not necessarily to punish the tort-feasor, how payment is accomplished (from liability insurance or other means) is irrelevant. To say that the wrongdoer is not concerned about a possible adverse negligence judgment would be a gross misstatement. Court cases are time-consuming for the defendant, and the possibility exists that the judgment will exceed the amount of insurance. Accident-prone individuals may find it difficult and expensive to buy liability limits beyond those offered under AIPs.

While critics of no-fault insurance admit the present tort system is not concerned with persons injured as a result of their own negligence, they say disability income and medical payment insurance may be purchased to cover these losses. Critics of the no-fault system argue that it would (1) reduce driver responsibility and hamper accident prevention techniques (the elimination of the risk of a lawsuit would affect care exercised by drivers, and the absence of need to determine fault would reduce efforts to find accident causes); (2) force motorists to buy insurance protection against careless conduct of others (the individual's right to sue is eliminated, and justice becomes mechanical and mass-produced); (3) at least partially eliminate recovery for pain and suffering (nearly half of all amounts paid under the tort system for auto bodily injury claims is for pain and suffering); (4) not reduce premiums to the degree claimed by advocates (the actuarial studies supporting claims of reduced cost are spurious); and (5) produce an inequitable rating structure (careless teenagers driving fast sports cars could demand lower premiums than careful parents driving station wagons because fault would not be a factor in the reparations system).

The principal supporters of a *pure* no-fault system (complete elimination of tort liability) are: Consumers Union, the 3-million-member National Council of Senior Citizens, various labor unions, the Risk and Insurance Management Society, Inc., and many established stock insurers and their trade association, the American Insurance Association. Opposed to *any* type of no-fault plan are the American Bar Association and the American Trial Lawyers Association. They have been accused of opposing no-fault legislation because it would eliminate a need for lawyers in settling auto claims. More than one sixth of the total income of American Bar Association members is derived from auto accident cases; a large percentage of practicing U.S. attorneys earn much of their income from these cases.

Current issues.   Although the no-fault concept itself is still being debated, 24 states as of early 1984 have established some form of no-fault auto insurance, and a federal no-fault law is still under discussion. Two current problems facing legislatures are the primacy issue and the applicability of no-fault insurance to property damage.

Primacy.   The primacy issue deals with the question of whether or not no-fault auto insurers should be the primary source of medical and income benefits for accident victims. To decrease claim costs and reduce auto liability premiums, most state no-fault laws seek to coordinate benefits for victims. Under the tort system, an injured party can collect payments from any and all available sources (group and private insurance plans, first-party auto insurance payments, Medicare, social security, and tort awards). This practice results in significant benefit duplication, and no-fault laws seek to eliminate this wasteful and unnecessary duplication. Auto insurers believe they are the ones to provide the primary coverage, while Blue Cross and Blue Shield organizations want their coverage to be primary, with auto insurance as excess coverage. The Blues' position is supported by organized labor.

Both groups argue strongly for their positions, but the preponderance of *objective* arguments seem to favor making auto insurance the primary coverage. The Blues have no experience in administering disability income payments, while auto insurers have had experience with both disability income and medical payments coverage. If the Blues were primary, auto insurers still would have to process all nonmedical expenses. An argument is that greater efficiency results if one insurer handles all related claims. Primary coverage by the Blues could create problems for injured insureds who had become ineligible for their group medical expense insurance; primary auto coverage would allow these insureds to avoid needless coverage gaps. Where health insurance is available for employees, primary coverage by the Blues would give employees a tax advantage because employees need not report as income premiums paid by employers for this insurance (see Chapter 19). However, employees must report as income employer-paid auto insurance premiums under employee benefit plans. And finally, if a *comprehensive national health insurance plan* is passed, some of its staggering cost could be shifted to the motoring public by making auto insurance primary.[6]

No-fault for property damage. Some states with modified no-fault laws have extended the no-fault principle to include property damage victims. The usual attempt to justify the practice is based on the assumption that no distinction exists in the problems of bodily injury and property damage reparations, and that the fault system is the main source of problems in compensating accident victims. But many of the system's shortcomings with respect to bodily injury claims do not apply to most property damage claims. One reason for instituting the no-fault bodily injury system is the elimination of benefit duplication. However, duplication has never been allowed for property damage benefits. Claim settlements for bodily injury cases often include amounts for pain and suffering, inconvenience, and loss of consortium. These general damage awards are not paid for property damage claims, making them easier to determine. Attorneys, heavily involved in bodily injury cases, are not used nearly so much for property damage disputes. For these reasons, little evidence supports the conclusion that a no-fault property damage system will result in cost savings to insurance buyers. In declaring a no-fault property damage statute unconstitutional, the Florida Supreme Court said that no case had been presented showing public necessity for the abolition of the right to sue for recovery of a property damage loss. At the present time it seems doubtful that such a case can be presented.[7]

Constitutionality. Several states have experienced problems relating to whether or not their no-fault laws are constitutional. As of January 1976, no-fault laws had been upheld by the supreme courts of eight states when the U.S. Supreme Court declined to hear a challenge to the constitutionality of such laws. The court dismissed an appeal from

---

[6] For a discussion of the primacy issue, see R. I. Mehr and M. H. Shumate, "Primacy in Automobile Bodily Injury Coverage," *The Journal of Risk and Insurance,* June 1975, pp. 216–20.

[7] R. I. Mehr and G. W. Eldred, "Should the 'No-Fault' Concept Be Applied to Automobile Property Damage?" *The Journal of Risk and Insurance,* March 1975, pp. 17–33.

a decision of the Connecticut Supreme Court upholding a no-fault law enacted there in 1972. In state supreme courts the vote frequently has been close.[8] Constitutional questions have been raised concerning the proposed national no-fault bill. The constitutional issues involved in no-fault auto insurance or in the abolition (or modification) of the tort system have by no means been solved. Workers' compensation laws, it will be recalled (Chapter 13), faced constitutional questions that eventually were resolved. A similar destiny may be in store for no-fault laws applying not only to auto liability but also to other forms of liability: products, malpractice, and so on.

Modified no-fault plans.   Major insurance company trade associations support a modified no-fault plan. Included in these associations are insurers that write a major share of the auto premiums in the United States. *Modified* no-fault laws are in effect in 12 states (now that Nevada has repealed its law). Plans approaching *pure* no-fault are in effect in three states (Michigan, New York, and Minnesota). Eight states have *add-on* no-fault laws, which in reality are *no* no-fault laws because the tort remedy remains in full. These laws require only that first-party coverage be added to auto policies.

Massachusetts.   In 1970, Massachusetts became the first state to pass a *modified* no-fault law. Its plan, effective in 1971, is not a pure no-fault plan because it preserves the fundamental characteristics of the tort system. Even in its modified form, the Massachusetts plan had strong critics (especially among trial lawyers) who, failing to keep the plan from being passed, unsuccessfully pressed for amendments to arouse industry opposition. In 1971, the Massachusetts Supreme Court upheld the no-fault law. The plaintiff (joined in opposing the law by the American Trial Lawyers Association and the Massachusetts Bar Association) argued that the law unconstitutionally deprived him of his right to recover by tort law.

Under the Massachusetts plan, the victim's own insurer provides compensation, regardless of fault, up to $2,000 for out-of-pocket expenses, including hospital bills and 75 percent of wages. The plan prohibits tort action for pain and suffering unless medical bills are more than $500 or disfigurement or death occurs. Late in 1971, the Massachusetts legislature extended the no-fault principle to property damage and made property damage liability insurance compulsory. In late 1976, the property damage section of the law was repealed (effective January 1, 1977) and claims involving property damage once again are subject to the tort liability system. Property damage liability insurance, with a minimum limit of $5,000, is required of all motorists subject to the law. The plan is compulsory for all autos registered in the state.

---

[8] The Supreme Court of Michigan in a 4–3 decision held that state's law unconstitutional but delayed the effective date of the decision (see Chapter 4, p. 82). Legislation was later passed that remedied the objections of the Michigan Supreme Court and allowed the no-fault law to continue in effect.

The plan's proponents believe that the main deficiencies of the present system can be overcome by shortening settlement delays through eliminating the need to establish fault for minor claims and cutting costs through elimination of legal services and overpayment of small claims. At the same time the plan maintains the major benefits of the present system: the recovery for pain and suffering as well as for economic losses in excess of no-fault benefits.

Michigan. In 1973, the most comprehensive no-fault plan in the United States (Michigan's) became effective. Liability insurance with minimum limits of $20,000/$40,000/$10,000 is mandatory. No threshold specifying a dollar amount of loss is set for determining when tort actions may be instigated. Instead, suits are allowed only when (1) economic loss exceeds the no-fault benefits discussed in the following paragraph, (2) death, serious impairment, or disfigurement occurs, or (3) the accident resulted from an intentional tort. The Michigan law was the first to use a "verbal threshold" to limit the amount payable for auto accident-related suits. Verbal threshold no-fault laws are distinguished by the absence of any reference to a stated dollar amount of loss to be met before tort action is allowed. Other states that use verbal thresholds in their no-fault laws have adopted variations of the criteria from the Michigan law.

The insurer pays *all* reasonable medical expenses incurred by the insured, including those for care, recovery, and rehabilitation. No time or amount limits are established for this coverage. Some insurers had warned that this unrestricted provision might cause "shocking" premium increases; they proposed that some limit, such as $100,000, be included. Reasons for initial insurer objections included the expected effects of inflation and the occurrence of many injuries to young children. Insurers believed that lifetime payments to these people would cause rates to increase dramatically.[9] Funeral expenses are paid up to $1,000, and loss of income is reimbursed up to 85 percent of earnings (maximum of $1,000 a month, subject to cost-of-living adjustments, for three years). Although awards payable under workers' compensation plans and social security are primary to no-fault benefits, no restriction is placed on duplicate benefits available from private health insurance plans. The insurer will pay benefits for "essential services" such as household help and child care up to a maximum of $20 a day for three years. Survivor and dependent benefits up to $1,475 a month for three years also are included. These benefits also increase with changes in the cost of living.

---

[9] However, Michigan's no-fault experience suggests that these subjective fears (though seemingly logical) were not warranted. *The Rutgers Law Review* (1977) measured the change in Michigan's auto personal injury premiums during 1972–77. The study found an 11 percent decrease in total personal injury premiums for both no-fault and fault-finding claims. Studies of Michigan's no-fault experience covering the period 1976–81 show a decrease in the number of personal injury claims, but an increase in the size of the average claim. By the end of the study period, personal injury premiums had begun to rise.

Other plans.   Modified no-fault plans usually prohibit certain persons from receiving no-fault benefits. These persons include those driving under the influence of liquor or drugs, those committing a felony or trying to avoid arrest, and those intentionally injuring themselves or others. The plans usually have pain and suffering damages based on a threshold; that is, no recovery is allowed for pain and suffering unless economic and medical losses exceed a given amount (the threshold).

The addition of no-fault benefits *(add-on-benefits)* to an insured's auto liability policy without impairing the right of the injured party to sue the person causing the loss is provided by several states. These add-on benefits are compulsory in some states and voluntary in other states. In essence, these plans grant expanded medical and disability benefit payments not found under traditional auto medical payments coverage. A system of subrogation is established in which the insurer paying no-fault benefits may recover against the negligent party. The laws usually require arbitration of disputes involving the question of liability or damages. Payments made under no-fault coverage are deducted from any damages awarded by arbitration or court action. The advantage claimed for superimposed first-party benefits on a fault system over a modified no-fault system is that it simplifies insurance pricing and forces those that present the greatest driving hazard to pay the highest share of auto accident costs. The argument is that a first-party coverage system when superimposed on the tort system has all the advantages of a modified no-fault system while preserving the concept of accountability for negligent driving.

Federal no-fault.   Several different no-fault bills have been considered at the federal level. The first national no-fault auto insurance measure was introduced in 1971 by Senators Hart of Michigan and Magnuson of Washington. The bill, which failed to pass, would have established a national compulsory no-fault system that would have paid all medical and rehabilitation expenses for accident victims. Lost wages also would have been reimbursed up to specified amounts. Bills introduced (but not adopted) in 1977 and 1978 would have established federal standards for state-administered no-fault automobile insurance plans. Each state could develop an independent plan if it met the minimum standards of the federal plan. As more than 1,600 insurance companies are opposed to the bills that have been introduced, passage in the near future of a federal plan seems unlikely.[10]

---

[10] For a simple review of no-fault, see Jeffrey O'Connell, "No-fault Insurance: What, Why, and Where," *The Annals of the American Academy of Political and Social Science* 443 (May 1979), pp. 72–81. For an extensive study of the auto injury compensation problem, see the two-volume work, *Automobile Injuries and Their Compensation in the United States,* published by the All-Industry Research Advisory Committee in March 1979 and distributed by the Research Department of the Alliance of American Insurers, 20 North Wacker Drive, Chicago, Ill. 60606.

Loss Prevention

Losses from auto accidents, including property damage, medical and legal costs, and income losses, total more than $60 billion annually and are increasing dramatically. Underwriting losses to insurers writing auto coverage have been high. Although the premium level has grown substantially, it has not kept pace with claims. Legislators, insurers, and insureds are deeply concerned with auto problems and are seeking solutions. Proposals aimed at loss prevention include improved car design, better drivers, improved highways, and more effective enforcement of traffic safety laws.

Traffic deaths have experienced some decline attributable to energy-saving measures either imposed on or voluntarily adhered to by drivers. Some of these factors are the 55-mph speed limit, car pooling, and a reduction in night driving. Nevertheless, economic losses arising from operation of autos continued their upward trend because of increased accident frequency (most driving is local and unaffected by speed limits) and inflation.

Better car design

The development of better car designs to reduce the severity of bodily injury losses and auto repair costs concerns insurers, government authorities, and consumer advocates. The traffic safety problem has become more acute with the trend toward smaller cars accelerated by rising gasoline prices. Small cars are more dangerous to passengers than are medium-sized and large autos. As one solution, safety experts and the auto insurance industry are pressing for mandatory use of passive restraint devices such as front seat air bags that inflate automatically. Some insurers offer rate reductions for cars equipped with these bags. Insurers also support federal legislation requiring front and rear bumpers to withstand impacts at speeds up to 5 mph. Some insurers believe the upper limit should be 10 mph. However, automakers object to these standards and continually push for time limit extensions to meet safety standards. What do a few lost lives mean if saving them works a hardship on the auto industry? After all, did not a GM executive say a number of years ago that what is good for General Motors is good for the country? Yet one must recognize that the slowness of automakers to respond is not so much a technological problem as a consumer indifference problem. One authority states that the public attitude toward highway safety and highway accidents is one of apathy and fatalism. Even with the evidence indicating the lifesaving capabilities of seat belts, over 80 percent of all drivers fail to use them regularly.

Improved highways

Better highway design is necessary to reduce losses from auto accidents. Steel and concrete sign supports, steel guardrail ends that act as spears, and concrete bridge railings are obstacles that contribute to high loss severity. Effective alternatives are breakaway signposts and energy-absorbing barriers. Cook County, Illinois (Chicago), implemented a plan using these alternatives, and the auto-accident fatality rate dropped to the lowest of any major U.S. city.

The driver

Mechanical failure accounts for less than 10 percent of auto accidents. Many safety experts believe one measure necessary to reduce losses is stricter licensing standards for drivers, plus the removal of habitual traffic offenders from the roads. Especially important is removal of intoxicated drivers. Some authorities believe mandatory jail sentences for persons convicted of drunken driving would effectively keep the drunk driver off the road. Every state has an "implied consent" statute whereby all motorists, when obtaining a driver's license, automatically consent to a test of their blood's alcoholic content at any time they are operating a motor vehicle. Other proposals include lowering the percent of alcohol required to declare a person legally drunk and an expanded information program on alcohol as a factor in auto accidents.

A number of civic groups have been formed to help in the fight against drunken driving. These organizations include groups such as RID (Remove Intoxicated Drivers), SADD (Students Against Drunk Drivers), and MADD (Mothers Against Drunk Drivers). One of their primary activities has been the continued lobbying of legislators and congressional representatives to stiffen penalties imposed for conviction of drunken driving. In addition, they have worked to raise the drinking age to 21. These efforts were rewarded in mid-1984 when the U.S. Congress passed a law requiring states to set 21 as the minimum legal drinking age, or face the possibility of losing federal highway funds. The law also provides incentives for states to establish tougher drunk driving laws and penalties. In mid-1983, 19 states were already using 21 as the drinking age for all alcoholic beverages. An additional 8 states had imposed restrictions on the type of beverages that could be legally sold to young people age 18 in some states, 19 or 20 in others. The new federal law allows these 8 states (plus the remaining 23) two years to adopt the age 21 limit, with incentives for states to act during the phase-in period. The use of federal highway funds as an incentive to obtain state action is similar to the strategy employed to get states to lower their speed limits to 55 miles per hour. If the states move as quickly to raise the drinking age as they did to lower their speed limits, the new age requirement likely will be in place nationwide before the end of 1985.

Safe-driver insurance plan.   Under the safe-driving rating plan, premiums are based upon the insured's conviction and accident record. Points are charged against the insured. The more serious the conviction or accident, the larger is the penalty. The experience period for rating varies among states, with two and three years the most common. The plan applies to liability, medical payments, and collision insurance, and is used with all types of auto policies.

Good-student discount plan. Because of the apparent connection between good grades and good driving habits, most automobile insurers offer substantial premium discounts for student drivers in the upper 20 percent of their class with a B average or better.

Law enforcement

In addition to intoxicated drivers, speeders and other traffic offenders account for most auto accidents. These facts indicate need for better traffic regulation enforcement and more stringent penalties for violators. Insurers also pay for losses caused by auto thefts. As a joint effort of six federal agencies, the Interagency Committee on Auto Theft was formed with the goal of reducing thefts by 50 percent. The group maintains that because three fourths of all thefts are by juveniles, losses could be significantly reduced by improving ignition and door locks. (No type of lock would deter the professional car thief.) Other suggestions are the enactment of state laws that provide for (1) uniform state automobile registration laws and title procedures, (2) prohibiting drivers from leaving unlocked cars or autos with keys in the ignition on public streets, and (3) making car theft a uniformly extraditable offense (extraditions are now possible only from Canada and Mexico).

Summary

1. All drivers have a liability exposure when operating a motor vehicle. They also may incur personal injury to themselves and physical damage to their cars. Auto insurance is available to protect against these loss exposures.
2. The personal auto policy (PAP) covers private passenger autos and light trucks owned by or leased to individuals or married couples.
3. The PAP protects an individual driving a nonowned automobile. Separate nonownership policies are available to extend nonowned coverage both for liability and physical damage. Nonownership insurance also is used to protect employers from liability resulting when employees use their own cars in their employer's service.
4. As most people believe all drivers should have access to auto insurance, states have set up Automobile Insurance Plans (AIPs) to assign extra-hazardous insureds on a premiums-written pro rata basis to insurers operating in the state. The expense and claims experience of these plans has been poor, so some states are experimenting with alternative solutions.
5. Special policies have been developed to insure all kinds of recreational vehicles.
6. In auto rating, 161 classifications are used, which group drivers

according to age, sex, marital status, and accident record, and classify cars according to their primary use (pleasure, business, transportation to and from work, and so on). Trucks are rated according to their size, intensity of usage, and radius of operation. Rates for public vehicles depend upon the vehicle type, size, and the territory involved.

7. Revision in auto insurance rating can be expected after a reevaluation of the factors currently used and as states eliminate sex as a rating factor.

8. Autos owned by partnerships or corporations must be insured under the business auto policy (BAP), which offers coverage more restricted in most instances than the PAP.

9. The garage liability policy protects against liability from bodily injury and property damage.

10. Property in the garage owner's care, custody or control must be protected with the garage keepers' legal liability form.

11. A basic problem in auto insurance is providing an effective and efficient system for compensating accident victims. Financial responsibility laws and compulsory insurance requirements help protect the public from financial loss caused by careless and financially irresponsible motorists. In some states unsatisfied-judgment funds pay victims unable to collect judgments from negligent drivers with insufficient resources. Uninsured motorists insurance also protects the innocent victim.

12. No-fault auto insurance is the most discussed solution. The basic philosophy of no-fault plans is that one should be compensated for medical expenses and income losses by one's own insurer, regardless of fault. Twenty-three states have adopted modified no-fault plans. Among the issues currently being debated are those of primacy, the applicability of the no-fault principle to property damage losses, and the constitutionality of no-fault laws of various types.

13. Losses from auto accidents total more than $60 billion each year and continue to increase. Proposed methods of preventing losses include improved car design, better drivers, improved highways, and more effective traffic law enforcement.

Questions for Review

1. What is an "automobile" for insurance purposes?
2. What is a JUA? How does it work?
3. Compare and contrast the BAP with the PAP.
4. Explain the need for nonownership coverage.
5. How do auto financial responsibility laws differ from compulsory auto insurance laws?
6. Discuss the arguments commonly used for and against no-fault insurance.

7. Explain the primacy issue with respect to no-fault insurance.

8. Give *specific* suggestions for reducing the frequency and severity of auto accidents.

Questions for Discussion

1. Auto underwriters classify drivers according to age, sex, marital status, and accident record. Is this procedure unduly discriminatory? What is your concept of "unduly discriminatory"? Can you suggest a better method? Explain.

2. Can automobile insurance plans be justified? Which, if any, of the alternatives being tested do you believe are better than AIPs? Why?

3. Do you believe that the no-fault principle could be successfully applied to nonauto liability exposures such as medical malpractice and product liability? Explain.

4. Michigan has the most comprehensive no-fault plan in the United States. Compare its plan to a pure no-fault plan. Which would you prefer? Why?

5. Does your state have a no-fault auto plan? If so, describe and evaluate it. What criteria and standards have you used for evaluation? If not, why not? Explain why you believe your state should or should not have an auto no-fault plan. What criteria and standards have you used in answering this question?

15

Crime, surety, miscellaneous, and multiple line coverages

Crime coverages protect against loss by burglary, robbery, theft, forgery, embezzlement, and other dishonest acts. Fidelity coverages protect the employer from employee dishonesty, while surety coverages guarantee the performance of an obligation assumed by the applicant. Miscellaneous coverages discussed include glass, boiler and machinery, credit, accounts receivable, valuable papers, title, municipal bond, mutual fund, and aviation insurance. Included in the discussion of multiple line coverages are the Special Multi-Perils program, the Businessowners program, and several specialized multiple line forms.

Crime Coverages

The discussion of crime coverages is organized in this chapter on the basis of the customer for whom coverage is written.

Crime coverages for business

A business's merchandise, furniture, fixtures, money, and securities are exposed to loss by burglary, robbery, larceny, embezzlement, and forgery.[1] Several policies are available to protect against these losses. Usually excluded are manuscripts, records, or accounts; glass, letterings, or ornamentation; loss due to fire; and loss caused by vandalism, malicious mischief, war, nuclear hazards, or dishonest acts of an associate or employee. Other policies cover these exposures. Most crime forms may be written as part of the Special Multi-Peril program and other multiple line contracts discussed later in this chapter.

Mercantile open-stock burglary policy. The mercantile open-stock burglary policy is written for businesses handling merchandise.

Perils. The policy covers actual or attempted burglary, robbery of guards, and damage other than fire caused by criminal action. Coverage for robbery and theft of merchandise may be added by endorsement. (See footnote 1 for insurance definition of these terms.) Although not considered burglary or robbery, loss caused by a person hiding on the premises and later breaking out is covered. For burglary coverage to apply, there must be visible signs of forcible entry or exit.

Property. Covered property includes merchandise, furniture, fixtures, and equipment that the insured owns or for which the insured is legally liable. Jewelry is covered for $50 per piece. Furs stolen from show windows by a person breaking the glass from outside the premises are excluded. The general crime exclusions apply, and premises damaged by burglars are covered if the insured is the owner or is liable.

Period. The policy covers only while the premises are closed and is effective (and expires) at noon at the address in the policy. The policy can be canceled by both the insured and insurer.

Hazards excluded. Coverage is suspended if there is a change in conditions contributing to the loss. War, fire, vandalism, malicious mischief, and dishonest acts of employees are excluded.

Amount. The policy has a coinsurance clause, but it is inoperative if the insurance amount at each location equals a designated amount. The *amount limit* is determined by the type of merchandise, whereas the territory determines the coinsurance *percentage.* Coinsurance requirements may be satisfied by meeting either the *amount* or the *percentage* requirement. The policy may be scheduled, with all premises designated and specific insurance amounts applying to each. Or it may be blanket, with the face amount applying to any location in the United States, Virgin Islands, Canal Zone, Puerto Rico, or Canada.

---

[1] The typical person makes little, if any, distinction among the terms *burglary, robbery, theft* and related terms. In insurance, however, these terms have specific meanings defined in the policy. Briefly, *burglary* is forcible entry to premises; *robbery* is forcible taking from a person; *theft* or *larceny* is felonious taking of property; *embezzlement* is fraudulent appropriation of property; and *forgery* is falsely making or altering a document.

Mercantile safe burglary policy.   Some businesses keep money and securities in safes, whereas others (jewelry stores) have large quantities of merchandise in safes. The safe burglary policy protects these firms against loss by forcible entry into safes, removal of the safe from the premises and for any damage that results from actual or attempted burglary. The policy contains the usual crime form exclusions and also excludes loss resulting from lock manipulation and loss while specified protection is not maintained. The rate for this policy depends upon type of business, territory, and type of safe. Rate credits are given for various protective devices.

Mercantile robbery policy.   Robbery is not covered by either the mercantile open-stock or mercantile safe burglary policies. The mercantile robbery policy covers loss by actual or attempted robbery of money, securities, inventory, and other property. Two coverages are available: inside and outside. Premises damage is covered if the insured is the owner or is liable. The inside section covers if the robbery is committed within the insured's premises. The outside section covers the property against the same perils, but only while conveyed by a messenger outside the premises.

Gasoline stations have a special problem. Attendants are likely to be held up while outside the station but on the property. The policy does not cover such losses unless specifically endorsed, and a 50 percent additional premium is paid. Another problem involves robbery from homes of employees empowered to take business proceeds home for the night. The policy can be endorsed to protect such funds from burglary, robbery or both.

Robbery is defined broadly to include (1) taking property by actual or threatened violence inflicted on a messenger or custodian; (2) taking property from a messenger or custodian who has been killed or rendered unconscious; (3) feloniously taking property in the presence of a messenger or custodian aware of the act; (4) kidnapping, meaning taking property from within the premises by use or threat of violence to compel a custodian or messenger while outside the premises to admit the criminal to the premises; and (5) stealing property from within a show window on the premises while regularly open for business, if the thief has broken the window from the outside. The latter two definitions apply to inside coverage only, the others to both inside and outside coverages.

Custodian is defined as "the insured, a partner therein or an officer thereof or any employee thereof who is in the regular service of and duly authorized by the insured to have the care and custody of the insured property within the premises, excluding any person while acting as a [guard], porter or janitor." Messengers similarly are defined for property outside the premises except that guards, porters, and janitors qualify as messengers if the insured so designates.

Inside and outside coverage may be purchased separately. The inside rate is determined by the type of business and territory, and discounts are given for various protective measures. The outside rate depends on the territory and number of messengers and accompanying guards.

Paymaster robbery policy. For most insureds, the only need for outside coverage is payroll protection. The paymaster robbery form covers the payroll from the time it is drawn from the bank until the workers are paid. It covers loss of money and checks intended solely for the insured's payroll, the wallet, bag, satchel, safe, or chest containing the payroll and all damage to the premises occasioned by robbery from a custodian engaged in regular payroll duties inside the premises. The policy also protects employees robbed of their pay on the premises on payday at the same time a robbery or attempted robbery from a custodian or messenger occurs. The form covers loss of payroll funds from a messenger outside the premises, and nonpayroll money and securities up to 10 percent of the payroll insurance. The 10 percent coverage is not additional insurance but a provision allowing the total amount to cover both payroll and a limited amount of other funds.

Money and securities broad-form policy. The safe burglary, mercantile robbery, and paymaster policies may be bought separately or in combination. Broader money and securities coverage than would be obtained under all three policies combined may be purchased through the money and securities broad-form policy. It has two insuring agreements (on and off premises), and either or both may be bought. The on-premises agreement covers: (1) loss of money and securities from within the premises or recognized places of safe deposit caused by destruction, disappearance, or wrongful abstraction; (2) loss of other property caused by safe burglary or robbery within the premises; (3) damage to a locked cash register, cash drawer, or cash box on the premises caused by a felonious entry or attempted entry into the container; and (4) damage to the premises caused by robbery, safe burglary, or burglarious entry or attempted entry into the premises if the insured owns or is liable for the premises.

The off-premises agreement covers all loss of money and securities outside the premises caused by destruction, disappearance, or wrongful abstraction while conveyed by a messenger or an armored car company or while within the home of any messenger; all loss to other property caused by robbery or attempted robbery outside the premises while such property is conveyed by a messenger or an armored car company, and theft while the property is in the messenger's home.

Insureds who cannot afford the broad form may still buy coverage against the destruction of money and securities by adding the money and securities destruction endorsement to the interior robbery, storekeepers', or office burglary and robbery policy. Destruction of money and securities on the premises during business hours and within a safe while the premises are closed is covered for a small additional premium.

Burglary special-coverage forms. An available burglary special-coverage form includes the basic crime insurance provisions and exclusions but, like the standard fire policy, requires an endorsement to complete coverage. It is used to combine coverages such as mercantile safe burglary and mercantile robbery and to schedule coverages such as paymaster robbery, paymaster broad form, and money and securities destruction. Coverage for many special risks such as church theft, employees' or students' property burglary or theft, gravestone theft, and vending-machine theft also may be included.

Package policies. The *storekeepers' burglary and robbery policy,* a package policy including seven coverages often required by shopkeepers, is available to small shop owners and covers: (1) inside robbery, (2) outside robbery, (3) kidnapping, (4) safe burglary, (5) theft of money and securities from a bank night depository or from within a messenger's home, (6) mercantile open-stock burglary and robbery of a guard, and (7) damage caused by actual or attempted robbery and burglary.[2] All seven coverages are provided in one insuring agreement, sold in $250 units with the limit applying separately to each coverage. The insured may buy one to four units.

The *office burglary and robbery policy* is intended for office building tenants who sell no merchandise. It is written only for those offices not on the same or contiguous ground where the insured has property for sale, manufacture, cleaning, repairing, processing, storage, or distribution. Coverages similar to those of the storekeepers' policy are offered, except that the open-stock burglary protection is replaced by a theft within premises clause covering loss of office furniture, fixtures, equipment, instruments, and supplies.

Crime coverages for banks. Crime insurance for banks is a specialized field. The introduction of the bankers' blanket bond by Lloyd's of London early in this century and its subsequent development in the United States have made obsolete many former separate bank coverages. Bank coverages written in volume today other than the blanket bond are the bank burglary and robbery policy and the safe-deposit box policy. The blanket bond is discussed later in this chapter.

The *bank excess burglary and robbery policy* may be written as primary coverage for smaller banks but is usually written as excess coverage for banks buying the blanket bond. Burglary, robbery or both can be bought. The burglary insuring agreement covers loss by burglary of money, securities, and other property from within specified safes or vaults. Damage by vandalism and malicious mischief also is covered. The robbery insuring agreement covers loss of money and securities by robbery, vandalism, and malicious mischief occurring on the premises. Premises damage, including equipment, is covered if the insured is the owner or is liable for the damage.

The *combination safe depository policy* may be used by the bank to cover its legal liability (coverage A) and to cover customers' property and the bank's equipment (coverage B). The bank is legally liable to

---

[2] Money and securities destruction protection may be added for a small additional premium per premises.

use care in holding goods of others in safe-deposit boxes. For customer relations, the bank may wish to reimburse boxholders for losses, even though no legal liability exists. The bank may purchase either or both coverages. Under coverage A, the insurer pays all sums that the insured becomes *legally obligated* to pay by reason of liability for loss of customers' property while in safe-deposit boxes in vaults on the premises, property stored in vaults on the premises for customers, and property temporarily elsewhere on the premises in the course of deposit in or removal from such boxes or vaults. The only exclusions are contractual liability and the nuclear hazard. As evidenced by a recent court decision, the circumstances in which legal liability exists may be expanded. A California bank was held liable for customer losses caused by a safe-deposit box burglary because the bank had advertised its boxes as "burglar proof" and "islands of absolute security." Coverage B covers actual or attempted burglary and robbery and damage to customers' property. Damage to the premises and equipment is covered only if caused by actual or attempted burglary, robbery, vandalism, or malicious mischief.

Crime coverages for individuals

Most personal theft coverage is written as part of the Homeowners policies, discussed in Chapters 7–10. Theft protection under the personal property floater is described in Chapter 12. The basic policy written specifically to protect individuals against theft is the personal theft policy.

The broad form personal theft policy. The broad form personal theft policy provides wide coverage against burglary, robbery, theft, and mysterious disappearance of property of the insured, the immediate family, servants, and guests. Two basic insuring agreements (A and B) are available. Coverage A may be purchased separately, but to buy coverage B at least $1,000 of A must be bought. Coverage A protects against theft from the insured's premises. This protection is extended to include theft from within any bank, trust company, safe-deposit company, public warehouse, or occupied dwelling not owned, occupied, or rented by the insured, if the insured placed the property there for safekeeping. Damage to property and premises caused by theft or attempted theft, vandalism, or malicious mischief also is covered. If losses occur in parts of premises unoccupied by the insured, property of guests is excluded. Coverage B includes the same perils away from the premises. It covers loss to personal property owned or used by the insured, a permanent member of the household, or a residence employee. The policy for coverages A and B excludes animals; aircraft, automobiles, motorcycles and their equipment; and articles held as samples for sale or delivery. Boat losses are limited to $500. Loss of securities is limited to $500 and loss of money to $100.

Coverage is written on three forms: specific, divided, and blanket. Under the specific form, certain articles are separately described and enumerated. Divided coverage insures jewelry and furs for one amount and all other property for another amount. The blanket form applies the face amount of insurance to pay losses of any type of property. The amount of insurance written for coverage B on any of the forms may not exceed the amount written under coverage A.

The limited form personal theft policy.   The limited form combining both on- and off-premises theft coverage may be written separately or endorsed to some other contract. At least $1,000 must be purchased. Theft, damage to premises caused by theft or attempted theft, and malicious damage to insured property or to the interior of the premises are covered. Mysterious disappearance is excluded. Property is not covered if taken from a dormitory, fraternity house, or sorority house. Loss of money is limited to $100 and securities to $500.

Safe-deposit box coverages.   The bank is liable for safe-deposit box losses only if it is negligent. Thus, most losses will not be recoverable from the bank. Box owners can insure burglary and robbery losses of all property in their leased boxes. Money is excluded but may be added by endorsement for an additional premium. Also covered is damage to property caused by actual or attempted burglary, robbery, vandalism, or malicious mischief. The coverage is written as an endorsement to the burglary special-coverage policy and may insure against burglary, robbery or both.

Federal crime program

During the 60s, the crime rate jumped in most categories. The FBI's statistics showed that property crimes increased 151 percent and robbery, 177 percent. Three fourths of all reported robberies occurred in cities of over 250,000 population. These cities also had a disproportionate share of auto thefts and burglaries. These developments led to dramatic rate increases and a severe reduction in the availability of crime insurance.

In 1971 a federal crime insurance program was launched to provide coverage in those states where needed. The plan resembles the FAIR plans (Chapter 11) in utilizing agents and brokers to sell the coverage. The Federal Insurance Agency determines the states where coverage is necessary. These states have the option to establish a pool arrangement or an assigned-risk plan in which all licensed property insurers operating in the state must participate. If a state does not set up a satisfactory program within the time limits, the federal government can write crime insurance directly in that state. Many states are reluctant to develop programs. Why should one state incur the expenses to establish a plan when others do not? If no state plan exists, the federal government writes the coverage and finances underwriting losses through reinsurance under HUD's riot reinsurance fund. By developing its own plan, a state is denied these federal funds, so it is not surprising that states do not have crime insurance programs. This understandable reaction by the states has led to the planned termination (currently scheduled to be considered by Congress in September 1985) of the riot reinsurance program.

Federal crime insurance is available in 24 states, Puerto Rico and Washington, D.C. Areas designated as "high risk" have to pay higher rates. In the "high-risk" category, for example, are Miami, New York, and Trenton. Chicago, St. Louis, and Atlanta are examples of cities in the "average-risk" group and have lower rates. The program provides both commercial and residential burglary and robbery insurance. The maximum coverage is $15,000 for commercial and $10,000 for residential exposures. The statute provides that "affordable rates" based on FBI statistics will be charged. All coverages have deductibles, and the insured must use protective devices and procedures to reduce loss.

The federal program has not had the impact many believe it should have. Only 20,000 residential policies were sold in its first three years. In fact, as of mid-1984 only 48,000 policies were in force (including both residential and commercial exposures). But most people agree crime insurance is needed. Agents have been accused of lack of interest in selling the coverage and failing to inform those needing protection. Agents believe that the coverage costs too much and that guidelines regarding mandatory use of protective devices are complicated.

Bonding

A bond is a contract binding one party financially for the performance by another of an agreed-upon obligation. A suretyship contract involves three parties: a principal who promises performance; a surety who guarantees fulfillment, and a third party, the obligee, to whom these promises are made. If the principal does not achieve as promised, the surety must indemnify the obligee. Bonds that guarantee the principal's honesty are *fidelity bonds,* and those guaranteeing that the principal will accomplish certain tasks are *surety bonds.* The surety under either type is called upon only if the principal fails to live up to the agreement.

The nature of bonding

Is bonding insurance? This question has raised much heat and produced little light. The arguments that surety bonding is not insurance usually include these points:

1. Bonding always involves three parties; insurance, two.
2. The bond principal is in full control, whereas the insured ideally has no control over the event causing the loss.
3. Losses are not expected in surety bonding. Premiums are service fees for the use of the surety's name; in insurance, losses are expected and reflected in the premiums.

4. In bonding, the principal is liable to the surety for losses paid; in insurance, the insured does not agree to reimburse the insurer.

In fidelity bonding, losses are anticipated and considered in the rate. Most authorities agree that fidelity bonding resembles insurance.

Fidelity bond coverages

Fidelity bonds are discussed under several categories: individual and schedule bonds, general blanket bonds, special blanket bonds, forgery insurance, and the comprehensive dishonesty, destruction, and disappearance (3-D) policy.

Individual and schedule bonds. Two general types of fidelity bonds are available: individual and schedule. Individual bonds cover a particular named person. Schedule bonds may be name or position schedules.

The *name schedule bond* in effect combines several individual bonds. Covered persons must be listed, including the coverage amount applying to each person. New employees may be added and former employees deleted at any time, but all covered employees must be listed.

The *position schedule bond* lists the positions, specifying the amount for which each is bonded, so it is unnecessary to notify the bonding company of employee turnover. No change is necessary in the bond unless the number of workers in a position changes. The position schedule bond may include only positions the employer wants covered; but all workers in a given position must be covered if any in that position is covered.

Bonds have no expiration date and are valid until cancelled. Thus, if a bond has been in force since 1910, a loss occurring in 1911 but not discovered until 1976 would be covered. One can easily determine that a house has burned before the fire policy expires. It may not be easy to discover a loss in the event of infidelity. Lynn may tap the till for several years before Ms. Wong discovers it. By then, the bond may have been cancelled. A time limit is set for losses to be discovered and reported. The time following cancellation during which losses may be discovered and the bonding company held liable is the cutoff period and will vary from six months to three years. However, the loss must have occurred while the bond was in effect.

If an employer terminates a schedule bond and buys a new one, continuity of coverage exists, because the company selling the new bond will pay newly discovered losses that occurred under the old bond. The new bond covers losses only to the extent that they would have been covered by the old bond if discovered during its life. But if a loss under the old bond is discovered during its cutoff period, the old bond must pay the loss even though the new bond is in effect.

General blanket bonds. General blanket fidelity bonds are *commercial blanket* and *blanket position.* Either is written for anyone ineligible for the bankers' or brokers' blanket bonds or any federal or other public official bonds. Because they offer broad coverage, blanket bonds are the most popular method of covering employee dishonesty. No list of persons or positions appears, as blanket coverage is provided uniformly to all persons in the insured's regular service,[3] compensated by salary, wages, or commission, whom the insured may govern and direct at all times in the performance of such service. Blanket coverage means that the full bond amount (penalty) is available to pay a loss no matter how many employees are involved. Brokers, factors, commission merchants, consignees, contractors, and similar representatives are ineligible.

The *commercial blanket bond* guarantees employees' honesty up to the bond penalty. Loss payment terminates coverage on the defaulting employee, but the coverage is automatically restored to the original amount and is available for future losses and existing undiscovered losses. The penalty of the commercial blanket bond is the maximum available for any one loss regardless of the number of employees involved. If a $50,000 bond is in force, and the discovery is made that one employee has stolen $30,000, the bond is cancelled instantly for this employee, but the $50,000 is restored for newly discovered losses caused by other employees. The primary commercial blanket bond is issued for a $10,000 minimum but may be increased in multiples of $2,500 to $25,000 and in $5,000 multiples thereafter for as large a penalty as the bonding company will write.

The *blanket position bond* guarantees each employee's honesty up to the bond's penalty. The bond is issued with a minimum penalty of $2,500 and is available in multiples of $2,500 to a maximum of $100,000. In contrast to the commercial blanket bond, the maximum liability of the bonding company for loss under this plan is the product of the number of employees involved in the crime times the penalty of the bond. Thus, if a merchant has a $10,000 blanket position bond and three employees are involved, a total of $30,000 is available to pay the loss. Payment terminates coverage on the defaulting employees but does not affect coverage on other employees.

The blanket position bond coverage sometimes leads insureds into self-deception. The merchant with the $2,500 blanket position bond may feel protected for losses larger than $2,500. However, coverage in excess of $2,500 exists only if several employees are involved in the default. One clerk operating alone for years may succeed in stealing $5,000. The bonding company, however, would pay only $2,500, leaving the merchant with a $2,500 net loss. Most blanket position bonds are written for a low penalty—not a wise decision, as most losses involve "lone wolves" and are not joint operations.[4] Many insurance advisers believe that a

---

[3] Directors and trustees not otherwise employed by the insured and partners of the insured are not covered.

[4] On the other hand, times may be changing: a loss to a large eastern manufacturer of electrical equipment involved 32 employees; a southern telephone office had a loss that involved nearly the entire staff. If these incidents reveal a trend, one can expect an increase in the rates charged for blanket position bonds. If the electrical company had owned a blanket position bond for a $10,000 penalty only, the bonding company could have been liable up to $320,000.

commercial blanket bond usually is preferable to a blanket position bond. Some firms prefer a blanket position bond with a minimum penalty and additional specific excess indemnity over the blanket coverage. Thus, a position schedule bond could be added to provide additional protection on certain "sensitive" positions. Other insureds prefer to buy a position schedule bond and add a commercial blanket bond as excess coverage. In either case, premiums are adjusted to prevent a double charge for coverage.

Blanket bonds for financial institutions.   Special blanket bonds are written for banks, brokerage houses, savings and loan associations, credit unions, and other financial institutions. Many of these bonds were written before the general blanket bonds were developed. The demand for a general blanket bond arose from the interest in the bankers' blanket bond. Blanket bonds indemnify for loss of money, securities, bullion, precious metals and articles made from precious metals, jewelry, watches, necklaces, bracelets, gems, precious and semiprecious stones, and specified classes of valuable documents. They are written for an indefinite period and continue until terminated. Each bond is written for a specific liability for a single loss. Any number of separate losses may be recovered, as upon discovery of a loss the bond is fully reinstated without charge.

By 1915 U.S. insurers had developed a *bankers' blanket bond* (known as Form 24) to compete with Lloyd's of London, originators of the bond in this country. The coverage includes many sections. Section A, fidelity, covers loss through dishonesty of employees. Section B, premises, covers loss of covered property through robbery, burglary, larceny, theft, false pretenses, holdup, mysterious disappearance, misplacement, damage, or destruction, while the property is in any covered office of the insured and any loss, except by fire, to the insured's offices, furnishings, fixtures, equipment, safes, and vaults from a covered peril. Property covered includes money, postage and revenue stamps, securities, precious metals, jewelry, watches, and gems. Section C, in transit, covers loss of the insured classes of property through robbery, larceny, theft, holdup, or negligence of messengers while the property is in transit. Section F covers redemption of U.S. savings bonds, and section G provides counterfeit currency coverage. Check and securities forgery are optional coverages, although they are printed as sections D and E. Coverage similar to bankers' blanket bonds is written for savings banks, stock brokerage firms, and investment banks by forms tailored to their needs.

Forgery insurance.   Any business may suffer financial loss because someone forges a signature to a check. Except for the coverage sold with the bankers' and other blanket bonds for financial institutions, the main forgery coverage offered is the *depositors' forgery bond*. This form, when covering outgoing items only, indemnifies the insured and any bank in which the insured has a checking or savings account for loss by forgery or alteration of any check, draft, promissory note, bill of exchange, or similar written order to pay money. The protection applies only to forgery of the insured's name. It does not apply to the insured's receipt of forged checks. Protection against incoming items can be insured under a separate agreement printed on the contract.

The *family forgery bond* is intended for individual use. Any individual is exposed to loss by forgery. The chance of loss is small, and so is the bond premium. Three basic coverages are included: outgoing instruments, incoming instruments, and loss from acceptance in good faith of counterfeit U.S. paper currency up to $50 in one transaction or $100 in the aggregate. The bond is written for a minimum of $1,000.

The 3-D policy. The comprehensive dishonesty, disappearance, and destruction (3-D) policy is a combination of fidelity and crime insurance designed to provide the widest possible protection. The basic form includes five standard insuring agreements plus 13 more under standard endorsements. The insured may select as many coverages as desired and elect the amounts to be applied to each. Coverage I is an employee dishonesty bond corresponding to either the commercial blanket bond or the blanket position bond. Coverage II is money and securities coverage inside the premises. Coverage III is coverage outside the premises. These latter two coverages are identical to the money and securities broad form discussed earlier. Coverage IV is money order and counterfeit paper currency coverage, protecting the insured against loss from acceptance in good faith or a worthless money order or counterfeit U.S. or Canadian paper currency. Coverage V is depositors' forgery coverage, corresponding to the depositors' forgery bond. If the insured has some of the coverages in force when purchasing the 3-D policy, a pickup rider provides automatic replacement of the specific policies as they expire, thus providing uninterrupted coverage without duplicating premiums.

The 13 additional coverages available through standard endorsements include incoming check forgery; burglary of merchandise; paymaster robbery, inside and outside premises; broad-form payroll, inside premises only; burglary and theft of merchandise; forgery of warehouse receipts; securities of lessees of safe-deposit box; burglary of office equipment; theft of office equipment; paymaster robbery inside premises; credit card forgery; and extortion. Each insuring agreement is separately rated, and the cost is the same as if bought individually.

The 3-D policy has three major advantages. First, all coverages are with the same insurer. As the coverages are closely related, legitimate claims may occur that are not easily attributable to a specific coverage. For example, a money loss may be the result of employee embezzlement or of theft by an outsider. If the fidelity bond is with one insurer and money and securities coverage with another, the loss cannot be paid until it is determined who is responsible for the loss. If both coverages are written by the same insurer, the insured can be indemnified promptly while the argument continues between the bonding and crime departments as to which one should be charged with the loss. A second advantage of the 3-D policy is that coverage is continuous. The lack of an expiration date eliminates the possibility of losses occurring under lapsed coverage. A final advantage is that including complete coverage against all business crimes in one package reduces the chance of ignoring important exposures.

Other comprehensive crime coverages.   Two other important comprehensive contracts are: the *broad-form storekeepers' policy* and the *blanket crime policy*. These forms differ from the 3-D as they are packaged rather than scheduled.

The *broad-form storekeepers' policy* is written for single stores with no more than four employees. It has nine insuring agreements providing protection by combining the blanket fidelity bond, money and securities broad form, mercantile open-stock burglary, depositors' forgery bond, money orders and counterfeit paper currency, damage to the insured's property by vandalism, malicious mischief, and other specified crimes. The policy may be written for minimums and maximums of $250 and $1,000 per insuring agreement. A $25 deductible, for which premiums are reduced 20 percent, may be used. Premiums are based on business class, territory, and amount of insurance.

The *blanket crime policy* includes five coverages written for a single limit. The coverages are those of the commercial blanket bond, money and securities broad form, money orders and counterfeit paper currency, and depositors' forgery insurance. Additional agreements may be endorsed as in the 3-D. The minimum coverage is $1,000. The premium is based on factors used in rating each coverage separately. While this policy offers blanket coverage on all insured perils, premises, all messengers, and so on, one drawback is that all coverages are written for the same amount. To expect the amount of fidelity exposure to be the same as the safe burglary exposure or the off-premises money and securities exposure is not logical.

Surety Bond Coverages

Surety bonding is the assumption of responsibility by one or more persons for fulfilling another's obligations. This guarantee originally was given by friends of the person whose obligations were guaranteed. Individuals persisted in giving surety in spite of the injunction of Proverbs 6:1–2 (Authorized [King James] Version), ". . . [I]f thou be surety for thy friend . . . thou art snared with the words of thy mouth, thou art taken with the words of thy mouth." These words are coupled with the warning that the price of giving surety is to lose one's shirt: "Take . . . [the] garment that is surety for a stranger" (Proverbs 20:16). Through the years, corporate suretyship has replaced personal suretyship. Today, personal surety has nearly disappeared. Surety bonds are classified into judicial, contract, license, official, and miscellaneous.

Judicial bonds

Some privileges or remedies are permitted by law only if a surety bond is furnished to protect the opposing litigant or other interested party. Judicial bonds are prescribed by law. The bonds are noncancellable and continue until the principal's obligation is discharged or until the bond is voided by the statute of limitations. Two general categories of judicial bonds are litigation and fiduciary.

Litigation bonds. Litigation bonds are required to be posted in the course of legal actions. A familiar type is the *bail bond,* used to secure the release of one arrested on a criminal charge. The bond guarantees that the accused will appear for trial. Upon failure to appear, the penalty of the bond becomes due. This surety bond often is written as personal rather than corporate suretyship.

A second litigation bond is the *appeal bond.*[5] If a person is dissatisfied with a court's decision and decides to appeal to a higher jurisdiction, a bond must be posted to guarantee that, if the appeal is lost, the original judgment and the costs of the appeal will be paid. As most appealed cases result in a confirmation of the lower court's decision, applicants for these bonds are carefully examined by the bonding companies. Full (100 percent) collateral often is required. Cash, U.S. government bonds, Treasury notes, or other obligations guaranteed as to principal and interest by the U.S. government are acceptable as collateral. In return for posting the collateral, the bonding company will charge a lower premium. The question arises: If cash equal to the bond's full penalty must be deposited, why buy a bond? Why not deposit the cash with the court? The answer is: (1) the court may be legally forced to demand a bond; (2) often it is easier to obtain return of the collateral from the insurer than from the courts, and (3) the service fee charged by courts for handling collateral may be more than the bond premium.

Fiduciary bonds. Fiduciary bonds provide indemnity if trustees, receivers, executors, or administrators controlling property through court order do not faithfully and honestly perform their duties.

Contract bonds

Many business situations arise in which signing a contract requires surety bonding. One example is a supply contract. A manufacturer contracting to supply semifinished articles to a finisher may be required to submit a *supply bond* guaranteeing that the contract terms will be fulfilled. The finisher depends on the contractor for a steady supply, and if it does not arrive, the finisher will incur additional expense. The bond guarantees the finisher indemnity if the goods are not delivered.

When a contractor bids on a building, often a *bid bond* must be posted, guaranteeing that if the bid is accepted, the contractor will sign the contract and furnish a *performance bond.* When a contract is awarded, the premium on the bid bond is credited toward the premium on the performance bond. Under a performance bond, the surety must complete

---

[5] A cynic defines "appeal" as "putting the dice in the cup for another throw."

the building if the contractor fails or pay the additional expense to find another contractor for the job. The surety also must pay income losses due to delays. A person borrowing money for the construction will need a *completion bond* to guarantee the lender that the building will have no mechanics' liens or other claims when transferred to the owner. The performance bond guarantees that the building will be erected according to the contract, but does not guarantee that the owner will protect creditors' rights. If the construction requires a loan, both a performance and a completion bond are needed.

Surety bonds essential to contractors have been denied to many black contractors, making it difficult for them to obtain construction contracts. According to many insurers, these applicants have been rejected only because of their lack of qualifications. Insurers have attempted to assist and train minority group contractors in efforts to qualify the unqualified, and increase their own business. In 1971 a federal program for bonding small and minority contractors was implemented under which the Small Business Administration guarantees participating surety companies up to 90 percent of a loss on a bid or performance bond issued to an eligible contractor.

License (or permit) bonds

License (or permit) bonds are required by law as conditions to be fulfilled to obtain a license for a particular business or a permit to exercise some specific privilege. These bonds are of two types. One provides payment to the licensing authority for loss resulting from operations permitted by law or from the violation of the principal's imposed duties. The other provides funds to compensate third parties in successful actions to recover loss resulting from the principal's breach of a legal obligation. The time covered by the bond is the term of the license or permit, but the right to file claims under any bond for losses sustained while the bond was in force continues for varying periods following termination.

One large group of bonds guarantees payment of taxes on processed articles. The brewers' bond, for example, guarantees payment of taxes assessed against brewers. Similar bonds are sold to manufacturers of cigars, cigarettes, playing cards, and other articles subject to excise taxes. A wide variety of license bonds is written to insure that laws and regulations pertaining to a certain business will be followed. Examples are the abattoir (slaughterhouse), detective, electrician, funeral director, hack driver, housewrecker, hunter, pawnbroker, peddler, public accountant, travel agent, and ticket broker bonds.

Official bonds

Bonds required of elected governmental officials are called *public official bonds*. The bond may be required by statutory provision, custom, or administrative ruling. The term of a public official bond usually corresponds with the official's term in office. The time limit for the discovery of loss may be prescribed by statute or by agreement between the surety and obligee. Sometimes these bonds are issued with no limitation as to time of loss discovery.

The *federal official* bond is required of any official of the federal government controlling certain kinds and quantities of federal property. The bond may name as the obligee the government or the superior to whom the employee is responsible.

Miscellaneous bonds

Some miscellaneous bonds are: the *depository bond,* bought by banks serving as official depositories of government funds; the *lost-instrument bond,* bought by owners of stocks, bonds, or similar instruments for replacement in event of loss and the *students' bond,* bought by those attending colleges that demand bonds guaranteeing payment of tuition, fees, room rent, board, and other bills, or to indemnify for damage to rooms, grounds, or school property.

Miscellaneous Coverages

A number of coverages written by "casualty insurers" are available that cannot be classified neatly as liability, auto, or crime insurance but nevertheless are important to those with the exposure that these forms are designed to protect. They are discussed here under the innocuous heading of "Miscellaneous Coverages" and are written by property and liability insurers.

Comprehensive glass insurance

The comprehensive glass insurance policy is almost completely comprehensive, as reimbursement is made for all glass breakage except that due to fire, war and associated perils, and nuclear energy. The policy covers: (1) damage to glass described in the declarations and to lettering and ornamentation *separately described therein on a valued basis,* caused by glass breakage (note the policy does not cover scratches), or chemicals accidentally or maliciously applied; (2) repairs or replacement of frames immediately encasing the glass when necessary because of covered damage; (3) installation of temporary plates in or boarding-up of openings containing the glass due to unavoidable delay in repairing or replacing the damaged glass; and (4) removal or replacement of obstructions other than window displays in replacing damaged glass, lettering, or ornamentation. The amount limit under divisions 2, 3, and 4 is $75 per occurrence at any location. Higher limits are available for an additional premium.

Rating of business glass is based on the size and type of glass, its setting, use and location in the building, and territory. Discounts are applied when glass is 100 square feet or more and can be replaced with two or more smaller plates. For residences, glass is covered without measurement or scheduling. The residence form limits recovery on any one glass category to $50, but this limitation may be removed. The residence premium is $6 a year. Most residential glass coverage today is written on a Homeowners form. Sometimes it is difficult to find an insurer for glass in inner cities.

Unlike most other insurance lines, glass losses usually are adjusted by replacing the damaged glass. This service is performed quickly and is a principal argument for buying the coverage.

Boiler and machinery insurance

Most property insurance contracts exclude steam boiler losses, leaving the protection to boiler and machinery policies (B&M). Insurers writing B&M are among the oldest in existence. In 1854 a group of interested English engineers and other formed an organization known as the "Huddersfield Association for the Prevention of Steam Boiler Explosions and for Effecting Economy in the Raising and Use of Steam." They inspected boilers to prevent explosions and to assure that boilers worked at peak efficiency. The company did not issue insurance policies. If a boiler did explode, it was jolly well too bad for the owner. In 1860 a group of engineers in Hartford familiar with the English company formed a similar organization known as the "Polytechnic Club," which, in 1866, organized the Hartford Steam Boiler Inspection and Insurance Company to locate latent causes of explosion and provide indemnity in case an explosion or related loss occurred. This company is still in business and writes only B&M. The tradition of B&M insurance continued, and today B&M insurers provide extensive safety engineering and inspection services. More of each premium dollar is spent for preventive measures than for losses. Losses are 20 to 25 percent of earned premiums compared with the 50 to 60 percent ratios in most property and liability lines. About 40 percent of the premium is used to pay for inspections. The loss preventive service is an important reason for buying B&M coverage.

Six basic coverages are offered: coverage A, damage to the insured's property; coverage B, expediting charges ($5,000 limit); coverage C, property damage liability; coverage D, bodily injury liability; coverage E, defense costs and supplementary payments; and coverage F, automatic coverage of additional insured objects acquired during the policy period. Coverage D may be excluded by endorsement with a premium reduction. The policy limit is the maximum amount payable per accident. However, the immediate medical and surgical relief of coverage D and the legal expenses and supplementary payments of coverage E are not subject to or deducted from this limit. The insurer pays losses first under A, then B and so on. If losses under A consume the limit, then nothing is available for B, C, or D. The premium for B&M insurance is based on the nature of the object insured and the number of locations involved.

One important exclusion is consequential damage. Boiler or machinery damage may cause property spoilage from lack of power, light, heat, steam, or refrigeration. These indirect losses are not covered by the basic policy. Consequential damage coverage may be endorsed on the basic policy or provided by separate contract. Another exclusion is loss caused by business interruption. This loss is covered by a boiler and machinery business interruption policy, which is available in two forms: the valued form, in which a stated amount is recovered for each day the business is inoperative, and the actual loss sustained form, similar to the usual business interruption forms described in Chapter 11. To collect the full face amount under the valued form, an insured need not prove the actual amount of loss, but only that operation is impossible. If only partial operation is feasible, a percentage of the insurance amount may be collected. Under the actual loss form, the loss amount must be proved. Coinsurance of 25 percent of potential daily loss is required in the actual loss form. Waiting periods (deductibles) are available with both forms. Many boiler accidents do not close the business but increase the cost of operation. Extra expense insurance protects against this contingency by loss indemnification for each hour that a boiler or other insured object is inoperative. If a boiler is only partly disabled, the hourly indemnity is paid pro rata. Power interruption insurance covers losses caused by public utility power interruption.

Credit insurance

Credit insurance protects certain businesses from excessive credit losses due to debtor insolvency. The protection is available to manufacturers, wholesalers, and service organizations. The coverage is unavailable to retailers. Protection does not extend to normal credit losses. The normal loss percentage is determined by the insured's experience or that of a similar business. If a manufacturer's line of business has a usual credit loss of 5 percent, a 5 percent credit loss is considered a normal operating cost. Credit insurance protects against only unusual credit losses.

Credit insurance also may provide for loss participation by the insured. When required, the percentage is usually 10 or 20 percent. Also used is an account limit based on the debtor's credit rating at the time of shipment. Legal insolvency or bankruptcy of a debtor is not required for a claim. Claims may occur when a debtor absconds, a sole debtor dies, a sole debtor is adjudged insane, a receiver is appointed, and so on. Most policies are written under the optional collection form. At the insured's option, past-due accounts may be turned over to the insurer for collection. The insurer charges a collection fee for this service. If the insurer fails to collect the accounts and the debtor is insolvent, the insurer must pay the insured. Credit insurance usually covers all accounts of the insured, although it is possible to insure only certain account classes or, in special cases, only a specific account. The rate base is the sales volume. Rates vary with the insured's loss experience and customer credit standing.

Accounts receivable insurance

If its accounts receivable records are lost or damaged, a firm may be unable to collect all outstanding accounts. Insurance is available to cover this loss and additional expenses that may result, such as extra collection expenses, cost of reconstructing records, and interest on money borrowed to offset impaired collections. The policy is written as all-risk coverage. Exclusions include dishonest acts of the insured, officer, director, or partner; loss caused by manipulation of records to conceal another dishonest act; loss due to bookkeeping, accounting, or billing mistakes; loss from electrical or magnetic injury of electronic recordings, except by lightning; the nuclear and war hazards; and loss for which proof is entirely dependent on an audit or inventory computation.

The accounts receivable policy usually is written on a monthly reporting form. A nonreporting form may be used if the insured has a credit history of at least two years and an exposure of not more than $100,000. Rate credits are given for record duplication and for keeping records in receptacles meeting certain requirements. A debit applies if records are kept in receptacles not qualifying for the net rate. Wholesalers, manufacturers, and insurance agents receive a 20 percent credit.

Valuable papers and records insurance

A business can insure inscribed documents and records, including books, maps, films, drawings, abstracts, deeds, mortgages, media for electronic data processing, and manuscripts against all risks, either on a scheduled or blanket basis under a valuable papers and records policy. Property insured on a scheduled basis is written for an agreed amount, while property insured on a blanket basis is covered for actual cash value. The exclusions are those found in inland marine policies, plus dishonesty of any insured, partner, officer, or director. Irreplaceable property is excluded under blanket coverage. It is covered when scheduled. For libraries, loss by failure of borrowers to return books or other documents is excluded. Rate credits of 10 to 40 percent are allowed if particular types of safes or vaults are used.

Title insurance

Ownership of real property usually is transferred by warranty deed. The buyer generally hires a lawyer to verify that the title is clear. Should the title prove cloudy, the buyer may not have a clear right to the property. Even if the buyer can prove ownership, the legal battle may be long and costly. Title insurance can be bought to protect against these costs, including the loss of the property because of rights inferior to those of another.

Title insurance is written by specialty insurers that search the title. If convinced that the title is clear, they issue the policy. The title is guaranteed until the policy is issued, and the policy is effective as long as the same person owns the property. Title insurance is bought not only by prospective owners of real property but also by those who make mortgage loans on real property. The title policy issued to mortgagees is similar to that written for owners.

Municipal Bond Insurance Association (MBIA)

The MBIA was formed in late 1973 to guarantee principal and interest payments for certain municipal bonds. Composed of four major insurers, the MBIA caters mostly to medium-quality bond issuers. Such issuers have the most to gain from the coverage, and their savings in borrowing costs more than offsets the insurance premiums. With the guarantee, many medium-quality issuers are able to boost their bond ratings to AAA.

Municipalities that issue insured bonds pay interest rates about one quarter of 1 percent below the rates paid on similar uninsured bonds. This quarter point advantage is also found when an insured portfolio of municipal bonds is compared to an unprotected portfolio. Insurance for a municipal bond fund is available only if all the bonds in the portfolio are insurable. Premiums must be paid in full in advance (i.e., when the bonds are first issued), and are based on the quality (financial strength of the issuing municipality), the amount of principal and the total interest charges. Rates are quoted in fixed dollars, and not on a percentage of the principal.

The market penetration for this coverage has been growing impressively. In 1979 only about 1 percent of new issues of municipal bonds were protected by municipal bond insurance. However, by 1983, nearly 15 percent of new issues were covered. With the current, relatively high-interest yields on municipals (in the 10 to 12 percent range) and the differential between insured and uninsured bonds, the cost for protection that guarantees principal and interest can be more than offset by interest savings.[6]

Mutual fund insurance

The insured mutual fund redemption value program (IMF) guarantees that if, at the end of the insured period, the value of the insured's mutual fund does not equal the amount invested, the insured will be reimbursed for the difference. An IMF account is subject to a minimum and maximum investment and a minimum period.

Aviation insurance

The bulk of aircraft insurance is written through groups of insurers banded together to form aircraft syndicates. The syndicates then operate

---

[6] Data for this section and a more detailed discussion of municipal bond insurance can be found in "Twelve Improvements in the Municipal Credit System," *The Quarterly Review* 8, no. 4 (Winter 1983–84), published by the Research and Statistics Function of the Federal Reserve Bank of New York, 33 Liberty St., New York, NY 10045.

as the aviation departments of the cooperating insurers. Aviation insurance is closely related to ocean marine and automobile insurance, as the aircraft owner needs physical damage and liability insurance.

Hull insurance.   Hull insurance is available on a specified-peril or all-risk basis and may cover the plane while (1) stationary only, (2) stationary or taxiing, or (3) on the ground or in flight. The policy generally contains a deductible of 5 to 10 percent of the insured value. Some policies are written on a participation form in which the insured pays a percentage (e.g., 25 percent) of each loss. Rates depend upon the size, use, type, and age of the plane, and the type and size of the deductible.

Aircraft liability insurance.   The pilot needs protection against liability suits arising from operation or ownership of the plane. Basic aviation policies do not automatically cover the passenger bodily injury hazard, although that coverage can be purchased by endorsement if desired. A pilot who flies planes belonging to others may buy liability insurance to cover the exposure while flying these planes. Rates vary as to whether the plane is used for pleasure or commercial pursuits and usually are on a per-plane basis. For large aircraft operators the rates may be based on the hours of flight. Airlines need passenger liability insurance, and these policies are rated on a per-seat basis for insureds with only a few planes and on a flight-hours basis for insureds operating many planes. A hangar keepers' legal liability policy is available to protect these operators from claims arising from losses that occur to planes left in their custody. This coverage is similar to the garage keepers' legal liability policy.

Medical payments.   Medical payments coverage for the pilot and passengers is available with passenger liability insurance. Limits per person range from $500 to $2,000, and payments are made regardless of liability. Covered expenses include reasonable medical, surgical, hospital, ambulance, professional nursing, and funeral costs.

Multiple Line Coverages

Will Rogers said, in discussing his Ziegfield Follies comedy routines, that if he needed any new jokes, he would "just get the late afternoon papers and read what Congress had done, and the audience would die laughing." Today it is easier to keep up with the activities of Congress than to keep abreast of all the changes that characterize multiple line insurance. An occasional agent may smile wanly as he opens a bulky package of instructions and new forms, but there has been no report of agents dying laughing.

Multiple line coverage must not be confused with other multiple line activity that has always existed. Agency and brokerage firms for years have marketed a full line of property liability coverages. Insurer groups composed of two or more separate companies commonly owned, managed, or controlled have operated for years. These groups usually include fire and casualty insurers that offer combination policies issued jointly. The combination auto policy is a classic example of two contracts in one document. The liability coverage was written by the casualty insurer, and the physical damage coverage was written by the fire insurer. The collision coverage was written by either. Multiple line coverage in this chapter is coverage of many perils, written by one insurer in one policy, that previously were covered in several policies written by fire and casualty insurers.

Historical Development

A brief sketch of the evolution of multiple line underwriting powers is outlined in Chapter 1. Since the 1950s, all nonlife insurers were granted multiple line underwriting powers if they met required financial standards. Previously, marine underwriters were the experimenters and innovators. The agreement embodied in the 1933 Nation-Wide definition of marine insurance (Chapter 12) slowed their efforts to write broader policies and put the industry back into tight compartments: fire, marine, and casualty.

With multiple line underwriting powers, insurers were freed from the bondage of compartmentalization. Qualified property liability insurers could combine their coverages into one policy. To exploit this opportunity, all an insurer needed for a multiple line package was a bundle of inland marine forms, some liability policies, a few crime insurance contracts, the standard fire policy, a pair of scissors, and a pot of paste. Initially, experimentation was complicated and inhibited by separate fire, marine, and casualty advisory and rating organizations. Each organization could file its own version of a multi-peril form or a variation of that filed by another organization. Individual insurers in some instances filed their own forms.

The Multi-Peril Insurance Rating Organization was organized to promulgate multiple line rates and forms, and the Interbureau Insurance Advisory Group was organized to coordinate rating bureaus operating on behalf of stock insurers. In 1957 these two groups were consolidated into the Multi-Peril Insurance Conference, an advisory organization with jurisdiction over all multiple coverages. This organization underwent several subsequent changes and since 1971 has been part of the Insurance Services Office (ISO).

Special Multi-Peril program

In 1960 the Inter-Regional Insurance Conference recommended a SMP program originally to provide broad coverage for business units whose principal business was providing services rather than manufacturing, processing, or merchandising. The first form developed was for motels. Later, five additional programs were developed: apartment, institutional, mercantile, office, and processing or service. The program has since been expanded to cover public institutions, condominiums, and manufacturing concerns.

At the present time, virtually any business is eligible for the SMP program. The exceptions are: (1) boarding or rooming houses and other residential premises containing fewer than three apartment units; (2) farms or farming operations; (3) grain elevators, grain tanks, and grain warehouses; (4) automobile filling or service stations; automobile repairing or rebuilding operations; automobile motor home, mobile home, and motorcycle dealers; parking lots or garages unless incidental to an otherwise eligible class; and (5) firms eligible for special rating plans, such as highly protected risks.

SMP policies have a common jacket that includes the policy face amount, insuring agreements, declarations, and provisions that apply either to the property (Section I) coverage or the liability (Section II) coverage. Four broad areas of coverage can be written under an SMP policy: Section I, property; Section II, liability; Section III, crime; and Section IV, boiler and machinery. Generally, an SMP policy must be written to include both property and liability insurance. In addition, the property coverage must apply to both the building and its contents if the insured has an insurable interest in them. Crime and boiler and machinery coverages are not mandatory under the program.

Under Section I, property coverage for buildings and contents may be written on either a named perils or "all-risk" basis. (As different forms are used for buildings and for contents, any combination of named perils and "all-risk" coverage may be written. For example, coverage on buildings can be "all-risk" even though coverage on contents is named peril.) Endorsements are available to tailor the SMP to the specific needs of the insured. The endorsements that may be added to Section I of the SMP include, for example, coverage for builders' risk, replacement cost, sprinkler leakage, business interruption (gross earnings or loss of earnings), extra expense, accounts receivable, fine arts, glass, mercantile open-stock burglary, mercantile robbery and safe burglary, outdoor signs, and valuable papers and records.

Liability coverage is provided in Section II of the SMP. A basic form that is unique to the SMP program, the SMP Liability Insurance Form, is a mandatory part of every SMP policy. The form provides coverage for liability arising out of the

> ownership, maintenance, or use of the insured premises and all operations necessary or incidental to the business of the named insured conducted at or from the insured premises. . . .

The form also provides coverage for medical payments and products and completed operations.

To obtain liability coverage broader than that offered under the basic form, standard monoline general liability endorsements (as discussed in Chapter 13) can be added. Thus, it is possible to achieve within the

SMP format the broad coverage offered by a comprehensive general liability policy.

Although the automobile hazard cannot be covered under an SMP policy, coverage can be provided for the employers' nonownership automobile liability exposure by adding the appropriate endorsements to the basic form.

Under Section III, crime coverage can be written for the following exposures: employee dishonesty, loss inside the premises, loss outside the premises, money orders and counterfeit paper currency, and depositors' forgery. The foregoing coverages are virtually identical to the coverage found in the comprehensive dishonesty, disappearance, and destruction (3-D) policy and the blanket crime policy discussed earlier in this chapter.

The boiler and machinery coverage afforded under Section IV of the SMP is similar to that of the standard boiler and machinery policy, also discussed earlier in this chapter. Endorsements are available that provide coverage for indirect and consequential losses associated with boiler and machinery hazards.

The anticipation is that in time most commercial coverage will be written under an SMP format or some other package program. For the insured the SMP generally is more efficient because it provides more coverage for less money, causes fewer problems of coverage gaps and overlaps, and eliminates problems in gray areas of determining which policy covers a particular loss. For the insurer, the SMP provides greater stability of loss experience as losses are spread over more perils, and a lower unit expense because the costs are spread over larger average-size policies. In exchange, the insured relinquishes some freedom in choosing among coverages.

Businessowners program

A "readable" package to serve businesses as Homeowners policies serve individuals was introduced by one insurer early in 1975. Intended mainly for medium and small firms, a similar plan, the Businessowners program, was introduced by ISO and became effective in March 1976. The program is designed to fill the needs of the multitude of small businesses that operate in this country. For larger business or for those requiring more flexibility in designing coverages, the SMP program is available.

Eligibility for the Businessowners program is determined by the physical size of the premises to be insured. The Businessowners policy may be used to insure buildings and building owners' personal property for the following classes of risks:

1. Apartment buildings that do not exceed six stories in height and contain no more than 60 dwelling units. Apartments that contain more than a total of 7,500 square feet of mercantile space are ineligible.

2. Office buildings occupied principally for office purposes that do not

exceed three stories in height or 100,000 square feet of total area. Office buildings that contain more than 7,500 square feet of mercantile space are ineligible.

3. Mercantile buildings occupied principally for mercantile purposes, where the principal business is the buying and selling of merchandise, that do not exceed 7,500 square feet in total area.

Tenants' personal property can be insured under a Businessowners policy if used in the following operations:

1. Offices that do not occupy more than 10,000 square feet in any one building.
2. Mercantile businesses that are engaged principally in the buying and selling of merchandise and that do not occupy more than 7,500 square feet in any one building.

Basement areas not open to the public are not used in computing floor area.

The Businessowners policy may not be written for the following classes:

1. Automotive repair or service stations: automobile, motor home, mobile home, and motorcycle dealers: parking lots or garages, unless incidental to another otherwise eligible class.
2. Bars, grills, and restaurants.
3. Condominiums.
4. Contractors.
5. Buildings occupied in whole or in part for manufacturing or processing.
6. Insureds whose business operation involves one or more locations used for manufacturing, processing, or servicing.
7. Owner's household personal property.
8. One- or two-family dwellings, unless of the garden apartment variety where multiple units are grouped within a single area and are under common ownership, management, and control.
9. Places of amusement.
10. Wholesalers.
11. Banks, building and loan associations, savings and loan associations; credit unions, stockbrokers, and similar financial institutions.

The Businessowners program has two self-contained forms: the Standard form and the Special form. The principal difference between the Standard and Special forms is that the former provides named perils property coverage, whereas the latter has "all risks" coverage. Section II of both forms provide comprehensive business liability coverage.

The property coverages of Section I are written without a coinsurance clause. However, the amount of insurance is expected to be the full replacement cost of the property. The Businessowners policy includes an automatic increase in insurance clause that will assist in maintaining insurance to value, assuming the initial value is correct when the policy is written. The clause increases the insurance on the building automatically every three months by 2 percent. The insured is offered the option of a higher quarterly percentage increase.

Replacement cost coverage is provided for all direct property damage, including buildings, stock, contents, and improvements and betterments. No reporting form is required for business personal property, as an automatic 25 percent increase is provided for seasonal variations.

Loss of income coverage is automatically included in the Businessowners policy. Coverage is provided for rental income, business interruption, and extra expenses necessarily incurred to resume normal business operations. The period of indemnity is based on the actual loss sustained for the time required to rebuild, repair, or replace the property, but not exceeding 12 consecutive months.

Although one of ISO's main objectives was to clarify policy wording, in at least one instance it has succeeded in doing the opposite. In the business interruption coverage agreement, the insurer agrees to pay for income losses "for only such length of time as would be required to resume normal business operations." The policy then defines the insured's normal business operations to be "the condition that would have existed had no loss occurred." Is this condition met when the physical facilities have been rebuilt *or* only after all customers have returned and earnings are at their level prior to the loss (as in Canada)? Or is the intended meaning somewhere in between these two extremes?

Several coverages not required are available as optional coverages for those insureds needing them: employee dishonesty, exterior signs, exterior grade floor glass, burglary and robbery (included in Special form), boiler and machinery, and earthquake damage.

The liability provisions in both the named perils and all-risk forms are identical and written as comprehensive general liability including both the completed operations and products hazard. In each form, the insured may choose between the basic per-occurrence limit of $300,000 and an optional $1 million limit. The liability coverage includes not only bodily injury and property damage, but also personal injury defined as injury arising out of false arrest, detention, or imprisonment, malicious prosecution, libel and slander, invasion of privacy, wrongful entry or eviction, and the invasion of the right of private occupancy.

Liability coverage is extended to the fire and explosion legal liability hazards but has a $50,000 per-occurrence limit. The medical payments coverage also is identical in both forms. This limit is $1,000 per person and $10,000 per accident. Various deductibles are available. The single package rate depends on the type of business, building, construction, and territory.

Miscellaneous multiple line coverages

Several multiple line forms designed to cover qualifying personal property are available for commercial risks. The following forms provide property coverage only. Liability coverage must be written under a separate policy.

The *commercial property form* is used to provide broad protection for the business personal property of retailers, wholesalers, and similar eligible business owners. For a tenant, coverage can be provided for the interest in improvement and betterments. The form is all risk, excluding perils such as flood, seepage and leakage, earthquake, war, mysterious disappearance, inherent vice, and employee dishonesty. Limited transit coverage is included in the form, as is limited extra-expense coverage.

The *office personal property form* provides similar coverage for most office exposures other than a doctor's or dentist's office exposure. The form provides all-risk coverage on business personal property on or off premises. Improvements and betterments are covered at the insured's option.

The *industrial property form* is designed for manufacturing and processing businesses. The form is available only to businesses with personal property at two or more locations. The form can be written either on a specified-perils or an all-risk basis.

The *public and institutional property* (PIP) forms provide broad coverage for churches, libraries, hospitals, government buildings, schools, and other public institutions. The PIP form gives blanket coverage for real and personal property against the basic fire and extended coverage perils. Vandalism, malicious mischief, and sprinkler leakage coverages are available by endorsement, or an all-risk endorsement may be purchased.

The *manufacturers' output policy* provides all-risk coverage to manufacturers for personal property *away* from the premises. Originally designed for auto manufacturers, its availability has been extended to more than 300 types of manufacturers. Excluded perils are identical with those of the commercial property form. Flood and earthquake coverage are available by endorsement. Property covered includes the insured's interest in improvements and betterments, plus personal property of others in the insured's care. The policy excludes most property excluded from the fire policy. Only direct losses are covered. The policy covers goods in the United States and goods in transit in Canada. It is written on an open basis without termination date and may be cancelled either by the insurer or insured upon 90 days' written notice. Four loss limits are established: losses per location, losses on conveyances, losses of property at conventions or fairs, and losses per flood if the policy is endorsed to cover the flood peril. The annual premium (subject to a $1,000 minimum) is determined on a reporting basis. Available deductibles range up to $5,000.

Summary

1. Crime coverages can be purchased to protect many types of firms and individuals against the perils of burglary, robbery, theft, forgery, embezzlement, and other dishonest acts.

2. The burglary special-coverage form includes basic policy provisions but requires an endorsement to complete the coverage. Some endorsements often used are those that protect against mercantile robbery or burglary, mercantile safe burglary, paymaster robbery, and money and securities destruction. All these coverages also can be obtained through separate policies, or as a part of multi-peril packages.

3. Package policies for storekeepers and offices are available that combine coverages most often needed by these enterprises.

4. Crime insurance for banks is a specialized field. Policies have been designed specifically to cover a bank's exposure to burglary, robbery, and legal liability for property in safe-deposit boxes. The banker's blanket bond protects against employee dishonesty.

5. Although most personal theft coverage now is written under the Homeowners policies, contracts still are available to protect individuals against crime losses. A potentially important coverage sometimes overlooked is safe-deposit box insurance, as the box owner (e.g., bank) probably will not be held liable for any losses to property within the rented box.

6. The federal crime insurance program began operation in 1971 to provide coverage at affordable rates where needed. Federal insurance is now (1984) available in 24 states, Puerto Rico, and the District of Columbia, but many potential insureds remain unaware of the program.

7. A bond is a contract binding one party financially for the performance by another of an agreed-upon obligation. Three parties are involved: one party, the *surety,* guarantees that the *principal* will fulfill an obligation for the *obligee.*

8. Bonds guaranteeing the principal's honesty are fidelity bonds and may list the names or the positions of all persons covered or offer blanket coverage for all employees of the insured. Special blanket bonds are available for banks, stockbrokers, and other financial institutions.

9. Bonds guaranteeing that the principal will perform certain obligations are *surety bonds.* Such bonds are often used in judicial situations (bail, appeal, and fiduciary bonds), with contracts (supply, bid, performance, and completion bonds), for elected governmental officials (public official and federal official bonds) and when licenses and permits are required by law.

10. Comprehensive glass insurance and boiler and machinery insurance are often bought because of auxiliary services offered by the insurer. For boilers and machinery, the insurer provides extensive safety engineering and inspection services to help prevent losses.

11. Coverage against unusual credit losses is available to manufacturers, wholesalers, and service organizations. Retailers are not eligible, but they can purchase accounts receivable insurance to protect against damage to their account records. Other valuable papers and records also can be insured.

12. An aircraft operator has both a physical damage and a liability exposure when piloting a plane. Special contracts are available to cover all aviation insurance needs.

13. The Special Multi-Peril (SMP) program was developed in 1960. The SMP policies combine property, liability, crime, and boiler and machinery coverages, and in time may replace most other business forms now available.

14. A special package plan designed specifically for small- and medium-sized businesses was introduced in 1975 to meet the need of eligible firms as Homeowners packages satisfy those of homeowners and tenants.

15. Special multiple line policies are available to protect personal property of retail and wholesale establishments, manufacturers, offices, and public and institutional organizations.

Questions for Review

1. What does the term "kidnapping" mean in connection with the mercantile robbery policy?

2. Give examples of insureds who have a crime exposure *(a)* on the premises only and *(b)* both on and off the premises.

3. How does the burglary special-coverage form resemble the standard fire policy?

4. Why have states been reluctant to develop crime insurance programs of their own?

5. Why do many insurance advisers believe that the commercial blanket bond usually should be purchased in preference to the blanket position bond?

6. Compare the blanket crime policy to the 3-D policy.

7. What is an appeal bond? When is it used?

8. What is a principal argument for the purchase of comprehensive glass insurance?

9. What coverages are available for aircraft owners and operators?

10. What innovations have arisen from permitting multiple line underwriting?

11. What are some advantages of the SMP program to the insured? To the insurer?

12. What point is made by describing the development of multiple line policies as "requiring some fire forms, a few marine contracts, some crime policies, some liability contracts, a pair of scissors, and a pot of paste"?

13. How does the standard Businessowners package differ from the special one?

Questions for Discussion

1. Why do insurers differentiate carefully among the terms *burglary, robbery* and *theft?* Could all three terms be replaced by the word "stealing"?

2. What factors do you believe are the most important in rating the money and securities broad-form policy?

3. Is bonding insurance? Are mutual fund and municipal bond insurance theoretically insurance? Explain.

4. Why are "normal" credit losses not covered by credit insurance policies?

5. Can an all lines policy as well as a multiple line policy be written? Why or why not? Would you recommend it? (An all lines policy combines property liability coverage with life insurance coverage.)

6. As some policies have been incorporated into the SMP program, why are the separate forms for these coverages still available?

7. What do you see in the future for all lines underwriting powers, considering that several large life insurers recently have formed property liability insurance subsidiaries and other large insurer groups for years have had life insurance subsidiaries?

Life insurance and annuities

Two basic contingencies people face are dying too soon or living too long. The latter does not mean living too long to suit themselves, but outliving their financial productivity or their ability to provide for their economic needs. The first contingency is physical death. Life insurance is a financial instrument for providing postdeath resources to support survivors or pay the obligations of the estate of the deceased. The second contingency is economic death. Economic death results from disabilities arising out of injuries or illnesses, or from compulsory retirement. Health insurance (discussed in Chapter 18) is designed to provide resources for an insured while disabled. Life annuities are financial instruments offering insureds lifetime postretirement income.

Development of Life Insurance

The origin of life insurance is not known. The Code of Hammurabi provided for an adoption annuity plan. A Babylonian could adopt a son and depend on the adopted son's legal obligation for parental support in old age. In early Greece some religious sects collected monthly subscriptions from devotees, who in turn were promised that the prescribed rituals would be performed at the insured's burial, and the *immediate* liquidity needs of survivors would be met. At least one temple society allowed members to borrow money under specific circumstances, thus providing an early instance of policy loans.

The Romans adopted Grecian art, literature, philosophy, and the religious societies' idea of furnishing burial insurance and funds for the most pressing postburial necessities of the deceased's family. A special society developed to insure soldiers and offered its members death benefits and old-age or disability pensions.

On June 18, 1536, Richard Martin, a marine underwriter who operated from the Old Drury Ale House in London, suggested to his underwriting companions they might include in their business the insurance of human life; in this case, a drinking companion, William Gybbons (described as "healthy of person, and apparently destined to live the full biblical 'three score and ten' "). Martin, with confidence in his judgment elevated either by a series of lucky underwritings or the ale, proposed to write a $2,000, 12-month policy on William Gybbons's life for an $80 premium. Fifteen underwriters participated. Mr. Gybbons accepted and, as fate would have it, died on May 29, 1537.

Richard Martin, his associates, and William Gybbons might forever have escaped historical notice if the underwriters were not so upset by their bad selection that they contested the claim. Their plea was that in insuring Gybbons for "a period of twelve months," they believed the contract would run 12 lunar months (28 days each) and that the policy had expired on May 10. The court, unimpressed by this argument, ordered the claim paid. To this day, courts continue to hold rigorously to the principle of interpreting any ambiguity in policies against the underwriters.

In 1698 the Mercers' Company of London inaugurated a plan to grant life annuities to beneficiaries of member insureds. The venture, undertaken at the instigation of a Lancashire divine, Dr. William Assheton, author of such delightful Calvinism as *The Certainty and Eternity of Hell Torments,* finally had to be bailed out by the government. The mortality table on which the Mercers' Company proceeded seems to have had little of the certainty the worthy doctor saw in Hell's Torments.

The Society of Assurance for Widows and Orphans, founded in 1699, is considered the first true life insurance association. All 2,000 members contributed $1.20 a week to create a fund of $2,400 payable at each member's death. The life insurance proposed by this mutual society included such modern features as the consideration of age and health in selecting insureds, exclusion of hazards such as military service, and a grace period for premium payments.

In 1706 Queen Anne issued a charter to the Amicable Society for a Perpetual Assurance Office. Notably it offered insurance for the whole of life rather than the usual specified term. Death payments varied with mortality and investment experience similar to the current variable annuity. Not until 100 years later did the society attempt to write coverage with a guaranteed fixed face amount. The Amicable was the first and last dominant group of individual underwriters, as opposed to corporate underwriters, in the life insurance industry. It was merged with the Norwich Union Life Office.

The oldest existing life insurer is the Society for the Equitable Assurance of Lives and Survivorships, commonly known as "Old Equitable." Founded in 1756 it began writing business in 1762. The company founders, Simpson and Dodson, were not pleased with the types of life insurance then available. Two choices were offered: short-term insurance without renewal privileges, or lifetime insurance but with the death benefit contingent upon funds available at the time of death. Simpson wanted to issue a policy for a stated amount for a level premium each year. Sufficient financiers were found to organize an insurer on the mutual plan.

The Old Equitable instituted practices that have become standard operating procedures. These included a 30-day grace period, a three-month reinstatement period, and a refund of premium overcharges. The major difference between the Old Equitable and the present-day life insurer was that the former did not use agents. To this day, Old Equitable does not employ agents; it sells insurance to those who come to buy.

The Scottish Widows' Fund and the Equitable Assurance of Edinburgh added surrender values in 1851 and paid dividends in the form of additional paid-up insurance, one of the modern dividend options.

Early development of life insurance in America

For many years after the founding of the New World colonies, insurance was written by alien underwriters, primarily English. American insurance did not develop until after the Revolution. However, a record exists of a public insurance office opening in Philadelphia in 1721. These offices were headquarters for marine underwriters who occasionally wrote life insurance. Such offices became common in the principal cities of the Atlantic seaboard. The usual life insurance policy was written for a 6- or 12-month term or for the duration of a sea voyage or some other perilous venture. Life insurance was purchased only for short-term, extrahazardous adventures, not for the everyday exposure to death. Life insurance was viewed with disfavor. As late as 1809 a Massachusetts court argued the legality and morality of life insurance.

The Corporation for the Relief of Poor and Distressed Presbyterian Ministers and for the Poor and Distressed Widows and Children of Presbyterian Ministers (the Presbyterian Ministers' Fund) was organized in 1759 by the Presbyterian Synod of Philadelphia. The Fund insured only clergy and used no agents. It is still operating but has expanded to insure other church members. This venture led to the formation, 10 years later, of the Episcopal Corporation.

In 1794 the Insurance Company of North America (INA) (now part of CIGNA Corporation) became the first American commercial corporation to insure lives. It wrote six life insurance policies in five years, all short-term shipmaster policies covering mariners against death while in pirate captivity, none of which produced a claim. A few years later INA dropped life insurance, until 1957 when the company again began writing life insurance, this time through a subsidiary. INA is now heavily involved in life insurance through Connecticut General Life Insurance Company, the CG part of CIGNA.

The first commercial company to write life insurance exclusively was the Pennsylvania Company for Insurance on Lives and Granting Annuities. Its first policy was issued in 1812. This company operates today, but only as a bank and trust business, long ago ceasing to write life insurance. The Pennsylvania Company was the first American insurer to use scientific underwriting principles. Most policies issued were term, with much less liberal provisions than those in today's policies.

Two large mutuals are distinguished as the oldest commercial insurers writing life insurance. The New England Mutual Life Insurance Company, chartered in 1835, is the oldest company in date of incorporation, although its first policy was not issued until 1844. Meanwhile the Mutual Life of New York (called MONY as a euphemism to suggest that the company deals in money), incorporated in 1842, had issued a policy in 1843, becoming the first of the current mutuals to begin operation.

Further development of life insurance

The mid-19th century produced Elizur Wright, called the father of legal reserve life insurance. Wright, a Yale graduate and mathematics teacher at Western Reserve College, was actively associated with abolitionist journals as a writer and editor. On a visit to the Royal Exchange in England, Wright witnessed the "slave auction" treatment of old men selling their insurance policies because they no longer could afford the premiums. These insureds stood on a platform so prospective purchasers could assess the likelihood of their longevity. The purchaser bought the policy for a small sum and continued premium payments hoping for the insured's early death. Wright became the champion of these "plundered policyholders." By 1850 Wright was a full-fledged lobbyist in the Massachusetts legislature, and a driving force behind the passage of a bill requiring life insurers to include in their financial statements the net liability on policies outstanding (called the legal reserve). The purpose was to facilitate judging insurer solvency.

In 1861 Wright succeeded in having the first nonforfeiture law passed. The law required insurers to provide term insurance, extending for a period that could be financed with 75 percent of the policy reserve, for policyowners discontinuing premium payments. In 1880 (two years before he died) Wright succeeded in his struggle to require insurers to return cash values to policyowners who lapsed their policies.

Wright was appointed one of the first Massachusetts insurance commissioners, in which capacity he irritated all who did not want sound life insurance practices. His annual reports as commissioner, and his legislative contributions were instrumental in putting the life insurance business on a scientific basis and laying the foundations for its future sound development.

The Armstrong investigation. In the final quarter of the 19th century, most life insurers adhered to the principles of honesty, integrity, and the sense of trusteeship which characterize the business today, but many insurers were guilty of sharp practices, extravagance, and autocratic disregard of policyowners' rights. As might be expected, these insurers frequently become insolvent. Beginning in 1877 failures occurred at the rate of nearly one a month.

In 1869 Equitable Life Assurance Society initiated a tontine policy, named after Lorenza Tonti who 200 years earlier had introduced the tontine system in France to help raise funds for the government. The life insurance tontine plan replaced annual dividends with deferred dividends. The insurer allocated a large part of each year's addition to surplus to a separate deferred dividend fund. If a policyholder continued a policy in force and lived until the end of the deferred dividend period, usually 10, 15, or 20 years, the dividend was shared with the other surviving policyowners. The more deaths and lapses, the larger would be each survivor's dividend. Also available was the option to sacrifice the right to cash surrender values in exchange for the right to share in forfeitures of lapsed policies if the policyowner stayed alive and continued the policy during the deferred period.

The tontine policy was designed to give policyowners who expected to outlive the deferred period and to keep their policies in force an opportunity to share in the forfeitures of those less fortunate. Elizur Wright viewed the tontine system as life insurance cannibalism to make the rich richer and the poor poorer. Such inequality was believed unessential to the fundamental purpose of life insurance—to pay policy proceeds at death—and was called an immoral speculation making a lottery of life insurance. Wright foresaw that tontine "kitties" would build huge sums which might tempt insurers to investment speculation.

Public resentment against life insurance reached a climax in demands for an investigation. In 1905 the New York legislature passed a concurrent resolution appointing the Armstrong Committee to

> examine into the business and affairs of the life insurance companies doing business in the State of New York, with reference to the investments, the relation of such companies to subsidiary corporations, the government and control of said companies, and any other phase of the life insurance business deemed by the committee to be proper, for the purpose of drafting and reporting to the next session of the legislature such a revision of laws relating to life insurance in this state as said committee may deem proper.

The committee, under Charles Evans Hughes, its chief counsel, made it clear that the institution of life insurance was not on trial.

The committee's investigations and recommendations can be summarized under four headings:

Control. The committee found that many directors did not hold the insurer's officers accountable. In mutual insurers the policyowners had no control.

Investments. The committee found that some life insurers also were in the banking business. Insurers with banking interests were engaging in practices favorable to banks, regardless of the best interests of policyowners. They were extravagant in building and maintaining home office buildings. The committee recommended prohibiting investment in corporate stocks.

Expenses. Extravagances were found in agents' commissions and officers' salaries.

Dividends. The committee opposed deferred dividends and recommended that if dividends are paid, they should be distributed on an annual basis.

A conference of governors and insurance commissioners held in 1906 resulted in appointment of a committee on Uniform Legislation, known as the Committee of Fifteen, to study methods of strengthening insurance regulation. Their work was reflected in the New York Insurance Code of 1906 that set the pattern for life insurance regulation throughout the United States. The end product of the Armstrong investigation was housecleaning in the industry and marked the maturing of the life insurance business.

Life insurance after World War I

The epidemic of influenza near the end of World War I put a greater strain on life insurers than did the war. Most deaths were among young persons, and insurers were forced to draw heavily on contingency funds to make payments. The depression of 1929 also caused some distress among life insurers. Many policies lapsed, and cash demands, both for surrender values and loans, increased dramatically. The business with the help of a favorable regulatory climate, for the most part was able to weather the storm.

Beginning in 1938 a congressional committee, the Temporary National Economic Committee, undertook a study of the concentration of economic power. Life insurance was one of the allegedly monopolistic institutions studied. While initiated to study life insurers as instruments of economic power, the investigation went far afield, covering technical operations of the insurance business. The committee's recommendations regarding life insurance dealt largely with the need for strengthening state regulation; better qualification, training, and methods of compensating agents; prohibiting an insurer from soliciting business by mail in states in which it is unlicensed, and prohibiting intercompany agreements that reduce competition.

In 1940, just before the United States entered World War II, Congress passed the National Service Life Insurance Act, designed to provide life insurance up to $10,000 for members of the armed forces. At the height of the war, about $125 billion of this insurance was in force. The amount fell to less than $40 billion by 1946. By the beginning of 1983, the amount of National Service Life Insurance in force dropped to $30.6 billion.

Recent trends in life insurance

Life insurance remains an important instrument in personal financial planning even with the enormous growth of employee pension plans and government social insurance plans. In the United States at the beginning of 1983 about $4.5 trillion of life insurance was in force, of which 46 percent was group insurance (excluding an additional 5 percent of group credit life). The Employee Retirement Income Security Act of 1974 provided tax incentives for individuals not covered by employee plans to save for retirement years and has resulted in increased purchases of life insurance and deferred annuities.

Life insurers must remain aware of the changing resources and needs of an increasingly knowledgeable buying public. Insurers are discovering a trend toward term insurance rather than permanent (whole life) insurance. Individuals also are seeking financial instruments which enable them to keep pace with inflation. Along with the variable annuity, insurers have introduced policies that tie the amount of proceeds to the official Consumer Price Index. Some insurers are offering variable life insurance and life cycle policies (both discussed in this chapter).

American citizens are becoming increasingly consumer oriented, and the life insurance industry is hardly a "sacred cow." The National Association of Insurance Commissioners (NAIC) approved the final draft of its Model Life Insurance Solicitation Regulation in June 1976. This bill requires insurers to supply specific cost information in the form of a "Policy Summary," and a life insurance "buyer's guide" to prospective applicants. The proposed buyer's guide attempts to educate applicants for insurance purchase decisions by including sections on the analysis of life insurance needs and how to make cost comparisons among policies. The 1983 revision of this regulation, the Life Insurance Disclosure Model Regulation, adds methods of cost disclosure to deal with new policies containing variable death benefits or cash values (e.g., universal life products), and policies that provide reduced rates to insureds who can show evidence of continued insurability (i.e., primarily still in good health, a nonhazardous occupation, and morally fit as defined by the insurer). The NAIC recommends using the surrender cost index, the net payment cost index, and the equivalent level annual dividend in making cost comparisons. As of early 1985, more than 30 states have enacted some form of the model bill, and other states are expected to join the list.

The Federal Trade Commission staff finds the NAIC Model Regulation helpful but inadequate. It wants to provide consumers with a more inclusive standard preliminary policy summary and buyer's guide, recommending use of a single index for comparing similar policies, and disclosure of comparative cost for the 20-year surrender cost index. (Life insurance cost comparisons are discussed in Chapter 21.) The proposed policy summary would include information showing how long the policy must be held before a policyowner could surrender it without financial loss and how policy benefits would compare to a program combining term insurance and a separate savings account. Thus, the FTC staff would incorporate a cost comparison using an average rate of return on the policy's "savings element." It also would require disclosure of cost information before the buyer signs the application. A serious defect in the staff proposal is its misdirected emphasis on life insurance as a savings medium and on its termination by surrender when by the staff's own admission life insurance should be purchased primarily for death protection. It follows that a disclosure index that measures the cost of a policy purchased for death protection should be included in the policy summary and buyer's guide.

Replacement of life policies is another area where increased regulation is expected. The NAIC adopted a model replacement bill in 1970 with amendments in 1978, which includes the following: the pros and cons of the proposed replacement for the buyer; a comparative information form covering a wide range of policy facts, including contract provisions and cost data; delivery of comprehensive policy summaries; and an exchange of disclosure information between replacing and replaced companies. Most states have passed this bill with various modifications.

Because insurance policies are not always easy to read by the layperson, some states have passed policy readability laws that are applicable to both life and nonlife insurance. Consumers will benefit from these laws which additional states are expected to enact. The purpose of a readability law is to force insurers to write (language used) and print (size of type used) policies a buyer will be able to read and understand. (Is this objective really possible, given the "why Johnny (or Janie) can't read" syndrome?)

Types of Life Insurance

In a motion picture, a southern grandam is quizzing her nephew, who is trying to sell her a life insurance policy. "Will this policy insure my living a day longer than the good Lord intends me to live?" she asks. The nephew replies that it does not. "Then," she says, "you should be ashamed of yourself. You're not selling life insurance; you're selling death insurance." This criticism is apropos even though one cannot condone the woman's condemnation of her nephew for a nomenclature he had no part in making. However, usage has firmly established the designation "life insurance" for those contracts which protect against financial losses from death. A person deciding to buy insurance protection is faced with the difficult problem of choosing from a host of life insurance policies. This chapter primarily discusses life insurance and annuity forms available. Some specific issues relating to buying life and health insurance are discussed in Chapter 21. Life insurance policies functionally are of three types: term insurance, endowment insurance, and whole life insurance.[1]

Term insurance

A term insurance policy is a contract between the insured and insurer whereby the insurer promises to pay the face amount of the policy to a third party (the beneficiary) if the insured dies within a specified time period. If the insured survives the period, the contract expires without value. The important and distinguishing features of term insurance are that contracts are for a fixed period, and little or no cash values are accumulated.

Forms. A variety of term forms is available. *Straight term* insurance is written for a year, or a specified number of years, and terminates automatically at the end of the designated period. Five-, 10- or 20-year policies, and term to age 65 or 70 are popular contracts. *Renewable term* insurance is a contract under which the insured may renew the policy before its expiration date, without again proving insurability. Thus, an insured could buy a 10-year renewable term policy permitting renewal for an additional 10 years. The premium charged on renewal will be higher than that charged originally, to reflect the higher probability of dying within the second 10 years. The policy usually provides for several renewal periods, or renewal up to a given age.

A similar policy is the *yearly renewable term policy* (sometimes called YRT, and also referred to as ART—annual renewable term). At the option of the insured and without evidence of continued insurability the policy may be renewed each year. The renewal privilege is limited to a specific number of years or to a specific age at which time the contract expires.

The high level of public acceptance of YRT as the ultimate in low-cost protection has led to extensive and fierce price competition among insurers writing this coverage. In an effort to keep their YRT products from being replaced by new, lower rate policies of competing carriers, some companies have introduced *re-entry* YRT. This form allows the insured to pay lower premiums after the second or third policy years if he or she can show evidence of continued insurability based on a new medical examination.

Convertible term policies are available that may be converted into

---

[1] Chapters 25 and 26 contain short discussions of the actuarial basis for life insurance. Chapter 25 discusses the calculation of the net single premium and the net level premium for whole life insurance. Chapter 26 discusses the computation of the life insurance policy reserve. Those readers who feel a need for a conceptual understanding of the actuarial basis for life insurance before studying the differences among the various types of policies are advised to study these sections now. Check the index for applicable pages.

whole life or endowment insurance within a specified period, without evidence of insurability.[2] Some insurers write a convertible term policy that automatically is converted at a specific date into a whole life policy called *automatically convertible term insurance.*

The renewable and convertible features may be combined into one policy, called renewable and convertible term. For example, a five-year renewable and convertible policy might be renewable until age 70 and convertible at any time before age 65. The usual form of term insurance is level term, under which the amount payable remains the same throughout the period. *Increasing* and *decreasing* term insurance also are available. Under decreasing term, the face amount of the policy reduces periodically (e.g., monthly or yearly). This policy is useful in furnishing low-cost protection during the child-rearing period. A form of decreasing term insurance coupled with whole life insurance called *family income insurance* is discussed later. Increasing term insurance provides for a policy amount which increases monthly or yearly. The policyowner can increase the amount of insurance without providing evidence of insurability. This policy is useful in protecting the policyowner from the effects of inflation. Increasing term added as a rider to whole life or endowment policies also can be used to provide additional insurance to fund policy gimmicks such as the return of premiums or the payment of the cash value in addition to the face amount of the policy upon the death of the insured.

Premiums.   Because the probability of death increases with age, premiums increase gradually with the applicant's age. However, at advanced ages premiums, reflecting much higher death rates, rise at a sharply increasing pace. Rather than pay increasing natural premiums, term insurance can be bought on a *level premium* plan under which premiums remain the same for each year throughout the life of the policy. The annual level premium for a five-year term policy written on a nonparticipating basis (i.e., paying no policyowners dividends) is about $2.16 per $1,000, at age 25; $3.04 at 35; and $6.84 at 45. Premiums are for convertible and renewable term policies.

Uses of term insurance.   Term insurance may be appropriate for any death protection need which is not of lifelong duration. A person with a 20-year mortgage loan can use decreasing term insurance wisely for additional death protection during the period of the mortgage loan. The insurance can be arranged so that when the mortgage loan is retired the term insurance expires. If the person dies before the mortgage loan is paid, the policy will provide funds to complete the payments.

Term insurance is widely used by young people who need more protection than they can afford through higher premium insurance. They can

---

[2] Whole life insurance consists of forms intended to provide lifetime protection, as distinguished from term policies intended to provide short-term protection. Endowment insurance provides a survival benefit upon termination of the policy period.

buy convertible term and convert to a whole life policy later if appropriate.

Buy term and invest the difference.   The suggestion often is made that term insurance should be purchased to provide pure protection and that the difference between the premium for the term policy and that for a like amount of whole life insurance should be placed in other savings media. For example, at age 25, the premium for a $100,000 continuous-premium whole life policy (premiums are paid until death) would be about $860 a year, "nonpar" (nonparticipating). The premium for $100,000 of one-year renewable term insurance would be about $180. If the insured purchased one-year term instead of continuous premium whole life, the death benefit would be the same for that year but the premium would be $680 less. This $680 could be put in some other savings medium and build emergency or retirement values independent of life insurance. The next year, at age 26, enough term insurance could be purchased to equal $100,000 when added to the $680 savings plus investment return. This process would continue each year reducing the insurance so that at death the insurance plus the accumulated savings will equal $100,000.

Three problems arise in this program. (1) Some people cannot save money unless compelled to do so. Life insurance premiums usually are budgeted as a debt, and a person generally will pay the premium if the money is at hand, while a savings deposit or the purchase of government bonds or mutual funds requires positive action each month. (2) Withdrawing from a savings account is easier than cashing in life insurance. Surrendering life insurance or borrowing its cash value is not undertaken as lightly as the withdrawal of savings. (3) Most people are not investment experts, and in an effort to improve investment yields some persons are tempted to speculate thus exposing their principal to losses. Furthermore, savers not psychologically attuned to fluctuating market prices of investments are likely to invest the "difference" in savings accounts. These accounts may not offer *after-tax yields* as high as can be obtained through cash value life insurance. A 1975 statement by Senator Phillip Hart, citing a study by the antitrust and monopoly subcommittee, indicated a wide range among insurers of rates of return on life insurance cash values. The rate earned on cash value life insurance depends also on the type of policy purchased, the age at which it is purchased and the number of years that the policy remains in force. Therefore, generalizations cannot be made about the rate of return on cash value life insurance. However, for the most part, if the policy is held for a long term, the rate of return in many cases would be comparable at least to that earned on passbook savings. As explained later, life insurance rates of return offer tax shelters. Nevertheless, the increased yields in recent years on corporate and government bonds, bank certificates of deposit, and tax-free municipal bonds have increased the relative attractiveness of these forms of savings media.

Persons who can successfully separate savings from life insurance (buy term insurance and successfully invest the difference) may gain worthwhile advantages if they are willing to sacrifice the advantages (discussed later) that accrue from combining savings and insurance.

In the present economy, two principal drawbacks to the use of life insurance cash values and other fixed dollar investments are their vulnerability to the inflation risk and their inability to give the investor a stake in a growing economy. A possible advantage of an "invest the difference" program is the opportunity it affords the saver to invest in equities—common stocks and real estate—the values of which are expected by some but not all financial experts to increase *over the long run* as the dollar loses some of its value. A further advantage is the opportunity it gives to invest in companies in "growth industries" where some experts anticipate attractive increases in profits and dividends. Some experts suggest that savings institutions and life insurers be required to place a sticker on savings passbooks and life insurance policies containing a warning that "savings through this instrument can be dangerous to your wealth."

As a fixed dollar savings medium, cash value life insurance offers some worthy features. Every state has a statute that to some extent protects life insurance cash values and life insurance proceeds from the insured's creditors (discussed later). Protection from claims of the beneficiary's creditors also may be arranged cost free by a spendthrift trust clause (also discussed later). Furthermore, income options are included in life policies under which cash values may be paid as a monthly income of a specified amount guaranteed for life. Settlement options (again discussed later) also are available for the beneficiary.

Life insurance as an investment has important income tax advantages. Interest earned on and added to cash values is not subject to federal income tax in the year earned. If paid as a death claim, the full proceeds are exempt from federal income tax. Interest earned under liquidating settlement options is exempt up to $1,000 a year if payable to a surviving spouse. If the policy is surrendered for its cash value, only that amount in excess of premiums paid is taxable as ordinary income.

An important advantage of combining savings with insurance is that the savings plan need not be interrupted during periods of total disability. A waiver of premium rider is available for a life policy under which premiums are waived, following the sixth month of an insured's total disability. The cash values grow as though the premiums were paid, thus preserving the planned retirement or emergency fund.

Endowment insurance

Endowment insurance is a contract under which the insurer promises to pay the beneficiary a stated sum if the insured dies during the policy term (called the "endowment period"), or to the insured if the endowment period is survived. Thus, under a $10,000, 20-year endowment policy, the insurer promises to pay $10,000 to the beneficiary if the insured dies at any time within the 20-year period or to the insured if alive at the end of the period.

Premiums. Premiums for endowment policies are high. Written on a nonparticipating basis the premium for an endowment at age 65, issued at age 25, is about $20 a year per $1,000. The premium for a 20-year endowment at age 25 is about $30 a year per $1,000. Endowment policies usually are issued on an annual level premium basis, although single-premium forms are available under which the insured pays the entire premium at the inception of the policy. The high initial outlay makes single-premium endowments impractical for most insurance buyers. Endowment policies also may be purchased on a level premium basis for a period shorter than the duration of the endowment.

Uses. The endowment policy is sometimes viewed as a savings account protected by life insurance. The insured knows that the face amount of the policy will be paid not later than the end of the endowment period. The insurer must charge premiums high enough to accumulate this amount when due. The high premium means that less death protection can be purchased with the money budgeted for life insurance. Therefore, endowment insurance is not recommended unless the death protection need is secondary.

Because endowment policies create large savings accumulations, they may be used to fund retirement income. As a person's most important need may be for death protection rather than survival protection, a danger is inherent in the endowment policy. Young people may be sold endowment insurance when they should buy term or whole life insurance. The lure of a lump sum of money 20 years hence causes people to lose sight of the basic purpose of life insurance: to provide an efficient predeath arrangement for an effective postdeath balance between resources needed and those available. The combination of high cost for protection and limited usefulness has caused a decline in the popularity of endowment insurance. During 1982 less than one half of 1 percent of the new insurance sold was endowment insurance. In fact endowment insurance has become so unpopular that many insurers do not include it in their rate manuals (or in their computerized rate quotations). However, they will write the policy if for some unknown reasons (i.e., unknown to the authors of this text) an eligible person applies for it.

Whole life insurance

Whole life insurance is the only form of permanent death protection; that is, the insured is covered for life. Whole life insurance can be viewed either as endowment at age 100 or term to age 100. To understand these statements some knowledge about life insurance premium calculations is necessary. The basic ratemaking tool in life insurance is the mortality table which shows the number of people who are expected to die at each age, from an arbitrary number living at the youngest age on the table. The table does not consider the extreme ages on the high side and assumes that all people die before their 100th birthday. Those who reach age 100 receive a check for the face amount of the policy, having survived the period the actuaries set as the maximum. For this reason, a whole life policy may be viewed as an endowment policy maturing at age 100. In computing the premium for a whole life policy, no allowance is made for a survivor benefit at the age 100 because all insureds are expected to be dead at that age. Thus, when survivors reaching age 100 are paid the policy face amount, these payments are in effect mortality and not survivorship payments. Therefore it is reasonable to view the whole life policy as term to age 100 with "death" payments made to those who reach that age. Thus, actuarially and conceptually, only two basic types of policies are written: term and endowment. Viewed functionally, however, a whole life policy is an endowment at age 100 because benefits are paid to those who die before age 100 and to those who survive to age 100.

Premiums. Premiums for whole life policies may be paid under the single-premium, limited payment, or continuous premium plan. The yearly premium which the insured must pay decreases as the length of the premium payment period increases. Premiums must be large enough so that when combined with accumulated investment earnings the insurer will have sufficient funds to pay expenses and honor all claims under the contract. The single-premium plan requires a large one-time initial cost. For example the single premium for a $10,000 "nonpar" whole life policy issued at age 25 is about $1,100.

Limited payment plans involve payment periods of 10, 15, or 20 years or to age 65, after which no further premiums are paid. (A policy that has not matured, and on which no additional premiums are due is called a "paid-up" policy.) The premium payment period is selected to meet the insured's need. The paid-up at age 65 plan has the advantage of relieving the insured of premium payments during retirement. For a $10,000 nonpar policy issued at age 25, annual premiums range from about $170 for a 20-pay life to about $125 for a policy paid up at age 65 (slightly higher for males and slightly lower for females, at least now [1985] and until sex is legislated out as a factor in insurance ratemaking).

The most common plan of whole life insurance is written on a continuous premium basis, variously known as an ordinary life policy, straight life policy or, as in this text, a continuous premium whole life policy. Under this plan, the policyowner pays a fixed annual premium for the life of the insured to retain the full face amount of insurance in force. The premium for a $10,000 nonpar whole life policy issued on the continuous premium plan at age 25 is about $110 annually.

Use of whole life insurance. As the only form of permanent death protection, whole life insurance provides resources after death regardless of when the insured dies. It also is used as a savings plan for financial emergencies or for funding a retirement income to supplement social security and employee retirement plans. The savings accumulation in a whole life policy is a function of the premium plan selected. The continuous premium form offers the lowest and the single-premium form the highest cash value per $1,000 of insurance.

For those seeking insurance protection for the whole of life, the continuous premium policy is attractive. If one is sure of dying early, term insurance offers the best bargain. If, on the other hand, one is convinced of outliving all dependents, no need exists for insurance, except to pay the cost of dying.[3] Under these conditions a continuous premium whole life policy taken late in life would be appropriate, and savings media other than life insurance cash values are more attractive. However, as no one can predict the time of any one individual's death, continuous premium whole life insurance provides a compromise. It contains a large amount of death protection per premium dollar and develops a cash value which represents an effective method of accumulating savings. Generally, when all death protection is bought using continuous premium whole life insurance (assuming that an adequate amount has been purchased), the cash value will provide a large part of planned retirement needs (inflation, of course, can upset the plan).

Term insurance is used to satisfy a temporary need for life insurance or to provide adequate death protection when the budget is too small for cash-value insurance. Endowment insurance is used to arrange for a fixed sum of money at a particular future date or upon the prior death of the insured. But the continuous premium whole life policy is the basic insurance coverage and the appropriate one in the majority of cases because it combines, to a moderate extent, the good features of both term and endowment insurance.

Like the payments, the use of limited pay life policies is limited. They overemphasize cash values at the expense of death protection. While life paid up at age 65 serves a useful function in completing premium payments before retirement, no use seems to be indicated for 20- or 30-pay life plans for the young family. Why should a couple just starting a family want to pay high premiums now to avoid paying premiums later when family responsibilities are reduced and their income is likely to be near its highest level? It does not make sense.

One use of the limited payment life policies is as a gift medium. A grandparent may wish to give a grandchild a policy and have it paid up when the grandchild reaches majority.

Term insurance is the most popular type of policy written, with about 57 percent of all ordinary life insurance (as distinguished from group and industrial insurance) currently being purchased on this plan. About 30 percent of the amount of ordinary insurance now purchased is continuous premium whole life. Limited payment life accounts for 4 percent, retirement income policies for 1 percent, and endowments for less than 1 percent of ordinary insurance purchases. The remaining 8 percent of the ordinary insurance purchased is a combination of term and whole life policies. Ordinary insurance purchases represent about 70 percent of all life insurance currently bought. Check the latest *Life Insurance Fact Book* to update these figures.

---

[3] For a discussion of items to be included in the cost of dying, see Robert I. Mehr and Sandra G. Gustavson, *Life Insurance Theory and Practice,* 3d ed. (Plano, Tex.: Business Publications, 1984), p. 488.

Universal life insurance

Universal life insurance, a new form of whole life insurance, was first sold in 1979. The primary reason for the development of this product was to address and overcome the disadvantages of whole life as seen by the advocates of the "buy term and invest the difference" philosophy. Universal life, in effect, allows the insured to apply the "buy term and invest the difference" concept by dividing the whole life contract into two components: savings and protection. The protection is provided by term insurance renewable to the end of life (i.e., to age 100). A savings fund is established from which premiums in excess of the amount required to pay the term insurance premiums may be invested and accumulated. Thus, the insured receives permanent protection as well as a savings account with potentially higher returns (see next paragraph) than those associated with the growth of cash values in a traditional whole life policy. Upon the death of the insured, both the term insurance proceeds and the savings accumulations are paid to the beneficiary.

Premium payments from the insured are, in effect, put into a savings fund. At the beginning of each month, enough money is taken from the fund to buy the term coverage for that month. The remainder of the money in the fund is invested, usually in high-grade corporate or government bonds or notes of short maturities. The initial premium payments must be sufficient to pay for an amount of term insurance equal to the desired face amount of the contract. Thereafter, annual payments by the insured need be sufficient, when added to the existing savings accumulations, only to purchase the term insurance. Whenever accumulations in the fund exceed the required term insurance premium, payments by the insured may be reduced or even discontinued. If the insured chooses to continue payments, they are added to the accumulation fund. Earnings are credited to the fund after the insurer's expenses have been deducted. The rate of growth sought for the fund is one that will make this type of savings competitive with other savings vehicles available to the insurance-buying public. The interest rate paid may be left to the discretion of the insurer or it may be tied to the rates on 13-week Treasury bills or some index that reflects movements in interest rates.

Death benefits may be level or increasing. Level death benefits are obtained by setting the amount of term insurance purchased equal to the difference between the face amount of the policy and the value of the fund. If instead, the amount of term insurance is held constant and equal to the policy face, the death payment can increase with the (hopefully) increasing value of the fund. In either case, the beneficiary receives both the term insurance proceeds and the value of the fund at the time of death.

Premiums. Universal life insurance plans have the potential to provide a nearly limitless choice of premium payment schemes. Although some insurers set minimum premium payment requirements (e.g., $25 per

payment regardless of the frequency), theoretically any system of premium payments discussed in the previous section could be used. In addition, when the savings fund is large enough to cover the cost of term
insurance, no premium payment is necessary. This seemingly ultimate
in premium flexibility however, has a price. An insured who pays only
the amount required for the term coverage during the early policy years,
is likely to find the rising cost of protection to be extremely expensive
if not unaffordable. Failure to pay premiums in excess of the cost of
term insurance will keep the savings fund from growing, thus hindering
its ability to offset the high protection costs at advanced ages. Fear of
the lack of discipline on the part of the insured in paying premiums
has led some observers to forecast high lapse rates for universal life
policies.[4] The "forced savings" advantage of traditional whole life may
not be an advantage of universal life. Only time will tell whether this
fear of lapsation is well founded. Most of the policies are less than three
years old, and, if lapses do become a problem, it is unlikely to be evident
before about the eighth or ninth policy year.

Another problem of the cost of universal life is the expense loading
used by the various insurers. Policy fees or extra first-year premiums
are used to help cover the cost of issuing the policy (including the agent's
commission). Companies generally guarantee a minimum interest rate
of 4 or 4.5 percent on the savings fund, and limit interest credits on
the first $1,000 in the fund to that minimum rate. Prospective buyers
should insist that prospective insurers disclose precisely how expense
charges are levied. Most sellers of universal life quote the interest rates
currently credited to savings funds on a gross basis (no pun intended)
and not on a net basis; that is, not after all expenses (i.e., the extra
first-year premium and, in some cases, a percentage charge made against
each payment) are deducted. This method of quoting interest rates misleads the buyer into thinking that a higher rate of return is paid than
is the case.

Uses of universal life insurance.   Universal life insurance, with its many
premium variations, can be used in nearly all situations where whole
life or term insurance are currently recommended (assuming, of course,
that the insurance company does not establish rules to diminish premium flexibility). Higher earnings on savings than earnings attributable
to cash value growth of traditional whole life contracts is the major
selling point for the new product. These two characteristics have made
universal life an immensely popular product. During 1982 alone, more
than 400,000 new universal policies were sold, bringing the premium
volume of these products to about 10 percent of all ordinary premiums.
In 1983, universal life insurance premiums reached 18.9 percent of new
ordinary premiums. Continued substantial growth is foreseen as interest
rates that are high relative to those of the not too distant past (but not
necessarily the future) remain prominent in the economy.

---

[4] An insurance policy is said to lapse when the insured stops paying premiums and policy
values are insufficient to provide continued protection.

Annuities

The life annuity has become an important instrument in planning financial security for old age. Increasing emphasis placed on individual pension plans resulting from the Employee Retirement Income Security Act of 1974 (see Chapter 19) explains much of the growth in individual annuities over the past 10 years. The life annuity is true life insurance. It is insurance against living too long—against outliving the periodic liquidation of accumulated capital. A life annuity is a contract that provides for a regular periodic income for the life of the annuitant.

The annuity principle

Each payment under a life annuity contract has three elements: principal, investment income, and insurance benefit. To illustrate, a principal sum of $11,013 is necessary to fund a life income of $1,000 a year for a man age 65 (more for a woman), assuming that the fund will earn 3 percent interest and that the group of insureds will die according to the 1949 Annuity Table. No allowance is made for expenses. A year later, only $10,611 would be necessary to fund the plan. Thus, $402 of principal ($11,013 − $10,611) is used during the first year. At 3 percent interest, the $11,013 earns $330.39, making a total of $732.39 from interest and principal. The remaining $267.61 needed for the $1,000 payment is the insurance benefit. The annuity insurance benefit is a survivorship benefit. Those who die during the year release their principal and accrued interest to be shared by those who survive. According to the assumed mortality table, enough people will die during their 65th year to release funds necessary to pay $267.61 to those who survive. For the second $1,000 payment, the insurance benefit will increase, whereas the amount of principal used and the interest earned will decrease, and so on.

Annuities may be classified according to (1) the number of lives covered, (2) how premiums are paid, (3) when benefits begin, (4) involvement of life contingencies, (5) how long (if at all) payments continue after a life annuitant's death, and (6) how benefit payments are measured.

The number of lives covered. Usually, the annuitant will be one individual, but not always. For example, the *joint and last survivor annuity* is available to cover two or more annuitants. Under this contract payments continue until the death of the last survivor. The joint and last survivor annuity may be used by a husband and wife to provide the survivor with an income. A man 65 and a woman 61 can buy a $500 a month joint and last survivor annuity for a premium of about $82,000. On the theory that two cannot live as cheaply as one, some joint and last survivorship annuities are written to provide for a one-third reduction upon the death of the first annuitant. Thus, rather than continue payments of $500 a month to the survivor, for the same premium the foregoing annuity might be written to pay $570 a month during the joint lifetime of the couple and $380 a month to the survivor.

How premiums are paid.   Two methods of paying premiums are possible: single premium and annual premiums. Annual premium annuities are a systematic method of planning for retirement income. Life insurance cash values and death proceeds frequently are converted to single-premium annuities through settlement options. Single-premium annuities are used extensively to fund employee retirement plans (Chapter 19).

When benefits begin.   Annuities are classified as immediate or deferred. Under an immediate annuity, payments begin at the end of the first income period following purchase. If the first payment is due at the beginning of the period, the annuity is called an annuity due. An immediate annuity usually is purchased with accumulated savings. An annuity due usually is purchased with life insurance proceeds or cash values. Premiums paid over a number of years purchase a deferred annuity; that is, annuity payments are deferred until retirement. Deferred annuities commonly are purchased on a single-premium basis in arranging employee pensions.

Involvement of life contingencies.   Payments may be continued only until the death of the annuitant, or for a designated period of years, irrespective of life or death. An annuity of the former type is called a life annuity. One of the latter type is called an "annuity certain." Life annuities are used as funding instruments for retirement plans, and annuities certain are used as settlement options under life insurance policies.

How long (if at all) payments continue after annuitant's death.   Life annuities are classified as straight life annuities or guaranteed minimum annuities. Under the straight life annuity the annuitant is paid until death. Upon death, no further payments are made. This type of annuity provides the highest periodic income per dollar of premium. Some annuitants elect to receive a smaller periodic payment in exchange for a guaranteed minimum return. The guarantee may be either a full refund of the invested principal (called a refund annuity) or a guaranteed minimum number of payments (called a life income period certain annuity).

Refund annuities are of two types: cash refund and installment refund. These two are alike in that they guarantee either the annuitant or beneficiary will receive payments totaling the full amount of the premium paid for the annuity. If the annuitant dies prior to receiving an amount equal to the full premium, under the cash refund the heirs will receive the balance in a lump sum whereas under the installment refund they will continue to receive the periodic annuity payments.

Under the period certain life annuity, the insurer promises to make a designated minimum number of annuity payments, whether the annuitant lives or not. After the guaranteed payments have been completed, the annuity payments will continue only as long as the annuitant remains alive.

How benefit payments are measured. Conventional annuities are expressed in terms of fixed dollars under which the annuitant is guaranteed a specified minimum number of dollars at each payment period regardless of the purchasing power of these dollars. If the annuity is written on a participating basis, the amount of each payment might be higher than the guaranteed minimum amount.

The variable annuity

In July 1952, the College Retirement Equities Fund (commonly called CREF) began issuing variable annuities for college teachers. Since then several life insurers have been formed to write variable annuities, and a number of established insurers offer them to the general public. Under the variable annuity the dollar amount of the periodic payments is based on the value of the assets in which annuity premiums are invested. These assets usually consist primarily of common stocks. Variable annuities pay a monthly amount which fluctuates according to investment results. The theory behind the variable annuity is that common stock prices and the cost of living will move in the same direction *over the long run,* thus giving the annuitant a nearly stable amount of purchasing power. However, changes in the market prices of common stocks and in cost of living are not perfectly correlated. Frequently they move in opposite directions, as illustrated in Figure 16–1. Yet, in the long run, a substantial correlation between common stock averages and the cost of living had been recorded before 1969. The long-term correlation thesis has failed the test miserably over recent years. In the 15-year period ending in 1983, the period from 1969 to 1972 showed the best correlation between the CPI and the S&P 500 stock index. During this period, the CPI steadily increased over these three years, and the S&P 500 index decreased 18 percent from 1969 to 1970 then rose 31 percent from 1970 to 1972. As Figure 16–1 demonstrates, the S&P 500 stock index fluctuated widely from 1969 to mid-1984 in spite of severe inflation near the latter stages of this period. Nevertheless, the dedicated variable annuity proponents (a declining breed) consider the decade of the 70s an aberration. They feel their position was at least partially vindicated by the return of a positive correlation between stock prices and consumer prices in 1983. But in 1984, they were back to square one with a declining stock market during much of 1984. However, the variable annuity seems to be in a state of limbo at the present time. Fixed dollar annuities with their high interest rates currently appear more attractive.

How the variable annuity works. Assume that a person age 35 buys a 30-year deferred variable life annuity with a monthly premium of $100. This $100 is used to purchase accumulation units, the current value of which depends on the value of the investment portfolio supporting

FIGURE 16–1

A comparison of the consumer price index and Standard & Poor's index of 500 stocks, 1969–1984

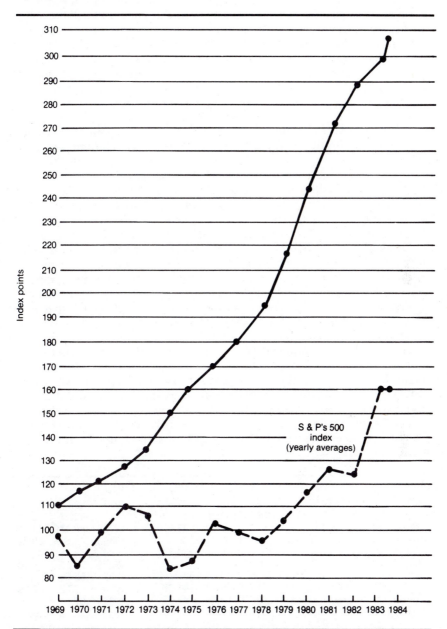

Note: The index values are yearly averages. Figures were obtained from *Standard and Poor's Current Statistics.*

the units. For example if the unit value is $10, 10 units are purchased the first month. In the second month if the unit value changes to $12, only 8.33 units are purchased. By age 65, 3,180 accumulation units will purchase a monthly life annuity of 300 units a month. The dollar value of the units, like the dollar value of the accumulation units, is determined by the value of the assets in the variable annuity fund. The first month, each of the 300 units may be worth $1.50, which gives the annuitant a monthly income of $450. The next month, the units may be worth $1.60 each, or perhaps only $1.40. In any case, the annuity payments vary with the dollar value of the investment portfolio. Variable annuities are written under an arrangement in which payments fluctuate not only with investment results but also with mortality and expense experience. Payments usually fluctuate monthly, but they may fluctuate yearly as in CREF.

Why a variable annuity? Two basic objectives of the variable annuity are (1) to give annuitants some protection against inflation and (2) to provide them an opportunity to share in the country's economic growth. CREF, before undertaking to offer a variable annuity, made impressive studies which seemed to indicate (if the past provides any basis on which to judge the future) the variable annuity *in the long run* will provide better results than a fixed dollar annuity. The question now appears to be how long is the long run!

The following are tabulations of the results of 32 years of experience with the variable annuity by CREF. These results appear to have supported CREF's expectation until 1973 after which the value of the annuity unit dropped nearly 39 percent in three years while consumer prices soared. But is three years a long run? Also how long a run does a retiree have? During this same three-year period, the accumulation unit dropped nearly 53 percent from its high to its low for the period. Again, perhaps these years hopefully will prove to be a severe aberration.

The accumulation unit was valued initially at $10 by CREF. Over its first 32 years, the dollar value of the CREF accumulation unit fluctuated as follows:

Year	High	Low	Year	High	Low	Year	High	Low
1952	$10.52	$ 9.59	1964	33.96	31.55	1976	42.66	39.69
1953	10.37	9.35	1965	39.08	34.83	1977	40.27	36.91
1954	14.85	10.74	1966	39.68	33.80	1978	42.17	34.96
1955	18.06	14.79	1967	43.78	38.55	1979	44.60	39.47
1956	20.83	17.30	1968	47.67	39.34	1980	53.19	40.33
1957	20.50	17.50	1969	45.25	40.19	1981	52.85	45.89
1958	24.36	17.92	1970	40.01	30.76	1982	55.73	42.41
1959	27.11	24.84	1971	45.23	41.37	1983	67.12	57.59
1960	27.24	24.84	1972	53.74	48.27	1984	67.04	60.35
1961	32.45	28.54	1973	50.36	41.30	1985	72.38	72.01*
1962	30.67	22.53	1974	40.83	25.39			
1963	30.83	26.80	1975	39.88	30.67			

* The high for 1985 was reached in February and the low, in January during the first three months of the year.

The annuity year (May through April) value of the CREF annuity unit has been as follows:

Year	Value	Year	Value	Year	Value
1952	$10.00	1964–65	26.48	1976–77	26.24
1953–54	9.46	1965–66	28.21	1977–78	24.80
1954–55	10.74	1966–67	30.43	1978–79	23.28
1955–56	14.11	1967–68	31.92	1979–80	27.28
1956–57	18.51	1968–69	29.90	1980–81	26.27
1957–58	16.88	1969–70	32.50	1981–82	35.86
1958–59	16.71	1970–71	28.91	1982–83	30.56
1959–60	22.03	1971–72	30.64	1983–84	42.52
1960–61	22.18	1972–73	35.74	1984–85	46.14
1961–62	26.25	1973–74	31.58		
1962–63	26.13	1974–75	26.21		
1963–64	22.68	1975–76	21.84		

Several objections to the variable annuity are noted. Aside from the lack of perfect positive correlation between stock prices and the cost of living, the cost of living for an individual annuitant does not fluctuate with an aggregate cost of living index. Additionally, annuitants may be upset when their annuity decreases with the market value of the investment portfolio. This latter objection is psychological as well as economic. In buying the variable annuity, the annuitants make the choice of taking fewer dollars when stock prices fall. When prices fall, variable annuitants may upbraid themselves for not electing fixed dollar annuity payments, and some of the less informed ones may even blame the insurer. Current long-term holders of variable annuities would have experienced a much higher rate of return on their money if they had purchased fixed dollar annuities.

Selection of the type of annuity

The purchase of a refund annuity for retirement purposes is difficult to justify. A retirement annuity is bought to maximize guaranteed income for life. Given that purpose, income should not be decreased by insisting on refund features or guaranteed payments. Yet, because of psychological considerations, sales of the straight life annuity lag behind other types of annuities. If the annuitant has a dependent spouse, protection should be provided by a joint and last survivor annuity rather than by refund features in a single life annuity. Other dependents may be protected better by life insurance than by refund clauses in annuity contracts.

As to fixed or variable annuities, the annuitant selects either a guaranteed fixed dollar income and accepts the risk of decreased purchasing power by inflation, or is willing to have the money income fluctuate, hoping, as a result, real income will fluctuate less. A balanced program may be desired in which case both variable and fixed dollar annuities can be bought.

Special-Purpose Policies

In addition to writing basic types of life insurance policies and annuities, life insurers offer several special policy forms. Many special forms combine basic policies into packages to meet particular life insurance needs. Other special forms reflect sales gimmicks not related to buyer needs. Often they are designed to confuse buyers seeking to compare prices and products of various insurers. The latter plans add more complication to an already difficult purchase decision problem faced by the life insurance buyer.

The family income policy

The family income policy provides a specified monthly income from the date of the insured's death until a future date *named in the policy* (this period is called the family income period). At that date, the policy's face amount is payable to the beneficiary. If the insured lives beyond that date, the beneficiary receives only the face amount of the policy upon the insured's death.

In structure, the traditional family income policy consists of whole life insurance and monthly decreasing term insurance. Upon the insured's death the proceeds of the whole life policy are held at interest by the insurer until the end of the family income period. The interest provides part of the family income payments and the decreasing term insurance provides the remainder. Each month the insured lives, less term insurance is needed to fund the income for the unexpired period, so *monthly* decreasing term is used.

The family income policy efficiently adds protection during the child-rearing period. Assume that a young parent wants to protect the family against financial losses resulting from the parent's death, and so buys a family income policy. The child is one year old, and the parent knows the spouse would need extra income until the child becomes financially independent. The policy may provide that if the parent dies at any time within the next 20 years, the spouse receives a monthly income of a stipulated amount (usually 1 percent of the policy's face amount) until the child is 21. At that time the face amount of the policy becomes payable to the surviving spouse. If the parent lives until the child is 21, upon the death of the insured only the face amount of the policy is paid, as the family income period would have expired.

The premium required to provide the necessary additional income for the child-rearing period solely with permanent insurance might be prohibitive for some families. About $20,000 of proceeds is needed to produce an income of $120 a month for 20 years. On a continuous premium whole life plan this amount would require an annual premium of about $270, nonparticipating at age 25. However, a traditional 1 percent of $12,000 family income policy issued at age 25 would require an annual premium of only about $175, nonparticipating.

The objectives of a family income policy also may be accomplished by using decreasing term insurance riders, usually with greater flexibility because of the wide choice of policies to which the rider may be added and the greater flexibility in the amounts of decreasing term insurance available.

The family maintenance policy

The family maintenance policy differs from the family income policy in that monthly payments continue for a fixed number of years *following* the insured's death, if the insured dies within that period. Assume that the parent buys a family maintenance instead of a family income policy. The beneficiary would receive payments for 20 years following the insured's death if the insured dies within 20 years. As in the family income policy, the face amount of the policy is payable at the expiration of the monthly payments.

In structure, the family maintenance policy is whole life insurance plus *level* term. The full amount of the initial term insurance will be necessary each year to provide the family maintenance income. As the family maintenance policy involves level rather than decreasing term, it requires a premium nearly one third higher than the premium for the family income policy. Because it includes level term insurance to meet what typically is a decreasing insurance need, legitimate uses of the family maintenance policy are limited.

Multiple protection policies

Multiple protection policies are whole life policies plus term insurance. A multiple protection policy provides a multiple of the face amount of the whole life policy if the insured dies within a specified period, but only the face amount if he or she dies after the expiration of the multiple protection period. The term expires after a specified number of years such as 10 or 15, or when the insured reaches a certain age; for example, 60 or 65. When the term insurance expires, the premium may be reduced to that for whole life, or it may be computed to remain level for the life of the policy. The principal advantage of multiple protection policies is that term insurance can be purchased at a premium lower than if brought independently. The nonpar rate quoted by one insurer for multiple protection to age 65 issued at age 25 is about $2 a thousand less than if term to 65 and continuous premium whole life were bought separately.

Mortgage protection policies

One important use of life insurance is protection against loss of mortgaged property if the mortgagor dies before the mortgage debt is paid. If the breadwinner dies, mortgage protection life insurance will provide the spouse with funds to continue mortgage payments and permit the family to retain the property. Mortgage protection policies are decreasing term policies in which the insurance amount approximately equals the unamortized portion of the mortgage. Some insurers issue a special mortgage protection form combining decreasing term insurance with small amounts of whole life insurance. When the mortgage loan is paid and the term insurance expires, the insured will retain a small amount of permanent insurance to pay property taxes and repairs. The premium is low, as with all decreasing term policies.

The difficulty of financing the purchase of a home during recent periods of unstable and relatively high mortgage interest rates, has produced a number of new types of mortgage loans. Changes in the outstanding loan balance under these new mortgages no longer follow the predictable pattern associated with fixed rate mortgages. Therefore, new mortgage protection plans must be developed to fit the requirements of mortgage loans where monthly payments and/or outstanding balances can increase or decrease.

The most popular of the new approaches is the *variable rate mortgage*. Monthly payments are adjusted at regular intervals to reflect interest rate changes according to a specified index. Limits in the size of payment adjustments (e.g., the payment increase is limited to $200 per month more than payments during the previous six-month period) and the interest rate adjustments (e.g., the interest rate charged may not exceed the initial rate, plus or minus 3 percent) are set out in the mortgage contract.

A *participating mortgage* allows the lender to participate in any appreciation in the value of the mortgaged home during the mortgage period. The principal is adjusted at stated intervals to reflect whatever value change that may have taken place. These mortgages are set up with a fixed interest rate (although a variable rate could be used) that is lower than concurrently available conventional fixed rate mortgages due to the use of the appreciation advantage (a.k.a. kicker or sweetener). If the home is sold before the mortgage is paid off, the lender shares in the appreciation according to the terms of the mortgage contract.

Under a *graduated payment mortgage,* monthly payment amounts increase at a specified rate and time for the first several years of the mortgage period. After the initial period, payments become level for the remainder of the life of the loan. Compared to a conventional fixed rate mortgage with the same interest rate, payments under the graduated payment mortgage start lower, but level off at an amount higher than payments on the conventional mortgage.

For each of the new mortgage contracts described above, an adjustable yearly renewable term life insurance contract can be used to pay a lump-sum benefit equal to the outstanding mortgage loan balance at the death of a breadwinner. Although adjustable term products have been available for nearly 15 years, their application to the mortgage protection problem has not been widespread. Moreover, many insurers already have products that allow sufficient flexibility in coverage amount (without requiring new evidence of insurability by the insured) to accommodate the mortgage protection needs where the outstanding loan balance can increase.

Unfortunately, insurance products designed to pay postdeath benefits in the form of monthly mortgage payments usually provide for level benefit payments only. Newly designed coverages are needed for mortgages that allow payment adjustments based on interest rate changes.

The family policy

With one policy and one premium, the family policy insures the lives of the entire family—father, mother, and eligible children. The policy is sold in units of $5,000, written on the life of the father and is usually continuous premium whole life insurance. Term insurance of $2,000 per unit is written on the mother's life if she is the same age as the father, more if younger and less if older. Term insurance for $1,000 per unit is written on the children usually until age 25. Children usually are excluded until they are 15 days old. The term insurance on the lives of family members usually ceases when the father reaches age 65. If the mother predeceases the father, the insurance on the life of the father is increased by $2,000 until age 65. If the father dies first, insurance on the other family members becomes paid up and remains in force until its scheduled termination date. The term insurance on the mother is convertible at the end of the term period for the full amount, and for the children up to five times its amount. If the mother is the principal breadwinner, then substitute the word "mother" for "father" and "father" for "mother" in this and the following paragraphs.

Family policies differ with various insurers. In some plans permanent insurance is written on the wife. Also the amount of insurance on family members may be a higher percent of the amount written on the husband. As in all special-purpose policies, plans have to be studied individually rather than relying on categorical descriptions.

Premiums.   The premium for the family policy is based on the father's age. The number of children has no effect. The age of the mother does not affect the premium but affects the amount of insurance on her life. The premium usually remains level until age 65, when it is reduced. One insurer's nonparticipating premium for the family policy at age 25 is $83.65 a unit. At age 65, the $83.65 premium is reduced to $63.30, the premium for $5,000 continuous premium whole life insurance.

Uses.   The principal advantage of the family policy is that it allows those who insist on insuring dependents' lives to do so at the lowest possible cost. The right to convert the insurance on the children's lives to five times its original amount protects the "insurability" of the children at a nominal premium.

The policy has appeal, which is unfortunate because it is particularly vulnerable to misuse. A family that can afford to spend only $83.65 a year for insurance should have more than $5,000 insurance on the father; and one that can spend $167.30 should have more than $10,000 on the father. An insurance program involving less whole life and more term insurance on the father may be more desirable. Nevertheless, the family policy represents about 7 percent of the policies and 9 percent of the amount of ordinary life insurance currently bought.

Joint life policy

Joint life policies are written with more than one named insured. Usually the joint life policy covers two persons, with the face amount payable upon the first death only. The premium for a joint life policy is based on the ages of the insureds, and is less than the cost of two individual policies.

Retirement income policy

A retirement income policy is a special form of endowment insurance at age 65 under which cash values will be sufficient to fund a $10 monthly lifetime income, 120 months certain per $1,000 of face amount. Because it takes more than $1,000 to fund the income, at some point the cash values of the policy exceed the amount of insurance. If the insured dies prior to retirement, the insured's beneficiary receives the face amount or cash value, whichever is higher.

Preferred risk

The "special deal" in life insurance is undoubtedly as old as the use of agents. Some agents convince customers that a "special proposition" is designed just for them. College students often are fed the story that they are in a "preferred risk" category, and some swallow it. Since the turn of the century, legitimate "specials" have been sold by life insurers under the name "preferred risk" policies. Recently competitive interest in this type of policy has increased.

"Preferred risk" at one time applied *only* to contracts issued to low-hazard applicants at less than standard rates. "Standard" applies to policies written on applicants whose health, habits, and occupations conform to the norms used in predicting mortality experience. An extra premium is charged for those who fail to meet these standards. Thus, the term "preferred risk" logically should be applied only, and in most cases is, to those whose health, habits, and occupations are better than standard. For example, a number of insurers give special rates to non-smokers and to persons who are physically trim. However, from some insurers "preferred risk" policies are available to other than low-hazard applicants at premiums below standard. Premium reduction is achieved in one or more ways: (1) requiring a large minimum policy; (2) reducing agents' commissions; (3) granting less favorable settlement options; (4) lowering expense loadings in participating plans thus reducing the gross premium but not necessarily the net premium, as the policy dividends may be reduced correspondingly; (5) paying a "surrender dividend," available only if the insured terminates the policy at the end of a stated number of years; and (6) providing lower cash surrender values. The first three items reduce the cost of the policy to the insurer. The fourth lowers the gross premium only, whereas the fifth makes the insurer appear to provide insurance at lower cost; but if the policy is not terminated before death, no surrender dividend is paid, so cost saving may prove an illusion. The sixth item offsets the premium reduction only if the insured surrenders the policy.

Guaranteed insurability agreements

Guaranteed insurability agreements introduced in 1957 have become widespread in the United States and Canada. Under the agreements the insured has an option to purchase additional insurance at specified times without evidence of insurability. Coverage is written as a rider to whole life or endowment plans usually for amounts equal to at least $5,000. The rider specifies the amount of insurance that can be purchased during each option period as the face amount of the basic policy or a specified maximum (e.g., $20,000), whichever is less.

Several option periods are offered, the number depending on the issue age of the basic policy. For example, if the policy is issued before age 25, the insured may purchase additional amounts of insurance at anytime within 60 days of the policy anniversaries nearest the insured's 25th, 28th, 31st, 34th, 37th, and 40th birthdays. If the basic policy is issued at age 31, only three option dates are available. The option usually is not written for applicants over age 37. Some companies allow additional options upon the occurrence of a specified event such as the marriage of the insured or the birth of a dependent. The options generally are not cumulative. Failure to exercise an option results in a loss of that option but does not affect subsequent ones. Any whole life or endowment plan written by the insurer may be bought under the option, and the premium is that for the attained age when the option is exercised.

Premiums. The option premium is expressed in terms of the basic amount of insurance and applies only to the maximum allowable. The annual premium varies widely among insurers but the mean is about $1.50 per $1,000 at age 25, payable with the regular premium until the option's expiration.

Uses. The guaranteed insurability option enables one to postpone the purchase of insurance without the risk of losing insurability when additional insurance is needed.

The principal drawback is that a basic whole life or endowment policy for a minimum of $5,000 usually is required. Many young people who could use guaranteed insurability riders cannot afford the necessary basic contract. For them protection during the early high-need, low-income years is best arranged with convertible term insurance. When adequate protection with the required basic policies is affordable, guaranteed insurability is practical. Some insurers allow the options to be exercised while the policy is on disability premium waiver (discussed later).

Variable life insurance

A variable life policy provides a *minimum* face amount of insurance but allows the policy proceeds to fluctuate beyond this amount based on the value of the investment portfolio supporting the policy. Cash values also fluctuate with investment values. As life insurance proceeds and cash values are tied to a portfolio of securities, the variable life policy uses some of the principles of the variable annuity. Variable life was not marketed in the United States until 1976, as legal problems first had to be solved. The product was originally introduced in Holland but because of special tax advantages enjoys its greatest popularity in England. This policy is designed to remedy the adverse effects of fixed dollar contracts in an inflationary economy, but it has yet to gain popularity in the United States. One disadvantage is that, in recent years, the stock market and the consumer price index have not consistently moved in the same direction, and the stock market has lagged considerably behind the cost of living.

Split-life insurance

Structurally split-life insurance involves a tie-in of two contracts, an annual premium retirement annuity and yearly renewable term insurance, allowing the insured to split the savings feature of life insurance from its protection. Up to $10,000 of term insurance can be purchased per $10 of annual annuity premiums. The term insurance may be renewed only if the annuity premium is paid. At age 65 when the annuity payout becomes effective, the term can be renewed until an advanced age (e.g., 95). The term insurance rate is low for each age, but the annuity price is high creating a package priced comparably to moderately priced whole life insurance. The annuity and the life insurance need not be purchased on the same life. The term insurance can be written for several lives (e.g., two or more children) thus providing the children with low-priced term insurance at the expense of a high-priced annuity paid for by the parent—a form of subsidy offered by the parent to the children. Split life is not approved in some states because of legal and tax questions and because of concern about its value to consumers.

The life cycle policy

A life cycle policy, introduced in the early 1970s, provides "flexibility" to meet the policyowner's varying needs throughout life. It switches between term and whole life insurance depending on the amount of premium a policyowner wants to pay. A computer program is used to vary cash values and other benefits as well as maturity dates consonant with the premium input as the insured passes through life and needs a change in insurance coverage. A number of variations exist among policies offered under the name of life cycle.

Adjustable life

The adjustable life insurance policy was introduced in the United States in 1971 and is now marketed by two insurance companies. Adjustable life reflects the changing needs of a policyowner and the policyowner's ability to pay for life insurance. A policyowner can elect to adjust the policy in any one of the following ways: (1) increase the face amount (subject in most cases to evidence of insurability), or decrease the face amount, (2) increase or decrease the premium level, and (3) pay an extra premium in addition to the scheduled premium. These adjustments could vary the policy between term insurance and whole life insurance one or more times. The adjustable life policy includes provisions to increase the face amount of the policy to reflect an increase in the cost of living without providing evidence of insurability.

The effective use of adjustable life by a policyowner will require ongoing services from a trained agent. Expansion in the marketing of this policy will be slow because of the expense and time involved in its development and implementation.

Indexed-linked policies

Insurers are now offering policies in which death benefits are linked to the official consumer price index (CPI). One insurer has introduced a whole life policy designed to help the policyowners protect the face amount of their insurance against the erosion of value caused by inflation. Additions based on the CPI are offered annually (when the index increases) beginning on the second policy anniversary. The maximum index addition is 15 percent of the face amount or $30,000, whichever is less. The minimum index addition is $500. Premiums are increased according to the size of the addition. The policyowner can stabilize the contract by declining an addition. Once an individual addition is not accepted, no further additions are offered the policyowner.

Another insurer has introduced a term policy which ties the face amount of the policy to the CPI. The policyowner's premium automatically would be adjusted to cover the new benefit.

Deposit term

Deposit term is appropriate for persons who intend to keep their policies in force and seek to avoid sharing the high cost of early termination by those that lapse their policies. Deposit term is a term policy with a required deposit premium the first year in excess of the cost of the term insurance. No early cash value and only a token cash value later is payable on the deposit premium until the end of the designated term period. At the end of the period the insurer offers a cash value, which includes interest earned and accumulation from persistency. Persistency values result because most of the deposit premium of those who lapse during the term period is retained by the insurer for distribution to those who persist. If death occurs prior to the term period, the deposit premium plus compound interest is paid as an additional death benefit.

Deposit term offers the insured three options at the end of the term period:

1. Automatic conversion of the policy into continuous premium whole life insurance or some other cash value form.
2. Renewal of the plan for additional term periods without evidence of insurability until a maximum specified age upon payment of another term deposit and the premium for the attained age at renewal.
3. Conversion of the policy to decreasing term to age 100.

Other special policies

A compendium of life insurance policies will list policies not discussed here. Types of policies are limited only by the imagination of the actuaries, creativity of insurer managements, and the flexibility of the regulatory authorities. Some additional special policies are the *survivorship policy,* under which a life income is paid to the originally named beneficiary (usually old) only if the insured (usually young) is survived; *coupon policy,* to which are attached coupons, one of which is redeemable in cash at the end of each policy year; and *modified life policy,* under which the premiums for whole life insurance are lower than the corresponding continuous premium policy during the first three to five years and higher thereafter.

Juvenile life insurance forms

Juvenile insurance is popular. About 14 percent of all ordinary policies currently purchased are on the lives of children under age 15, and these policies make up about 5.4 percent of the dollar amount of ordinary life insurance purchases. The advisability of insuring the lives of children is discussed in Chapter 21, where the point is made that premium dollars usually are more efficiently used to provide additional life insurance on the working parent or parents. Two special policies have been developed exclusively for insuring children: the graded benefit plan and the "jumping juvenile" plan.

Graded benefit plan. Under the graded benefit plan, the policy face amount is scheduled to increase yearly to a stated maximum. For example, a juvenile policy issued on Sara Ann Dippidy, age two, provides that if she dies during the first policy year the death benefit will be $2,000. If she dies in the second year, the death benefit will be $3,000.

For the fourth year, $4,000 will be paid. If Sara lives beyond this period, the face amount of $5,000 would be paid at death.

"Jumping juvenile."   A "jumping juvenile" policy is issued in units of $1,000 automatically jumping to $5,000 with no increase in premium when the insured reaches age 21. The basic policy usually is endowment at age 65, life paid up at age 65, or continuous premium whole life. The purposes are to pay expenses of the death of a child and to offer a large amount of insurance at a time when the child may soon have family responsibilities.

Summary

1. Three basic types of life insurance are term, endowment, and whole life insurance. In addition, life insurers write a variety of annuities and special-purpose policies.
2. Term insurance provides death protection for a specified period of time, at the end of which the coverage expires without value. Term insurance may be short term, long term, renewable, convertible, level, increasing, or decreasing. Term may be appropriate for protection needs that do not extend for the life of the insured.
3. Endowment insurance also provides death protection for a specified period only, but unlike term, if the insureds survive the period, they are paid the policy face amount. Endowment often is viewed as a savings plan protected by life insurance. Its uses are as a gift medium, a savings medium for a particular purpose (an exotic vacation), or as a method of funding retirement income.
4. Whole life insurance offers permanent death protection, and may be classified by the method of paying premiums: single premium, continuous premium, or limited payment periods such as 20 years or to age 65.
5. Universal life insurance provides permanent or temporary protection according to the incidence and amount of premium payments. Under this plan a savings fund is established in order to separate and enhance policy values during the insured's life-time and to increase benefits at death.
6. Annuities provide a regular periodic income for the life of an annuitant. Annuities may include one or more lives. They may be written as immediate or deferred and with a single premium or a series of annual premiums. During the payout period the annuity may be payable for life (a life annuity) or for a specified number of years independent of the annuitant's survival (an annuity certain). When written for life, the annuity may guarantee a specified minimum amount of payments (a life annuity with a minimum period certain or refund annuity), or the annuity may cease upon the death of the annuitant (a straight life annuity). Furthermore the annuity payout may be paid in fixed dollars (conventional annuity) or variable dol-

lars fluctuating with the insured's investment portfolio supporting the annuity (variable annuity).

7. Life insurance and annuities may be combined in one contract to form special-purpose policies to meet specific needs of insureds; for example, the family income policy uses whole life insurance and decreasing term insurance and an annuity certain payout. They may also be written as tie-in contracts as in the split-life plan offering an annual premium retirement annuity along with yearly renewable term insurance, the latter on the same or different persons.

Questions for Review

1. How does the length of time a life insurance policy is in force affect the true rate of return on its "savings element"? What other factors affect the true rate of return? Explain.

2. Which is more reasonable, to view the whole life policy as term *to* age 100 or to view it as endowment *at* age 100? Explain.

3. Is the family income policy or family maintenance policy more appropriate for providing income during the child-rearing years? Why?

4. What are the arguments for and against "buy-term-and-invest-the-difference?"

5. Explain the variable annuity and the theory supporting it. Is the concept of a variable life policy new? Explain. (Hint: refer to the historical discussion in the chapter.)

6. Explain the concept of survivorship benefits. How do they affect the amount of monthly income paid under various types of annuities?

7. Why is William Gybbons so important a person in life insurance history?

8. What advantages and limitations do you see in the split-life policy, the family policy, the limited payment life policy, and the endowment policy?

9. What is the difference between an immediate annuity and an annuity due? Under what circumstances is each used?

10. Three types of term insurance are level, increasing, and decreasing term. Illustrate by use of examples situations in which each type is appropriately used.

Questions for Discussion

1. Design a life insurance policy benefit schedule for a breadwinner age 25 that will serve the insured's life insurance needs for life.

2. Life insurance agents generally are paid less commission on some policies than others. Could this discriminatory treatment create a problem for the buyer? Can you suggest a remedy?

3. What is a mutual fund? Do you believe that mutual funds are in competition with life insurers?

4. Life insurance held per family is about double the annual disposable income per family. Is this the right amount of life insurance for a family to hold? Can you think of reasons why these figures may be misleading?

5. Many insurers emphasize the investment aspects of life insurance rather than protection against financial loss from death. Does this emphasis do justice to the product? Does it do justice to the customer?

6. Do you believe the theory behind the variable annuity is sound? Discuss.

7. Do you agree with the theory supporting the variable annuity discussed in question 5 in Questions for Review?

8. What do you consider the most significant development discussed in the section dealing with life insurance history? Why?

Life insurance contracts:
Riders and provisions

People buy life insurance for three reasons: to protect dependents against the financial effects of the insured's death, to provide for old-age dependency, and to use the "compulsory savings" feature of life insurance. To decide on the "best policy," an individual must decide which of the three purposes is most important. Table 17–1 shows the death, retirement value, and savings feature in various types of policies that can be bought for a premium of $250 a year at age 25. The purpose of the table is to show the meaningful relationships, and not to reflect current rates which vary widely among insurers and over time. Price variations are discussed in Chapter 21. The best policy is one that gives the combination of savings and protection desired; it is the subject of Chapter 21.

Life Insurance Riders

Supplemental agreements are frequently made part of life insurance policies. Some add more life insurance, such as level, increasing, or decreasing term to a basic whole life or endowment policy. Others may add total disability benefits or accidental death benefits, discussed in Chapter 18. In addition to the level term and family income riders previ-

TABLE 17–1
Death, savings, and retirement values of popular policies based on annual premium outlay of $250, issue age 25, nonpar

Type of policy	Age	Death protection	Savings (cash value) end of 20 years	Cash value at 65	Monthly life income (10 years certain at age 65)
Yearly renewable and con-					
vertible term	25	$193,966	0	0	0
	40	125,698	0	0	0
	50	25,656	0	0	0
	60	10,781	0	0	0
Five-year renewable and					
convertible term	25	182,540	0	0	0
	30	163,121	0	0	0
	35	129,944	0	0	0
	45	51,339	0	0	0
Universal life:					
guaranteed rate*		26,300	$4,900	$11,500	$ 71.65
8 percent interest rate†		83,400	6,798	25,900	284.90
10 percent interest rate†		109,000	6,355	27,848	306.33
Continuous premium					
whole life		24,530	4,832	12,756	85.46
Whole life paid up					
at 65		21,095	4,683	13,163	88.19
Retirement income at					
65 (male)		8,545‡	4,949	13,867	92.91
20-pay life		15,016	5,571	9,370	62.78

* These figures are based on the low guaranteed rate of 4 percent. The amounts paid currently are much larger because of the high interest rates available in today's market.

† These figures are based on obtaining the stated interest rate for a long period of time, and therefore should be considered speculative.

‡ Or the cash value when it exceeds the face amount of insurance.

ously mentioned, other standardized riders include waiver of premium, return of premium, return of cash value, payor benefits, and the cost-of-living rider.

Waiver of premium

Waiver of premium provides that in case of total disability, the insured is relieved of the obligation to continue premium payments after a six-month waiting period. The common practice is to refund premiums paid during the six-month waiting period. The policy continues as if premiums were paid. The cost is low, the coverage essential, and the rider nearly universally available.

Return of premium rider

The return of premium rider usually provides that if the insured dies within the first 20 policy years, the insurer will pay the beneficiary both the face amount of the policy and the total premiums paid by the insured. The rider is not issued on limited payment or endowment policies with premium-paying periods shorter than 20 years. The rider in effect is increasing term insurance. If the insured survives the 20-year period, the rider expires, and the policy continues in its basic form.

Cash value rider

The cash value rider provides for the return of the cash value of the policy at death, thus giving the beneficiary not only the face amount of the policy but also its predeath cash value. These riders are used to satisfy those who fail to understand why upon their death "their cash values" are "confiscated" by the insurer. The rider also offers those who want to increase their insurance the opportunity to buy protection at a relatively low premium.

Payor benefit rider

The payor benefit agreement is used with juvenile insurance and is similar to the waiver of premium rider. In this case, the death or disability of the insured's parents causes premiums to be waived. Suppose a parent has insured a child's life. If a payor benefit rider is attached, the parent's death or total disability would waive the premiums on the child's policy until the child reaches 25 (or some other predetermined age). Then the child can either pay the premiums or accept one of the nonforfeiture options. The annual premium for the benefit depends on the policy type and the ages of the insured and the payor.

Cost-of-living rider

Some insurers offer a rider under which the amount of insurance increases or decreases to reflect cost-of-living changes as measured by the consumer price index (CPI). A maximum is placed on the amount by which the insurance may be increased. These riders offer one-year term insurance as an addition to the amount of the basic policy. Thus, if the rider is used with a $50,000 whole life policy and the CPI advances 5 percent during the year, $2,500 of one-year term insurance is written automatically for the next year without evidence of insurability. The insured is billed for the additional coverage. If the CPI falls, the amount of one-year term insurance is decreased proportionately. Only the amount of insurance provided by the cost-of-living rider is subject to change. The amount of the basic policy is unaffected by fluctuations in the CPI.

Classes of Life Insurance

As distinguished from *types,* several *classes* of life insurance are written. These classes are ordinary, industrial, and group. They differ in type of customers, policy amounts, cash values, methods of computing and collecting premiums, underwriting standards, and marketing methods. The division line between industrial and ordinary insurance is muddled because different states and different insurers have their own definitions of the terms.

Ordinary life insurance

Ordinary life usually is issued in amounts of $1,000 or more with premiums payable annually, semiannually, quarterly, or monthly. The ordinary department of most life insurers is their largest department and many insurers write only ordinary life insurance. All life insurance types previously discussed are available through the ordinary departments of life insurers. Ordinary insurance accounts for nearly 50 percent of life insurance in force in the United States and about 72 percent of the insurance currently purchased. Mass-marketed or wholesale insurance is a form of ordinary insurance that has been increasing in importance. Although sold to members of a group, the sale is on an individual basis and usually written as automatically renewable term insurance.

Industrial life insurance

Industrial life insurance usually is written with face amounts less than $1,000. Premiums generally are payable weekly or at some other time interval less than one month and are collected at the insured's home by an agent referred to as a "debit man." Although many of the same types of policies are written in industrial insurance as in ordinary insurance, limited payment, whole life accounts for about 70 percent of the industrial life insurance in force. Expansion of government social insurance, increased affluence, and the exit from the market of some large insurers have contributed to the declining popularity of industrial life insurance. Presently industrial insurance equals less than 1 percent of the life insurance in force in the United States compared with 9 percent 25 years earlier and 31 percent 45 years ago.

Premiums charged for industrial insurance generally are higher than those charged for ordinary insurance for three reasons: higher administration costs per dollar of insurance, higher mortality rates for persons covered (more liberal underwriting standards are applied in industrial than in ordinary insurance), and greater lapse rates. The cost of selling and administering a policy exceeds the first premium. The excess cost is recaptured from subsequent premiums. If large numbers of persons buy policies and keep them in force only a short time, the insurer cannot recover acquisition costs for that business and must shift these costs to those who retain their insurance (see Chapter 26). In a study released in 1979 by the Federal Trade Commission, industrial insurance was severely attacked for its excessive costs and the sales tactics used by some agents to persuade unknowledgeable persons to purchase an excessive number of policies.

Group life insurance

Group life insurance is life insurance, usually issued without medical examination, on a group of persons under a master policy, with members of the group receiving certificates of participation. Group life including credit life equals about 50 percent of the life insurance in force in the United States. Group life and other group coverages are discussed in Chapter 21.

The Life Insurance Contract

Although no nationwide uniformity exists in their wording, all life policies contain certain basic provisions, called general policy provisions, appearing in various forms. Also three important types of options are available in most life policies: nonforfeiture options, dividend options, and settlement options.

The first page of the typical life policy contains a statement of the insuring agreement between the insured and the insurer. The beneficiary's name is stated on the front page, and the policy declares that provisions attached are part of the contract. The amount of premium to be paid each payment period may be stated. At the bottom are signatures of authorized company officials, usually the president, secretary, and registrar. Next are two types of general policy provisions: those required by state law, and those not prohibited by law which the insurer chooses to include.

Decisions by the insured

The insured must make certain decisions relating to beneficiary designation, ownership, and policy options. Qualified agents help the insured make efficient decisions.

Beneficiary designations. The insured must name one or more beneficiaries to receive the proceeds of the policy upon death. Insureds may designate third parties as beneficiaries or may have the proceeds paid to their estates. The designation may be either revocable or irrevocable. If revocable the insured may change the beneficiary and may also transfer, assign, or surrender the policy. If irrevocable the beneficiary has a vested right in the policy, and the insured may not assign the policy or borrow on it without the consent of the beneficiary. An irrevocable beneficiary designation may be either reversionary or absolute. If reversionary, the policy rights revert to the insured if the beneficiary dies first. If absolute the value of the policy is included in the beneficiary's estate for the beneficiary's heirs. These heirs may keep the policy in force or surrender it for its cash value.

The beneficiary clause is the one provision the insured writes. The beneficiary designation should be precise so that no doubt exists as to exactly who is to receive the policy proceeds. For example, the primary beneficiary designation of "wife of the insured" is not sufficiently precise as, prior to the death of the insured, more than one person may fit this description. (It is also insufficient to specify "first wife of the insured" as there may be more than one who considers herself to be the "Number 1" wife.) Full, proper names, including maiden names for women, should accompany the "wife of the insured" designation. This also helps avoid problems that arise where a man has named his wife as the beneficiary, then is divorced and remarries a woman who has the same first name as his former wife.

In addition, use of the phrase "children of the insured" can lead to problems. How is the share of death benefits to be divided if an insured parent outlives one of the children? What about legally adopted children, and children born after the designation was made? And what about children of a spouse who are not children of the insured? The designation, "children of the insured and Lula May Schichelgrubber, including those legally adopted, *per stirpes,*" can be used to solve these problems. *Per stirpes* means that children of a deceased child-beneficiary will share their parent's portion of the proceeds equally. Thus, an insured could use this designation to pay proceeds to his or her three children. If one of the beneficiaries is deceased at the time of the insured's death, that beneficiary's two children would share one third of the policy's death benefit (i.e., each would get one sixth of the total death benefit).

Secondary beneficiaries should be named in the event the primary beneficiaries do not survive the insured. As in the primary beneficiary designation, the secondary beneficiary designation should be precise and complete. In cases where disputes arise among beneficiaries or potential beneficiaries, the insurer can use the equitable remedy of interpleader and pay the proceeds directly to a court of law. The court then determines the disposition of the death benefits. The insurer is thereby relieved of the responsibility of deciding the validity of the various claims.

Ownership.   Generally, under ordinary life insurance the insured also is the owner of the policy. However estate planning considerations may dictate that someone other than the insured own the policy. Proceeds of life insurance policies are included in the taxable estate of the insured unless the insured has relinquished all the incidents of ownership in the policy (among which are the right to assign the policy or change the beneficiary). When someone other than the insured owns the policy, a successor owner should be named in the event the insured survives the owner.

Policy options.   Life insurance policies generally offer three sets of options: nonforfeiture, dividend, and settlement options. Nonforfeiture options are found only in cash value policies.

Nonforfeiture options.   If the insured wishes to discontinue premium payments, three choices are available: surrender the policy for its cash value; convert the policy to a paid-up policy of the same type, but for a reduced face amount; or convert the contract to a paid-up term policy for the full face of the policy, but for a period usually shorter than the original policy. This latter option is called extended term insurance.

Assume that Peter Colwell bought a $50,000 continuous premium whole life policy when he was 20 years old, paid premiums for 10 years, then decided to discontinue payments. The value of his options are as follows: $2,907 in cash (or in annuity payments); a fully paid-up whole life policy for $12,450, or $50,000 of term insurance for 18 years and 204 days.

Most policies have an automatic option providing that if premium payments are discontinued, the policy will be changed to extended term insurance if the insured fails to elect another method.

Dividends and dividend options. In 1983 more than $8 billion were paid as dividends to owners of participating policies. Virtually all mutual policies are participating. Stock insurers may issue both nonparticipating and participating policies, but most stock insurers issue only nonparticipating policies. The source of dividends and their determination are discussed in Chapter 26.

In the absence of the insured's election, dividends are *paid in cash*. However, generally no money is transferred. The insurer applies the cash dividend toward the next premium payment. Cash is paid to the policyowner only under paid-up policies. Cash is the most widely used dividend option.

Dividends may be *accumulated at interest*. In this event, the insurer retains the dividends and accumulates them at not less than the interest rate specified in the policy. Excess interest will be credited if earned.

Dividends may be used to buy *paid-up additions* to the policy at *net* rates. Thus, under a five-year-old continuous premium whole life policy, a $2.42 dividend would buy $11.00 of paid-up whole life insurance at age 25. If the insured is age 40 when the dividend is received, the amount of paid-up addition would be only $8.12, as the insurance cost is higher at age 40. Paid-up additions are an inexpensive way to acquire additional insurance. This option may be selected for current dividends at any time without proof of insurability.

A fourth dividend option is *one-year term insurance*. Under the one-year term option, the amount of insurance that can be purchased usually is restricted to an amount equal to the cash value of the policy. Dividends in excess of that required to purchase term insurance may be paid under one of the other options.

A fifth option is the *"accelerative" endowment* option, under which dividends are added directly to the policy reserve. When the reserve value equals the policy face amount, the policy matures as an endowment. By adding the dividend to the reserve, the amount payable at the death of the insured is not increased although the cash values increase. (Under the accumulation at interest option, the death payment includes the policy proceeds *and* the accumulated dividends.) In exchange for forfeiture of dividend accumulations at death, the insured receives additional survivorship benefits to be added to the reserve, thus accelerating the time when the reserve equals the policy face and matures the policy as an endowment. (The option also allows the policy to become paid up at an earlier date.) This option is not usually printed in the policy.

If additional death protection is desired, either the paid-up insurance or the one-year term dividend option should be selected. An insured more interested in a savings fund or retirement income might choose the accumulate at interest dividend option or the accelerative endowment. However, reconsideration could lead to a different answer. Interest paid on dividend accumulations is taxable as income, but many insureds failed to report this interest either deliberately or unknowingly. The problem presumably was remedied when regulations were established requiring the insurer to report interest payments to both the recipient and the Internal Revenue Service (IRS). However, annual increases in the cash value of the paid-up additions are not subject to current income taxation. So, the insured who is more interested in savings than in death protection may elect paid-up additions or the accelerative endowment option for tax reasons, or perhaps may withdraw the dividend payments for investment elsewhere for higher investment yields.

Policyowners currently take about 36 percent of dividend distributions in the form of cash or as payment on their premiums; they leave 26 percent with the insurers at interest under the accumulation at interest or the accelerative endowment option; and they use 38 percent to buy additional insurance under the one-year term option or the paid-up insurance option.

Settlement options.   The basic method of settling proceeds of a life policy is a lump sum and this is the method used in the great majority of settlements. But for those interested in providing beneficiaries (or themselves) income payments, interest only and annuity options are offered in nearly every policy. The annuity options are installments for a fixed period, installments of a fixed amount, and a life income.

Under the *interest only* option the insurer retains the policy proceeds and pays the beneficiary interest earned. A minimum interest rate is guaranteed, with the actual interest payment a function of the amount the insurer earns. Many policies written today *promise* 2.5 to 4 percent, but most insurers pay much higher interest rates.

Installments for a fixed period is a settlement option under which the proceeds of the policy (principal and interest) are paid in a fixed number of monthly, quarterly, or annual installments. The guaranteed amount of each payment per $1,000 of proceeds is a function of the period over which payments are continued. This option is an annuity certain. The payments continue until the required number of installments has been paid, regardless whether the annuitant survives. For example, a minimum monthly installment of $17.70 per $1,000 of insurance proceeds is guaranteed for a five-year period, assuming 2.5 percent interest. If the payments are guaranteed for 10 years, the minimum monthly amount is $9.39. Thus, a $100,000 policy guarantees $939 a month for 10 years. In the likely event the insurer earns more than the assumed 2.5 percent and the settlements are participating, the monthly payments are increased to more than $939. A loan outstanding against the policy reduces the guaranteed payments to less than $939.

Under the *installments-for-a-fixed-amount* option the insurer pays a monthly benefit of a predetermined amount and continues the payments until the policy proceeds are exhausted. The duration of the payments is determined by the amount of each guaranteed payment. For example, a beneficiary can be guaranteed $100 a month for a minimum of nine years and six months from $10,000 of insurance proceeds (assuming interest at 3 percent). The difference between the fixed amount option and the fixed period option is that in the former the amount of each payment is guaranteed, and in the latter the period over which payments are to be made is guaranteed. In the fixed amount option, if the settlement is participating, dividends are used to extend the period rather than increase the amount of each payment. Loans outstanding against the policy reduce the benefit period, not the amount of each payment.

The *life income option* is equivalent to using insurance proceeds to buy a life annuity. In the typical life income option, the insurer promises to continue income payments, usually for a guaranteed period and thereafter for the life of the annuitant. The guarantee period usually ranges from 5 to 20 years. Although a life income is ideal, the amount of insurance proceeds required to make this option practical is large especially for young beneficiaries. For a beneficiary age 35, $1,000 of insurance proceeds pays a *guaranteed* income of only about $3.36 a month under a 10-year certain and life thereafter option. About $300,000 of insurance would be necessary to guarantee an income of $1,000 a month. (The $300,000 invested in a passbook savings and loan account currently pays about $1,370 a month without liquidating principal.) The insurer pays a dividend on participating options, and to be more competitive, many allow the purchase of life annuities at current *net* rates; that is, without the expense addition. The insured or beneficiary is advised in any case to engage in comparative shopping in the financial markets before choosing a settlement option. Although a life income is desirable, a livable income for a few years, during the time necessary for the children to become self-supporting, may be better than an inadequate income for life. The life income option may be considered for older people. If the beneficiary is age 65 when the income becomes payable, a monthly lifetime income of about $5.50 a month, 10 years certain (more for a male), would be guaranteed for each $1,000 of insurance. In this case $300,000 of life insurance would guarantee a lifetime income of $1,650 a month, still not competitively attractive unless increased by dividends.

An important option which may be included in the policy or as a rider upon request is the *joint and last survivorship option,* under which a minimum periodic income is guaranteed during the joint lifetime of two or more persons and throughout the lifetime of the survivor. This option is used more frequently for distributing cash values to the insured and spouse as a retirement income than as a method of settling the proceeds of a policy paid at the insured's death. Under this option each $1,000 of cash values or endowment proceeds guarantees a man and woman, both age 65, $4.90 a month as long as either is alive. If the couple agree to reduce the income by one third after the first death, the option will guarantee $5.72 a month while both are alive and $3.81 to the survivor. Unless enhanced by participating dividends or written at current annuity rates, these values are not necessarily attractive when compared with other investments that preserve the principal. Furthermore some insurers offer better annuity rates than others, so the insured or beneficiary insisting on annuity settlements is again advised to engage in comparative shopping among insurers. One advantage of using settlement options following death, at least for part of the proceeds, is that the surviving spouse receives $1,000 of interest income from liquidating options income tax free. Therefore the after-tax return on other investments for part of the proceeds may be less attractive.

Other policy provisions

In addition to ownership, beneficiary designation, and settlement options (which are determined by the insured), life insurance policies contain provisions required by law, provisions permitted by law, and other general policy provisions.

Provisions required by state law. The various states require that insurers include policy provisions concerning incontestability, misstatement of age or sex, deferment, nonforfeiture values, loan values, grace periods, and reinstatement.

Incontestability. The incontestability clause prohibits the insurer, after a period of time, to contest the policy on the basis of statements made in the application or concealment of facts. A typical clause is: "This policy shall be incontestable after it has been in force during the lifetime of the insured for a period of two years from its date of issue except for nonpayment of premiums." The courts have interpreted the clause liberally, allowing it to become an agreement to disregard fraud. Although social and economic justification exists for incontestability in life insurance, no generally accepted legal explanation is available for either the incontestable clause or court decisions upholding it. The law usually holds that an agreement to disregard fraud violates public policy, and hence is void. Thus the incontestable clause is an anomaly among contract provisions and is peculiar to life insurance. The clause is justified because of the impracticability of assembling evidence and witnesses many years after the policy is issued. Defense against fraud is especially difficult if it must be made by a beneficiary after the death of the suspected insured. The clause is valuable to the beneficiary in preventing delayed settlements resulting from long and costly court action.

Misstatement of age and sex.   The incontestability clause does not excuse the misstatement of age or sex of the insured, as they are primary life insurance rating factors. If the insured misstates age or sex, an adjustment is made in the policy proceeds. The beneficiary is paid the amount of insurance which the premiums paid would have purchased if the age or sex had been stated correctly. Thus, if a man aged 30 states his age as 25 when buying a $50,000 whole life policy and this misstatement is discovered, the insurance proceeds will be reduced to $41,055—the amount of insurance the premiums paid would have bought at age 30. If sex also was misstated, the face amount of the policy would be reduced to $45,202, the amount of continuous premium whole life insurance that would have been bought by a woman age 30 for the premiums charged a man aged 25.

Deferment clause.   In the 1930s some insurers were financially embarrassed when many policyowners wanted to borrow or withdraw the cash values of their policies at the same time. The difficulty was that the insurers could not liquidate other resources quickly without suffering substantial losses. Since then life insurers have been required to include a clause giving them the right to defer the payment of the cash or loan value of a policy for a period not to exceed six months unless the loan is for renewal premiums. The clause does not apply to proceeds payable in cash at death, although it may apply to the withdrawal of proceeds retained at interest or to commutations of guaranteed installments under settlement options.

Nonforfeiture values.   Except for short period term insurance, every life insurance policy has a cash value after it has been in force for a minimum of one, two, or sometimes three years. The cash value is available to the insured when the insurance is discontinued. As the insured does not forfeit cash value rights in the policy if premium payments are discontinued, these rights are called "nonforfeiture values." The options that the insureds have under the nonforfeiture clause have been discussed.

Loan values.   If the insured needs money but does not want to terminate the insurance, a loan can be arranged from the insurer up to the cash value of the policy. The insurer lends the money at the guaranteed policy rate. This guaranteed rate is 5 or 6 percent on older policies, but many insurers have increased the guaranteed rate to 8 percent on recently issued policies in those states where it is allowed. (Some insurers offer owners of older policies the option of changing the guaranteed loan rate from 5 or 6 percent to 8 percent in exchange for higher policy dividends.) Interest not paid is added to the principal; if total indebtedness equals or exceeds the cash value, nonpayment of interest renders the policy invalid 30 days after notice is mailed to the insured. At first glance it seems unfair that insureds must pay interest to borrow what they consider to be their own money. However, the insurer had taken into consideration the investment income on this money in computing the premium; therefore if the policyowner withdraws the money, the insurer must be compensated for the lost investment income.

The original purpose of policy loans was to provide a source of funds to the insured, based on the security of the policy's cash value, primarily for emergencies. In recent years sophisticated policyowners have used the policy loan as a method of adverse investment selection against the insurer. With the financial markets providing rates of return in excess of the 5 to 6 percent policy loan charge, a number of policyowners borrowed against their policies at these rates and invested in short-term financial paper at higher rates to earn a profit. For the 10-year period ending in 1974, policy loans increased from 4.8 percent of insurers' assets to 8.7 percent, an 80 percent increase. The dollar amount of policy loans increased nearly 200 percent. To honor their obligations to make policy loans and at the same time have funds available for advance loan commitments, some insurers had to borrow money at rates in excess of the amount charged for policy loans. To reduce the incentive for adverse investment selection, a number of insurers changed to a variable policy loan rate up to 8 percent on new policies.

The Model Policy Loan Interest Rate Bill proposed by the NAIC in 1981 permits insurers to use either a maximum loan rate of 8 percent, or a variable rate indexed to the Moody's Corporate Bond Yield Average— Monthly Average Corporates. In the latter case, the interest rate may not exceed the rate used to determine cash values by more than 1 percent. About 82 percent of the states had adopted this or similar legislation by mid-1982. Policy loans had decreased from 8.5 percent of insurers assets in 1975 to 8 percent in 1979, based on the increased use of an 8 percent loan rate. However, even the new legislation has not solved the insurers' problem, as policy loans reached 9 percent of assets by the end of 1982.

Grace and reinstatement. Every life policy provides a grace period of 30 or 31 days following the premium due date. If the premium is paid within this period, the policy continues in effect. If payment is not made by the end of the grace period, policies without a cash value terminate. Those policies with a cash value will be placed on the appropriate nonforfeiture option. If death occurs during the grace period, the premium due is deducted from the proceeds.

For lapsed policies, the terminating policyowners have a period to reinstate the policy upon payment of premium arrears and upon proof of insurability if the policy has not been surrendered to the insurer for cash. The length of the reinstatement period varies among insurers, but usually is three to five years. If the policy lapsed recently, the proof of insurability requirement may consist only of a simple statement by the policyowners; otherwise a medical examination may be required.

Permissible provisions. State laws permit insurers to include policy restrictions for suicide, aviation, and war. A suicide restriction is included in nearly every ordinary life policy. An aviation exclusion seldom is found and the war clause is contained in policies issued during a war or a threat of a war.

Suicide. If the insured commits suicide within two years (one year, in some policies) from the inception of the policy, the liability of the insurer is limited to a return of premiums. Insurers, in the absence of this clause, would be subject to severe adverse selection.

Aviation. As a rule, insurers do not use aviation exclusion clauses. Instead they prefer to increase premiums to reflect the increased hazard. Nevertheless, four types of aviation clauses may be found in existing policies: an exclusion of all aviation deaths except those of fare-paying passengers on regularly scheduled airlines; exclusion of deaths in military aircraft only; exclusion of pilots, crew members, or student pilots; and aviation death while on military maneuvers. The first and third clauses rarely are used and the second and fourth rarely are included in policies issued during peacetime.

War. War clauses vary widely, ranging from absolute prohibition of payment if the insured was in the armed forces at the time of death to a clause which denies payment only if the insured's death resulted from war. In any case, the insurer will refund the premium or an amount equal to the policy reserve.

Other general provisions. Several other provisions necessary for the protection of the insurer or the insured are included.

Deduction of indebtedness. Indebtedness to the insurer under a policy loan will be deducted from the proceeds of the policy at death, or from the cash value upon surrender. In most older policies, indebtedness also included payment of remaining quarterly premiums if the insured died before the fourth quarterly payment was made. Postmortem collections of fractional premiums have been discontinued by nearly all insurers, and many insurers refund premiums for the unexpired period if the insured dies after paying the premium.

Change of beneficiary. A beneficiary is named in the application for a life policy. The applicant usually reserves the right to change the beneficiary. Under the typical beneficiary clause the policy must be returned to the insurer's home office with a written request for a change in the beneficiary designation.

Assignment. Unlike property insurance, the consent of the insurer to the assignment of a life insurance contract is not needed. However, the insurer stipulates that it "shall not be charged with notice of assignment of and interest in this policy until the original assignment or a duplicate has been filed with the company at its home office. The company assumes no responsibility as to the validity or effect of any assignment." This provision means that an insurer probably will not be held liable if it pays proceeds to the beneficiary and later learns the policy was assigned to a third party. (The use of the word "probably" is not meant to be a weasel word, but to indicate that one never knows how a court will react to a given case. A juridical risk always exists in the interpretation of a contract.) The assignee takes precedence over the beneficiary if the insurer knows of the assignment, but the insurer probably cannot be held responsible if it unknowingly pays the proceeds to the beneficiary at the assignee's expense.

Third-Party Rights in Life Insurance

Beneficiaries and creditors have important rights in life insurance.

Rights of the beneficiary

The rights of a beneficiary are determined by the type of beneficiary designation and by the ownership of the policy. If the beneficiary is the policyowner, he or she can exercise all policy rights including policy loans and assignments regardless of the type of beneficiary designation. If the beneficiary is not the owner but is revocably designated, he or she has only a future interest in the policy. If irrevocably designated the beneficiary has a "vested interest" in the policy and must give the insured permission for policy loans, assignment, and any other action relating to the policy.

Rights of creditors

When the courts are asked to determine issues involving creditor rights in life insurance, generally they hold that rights of the insured's or beneficiary's creditors in the proceeds or cash value depend on the beneficiary designation, on whether the insured is in bankruptcy proceedings, and on the interpretation of applicable state statutes governing the exemption of life insurance policy values from creditor claims.

Policies payable to the insured or the estate. A life insurance policy payable to the insured or to the estate can be seized by the insured's creditors when the policy matures. The cash value of the policy before maturity generally is not available to the insured's creditors if the right to have the cash value paid is an option to be exercised only by the insured. The insurer has no obligation to pay this value until the insured elects the option. The attaching creditors cannot exercise the option and most courts will not force the insured to do so. Creditors in this instance can claim the cash value only by formal bankruptcy proceedings.

Policies payable to a named beneficiary. When the policy is payable to a named beneficiary, the question is: Has the beneficiary been named irrevocably? If the beneficiary is irrevocable, the cash value is not available to the insured's creditors, unless the beneficiary acted in bad faith (fraudulently) by paying premiums or transferring the policy ownership while insolvent, or by paying premiums with embezzled funds. If the beneficiary is named revocably, the insured's creditors can claim the cash value only through formal bankruptcy proceedings. Upon the death of the insured, the policy proceeds belong to the beneficiary regardless of the type of beneficiary designation, and the insured's creditors have no interest in them, except the federal government, which can collect tax obligations of the insured, up to the amount of the policy's cash value immediately before the insured's death.

Spendthrift trust clause. Generally, state exemption statutes apply only to creditors of the insured. However, the insured may arrange to protect policy proceeds from creditors of the beneficiary by a spendthrift trust clause in the settlement agreement. Under this clause, the benefits payable to the beneficiary shall not be assignable or transferable nor subject to commutation, incumbrance, legal process, execution, garnishment, or attachment proceeding. To use the spendthrift clause, the insured must elect an installment settlement option. The clause protects from creditors only the proceeds held for the beneficiary. When the funds are paid to the beneficiary, creditors are free to take action to recover the amount that has not been spent.

Statutes exempting life insurance from creditors. Nearly every state has a law exempting life insurance from claims of creditors, and these statutes take precedence over the Federal Bankruptcy Act. The statutes protect cash values of unmatured policies from the insured's creditors. In some cases they exempt only policies payable to the insured's spouse and children, but in a few cases the exemption covers all named beneficiaries other than the insured.

Section 70a of the Federal Bankruptcy Act states: "When any bankrupt who is a natural person shall have any insurance policy which has a cash surrender value . . . he [or she] may, within 30 days after the cash surrender value has been ascertained and stated to the trustee . . . pay or secure to the trustee the sum so ascertained and stated and continue such policy free from the claims of the creditors." Thus a bankrupted insured can keep the policy in force if a trustee is paid an amount equal to its cash value. A policy loan is a source of funds open to the insured to satisfy this option.

Summary

1. Typical riders that can be attached to life insurance policies include those which provide for accidental death benefits, waiver of pre-

mium in the event of total disability, return of premiums, return of cash values, cost-of-living increases and payor benefits written in connection with juvenile policies.

2. Life insurance policies may be classified as ordinary (individual policies for at least $1,000 and premium payment periods at least monthly), industrial (policies for face amounts less than $1,000 and premiums paid weekly), or group insurance (the group, not the individual, is underwritten).

3. Life insurance policies usually contain policy options requiring decisions by the insured. Participating policies offer dividend options; cash value policies have nonforfeiture options, and nearly all policies include settlement options.

4. Although life insurance premiums increase with age, an insured does not save money by buying early because their payments would be made for protection not needed. Insurance cost is lowest if an individual purchases life insurance just before becoming uninsurable, but that time is not known. So it is best to purchase life insurance when a need exists.

5. State laws require that insurers include provisions in life policies concerning incontestability, misstatement of age or sex, deferment, nonforfeiture values, loan values, and a grace period for payment of premium and reinstatement.

6. The insured must make decisions regarding beneficiary designations and policy ownership as well as how to use settlement options, dividend options, and nonforfeiture options.

7. Additional provisions found in a life insurance policy include suicide clauses, war clauses, aviation clauses, change of beneficiary clauses, and assignment clauses.

8. Life insurance is accorded special protection from creditor claims against the insured both by federal and state law. The policy payout provision can include a spendthrift trust clause to protect the insurance proceeds against the claims of the beneficiaries' creditors.

Questions for Review

1. When the policy is participating, explain how dividends affect the payments received by a beneficiary under the various settlement options. What else affects these payments?

2. Under what conditions should the policyowner be someone other than the subject of the insurance?

3. Why must an insured prove insurability to select the one-year term dividend option if not originally selected?

4. What rights do creditors of the insured have in the cash value of a life insurance policy? The proceeds of the policy?

5. Explain why the insured or beneficiary should engage in comparative shopping in the financial markets and among insurers before selecting a settlement option.

6. Explain why a guaranteed policy loan rate may lead to adverse investment selection against the insurer. What steps have been taken to discourage this adverse selection? Why must insureds pay interest to "borrow their own funds"?

Questions for Discussion

1. How has the growth of government social insurance programs and employee benefit plans affected people's need for individual life insurance? (Consider both the amount needed and the type needed.)

2. Assume that a life insurance agent contacts you and you ask to see the best policy. What type policy might normally be suggested? Why? What do you think the answer *should* be?

3. In question 6 in "Questions for Review," why is "borrow their own funds" in quotes?

4. Suggest arguments for and against exemption of life insurance death benefits from creditors. What argument can be made for and against exemption of life insurance cash values from creditors? Discuss, considering creditors of the insured and of the beneficiaries.

18

Health insurance

Health insurance pays the cost of hospital and medical expenses and offsets income losses arising from accidental injury or sickness. Nearly 90 percent of U.S. citizens are protected by private health insurance, and 30 percent of the premiums paid to life insurers is for health insurance. Yet the coverage generally is inadequate, and that concerns the government. Families able to assume the medical care and disability income risk are limited to the independently wealthy. Currently resources for medical care and disability income are provided through public plans (Chapter 20), employee benefits plans (Chapter 19), and individual health insurance plans.

Extensive discussions of the possibility of national health insurance continue in the United States into the 1980s, a discussion that has reached varying degrees of intensity since the 1930s. Currently, the discussion is crawling at a snail's pace because few of the avid proponents expect any action on the issue until the huge federal budget deficit is brought under control, an unlikely event unless dependable assurances of worldwide peace over the near- and long-term future are forthcoming. The fear that national health insurance would compound the federal deficit eliminates it as a viable solution at this time to health care financing. The priorities appear to be self-preservation of the country as a nation rather than spending to solve what are admitted to be serious or even critical social problems. A number of people, however, believe that the United States can handle both sets of problems without destroying its economy and the individual initiative and incentives that make it work.

Many Americans view the lack of adequate health care for all citizens as a matter of national shame. Over the years a wide variety of health care proposals have been brought before Congress, and in the late 1970s it seemed to many that national health insurance was imminent. However, most observers believe that spiralling health care costs must be controlled before implementing a national health insurance proposal. Several of these proposals are discussed in Chapter 20.

Historical Development of Health Insurance

Among the first modern health insurance policies were those written by the Railway Passengers' Assurance Company of London, which began insuring railway passengers in 1848. By 1852 the company extended coverage to include all accidents.

American health insurance originated with the Massachusetts Health Insurance Company of Boston in 1847 and the Franklin Health Assurance Company of Massachusetts in 1850. The Franklin wrote insurance on travelers. The policies were full of restrictions but premiums were low. James G. Batterson, a stonecutter from Hartford, bought a policy from the Railway Passengers' Assurance Company while traveling in England. This type of policy so impressed him that on returning to Hartford, he formed the Travelers Insurance Company of Hartford in 1863. At first, the insurer sold travel policies only. In 1864 its charter was amended to permit sale of all types of accident policies. In the same year, the first accident policy was written, an oral one to insure James Bolter on a walk from his home to the Hartford post office, two blocks away. The premium was $0.02. Bolter made the trip safely, and from this humble beginning the present Travelers has grown.

As American society became less rural and less family oriented and as individuals became more concerned with protection against economic loss, health insurance expanded.

Accident insurance

Accident insurance became popular in the mid-1800s because of frequent rail and steamboat accidents. Soon after the first U.S. accident insurer was organized in 1850, coverage was offered for nearly any accident. Today accident insurers offer the following coverages: loss of life, dismemberment and loss of sight, weekly indemnity for total and for partial disability, special indemnity for fractures or dislocations, multiple benefits (double or more) for some uncommon accidents, medical expenses, and waiver of premium for total disability. These benefits often are scheduled and rated separately, making it possible to select only the coverages needed.

Sickness insurance

Although the first U.S. health insurer was organized in 1847, substantial growth did not develop until late in the century. The early policies provided no medical expense protection, covering only income lost from disability arising from a restricted list of diseases. Through the years the list expanded. During the depression of the 1930s health insurers experienced a moral hazard when many policyowners feigned sickness to collect benefits during high unemployment years, leading many insurers to discontinue writing the coverage. Not until the 1950s did the writing of disability income coverage again interest insurers.

Sickness insurance written today offers an array of coverages: total disability; expenses for hospital, surgical, medical, and nursing care; and waiver of premium for total disability. Over the years coverages have been broadened to include payments for nursing home care, mental illness, alcoholism, drug addiction, out-of-hospital drugs, vision care, dental care, and rehabilitation.

The uniform provisions

In 1908 the New York superintendent of insurance appointed a committee to standardize health insurance. A similar committee was appointed by the National Association of Insurance Commissioners (NAIC). The committees together drafted a set of standard provisions recommended to and adopted by the states. The original recommendation required that 15 provisions be included verbatim in all health policies. Five optional provisions were available for use if the policy covered these items. The standard provisions dealt with matters such as policy changes, reinstatement after a lapse, other insurance, cancellation by the insured, examination or autopsy, and claims settlement. Amendments by various states to the standard-provisions law diminished the degree of uniformity among them. In 1950, the NAIC recommended a Uniform Individual Accident and Sickness Policy Provisions Law for adoption by the states. The law contains 12 mandatory and 11 optional provisions.[1] These provisions are discussed later in this chapter.

Recent trends in health insurance

The health insurance industry, along with the consuming public, cannot ignore the increasing costs of medical care. Health care costs increased 53 percent from 1972 to 1977, decreased slightly in 1978, but

---

[1] The 12 mandatory and 11 optional provisions are discussed in Robert I. Mehr and Sandra G. Gustavson, *Life Insurance Theory and Practice,* 3d ed. (Plano, Texas: Business Publications, 1984), pp. 267–72.

resumed their upward spiral in 1979 and on into 1980. The Carter Administration was unsuccessful in its attempt to pass a mandatory cost containment bill through Congress in 1978.

In the area of health care cost control, many empathetic patient-oriented physicians (as contrasted to the large number of money-oriented ones who seemingly make these controls necessary) conscientiously and rightly are concerned about what they consider to be unwarranted emphasis on health care economy at the expense of adequate and humane health care treatment. This feeling is true especially for older patients who are unable to undergo necessary treatment in the doctor's office or who are unfit to be discharged from the hospital "before their time." In 1982, however, the Tax Equity and Fiscal Responsibility Act (TEFRA) established federal standards of cost containment for hospitals serving Medicare patients. In addition, a voluntary effort by hospitals to reduce their costs has been in effect since 1977.

Many health insurers have instituted programs in an attempt to decrease health care expenditures. Insurers have updated benefits to include coverage for less expensive care at home, care in nursing and convalescent homes, care in out-patient wards, preadmission testing, well-baby preventive care, discouragement of elective surgery, and the encouragement of second opinions in other surgery cases. (In one study of cases where patients requested second opinions, nearly 18 percent of the proposed operations were found to be unnecessary.) Some insurers encourage the use of out-patient surgical facilities to eliminate unnecessary hospital confinements. Insurers also are giving increased attention to health education. An advertising campaign encourages people to accept more personal responsibility for good health, to follow better living habits, and to think twice about incurring possible unnecessary medical expenses. *Excessive* health care charges are reviewed and trimmed by some insurers through the tightening of claims practices.

Types of Health Insurance Coverages

Health insurance coverages may be classified as to the nature of the peril, type of loss covered, basis of loss payments, breadth of benefit provisions, and underwriting standards.

Nature of the peril

Based on the nature of the peril, health insurance covers accident (loss by accidental bodily injury) and sickness (loss by disease). Illness coverage does not include accidental bodily injury but does include mental illness. Sickness insurance may provide benefits for time lost or expenses incurred by pregnancy and for preventive and diagnostic medicine. Accident insurance may be written separately or combined with sickness coverage. Sickness insurance is rarely sold separately except for medical care expenses covering "dread diseases."

Type of losses covered

Health policies classified as to losses covered are: income coverages; coverage for loss of life, sight, or limb; and medical expense coverages.

Income coverages. Accident and sickness policies are written to provide a stated weekly sum if the insured is disabled. Accident (and sometimes sickness) policies may be written to provide a smaller sum for partial disability. If the insured suffers certain fractures or dislocations, many accident policies offer the option of a lump-sum settlement in lieu of income payments. Under more liberal policies the elective benefit (i.e., the lump-sum settlement) is the minimum benefit. Thus, if the insured is disabled long enough to collect more than the minimum benefit, the higher total benefit will be paid. For example, if the elective benefit is $4,000 and the disability income benefit is $1,000 a week for 6 months, the insured would collect $4,000 if disabled for 4 weeks or less, but would collect $26,000 if the disability lasted 26 weeks, the duration of the benefit period.

Disability income protection may be short term or long term (benefit periods in excess of two years). Only one of five disability income policies is long term. Some insurers offer cash value disability income policies providing a refund of premiums if an insured receives in benefits less than the amount paid in premiums. Income coverages are written both on an individual and a group basis.

Loss of life, sight, or limb. Accident policies provide for a "capital sum" payment to the beneficiary if the insured dies accidentally. Most accident policies also provide payment for accidental loss of limb or sight. Accidental death and dismemberment benefits are the least expensive health coverage, but also are the least important. Death benefits are best bought through life insurance, as both natural and accidental deaths would be covered. Because disability income coverage provides protection against losses caused by a disabling dismemberment or loss of sight, loss of life, sight or limb coverage appears to be unnecessary.

Medical expense coverages. Health insurance policies are available to cover expenses ranging from the simple hospital policy providing a limited amount per day for hospital room and board and an additional limit (10 or 20 times the daily room and board rate, for example) for ancillary hospital expenses, to the major medical policy covering most medical costs involved in an accident or illness. Expense coverage may be scheduled or blanket. If scheduled, the maximum amounts paid for hospital room and board, miscellaneous hospital expenses, and for surgical procedures are listed, as are the maximum amounts paid for nursing fees, physicians' fees, and other expenses. If the coverage is blanket, a maximum amount is specified for necessary and reasonable medical expenses. Medical expense coverage offered with accidental insurance usually is written blanket, whereas basic medical benefits under sickness policies usually are scheduled.

Most health expense coverage is written independently of disability income protection. Hospital insurance is the most popular type of health coverage, followed by surgical expense, regular medical expense (written to cover physicians' bills), and major medical expense. The number of persons with major medical insurance has increased 12 percent in the past five years compared with an increase of only slightly more than 5 percent for those covered under hospital insurance. The benefits paid under major medical coverage include expenses incurred for nearly all health care prescribed by a physician, subject to a deductible and participation percentage discussed later. Expense coverages are written on an individual, family, or group basis.

Basis of loss payments

Because health insurance need not be indemnity contracts, loss payments are not restricted to actual losses incurred. Health coverage is written on one of three bases: valued forms, reimbursement forms, and service forms.

Valued forms. Disability income is written to pay a specified amount per week (or month) for a given benefit period. Specific benefit schedules are established for accidental death and dismemberment losses. Some hospital policies provide a flat amount per day for a maximum number of days while the insured is hospitalized. The benefit instead may be expressed as a weekly or monthly benefit.

Reimbursement forms. More common in expense benefits coverage is a maximum allowance, with the insurer paying only the actual and necessary charges incurred, up to the allowable limits. If the charges are more than the policy limits, the insured bears the excess.

Service forms. Under the "service incurred" plan, payments are made directly to the hospital and doctors for services rendered. This payment arrangement is found in Blue Cross (hospital) and Blue Shield (physicians and surgeons) plans, as well as in some independent plans, health maintenance organization plans (HMOs), and in some insurer plans. Because excessive utilization of medical services has made the service form plan too expensive, it has been discontinued by some Blue Cross and Blue Shield groups. Excessive utilization results from a combination of factors including the practice of defensive medicine in reaction to increasing medical malpractice claims, malingering by patients, and the convenience of the physician.

Breadth of benefit provisions

No health policy is free of limitations, but some forms have more than others. A policy containing unusual exclusions, limitations, reductions, or restrictive conditions is called a limited policy.

Under limited health policies insurers pay only if the insured is injured in specially designated accidents or incurs specified illnesses. Some insurers pay only for accidental death. (One underwriter has characterized limited policies as paying benefits only if the insured is kicked to death by a goose in a Pullman car.) As a circulation booster, newspapers have offered limited accident policies with newspaper subscriptions for a nominal charge. Coverage usually is limited to a small list of accidents with benefits graded by accident with higher benefits for less frequent accidents and lower for more common types. Those reading their junk mail will note circulars peddling these policies.

Various types of travel accident policies are written ranging from specific and limited policies providing coverage for one trip by a designated common carrier (the type often sold at airports) to the comprehensive travel policies mass marketed through associations and credit card companies.

Dread disease policies offer coverage on a blanket basis for medical expenses arising from certain diseases (some of which are rare) such as cancer, poliomyelitis, leukemia, encephalitis, scarlet fever, spinal meningitis, tetanus, diphtheria, multiple sclerosis, smallpox, elephantiasis, rabies, and tularemia. Because of the broad coverage of major medical insurance, dread disease policies are losing their appeal. An example of the value (or lack thereof) of some limited policies may be observed in the standard operating procedures of one major health insurer. This insurer agrees to pay 100 percent of the health care expenses of cancer patients who are covered under one of the carrier's group insurance contracts. Other illnesses require the patient to pay a deductible plus a portion of all costs over the deductible and less than $5,000. The insurer does not charge the group an extra premium to include this feature in the group contract.

Most limited policies create misunderstanding. Often the large capital and principal sum benefits for rare accidents, such as those involving a common carrier, are emphasized in the sales pitch while the minor benefits payable for more common accidents are mentioned casually, if at all. Because the public always is looking for bargains in insurance, as in everything else, many persons are prompted to purchase limited policies in lieu of broader coverage. The lower premiums for limited policies do not make them a bargain. In fact, they are more expensive for what is offered than a quality health insurance policy, as is often the case in other so-called bargain goods and services. Many states require that limited policies include a warning overprinted on the policy face in large red letters, worded in some form such as "THIS IS A LIMITED POLICY. READ ITS PROVISIONS CAREFULLY." This advice is good for *any* policy.

Limited accident forms available include those covering occupational accidents only, vacation accidents, accidents while participating in specified sports activity, injuries incurred while serving with a volunteer fire department, home accidents, and school accidents.

Underwriting standards

Not all prospective insureds meet the insurer's underwriting requirements for standard policies at standard rates. Policies for these persons are classified as: older age, substandard (or extra risk), and special risk. In addition, a special policy is written for business overhead expense.

Older age policies. Older age policies are contracts issued beyond the normal insuring age of 60. A person age 65 eligible for Medicare still needs private coverage. Over 15.6 million people 65 and over own private health insurance to supplement Medicare. Many insurers write policies to fill gaps in Medicare without creating overlaps. An appropriate medical expense policy for persons at least age 65 and covered under basic and supplementary Medicare plans includes items such as the initial $356 ($144)[2] hospital expense; the $89 ($36) a day charge after 60 days; the $178 ($72) a day charge while utilizing the 60-day lifetime reserve and the full charge thereafter; the $44.50 ($18) a day charge for nursing home care after 20 days through 100th day; private nursing; self-administered prescribed drugs; extended psychiatric services (beyond a lifetime total of 190 days); extended care (beyond 100 days) in a nursing home; the $75 ($60) deductible applicable for each calendar year under the Medicare supplementary plan; 20 percent of the medical bills payable under the Medicare supplementary plan; and all amounts in excess of $250 annually for psychiatric or mental treatment. Some insurers have been using pressure tactics to sell older people highly restrictive policies at excessive rates. After thorough investigations, several states have taken regulatory action to eliminate these abuses. A person may be able to purchase an attractive older age health policy, but usually more liberal protection can be obtained by buying a lifetime-guaranteed renewable policy at a young age.

Substandard policies. Substandard (or qualified impairment) policies for physically impaired persons usually are written for those with an arrested serious illness such as cancer or heart trouble. In some policies, coverage includes recurrence of the impairment but for a benefit level lower than for other illnesses. Generally a higher premium is charged, or a waiver of medical conditions is required. These policies may cover both income and expense losses.

Special-risk policies. Special-risk policies cover hazards excluded in usual health policies, such as war, accidents to those involved in dangerous scientific experiments, moon travel, and most other hazards within the realm of imagination. Many persons with incomes dependent upon

---

[2] The figures for Medicare in the foregoing paragraph show those for 1984 with the amounts for 1979 in parentheses to dramatize the massive five-year increases in the dollar amounts of the burden to be paid by the Medicare patient—increases of nearly 150 percent. Increases in the "noncovered" expenses are expected to continue. For current figures, check with the local social security office.

some special talent or personal characteristic buy high-benefit limit special-risk forms to insure their exposure. Lloyd's of London provides underwriting facilities for many of these exposures.

Business overhead expense policies. Business overhead health insurance is a special form of disability income coverage written for a business or professional person to provide resources to pay such business expenses as rent, taxes, utilities, clerical salaries, and insurance premiums that continue while the insured is disabled. The insurer reimburses the insured only for expenses incurred, subject to policy limits. When used, the premiums paid are tax deductible, and the proceeds are reportable as income. Normally, premiums paid by an individual for disability income insurance are not deductible, and the policy proceeds are not reportable as taxable income.

The Health Insurance Contract

Health insurance policies are discussed in three parts: the requirements of the Uniform Provisions Act, the application, and coverage analysis.

The requirements of the Uniform Provisions Act

The Uniform Provisions Act contains 12 mandatory and 11 optional provisions to be included in a health insurance contract. The 12 *mandatory* provisions deal with (1) the entire contract and change provisions, (2) time limit for certain defenses, (3) premium grace period, (4) policy reinstatement, (5) claim notice, (6) claim forms, (7) proof of loss, (8) time limit for paying claims, (9) beneficiaries, (10) physical examination and autopsy, (11) time limit for legal action, and (12) beneficiary change. The *optional* provisions deal with *(a)* occupation change, *(b)* age misstatement, *(c)* other insurance with same insurer, *(d)* expense insurance with other insurers, *(e)* income insurance with other insurers, *(f)* relation of earnings to insurance, *(g)* unpaid premiums, *(h)* cancellation, *(i)* conformity with state statutes, *(j)* illegal occupation, and *(k)* intoxicants and narcotics. Optional provisions *a, b, f,* and *i* are the most common. The uniform provisions must be followed "in substance" only. Any wording may be used if the policyowner is given the required protection. Many insurers use provisions more favorable to policyowners than the law demands. The uniform provisions appear in most policies under the label of "general provisions," "required provisions," or some similar term. The insurer, with the approval of the commissioner, may modify or omit any mandatory provision inapplicable to or inconsistent with the coverage offered in the contract.

In addition to mandatory and optional provisions, the Uniform Provisions Act includes other health insurance policy requirements such as: the entire monetary and other considerations must be expressed in the policy; the type used in the policy must be at least 10 point[3] and must not give undue prominence to any portion of the text; general exceptions and reductions shall be grouped under a descriptive head; a policy in violation of the act shall be construed to conform to the act; no policy provision can restrict or modify the provisions of the act; supplying claim forms, acknowledgement of notice of claim, and investigation of a claim are not waivers of defense against the claim; the policy remains in force for any part of a policy term that exceeds the age limit, and acceptance of a premium after that term keeps the policy in force, subject to any cancellation provisions in the policy; if misstatement of age leads the insurer to accept premiums beyond the age limit, liability is limited to a premium refund; and the act does not apply to workers' compensation, reinsurance, blanket or group coverage, or life insurance or annuity riders covering total disability.

The application

The application for a health policy closely resembles a life insurance nonmedical application,[4] with the usual questions concerning name, address, employer, and occupation. The insured must reveal the health insurance owned or applied for and the amount of claims made for injury or sickness giving the insurer's names. The applicant must specify the nature of any medical or surgical advice or treatment received in the past five years. Any life or health insurance which has been declined, cancelled, postponed, refused, rated "extra risk," or renewal denied must be listed. The applicant also is asked about experience with a long list of health conditions, including ulcers, heart trouble, diabetes, tuberculosis, and blood pressure. The application usually is attached to the policy, making it a part of the contract.

Analysis of the coverage

Health insurance coverage may be analyzed using the technique outlined in Chapters 7 through 9.

Perils. Health insurance covers the perils of bodily injury and sickness subject to limitations. For example, accident coverage usually excludes suicide and injuries intentionally self-inflicted, and sickness coverage

---

[3] Ten point type is one point larger than the type used in the body of this book.

[4] Not all health policies have elaborate application forms. For example, the following is the application for the accident policy in Illinois.

As required by the Laws of the State of Illinois, the following application must be completed by the applicant for this insurance.
I hearby apply for this Policy, to be based on the following statement: What is your full name? _____
_____

may exclude mental illness, pregnancy, childbirth, and miscarriage. Frequently, expense reimbursement coverage excludes charges incurred for injuries sustained or sickness contracted if benefits are due under workers' compensation or a similar law, and for services and facilities provided by or in a federally owned or operated hospital. This latter exclusion has received criticism from government sources because thousands of patients with private insurance are treated annually at veterans hospitals without reimbursement to the government for these services.

Losses.   Health policies cover physicians, surgeons, hospital, nursing, and medical expenses, and real or presumed earnings lost because of accident or illness. Accidental loss of life, sight, or limbs is covered. Major medical policies may exclude losses such as dental work, eye examinations, glasses, hearing aids, cosmetic surgery, or plastic surgery, except if necessary to repair bodily damage caused solely by an injury covered in the policy. Except for local ambulance service, transportation expenses usually are not covered. Because of competitive and social pressures the number of excluded perils, hazards, and losses has decreased substantially over the years.

Persons.   Health policies cover only the named insured for income loss but usually includes medical expense coverage for eligible family members (spouses and unmarried children usually at least 14 days old and under age 21).

Where.   The coverage generally applies anywhere in the world, although some policies exclude injuries or illnesses contracted outside a given territory. Several factors justify territorial exclusions: morbidity (sickness) rates are higher in some countries, political conditions are less stable in some areas giving rise to a greater accident hazard, and living costs are sufficiently low in a few areas so that a modest amount of disability income is attractive, thereby creating a moral hazard.

When.   The coverage typically is written on an annual basis, with renewal at the insurer's option. The policy begins and ends at 12:01 A.M. at the insured's residence. Many insurers write contracts renewable at the insured's option up to a stated age (usually 65).

Most health policies do not cover preexisting conditions.[5] The injury or illness must occur while the policy is in force. As a precaution, a "probationary" period sometimes is included limiting sickness coverage to illness contracted after an initial period (e.g., 15 days) from the policy date. Maternity benefits usually are not effective until the policy has been in force 10 months. Illnesses beyond the policy period are covered if incurred during the policy period. Surgical coverage provides pay-

---

[5] Group health policies usually cover preexisting conditions because adverse selection is no problem. All eligible employees are covered automatically under a noncontributory plan, and under a contributory plan, 75 percent must participate.

ments for surgery performed within 90 days after the policy term, if performed during a period of continuous total disability commencing while the policy is in force.

Hazards. Health policies usually exclude some specified hazards. Typical exclusions are war and acts of war, declared or undeclared, and accidents or illnesses suffered during military service. Noncommercial aviation activity may be excluded, although the trend is to omit this exclusion. Injuries contributed to by bodily or mental infirmity, hernia, ptomaines, bacterial infection, disease, medical, or surgical treatment (except infection resulting from an injury, such as blood poisoning from a wound) generally are excluded from accident coverage. Sickness caused by accidental injury, or sickness for a period during which indemnity is payable for accidental injury, generally is excluded from sickness coverage.

Amounts. Health insurance policies may have several limits, each applying to a different coverage. For example, the policy may provide for weekly indemnity of specific amounts for total (or partial) disability caused by accident or sickness, and a designated amount for loss of life, sight, dismemberment, fractures, or dislocations arising from accidents. Multiple indemnity may be paid for specified accidents and an amount may be scheduled to pay the insured's medical expenses arising from a covered accident or illness. Medical expense coverage may be written on a scheduled or blanket basis.

Dismemberment and fractures. In some policies, dismemberment and loss of sight benefits are a sum equal to total disability weekly indemnity payments for a given number of weeks, such as 208 weeks for loss of both hands, 104 weeks for loss of one hand, and 52 weeks for loss of a thumb and index finger of either hand. In others, these benefits are a percentage of the accidental death benefits. Benefit levels are the same either way. Specific indemnities may be scheduled for fractures and dislocations, for example, $800 for a thigh fracture and $400 for a dislocated knee joint. These benefits also may be an amount equal to the sum of a given number of weekly indemnity payments.

Disability income. Monthly indemnity payments for total and partial disability involve three dimensions: the amount of the monthly payments, the maximum duration of payments, and the length of the waiting period. Partial disability payments, when covered, will be smaller— about 50 percent of total disability.

Residual disability benefits also are smaller than total disability benefits, but, rather than having payments based on a fixed percentage of total disability payments (as is the case with partial disability benefits), residual disability payments are determined according to the amount of work income received by a partially disabled insured. For example, Joy Grimes had a disability income policy that provided $1,300 per month during periods of total disability. Prior to her disability, Ms. Grimes earned $2,600 per month. She was totally disabled for four months, and then took a part-time job paying $1,000 per month until she was able to return to a full-time position. As the insurance policy's total disability benefits covered one half of her pre-disability income, the residual disability payments use the same proportion but are based on the difference between her part-time and preloss incomes. While totally disabled, Joy received $1,300 per month, or one half of her previous $2,600 monthly earnings. Residual disability benefits provided payments equal to one half of the difference between her preloss income of $2,600 and her postloss income of $1,000, or $800 per month. Thus, she received $1,800 per month from the part-time work plus residual disability payments. This amount was greater than her total disability payments (she was thereby encouraged to work at least part-time as soon as she was no longer totally disabled), but less than she would earn on a full-time basis (another encouragement to recover completely and return to her preloss position and income).

Premium reduction is possible if the insured accepts a 180-day elimination period ($9.12, 24 percent less than the 90-day rate). Additional savings are available as a few companies offer 365-, 730-, and even 1,825-day waiting periods. These longer elimination periods can be useful in integrating a personal disability income program with an employer-sponsored plan containing a two-to-five-year benefit period. (If a leap year is included in the waiting period, as it always will in an 1,825-day waiting period, the insured gains one day of overlapping coverage with the employer-sponsored plan, an important point, isn't it, because of its value in playing the game of trivia.)

The maximum payment duration varies according to the type and nature of the disability. The policy might provide lifetime payments for accident but only two years for sickness or five years for accident and one year for sickness, or the same limits may apply for both accident and sickness. A sickness policy might provide benefits up to one year for a nonconfining sickness (insured not confined to the house), and lifetime benefits for a confining sickness. The maximum benefit period usually is less for partial than for total disability.

Accident insurance may be written with no waiting period (elimination period), but one is usually required in sickness insurance. The elimination period generally is defined in the policy as the number of days of continuous total disability (7, 14, 30, 60, 90, and 180 days are common) for which no indemnity is payable. The premium decreases substantially with an increase in the elimination period. For example, the annual premiums quoted by one insurer for a $100 monthly disability income policy with benefits payable five years for sickness and lifetime for accidents are $32.04 if accident payments begin immediately and sickness payments after a 7-day waiting period, $24.12 (a decrease of 25 percent) if a 14-day elimination period is used for both, $19.08 (an additional savings of 21 percent) if the waiting period is 30 days, and $12.00 (a further saving of 37 percent) for a dual elimination period of 90 days.

Provisions frequently are made for recurrent disabilities. If the insured resumes regular work for a continuous period of six months, a subsequent disability from the same cause is considered a new disability period and will reinstate the maximum indemnity period and also the elimination period. If the subsequent work period is less than six months, neither the maximum nor the elimination period is restored.

Medical care coverage. Medical care insurance involves four types of coverages: hospital, surgical, medical expense, and major medical.

Some basic hospital insurance provides payment for room and board up to a maximum daily amount and a maximum number of days. Others provide full coverage for room and board without a daily limit but restrict the service to a given class, such as semiprivate rooms. Necessary hospital extras usually are covered up to a stated maximum. A separate limit may be available for maternity benefits, sometimes 10 times the daily room and board rate, payable in one sum. When an insured has nonconfining hospital emergency treatment for accidental injury, some hospital policies provide up to a given multiple (commonly three) of the daily room and board benefit if treatment is received within 24 hours of the accident. Nursing expenses are covered by some hospital forms but may apply only while the insured is in the hospital. However, the trend is to extend these benefits to home nursing care.

Surgical expense benefits are scheduled. Over 35 procedures will be listed, ranging from the maximum benefit for cutting into the cranial cavity or the removal of a lung, to 10 percent of the maximum for suturing a wound. The schedule is referred to in terms of its maximum benefits, such as a $500 or $1,000 surgical schedule.

Medical expense coverage is written to pay physicians' bills other than surgery. The policy may provide medical expenses regardless of disability, or it may cover expenses only while the insured is disabled. In some contracts, medical expenses are covered only while the policyowner is hospitalized. Medical expense coverage may be subject to one (or more) of three limitations: (1) the first few physician calls are excluded, (2) the amount payable per call or per day is limited, or (3) the aggregate amount payable is limited. Benefits either blanket or scheduled may be added to most medical expense plans for diagnostic procedures. Some plans offer medical expense coverage on a service-incurred basis under which participating physicians agree that the plan's payment to the doctor constitutes full payment for persons with incomes below a certain amount.

Major medical limits are discussed under six headings: (1) deductibles, (2) benefit periods, (3) maximums, (4) participation, (5) covered charges, and (6) specific diseases.

1. Deductibles. The deductible may apply to each family member or to the family as a unit. In the former case, if covered charges resulting from the same accidents are incurred by two or more family members, usually only one deductible applies to the combined charges. The deductible may be a benefit year deductible, under which the insurer is liable if covered charges incurred within a period of 12 consecutive months exceed the deductible amount. In some policies, the deductible applies to each disability rather than to a given period. In others, deductibles are cumulative over a calendar year rather than over any 12-month period. Because many families budget monthly, some insurers write a monthly deductible plan.

2. *Benefit periods.* The policy may provide payment only for those covered charges incurred within one year after the deductible is exceeded, unless the insured is still hospital confined. The deductible again becomes operative when the benefit period expires. In some policies benefit periods run for two or even three years. Benefit periods are not used in some policies. Instead the insurer relies on the maximum amount payable to control liability.

3. *Maximums.* The policy will limit liability, such as $50,000 for each disability. In some plans, the limit applies to a year rather than a disability. The year may be a calendar or benefit year. Other plans have lifetime or aggregate limits. Under these plans, the insured, if insurable, usually may reinstate the aggregate limit after receiving a given amount of benefits. Aggregate limits are used more often than annual limits, but less often than per-disability limits.

4. *Participation.* Participation provisions of 20 to 25 percent usually are included in major medical policies. Under these provisions the insurer will pay 75 to 80 percent of the covered charges in excess of the deductible. If a person with a $250 deductible and a 25 percent participation on a $50,000 major medical policy has covered medical expenses of $32,250, the insurer pays $24,000, and the insured absorbs $8,250 ($250 deductible plus 25 percent of $32,000, or $8,000 participation). Participation is used to control overutilization of medical facilities, but as shown in the foregoing example it can produce a burden to the insured. Therefore, in some policies, the participation provision applies only to part of the expenses, the first $5,000, for example.

5. *Covered charges.* Covered charges in major medical insurance generally include *reasonable* charges incurred by a family member for *necessary* medical or surgical treatment, services, or supplies prescribed by the physician or surgeon and furnished directly to the family member. *Rental charges* for a wheelchair, hospital-type bed, or iron lung are covered. Expenses for treatment of pregnancy complications are covered for amounts in excess of those charged in the absence of complications.

6. *Specific diseases.* Under some major medical policies, if a family member contracts one of a list of rare diseases discussed earlier, the insurer pays 100 percent of all covered charges incurred over a three-year period subject to the policy's maximum liability limit. The effect is to extend the benefit period to three years and to waive the deductible and participation. Transportation of the patient by commercial airline or railroad (if one can be found) to a hospital or sanitarium qualified to provide necessary initial treatment is covered.

Guideposts for Buying Health Insurance

Health insurers offer a wide variety of coverages. In choosing among them, a set of guideposts for making intelligent health insurance buying decisions is useful.

Points of comparison of policies

In comparing policies, the buyer should consider the following: (1) the insurer, (2) accident definition, (3) exclusions, (4) disability definition, (5) dismemberment provisions, (6) waiting period, (7) waiver of premium, (8) disability income benefit period, (9) renewal and cancellation provisions, (10) change of occupation, (11) medical expense provisions, and (12) cost.

The insurer. Health insurance frequently is solicited by mail. Although many legitimate insurers use mail solicitation, fly-by-night insurers thrive on mail-order business. An important rule in health insurance buying is to deal only with insurers licensed by one's own state. The problems that can arise in transacting business with an unlicensed insurer is discussed in Chapter 28. Health insurance shoppers should not overlook such plans as Blue Cross-Blue Shield and Health Maintenance Organizations (Chapter 22).

Definition of accident. Strictly worded accident policies state that payments are made only if the injury is caused by "accidental means." Liberally worded ones provide payments for losses due to "accidental bodily injury." This distinction is so widely misunderstood that courts frequently ignore it. An accidental means clause requires the injury to result from *causes* that were accidental. Thus, if the insured ruptures a blood vessel while carrying heavy textbooks, an accidental means policy would not cover the injury, as its cause was not accidental. The cause of the injury was carrying the books, which was the insured's intention. If the insured drops the books on a foot, breaking a blood vessel, the injury is covered by an accidental means insuring clause, as the latter action is not one the insured intended. Carrying the books is intended; dropping them is the accidental means causing the injury. Suicide while insane has been construed to be death by accidental means.[6] For this reason, most accident policies providing death benefits exclude suicide.

In a policy covering accidental bodily injury, payment is made if the injury was unexpected and unintended, even though the act causing the injury was not unusual, unexpected, or unforeseen. Thus, if the policy contains an accidental-bodily-injury insuring agreement, the insured

---

[6] Under Missouri law any suicide is assumed to have occurred in a moment of temporary or permanent insanity; thus, in Missouri, any suicidal death is deemed to be caused by accidental means. Presumably the law is based on the theory that anyone fortunate enough to live in Missouri would be crazy to kill himself.

would be indemnified for the ruptured blood vessel caused by carrying the books. For accidental-bodily injury the result must not be anticipated by the insured. Competition among insurers has resulted in less frequent use of accidental means policies. However, some limited policies and life insurance double indemnity riders include accidental means insuring agreements.

Most accident policies contain the wording, "directly and independently of all other causes." This clause is designed to allow the insurer to avoid claims under an accident policy for a loss due to an underlying health condition combined with a minor or imagined accident. If a student has a fainting spell, falls down a flight of stairs, and suffers a back injury, the injury has not been incurred directly and independently of all other causes, and the accident insurer presumably would not be liable.

Exclusions.   The fewer the exclusions, the better the policy. Intentional self-inflicted injuries and war-connected disabilities usually are excluded from coverage. More restrictive policies exclude coverage while the insured is outside the United States and Canada. Some exclude disability resulting from law violations (except traffic violations).

Definition of disability.   Some policies require that the disability begin within a specified period from the date of the accident. The most liberal policies have no such requirement.

Total disability.   Total disability is not uniformly defined. Its definition is important in any policy covering loss of time benefits. One insurer defines total disability liberally.

> Total disability means the complete inability of the insured to perform the duties of his [her] regular occupation, except that after the indemnity has been paid for 60 months of any continuous disability, then for the remainder of the period of disability after the said 60 months, "total disability" shall mean the complete inability of the insured to perform the duties of any occupation for which he [she] is reasonably fitted by training and experience.

Some insurers in defining total disability add "and does not engage in any occupation for wages or profit" after the words "regular occupation." This addition excludes benefit payments to insureds who accept positions when unable to perform their own regular occupation, such as professors who lose their voices and accept research assignments.

Once, "total disability" was defined as the inability to engage in any occupation for wages or profit (modified by the courts to include "for which reasonably fitted" and now usually so defined in the contract). Later, a one-year own occupation clause was added. Although the "own occupation" definition originally was one or two years, a five-year definition is widely available and the trend is toward increasing the period beyond five years, even to the length of the benefit period.

Some policies contain more restricted definitions of total disability. A policy might require the insured to be under a physician's regular care. This provision has been invalidated to some degree by court decisions holding that if competent medical testimony shows that the disabling condition cannot be treated or improved by regular medical care, the requirement is meaningless. Other policies require the insured to be house confined (continuously within doors) for benefits beyond one or two years. Absence for brief periods to consult physicians or for hospital examinations does not violate the house confinement restriction. Policies requiring house confinement are rare. House confinement-insuring agreements should be avoided. One should be allowed to take advantage of a physician's recommendation of an ocean cruise or a visit to a health resort without loss of disability income insurance proceeds.

Health insurance policies define other terms, such as hospital, loss of member, convalescent home, and benefit period to clarify the insurer's intentions.

Provisions for dismemberment, specified fractures, and dislocations. As noted, some disability income policies provide that in the event of dismemberment or other specified losses the insurer pays a lump-sum benefit in lieu of periodic indemnity payments. In other policies, the insured may elect either a lump-sum benefit or periodic disability income payments. Lump-sum benefits are usually limited to the amount of disability income payable for four years. Thus the insured may make a disadvantageous election. More liberal policies make lump-sum benefits the minimum to be paid. In even more liberal policies, certain dismemberments are considered permanent disability and the periodic disability income payment is continued for the maximum income period. In choosing a policy, the most liberal provision should be selected as its cost is insignificant.

Waiting or elimination period. A waiting period as long as the insured can afford to be without earned income should be selected, subject to the consideration that premium reductions for waiting periods beyond 180 days are minor.

Waiver of premium. The use of waiver of premium in life insurance is discussed in Chapter 17. In purchasing *disability income* insurance the insured should buy a policy containing a waiver of premium provision. The waiver of premium provision requires a period of total disability of a stated duration, usually 90 days, before premiums will be waived. In some policies, the insurer agrees to refund premiums paid during the 90-day waiting period. A provision for waiver of premium in the event of disability is rarely found in *medical expense* coverage.

The disability income benefit period. Disability income policies usually contain a limitation on the aggregate benefits to be paid. Less liberal policies state that "the total income paid throughout the life of this policy shall not exceed __ months *in the aggregate.*" Liberal policies state: "The total monthly indemnity shall not exceed __ months during *any continuous disability.*" Any subsequent disability is regarded as a new period of disability. This latter clause permits the insured a fresh start with full limits reinstated for each new disability.

The length of disability income benefit periods varies among policies. Some offer lifetime accident benefits and a sickness benefit for a limited duration—1, 2, 5, or 10 years. Others limit the benefit period for both accident and sickness to 1, 5, or 10 years, or to age 65. Still others provide lifetime benefits for both accidents and sickness but limit sickness benefits to confining illnesses beyond an initial period of one or two years. The ideal is a benefit period extending to age 65 or 70 for accident and sickness, to integrate disability income with a retirement income program based on retirement income insurance protected by a disability waiver of premium rider.

Provisions regarding renewal and cancellation.   Health insurance contracts may contain one of a variety of clauses specifying the insured's rights to retain the policy in force. The most favorable (and most expensive) is the noncancellable policy under which the insurer agrees to continue the policy in force with no change in premium until the insured reaches a specified age (typically 65). The least favorable (and least expensive) is the cancellable policy under which the insurer may terminate the insurance by giving written notice to the insured. The insured may also cancel the policy. In between these extremes, moving from the most desirable for the insured to the least desirable, are the guaranteed renewable, conditionally renewable, optionally renewable, and term. The term policy has no provision for cancellation. A travel accident policy purchased at the airport provides an example of a term policy. Figure 18–1 shows the respective rights of the insured and insurer under the *four continuation* provisions. The figure does not include cancellable or term policies because they have no continuation provisions.

Change of occupation.   Health insurance premiums vary with the insured's occupation. One insurer uses five occupational rating classes. For example, class 4A includes accountants and lawyers and class B includes laborers doing heavy manual work and bartenders. The rate at age 30 per $100 a month for a benefit period of up to five years with a 60-day elimination period is 29 percent higher for a worker in class B than for a worker in class 4A. Most health insurers specify that benefits will decrease if the insured changes to a more hazardous occupation. More liberal policies contain no such provision. An accountant, who had bought the foregoing policy and then became a bartender would, if injured, collect only 71 percent of expected income if the policy contained the more stringent occupation clause.

Medical expense provisions.   Because protection against potential large losses should be bought before smaller losses are covered, major medical

FIGURE 18–1

An analysis of continuation provisions in health insurance policies

Continuation provision	Insured's rights concerning renewal and premiums	Insurer's rights concerning renewal and premiums	Types of policies using this provision
Noncancellable	The insured is guaranteed renewal up to an age specified in the policy at premium rates guaranteed in the policy.	The insurer may cancel only for nonpayment of premiums.	Used to a decreasing extent in disability income policies but rarely in hospital expense policies. Highest initial premium.
Guaranteed renewable	The insured is guaranteed renewal up to an age specified in the policy. Premium rates are not guaranteed.	The insurer may increase premiums but only for the entire class of insureds, not for an individual insured. Some policies provide the fixed premium guarantee of the noncancellable form but only to a specified age.	Used for both income and expense coverages. Lower initial premium as insurer does not have to guarantee the premium.
Conditionally renewable	The insured is usually assured that renewal will not be denied solely on the basis of deterioration in health.	The insurer reserves the right to renew and adjust premiums although in some policies the insurer may deny renewal only if it declines to renew all policies of the same class.	Used for both income and expense coverages. Lower cost because of fewer insurer guarantees.
Optionally renewable	The insured has no rights concerning renewal or premium levels.	The insurer may deny renewal, increase premiums for all or any of the classes of insureds, and add restrictive policy conditions.	It is the most common provision in both income and expense coverages. It also has the lowest initial premium.

insurance should have priority over basic hospital, surgical, and medical coverage. The most important considerations in purchasing major medical insurance are the maximum limit, the deductible, and the participation percentage. The insured should determine if the maximum applies to each illness or accident, to a policy or a benefit year, or for a lifetime. The aggregate lifetime maximum is the least liberal. The variety of deductibles found in medical expense coverages is discussed earlier in this chapter. A logical deductible arrangement involves a yearly amount under which all family medical expenses are included, although an extended illness will result in additional payments of the deductible over the following years. The amount of the deductible should be low enough not to be burdensome but high enough to release premiums to make high maximum limits affordable. A plan that should be considered is the family budget deductible, under which the insured is covered for monthly family medical expenses in excess of a given amount up to a maximum limit for each family member. The maximum limit should be as high as the insured can afford because of increasing medical care costs. The participation provision should be limited to a minimum amount, say 25 percent of covered expenses in excess of the deductible, but in no event more than $2,500; that is, the insured should participate in covered expenses only up to 25 percent of $10,000 after bearing the deductible.

Cost. Wide variations exist among premiums for similar coverages. Therefore, the wise person seeking health insurance (and other types of insurance, also) realizes the importance of "shopping around" among reputable insurers to obtain a favorable combination of premiums and benefits. However, as both policy provisions and premiums differ greatly, the comparative health insurance shopper must consider the guideposts just presented in evaluating the price of the insurance. A low premium for low-quality coverage may, in fact, be more costly than a higher premium for better coverage. Budget restrictions, however, may force the buyer to settle for less than the best coverage. Nevertheless, buyers will find "bargains" among policies of all quality.

Several buyers' guides to the purchase of health insurance have been published, with price the major concern. The Pennsylvania Insurance Department, a pioneer in the field of consumer interest, has published such a guide. This guide may be purchased from the department at a nominal cost. It must be studied closely where the reported comparisons do not reflect products of similar quality. Also prices and quality change so that the buyer will need to check whether the information is current and update it where necessary.

Use of the guideposts

The foregoing 12 guideposts to the purchase of health insurance appear logical, and in some cases simple. Their apparent simplicity can be deceiving. The many variables make it difficult for the health insurance buyer to be completely certain the "best" decision has been made. The peace of mind solution to this problem is for the buyer to seek a "sensible" or "good" solution after considering needs, ability to pay, available products, and prices and not worry whether the "best" selection has been made. Who really knows what is the best selection? The best decision is one logically made based on the facts at hand and the state of the decision-makers' knowledge. A good agent may be of help if s/he knows the market and can answer questions satisfactorily based on these guideposts. The main use of the guideposts is to arm the buyer with questions to ask before making important decisions about health insurance purchases.

Summary

1. Benefits under health insurance are of two types; loss of income and medical expense. Health policies are further classified as to the basis of payment (valued, service, or reimbursement), the breadth of benefit provisions, and underwriting standards (older age, substandard, special risk, and business overhead expense).
2. Health insurance contracts generally are subject to the same rules of interpretation that courts apply to other insurance contracts. However, a few problems of interpretation are unique to health insurance. These problems include the question of accidental means versus accidental injury (becoming less important because of court interpretations) and the meaning of disability, also modified by the courts to differ from the wording of the policy.
3. No standard policy exists in health insurance but certain "uniform" provisions are required. One buying health insurance must be wary of pitfalls because of the wide variations among policies.
4. A set of guidelines for policy selection are offered. The buyer is advised to purchase insurance from a reputable insurer licensed in one's home state and to select the optimal combination of benefits and premiums, carefully comparing policy provisions.
5. Buyers' guides are published by some state insurance departments. The Pennsylvania Insurance Department was a pioneer in buyers' guides. Buyers' guides must be used with caution.
6. For the typical health insurance buyer, a combination of major medical expense insurance with affordable deductibles, participation arrangements, and maximums coupled with disability income protection with an affordable waiting period, benefit level, and benefit duration period (usually to age 65 or 70 to integrate with a retirement program) is the ideal. Budget considerations might require the buyer to settle for less. Individual health coverage must be integrated with group coverage and social security.

Questions for Review

1. What types of losses are covered by health insurance?
2. Explain the important considerations involved in selecting health insurance policies from among the many on the market.
3. The rising health care cost concerns the government, insurers, and health care providers. Explain how each of these parties attempts to reduce the cost.
4. How does accidental means differ from accidental injury? How important is this distinction in health insurance?
5. Define the three bases for payment under health insurance contracts.
6. Explain how health insurers attempt to meet the needs of prospective insureds who fail to meet the insurer's normal underwriting standards?

7. In terms of the procedure for analyzing insurance contracts discussed in Chapters 7 through 9, compare a health policy covering disability income with one covering medical expense.

8. Compare the continuation provisions available with health insurance policies in terms of the rights of the insured and the insurer.

9. How should the guidelines for buying health insurance be used by the prospective insured?

10. Explain the various ways in which disability is defined in health insurance policies. What role have the courts played in clarifying these definitions?

11. Explain the difference in the various methods of expressing deductibles, participation limits, and maximum limits in major medical policies.

Questions for Discussion

1. It is said that dollars spent on life insurance for dependents are dollars often ill-spent. Is this statement true of money spent on health insurance? Discuss.

2. Do you perceive a need for new types of health coverage? Explain.

3. What is the rationale for providing participation clauses in medical policies? Can you suggest a better alternative?

4. Under some health policies the insurer promises to pay for medical attention if the insured is sick and to refund the premiums if the insured remains well. Is this arrangement too good to be true? Explain.

5. Which of the many solutions to the "health care payment problem" do you favor? Why? Why is there a "health care payment problem"?

6. Do all medical expenses currently insured strictly qualify as insurable? If not, how can the coverages be written? Why are these coverages written?

7. Would you favor inclusion of some form of "other insurance" clause in individual health insurance contracts? Explain. If so, what form would you suggest? Why? Has "no-fault" automobile insurance coverage caused persons to focus on this issue? Explain.

8. Why do persons buy limited health insurance policies? Why do they buy "first dollar" medical coverage? Does it seem logical?

9. Explain the variations that should be considered by the insurance buyer in choosing deductibles (amounts and types), participation percentages (amounts and limits), and maximums (amounts and method of expression) in purchasing major medical insurance. Explain the factors that should be considered by the insurance buyer in choosing waiting periods, benefit levels, and length of benefit periods in purchasing disability income insurance.

10. Explain three possible sources of dispute between the insurer and the insured arising from health policies that could reach the courts. In each case, is it possible to write the policy to avoid the dispute? If not, why not? If so, how would you suggest the policy be rewritten?

Employee benefit plans:
Group insurance and pensions

Employee benefit plans may be defined as:

> . . . any type of plan sponsored or initiated unilaterally or jointly by employers and employees and providing benefits that stem from the employment relationship and that are not underwritten or paid directly by government. . . . The intent is to include plans that provide in an orderly, predetermined fashion for (1) income maintenance during periods when regular earnings are cut off because of death, accident, sickness, retirement, or unemployment and (2) benefits to meet expenses associated with illness or injury.[1]

Employee benefit plans have been growing at a rapid rate. During the 15-year period ending January 1, 1982, employee benefit coverage for survivors, medical care, disability income, retirement income, and severance pay increased from about 27 cents to 37 cents of the payroll dollar. Employee benefit plans are growing in breadth and depth. Medical care plans have expanded to include dental and visual care, mental health treatment, and prescription drugs. Also expanding are long-term

---

[1] *Social Security Bulletin,* monthly. (The employee benefits article usually is published in the April issue.) A broader definition of employee benefit plans would include paid vacations, company recreational facilities, prepaid legal services, school tuition, and any other nonwage benefit provided by an employer.

disability income benefits, retirement benefits for the widow (or widower) of an employee who dies before retirement age, and the accumulation of retirement pension credits for disabled employees. Now in the early stages of development are such benefits as prepaid legal aid and instruction programs in transcendental meditation (TM). A recent study concludes that TM increases individual productivity. A growing number of large and small companies have begun subsidizing TM courses for their executives and employees to reduce tension and improve interpersonal relations among employees. In addition to new benefits, traditional benefits such as hospital care, short-term disability income, and retirement plans are being liberalized. Finally, legislation has imposed additional specific criteria and standards on such plans.

This chapter is concerned with the insurer's role in employee benefit plans, including group life and health insurance, retirement benefits, group property and liability insurance, and prepaid legal care.

Reasons for Using Employee Benefit Plans

Three primary reasons for private employee benefit plans are to improve industrial relations, meet union demands, and satisfy the desire of employers and key employees to provide for their own insurance and retirement needs at low cost.

The relationships between employee benefit plans and employee morale and productivity is not clear. The argument is made that employee benefit plans enable employers to attract better employees, reduce employee turnover, and improve employee morale and efficiency. However, the empirical data upon which these arguments are based are questionable. Today, employee benefit plans are so widespread that they offer little contrast. An employer's lack of an adequate plan may be a dissatisfier, but the presence of a good plan will not lead necessarily to greater employee satisfaction, morale, and productivity.

Since 1948 when the National Labor Relations Board ruled that insurance and pensions were subject to collective bargaining, these benefits have been important union demands, and these demands are a main reason why employers have such plans. Some plans result from executives' desires for insurance at premiums lower than those charged for individual insurance, and group insurance is especially attractive to uninsurable executives. Favorable tax treatment of employer-financed employee life, health, and retirement programs is another incentive. Employee benefit plan tax advantages are discussed later.

Group Insurance

Group insurance is private insurance with some social insurance characteristics. The purpose of group insurance is similar to that of social insurance, but in its use of insurance principles, it is similar to individual insurance. In group insurance, the underwriting unit is the group and not each individual. Selection and rating are based on the group as a whole, and the policy is issued to the group. The members are not contracting parties. They are issued participation certificates and booklets describing coverage in the master policy.

Group insurance has experienced phenomenal growth in the United States over the years. In the decade ending in 1982, group life insurance increased over 300 percent, representing about 46 percent of all life insurance in force. Group insurance accounts for nearly 87 percent of health insurance premiums. Total premiums for group health insurance have increased more than 400 percent during the past 10 years. Group annuities also have grown substantially. In the past decade, the current and future group annuity income has more than doubled and is now nearly 60 percent of the annuity income in the United States provided through life insurers.

Distinguishing features of group insurance

Several features distinguish group insurance from individual insurance.

Distribution of cost. As a rule, group members do not bear the full insurance cost. Employers generally are required by statutes or insurer underwriting rules to assume part of the premium. Without employer contributions, premiums charged each employee would increase with age and become prohibitive. Charging employees the group average rate would not succeed, as younger employees would have to pay more for insurance than it would cost if they bought it individually. When the employee must bear part of the cost of the life insurance, contributions usually range from 50 to 60 cents monthly per $1,000 of insurance. Even so, employees under age 48 find this rate no bargain, as they can buy from some insurers individually issued nonparticipating yearly renewable term insurance initially for less than $6 annually per $1,000. However, to assure eligibility at bargain rates when they pass age 48, they are advised to participate during the early years.

As health insurance premiums do not increase sharply with age, average rates can be charged without creating serious inequities between age-groups. Marketing and administrative economies usually permit average group premiums per employee to be below individual premiums. Nevertheless, in most health plans employers will pay at least part of the premium. The trend is for employers to pay a large part of the cost.

No individual choice as to benefit levels. Individuals usually have no choice of amounts of insurance purchased. They receive the amounts determined by benefit formulas to eliminate selection against the insurer, which could occur if those in poor health were allowed disproportionately large amounts of insurance. Because large groups are partly self-rated[2] (the degree of self-rating depends on the group size), adverse selection could result in selection against the group, rather than against the insurer.

Lower cost. Group insurance generally provides low-cost insurance for several reasons: (1) group insurance is written without individual selection, removing a source of underwriting expense; (2) commissions are lower as they are on a sliding scale, with the percentage decreasing with premium size; (3) employers may handle much of the administration, and these costs are lower in group insurance; and (4) an income tax advantage reduces the effective cost of group term life insurance because premiums paid by employers for employee group life insurance normally are deductible by employers, without employees reporting them as income unless the amount exceeds $50,000 or the plan discriminates in favor of key employees.[3] The cost of the amount in excess of $50,000 must be included in the insured's gross income, but in computing this cost the Internal Revenue Service's (IRS) low-premium rate table is used. Payments made by employers to fund qualified pension plans (those approved by the IRS) and employee health plans are deductible as a business expense without employees reporting them as income.

Group insurance principles

Several principles apply in underwriting group insurance. These principles either are required by state statutes or determined by the insurer's underwriting standards coupled with the insurer's desire to maintain or improve its market position.

The group to be insured must have some common purpose other than obtaining insurance. Groups organized solely for insurance would likely exhibit adverse selection by including excessive numbers of participants in poor health or who engage in hazardous occupations, thus increasing the cost. Further, high costs would certainly drive away those with desirable characteristics (i.e., in good health and engaged in safer occupations), and might cause the insurer to discontinue the group.

The group should be large enough to reduce adverse selection and to achieve economies of administration. The larger the group, the less likelihood that the principal motive for group insurance is to obtain coverage on those otherwise uninsurable. The minimum number of persons needed for a group has decreased over the years, indicating insurers are paying less attention to this principle. The desire to expand group business has led insurers to seek other ways of handling the adverse effects of covering small groups.

To decrease adverse selection, little choice is given to members cov-

---

[2] The experience of the group will affect the ultimate amount charged the group.

[3] The Tax Equity and Fiscal Responsibility Act of 1982 (TEFRA) removes the tax advantages if the plan discriminates in favor of key employees. A more detailed discussion of the applicable TEFRA rules is found in Robert I. Mehr and Sandra G. Gustavson, *Life Insurance Theory and Practice,* 3d ed. (Plano, Texas: Business Publications, 1984), p. 317.

ered by requiring 100 percent participation if noncontributory (employer pays all) and 75 percent if contributory (employee pays part).

For life insurance the ideal group is fluid, with younger persons entering as older ones depart; otherwise the cost will become prohibitive.

A disproportionate amount of insurance should not be given to a few group members. The insurance on participants should relate in some way to the amount written for a typical employee, the size of the group, and the amount written for the group. Disproportionate amounts for a participant interfere with successful application of group selection and rating techniques. Eligible members not joining the plan shortly after qualifying should not be allowed in the plan later without evidence of insurability.

The foregoing principles adhered to by the insurer depend upon what the law allows and the insurer's underwriting philosophy. To what extent an insurer is willing to compromise to gain business poses an important question. Activity in the group business indicates that the strong desire to expand group coverage overrides the will to preserve what seems to be important group insurance underwriting principles.

Group insurers insist they can prevent adverse selection without requiring large groups or restricting the spread in insurance amounts by requiring evidence of insurability of employees scheduled for higher coverage. In some cases individual group members are investigated before the group is accepted.

Group underwriters are not interested in the individuals participating in the plan, but whether the group can be insured. Emphasis is placed on a sound group plan, rather than accepting or rejecting the group. Group insurance assumes that if the group is selected, no need exists to select individuals and that group loss experience will approximate that of a similar number of individually selected lives.

Group Life Insurance

In 1911 the Pantasote Leather Company bought for its workers a group life policy that was the first ever written, although, since 1910 the Equitable Life Assurance Society of New York had been trying to sell Montgomery Ward and Company a similar policy. This policy was sold in 1912, and the Equitable formed a group insurance department. Over 90 percent of the master group life policies now in force cover employer-employee groups.

State regulation

The National Association of Insurance Commissioners (NAIC) in 1917 developed the first standard definition of group life insurance and the first standard policy provisions. Soon thereafter, New York and several other industrial states established group life insurance laws. The original definition and standard provisions, revised over time, form the basis for group life insurance laws in many states, sometimes verbatim and sometimes with modifications.

Model group life insurance definition.   The model group life definition of the NAIC limits the groups eligible for life insurance including, among others, employees of single employers, multiple-employer groups, labor union groups, debtors of a common creditor, and members of an association. In addition to those prescribed by the model definition, other groups have been made eligible in various states, such as the state police, full-time reservists of the army and the National Guard, part-time reservists, veterans, and certain cooperatives.

The definition prescribes the minimum lives to be covered as 10 for employees of a single employer, 100 for multiple-employer groups, 25 for labor unions, and at least 100 new entrants a year for creditors' groups. No state has a minimum over 25 for single-employer groups. Many have no minimum. If the plan is noncontributory, the definition requires all eligible members to be covered. If contributory, 75 percent must be insured. The definition specifies employees eligible for coverage under employee groups. Corporation directors, partners, and proprietors are eligible only if they are bona fide employees.

The definition requires that employers share part of the cost and that insurance amounts preclude individual selection.

The definition limits the maximum on one life to $20,000 or 150 percent of compensation, whichever is larger, with a maximum of $40,000. This limit, known as the $20,000/$40,000 limit, is nearly extinct. Only three states still use limits and these range up to $100,000. The rest of the states impose no limit on the amount of group life insurance that may be written on one life. Limits had been established principally by pressure of agent associations to protect markets for individual policies. Obviously, the agent groups lost the fight. In 1982 primarily as a result of state actions to lift the limits, the NAIC revised their model definition and currently limit only dependent coverage, which is set at 50 percent of the amount covering the group member.

Standard provisions.   The model group law requires the following provisions in the master contract:

1. A grace period of 31 days for payment of premiums.
2. The incontestability of the master policy after two years from issue date and incontestability of the insurance on any employee's life two years after the effective coverage date.
3. The application, if any, shall be attached to the policy.
4. The participants' statements shall be representations.
5. The conditions under which insurers may require evidence of insurability. The custom is to require evidence of insurability if the employee does not join the plan within a designated period (often 31 days) after becoming eligible.
6. The handling of misstatement of age. Participants in a group life

program usually pay the same premium per $1,000 of coverage. So the custom is to adjust the premium rather than the benefit if age is misstated. The benefit is adjusted only in plans where the benefit formula is based on age.

7. A facility of payment clause allowing the insurer, in event no named beneficiary is living at the participant's death, to pay the policy proceeds to surviving close relatives or the employee's executors.

8. A clause requiring issuance of participation certificates to employees stating insurance benefits, the beneficiary, and the participant's rights in case of termination of employment or of the group contract.

9. A clause allowing the participant upon withdrawal from the group to convert the coverage to individual insurance of any type except term, without evidence of insurability. The premium shall be the one currently charged by the insurer for a person of the employee's sex and age. The conversion time limit is 31 days, and if the employee dies during that period without having converted, the beneficiary is entitled to the full death benefit under the group policy.

10. A clause requiring that if the master policy is terminated, every person insured for at least five years is entitled to convert up to $2,000 within 31 days, without furnishing evidence of insurability. The 31-day extended death benefit also applies under this provision.

11. Master policies written on other than a term basis must contain equitable nonforfeitable provisions.

Policy provisions

In addition to the standard provisions, the typical master policy provides that the group life insurance coverage may be continued for employees during layoffs and leaves of absence if these periods are simply interruptions of full-time and continuous employment; and that employees will not be deprived of coverage because of a clerical error such as the failure to notify the insurer of the employee's eligibility.

Group policies currently issued often provide that if an employee is totally disabled before age 60, the insurance will continue as long as the employee is totally disabled ("wholly prevented from engaging in any occupation for pay or profit"). This provision is the waiver of premium clause used in many individual policies. Some group contracts have a maturity value disability provision granting an employee the policy proceeds in the event of a total disability, usually before age 60. A third type of disability clause is an extended death benefit providing that if the participant dies within one year after employment termination, the insurance is paid, if the employee had been continuously and totally disabled since leaving employment and was under 65 at death.

In most instances, the beneficiary is permitted to elect an installment settlement, although the lifetime income option may not be available. The amounts payable usually are governed by the insurer's current rate when the option is selected.

The most frequent methods of determining the insurance amount for participants include: (1) a flat amount is made available for everyone; (2) a flat amount is provided such as $10,000 of insurance for workers in a wage bracket less than $15,000 a year, $15,000 for those earning from $15,000 to $24,999, and so on; (3) a multiple of the employee's earnings, such as one and one half or two times annual earnings; (4) job classifications are used and a flat insurance amount is provided for all workers in each category; (5) length of service is used (new employees might be given $10,000 of insurance, with the amount increasing $10,000 after each five years to a maximum of $50,000); and (6) combinations of the foregoing methods.

A seventh plan, a modification now in use and having merit, is that adopted by Montgomery Ward in its initial group program (1912) but later abandoned for a less expensive form common at the time. The plan provided a $100 burial benefit and one year's salary up to a maximum of $3,000 to the estate of an employee with no dependents. For an employee with dependents, the dependent received a four-year annuity and for life thereafter an amount equal to 25 percent of the employee's predeath salary. The income ceased on the spouse's remarriage.

Benefit levels for older participants may be decreased as set forth by the Department of Labor pursuant to the Age Discrimination in Employment Act. Although the act prohibits total benefit removal before age 70, it does allow for a reasonable reduction in group life coverage at age 65. Either an 8 or 9 percent annual decrease beginning at age 65 or a 35 or 40 percent one-time reduction is permissible.

Most group life plans provide lump-sum benefits (payable under *optional* settlement arrangements). However, some recent plans have replaced lump-sum payments with survivor income benefits designed to meet continuing family income needs.

The employer need not insure all workers. Coverage may be limited to specific classes of employees. The employee usually is given the right to name or change a beneficiary at any time. The statutes prohibit naming the employer as beneficiary. The master policy usually provides that an employee's insurance certificate shall not be assignable. However, to remove the proceeds of group life from their taxable estates, participants have assigned group certificates. Several court decisions and the elimination of assignment restrictions from many group policies have resulted in liberalizing certificate assignments. The employer must maintain a list of participants, including the coverage date, coverage changes, and coverage amount. Premiums may be paid monthly, quarterly, semiannually, or annually, in advance and are determined by the participants' ages and work performed by the group. Dividends or retroactive premium adjustments are given the employer based on the group's experience. Typically, group life is written on a one-year renewable term basis with renewal contingent upon premium payment, coverage of 75 percent of workers (100 percent if noncontributory), and continued coverage of the minimum workers required. Rates may be changed at the beginning of a policy year. The policy usually provides that from time to time all new eligible employees and other eligible members wanting the coverage shall be added.

Types of group life insurance coverage

Although most group life covers the employee's life, coverage in some states can be written to include *dependents*. Furthermore while most group life is written on a term basis, some plans are written on a *permanent* basis. Another type of group life, *group credit insurance,* is available to lending institutions and those making installment sales to insure their debtors' lives. Finally, some group principles are used in *wholesale* insurance to cover groups ineligible for true group because of failure to satisfy the minimum number of lives required or because of excessive flexibility in plan design.

Dependents' coverage. Group life is extended to employees' dependents to provide funds for funeral expenses when a dependent dies. Some states forbid dependents' life coverage and, in those states where allowed, insurers generally will not write it for small groups. The amount written usually is small—$2,000 for the spouse with a smaller amount for children. The younger the child, the lower is the amount of insurance. Premiums paid by employers for dependents' life insurance must be reported as taxable income to employees if the amount of insurance exceeds $2,000. This coverage customarily is written on an employee-pay-all basis. About 10 percent of the master policies include dependents' coverage. Survivorship benefit coverage also is offered in some group life insurance plans. This coverage provides for a continuing monthly benefit to the surviving spouse, usually for a period equal to the employee's length of service and for an amount related to the income of the employee. Payments may be made as long as the survivor lives or to the age at which normal social security retirement payments become available or, earlier if the survivor remarries. In the event of the spouse's death, contingent benefits to dependent children also are available.

Group permanent plans. Under group permanent plans, at least a portion of group life protection is bought using whole life forms. A group plan with some paid-up life insurance guarantees at least some coverage for retired employees. Section 79 of the Internal Revenue Code requires that permanent insurance policies meet specific requirements in order to be taxed as group term life insurance. The requirements are: (1) that the part of the death benefit which is group term must be specified; (2) that the death benefit under the group term must be at least as much as the difference between the total death benefit under the policy and the employee's "deemed death benefit" at the end of the policy year;[4]

---

[4] The deemed death benefit is the ratio R/Y, where R is the net level premium reserve or the cash value of the policy at the end of the policy year, whichever is the greater, and Y is the net single premium for $1 of permanent insurance at the insured's attained age at the end of the policy year. For example, the per $1,000 net level premium reserve at ages 40 and 50 are $151.80 and $292.90, respectively, assuming an entry age of 25. The net single premium for $1 of permanent insurance at age 40 is 32 cents, and at age 50 is 43 cents. Thus, the deemed death benefits at ages 40 and 50 are $474.38 (= $151.80 ÷ .32) and $681.16 (= $292.90 ÷ .43), respectively.

and (3) that the group term death benefit is not reduced because of an employee's election to decline or drop the permanent death protection. If an employee must purchase any other benefit together with life insurance, it does not qualify as group term, with the exception of employee participation under a qualified contributory plan or a health plan. Permanent group life plans account for less than 1 percent of the group life in force.

Two principal types of group permanent plans are used.

The level premium group permanent plan.   The level premium plan was introduced in 1913 to fund pension plans. Because of a 1950 adverse tax ruling making premiums paid by employers for permanent life insurance taxable income to the employee, level premium group permanent is rarely used and then only to fund qualified pension plans in which case only a small part of the premium is currently taxable to the employee. The employee is taxed on the cost of the life insurance computed by applying the IRS table of term insurance rates to an amount equal to the difference between the face amount and cash value of the insurance. At termination of employment, the employee may take the policy's cash value, a paid-up policy for a reduced amount, a paid-up term policy for the full amount but for a specified period, or continue the full face amount by paying the full premium.

Unit purchase plan.   The unit purchase plan, developed in 1941, combines employer-financed decreasing term insurance and employee-financed paid-up units of whole life insurance. If a 25-year-old employee contributes $1.30 a month per $1,000 of insurance, that amount purchases, say, $63 of paid-up insurance. The employer buys $937 of one-year term insurance (per $1,000 of coverage). The second year, the employee's contribution buys $61, increasing the total to $124. The employer will buy $876 of one-year term insurance. When the employee terminates employment, the paid-up units are retained. As the employer buys group term, no tax problems arise.

The unit purchase plan funds a paid-up policy for employees at retirement, whereas level premium group permanent funds retirement income benefits under qualified pension plans.

Group credit insurance.   The first group credit insurance policy was issued in 1930 to the National City Bank of New York covering debtors with unsecured loans. Group credit insurance is used by merchants making installment sales, credit unions, finance companies, banks, lenders on real estate mortgages, and other creditors to cover the debtors' lives. The proceeds are used to cancel the balance of the debt at the debtor's death. The insurance, therefore, protects the borrower, the family, and the lender. Group credit life insurance in force has substantially increased during the past decade.

Generally group credit life insurance premiums are paid by the debtor to the creditor and usually are excessive. The premium is negotiated between the insurer and lender, with the objective of obtaining high profits to the lender from substantial revenues from this coverage. The borrower primarily is interested in the loan, and thus generally will pay for the insurance. This suggests competition among insurers (for the creditors' business) contrary to public interest—reverse competition leading to higher prices for debtors and more revenue for creditors. Both state and federal governments are trying to help the borrower through credit insurance price regulation.

When group credit life premiums are paid by the creditor instead of the debtor, the cost of the coverage is included in the quoted annual percentage rate (APR) as are other expense loadings of the lender. As competition among lenders generally is based on the APR, this approach encourages the lender to find a financially sound insurer (one that can and will pay claims) with low rates. Thus competition can help reduce premiums instead of raising them.

Wholesale life insurance.   Wholesale life insurance is an adaptation of group insurance principles to cases ineligible for true group insurance. No master policy is used, and participants receive individual policies, issued after applications are approved. The insurer may reject an applicant failing to meet its standards for insurability. In a small group, even one or two substandard lives can lead to excessive mortality costs. As in group insurance, however, each participant's insurance amount is determined by formula. Wholesale insurance allows employers to give employees most of the group insurance advantages. Generally wholesale plans are written on a yearly renewable term basis.

Group Health Insurance

Group health insurance is similar to group life. The differences are in the perils covered and the broader definition of eligible groups.

State regulation

Group health insurance developed without special legislation. Insurers had to comply only with general statutes relating to insurance until 1937, when Illinois enacted the first state group insurance law.

The model bills of the Health Insurance Association of America (HIA) and the NAIC serve as the basis for state group health legislation. These laws include a definition of group health insurance and several standard policy provisions.

Definition of group health insurance.   The HIA definition designates no minimum number for the group, whereas the NAIC bill requires 25 lives. A significant number of states require minimums less than NAIC standards. In the remaining states the insurers set the minimum. The HIA bill has no minimum participation, whereas the NAIC bill specifies a 75 percent minimum participation requirement for contributory plans and 100 percent for noncontributory ones.

The eligible groups are less restricted than those for group life insurance. The HIA bill provides that any organization eligible for group life also is eligible for group health insurance, and eligibility extends to any association organized for purposes other than obtaining insurance. The group health insurance definitions are sufficiently broad to include dependents' coverage. In no group health policy can the employer or association be named as beneficiary.

Insurers are freer in writing group health than group life because insurance agents did not lobby for restrictions on group health coverage. The public's interest in health insurance was lacking when group health insurance was introduced, so the agents did nothing to protect the small market for individual health insurance. Major health insurance competition developed from organizations similar to Blue Cross operating on the group principle. Insurers believed this competition could be met by developing competitive group contracts.

Standard provisions for group health insurance. The HIA bill contains only three standard provisions: (1) no statement made can be used to avoid the insurance unless in writing, and these statements shall be interpreted as representation; (2) each group member must receive a summary statement of coverage, and (3) eligible new members or dependents may be added to the group in accordance with the policy terms. Standard provisions are required in a majority of states. Some states, for example, require a provision stating conditions under which the insurer may decline to renew the policy.

Group health and individual health contracts distinguished

Group health insurance differs from individual coverage as follows:

1. Group health often covers off-the-job accidents only, except for long-term disability coverage. Workers' compensation insurance is designed to cover on-the-job accidents. Occupational sicknesses usually are not covered by group health if they are covered under the state workers' compensation law. Some employers include coverage for on-the-job accidents and occupational illnesses in amounts sufficient to equalize on-the-job with off-the-job benefits.

2. State laws require uniform provisions in individual health policies, but not group policies. Many uniform provisions relate to loss adjustment and thus would not apply to group coverages.

3. The prorating clause for benefits received from other insurance usually is omitted in group contracts. Instead a "coordination of benefits clause" commonly is included to reduce excessive payments. These clauses, also known as antiduplication clauses, restrict benefits payable to employees by other group policies. Where a working couple both are covered under their own employer's contract and, as spouses, under each

other's insurance, the coverage afforded spouses is treated as excess to be applied after the primary coverage is exhausted.

Types of coverages

Many of the same coverages are available under individual health and group contracts. Coverage frequently written under group policies are: disability income, accidental death and dismemberment, hospital expense, surgical expense, nursing home care, psychiatric expense, major medical expense, dental care, vision care, and out-of-hospital drugs. A few are written almost entirely on a group basis. Measured by number of persons covered, group insurance accounts for nearly 74 percent of major medical insurance, 71 percent of dental care coverage, and most of the vision care coverage. The impetus for the development of the latter two coverages comes from (1) employers' views that good dental and vision care contribute to working efficiency and (2) unions' claims that no medical care protection is adequate without these coverages. The pioneering of all three coverages was done by group insurers. Since their introduction, these plans have been made available in many other private and independent plans (i.e., through medical society programs and health maintenance organizations).

Disability income benefits have expanded to treat pregnancy as a temporary disability. Insurers (and often employers who pay the bill) argue that pregnancy differs from illnesses because it is common to women only and is assumed to be voluntary. However, the court ruled that (1) exclusion of pregnancy from disability plans discriminates against women and (2) "voluntarism is no basis to justify disparate treatment of pregnancy." (Medical care coverages, discussed in Chapter 18, are referred to later in this chapter.)

Some people would favor covering only accidental pregnancies if claim adjusters were capable of separating intended from unintended pregnancies, because to cover an expected condition is contrary to the insurance principle. However, guidelines designed by the Equal Employment Opportunity Commission provide that employers offer coverage and benefits for pregnancy-related conditions in an amount equal to those for other health-related conditions, if the employer has an employee health benefit plan. An exception is coverage of hospital and medical expenses for abortion not caused by medical complications.[5] Also, employers are required to provide for the pregnancy-related expenses of employees' wives if they offer coverage for dependents in their employee health benefit plans. (Some employers argue against these guidelines on the grounds that the EEOC has no legal authority to require these benefits.)

---

[5] A few carriers do however cover the cost of abortions when pregnancies also are covered. The reasoning behind such payments may be based on the relative costs of the two procedures, and/or on the idea of leaving the decision to those involved.

Franchise (wholesale) health insurance

Franchise health insurance, the equivalent of wholesale life insurance, is designed for an employee group too small to qualify for group health insurance. Individual policies are issued, and individual selection is practiced. Thus, this policy is not true group insurance. The coverage is nonoccupational. The premium is less than for individual policies, but more than for group coverage. Franchise insurance is mass marketed to association members and credit card holders; administrative techniques usually associated with group insurance are utilized.

Blanket health policies

A blanket health policy protects all group members against the insured perils. Blanket insurance differs from group insurance in that no insured is named and no certificates are issued. Examples of groups written under blanket policies are students at a college, spectators at a sports attraction, members of a football squad, and campers at a camp. In general, the blanket group membership changes frequently, and the policy covers the changing membership.

Group credit health insurance

Group credit health insurance can be purchased to pay a disabled debtor's payments until recovery or until the debt is paid. In some plans, benefits are payable retroactively to the debtor's first day of disability if the disability is continuous for a given period. In other plans, benefits are paid only for the period following the waiting period. Retroactive payments can lead to malingering, so the tendency is to avoid them.

Cost of group health insurance

To generalize on the cost of group health insurance is difficult because of so many variables. Each plan is different. Competition is keen, and each insurer determines its own rates. Even initial rates are misleading, for the net cost after dividends or rate credits is the important consideration. Initial rates vary with the age distribution, occupations covered, proportion of females in the group (women have about twice as much time loss through sickness as men), variations in medical care costs in different localities, and in major medical, the earnings levels of the members. High-income people demand higher-priced medical services and may be charged more than low-income persons for the same service.

Private Pension Plans

Over 50 million wage and salaried employees are enrolled in 600,000 private pension plans. Employers and employees are contributing more than $45 billion annually to private pension plans, and retirement benefits paid amount to more than $17 billion annually. Private pension plan assets equal $500 billion. More than 8 million retired workers (or their survivors) are receiving benefits under these plans.

The Employee Retirement Income Security Act of 1974 (ERISA) prescribes standards for funding, participation, vesting, termination insurance, disclosure, fiduciary responsibility, and tax treatment of private pension plans. Prior to ERISA, assets to fund private pensions were the largest private fund accumulation not subject to strict federal regulation. Pension plans qualified under the IRC and its interpretative rulings receive favorable income tax treatment.

Funding

To provide employees with maximum security, private pension plans require realistic actuarial estimates of future benefits, costs and provisions for accumulating funds for benefits as they become due. Funded pension plans are those for which an amount in excess of that needed to pay current benefits to retired employees is accumulated by the employer with a trustee (usually a bank) or an insurer. How much is accumulated in excess of current disbursements is a function of the funding method used. In the absence of a sound funding method, advance funding does not adequately protect employee pension expectations. The funding provisions of ERISA require immediate full funding of current service cost and full funding over a maximum specified period of accrued past service liability. Plans operating as of January 1, 1974 have 40 years and new plans have 30 years to amortize accrued past service liability. An excise tax is imposed on underfunded plans. *Reasonable* actuarial assumptions and *reasonable* asset valuation methods are required.[6] A plan must be valued at least every three years.

Actuarial soundness for pensions relates both to funding methods and actuarial assumptions used in valuing accumulating liabilities for current service and past service credits. Actuarial soundness requires *reasonable* assumptions of mortality, interest, expenses, turnover, and other items used in projecting the potential liability (cost) under a plan. Actuarial opinions vary widely as to reasonable sets of assumptions. Actuarial soundness also relates to methods used in valuing pension funds assets.

Aside from offering some protection to employees, advance funding provides income tax advantages to plans approved by the IRS. These advantages result in a reduction in the cost of providing employee pensions. The advantage to employers is that investment income earned

---

[6] The concept of reasonable actuarial assumptions is not a precise one. The term has been given various interpretations even among those whose understanding of "actuarial soundness" is more sophisticated than that of the typical business financial officer, accountant, lawyer, or labor relations expert who superficially has concluded that "our plan must be actuarially sound." For a still *current* discussion of actuarial soundness in pension plans, see Dorrance C. Bronson, *Concepts of Actuarial Soundness in Pension Plans* (Homewood, Ill.: Richard D. Irwin, 1957).

on funds deposited with the insurer or trustee accrues income tax free.[7] Advance funding also allows employers to charge as a tax deductible business expense the cost of current service benefits in the year incurred and the cost of past service in the years funded. Under some funding methods, the employers' annual deduction for contributions to fund past service benefits is limited to 10 percent of the initial past service liability.

Another advantage of advance funding is that pension benefits may be increased without increasing employers' cost by requiring employees to share in the financing. Also, an advance funding advantage is the flexibility given employers in financing. During periods of reduced cash flows (or great cash needs), payments to a fund usually can be reduced or postponed with little repercussions. However, a reduction or postponement must not violate ERISA standards.

ERISA allows a 40-year amortization funding period for Taft-Hartley (multiemployer) plans because they are unique. Also, some plans are relieved of amortization requirements either by waiver or variance if the participants' interest is served. ERISA established a "funding standard account" to facilitate employer compliance and began enrolling actuaries to practice before the IRS.

Funding agencies

When a bank or individual trustee is the funding agency, the plan is called a *trust fund plan*. When a life insurer is the funding agency, the plan is called *insured*. When both agencies are used, the plan is called *split-funded*.

Trust fund plans.   Trust funds are the oldest type of funded private pension plans. In trust fund plans, the employer deposits contributions with the trustee, who invests them and pays the benefits. This plan may be used either by an employer with a large enough number of employees to be able to predict with an acceptable degree of confidence the mortality rate among employees or by employers strong enough financially to retain the risk of adverse mortality fluctuations. The trust fund plan is a popular funding agency among multiemployer and union pension plans.

Insured plans.   In an insured plan, the employer pays the contributions to an insurer, who invests them and pays the benefits. The insurer makes certain guarantees depending on the type of insurance contract (technically known as a *funding instrument*) selected.

Contracts with insurers acting as pension funding agencies are broadly classified into (1) those under which the funds are used to finance the purchase of cash value life insurance or deferred annuities for each participating employee when paid to the insurer; and (2) those under

---

[7] Additional tax advantages (income, estate, and gift) accruing to employees under certain conditions are discussed later.

which the funds accumulate (as in trust fund plans) and later are used to purchase immediate annuities for retiring employees or finance benefits payable to terminating employees. Contracts of the first type (technically called *allocated funding instruments*) are of three forms: individual life or annuity contracts; group permanent life; and group deferred annuities. Contracts of the second type (technically known as *unallocated funding instruments*) are group deposit administration contracts, immediate participation guarantee plans, and guaranteed investment contracts. Unallocated funding instruments grew from insurers' efforts to improve their competitive position with banks as pension funding agencies.

Individual policy plans. Some retirement plans are funded through individual policies, frequently plans involving a small number of employees, averaging less than 10. The number of individual policy plans continues to grow, in spite of the willingness of some insurers to write group annuities for very small groups.

The administration of a qualified individual policy plan is by a trustee operating under the same agreement that includes the plan's provisions. Employers frequently designate one of their executives as trustee to receive the contributions, apply for the policies, retain them, and pay the premiums. The insurer usually pays the benefits to the workers.

In individual policy pension plans, interest, mortality, and expense rates are guaranteed for the lifetime of each policy. Thus, the employers' maximum cost for each employee's pension is guaranteed when the policy is purchased. The maximum cost of additional coverage for present employees or for new ones depends on the insurer's premium at the time the additional policies are purchased.

Group permanent life insurance. Group permanent life is written as retirement income insurance when an objective is to fund pensions. Premiums are paid to the insurer, who pays the benefits to employees on retirement. Guarantees are similar to those in individual policy plans, with the additional guarantee that initial rates are applicable to purchases of additional units during the first several years of the master contract. Rather than combine the funding of death protection and qualified retirement plans through the use of group permanent, the simpler approach is to provide survivor benefits through group term life insurance and pension benefits through group annuity contracts.

Group deferred annuities. Group deferred annuity plans, first written in 1921, provide the closest approximation of group principles to pensions. Some insurers will write group deferred annuities for as few as 10 or even fewer employees. Insurers might establish minimum total premiums or minimum premiums per life as an eligibility standard to assure adequate size. These underwriting rules are established to provide adequate administration funds rather than to prevent adverse selection. A separate contract charge sometimes is made for a small group or for relaxed underwriting standards.

Typical group deferred annuity plans provide for purchase of specified amounts of fully paid deferred annuity units each year for eligible employees. The units are single-premium deferred annuities. If a fully paid deferred annuity of $30 a month is purchased each year, an employee who has 35 years of service at retirement will have a guaranteed retirement income of $1,050 a month. Group deferred annuity rates usually are guaranteed for five years; that is, all paid-up units purchased during the first five years after the master contract is issued may be purchased at the initial rates. Then the rate scale is subject to change annually, sometimes less frequently. Under some plans, ownership of paid-up annuity units vests immediately in the employee.[8] Under other plans, vesting occurs only after the employee has worked for a designated period. Vesting usually provides employees with paid-up pension benefits that are available only at the earliest retirement age.

Deposit administration plans.   Under the deposit administration plan (DA) introduced in 1929, units of an annuity are not purchased immediately with each contribution. Instead, the insurer accumulates the deposits to buy annuities for employees at retirement. Before retirement, the position of the employee is similar to that under a trust fund plan. After retirement, the position is the same as under a group deferred annuity because at that time the funds are "transferred" from the DA account and used to "purchase" a single-premium retirement annuity for the employee. For the conventional DA plan, interest rates and annuity purchase rates are guaranteed for funds deposited during the five years following issuance of the master contract. Then lifetime interest and annuity purchase guarantees for funds deposited each year may be changed.

The *immediate participation guarantee plan* (IPG), a variation of the DA plan, was introduced in 1950. Under the IPG, the fund is credited annually with the net rate of interest earned by the insurer. The fund is charged annually with administration expenses and credited or charged with mortality gains or losses. At retirement, the employee receives the pension directly from the fund (theoretically, one-year temporary life annuities are purchased yearly). The plan then participates immediately and fully in its own favorable or unfavorable experience. No contributions need be made to the insurer's contingency fund. The plan is unaffected by the insurer's dividend formula.

The IPG is similar to trust fund plans with the following exceptions: (1) Under the IPG plan, one-year temporary life annuities theoretically are purchased each year as new contracts, whereas under trust fund plans the trustees purchase single-premium life annuities, if annuities are used. (2) If the DA fund should fall to an amount barely adequate

---

[8] Vesting describes rights of a pension plan participant who leaves the group prior to retirement. The major concern of the terminating member is the vesting or ownership rights to contributions made by the employer on his or her behalf.

to fully fund annuities for retired employees, the combined contributions of the employer and retired employee generally are used to purchase annuities to continue full payments to those already retired. For those not yet retired, employee contributions are returned in cash or as paid-up annuities. Employer contributions will be used either to continue the fund and provide reduced benefits or to purchase single-premium annuities for eligible employees on a pro-rata basis.

A minimum interest rate usually is guaranteed. The contract describes the basis for crediting interest earned. In some plans the interest credited is related to the *average net rate earned* by the insurer's total investment portfolio. The newer method, *the investment year* or *new money approach,* is to relate interest directly to that earned on the deposited funds. (These two methods of allocating interest are found in dividend formulas used in rate adjustments in conventional DA plans.)

Separate or segregated accounts are another variation of the DA plan, introduced in 1961. The separate account is designed for employers who want to invest a part of their deposits in equities without subjecting their funds to the restrictive regulations applicable to the insurer's general assets. The separate accounts are maintained by the insurer who selects the investments. Generally the accounts are pooled for all employers, although some insurers maintain individual accounts for plans involving sums large enough for diversified investment portfolios. The insurer may maintain pooled accounts for common stocks, real estate mortgages, and corporate bonds, and the employer can determine how the contributions are spread among these three accounts.

When individual accounts are used, the employer specifies the investment diversity but the insurer retains the responsibility of choosing particular investments to purchase. In contributory plans, only employer contributions can be placed in segregated accounts. The Securities and Exchange Commission requires that employee contributions be included in the insurer's general investment funds to be accumulated at a guaranteed minimum rate of interest. No investment guarantees are made on the separate accounts; however, annuity purchase rates are guaranteed just as in IPG plans.

Unallocated funding instruments are the most popular in terms of the number of covered persons. Individual policy pension trusts, group permanent, and other plans account for less than 10 percent of the number of people covered by insured plans.

Termination of plans

Upon termination of plans, the funds are allocated to employees according to their equitable interest. The termination provisions must not result in discrimination in favor of officers, stockholders, and highly paid employees. ERISA provides for the following order of priorities in allocating benefits among employees:

1. Voluntary employee contributions.
2. Mandatory employee contributions.

3. Benefits for employees who have been retired for at least three years or who were eligible to retire at least three years before the plan's termination date. (The provisions of the plan in effect five years prior to the plan's termination date are used to determine the amount of these benefits.)
4. All other benefits guaranteed by the Pension Benefit Guaranty Corporation (PBGC).
5. All other vested benefits.
6. All other benefits accrued under the plan.

If, because of actuarial error, funds remain after satisfying the foregoing priorities, these funds may be recaptured by the employer.

Decisions in Establishing Employee Benefit Plans

Many decisions must be made in designing employee benefit plans. In this section some of the more important ones are identified.

Contributory or noncontributory

When employee benefit plans are installed, a decision must be made whether the program's cost should be paid entirely by the employer or if the employee should contribute. The issues of administration and cost must be considered in answering this question.

The noncontributory plan has the advantage of *administrative* ease. In most group arrangements, if the plan is contributory, at least 75 percent of eligible group members must elect to be covered for the plan to be installed. A noncontributory plan automatically covers everyone without pressuring employees. The noncontributory plan eliminates paper work involved in withholding funds from participating employees and reduces clerical errors. Noncontributory plans are significantly more popular than contributory plans.

Some *cost* considerations favor contributory plans. More attractive benefits can be offered employees for each employer dollar. The additional benefits purchased through employee contributions usually are better than the employee could purchase individually for the same money. But income tax considerations favor noncontributory plans. The employer may deduct as necessary business expenses premiums paid for group life and health insurance and contributions made to qualified pension plans. The employee does not have to report the employer's group insurance premiums or pension contributions as current income except those premiums used to purchase life insurance in excess of $50,000. Benefits from life and medical care insurance are income tax free. Therefore, income tax-free death and medical benefits are purchased with pretax dollars under noncontributory plans.

Disability and retirement income benefits under a noncontributory plan are reportable as income to the employee when received. However, eligible employees may exclude disability income up to $100 a week.[9] When pension benefits are paid, the retired employee usually will have a double exemption (taxpayers beyond age 65 claim an extra exemption) and probably a lower income. Consequently, these benefits likely are taxed at a lower marginal tax rate.

Before the Tax Reform Act of 1969, if an employee on termination of employment, or the beneficiary upon the employee's death, received all accumulated benefits in one taxable year from a qualified plan, these funds were taxed as capital gains rather than as normal income. With the Tax Reform Act of 1969 and ERISA, the treatment of lump-sum distributions in one taxable year has become complicated. In 1974 these distributions were split into pre-1974 capital gains, and post-1973 ordinary income. No capital gains are accrued after 1973. The ordinary income portion of the distribution is accorded a 10-year rather than the previous 7-year averaging treatment. The present income tax status of lump-sum distributions from qualified pension plans is as follows: the measure of capital gains is the excess of the payment received over the consideration paid by the employee participant. The 1969 Tax Reform Act precludes from capital gains treatment that portion of the distribution representing benefits accrued for plan years beginning after December 31, 1969. That part of the distribution representing employer contributions for years prior to 1974 and all investment earnings accrued until 1974 is taxed as a long-term capital gain. The amount remaining is taxed as ordinary income, subject to the aforementioned 10-year averaging rule. Taxpayers who find it disadvantageous to divide the accumulated benefits into capital gain and ordinary income may elect irrevocably to report all lump-sum benefits as ordinary income and apply the 10-year averaging rule.

Specification of employee benefit plans

What benefits should be included in employee benefit plans, who should be entitled to these benefits, and what should be the benefit level? Most programs include life insurance, accidental death and dismemberment benefits, hospital care, surgical expense, and regular medical expense. More than half the plans based on people covered include pension benefits. Major medical benefits are standard in a majority of firms, and more than one half include loss of income protection. Certain decisions peculiar to each benefit will have to be made, as well as decisions

---

[9] Employees may exclude disability income up to $100 a week only if (1) they are under age 65, (2) have not reached mandatory retirement age, and (3) are permanently and totally disabled when retired. Payments are excluded up to $5,200 a year if the recipient's adjusted gross income, including disability payments, does not exceed $15,000. If the recipient's income is in excess of $15,000 annually, the $5,200 deduction is reduced dollar for dollar. Thus if the retirement disability income payee has an adjusted gross income of $18,000 annually, including $5,200 of disability income, only $2,200 may be deducted by the employer. The exclusion would be phased out entirely if the adjusted gross income annually plus $5,200 of disability income is greater than $20,200. When advantageous, the recipient may elect to have qualified disability income taxed as retirement income.

common to all benefits. To simplify the presentation, life and health benefits are considered, followed by retirement benefits.

Group life and health benefits.   Several issues need to be decided in planning an employee group life and health insurance program.

Eligibility requirements.   To be eligible for coverage under group life and health plans, employees usually must be regular and full time, actively at work and have served a job probationary period. A minimum number of hours worked per week usually is the test for full-time regular employees. The probationary period customarily ranges from one to three months. Two special groups need to be considered: employees temporarily separated from employment, and retired employees. A limit frequently is placed on the length of time that coverage can be continued on an employee temporarily laid off or on leave of absence. Although the cost is high, the trend is toward extending group life and medical care coverage to retired people. The employer usually pays the entire cost, but benefit levels are reduced to control costs. As noted, life insurance for retired people occasionally is handled through group permanent, and consideration has been given to group medical care coverage that can be fully funded by retirement age. Medical care benefits provided for the aged under employee benefit plans usually are integrated with Medicare (discussed in Chapters 18 and 20).

Benefit structure.   After determining the amount that can be budgeted for employee benefits, an allocation of funds among types of benefits and employees is necessary. For *group life insurance,* establishing the benefit structure involves two decisions: the benefit level and whether dependents are to be covered. The various bases upon which benefit levels are determined have been discussed, and the one, or combination that best fits the plan's objective, must be selected. The practice of including dependents' coverage is not common, and little seems to recommend it. The employer, however, might wish to include dependents' coverage in a contributory plan because the dependents' coverage financing can be arranged so as to reduce the employer's cost.

For *health insurance,* the decisions are more numerous. One is the types of health coverages to include. The principal coverages written under group health contracts have been discussed and include disability income, accidental death and dismemberment, hospital expense, surgical expense, major medical, dental care, vision care, psychiatric expense, and out-of-hospital drugs. According to sound insurance-buying theory, only disability income insurance with a waiting period and major medical insurance with a deductible should be considered, because they exclude small losses. But many employees fail to appreciate plans that do not pay some of the small and frequent expenses. Furthermore, the advantage of having medical bills paid by the employer with tax deductible dollars often is a practical consideration.

Plan specifications must be made for each coverage selected. In *disability income plans* the following specifications are needed:

1. Disabilities covered. Should the plan cover both occupational and nonoccupational injury and illness? Most plans are nonoccupational because workers' compensation benefits are paid for on-the-job losses.

2. Length of the waiting period. The common pattern is a seven-day waiting period for sickness, but no waiting period for accidents.

3. Duration of the benefit period. The usual benefit periods are 13 and 26 weeks, although a trend toward longer durations is evident with a number of plans providing benefits for one or more years. Disability income payable to age 65 is a major development.

4. Benefit levels. A benefit schedule for each wage bracket, usually not more than two thirds nor less than one half of salary is common. Benefits also may be based on job classification, length of service, a flat amount for all employees, or some combination of two or more of these factors.

Accidental death and dismemberment benefits frequently are included in a group insurance program and usually are paid for both occupational and nonoccupational injuries. The coverage is attractive because high dollar amounts can be purchased with low premiums. Employees overvalue these benefits. The traumatic nature of accidental death and dismemberment gives the coverage psychological appeal. The basic decision is the benefit level. Usually it is the same as that for group life insurance. Dismemberment benefits are commonly related to accidental death benefits by a percentage. For example, the loss of both feet, hands, or eyes might produce a benefit equal to 100 percent of the accidental death benefits, or 50 percent for the loss of one foot, hand, or eye.

In *hospital insurance,* the principal decision also concerns benefit levels. Customarily all employees receive the same benefits. Hospital room and board may be covered for actual costs up to a given dollar amount per day, or ideally the coverage may be for the cost of a semiprivate room. The coverage is subject to a specified number of days, most commonly 120 to 365. Miscellaneous hospital expense benefits usually are 15 or 20 times the daily room and board rate. Miscellaneous hospital expense includes expenses incurred during hospital confinement or confinement as a resident patient (i.e., laboratory or X-ray service). For miscellaneous hospital expenses in excess of the basic amount, the trend is to grant an additional amount equal to the basic amount, but on a participation basis, usually 80 percent. Group hospital expense insurance, in contrast to group life insurance, usually extends coverage to dependents of covered employees. In some cases when the employee's coverage is written on a noncontributory basis, dependents' coverage is written on a contributory basis.

In *surgical expense* coverage, schedules commonly list benefits for specific operations. Nearly one half of covered persons have schedules with maximum benefits of $1,000 or more. Specific amounts may be paid for anesthesiologists and anesthetics in addition to surgery. The major decision to be made is the maximum surgical schedule. The cost of surgical procedures in the community influences this decision. Surgery coverage usually is for reasonable and necessary charges, and some policies do not include limiting schedules.

Physicians expense coverage provides for payment of doctors' fees for services other than surgery. These services include home, office, and hospital visits. Some plans also may cover expenses of diagnostic X-rays and laboratory tests up to a specified amount.

Major medical requires a number of choices: Should the plan be in addition to a basic plan, as is most common? What type of deductible should be used: initial, corridor, or integrated? Under the *initial deductible,* the insured pays the first $250 or so and the insurer pays the rest, up to the policy limit and participation percentage. The deductible frequently is offset by hospital, surgical, and medical expense insurance. The *corridor deductible,* usually $100, is applied after the basic plan benefits are exhausted. Under an *integrated deductible* the basic plan or some dollar amount, whichever is higher, is the deductible. The integrated deductible is the most common. What size deductible (flat amount or percentage of earnings) is appropriate, and should it be per case, per benefit period, per calendar year, or on a family budget basis? Most common is a flat deductible usually applied to a benefit period or a calendar year rather than each disability. What should be the participation level? Usually the employee must pay 20 percent. Most plans limit the participation to those expenses under a specified amount, such as the first $5,000. What should be the benefit limit, and should it be per illness, per policy, or calendar year, per benefit year, per lifetime, or some combination of these limits? A common maximum is $250,000 per illness or injury, and many plans use maximums of $1 million or no limit at all. What expenses should be excluded? Usual exclusions are expenses covered under other insurance, cosmetic surgery, and workers' compensation.

Currently nearly all health plans cover in-hospital treatment for nervous and mental disorders, and more than 92 percent cover out-of-hospital treatment for mental illness. Prescription drugs usually are covered with a calendar year the most common deductible. Should coverage be extended to vision care? (Arguments for this coverage are that employers benefit if employees have good vision and the employee benefits by having the employer pay the cost of vision care with pretax dollars.) Usually benefits are low and a deductible is used. However, an increasing number of the plans offer vision care. A number of plans offer coverage for nursing home care as continuing efforts are made to control hospital costs by providing care in adequate nursing homes.

Dental care insurance usually covers 50 to 80 percent of reasonable and customary charges for diagnosis (oral examinations, X-rays), preventive, restoration, orthodontics, root canal therapy, and gum disease treatment. Benefits usually are $500 to $1,000 per individual for a calendar year and are subject to internal limits for various procedures. Although they have no colorful symbol such as a Blue Cross or a Blue

Shield, dental associations offer group dental care coverage on a prepaid basis, frequently more liberal than that written by commercial insurers. Nevertheless, commercial insurers cover over 70 percent of the 86 million persons who have group dental coverage.

Medical expense coverage may be reduced for workers age 65 and over without violating the requirements of the Age Discrimination in Employment Act. The plan usually provides for integration of group benefits with benefits available to older employees under Medicare. Disability income benefits may also be reduced. However, compliance with the act requires that reductions in either type of plan be justified according to cost data. Further, for employers with more than 25 employees, the Tax Equity and Fiscal Responsibility Act of 1982 (TEFRA) requires the same health benefits be made available to older workers (age 65 through 69) and their dependents as are available to employees under age 65. Medicare payments are made secondary to the health benefits of older workers who choose to join the employer's plan.

Funding the benefits. In group life and disability income coverage, the employer may pay claims directly as they occur or may use a commercial insurer. The decision hinges on whether the employer can assume the risk in handling the plan and if the plan can be administered at a cost lower than that charged by insurers.

If death benefits are insured, the employee's spouse has an income tax advantage. Death benefits paid by life insurers are not subject to federal income taxes. However, payments made directly by an employer on behalf of a deceased employee are taxable as income subject to a $5,000 spouse exclusion.

The alternatives to commercial insurance in funding medical care plans are Blue Cross and Blue Shield or similar independent plans, health maintenance organizations, and self-insurance. In choosing between the "Blues" and commercial insurers several competitive factors may be of concern. The "Blues," because of their not-for-profit status, have tax advantages in nearly all states, thereby gaining a cost advantage. To meet insurer competition, the "Blues" are offering experience rating plans. Still, insurers may have an advantage. If the entire group package (life, disability income, and health expenses) is underwritten by an insurer, a broader base is achieved, giving greater weight to the group's own experience in determining the premium. The underwriting philosophies of the "Blues" and the insurers must be considered to determine if one or both will write the plan according to desired specifications. Health maintenance organizations offer employees economies and may be used where employees are willing to restrict medical care service to one clinic.

A number of employers self-insure (or assume the risk of) their medical expense plans, particularly when these plans do not involve major medical expenses. Losses under basic plans usually occur with sufficient frequency for predictability within a range small enough to qualify for self-insurance without large numbers of employees. Loss severity is low enough so that the acceptable range of predictability can be wide. Most employers, however, prefer not to self-insure. They like claims to be administered (or at least to give the appearance that claims are administered) by an insurer so as not to endanger employee relations when a claim is denied.

Group retirement benefits. Retirement plans are more complex than group life and health plans. In addition to restraining tax considerations, discussed later, questions of finance and employee relations must be weighed. ERISA, the IRC, and the IRS rulings set forth broad requirements for a qualified pension plan. (Briefly, a qualified pension plan permits the employer to report contributions to the plan as deductible business expenses for federal income tax purposes. In addition, employees do not report the contributions as part of their taxable income until the funds become available to them upon retirement.) Basic decisions relating to pension plans that must be made are employee eligibility qualifications, conditions under which benefits are payable, benefit levels, and types of benefits. Requirements for qualifying pensions do not specify the precise funding policy but they do establish minimum and maximum funding standards. Cost, competitive conditions in the labor market, and the desire for an effective personnel and employee relations policy are important considerations in designing retirement benefit plans.

A qualified retirement plan must meet the following requirements: (1) established by the employer; (2) for the exclusive benefit of employees and their beneficiaries; (3) written; (4) permanent; (5) communicated to the employees; (6) financed by contributions made by the employer, the employee, or both; (7) nondiscriminatory with respect to coverage or benefits; (8) based on a defined contribution or defined benefit formula; and (9) no possibility of a reversion of contributions to the employer prior to the satisfaction of all liabilities to employees, or any other fund diversion for the benefit of other than employees.

Eligibility of coverage. Under the IRC provisions a qualified plan must be for the benefit of employees (and their beneficiaries) in general, not for specific ones. The plan therefore must meet one of the following tests: (1) at least 70 percent of all employees (or 80 percent of all eligible employees provided that in a contributory plan 70 percent or more are eligible) must be covered or (2) if only specific classes of employees are covered, such classification must not discriminate in favor of officers, stockholders, supervisors, or high-salaried employees. Plans meeting the percentage test automatically satisfy the coverage requirement of the IRS. Those plans that fail to meet the percentage test can qualify by meeting the classification test. In this event the plan is subject to the discretionary power of the IRS. For the classification test nearly any classification is acceptable if it does not violate the nondiscriminatory requirement. One classification not permitted is that of union employees only or nonunion employees only.

ERISA requires that employees age 21 with one year of service be covered. However, three years of service can be required if employer contributions are immediately 100 percent vested (vesting is discussed later). Employees within five years of normal retirement age may be excluded in defined benefit plans (discussed later).

Among the common eligibility standards in pension plans is that employees be actively employed on a full-time basis. However, ERISA has eliminated many of the former restrictive participation requirements and has improved the status of part-time and seasonal employees and reemployed participants. Some plans require no probation period for eligibility, particularly collectively bargained plans.

Eligibility for benefits. Pension plans may specify a normal retirement age at which an employee is eligible for full benefits and a compulsory retirement age. Following the social security example, most plans designate age 65 for normal retirement. Because federal legislation in many cases prohibit compulsory retirement before age 70, that age (or one beyond) is set for compulsory retirement. In some industries or occupations where age 65 seems inappropriate, the normal retirement age may be lower. Flexibility in the retirement age is provided in some plans by allowing earlier retirement (e.g., age 55 or 60), usually at a reduced benefit and by allowing delayed retirement under certain conditions. If early retirement is at the employer's insistence, benefits are not reduced. For delayed retirements, employees may be entitled to an increased pension, but usually no additional pension credits accumulate beyond the normal retirement age.

Benefit levels. Pension benefits usually are of the conventional type providing fixed dollar payments. However, some plans incorporate the variable annuity principle under which each periodic payment is a function of the investment performance of the pension fund. Several types of benefit formulas are used. They establish either a defined benefit for the employee or a defined contribution from the employer (and sometimes from the employee). *Defined benefit formulas* are the flat amount, the flat percentage of earnings, the flat amount unit benefit (flat amount per year of service), and the percentage unit benefit (percentage of earnings per year of service). *Defined contribution formulas* are known as money-purchase formulas.

Under the *flat amount formula* all participants are given the same benefit regardless of earnings, age, and years of service. The flat amount formula is used in a number of negotiated plans. The *flat percentage formula* relates benefits to earnings but not years of service. Under the flat percentage formula a pension equal to a percentage of an employee's average annual wage is paid to all employees completing a minimum number of years of credited service. The formula provides no benefit increase for time worked in excess of the minimum. Employees who fail to meet the minimum service required are given a proportionately reduced pension. The exact percentage used and the average compensation to which the percentage applies vary widely among plans.

The *flat amount unit benefit formula* relates pension benefits to years of service but not to earnings. Under this plan the employee is given one unit of benefit per month for each year of credited service. The flat amount unit benefit formula is used in negotiated plans. The unit benefit formula may be used to relate benefits to years of service and earnings by using a percentage formula. Under the *percentage unit benefit plan,* the employee is given a percentage of earnings for each year of service.

When an established company installs a pension plan, many employees who have accumulated years of service will be on the payroll. These service years usually are rewarded at a lower rate than are service years after the plan is effective. The differential is justified by the higher cost of past service benefits. The cost is greater because interest and survivorship play a significant role in pension financing. No interest or survivorship benefits will be earned on unfunded past service benefits. Furthermore, in contributory plans, a differential between past service and current service is justified because past service benefits must be financed entirely by the employer.

The discrimination against past service may be only illusory if the benefit amount is to be based on the earnings in the year in which the unit is applied. The percent used to determine the amount of the past service benefit is applied to the employee's current earnings at the time the plan is installed, rather than to the amount earned while rendering the service. Because of normal increases in earnings over the years, the higher base will compensate to some extent for the lower rate.

Limitations may be placed on past service credits by ignoring some past service credits, counting only those earned beyond a specific age or eliminating the first years of past service. Some plans may grant no past service credit, handling the problem by placing a floor on the amount of pension benefits.

In some unit benefit formulas, a higher percentage is applied to annual earnings in excess of the amount covered by social security. Pension formulas that take into consideration benefits payable under social security are called integrated plans. Under IRS regulations two types of integrated plans are approved: the offset and the excess plan.

The *offset* plan provides that at retirement age the benefits otherwise provided to employees under the formula are reduced by a percentage of the employee's social security benefit. Thus, as social security benefits are increased, employees receive only a fraction of that increase because it offsets most of what the employer otherwise must pay. The offset plan is seldom used because of lack of employee appeal.

An *excess* plan covers employees only if their annual earnings exceed a given amount, usually the maximum wage base for social security when the plan is established or revised. The excess plan is the popular method of integrating private pension plans with social security. Special IRS rules must be followed in establishing benefit formulas under qualified integrated plans.

The earnings to which the percentage is applied in determining the pension amount may be the compensation earned during the year in which the benefit is accumulated (career average) or earnings during the last few years before retirement (final average). Because inflation has made career-average benefits inadequate, the final average earnings formula is more popular.

Under the flat amount, flat percentage, and unit benefit formulas, the benefits are determined in advance by fixed formulas. The projected cost fluctuates according to interest, mortality, expense, and employee turnover assumptions; funding methods used; employee population data; and, in many plans, trends in salary and wage scales and the ages at which employees choose to retire.

Some business firms are willing to give employees a pension only if the costs can be budgeted in advance and related to unit production cost. These firms use the *money-purchase formula*. Under this plan a percentage of the worker's pay (or a flat amount) is contributed by the employer and sometimes matched by the employee. The contributions may be based on the earnings in excess of a set amount. The retirement benefit is determined by how much the contributions will buy. The retirement annuity purchased with the same contribution each year will decrease as the employee grows older. (A deferred annuity at age 65 costs more per $10 of benefit when purchased at age 40 than when purchased at 35.) Higher contributions produced by increased earnings may to some degree offset the normal cost increase from advancing age. The employee, however, bears the risk of an increase in the insurer's annuity rate scale.

While the definite cost associated with the money-purchase plan appeals to the employer, the absence of a definite benefit formula is unattractive to employees, particularly those with a long past service record (contributions made for past service will not purchase comparable benefits at the employee's current age) and to employees who join the plan at advanced ages (contributions for them will be made for fewer years, and because of their advancing ages, these contributions purchase smaller and smaller benefits). To make the money-purchase plan more palatable to these employees, some employers apply the formula only to current service, handling past service by a unit benefit formula or a minimum benefit. For employees who enter the program at older ages, a higher percentage of earnings may be contributed than for those who enter when younger.

Some employers prefer to relate their contributions for employee retirement benefits to profits rather than to payroll, especially if profits fluctuate widely.[10] These plans are called *deferred profit-sharing* plans. How much of the company's profit will be used to finance retirement benefits will vary among companies. However, a qualified profit-sharing plan must meet the same participation, vesting, benefit, lump-sum distri-

---

[10] Qualification requirements under the IRS will not allow a deferred profit-sharing plan to handle adequately retirement needs of employees who are near retirement when the plan is installed. The amount of profits contributed to the plan cannot be allocated to employees on the basis of the participants' ages.

bution, fiduciary, and disclosure standards of qualified pension plans as outlined in the IRC and ERISA.

Some companies will have no formula, leaving the amount of the contribution to be determined by management on a year-to-year basis. The IRS, however, requires frequent and recurring contributions. Other companies will use a formula: a percentage of gross profits, a percentage of net profits, a percentage of the profits available after the payment of a minimum dividend on common stock, a percentage of the net profits available after deducting a fixed percentage of invested capital, or a graded percentage of net profits.[11] If the employee has to accept a deferred profit-sharing plan rather than a bona fide pension plan, at least a formula plan rather than a discretionary one should be installed. In some deferred profit-sharing plans, employees are required to contribute if they wish to participate.

The IRS requires a definite predetermined formula for allocating among the employees the profits apportioned to the fund. Allocation formulas usually consider earnings and service. A system of points may be used for each service year and each $100 of annual earnings.

The retirement benefit available is determined as in the money-purchase pension plan. A money-purchase group annuity can be used, under which single-premium deferred retirement annuities are purchased for eligible employees periodically or the funds may be accumulated and invested by an insurer or trustee. At retirement, the trustee or insurer can either pay the employee an actuarially determined income or purchase an immediate annuity.[12]

Regardless of the formula used to compute retirement benefits, pension experts agree that retirement income should be 70 to 75 percent of preretirement income. But if the benefit is fixed throughout retirement, the retired employee is exposed to loss of purchasing power and denied the opportunity to share in an increasing standard of living arising out of a growing economy. Variable pensions with cost-of-living adjustments are growing in popularity as labor and management accept the thesis that the economy has built-in inflationary biases and give consideration to solving the difficulties that inflation and growth create for persons living on pension incomes.

Annual retirement income benefits provided by *employer* contributions under a defined benefit plan are limited by ERISA and TEFRA to the smaller of (1) 100 percent of the participant's average compensa-

---

[11] IRS will not allow contributions in excess of 15 percent of the total compensation paid to participating employees to be deducted in one year. If the amount of the contribution in any year is less than, or greater than, this limit, a credit or contribution carry-over is allowed. The maximum credit carry-over that can be absorbed in one year is 10 percent, limiting the total amount deductible to 25 percent. However, the use of contribution carry-overs still is limited to the annual maximum of 15 percent of total compensation paid for the year.

[12] The funds may be used by the trustee when received to buy individual life insurance on participating employees but the insurance must be incidental and subordinate to retirement benefits. If not, the plan's tax advantages will be forfeited. Only part of the funds should be used to purchase the contracts so that some funds are retained to continue the premium payments in the years that the profit shares fall short of premium commitments.

tion for the three highest consecutive years, or (2) $90,000. For defined contribution plans, including profit sharing, the annual addition to a participant's account is limited to the *smaller* of (1) 25 percent of the participant's annual compensation or (2) $30,000. Inflationary changes in the dollar amounts are determined by a formula that modifies the social security inflation adjustment factor. The figures were originally set in 1975 at $75,000 and $25,000 respectively, then adjusted for inflation from 1976 through 1982 using the annual social security adjustment factors without modification. These factors, however, produced such high amounts ($136,425 and $45,475 respectively, by 1982) that Congress acted, as part of TEFRA, to reduce the amounts, to require a temporary freeze on automatic changes, and to develop a formula for the modification of the social security inflation factors for postfreeze adjustments. The new adjustment formula applies to post-1984 inflation, but may not be used for any plan year that starts before January 1, 1986.

The participant's "account addition" in a defined contribution plan includes the employer contribution, the lesser of one half of the employee contributions, or the amount of employee contributions in excess of 6 percent of the compensation and forfeitures added to the account for the year. (Forfeitures result from the allocation of survivor benefits to the employee's account and are derived from funds released from participants' termination by death or resignation.) If an employee participates in both a defined benefit and a defined contributions plan, total benefits are limited to the lesser of 125 percent (140 percent prior to the enactment of TEFRA) of the combined dollar limits, or 140 percent of the mandated maximum percentages for the two plans.

Types of benefits.   Although a qualified pension plan must be primarily for retirement benefits, other benefits may be included.

1.   Vesting.   A decision must be made on vesting provisions. If the plan is fully vested, a terminating employee retains the accumulated equity in the plan both from employer and employee contributions. An ERISA requirement is that a participant's rights to accrued benefits from employee contributions be nonforfeitable. In *defined contribution* plans, the employees must have a right to their contributions plus earnings on their account. In *defined benefit* plans, the employee is entitled to (1) mandatory employee contributions and (2) interest under the plan's rate before the effective vesting date and 5 percent thereafter.

For employer contributions, ERISA provides three minimum vesting standards: the 10-year rule, the graded 5–15, and the rule of 45. The 10-year rule grants employees full vesting after 10 years of service. The graded 5–15-year vesting standard requires 25 percent vesting after 5 years of service; then 5 percent a year, reaching 50 percent after 10 years of service; then 10 percent a year, arriving at 100 percent after 15 years of service. The rule of 45 requires 50 percent vesting after 10 years of service or when the employee's age plus service years equal 45, then 10 percent a year for 5 years, at which time 100 percent vesting is achieved. If the employee has 10 years of service, 50 percent vesting must be granted immediately regardless of the age-plus-service figure and increased 10 percent for each additional year thereafter.

The principal advantages to the employer of restricted vesting are (1) lower costs resulting from forfeiture of nonvested benefits when employees withdraw their contributions upon termination of employment and (2) the incentive that it offers for lower employee turnover. The employer must weigh these advantages against the social considerations that make liberal vesting desirable. An objective is to select the permissible vesting arrangement that would cause the least sacrifice of other employee benefits.

An employee's vested benefits from employer contributions may be forfeited if the employee dies (unless a joint and survivor option is in effect) or if the employee withdraws contributions from a contributory plan less than 50 percent vested. However, the employee may "buy back" and restore forfeited benefits by repaying the withdrawn contributions. The IRS may require more rapid vesting in plans to cure a pattern of employer abuse or prevent discrimination in favor of officers, shareholders, or executives. The IRS issued regulations that seemed to prevent many pension plans from using any of the three ERISA vesting rules. The IRS said that it would require a fourth standard—the 4–40 rule, under which a plan must be 40 percent vested for a participant after four years of service, 45 percent after five years, 50 percent after six years and then 10 percent additional for each of the next five years. The purpose of the regulation is to prevent "actual or potential discrimination" in favor of "highly compensated participants" against the "rank and file" participants. The IRS requires the 4–40 vesting rule to qualify plans that cannot pass the discrimination tests. Multiemployers can be exempt from the discrimination tests if these tests are "unduly burdensome." The vesting standards of ERISA are required for pension plan qualification with the IRS. In addition, most nonqualified plans also must adhere to the ERISA standards.

2. Death benefits. Under contributory plans, payments equal to the employee's nonforfeitable interest are made to the employee's beneficiary if the employee dies before retirement. Occasionally a *true death benefit* is provided in both contributory and noncontributory plans, but death benefits more commonly are arranged through group life insurance plans. When the pension is funded through individual life insurance policies, death payments usually are a fundamental part of the plan. According to ERISA requirements, pension plans must make available to married participants a joint and 50 percent survivorship annuity for the spouse. The annuity is optional for the participant who has attained the earliest retirement age under the plan. However, the payment plan is automatic for employees attaining normal retirement age unless a contrary election is made. The cost of this benefit is paid by the participant through a reduced pension.

3. Disability benefits. Long-term disability income benefits sometimes are included in pension plans, although many planners are reluctant to do so because these benefits increase pension costs and are difficult to administer. When disability benefits are included, safeguards are used to protect against adverse selection and faked claims. These safeguards include a long service eligibility period, a precise disability definition, low benefits, and periodic checkups following disability.

4. *Medical expenses.* Some pension plans provide medical expense benefits for *retired* employees, their spouses, and dependents. These plans incorporate provisions for accumulating funds for medical benefits for retired employees. Such funds are used to pay medical expenses up to the amounts specified in the plan or to pay premiums on behalf of retired employees for group health insurance or voluntary supplementary medical insurance available under Medicare. The payment of these expenses from qualified pension funds is not treated as taxable income to the participant, an additional tax advantage of qualified plans.

Funding the benefits. Management must decide if the funding agency is to be a trust company (e.g., bank) or an insurance company. If insurance is used, a choice of various funding instruments is available, each having its special use.

If the pension group is large enough, a trust fund plan can be used. The factors considered in choosing between insured and trust fund plans are the: (1) degree of freedom desired in investment decisions, (2) plan administration cost, (3) importance of the insurer's services in administering benefits to widely scattered retired employees, (4) importance of investment guarantees, (5) importance of mortality guarantees, (6) freedom desired in actuarial assumptions and funding method, (7) concern about fiduciary liability under ERISA, and (8) freedom desired in benefit design. All these factors should be considered not only in choosing between an insured and a trust fund plan but also in choosing among the several types of insured plans.

It is possible to have the advantages (and disadvantages) of both insured and trust fund plans by use of the split-funding approach. As the name implies, split-funding involves the use of both a trust fund and an insurer with the pension funds divided.

Plan termination insurance. Plan termination insurance (PTI) guarantees qualified defined benefit pensions up to a specified amount despite inadequate funding. The Pension Benefit Guaranty Corporation (PBGC), operating within the U.S. Labor Department, administers PTI, collects the premiums from employers, and guarantees payment of covered nonforfeitable benefits. All benefits under a plan or plan amendment in effect for five years at termination are covered. If the plan has fewer than five years of operation, the benefits covered are the larger of 20 percent of the benefit or $20 per month times the number of years the plan was in effect. The limitation on monthly benefits guaranteed is the smaller of 100 percent of the participant's average monthly income during the five-consecutive-year period of highest income or $750, adjusted by the ratio that the social security wage base in effect at termination bears to the 1974 wage base of $13,200 (this $750 became $2,199 in 1985). The original first-year premium was $1 per participant in a single-employer plan and 50 cents per participant in a multiemployer plan. The premium for single-employer plans was increased to $2.60 as over 18,000 insured plans were terminated during the first four years of the PBGC's existence. The PBGC has requested Congress to authorize a further increase to $6.00. Whether the $6.00 figure or some formula-based amount (also requested by the PBGC) will be adopted is subject to speculation. However, rates appear certain to rise in the wake of plan terminations such as that of Braniff Airlines with over 9,000 covered employees and an estimated $50 million in unfunded pension liabilities. The employer is held liable for 100 percent of the underfunding up to 30 percent of its net worth. The PBGC has a lien against the employer's assets for this amount. However, the PBGC must provide insurance for coverage of the employer's 30 percent residual liability, but such coverage will not be effective until premiums are paid for five years.

Fiduciary responsibilities.   Under ERISA a plan must designate a fiduciary to administer its operation. Persons exercising discretionary authority or management control over the plan or its assets are fiduciaries, regardless of their formal titles. Fiduciaries are responsible for compliance with the laws and must use the "care, skill, prudence, and diligence . . . [of] a prudent. . . [person] acting in a like capacity. . . for the purpose of providing benefits to participants and beneficiaries and defraying reasonable plan administrative expenses." Furthermore, fiduciaries have the responsibility to diversify assets and refrain from "prohibited transactions" such as conflict of interest situations. The U.S. Department of Labor is charged with interpreting regulations, and fiduciaries are held personally liable if these regulations are violated. Fiduciary liability insurance is discussed in Chapter 13.

Disclosure.   Plan administrators must file annual reports with the Department of Labor and with participants and beneficiaries. Annual reporting to the IRS also is required. Furthermore, the plan administrators must file with the secretary of labor and furnish participants a plan description initially and at least every five years thereafter, plan amendments, annual financial report, any plans for termination, and a statement of active participants' rights. The plan administrators also must allow inspection of the complete annual report on request.

Individual retirement account.   An individual may set up a retirement savings program, known as an Individual Retirement Account (IRA). The funds may be invested in a trusteed account, custodial account, annuity contract, or qualified retirement bond. The maximum deductible contribution is $2,000. Furthermore, if a terminating employee's plan permits, the vested amount from employer contributions may be transferred into an IRA. This transfer is called a tax-free rollover to IRA because if the transfer is complete within 60 days after the funds are available, no income tax is payable on the transfer. Furthermore, tax deductions are allowed for contributions made for the nonworking spouse of an employee eligible for an IRA. An additional $250 is allowed for a spousal IRA, increasing the maximum to $2,250, but that amount still may not exceed 100 percent of the earned income of the working spouse.

Simplified employee pensions. Prior to 1984 employers were allowed to contribute the lesser of $15,000 ($7,500 before 1982) or 15 percent of compensation to an employee's IRA. Restrictions on this plan, called a simplified employee pension (SEP), were liberalized for 1984 to allow increased employer contributions. Under the new provisions, the employer can contribute the lesser of $30,000 or 25 percent of the employee's compensation. However, unlike non-SEP IRA-funded plans, SEPs are not allowed to discriminate with respect to either participation or contribution amounts. The more liberal contribution limits bring SEPs in line with new limits for Keogh plans.

Self-employment (Keogh) retirement plan. Self-employed persons are allowed by the IRC to cover themselves for retirement plans under a pension or profit-sharing arrangement, subject to special rules relating to coverage of their employees. The maximum annual deductions under an approved "Keogh" plan are the lesser of $30,000 or 25 percent of compensation for defined contribution plans, and the lesser of the amount required to fund $90,000 of annual retirement income or 100 percent of the employee's average income over the three highest income years for defined benefit plans. After 1986 the dollar amounts of these limitations will be allowed to increase on the same basis as the qualified pension plans discussed earlier. When a self-employed person with employees establishes a Keogh plan, those employees who meet the minimum eligibility requirements must be included. Numerous restrictions and limitations applicable to Keogh plans prior to 1984 were repealed by TEFRA. The trend toward higher limits for SEPs and Keogh plans represents a congressional effort to treat them on a more equitable basis with the qualified pension programs.

Group Property and Liability Insurance

Group property liability insurance as an employee benefit is receiving attention by both insurers and insureds. A relatively small but growing percentage of homeowners and personal auto insurance is written on a group basis. When the major obstacles to writing group property liability insurance are overcome, this coverage can be expected to grow considerably. These major obstacles have been opposition from independent insurance agents and restrictive state regulation.

Attitudes and objectives

A management consultant firm hired by the National Association of Insurance Agents told independent agents to "accept the reality of group plans and their probable growth," and that "a negative attitude will not work toward their best long-term interest." The objective of group property insurance is to give quality insurance at the lowest possible rate by reducing distribution and administration costs. This reduction is accomplished primarily by a reduction in, or elimination of, agents' commissions and reduced cost of administrative overhead. One insurer writing group-rated insurance in Michigan has reduced auto insurance cost to group members by more than 15 percent. The National Educational Association offers group homeowners insurance to its members at a substantially lower rate than that of individual policies. Other advantages claimed for group property liability insurance are better service to policyowners, greater potential for innovation, increased opportunity for loss prevention activity, payroll deduction convenience, and ease of integration with other employee benefits.

Limitations

Some agents say that considerable structural change would be necessary in insurance for the extension of group principles to property liability coverages. They argue that extensive writing of group property liability insurance would lead to scrapping the agency system. Sufficient commission dollars would not be available to pay for services presently demanded of agents. Loss adjustment expenses would mount, and to retain the group, insurers might resort to lax claims administration, eventually leading to higher premiums. Other arguments offered are that group property liability insurance adversely affects small insurers, restricts the market for nongroup members, reduces coverage flexibility, and undermines the credibility of statistics for nongroup members. In the early days of group life insurance dire results were predicted for that industry by those who stood to lose by the growth of the group marketing concept. But the life insurance industry and its agents have survived. However, the personal lines property liability agent may not fare as well as his life insurance counterpart. The market for auto and Homeowners insurance is finite. That is, an individual's total needs for these coverages can be satisfied with group insurance. Yet an individual's need for life insurance is rarely fulfilled with group life insurance alone. Thus, while expansion of the group marketing concept can adversely affect the personal lines property liability agent, nothing suggests that the industry would be severely hurt. The insurance must be provided, regardless of the marketing technique used for its distributin.

The legal climate

Antidiscrimination laws and fictitious grouping laws have been the primary legislative blocks to group property liability underwriting. Both laws have been administered and enforced much more stringently for group property liability insurance than for group life and health insurance. Under the "fictitious group" law, groups formed primarily to buy insurance may not be underwritten for fear of the resulting adverse selection. Curiously, this law has been used to deny an employer the right to purchase group property liability insurance for employees. The antidiscriminatory law requires insurance rates to be the same for individuals with identical rating characteristics. However, in writing group life and health insurance, the question of rate discrimination is not an issue. The social value of group life and health coverages has been recognized. The fundamental question is whether group property liability insurance also has a social value.

The regulatory climate has improved considerably for the mass merchandising of group property liability insurance as states have repealed "fictitious group" laws and regulations. The result is that most states now permit mass merchandising of group property liability insurance. Nevertheless, laws and regulations still create a problem for writing true group property liability insurance. *True group* means group underwriting rather than underwriting individuals within a group.

Underwriting true group property liability insurance either is illegal under state law, not permitted by state insurance commissioners, or discouraged by commissioners. An increasing number of exceptions are noted.

The icebreaking example came in 1968 when the Michigan Insurance Bureau approved a true group property liability plan for autos and the Michigan attorney general did not challenge its legality. The group is rated, and all participating employees pay the same premium for the same protection regardless of age, sex, residence, or auto. Dividends are returned to the group, based on experience rating. In the specific plan approved, both the employer and employee contribute. The employer is issued a master policy, and "certificates of participation" are given to covered employees. However, unlike group life and health insurance, an employee with a bad driving record may be segregated for special treatment.

A survey of union representatives indicated they believed property liability insurance was a fringe benefit to be considered for members but did not assign it a high priority. Nevertheless, some small unions have negotiated successfully for auto coverage. Some observers believe that as more states pass modified no-fault auto accident reparations laws or mandatory first-party auto accident insurance laws, group auto insurance will be a logical fringe benefit for employees. If employers do not pay a part of the premium, this coverage would have little appeal to some buyers, because even with true group rates premiums may be in excess of those charged by some auto insurers with strict underwriting standards. Income tax treatment similar to that given group life and health insurance would stimulate the growth of group property liability insurance as an employee benefit.

Prepaid Legal Insurance

Prepaid legal service insurance plans provide group members coverage for legal fees up to specified maximums. Five phases of legal work are covered: civil, criminal, clerical, counseling, and preventive law (e.g., annual legal checkup). Prepaid legal service plans first developed in the early 1900s, but have only recently gained popularity. A number of plans now in operation are offered by various groups, including labor unions, consumer groups, teacher associations, credit unions, bar associations, private firms, and insurers. Among other considerations (insurer efficiency, profit goals, and so on), the cost of coverage is a function of the benefits offered. However, much of the insurance activity remains in the infancy stages.

About 5 million workers and dependents are covered by prepaid legal plans providing legal services for an average cost of about $120 a year per covered worker. The plans have been less popular than expected due primarily to the increased cost of other employee benefit programs, notably the cost of group health insurance. Also no one aggressively markets these plans. If large insurers become interested in full-blown plans and seek to market them, they may increase in numbers. Several such insurers are attempting to sell these full-scale plans in California. In the meantime a minilegal service plan called Advice and Referral is growing rapidly. These plans provide consultation and limited follow-up such as an attorney's letter. The law firm bills the employee for any additional work on an hourly basis. These plans cost about $20 per year.

Regulation

As to whether prepaid legal expense plans are considered insurance, courts have expressed different opinions arising from conflicting views about (1) the principle of indemnity, (2) the transfer of risk, and (3) fortuitous events. The end result has been that some states permit insurers to write prepaid legal expense plans, but only on an individual basis. Other states do not allow prepaid legal insurance, whereas still other states allow insurers to write the coverage on both an individual and a group basis. Contributions by employers to qualified legal expense plans are deductible as a business expense without requiring employees to report as taxable income either these contributions or the value of the legal service provided. The tax advantage applies to employer contribution on behalf of employees, their spouses, and their dependents. For a plan to qualify: (1) the plan must be written separately from other employee benefit plans, (2) the plan must be initiated by an employer, (3) the plan must be for the exclusive benefit of employees, their spouses, or dependents, (4) benefits must be specified, (5) the benefits must provide for personal legal services only, (6) legal fees must be prepaid in whole or in part by the employer, and (7) the plan must be administered by a tax-exempt organization. (Any organization or trust whose exclusive function is to administer qualified legal-expense plans is treated as a tax-exempt organization.)

Prepaid legal expense plans are subject to federal regulation under ERISA. ERISA preempts state laws and provides the fiduciary standards and the reporting and filing requirements. State regulators would prefer to have plans file informational statements with them. Some states exempt qualified plans under ERISA from filing, but other states ask for a duplicate copy of the plan's ERISA filing. Federal control began with a 1973 amendment to the Taft-Hartley Act making legal services an employee benefit subject to collective bargaining, with the employer sharing the cost.

However, legal benefits cannot be used to bring a legal action against an employer or labor organization or to aid labor unions in proceedings barred by the Labor-Management Reporting and Disclosure Act of 1959. The Welfare and Pension Plans Disclosure Act was revised by ERISA to include prepaid legal services as an employee benefit. This legislation further extended federal control into the legal benefits area.

While the rationale for prepaid legal service plans is to help middle-income persons (the poor receive free legal aid, and the wealthy can afford to pay), the profit motive is the primary incentive. Legal insurance offers an additional source of income to insurers and a solution to the exploding lawyer population. Many persons question the need for legal insurance. One professor calls prepaid legal service plans the "most overstudied nonevent of our time."

Summary

1. Protection against income loss brought on by premature death, disability or old-age retirement is handled in the United States by three methods: individual, social, and group insurance. Group insurance is life, health, or retirement income insurance usually issued to a group without medical examination under a master policy.
2. Group is distinguished from individual insurance as follows:
   a. More than one person is insured under a group master policy.
   b. Employers generally share in a group plan's cost.
   c. Individual members usually have no choice as to group benefit levels.
   d. Group sales commissions are lower than those for individual policies.
   e. Employers handle much of the administrative work in group insurance.
   f. Group administrative costs generally are lower.
   g. Group insurance provides special tax advantages to the employer and employees.
3. The group most often will be employees of a particular employer, but policies are written on other groups such as labor unions and creditor groups. However, the group must have some common purpose other than that of obtaining insurance.
4. As medical examinations usually are not required, adverse selection against the insurer or group is avoided by requiring a large participation percentage in the program by the group. Furthermore, the protection amount granted is decided by means beyond the workers'

control to prevent those in poor health from obtaining unusually large insurance amounts. In addition, when the group qualifies for experience rating, such rating may encourage the group to avoid excessive adverse selection (other and more compelling reasons exist for insurers to use experience rating; for example, to meet competition from self-insurers and other insurers).

5. Group life insurance was the first standardized group coverage. Most group life insurance is written on a yearly renewable term basis. The protection is virtually identical with that provided by individual term insurance. Upon employment termination an employee can convert the group policy to any type of permanent insurance without evidence of insurability.

6. Group credit insurance is used by creditors to cover lives of unsecured debtors. The policy cost usually is considered part of the debtor's loan cost. Reverse competition in group credit insurance means high cost to the borrower and high profits to the lender.

7. The group insurance cost often is substantially below that of similar protection purchased on an individual basis because acquisition costs are lower and the employer does much of the administrative work. Many group plans are noncontributory, and in the contributory plans the employee's premium generally is limited to 50 or 60 cents a month per $1,000 of coverage, which is usually a favorable rate except for employees under age, say, 48.

8. Group health coverage most often provides benefits for accidental death and dismemberment, hospital expenses, and surgical fees. Also included may be disability income, nursing home care, major medical, dental care, out-of-hospital drugs, vision care, and psychiatric care. Group health insurance cost is less than the cost of similar protection obtained through individual policies, for the same reasons that group life insurance is less expensive.

9. Three primary reasons for employee benefit plans are to improve industrial relations, meet union demands, and satisfy the employers' desires to provide their own personal life and health insurance and retirement needs at low cost.

10. The Employee Retirement Income Security Act of 1974 (ERISA), the Tax Equity and Fiscal Responsibility Act (TEFRA), the IRC, and the IRS prescribe standards for funding, participation, vesting, plan termination, disclosure, fiduciary responsibility, and tax treatment for pension and profit-sharing plans.

11. Insured pension plans are administered by insurers and trust fund plans are administered by banks or other reliable institutions or persons, known as trustees.

12. Although primarily for retirement benefits, pension plans may include other benefits consisting of spouses' pensions, medical coverage for retired employees, disability coverage, and incidental life insurance.

13. In designing employee benefit plans, several decisions must be made:

a. The appropriate benefits offered in terms of union demands and employers' finances.

b. The financing method.

c. Eligibility standards.

d. Benefit structure.

e. Funding agency.

f. Funding instruments.

14. Various criteria and standards are established for qualifying a pension plan and are designed to protect the interest of employee participants and eliminate unreasonable discrimination in favor of higher paid employees and owners.

15. Under group property and liability insurance the individual rather than the group often is the underwriting unit. It appears that increased union interest and the passage of more auto reparation reform laws may lead to a substantial growth of true group property liability insurance as states improve the regulatory climate.

16. Prepaid legal service insurance plans offer group coverage for legal fees primarily in five legal areas: civil, criminal, clerical, counseling, and preventive law.

Questions for Review

1. Explain why group life and health insurance costs less than insurance sold on an individual policy basis. Do individuals in a group plan have a choice as to the amount of coverage they may buy? Why or why not?

2. Would an employee's group health insurance coverage likely cover on-the-job accidents? Should on-the-job coverage be offered under group health coverage? Explain.

3. Certain insurance coverages previously unavailable have been included in group insurance plans. Explain the nature of the coverages and suggest reasons for their introduction and development.

4. What factors distinguish group insurance from individual coverage? Which distinguishing factors are necessary to make the group insurance principle effective? Which are necessary for administrative reasons? Explain.

5. Explain the various group life coverages offered by insurers. Are these coverage needs more adequately fulfilled under group insurance than under individual policies? Explain.

6. How does group health insurance differ from individual coverage? Give the reasons for these differences.

7. What effect has the Employee Retirement Income Security Act (ERISA) had on employee pension and profit-sharing plans with respect to plan design and administration?

8. What criteria and standards are necessary for qualifying a pension plan under the IRC? What advantages are offered qualified plans? Explain.

9. Explain the three minimum vesting alternatives permitted by ERISA. What advantages are offered by each vesting provision? What objectives should

be considered in selecting among these alternatives? Does the IRS have any jurisdiction over vesting requirements? Explain.

10. Explain the funding requirements under ERISA. Do they offer any flexibility? Explain.

11. What are the advantages and disadvantages of fully funding and fully vesting pension plans? Distinguish between allocated or unallocated funding instruments. Which type of funding instrument is likely to be used by trust fund plans? Explain.

12. What is the objective of prepaid legal insurance? What is the federal government's role in the development of these plans? Do the state governments have a role? Discuss. What other groups are involved? Why?

13. What accounts for the wide disparity between the amount of group life and health insurance and the amount of group property liability insurance written? Explain.

14. Explain the benefits offered under IRA plans. Who are eligible for these plans and for how much? What benefits are offered under the Keogh plan? Who are eligible and for how much?

15. Explain the importance of proper actuarial assumptions in valuing pension liabilities. What is the importance of reasonable valuation standards for pension fund assets?

Questions for Discussion

1. Although group life and health insurance is widely written, group auto insurance has been offered only to a small number of employees. Why? Do you anticipate change? Why or why not?

2. Employers' contributions are necessary for the successful operation of a group life insurance program as an employee benefit plan. Employers' contributions are not needed for the successful operation of a group health employee benefit plan. Explain why you agree or disagree with these two statements.

3. In programming life and health insurance, should group life and health be given the same consideration as individual policies?

4. Some critics of the life insurance industry feel more price competition exists in group life than in individual life insurance. Is this observation true? Why or why not? If not, should it be true? Explain.

5. Group life and health insurance plans, as well as pension plans, often are regarded as fringe benefits. Does this mean they are employer gratuities rather than earned wages? If they are regarded as earned, what implications does this have for employees who are on strike? Do employers expect any benefits from granting employee benefit plans? If so, why are they not also called employer benefit plans? Explain.

6. What developments in the past 100 years have contributed to the increased need for retirement plans?

7. Group dental and vision care insurance has increased in popularity. Do you believe these coverages are true insurance or simply another employee fringe benefit? Can they be justified even though you conclude that they are not true insurance?

8. Some persons believe that ERISA discourages many employers from instituting any retirement plan and continuing existing plans. Do you agree with these ERISA doubters? Explain.

9. Would an employee benefit plan fully serve its purpose without ERISA's requirement of plan termination insurance? Why or why not?

10. Group property liability insurance has been a subject of strict regulation. Do you believe this regulation is in the public interest? What changes do you believe are necessary in group property liability insurance regulation?

11. Do you believe that group legal insurance is for the benefit of insureds, insurers, lawyers, or a combination of the three? If you believe the benefit primarily is for other than the insureds, do you believe this benefit is necessarily contrary to the public interest? Explain.

12. Do you believe the U.S. government has moved far enough, too far, or not far enough in its pension laws? Explain.

13. Why is it so difficult to determine the adequacy of the funding of a pension plan? Can you suggest a way to make it less difficult? Explain.

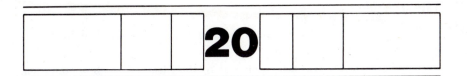

20

Social insurance

The government insures more persons than do private insurers. Broad governmental schemes to provide income for old age, unemployment, death, and disability and to pay the cost of medical care are called *social insurance*.

The Nature of a Social Insurance System

Broadly conceived, social insurance covers social risks, which are whatever a particular society views them to be at a given time. Whether the burden of medical care is a social risk has been debated in the United States for years. Now it is accepted as one for the aged and for the long-term disabled who meet specified criteria discussed later, and eventually may be treated as a social risk for everyone. Replacement of some liability exposures in part or in full with no-fault laws expands the number of risks which society considers to be social risks. Thus social risks change over time.

Definition of social insurance

The Commission of Insurance Terminology has defined social insurance as follows:

> A device for the pooling of risks by their transfer to an organization, usually governmental, that is required by law to provide pecuniary or service benefits to or on behalf of covered persons upon the occurrence of certain predesignated losses under all of the following conditions: 1. Coverage is compulsory by law in virtually all instances; 2. Eligibility for benefits is derived, in fact or in effect, from contributions having been made to the program by or in respect of the claimant or the person as to whom the claimant is a dependent; there is no requirement that the individual demonstrate inadequate financial resources, although a dependency status may need to be established; 3. The method for determining the benefits is prescribed by law; 4. The benefits for any individual are not usually directly related to contributions made by or in respect of him [or her] but instead usually redistribute income so as to favor certain groups such as those with low former wages or a large number of dependents; 5. There is a definite plan for financing the benefits that is designed to be adequate in terms of long-range considerations; 6. The cost is borne primarily by contributions which are usually made by covered persons, their employers, or both; 7. The plan is administered or at least supervised by the government; 8. The plan is not established by the government solely for its present or former employees.

The following discussion suggests that the social security system may violate the foregoing definition in several respects.

Kinds of social insurance in the United States

Social insurance in the United States includes the federal social security system with its old-age, survivors', disability, and health care coverages and the state systems of unemployment compensation, workers' compensation, and temporary disability plans. (Workers' compensation is discussed in Chapter 13.) Other forms of insurance are available under government auspices. These include crop, war damage (including aircraft), flood, auto accident (Puerto Rico), life (Wisconsin), and crime insurance. Also written are various government reinsurance plans. Several government-sponsored plans are discussed in Chapters 11, 15, and 22.

The Need for Social Insurance

Why are social insurance programs regarded as a government obligation? The reasons are discussed under three headings: economic changes, increasing age of the population, and social change.

Economic changes

In earlier cultures society saw no need for social insurance. Most people were self-employed. Individuals hunted food for themselves and their families. Unemployment and laziness were synonymous. Anyone wishing to follow usual economic pursuits could do so. Among many primitive peoples, the economic problem of old age presented no difficulties. The perils of the jungle, as well as those of disease, resulted in a low rate of longevity. The typical child at birth could expect a short lifetime. A few hardy ones might survive to an age when they could no longer provide for themselves. In the earliest cultures, the individual would starve to death upon reaching an age beyond self-sufficiency, unless some charitable friend or relative was willing to assume the burden of care. Some tribes are reputed to have solved the problem by killing the aged.

During the Middle Ages problems of unemployment and dependent old age did not exist. In the secular world, the lord of the manor provided the necessities of life for the serfs in return for their full-time services. In old age, tasks suited to a person's declining productive powers were found. The church made similar provisions for its clergy. However, as towns expanded, difficulties arose. Serfs found ways to leave their bondage, work for themselves, and retain the profits. This new freedom brought the responsibility for persons to support themselves, the significance of which was not felt for centuries. As long as agricultural pursuits and handicrafts were the principal occupations, the problems of unemployment or old-age dependency were only slightly more important than during prehistoric times. Families or guilds were tightly knit economic units. The sick and old were cared for by the family. As long as self-contained economic groups remained, economic problems of unemployment and old age were in the background.

With the factory system, the Industrial Revolution, and the end of the family as the principal economic unit, the problem of unemployment became serious. The family no longer produced sufficient goods for self-maintenance. Workers, producing articles belonging to factory owners, traded money wages for goods and services to meet their families' economic needs. Eventually nearly every member of society received a money wage for performing a particular task. Workers became divorced from their products.

This economic development has been of critical importance in world economic growth, but at the cost of exposing workers to the mercy of changes in the nature and growth of economic activity, making them what may be termed "wage slaves" and victims of the business cycle. Until the end of the 19th century, an unemployed worker and family in the United States could go west and homestead a plot of government land. The frontier offered an economic safety valve for the unemployed. Now, even that opportunity is denied, making other ways of dealing with the unemployed necessary.

Increasing age of the population

Along with the end of the family as a self-supporting economic unit has come the additional problem of increased numbers of persons reaching old age. The United States at one time had a young population. In those days the percentage of the population more than 65 years old was about 1 percent. By 1870, 1.7 percent was over 65, and by 1980 the figure increased to about 11 percent. Between 1900 and 1980, the U.S. population nearly tripled, but persons over age 65 increased more than eightfold.

Much of the higher percentage of old people is due to a long-term declining birthrate. The number of births per thousand of population during the early days of the Republic was about 55, whereas in recent years that figure declined to about 15. Economic pressures requiring two-career families, the rising career orientation among women, and ecological concerns over population problems may continue to depress the birthrate. Improvements in medical science also have influenced the increased number of old people. Although the maximum life span has not lengthened significantly, more people are living to become old. Life expectancy at birth for males has increased from 46 years in 1900 to 70.3 years today. The life expectancy for females is 77.9 years. The chance of a typical male college sophomore in 1900 of reaching age 65 was 1 in 2; today the sophomore is a 3-to-1 favorite. Upon reaching age 65 in 1900 a man had a life expectancy of 11.5 years; today the man would have a life expectancy of 14.3 years, a woman 18.7 years. Actuaries expect mortality experience to continue to improve.

Social change

As a result of economic change and the increase in the number of the elderly, changes have occurred in society that make old-age problems more acute. The social unity of the family has changed. Aged parents who could participate in the economic life of the family used to be a welcome adjunct. Today, however, the aged have few ways to contribute economically to the family, and thus have become an unwelcome burden. As a young man in George Ade's *Fables in Slang* muses about his father: "Here is an Ancient Party without any Assets, who lives with me Week in and Week out and doesn't pay any board. He is getting too Old and Wobbly to do Odd Jobs around the Place, and it looks to me like an awful Imposition."

Even the performance of domestic tasks by an older woman no longer is as welcome as in the past. The changes in modern living require less from the homemaker than before. At one time a grandmother would be welcome in the home to help with laundry, cooking, housecleaning, and child care. These tasks have been so reduced by modern appliances, convenient precooked frozen dinners (frequently more tasty than grandmother could prepare), attractive easy-to-care-for modern living quarters, and widespread government-sponsored day-care centers as to render grandmother technically obsolete. Rather than a welcome guest, she has become a burden.

In former days, two people reaching age 65 might have a family of 4 to 10 children who could pool resources to provide a comfortable old age for their parents, without undue hardship falling on one child. With decreased family size, however, parents are likely to have only two children to help them. Even a *willing* only child has difficulty providing adequate support both for parents and a young family.

Another factor adding to old-age distress has been the common acceptance of retirement at age 65. The findings of current surveys suggest that the recent federal legislation prohibiting mandatory retirement for most workers, prior to age 70 is destroying the magic of 65 as the retirement age, thus decreasing the cost of providing retirement income benefits. Even so, most private pension plans do not provide adequate protection against the high level of inflation that this country has experienced in recent years. More flexible retirement programs, including options for continued part-time or less demanding work for older employees, not only would help to alleviate old-age support but also relieve the mental anguish caused by depriving an older person of an active work life.

Social insurance operates where compulsory coverage seems to be the only way of extending protection to large segments of the population. Experience has shown that without governmental assistance much of the population will not, or cannot, provide financial protection for themselves and their families for old age, death, disability, and unemployment. This observation also has become apparent at a time when more and more people view old-age support, medical payments, unemployment compensation, and disability payments as the responsibility of the government rather than the individual. Many Americans no longer view the function of government as solely that of providing a stable environment for the operation of individual initiative, but instead view the government function also as one of direct responsibility for the financial security and happiness of all Americans. This attitude, along with the political popularity of governmental assistance programs, has resulted in their expansion until many observers are questioning whether the benefits of such social programs justify the costs.

This chapter discusses old-age, survivors, disability, and health insurance; unemployment compensation; temporary disability income benefit plans; and national health insurance proposals.

Old-Age, Survivors, Disability and Health Insurance (OASDHI)

Many private corporations provide retirement income, disability income, survivorship payments, and medical care benefits for workers and their families (Chapter 19). Annuities for federal civil service workers were provided by a congressional act in 1920, and annuities are granted to qualified retired members of the armed forces. Railroad employees are insured under the Railroad Retirement Act, and many states and political subdivisions have provided annuity plans for employees. Recent estimates show more than 50 million people covered by private pensions, 1.4 million by the Railroad Retirement Act, and more than 19 million by federal, state, and local government plans.

Under the Social Security Act, benefits may be classified as either public assistance or social insurance. Public assistance benefits are disbursed on the basis of need; insurance payments are made to those entitled to them, regardless of need. About 36 million receive monthly benefits and about 116 million work in covered employment in a typical year. Over 15 million people are receiving public assistance cash payments.

Public assistance programs

The Social Security Act of 1935 encouraged a system of state plans for assistance to the needy aged (OAA). The states were permitted wide freedom in formulating plans within limits of certain broad principles. These principles required that the program be statewide and that the state consider other income of an old person. The state was required to participate financially in the program (so it could not require all money to be furnished by local governments), although the exact amount of participation was not specified in the act.

Under the 1935 act, the federal government agreed to pay a subsidy to each qualifying state equal to one half the amount given to each needy person over age 65. A maximum of $15 per month of federal funds per recipient was paid. The federal government also agreed to give the state an additional amount equal to 5 percent of this subsidy for administrative costs. The maximum dollar amount of federal participation was increased several times by Congress.

The initial assistance programs included aid not only to the aged but also to families with dependent children (AFDC) and to the blind (AB). In 1950 aid to the permanently and totally disabled (APTD) was added. In 1960 amendments to the Social Security Act provided federal matching funds for states to improve medical care programs for aged persons receiving old-age assistance, and to provide funds for other aged persons unable to pay for medical care.

The 1972 amendments to the Social Security Act established the Supplemental Security Income program (SSI) to replace federal grants to states for care of the aged, blind, and permanently and totally disabled. The program is administered by the Social Security Administration and financed by general revenues of the U.S. Treasury. The states are allowed to supplement federal payments if they wish. The SSI program established basic benefit standards for eligible aged, blind, and disabled persons. The eligibility of applicants is based upon need rather than contributions. The extent of state supplementary payments differs widely. States may administer supplementary payments themselves or allow the Social Security Administration to administer them, thus shifting these costs to the federal government.

The theory behind the SSI program is to provide a benefit program with national uniformity as to eligibility standards and benefit levels. The previously existing state programs of OAA, AB, and APTD varied greatly. The average benefit levels had been $83 per month nationwide. Individual state averages, however, ranged from $56 to $121 per month.

Title XIX of the Social Security Act created a separate medical assistance program (Medicaid) in 1965, which replaced all other medical assistance programs in 1970. Payments are made direct to the vendors of the service (hospitals, physicians, and druggists, for example). Under this program, as a minimum states must cover inpatient and outpatient hospital care, skilled nursing home care, laboratory and X-ray services, and physicians' services. However, most states go beyond the minimum requirement and cover dental care, prescription drugs, eyeglasses, and prosthetic devices. The public assistance programs (SSI, Medicaid, and state supplemental payments) are not insurance programs. They are not based upon contributions, but rather are payments based upon need.

The insurance coverage

In contrast to the assistance program, the federal Old-Age, Survivors, Disability, and Health Insurance program (OASDHI) establishes a system of social insurance administered by the federal government. Benefits are determined on the basis of earnings and are financed by a tax on wages, levied on each insured worker and employer. For 1984 the first $37,800 of each individual's annual wage was subject to the tax. The maximum annual taxable wage is subject to automatic increases based on increases in nationwide average wages. The life expectancy of social security tax schedules is extremely short. The tax rate in 1984 was 6.7 percent from employees and 7 percent from employers. For the self-employed, the rate was 14 percent. Rates are scheduled to be raised gradually until 1990, when they will be 7.65 percent for employees and employers alike, and 15.30 percent for the self-employed. These contribution rates are those set by the 1983 act. Who knows what they will be in years to come or even before this text is released? Up-to-date information on social security might be found by telephoning the local social security office, assuming a knowledgeable person answers the phone. The system is nationwide and in nearly all instances is compulsory. Although defined by law rather than contract, the coverage can be analyzed using the techniques developed in Chapters 7 through 9. The reader is advised to check the law for current coverage and amounts—a difficult assignment for most people. This analysis is based on the law in effect in mid-1984.

Perils. The perils covered are death, injury, sickness, and old-age dependency.

Losses. Losses covered are earned income and cost of medical care for the aged. When the insured reaches age 70, the loss covered is the *presumed* loss of earned income, as no reduction is made for income earned after that age.

Persons covered. Coverage is provided for insured workers and their dependents. Nearly every worker (more than 90 percent of all employed persons) in the United States is covered, except some governmental employees; college students working for sororities, fraternities, the college or a college club; some members of religious orders who have taken vows of poverty; student nurses; inmates of penal institutions; newspaper carriers under age 18; individuals employed by their spouses; and minors employed by their parents. The Social Security Amendments of 1983 brought all newly hired federal employees under OASDHI, leaving only those hired prior to January 1, 1984 with their own retirement program. This amendment also includes coverage of employees of charitable, religious, or educational nonprofit organizations on a compulsory basis. Many state and local government employees are covered by the act through agreement entered into by the state with the secretary of health, education, and welfare. Members of the armed forces became covered in 1957.

The social security system provides three types of insured status: fully insured, currently insured, and disability. The insured status of the worker determines those benefits for which the worker is eligible, as shown in Table 20–1.

To be *fully insured,* workers must have one of the following: (1) a minimum of 6 quarters of coverage with one quarter of coverage for each calendar year elapsing *after* 1950 (or the quarter in which they

TABLE 20–1
Types of cash benefits

Retirement	
Monthly payments to	If worker is
Worker and spouse and/or child*	Fully insured.
Survivors	
Monthly payments to	If at death worker is
Widow or widower 60 or over or disabled widow or widower 50–59*	Fully insured.
Widow or widower (regardless of age) if caring for child under 18 or disabled and entitled to benefits*	Either fully or currently insured.
Dependent child	Either fully or currently insured.
Dependent parent at 62	Fully insured.
Lump-sum death payment	Either fully or currently insured.
Disability	
Monthly payments to	If worker is
Worker and the worker's dependents if worker is disabled	Fully insured and worker has at least 20 quarters of coverage in the 40-quarter period ending with the current quarter.†

* Under certain conditions payments can also be made to the worker's divorced spouse or surviving divorced spouse.
† If disabled before age 31, worker qualifies with (1) a minimum of 6 quarters of coverage and (2) coverage for one half of quarters elapsing after age 21 until disabled or, for those disabled before age 24, 6 quarters of coverage in the last 12 quarters.

reached age 21 if later) and *before* the year of death or disability or the year in which they reach age 62 or (2) 40 quarters of coverage. For the years before 1978, a quarter of coverage was earned for:

1. An individual who has been paid $50 or more in wages for covered employment in a calendar quarter.
2. An agricultural worker (after 1954) who has been credited with $100 or more cash wages in a calendar quarter.
3. An individual who has been credited with $100 or more self-employment income in a calendar quarter, but a self-employed person must have at least $400 in net earnings from self-employment in a taxable year after 1950 to earn any quarters of coverage for that year.

For 1978 all workers received one quarter of credit for each $250 of annual earnings. Self-employed workers still needed to have a minimum of $400 in net earnings from self-employment in a year to qualify for any quarters of coverage for the year. For the years following 1978, the $250 earnings measure automatically increases annually in line with increases in average wages. For 1984 the amount increased to $390. In no event will a worker be credited with more than four quarters in one year.

To be *currently insured,* the worker must have at least 6 quarters of coverage out of the last 13 quarters ending with the quarter of death. This status only applies to death benefits for surviving spouses and children.

Conditions suspending benefits. Persons receiving old-age benefits, their eligible dependents, and eligible survivors of insured workers may lose some benefits if they receive certain wages or net self-employed income. Payees under age 65 may earn up to $5,160 (1984) a year as wages or self-employment income in any employment without a reduction in benefits. For payees age 65 to 69, the maximum earnings allowed without a reduction in benefits is $6,960 (1984). For earnings in excess of these amounts, the individual loses benefits equal to half the excess. The 1983 Amendments liberalize the excess earnings test for years 1990 and beyond by reducing lost benefits to one third of excess earnings. Investment income is not considered earned income. Upon attaining age 70, full benefits are payable regardless of the payee's earnings. The maximum levels of exempt earnings automatically increase each year, according to changes in national average earnings.

Amounts. The primary insurance amount (PIA) is the basis for all calculations used to determine benefit amounts following the death, disability, or retirement of a covered worker. The 1977 Amendments to the Social Security Act corrected a serious error that had been made in 1972, one that, in effect, double-indexed social security benefits. In their attempt to increase benefit levels automatically to offset inflation, legislative drafters overlooked the relationship between inflation and wage levels. Inflation-induced increases in wage levels by themselves produce higher benefit levels for future beneficiaries. To correct this error, a dramatic change was made in the method of calculating the PIA the amount of monthly payment for which a worker would be eligible at age 65. During a transition period from 1979 to 1984, each eligible worker reaching age 62 receives the *higher* of the benefit derived under the old average monthly wage (AMW) system frozen at the benefit level as of the end of 1978 or the revised average indexed monthly earnings (AIME) formula.

The first step in obtaining the PIA under the former AMW system is to calculate the AMW. To determine the worker's average monthly wage, divide the sum of covered wages and self-employment income in the *benefit computation years* by the number of months in those years. The *benefit computation years* begin with December 31, 1950, or the year the worker becomes age 21 if later, and end with the year *prior* to death or the year *prior* to reaching age 62 or becoming disabled. This elapsed period is reduced by five years plus the number of years falling *wholly or partly* within a period of disability. The benefit computation years are the years of highest earnings taken from the *computation base years*. The computation base years start with 1951 and end with the year in which the worker dies or becomes entitled to retirement or disability benefits.

After the AMW for the appropriate years is determined, a social security benefits table is used to determine the PIA. These tables are updated annually. Current tables should be obtainable from the local social security office.

If a worker becomes disabled or dies before age 62 in the transitional period 1979 to 1984, the new wage-indexed formula automatically will apply. If, however, a worker becomes eligible for benefits by reaching age 62 during this period, then the PIA is calculated by both the AMW method and the AIME formula, and the one yielding the higher value is applied.

The AIME formula adjusts the actual covered earnings of each worker to a more nearly current level. The calculation involves multiplying the worker's actual covered earnings each year by a specified ratio. This ratio is the average earnings for the second year prior to the year in which he or she reaches age 62, becomes disabled, or dies, to the average wages in the year to be indexed. For example, the average earnings were $13,773.10 in 1981 and $2,799.16 in 1951. If this worker attained age 62 in 1983 and earned at least $3,600 in 1951, the maximum covered earnings for that year, the indexed earnings would be:

$$\$3,600 \times \frac{\$13,773.10}{\$2,799.16} = \$17,713.59$$

Each year since 1950 must be indexed to the second year before the worker retired, became disabled, or died. A table of these ratios is useful in the determination of a worker's AIME. Table 20–2 shows the ratios for a worker whose eligibility began in 1983.

TABLE 20–2
Maximum covered earnings levels under the OASDI
retirement program

	(1) Maximum covered earnings	(2) Average earnings ratio	(3) Maximum possible indexed earnings to 1981 earnings level
1951	$ 3,600	4.92	$17,714
1952	3,600	4.63	16,676
1953	3,600	4.39	15,794
1954	3,600	4.36	15,713
1955	4,200	4.17	17,522
1956	4,200	3.90	16,376
1957	4,200	3.78	15,885
1958	4,200	3.75	15,746
1959	4,800	3.57	17,146
1960	4,800	3.44	16,498
1961	4,800	3.37	16,177
1962	4,800	3.21	15,405
1963	4,800	3.13	15,037
1964	4,800	3.01	14,446
1965	4,800	2.96	14,191
1966	6,600	2.79	18,407
1967	6,600	2.64	17,436
1968	7,800	2.47	19,281
1969	7,800	2.34	18,228
1970	7,800	2.23	17,366
1971	7,800	2.11	16,535
1972	9,000	1.93	17,376
1973	10,800	1.82	19,624
1974	13,200	1.72	22,639
1975	14,100	1.60	22,501
1976	15,300	1.49	22,840
1977	16,500	1.41	23,238
1978	17,700	1.30	23,094
1979	22,900	1.20	27,476
1980	25,900	1.10	28,507
1981	29,700	1.00	29,700
1982	32,400	1.00	32,400
1983	35,700	1.00	35,700
1984	37,800	1.00	37,800
1985*	39,600	1.00	39,600

* Figures for 1985 are based on assumptions specified in the 1984 Report of the Board of Trustees of the Social Security Funds.

After the indexed earnings are obtained, the benefit computation years must be chosen. The number of benefit computation years is determined in the same manner as for the AMW system. The benefit computation years are the years of highest *indexed* earnings and will not necessarily include the same years as those counted using the previous method. The average indexed monthly earnings are calculated by dividing the sum of the indexed earnings for the benefit computation years by the number of months in those years.

The following formula rather than a benefits table is used to determine the PIA when the PIA is computed from average indexed monthly earnings (using 1983 values):

90% of the first $254 of average indexed monthly earnings,

plus

32% of the next $1,274 of average indexed monthly earnings,

plus

15% of any average indexed monthly earnings in excess of $1,528.

Any applicable inflation adjustments must be added to the formula determined amount.

An example may clarify the two methods of calculating the PIA. Consider the case of Professor Kingsfield, who becomes 65 years old in January 1986. He has earned at least the maximum covered earnings in each year since 1950, and decides to retire at age 65. The benefit computation years start with 1951 and continue through 1982, the year before Kingsfield reached age 62. Thus the number of elapsed years is 32. This number is reduced by 5, plus any years in which the professor was disabled. Assume no years of disability for this example. For Kingsfield the number of benefit computation years then is 32 minus 5, or 27.

To compute the AMW for the first option, use the 27 years of highest covered earnings between 1950 and the year Kingsfield becomes 62. The maximum covered earnings are listed in Table 20–2. Prior to the establishment of the frozen AMW method, the 27 years of highest covered earnings since 1950 (i.e., through 1985) would have been used. However, under this method, the computation base years do not include the year in which the worker becomes 62 or any subsequent year. In the present example, the 27 years of highest earnings are 1956 through 1982. The total covered earnings during that period were $298,100. The AMW is:

$$\frac{\$298,100}{27 \times 12} = \$920.06, \text{ which is always rounded down to an even dollar (i.e., \$920).}$$

Based on the social security benefits table in effect in December, 1979, the PIA for an AMW of $920 is $559.30. This amount is increased by the benefit adjustments for December 1983, and all subsequent adjustments.

The alternative calculation is the AIME formula. The same number of benefit computation years that were calculated in the first option, 27, apply to this method. However, for this formula, the computation base years are 1951 through 1985. The indexed earnings are calculated by multiplying the covered earnings by the ratio of the average earnings in 1981 (the second year prior to the one in which Kingsfield reaches 62) to the average earnings in the year indexed. The average earnings ratios for the years 1951 through 1981 are listed in column 2 of Table 20–2. In column 3, the maximum possible indexed earnings for Prof. Kingsfield are shown. The earnings for the years 1982 to 1985 are not indexed but are the earnings shown in column 1.

The 27 years of highest earnings in this example are 1951, 1952, 1955, 1956, 1959 through 1961, and 1966 through 1985. The total covered indexed earnings are $607,557. The average indexed monthly earnings are:

$$\frac{\$607,557}{27 \times 12} = \$1,875$$

The PIA is determined by the formula applicable to those attaining age 62 in 1983:

90% of the first $254 or	$228.60
plus 32% of the next $1,274 or	407.68
plus 15% of the amount over $1,528 or	52.05
	$688.33, which is rounded to $688.30.

In this example the PIA is $688.30. As this amount exceeds the PIA of the first option ($559.30), Kingsfield would receive a monthly retirement benefit based on the $688.30. PIAs under each option are adjusted by the automatic benefit adjustments for inflation made for years 1983 and thereafter. The 1983 Amendments Act delayed a 3.5 percent increase scheduled for June 1983 until December 1983. Therefore, Kingsfield's PIA of $688.30 is increased by the December 1983 adjustment to $712.30, and must also be increased by the adjustments in December of 1984 and 1985. Automatic benefit adjustments are used to increase payments when inflation has caused an increase in the consumer price index. Adjustments take effect in January based on the annual change reflected in the CPI as measured at the end of the third quarter of the current year. Again, because social security benefit formulas and levels are subject to rapid change, an individual should check with the local social security office in an attempt to obtain up-to-date information.

Losses. Losses covered include retirement income, disability, dependents' loss of support, and medical expenses for those reaching age 65 or receiving disability benefits for at least 24 consecutive months.

Retirement benefits. A *fully insured* worker retiring at age 65 is entitled to a monthly benefit equal to the PIA. An eligible worker may elect to retire as early as age 62 with reduced benefits of five ninths of 1 percent for each month of retirement before age 65. Thus, a worker retiring at age 62 receives 80 percent [1 − 5/9 × .01 = 36] of the PIA. If the worker delays retirement beyond age 65, an increase of one quarter of 1 percent of the PIA is paid for each month retirement is delayed, or 3 percent for each year of delay, up to age 70 (72 prior to 1983). The 1983 act gradually increases this "delayed retirement credit" to 8 percent beginning with those who reach age 65 in 1990 and thereafter. Further, the "normal retirement age" will be gradually increased from the present age 65 for those born before 1938, to 67 for workers born after 1959.

1. Wives' or husbands' benefits. If a fully insured worker reaching retirement age has an eligible spouse 65 or older, the spouse receives a monthly payment equal to one half the PIA. A spouse aged 62 to 64 is entitled to reduced benefits. If the spouse of a fully insured worker also is fully insured, the payment will be the larger of the two amounts to which the recipient is entitled. A spouse of any age receives a benefit equal to 50 percent of the worker's PIA if an eligible child under 16 or disabled is in his or her care.

2. Dependent children. If a fully insured worker retires at 62 or later, any unmarried children under 18 (or permanently and totally disabled before age 22 or age 18 and enrolled in elementary or secondary school) may receive a monthly payment equal to one half of the parent's PIA. Stepchildren, adopted children, and certain illegitimate children are covered provided they achieve that status at least one year before the benefits begin.

Disability benefits. Two principal disability provisions affect fully insured workers: a disability "freeze" preserves the worker's insured status and benefit level during the disability period; and monthly disability benefits are paid eligible workers after a five-month waiting period during disability periods before age 65. "Disability" is defined as the inability to engage in substantial gainful activity by reason of medically determinable physical or mental impairment that can be expected to result in death or that has continued or can be expected to continue for at least 12 months.

After the five-month waiting period, the applicant receives the PIA calculated as of the date the application was filed. If a worker becomes disabled a second time within five years of a prior disability, no additional waiting period is required. Disability benefits continue for two months following the insured worker's recovery. If the disabled worker is paid workers' compensation benefits, social security payments are reduced, if necessary, to keep the sum of the two below 80 percent of earned income before disability. Spouses and children of disabled workers receive the same monthly benefits as if the worker were retired.

Survivor benefits. Important benefits are available to widows, widowers, mothers or fathers of dependent children, dependent children, and dependent parents of a deceased covered worker. Widows', widowers', and parents' benefits are payable only if they survive a fully insured worker. The mothers', fathers', and children's benefits, and the lumpsum death benefit are payable if the deceased was either fully or currently insured.

1. Widows and widowers. A widow or widower who is at least 65 is entitled to a benefit equal to the spouse's PIA. Should he or she remarry, the benefit is not reduced. A widow or widower may elect to receive a reduced benefit at age 60. If the surviving spouse is disabled, he or she may receive a retirement benefit of 71.5 percent of the full benefit (up from 50 percent prior to 1984) at age 50.

2. Mothers or fathers of dependent children. Widows or widowers of any age who have dependent children in their care are entitled to the mothers' or fathers' benefits until the youngest child reaches age 16. This benefit equals 75 percent of the PIA.

3. Children. Children under age 18 (any age if disabled before 22) who are unmarried are entitled to receive a benefit equal to 75 percent of the parent's PIA. Prior to 1982, unmarried full-time students under age 22 retained the children's benefit. However, an amendment enacted in late 1981 required this benefit to be phased out over a 44-month period ending April 30, 1985.

4. Parents. A benefit equal to 82.5 percent of the PIA is payable to a parent aged 62 receiving half support from a fully insured worker. If two parents are eligible, each receives 75 percent of the PIA.

5. Lump-sum death benefit. If an insured worker dies, $255 is payable to the surviving spouse or to a child of the deceased. The benefit is not available to anyone else, and the recipient must be receiving monthly benefits (or be eligible for such benefits at a later date) based on the worker's coverage.

Total income benefits based on one worker's PIA are subject to a maximum limitation determined according to a formula. The formula is illustrated below using the PIA of $688.30 calculated for Professor Kingsfield who first became eligible in 1983 (the year he reached age 62).

150 percent of the first $324 of PIA	$ 486.00
272 percent of the next $144 of PIA	391.68
134 percent of the next $142 of PIA	190.28
175 percent of the excess over $610	137.03
	$1,204.99 (or when rounded to the next lowest dime, $1,204.90.)

Thus, $1,204.90 is the maximum monthly benefit available for a surviving family of three or more members. However, maximum family benefits based on a worker's disability are limited to the lesser of 85 percent of the AIME, or 150 percent of the PIA. A minimum family benefit of $274 per month following death or retirement, and $183 monthly after a disability were paid during 1983, but only to those who became eligible before 1980. No minimums apply to persons or families who became eligible after 1981. These amounts (including the family maximum) were increased by 3.5 percent, the December 1983 automatic inflation adjustment.

To receive benefits, the insured worker must file an application and submit proof of age. Benefits available to widows, widowers, parents, or dependent children also are available only upon formal application.

Taxes on monthly benefits. Beginning with 1984, social security benefits became subject to federal income taxes for the first time. The Amendments of 1983 specified that up to one half of social security payments may be taxed when one half of these benefits plus other income exceed a base amount. The amount of excess is determined by adding the recipient's adjusted gross income (from the IRS Form 1040) and interest received on tax-exempt bonds to half of the social security benefits for the year. If this sum exceeds $25,000 for an individual or $32,000 for a married couple filing a joint tax return (or zero for a married couple who file separately), a portion of the social security benefit becomes taxable. The amount of this addition to taxable income is limited to the smaller of one half of the benefits received, or one half of the amount in excess of the base income. The following examples illustrate the effects of this new tax on income.

Example A. Charles "Beatle" Bailey and his wife Sandra, both age 67, had $33,000 of taxable pension income, $2,000 of interest on tax-free municipal bonds and received $6,000 in social security retirement benefits. Their adjusted gross income (AGI) for 1984 was $26,000. To determine if a portion of the social security benefits was taxable, find the total of one half of these payments ($3,000), the tax-free interest received ($2,000) and the AGI ($26,000).

$$\$3,000 + \$2,000 + \$26,000 = \$31,000$$

As their sum was less than $32,000, and the Baileys filed a joint return, no portion of the social security benefits was taxable.

Example B. Art and Kay Parker had a 1984 AGI of $28,000, $5,000 of tax-exempt interest and $8,000 of social security benefits.

$$\$28,000 + \quad \$5,000 \quad + \quad \$4,000 \quad = \$37,000$$
$$(AGI) \quad (Interest) \quad (\tfrac{1}{2} \text{ of SS})$$

As the total exceeded the $32,000 base amount, the lesser of (*a*) one half the excess over the base (half of $37,000 − $32,000, or $2,500), and (*b*) one half of the social security benefits received ($4,000) was added to the Parkers' taxable income. Thus, their taxable income was increased by $2,500.

Medicare benefits.   Medical care benefits are available for those attaining age 65, and who are eligible to receive benefits under the Social Security Act or the Railroad Retirement Act. Provision is made for two types of coverages: basic hospital insurance to pay most hospital expenses, skilled nursing home expenses, home health care expenses, and expenses of hospice facilities for terminally ill patients, and supplementary medical insurance to pay part of doctors' fees and certain other medical expenses. The basic hospital insurance also covers workers under age 65 if they have been entitled to at least 24 months of disability benefits.

The *basic hospital services* program provides the following benefits:

1. A maximum of 60 days in a participating hospital, subject to a $356 (1984) deductible per illness and then all but $89 (1984) a day for an additional 30 days. This benefit is paid for each "spell of illness"; that is, the period beginning with hospital admission and ending after the patient leaves the hospital or nursing home for 60 consecutive days. An additional 60-day lifetime reserve is available at a $178 (1984) daily cost to the patient. Benefits for psychiatric hospital services are subject to a lifetime limit of 190 days.
2. Up to 20 days in a skilled nursing home, and all but $44.50 (1984) per day for an additional period of 80 days for each spell of illness after a stay of at least 3 days in the hospital and within 14 days of discharge, but only for continued treatment of the medical condition involved in the hospital stay.
3. Unlimited home health visits by nurses, physical therapists, or other health care professionals from qualified home health agencies (excluding doctors).
4. Hospice care for terminally ill patients became available on November 1, 1983 for beneficiaries with life expectancies of six months or less. The coverage is elective because other Medicare benefits (except for the cost of physicians' care) must be discontinued when hospice care is chosen. The future of hospice care is uncertain. It is scheduled to terminate October 1, 1986 unless Congress enacts an extension of the benefit.

The benefit payments for hospital or nursing home service covers semiprivate accommodations unless a private room is medically indicated, plus the cost of the usual auxiliary services such as drugs and supplies. The patient pays for the first three pints of blood needed, unless replaced. In addition, deductibles and participation rates increase as medical costs continue to increase. The secretary of the Department of Health and Human Services (HHS) is required by law to make annual reviews of Medicare costs and adjusts the basic plan deductibles if necessary. The increase to $356 in 1984 was from $304 in 1983, an increase of about 17 percent. The law requires that when the hospital deductible changes, comparable changes should be made in the amount Medicare patients pay toward hospital stays of more than 60 days, charges for remaining in a skilled nursing home for more than 20 days and the amount the patient will pay for each of the "lifetime reserve" days used. So these costs also increased about 17 percent.

The *supplementary medical insurance* is voluntary and costs the participant $14.60 a month during 1984. The federal government matches this amount from general revenues. The secretary of health and human services may increase the rate if it proves inadequate. The original cost in 1966 was $3 per person, and deductibles were lower. As the cost of medical care continues its upward spiral, further substantial premium increases and higher deductibles can be expected. The supplementary medical insurance plan is administered by private insurers under contract with the federal government. Those entitled to hospitalization insurance are automatically enrolled in the supplementary plan. However, as the plan is voluntary, they may refuse to be covered. Those over 65 who are not eligible for the basic plan, may join it and then take the supplementary coverage as well by applying for the protection and paying a monthly premium of $155 (for 1984) in addition to the $14.60 supplementary premium.

The supplementary medical insurance program provides the following benefits:

1. Physicians' and surgeons' fees at home, at the doctor's office, or in the hospital unless otherwise extended. Annual payments for psychiatric care are limited to $250 or 50 percent of the incurred expenses, whichever is less.
2. Unlimited home health visits under an approved home health plan each year without prior hospitalization.
3. The cost of outpatient diagnostic tests in a hospital.
4. A number of other medical and health services such as prescription and nonprescription drugs not self-administered, X-ray treatment, surgical dressings, and rental of medical equipment.

Benefits are subject to a $75 annual deductible and 20 percent participation by the patient. Benefit 3 (above) covers all charges fully, and is not subject to either the deductible or the participation requirement.

The Social Security Leviathan

The social security system is an instructive case study for analysis of the democratic political process, involving the often conflicting aims of government largess and fiscal responsibility, the uncertainties of economic and demographic forecasting, and the limits of news media in informing the general public accurately about important and complicated issues.

Social security and politics—Siamese twins

The desire of politicians to gain popularity in election years is illustrated by successive preelection increases in social security benefits. The need to maintain fiscal responsibility more often is met by postelection increases in contributions. Numerous forecasts by actuaries and economists about rates of inflation in wages and prices, birthrates, and early retirement proclivities have been proved erroneous, generally on the side of overoptimism. The response of the news media has ranged from sensational headlines of a $4.3 trillion unfunded liability to calm acceptance of misleading statements by government officials that all is well. The social security issue is as complicated as any issue facing elected officials. The impact of any changes in the program will affect directly all current and future workers paying social security taxes and all current and future beneficiaries. With more than 90 percent of the work force covered by social security, and about 36 million current beneficiaries, the impact of social security is nearly universal.

Perhaps the greatest irony concerning social security was the fact that, prior to 1984, federal civilian government workers, including the legislators who determined benefit and contribution levels and the employees of the Social Security Administration did not pay social security taxes on such employment or receive benefits therefrom. Federal workers had their own separate retirement program that, in many cases, was even more generous than generally was available to workers in the private sector from OASDHI plus private pension plans. The Social Security Amendments of 1983 changed this by requiring all new federal employees hired in 1984 and thereafter to be covered by social security rather than one of the government programs. In addition, as of January 1, 1984, social security coverage is mandatory for all members of Congress, federal judges, the president and vice president, other high-level political employees and any employees of the legislative branch not participating in a government retirement program on December 31, 1983. The hope is that the long-run financial future of the social security system may become less uncertain if the originators and administrators are participants in the program, and thus must rely on the system for their own retirement benefits.

Brief history of the social security system

When the social security system was developed in 1935, it was established as a program to provide minor supplementary retirement assistance to a small portion of the working population, which was attempting to recover from the effects of the Great Depression. The 1935 act provided retirement coverage for workers in industry and commerce. The initial benefit formula, which never went into effect because changes were enacted before the first benefits became payable, would have provided to eligible retired workers a monthly benefit of $10 to

$85, depending upon cumulative wage credits. The employer and employee were each taxed 1 percent of the first $3,000 of annual earnings in 1937–39, for a maximum total annual contribution of $60, but with the rate scheduled to rise to 3 percent in 1949. At least 17 amendments to the Social Security Act have been enacted since then, which in nearly all cases tended to: (1) provide benefits for additional categories of recipients, (2) increase the level of benefits, and (3) increase the level of contributions.

The major increases in the categories of recipients were in 1939, when dependents and survivors were included, and in 1956, when the disabled were added. Monthly benefit levels as measured by the PIA have increased from the initial levels of $10 to $85 to the levels that reached $703.60 (no statutory minimum applies after 1981) in early 1984 for those attaining age 62 in 1981, with further increases in line with adjustments for the rate of inflation automatically provided. The period of greatest benefit escalation was 1970–72, when benefit levels were increased 51.8 percent as compared with a cost-of-living increase from February 1968 (the last previous increase) to September 1972 (the last increase in that period) of 23.4 percent. Many of the financing problems described later developed because of these excessive benefit increases.

The maximum level of contributions has grown at a rate even faster than the level of benefits. Table 20–3 lists the maximum contributions for employees, the combined contributions of employees and employers, and the maximum contributions by the self-employed for each year since the inception of the social security program. The maximum tax is paid by any worker earning the maximum covered earnings listed in Table 20–2. The tax on earnings lower than the maximum would be proportionately lower. The maximum contribution level for an employee has increased from $30 to $2,532.60 in 1984, an increase of 8,442 percent (note that the consumer price index has increased from 43 in 1937 to 310 in 1984, an increase of 621 percent). With increases of this magnitude, one should not be surprised by the taxpayers' concern about the issue of social security financing.

In 1984, social security provided benefits to approximately 36 million beneficiaries each month at a rate averaging about $13 billion monthly. The average monthly retirement benefit in early 1984 was about $442.04, and the average disability benefit was about $455.48 monthly. Social security taxes collected in early 1984 averaged approximately $13.5 billion, slightly more than the benefits. As social security taxes are based on gross earnings, many families pay more in social security taxes than in federal income taxes.

Current financial status of the social security system

Expert opinion of the financial condition of the social security system, prior to the passage of the Social Security Amendments of 1983, was generally that if changes were not made immediately, the system would collapse. Its survival would depend on massive subsidies from general

TABLE 20–3
Maximum annual taxes payable under OASDI and HI

Year	Maximum for employees	Combined maximum for employers and employees	Maximum for self-employed
1937–49	$ 30.00	$ 60.00	No coverage
1950	45.00	90.00	No coverage
1951–53	54.00	108.00	81.00
1954	72.00	144.00	108.00
1955–56	84.00	168.00	126.00
1957–58	94.50	189.00	141.75
1959	120.00	240.00	180.00
1960–61	144.00	288.00	216.00
1962	150.00	300.00	255.60
1963–65	174.00	348.00	259.20
1966	277.20	554.40	405.90
1967	290.40	580.80	422.40
1968	343.20	686.40	499.20
1969–70	374.40	748.80	538.20
1971	405.60	811.20	585.00
1972	468.00	936.00	675.00
1973	631.80	1,273.60	864.00
1974	772.20	1,544.40	1,042.80
1975	824.85	1,649.70	1,113.90
1976	895.05	1,790.10	1,208.70
1977	965.25	1,930.50	1,303.50
1978	1,070.85	2,141.70	1,433.70
1979	1,403.77	2,807.54	1,854.90
1980	1,587.67	3,175.34	2,097.90
1981	1,975.05	3,950.10	2,762.10
1982	2,170.80	4,341.60	3,029.40
1983	2,391.90	4,783.80	3,337.95
1984	2,532.60*	5,178.60	4,271.40
1985†	2,791.80	5,583.60	4,672.80

* Amount shown was reduced to reflect a 0.3 percent tax credit for 1984. Self-employed amounts reflect a tax credit in 1984 and 1985 of 2.7 and 2.3 percent respectively.
† Amounts for 1985 are based on assumptions in the 1984 Report of the Board of Trustees of the Social Security Funds, and reflect tax credits available.

revenues or other funds—an entirely accurate prophecy which was confirmed in 1982 when the trust fund balance of the Old-Age and Survivors Insurance (OASI) got so low that it was forced to borrow $5.1 billion and $12.4 billion from the Disability Insurance (DI) and Hospital Insurance (HI) trust accounts, respectively. These borrowings and the widespread public questioning of the dependability of social security prompted a bipartisan movement in Congress and in the executive branch of government to remedy the situation. The National Commission on Social Security Reform was appointed to study the problem and propose solutions. Based on the Commission's recommendations, Congress passed and the president signed the Social Security Amendments of 1983. Sweeping changes required under the act to bolster the financial position of social security were so extensive as to produce some critics who believe the system will be overfunded by as early as 1990. In fact, few experts dispute the claim of the amendments' writers that, based on the reasonable performance of the national economy in the next few years, the system's financial strength is likely assured for the next 75 years.

Addressing the problems. The 1983 act includes major changes in (1) contributions, (2) covered workers, (3) benefit amounts, (4) benefit eligibility, and (5) internal financial procedures to be adopted for the administration of social security trust funds. A number of these topics have been discussed in earlier sections of this chapter.

Contributions. Although the Social Security Amendments Act of 1977 had already begun the phase-in of higher social security taxes, the 1983 Act accelerated the pace. The total contribution rate from employers and employees will reach the 15 percent level in 1988 instead of 1990 as originally scheduled.

Covered workers. Federal employees are finally required to participate in social security, a move expected to add more than $22 billion to the system's revenues by 1990. In addition, the right of state and local governmental units to leave the program by giving two years notice to the Social Security Administration was rescinded, thus preventing future defections.

Benefit amounts. Benefits are not reduced under the 1983 act (a political "no–no" of the first order), but allowed to grow only at a reduced rate. The cost-of-living adjustment (COLA) scheduled for June 1983 was delayed for six months, making the 3.5 percent increase in benefits effective in December 1983 for January 1984 benefit checks. Future COLA's will be indexed to the lower of the increase in the CPI or the increase in the wage index (instead of to the CPI only) if trust funds fall below 20 percent of the next year's estimated benefit payments.

Beginning in 1984, benefits are subject to federal income tax when payments and other income reach specified levels. The act also encourages workers to remain in the work force beyond age 65 by increasing the payments to those who retire late. However, social security retirement benefits will be offset for workers who "double-dip" and receive pension benefits from a public pension as well as social security.

Eligibility for benefits. A gradual increase in the age at which full retirement benefits become payable is scheduled to begin in 2003. At that time, two months will be added to the normal retirement age of 65 for each of the next six years. This increase will bring the retirement age to 66 for workers born after 1943. The same process will be used again, starting in 2021, to raise the age requirement to 67 by 2027. The late 1981 Amendments Act had already curtailed the eligibility of student dependents for payments to age 22, and of parents of dependents over age 15.

Although the foregoing measures represent more restrictive eligibility standards, two major types of less restrictive standards were also enacted. First, when specified requirements are met, the act allows benefits to be paid (or continue to be paid) to divorced spouses age 61 and over who remarry after they became eligible based on the former mate's coverage. Second, some gender based aspects of eligibility were changed to equalize the treatment of males and females.

Internal financial procedures.   So-called fail-safe mechanisms were added by the 1983 Amendments to establish restrictions and guidelines for the administration and handling of social security trust funds. These changes provide for faster collection of contributions and specific regulations on interfund borrowing such as took place in 1982. In addition, revenues from income taxes paid on social security benefits are earmarked for the OASDI trust funds.

Outlook for the future.   The financial prognosis for the system from the present to 1990 is good, although much depends on the general economic conditions of the period. Observers believe that, barring a major downturn in current trends, OASI should be able to repay the loans (including interest) to the DI and HI trust funds in the period 1986 to 1988. Thereafter, a surplus should begin to develop about 1990.

Long-term (75 years) forecasts by the Social Security Administration's actuaries indicate the building of a substantial surplus accumulation after 1990. If the short-term performance of the economy provides a pre-1990 surplus in the OASI trust fund, experts believe the system will then be able to withstand future economic hard times without resorting to drastic, quick-fix actions. (Hopefully, if large accumulations do arise, Congress will have the good sense to leave the funds alone, and prevent the need for future sweeping changes to keep the system viable.)

The problems of social security have not all been solved. For example, many working wives who contribute to social security will get little or no benefit from their contributions. As many of these women have income substantially lower than that of their husbands, their benefits will be based entirely on his PIA. Hence, their benefits are exactly the same as would have been the case had they not had an income and contributed nothing. In view of the fact that, in mid-1984, the percentage of white males in the work force fell below 50 percent (the first time in our history), it seems likely that this and other inequalities will be subjects of amendments in the near future.

Yet, some of the major problems facing the social security system were addressed by Congress in the 1983 act. The "baby boom" generation, born following World War II, loomed large on the system's financial horizon, and so threatened the financial integrity that Congress was forced to confront the problems and act. Now, however, instead of being threatened by the "baby boomers" and other problems (lower birthrates and increasing life spans—consequently fewer workers to support greater numbers of OASDHI beneficiaries) the system is capable of handling these situations without continual stopgap amendments to maintain its solvency and dependability.

Unemployment Compensation

In contrast to old-age, survivors', disability, and health insurance, unemployment compensation is not financed or administered primarily by the federal government, but rather by the states with some federal participation. The Federal Unemployment Tax Act provides for a 3.5 percent levy against covered employers on the first $7,000 earned by each employee. However, employers may credit toward the federal tax any tax paid to a state under a federally approved state unemployment compensation plan. Employers also may credit toward the federal tax any state tax savings produced by a favorable experience rating. However, the total credit may not exceed 2.7 percent of the applicable currently taxable wages. The remainder of the tax, 0.8 percent, is collected by the federal government to offset the cost of federal and state administrative expenses relating to the unemployment compensation program and to strengthen reserves of state programs where needed. The federal government's portion of the tax was to decline to the normal level of 0.5 percent when the trust fund repaid loans from the U.S. Treasury used to finance a special extension of benefits enacted during the 1975–1977 period of high unemployment. The continued pressure on the trust funds has prompted federal action to raise the tax again. A new tax rate of 6 percent (plus 0.2 percent for extended benefits) applies to wages paid in 1985 and thereafter. A 5.4 percent tax credit accompanies the new rate. The maximum number of weeks of benefits during the 1975–1977 period was increased from 39 to 65.

Employers covered by the federal law include industrial and commercial employers, certain state employers, and nonprofit groups who employ at least one worker for 20 or more weeks, or who pay wages of $1,500 or more, in a quarter of a current or previous calendar year. Also, 30 states in 1984 have a higher unemployment insurance taxable wage base than $7,000. (Alaska has a taxable wage base of $21,400; Hawaii, $14,600; Idaho, $14,400; and Utah, $13,300.)

The state-collected unemployment insurance taxes are held by the U.S. Treasury in a reserve fund where separate state accounts are maintained. Although, in the early years of the program, the fund exceeded three times the annual benefits paid, observers estimated that as of 1980, only one state held reserves greater than one and a half times the annual benefit paid.

Coverage provisions

Except for a few federal administrative regulations, states can design their own unemployment insurance programs, including questions of coverage, benefits, eligibility, and financing. Most states include only employments covered by the federal law. As a result, domestic servants, some farm workers, some government workers, and casual laborers are not covered. About two thirds of all workers are covered by the current program. Railroad employees have their own unemployment compensation system.

Variations are found among state systems. Hawaii covers agricultural workers. Domestic servants are covered in three states, Alabama, Hawaii, and New York. In some states a minimum payroll is required, and in most states a minimum employment period is required before an employee is covered.

Benefits

Unemployment compensation theoretically is designed to pay the unemployed worker a weekly benefit equal roughly to half of the wage the worker earned while employed but limited to no more than half the average weekly wage in the state. Many government officials, however, have been urging an unemployment benefit up to two thirds of the statewide average wage. Although recent liberalization has been made, a comparison of current state laws with those in effect during 1939 shows that increases have not kept pace with rising earnings over this 45-year period.

The method of determining weekly benefits varies among states. The majority use the "high quarter" basis, in which a given percentage or fraction is applied to the high earnings quarter of the base period to determine the weekly benefit. Some states use a schedule weighted to give higher proportional benefits to lower paid workers. The typical benefit duration period is 26 weeks. The current average (1983) weekly benefit payable is $123. During 1983, $18.6 billion in benefits were paid.

In 1958 Congress passed the Temporary Unemployment Compensation Act, which allowed states to extend benefits for a period equal to 50 percent of the normal duration, and shift to the federal government the financial burden of these additional payments through repayable federal advances. Since that time the federal government has frequently extended benefit periods during times of economic hardship.

In most states, the maximum regular duration of benefits is 26 weeks, but a few states have regular durations in excess of 26 weeks. The Federal-State Extended Unemployment Compensation Act of 1970 established a permanent program for extending benefit durations during periods of high unemployment. The extended benefits under this program (called EB) are for 13 weeks and are triggered into action by high state or national unemployment rates. The trigger rates originally were set at 120 percent of the prior two years' insured unemployment average in each state. The 120 percent requirement has been suspended by various temporary acts since October 1972. The unemployment rate used is not the standard rate released by the Department of Labor, but the unemployment rate among those individuals covered under the state's unemployment compensation act.

The Emergency Unemployment Compensation Act of 1974 was enacted in light of the highest unemployment rates since World War II. It established a two-year program, triggered by the same unemployment rates specified in the 1970 act. This act extended individual benefits for half of the regular duration, not to exceed 13 weeks. Benefits are financed by the federal government and called Federal Supplementary Benefits (FSB). The FSB in addition to EB and regular state benefits increased the maximum benefit duration for an individual to 52 weeks in most states, longer in some states.

The Tax Reduction Act of 1975 provided Amended Federal Supplemental Benefits (AFSB) extending benefits another 13 weeks, bringing the total possible benefit period in most states to 65 weeks. This law expired June 30, 1975. The AFSB were paid solely by the federal government, as were the FSB.

The Emergency Compensation and Special Unemployment Assistance Act of 1975 extended and modified the FSB and AFSB acts. The act extended the maximum 26 weeks of emergency benefits (for a total of 65 weeks) through December 31, 1975, but modified the trigger system controlling benefit availability. After December 31, 1975, FSB were payable for 26 weeks if a state's unemployment rate averaged greater than 6 percent for 13 consecutive weeks, thus waiving the 120 percent rule. If a state's unemployment rate was between 5 and 6 percent, 13 weeks of FSB may have been paid. This law was effective until December 31, 1977.

The Emergency Jobs and Unemployment Assistance Act of 1974 also established a temporary one-year program to provide 26 weeks of benefits to workers not eligible for state benefits, called Special Unemployment Assistance (SUA). The Emergency Compensation and Special Unemployment Assistance Act of 1975 extended the SUA program until March 31, 1977. The SUA payments were 100 percent federally financed. During the economic problems of the mid-1970s, 25 states borrowed funds from the federal government to meet benefit payments. As of early 1979, barring another major increase in unemployment, most states were expected to repay these debts by 1981.

It should be apparent that the federal government is highly responsive to the needs of the unemployed, if not in providing jobs at least in assisting those without them. If high unemployment is experienced in the 1980s, continued modification of federal unemployment compensation laws can be expected. Some authorities believe that the federal government should provide jobs rather than attractive unemployment benefits. They believe that the job approach would be more economical, better psychologically, and more palatable socially.

Eligibility for benefits

The federal act requires that no worker can be denied benefits for refusal to accept a job where wages are substantially lower than wages for similar work in the same area, where a strike is in progress, or where acceptance of the job would mean joining a company union or signing a "yellow-dog" contract; that is, a contract prohibiting the worker from joining a union.[1] Neither can a worker be denied eligibility while attending, under specified conditions, vocational training courses approved by the head of the employment security agency.

State unemployment compensation laws contain both *positive* and *negative* tests for determining eligibility for benefits. Positive tests include the following: the worker must (1) have been employed for a designated number of weeks by an employer subject to the act, (2) be registered for work, (3) file a claim for benefits, (4) be able to work, (5) be available for work, and (6) meet the waiting-period requirements.

The states have provisions relating to waiting periods, definitions of "suitable work," and basic conditions relating to the amount of earnings necessary for a worker to qualify for benefits.

Seven states require no waiting period. The remaining 43 require a waiting period to reduce moral hazard and to prevent insureds from filing claims for small affordable losses. In many states applicants are subject only to one waiting period in a benefit year.

To receive benefits, workers also must have worked in employment covered by the act. The states provide that the worker must prove presence in the labor market by having earned a given amount of wages in some prior period, usually referred to as the "base period." This amount usually is 20 to 30 times the weekly benefit amount. The purpose of requiring a specified amount of earnings is to restrict coverage to those who are genuine members of the labor force. This system generally excludes part-time and low-paid workers whose average weekly wage is less than the state's minimum benefit.

Certain conditions provide a basis for denying benefits. The following are principal types of negative tests: the claimant (1) is receiving severance pay from a former employer; (2) is receiving workers' compensation benefits; (3) is receiving federal old-age insurance benefits (if more than the unemployment compensation fund); (4) voluntarily quits the job without just cause; (5) was discharged for just cause; (6) refuses "suitable" work; or (7) fails to comply with the rules and regulations prescribed by law. Until recently, under most state laws, women who left their jobs for marital reasons or as a result of pregnancy were denied unemployment compensation. However, current federal minimum standards for the states' unemployment insurance law prohibits the use of an eligibility standard under which benefits can be denied solely on the basis of pregnancy or the termination of a pregnancy.

Financing

Except in three states (Alabama, Alaska, and New Jersey) where employee contributions are required, unemployment insurance is financed entirely by taxes levied on the employer. Alabama provides for the elimi-

---

[1] "Yellow-dog" contracts are outlawed under other federal statutes.

nation of the employee tax whenever state funds rise above a specified amount.

Although a tax of 3.5 percent of covered payroll is provided under federal law to pay benefits, most employers pay much less than that amount, because the federal law allows experience rating. To treat employers with stable employment experience equitably, credits are permitted in all states for employers showing regularized employment records. The purpose of the credits is to reduce payroll taxes paid by employers with stable employment records. In practice, however, the effect often is to reduce contributions during general economic prosperity with little influence on employment policy. In some states the minimum experience rate is zero. Employers qualifying for the maximum experience credit in these states are required to pay only the 0.8 percent levied for administration and reserve strengthening. The merits of experience rating in unemployment compensation insurance are widely and vigorously debated, but the system seems to be in little danger of abandonment.

Frequent changes are made in the state unemployment insurance laws. These changes cover nearly all important areas, including benefit amounts, financing, eligibility requirements, and coverage. Up-to-date information on unemployment insurance is available from the local office of the state's division of unemployment compensation.

Temporary Disability Income Benefit Plans

Temporary disability benefit plans, often called "cash sickness plans," provide partial replacement of lost wages for a limited period in which a worker is out of work because of sickness or injury unrelated to employment. In effect, these plans are compulsory group health plans similar to the voluntary plans in effect in many businesses.

Temporary disability benefit plans have been adopted in six jurisdictions. Rhode Island passed its act in 1942, California in 1946, New Jersey in 1948, New York in 1949, Puerto Rico in 1968, and Hawaii in 1969.

Rhode Island has a compulsory state fund, meaning that each employer required by law to participate must be covered by state insurance. In four jurisdictions private insurers are allowed to compete with state funds. Hawaii has no state fund for general claim payment, but a special fund is available to pay workers of bankrupt firms and workers who became disabled while unemployed.

Altogether, nearly 30 percent of all wage and salaried workers in private industry in the United States are covered by a state temporary disability income benefit plan.

Finance

Employees contribute to the cost of the plans in all six jurisdictions. In two of them, California and Rhode Island, *only* employees contribute.

The rate varies from one half of 1 percent of the first $60 of weekly wages in New York to one half of 1 percent of the first $9,000 of annual wages in Puerto Rico. In New Jersey, the worker pays 0.5 percent of the first $6,200 of annual wages, and the employer pays one half of 1 percent on the same base, if the insurer is the state fund. If a private insurer is used, the employer pays the balance of the cost of benefits, if any. In New York, if the contribution of the worker is not sufficient, the employer pays the balance.

Eligibility

Generally, employers who must participate in state unemployment compensation systems must also participate in the temporary disability income system. Those excluded are workers in agriculture (covered, however, in Hawaii and Puerto Rico), domestic service (covered, however, in New York), government service, and railroad workers.

Benefits

A seven-day waiting period is imposed in each of the six jurisdictions. In California and Puerto Rico, however, the waiting period is waived if the insured is confined to a hospital. In all but Rhode Island, the waiting period is for each disability; in Rhode Island it is for each benefit year. In New Jersey, payment of benefits for the waiting period is retroactive after three consecutive weeks of payments.

Table 20–4 shows the principal provisions of the six temporary disability insurance laws.

The future of temporary disability laws

Although nonoccupational temporary disability benefit plans have been discussed in many state legislatures over the past 30 years, only Puerto Rico and Hawaii have enacted plans since 1949. Reasons advanced to explain the slow growth of state plans include the reluctance of lawmakers to burden employees and employers with more taxes, and the success of unions through collective bargaining in gaining temporary disability income benefits for their members. Approximately two thirds of the work force now has some form of nonoccupational temporary disability income coverage, either compulsory, union bargained, or unilaterally installed by employers. However, some persons believe that more employees should be covered and advocate that OASDHI be expanded to provide for nonoccupational temporary disability income benefits.

National Health Insurance

National health insurance (NHI) proposals have received much attention over the past several decades. In this section the need for some

TABLE 20–4
Selected benefit provisions under temporary disability insurance laws

Jurisdiction	Weekly benefit for disability			Duration of benefits (weeks)
	Computation	Minimum	Maximum	
California	1/21–1/23 of high-quarter wages	$50	$224	6–39*
New Jersey	66 ⅔% of average weekly wage	$20	66⅔% of average weekly wage of all covered workers ($70)	8–26
New York	50% of average weekly wage	$20†	$135	26
Rhode Island	55% of average weekly wage, plus $5 for each dependent up to $20	$37‡	60% of state's average weekly wage in preceding calendar year ($162)	12–26
Hawaii	55% of average weekly wage	Average weekly wage if below $14	66⅔% of state's average weekly wage ($177)	26
Puerto Rico	1/11–1/26 of high-quarter wages up to weekly benefit amount of $59, for benefits above $59 under schedule provided by law	$ 7	$104§	26

* During 1984–86 formula establishes duration to be the lesser of 52 weeks or total of claimant's wages in the base period.
† Average weekly wage if less than $20.
‡ Exclusive of dependents' allowances.
§ The maximum for agricultural workers is $50.

form of NHI, basic principles for an NHI plan, provisions from three bills introduced in 1978 and 1979, and the outlook for the passage of an NHI plan are briefly reviewed.

The need for NHI coverage

The philosophy behind NHI proposals is that every American should have access to quality health care regardless of income, age, or residence. Advocates of NHI maintain that the present U.S. health care system does not accomplish this objective, insisting that many Americans cannot obtain satisfactory health care solely because they cannot afford it. Advocates of NHI also point out that although most Americans have some form of private health insurance, the coverage often is inadequate. Also, over 35 million Americans, nearly 16 percent of the population, have no health insurance at all.

Rising health care costs also have given impetus to NHI legislation.

A serious illness currently could bankrupt many American families and put severe financial strain upon the remainder. Most observers do not believe in continuing a system in which individual families can be financially ruined because a family member becomes ill or is injured.

Basic principles for a NHI plan

Proponents of NHI generally agree on the criteria for a NHI plan but not necessarily on the standards to be applied in developing a specific plan. The main differences among proposed plans concern breadth of coverage, financing, and the timetable for putting the plans into effect. One plan would phase in the benefits over several years, while under another plan, the benefits would come into effect all at one time. Conflicts among standards to be applied need to be resolved before any NHI proposal can be passed.

Basic principles for a NHI plan include: (1) every American should have access to adequate health care; (2) quality of coverage should not differ on the basis of a person's income; (3) the plan should not provide for unnecessary government interference into the private insurance system (what is unnecessary interference is a highly debatable matter!); (4) the plan must avoid the establishment of a gigantic federal bureaucracy (both suppliers and users of medical services want as much freedom as is consistent with operating efficiency, but room for disagreement exists as to what constitutes operating efficiency); (5) the plan's financing should not be financially burdensome on the highly taxed lower- and middle-income classes; and (6) the plan design must consider the program's cost and its effects on the present health care system by building into the plan appropriate controls to prevent overutilization.

Major NHI proposals

Many NHI programs were introduced in Congress during 1978 and 1979. Observers generally agree that the bill that eventually will be passed will be a compromise consisting of parts of several bills. Three of these bills are discussed here: the Kennedy bill, the Long bill, and a competition-based plan. These three bills offer a broad picture of the types of bills introduced.

The Kennedy bill. Sen. Edward Kennedy's Health Care for All Americans Act would provide comprehensive benefits for every resident of the United States through mandated health insurance plans, with federal financing of coverage for the poor, the unemployed, and the aged. Most of the coverages and benefits would come into effect all at once, two years after enactment of this legislation. The public would obtain health insurance coverage through Blue Cross and Blue Shield facilities, private health insurers, and Health Maintenance Organizations. The Kennedy plan would be administered by a public authority, which would assure universal coverage for all Americans. Individual insurance companies and individual Blue Cross and Blue Shield plans would be subject to certification requirements and regulations established by the public authority.

The Kennedy bill would be financed through a combination of employer and employee contributions, with federal general revenue support for the poor and unemployed and for improvement of the Medicare program. The employer's contribution would be a premium paid to an insurer and based on the total payroll. All employees will pay the same rate (i.e., the risk is not experience rated). This premium would cover the full costs of the covered benefits. Employees could be required to pay up to 35 percent of the premium costs.

The Kennedy bill includes built-in cost controls. When the bill was enacted, budget caps would immediately be used to control hospital and physician costs. After the benefits began, the public authority would control costs through prospective budgeting of hospital and physician expenditures. Hospitals and doctors would be paid on the basis of prenegotiated amounts. Kennedy believes that the total cost of health care would be less within a few years after this national health insurance program is enacted than they would be under current programs because of the immediate and long-range cost controls applied.

The Kennedy bill is backed by organized labor, which favors the comprehensive provisions. However, the American Medical Association believes that Kennedy's program would bring about total federal domination of health care in this country, which the AMA believes is not in the public interest. Another criticism of Kennedy's bill is that the absence of deductibles and coinsurance might lead to an unnecessary overuse of facilities and services. Many observers object to the inclusion of prospective budgeting of hospitals and doctors as the method of containing health care costs. They believe it to be an unrealistic and unnecessary measure, as the current voluntary effort has been successful in reducing the rate of increase in hospital expenditures.

The Long bill. The Long bill would provide catastrophic health insurance protection for all legal U.S. residents and would establish a national system of coverage for low-income persons to replace Medicaid. Catastrophic health insurance would be provided through one of two plans: (1) a federally administered public plan for the unemployed, welfare recipients, the aged, and persons who do not obtain private insurance coverage, and (2) a private catastrophic insurance plan allowed as an option for employers and the self-employed. Employers and the self-employed would be required to provide and pay the full cost of catastrophic protection for their employees.

The catastrophic health insurance plan would provide benefits similar to those currently given under Medicare, but only after an individual had been hospitalized for 60 days or had incurred $2,000 in medical expenses other than hospital costs. This plan would be financed by a 1 percent tax on the payroll of employers. Employers who opted for a private rather than a public plan would have the amount of the premium for the private coverage deducted from the 1 percent payroll tax. The public catastrophic insurance plan would be administered by the health care financing administration in a manner similar to the administration of Medicare. The private catastrophic plan would be administered by a qualified private insurer of the employer's choice. (A qualified insurer would have to meet certain federal requirements.)

The medical assistance plan would provide basic health insurance protection for low-income persons and would be financed by general revenues and state funds. This plan would be administered by the secretary of HHS. The secretary would use private insurers as intermediaries responsible for the administration of claims and payments to providers of health services.

The Long bill also provides for a voluntary federal certification program for basic private health insurance to encourage private insurers to make basic coverage (supplemental to the catastrophic program) available to all sections of the country. If private insurers failed to make basic private health insurance available in any state, the secretary of HHS would be able, three years after the enactment of the program, to offer a standard health insurance policy to individuals and families living in that state.

Competition-based plans.   The Kennedy and Long proposals represent opposite ends of the spectrum of NHI—the former a comprehensive "womb to the tomb" approach, and the latter a single-faceted catastrophic loss coverage. More recent discussion (that is, what little discussion that has taken place) has centered on competition-based plans which depend on market forces to control and determine health care costs. Proponents of competition-based plans believe the current system or one of the other proposals will exacerbate the problem of inflation in the cost of health care. Their position is based on three major criticisms of other approaches.

First, most consumers pay medical costs only indirectly through a governmental agency or insurance plan. Thus, at the time of illness, there is no incentive to keep the cost down as the bill, in the eyes of the consumer, has already been paid. Second, the reimbursement system of cost recovery by physicians and hospitals allows them to operate (no pun intended) on a "cost-plus" basis, and discourages the use of efficient, cost-effective procedures. Third, the sharing of health costs by employers with the government through tax deductions on employer payments for employee health care reduces the effect of high health insurance premiums. Employers are not encouraged to find the best, low-cost plan because the government shares in the expense thereby partially shielding the employer and employee (employer payments do not constitute taxable income to the employee) from the financial impact of a high-cost program.

Changes envisioned by proponents of a competitive program would provide for: (1) a restructuring of the tax treatment of employer paid health care expenses, (2) a number of health care plans for employees to choose from, ranging from low-cost basic coverage to high-cost comprehensive protection (with the difference in cost going to the employee who has the low-cost coverage), (3) cost to be shared by the employer, who pays an equal amount toward each employee's coverage, and the employee, who pays a deductible and participates in costs over the deductible, and (4) the administration would remain in the private sector with the secretary of HHS charged with the responsibility for establishing minimum coverages and guidelines for insurers.

Outlook on NHI passage

It appears that one of these days, but who knows when, the United States will have some form of "acceptable" NHI because of the mounting cost of health care in the United States plus the inadequate medical treatment that many of its citizens receive. The fact that the present systems (federal and private) do not provide all segments of the public the most efficient and highest level of medical care scientifically and technologically possible has many clamoring for a complete national health care plan operated by the federal government or a reasonable compromise involving all segments of the health care industry. One must not expect NHI to solve all the current health care delivery problems without creating new, possibly unforeseen ones.

Between 1970 and 1981 the total national bill for health care increased almost fourfold for diverse and yet often interrelated causes. The high cost and growing supply of doctors have been an important factor. Medical schools have expanded their facilities and enrollment, and as a result, some observers are predicting a doctor surplus by 1990. This surplus is a problem because in medicine, the laws of supply and demand do not work. As the number of medical practitioners increases, the costs of medical care go up, not down. The increase in the number of doctors has not relieved the shortages in some fields of medicine and in some parts of the country. Ninety percent of the new physicians decide to practice in urban areas, where only 75 percent of the population lives, despite federal programs designed to encourage physicians to locate in medically underserved parts of the country. It is estimated that more than 25 million Americans now live in inner-city and rural areas designated as "health manpower shortage areas."

Other contributing factors to high medical costs involve the expensive equipment that hospitals provide and the costly procedure of keeping patients with severe conditions alive. Many specialized pieces of lifesaving equipment have price tags ranging from several hundred thousand to over $1 million. As the total burden of these expenses cannot be borne by those who directly benefit from them, all persons who use the hospitals must pay through higher costs. Duplication of expensive equipment by neighboring hospitals for prestige also is a contributing factor to high cost.

Many studies of medical practices suggest that high medical costs can be attributed to the archaic manner in which medical expenses are computed. The "fee-for-service" or piecework basis on which doctors are provided their compensation offers incentives to prescribe more treatment than is necessary. Even when the doctor has good motives (which undoubtedly the majority do), the threat of a malpractice suit may lead to overtesting and diagnosis and thus higher costs. Studies have suggested that many doctors resort too quickly to the surgical knife for "remunerectomies"—appendectomies, tonsillectomies, and hysterectomies, said to be performed primarily for the fee involved.

Much of the blame for high medical costs has been placed on the insurers, including the "Blues" and the federal government. Over 70 percent of all medical bills are paid by these institutions, but none has made any *substantial* effort to scrutinize the expenses for which they are paying, and instead they are simply functioning as a cost pass-through mechanism. The practice of reimbursing hospitals on a cost-plus basis is an open invitation to inefficiency. Insurers should take the lead in bearing their part of the responsibility for encouraging innovation in health care.

Solutions. Solutions to the problem of rising costs and inadequate treatment have been suggested by many different sources. In addition to NHI, some have suggested wider use of group practice plans (also called health maintenance organizations or HMOs). The largest is the Kaiser Foundation Program with 2 million members, originally designed as a method to provide medical care for the Kaiser Corporation employees, many of whom lived and worked in remote locations. The foundation now owns a network of hospitals and outpatient clinics in Oregon, California, and Hawaii. The members pay a monthly fee and are entitled to a wide range of medical services. Contrary to private health insurance, the theory of group practice plans is to place great emphasis on preventive medicine.

Overall, the plans appear to provide high-quality service at costs that average 15 to 20 percent lower than the average for the areas in which they operate. Length of hospital confinements also has been below average, partially because the emphasis on preventive medicine reduces the number of serious illnesses incurred.

Although the Kennedy and Long proposals were originated and considered in the decade of the 1970s, except for the occasional competition-based proposal, activity on NHI has been almost nonexistent in the 1980s. Health care costs have continued to climb at a rate above (sometimes double) the rate of increase in the consumer price index. It now appears (late 1984), due to the high cost of any NHI proposal with enough appeal to get through Congress, the adverse effects on the federal deficit will cause further consideration of NHI to be put off until the deficit problem is handled.

Regardless of which NHI plan or combination of plans eventually is adopted, several basic criteria must be met. The plan, although dealing with an emotional subject (sickness), should be based on rational solutions and must be much more than a financing plan. The errors encountered with Medicare and Medicaid should not be repeated. Insurance coverage must be written to reward economies of operation and not provide incentives for inefficiencies. Spending for high-cost exotic treatments should be used only in necessary cases. Investment in infrequently used expensive equipment should be spread to benefit all needing it. Computers and scientific planning must be utilized to a greater extent, with more emphasis on coordination of facilities among hospitals. Doctors should be relieved of nonmedical duties. Professional managers should be more involved in hospital policymaking, and many new methods of cost cutting without quality reduction must be introduced. Greater emphasis must be placed on preventive medicine, prompt treatment, and rehabilitation for all classes of people. Education programs should be expanded to aid in meeting this objective. Insurance policy contracts should be redesigned to ease the burden of the participation feature and deductibles on the insured. Some progress already has been made in this area. The use of on-line computers for diagnostic work and to recommend treatment for patients many miles away from major medical centers should be encouraged. More emphasis should be given to ambulatory care and organized home care service as well as to other facilities less costly than hospitals, such as the OEO's health centers which, in addition to treating the illness of the poor, prevent the spread of those environmental factors that contribute to disease and sickness. Better transportation facilities should be provided for those unable to obtain local medical assistance. Greater use of paraprofessionals to perform portions of work that are significantly below an M.D.'s level of skill is also needed. More effort is needed to develop Professional Standards Review Organizations (PSROs) to check the quality and need of care given patients under both government and private programs. The PSROs were created by the 1972 social security amendments to monitor government programs.

In summary, what is needed in the health care delivery system is action to improve health labor force supply and efficiency, to develop ambulatory health care services, to improve comprehensive health planning, to establish national health care goals and priorities, to create controls on health care and quality, and to grant comprehensive health insurance for all.

Summary

1. Social insurance covers social risks; that is, whatever a particular society considers to be a social risk. Risks classified as social have grown over the past decades. This growth can be expected to continue in the future.
2. Earlier cultures felt no need for social insurance, as unemployment and old age were not problems. The unemployed did not exist or else starved, and few persons survived to reach old age. Economic development and social change have since increased the incidence

of unemployment and old age. Attitudes also have changed so that a prime function of government is viewed as that of assuming responsibility for these two problems.

3. The social security system provides both public assistance payments based upon need (SSI) and social insurance payments made to persons entitled to them, regardless of need (OASDHI).

4. Supplemental Security Income payments consist of basic income payments to needy persons, including the blind, aged, disabled, and dependent children. The Medicaid program also pays certain medical expenses for those unable to pay.

5. Old-age, survivors, disability, and health insurance benefits include payments to covered workers and their dependents. These benefit payments protect against losses to the covered worker caused by retirement and disability. Benefits also protect dependents against income loss caused by death, disability, or retirement of a covered worker. Furthermore, OASDHI benefits help defray the cost of medical care to persons over 65 and to long-term disabled persons.

6. Enactment of the Social Security Amendments of 1983 sharply enhanced the financial future of the social security system. Despite past problems, the current outlook for the financial prospects for the system is good, barring dramatic economic reversals in the near term (prior to 1990).

7. The solution to the financing problems of the social security system included raising tax levels, reducing benefit levels, and reducing the number of beneficiaries by restricting coverage.

8. In contrast to OASDHI, unemployment insurance is financed primarily by state taxes on covered employers to provide compensation during normal times for periods usually up to 26 weeks of individual unemployment. The states have been given wide authority in designing their own systems, and state plans vary accordingly.

9. Since 1970 temporary emergency unemployment acts have been enacted several times by the federal government to extend benefits beyond the basic 26 weeks during times of high national or state unemployment. These extended benefits are financed largely by the federal government out of general revenues. If substantial unemployment persists into the future, further modifications and extensions of federal "emergency" laws can be expected.

10. Five states and Puerto Rico have enacted temporary disability income plans to provide payments to workers disabled because of sickness or injury not arising from employment. More states have not enacted such laws for various reasons, the main one being that unions have been successful in getting employers to provide this type of protection without state compulsion.

11. Numerous national health insurance proposals have been introduced in Congress during the past 15 years. The principle behind these proposals is that every American has the right to adequate health care regardless of age or income, or increasing health care cost. The Kennedy bill would provide comprehensive benefits for

every resident of the United States. The Long bill would provide catastrophic health insurance protection for all legal U.S. residents. Competition-based plans would depend on market forces to provide health care efficiently—a goal to be achieved, in part, with a restructuring of the tax treatment of health insurance premiums.

12. The future of national health insurance is uncertain as to the type of plan which will be enacted and the date of enactment. Some form of national health insurance protection in all likelihood eventually will be enacted, probably starting with a modest plan and later expanding to become more nearly comprehensive.

Questions for Review

1. Is all insurance written by government (state or federal) social insurance? Explain. Is any type of social insurance written by private insurers? Explain.

2. Review the definition of social insurance presented in this chapter and analyze the programs discussed as to whether they adhere to the definition.

3. How does a person achieve eligibility for public assistance payments? For social insurance payments?

4. What types of benefits are paid under OASDHI? To whom are the benefits paid?

5. How does the administration and financing of unemployment compensation differ from OASDHI?

6. What are the requirements under social security for a person to be fully insured? Currently insured?

7. What serious error was made in the 1972 Amendment to the Social Security Act? How does the 1977 Amendment to the act correct the error? Explain.

8. The Social Security Act has been amended numerous times since its passage in 1935. In broad terms, explain the nature and purposes of these frequent amendments.

9. The current social security system is widely recognized as financially unsound. Explain why you agree or disagree with this statement. Would your answer have been different in 1981? Explain.

10. What states have adopted temporary disability benefit plans? What reasons have kept other states from adopting such plans?

11. Discuss the differences among the three national health insurance proposals presented in the text as to benefits, financing, and effect on private health insurers.

12. What reasons are expounded by proponents of NHI for the necessity of such a system?

13. What factors have influenced the expansion of social insurance systems during the 20th century?

14. Do you consider it unlucky for this Chapter to have 13 questions? Do you believe the addition of this question suggests superstition on the part of the author?

Questions for Discussion

1. In a completely socialized society would there be any need for social insurance? In a completely capitalistic one, is there a need?

2. Would it be advisable for private insurers to write unemployment insurance? Why or why not?

3. Originally, OASDHI benefits were designed to provide a floor of protection. What does this mean? Is this concept desirable? Do OASDHI benefits currently provide only a floor of protection? Discuss.

4. Why might providing jobs be better than providing unemployment benefits during a recession accompanied by inflation? How should these jobs be provided?

5. "Unemployment compensation benefits are too high and, therefore, impede a return to full employment." What does this statement mean? What policy implications might it provide if it is correct? Discuss.

6. "People living on social security payments are at the poverty level. Benefits should be increased, and the young taxpayer should bear the burden." Discuss the above statement, including your own opinion of its validity.

7. "Compulsory social insurance systems (social security or national health insurance) limit personal freedom by requiring a person to make payments to a governmental organization in specified amounts rather than allowing individuals to plan their own insurance protection." Discuss the foregoing statement. Is it possible to make social insurance optional? What problems might arise if this were done? Discuss.

Buying insurance

In insurance as in other business circles much is heard of the art of selling. Considerable time and money have been devoted to sales promotion. But in this age of consumerism more attention is devoted to discriminating buying. Many readers' only experience with insurance will be as buyers. Those readers who become insurance sellers will succeed through an appreciation of their customers' problems and an understanding of various insurance solutions.

Principles of Insurance Buying

Insurance should be bought on sound theory. As with all theories, several principles must be considered.

The large-loss principle

The basic insurance principle is the substitution of a *small* certain cost for a *large* uncertain one. Many insurance buyers seem to avoid this principle and substitute small certain costs for *small* uncertain ones! As one agent remarked, "People are not smart insurance buyers.

Sure, they *ought* to buy insurance protection against the large losses rather than small ones; but many times the only way to get them to buy protection against catastrophic losses is by tying it in with protection against the small losses, too."

Curious buying principles often are found in auto insurance. Some people carry low deductible collision coverage at the expense of more essential protection. If a person loses an auto by fire, theft, or collision, the most that can be lost is the value of the car. But if someone is injured by the car, the driver can lose all property owned, as well as future income. Yet, some people who cannot afford both physical damage and liability insurance buy physical damage and leave liability uninsured.[1]

Why do so many intelligent people suddenly seem so ignorant when buying insurance? Perhaps the more frequent the losses, the more aware they are of the perils producing them. They may want to insure only against losses that are likely to occur. Insurance of small losses is uneconomical. The cost of writing the coverage, when added to the loss cost, makes the insurance too expensive. Moreover, when losses are regular they can be viewed as expenses. Insuring them becomes unnecessary *unless valuable special-service features are associated with the coverage, or unless the coverage is required by law or contract.*

In purchasing insurance, too much weight may be given to the *probable chance or even cause of loss* and not enough to the *possible size of loss*. If a $40,000 loss would ruin a family, why does it matter if the loss has only a 0.01 percent chance of occurring or if it is caused by fire, windstorm, illness, death, or an adverse legal judgment?

Gradation of insurance coverages

After analyzing her loss exposures as discussed in Chapters 3 and 4, Mary realizes she cannot afford all the insurance she desires. Thus, she classifies her exposures and finds she *can* afford what she considers the most essential coverages.

Essential coverage. An important principle of insurance buying is to buy protection first against all losses which potentially are so large as to be financially disastrous. Insurance against these losses is essential. Severity of a possible loss, not frequency, should be the determining factor. Insurance *might* be considered even if the chance of loss is negligible. Consider the following story concerning the experience of one harried insurance agency manager:

> I remember a case called The Loss That Could Never Happen. A number of years ago we were asked to insure a collection of fine Egyptian statuary, and John Rogers, who's our partner in charge of Fine Arts and Special Risks, sent young Ad Taylor out to survey the place. Taylor came back

---

[1] Finance companies frequently require physical damage insurance on financed autos. They do not require liability insurance. Many car owners believe they have all the insurance needed when satisfying finance companies' standards.

and said, "Mr. Rogers, if I ever saw a perfect risk, this is it. The statues are six feet high and weigh a ton or more each. Frankly I don't see how they ever got them in there and it would take a railway car to get them out. They're housed in a separate fireproof building and anyway, they're stone and they can't burn. And they have a watchman and dogs around the place. There hasn't been an earthquake in Jersey for as long as I can remember and meteorites don't scare me. What could possibly happen to them?"

We underwrote that risk and practically no sooner had we done so than we had to write out a check for close to $500,000 for a total loss. It seems the statues were waxed to keep them at a high finish and one day a little fire broke out in a bundle of old rags they kept around for that purpose. The fire got going on the wax and the next thing you know, the statues are red hot. Then the firemen came and sprayed the darn things. Inside of two minutes those statues had split into pieces you could pick up in your hand.

However, in spite of this experience the suggestion is not made that all remote chances of loss be insured. One would not be expected to insure against volcanic eruptions in Chicago.

The decision to insure may not rest with the insured. Some insurance is essential because it is required by contract; other types are required by law. When property is mortgaged, fire insurance usually is required by the mortgagee. Some labor contracts require the employer to buy group life and health insurance and annuities. Workers' compensation insurance usually is required by law. Most jurisdictions require some proof of financial responsibility in the event of an auto accident involving liability—usually satisfied by insurance. When required, insurance coverage becomes essential regardless of the large-loss principle.

Desirable coverage. Some losses which cannot be financed from current income are not large enough to cause bankruptcy for a business or family. They may seriously impair accumulated savings or saddle a business or family with a burdensome debt. Insurance against these losses is desirable if the budget can provide more than essential coverage.

Available coverage. If the insured's budget is not exhausted after buying the desirable coverages, available coverages may be bought. Included in this class is insurance against small losses that can be paid from current income or retained earnings. Few businesses can afford the luxury of insurance simply because it is available; nor would the purchase be wise except for those with abnormally high risk-aversion factors. In nearly all families, every available premium dollar is needed for insurance necessities; and still some important exposures might not be covered.

Boundaries between the classes. The boundaries between the classes are highly variable. They depend on the insured's property, income, financial status, responsibilities, desires, and attitude toward loss assumption. Coverage that was essential last year logically may be only desirable coverage this year and simply available coverage next year.

Liability protection always is essential coverage as claims may arise at any time from various sources and for large amounts. Bodily injury damage claims resulting in awards over $100,000 are common, and accidents involving several persons can produce claims for millions of dollars.[2] Liability claims could exceed total business assets, and except for certain exemptions a person's entire property can be attached to pay a liability judgment. The future also can be "mortgaged." Garnishment of wages and liens against property acquired in the future reduce chances of financial growth.

To some families a $950 hospital bill might be enough to make hospital insurance desirable. Others might be able to absorb the expense. Auto physical damage insurance might be desirable for middle-income families; but high-income families might ignore the coverage and share losses with the government by deducting them from taxable income. However, the income tax rules concerning deductibility of casualty losses were tightened under the Tax Equity and Fiscal Responsibility Act of 1982 (TEFRA). Under prior law, that portion of each loss in excess of $100 was deductible. This $100 limit per incident remains under the new law, but losses are not deductible unless the aggregate of all losses exceeds 10 percent of the taxpayer's adjusted gross income. The effect is to further limit the number of families who are able to justify ignoring the purchase of insurance coverage. The important measure of a large loss is the relationship of the possible loss to free assets, not the absolute amount of the loss. The less affluent the business or family, the greater is the number of essential and desirable coverages, and the smaller the insurance budget. This fact creates an insurance planning dilemma. Those who need certain coverages cannot afford them, and those who can afford them do not need them.

The loss unit concept. In determining whether insurance is essential, desirable, or available, the loss unit concept is helpful. A loss unit is defined as the aggregate losses resulting from a single event. A peril can cause a loss which develops into catastrophic proportions. For example, a steam boiler explosion can cause an *aggregate* loss which would cripple a business, although several individual losses composing the aggregate might be handled along without stress. The maximum potential loss from this event would be the sum of the potential damage to the boiler, direct damage to the building, direct and consequential damage to contents, profit losses from business interruption, compensation payments to injured employees, judgments at law for bodily injuries and property damage, and loss of service of key persons injured or killed in the explosion. Of course, the explosion is unlikely to occur, and any loss sustained is unlikely to be the estimated maximum potential. The probability that a large loss will *not* occur should not be a controlling

---

[2] A court recently awarded damages for over $10 million in a case involving only one injured person.

factor in insurance buying. In deciding what losses *not* to insure, the buyer must consider the loss unit concept and the reality that the same free assets which may be used to offset *uninsured* losses also must be used to offset *uninsurable* losses. Because these assets may be needed to cover business reverses or family unemployment, they may be unavailable to meet losses which could have been insured.

Integrated insurance planning

Insurance buying is a budgeting problem. The insurance budget should be overall, not separate for each coverage. Insurance planning involves integrating all coverages: life, health, property, and liability; otherwise premium dollars will not be used efficiently. The danger inherent in nonintegrated planning is that a policy is bought because it fills a particular need, without consideration of priorities. Some family finance authorities, however, do not advocate a separate insurance budget. They suggest that auto insurance be included in the transportation budget, Homeowners insurance in the housing budget, and life insurance in the savings budget. This view can be defended, but it does not force the buyer to think in terms of buying insurance on a "first needs first" basis. Integrated insurance planning for a business is different. The use of profit centers may force efficiency-conscious managers to consider alternatives to insurance as a risk management device. Top management also may consider pure risk more carefully in planning new ventures.

Life Insurance Costs

Many insurance solutions to life and health exposures introduced in Chapter 3 are discussed later in this chapter. When buyers have decided on the best policies for their needs, their buying problem still is not solved. Costs vary widely among life insurers for essentially identical coverage. The price of life insurance is the amount the insured pays less that returned, but many methods of evaluating these two quantities are available.

The traditional net cost method

The traditional method of comparing life insurance costs has been to take the sum of all the premiums for a specified period (usually 10 or 20 years) *less* the cash value at the end of the period, the sum of the policy dividends for that period, if any, based on the insurer's current dividend scale, and the current applicable terminal dividend, if any. The result, either positive or negative, is divided first by the number of years in the illustrated period and then by the number of thousands in the face amount of the policy to produce the net cost per $1,000 per year. Assume that a prospective insured compares the costs of a $10,000 continuous premium whole life policy with a similar policy issued by a competing insurer. Assume that the sum of all premiums for the initial 20 policy years is $2,642; total dividends based on the current scale are $599; the cash value at the end of 20 years is $2,294; and the terminal dividend is $65. The traditional net cost per year would equal:

$$\frac{\$2,642 - (\$599 + \$2,294 + \$65)}{20 \times 10} = \frac{-\$316}{200} = -\$1.58 \text{ per } \$1,000 \text{ per year.}$$

Thus, the prospective buyer would use the figure −$1.58 per $1,000 per year in comparing the cost of that policy with another similar policy.

This method of computing the cost of an insurance policy is subject to major criticism. First, the assumption is made that current dividends will remain unchanged, although future dividends are unknown. Second, the interest the buyer could have earned on money invested elsewhere (known as the time value of money) is ignored. Thus, lower costs are shown for par than for nonpar policies. Third, the concept is founded on the assumption the policyowner will keep the policy in force for exactly the specified time period used in the illustration. Any change will vary the cost of the insurance. And fourth, it implies that insurance is provided for the specified period for practically no cost and even at a profit for the insured. Prospective buyers have been told their insurance not only is free but that the insurer will pay them to own it; for example, as shown in the foregoing illustration.

The surrender cost index

The surrender cost index (originally called the interest adjusted method) resembles the traditional cost concept but overcomes some of the major deficiencies. The surrender cost index differs from the traditional method in three respects: (1) instead of multiplying the number of payments by the premium amount, the premiums are accumulated at interest, (2) dividends also are accumulated at interest, and (3) instead of dividing the total by 20 (for a 20-year comparison), the amount of accumulated premiums less accumulated dividends, cash value at the end of the period, and any terminal dividend are divided by the amount to which one per annum payable in advance will accumulate in 20 years at the assumed interest rate.

This formula produces a higher, but more accurate cost estimate. Using the previous example and 5 percent interest with the surrender cost index, accumulated premiums equal $4,586, accumulated dividends equal $824, and the amount of one per annum paid at the beginning of each year for 20 years will accumulate to 34.719. The cost per year per $1,000 equals:

$$\frac{\$4,586 - (\$824 + \$2,294 + \$65)}{10 \times 34.719} = \frac{\$1,403}{347.19} = \$4.04 \text{ per } \$1,000 \text{ per year.}$$

This figure compares to a − $1.58 cost under the traditional method. The surrender cost index takes into account the time value of money, which was one of the deficiencies of the traditional method. However, some of the criticisms made against the traditional method still apply to the surrender cost index; namely (1) the current dividend scale is used to compute the cost, and (2) the assumption is made that the policyowner will surrender the policy after the specified period. A change in either of these factors will change the surrender cost of the policy.

The net payment cost index

The net payment cost index is calculated in the same manner as the surrender cost index, except that the cash value at the end of the specified period and the terminal dividend are not subtracted from the accumulated premiums. Using this method for the previous example, the net payment cost index for the policy per $1,000 equals:

$$\frac{\$4,586 - \$824}{34.719 \times 10} = \frac{\$3,762}{347.19} = \$10.84 \text{ per } \$1,000 \text{ per year.}$$

This cost index does not assume that the prospective buyer will surrender the policy after the specified period; rather, the net payment cost index shows how much a policyowner will have to pay to keep the policy in force for the specified period.

Equivalent level annual dividend

The equivalent level annual dividend (ELAD) shows the role of dividends in determining the cost of a *participating* policy. The total costs of similar policies before deducting the dividends can be compared by adding the policy's ELAD to its cost index. The ELAD is calculated by accumulating the illustrated dividends for a given period at interest and dividing by the amount to which one per annum payable in advance will accumulate over the specified period at the assumed interest rate and by the number of 1,000s in the face amount. Continuing with the same example, the calculation is:

$$\frac{\$824}{10 \times 34.719} = \$2.37.$$

Thus, $2.37 can be added either to the surrender cost index or the net payment cost index to find the total cost of the policy before deducting the dividends. This total can be used in comparing the costs of other par policies or in comparing a par to a nonpar policy.

For example, assume the following 20-year cost indexes for companies A, B, and C for a $10,000 continuous premium whole life policy. A and B are par policies so the ELADs are given for them. Because Company C's is nonpar and thus pays no dividends, it has no ELAD.

	Company		
	A	B	C
Surrender cost index	$4.04	$5.52	$5.88
Equivalent level annual dividend	2.37	4.18	—
Total cost	$6.41	$9.70	$5.88

When only the surrender cost indexes are compared, Company A's policy appears to be the best buy; if the total cost figures are compared, Company C's nonpar policy *would seem* to have the lower cost. *But* Company C's policy will have the lowest cost *only* in the event that the ELADs for companies A and B (using the actual dividend paid) are less than $0.53 and $3.82, respectively ($6.41 − $5.88 = $0.53 and $9.70 − $5.88 = $3.82). Between the par policies of companies A and B, Company A's policy seems to have the lower cost. However, the actual cost of each policy will depend on the amount of dividends paid to the policyowner. Similar comparisons can be made using the net payments cost index.

In assessing the probable cost of participating insurance, the buyers must judge the relative abilities of participating insurers to maintain or improve their present policy dividend schedules. The importance of the policy dividend in arriving at the surrender cost index and the net payment cost index is measured by the equivalent level annual dividend. Participating policies with lower equivalent level annual dividends and lower cost indexes (Company A as compared to Company B, for example) present less risk to the buyer in relying on the cost indexes. Note that 63 percent of the surrender cost index for Company A's policy (4.04 ÷ 6.41) is guaranteed whereas only 57 percent of the surrender cost index for Company B's policy (5.52 ÷ 9.70) is guaranteed. All the surrender cost index for Company C's policy is guaranteed, as it is a nonpar policy.

Average annual rate of return

The average annual rate of return on a cash value life insurance policy can be determined by using a method developed by M. Albert Linton. The Linton technique attempts to determine the annual rate of compound interest that must be earned on a separate investment fund so that the fund will equal the guaranteed cash value of a life insurance policy at the end of a specified period. The amount deposited in the savings fund each year is assumed to be equal to the annual premium for a cash value life insurance policy less a prescribed assumed premium payable for yearly renewable term insurance. The amount of yearly renewable term insurance purchased is an amount which, when added to the separate savings fund, equals the face amount of the permanent life insurance policy.

The calculations for the rate of return require much trial and error.

Various rates of return are tried until the rate is found that creates equivalence between the assumed accumulated fund and the guaranteed policy cash value at the end of the period selected.

The average annual rate of return provides information to buyers seeking to purchase life insurance as an investment. A buyer interested in life insurance as an investment can use this method to compare the rates of return of two different life insurance policies or to compare the rates of return of a cash value life insurance policy and "a buy term and invest the difference" plan, as discussed in Chapter 19.[3] Some persons advocate using the rate of return method as a basis for policy cost comparisons: a policy showing a high rate of return is regarded as a low priced policy and vice versa.

Retention method

The insurer's retention is the amount of the insured's premium the insurer keeps for expenses and profits. Under the retention method, the present expected value of future policy benefits (the amount the insured is expected to receive; i.e., death protection, savings, and dividends discounted for interest, mortality, and lapsation) is subtracted from the present expected value of future premium (the amount the policyowner is expected to pay; i.e., future premiums discounted for interest, mortality, and lapsation) to obtain the insurer's retention. Prospective buyers should purchase policies from insurers with low retentions.

Criticisms of the retention method are its complexity, reliance on separating the policy into protection and savings elements, use of group average mortality and lapse assumptions which may be inappropriate for any individual, and its limited value for use with participating policies for long durations because dividends are illustrated, not guaranteed.

Use of the cost comparison methods

After studying six different cost comparison methods, one might be concerned as to which methods, if any, are worthwhile. All of them, with the exception of the traditional net cost method, could be useful to a prospective purchaser. (The traditional net cost method patently is more misleading than helpful to a consumer.) The purchaser should use the method which satisfies his or her needs. For example, a buyer who plans to keep the policy in force should use the net payment cost index instead of the surrender cost index. To compare the total cost of a participating policy to a nonparticipating policy, the purchaser should use the equivalent level annual dividend with the surrender cost index and with the net payment cost index.

The consumer might believe the use of *all* the methods will generate

---

[3] Buyers of life insurance should remember: life insurance products are (or should be) designed primarily to provide postdeath protection. When a mistake is made in the purchase of a life or annuity contract, the purchase decision is usually based on the investment aspects of the product rather than on its protective features.

the best purchase decision. Instead, utilizing all the methods might lead the purchaser into a dilemma: some of the methods might favor one insurer's policy while the others will favor another insurer. Another problem might be that of determining the rate of return and the insurer's retention, as these are complex methods. The rate of return problem will be crudely solved if the staff of the Federal Trade Commission succeeds in its efforts to encourage states to require agents to provide this information to perspective buyers. (See Chapter 16.)

The purchaser also must realize that the cost of the policy is not the only aspect to consider when purchasing life insurance. The buyer must investigate and compare the quality of services offered by insurers, their financial standings, and the provisions of the policy under consideration. In the wake of the *Baldwin United* case, emphasis on the financial standing of the insurer should be increased. As noted in Chapter 29, the buyer cannot expect an underpaid and understaffed state insurance department to recognize and rectify problems of financial strength in time to prevent an unsound company from causing financial harm to some policyowners.

Business Insurance Needs

Business loss exposures are analyzed in Chapters 3 and 4. Property and liability insurance needs vary with the industry and the individual firm. A firm's life and health exposures also can be handled by insurance.

Property and liability insurance

Most property and liability exposures can be discovered using the process outlined in Chapters 3 and 4. Although insurance can be purchased to cover these loss exposures in many cases, more efficient management tools may be warranted. Each firm must determine its available resources in case of loss. Funds from within the firm as well as its credit resources should be considered. If gaps exist between needed and available resources, insurance can be purchased to fill them. Available policies and their uses are discussed in Chapters 11–15.

Key employee insurance

Key personnel are employees whose loss might materially affect the firm's profit. Key employee indemnification insurance is a simple coverage. Usually life and disability income policies are bought and owned by the employer, and when a key employee is lost through disability or death, the proceeds are paid to the firm. The premiums are not tax deductible nor are the policy proceeds taxable. A common form of key employee health insurance is written on and payable to the employee. The employer pays the premium. The purpose of the coverage is to attract and retain key workers by continuing the salaries if they are disabled and paying their medical expenses. The employer can deduct the premium for disability income insurance payable to the employee, and the employee does not have to report the premium as taxable income.

Individual medical expense policies bought by an employer for a key employee are treated the same as group insurance for income tax purposes. The key employee can be made the beneficiary of an employer-financed policy, and the premiums paid are deductible by the employer and not reported as income by the employee. The proceeds of the policy are not taxed if they constitute medical or hospital expense reimbursement. Life insurance also can be used to attract and retain key employees through life insurance funded salary continuation plans, split-dollar plans, and deferred compensation plans.

Salary continuation plans. The employer can continue the employee's salary for a period after the worker's death. This benefit can be arranged in advance under a written contract funded by the employer through life insurance. The employer should be named as beneficiary as the proceeds payable at the employee's death are not taxed. When the firm pays the employee's beneficiary, that amount can be deducted by the employer as a business expense, and the first $5,000 paid is not taxable income.

Split-dollar plans. Under split-dollar life insurance, the employer buys either a whole life or endowment policy on the employee's life. The employer pays that part of the premium equal to the yearly increase in the cash value, and the employee pays the remainder. After several years, when the annual cash value increases exceed the premium, the employer pays the entire premium. Upon the employee's death, the employer receives an amount equal to the policy's cash value, and the employee's beneficiaries receive the remainder. Thus, the employer is reimbursed for contributions, and the employee receives essentially low-cost, decreasing term insurance. When used with participating insurance, the one-year term dividend option can guarantee the beneficiaries the full face amount of the insurance if the employee dies while the option is effective. Nonparticipating policies may include the return of cash value rider to accomplish the same purpose as the one-year-term dividend option. The "measurable economic benefit" received by the employee is computed using IRS tables and is taxable as current income. The employer cannot deduct premiums paid, but the proceeds are not taxable.

Deferred compensation plans. With progressive income tax rates, "raises" will result in relatively small increases in net pay to employees in high-income brackets. Plans often are attractive which defer additional compensation to the future, when income probably will be taxed in lower brackets and the age-65-or-over double exemption applies. Cash value life insurance can fund a deferred compensation plan, but the plan must be set up with care, because of the "theory of constructive receipt." The IRS has ruled that amounts the employee can draw currently are considered as actually paid and are taxable in the year earned. To defer the taxes until the funds are received, the deferred compensation must be conditional; that is, the payments must be subject to a condition such as a promise not to work for competitors. A conditional plan may be secured by insurance or another funding device. However, the IRS holds that an unsecured promise of future income is not considered current taxable income to the employee, even though the right to that compensation is unconditional. Thus, if insurance is used to fund an unconditional plan, the plan and insurance must be separate and unrelated.

Sole proprietorship insurance

The loss exposures peculiar to the sole proprietorship were examined in Chapter 3. Life and health insurance can function as a risk management tool in dealing with some of these exposures.

A sole proprietor may need life insurance to provide funds to protect the personal estate against business debts. If the sole proprietor has no suitable heirs to whom the business may be left and the business is worth more as a going concern than the amount of its forced liquidated assets, as is the usual case, the sole proprietor may want to find a buyer to purchase the business at a fair price upon the owner's death. In this instance, a buy-out agreement with a key employee may offer a solution, with the key employee buying life and disability income insurance on the sole proprietor for amounts necessary to fund the buy-out agreement at the agreed-upon price. The insurance would be owned and purchased by the employee. The premiums would not be tax deductible nor would the proceeds be taxable. The sole proprietor could develop an equitable arrangement to help the employee pay premiums if a problem exists. To offset the loss of an owner who also is a key person, adequate insurance should be purchased to preserve the value of the business following the loss of the owner's services. If the proprietor becomes *temporarily* disabled, disability income insurance can help pay for needed extra help and offset an anticipated earnings drop caused by the owner's absence. The policy can be written with a waiting period for the number of days the business can function during the proprietor's absence without serious loss. Again, premiums paid are not tax deductible nor are insurance payments reportable as taxable income.

Partnership insurance

Disability and life insurance also are important risk management tools for partnerships. After the partners decide the period the partnership can compensate disabled partners from partnership funds (considering the temporary loss of the partners' services), disability income coverage can be purchased on the partners to extend the benefits for a "reasonable period." If the disability is long term, the partnership may want to buy the interest of the disabled partner. Similarly, if a partner dies, the surviving partners may want to buy the interest of the deceased partner. A mandatory buy-and-sell agreement offers a sensible solution to the problem especially when funded by life and disability income insurance. The simplest arrangement is a "cross-purchase" plan under which each partner owns and buys the insurance on the other partners. Sometimes, the "partnership entity" plan under which the partnership owns the policies on each partner is more advantageous. This latter plan is simpler when the number of partners is large, as fewer policies are required.[4]

Close corporation insurance

If an employee stockholder becomes disabled, the disability will create the same problems as that of a disabled partner. The recommended disability insurance and its arrangement are identical in most respects with those used for a partnership. As the corporation's existence is not affected by a shareholder's death, the heirs may legally sell their shares to anyone unless the corporation's bylaws provide otherwise as in closely held corporations. Often the surviving shareholders or the corporation may wish to buy the shares of a previously active stockholder who dies or becomes totally disabled. Life and disability income insurance can provide the money for this purchase. If a state permits the corporation to purchase its own stock, the best insurance arrangement may be to have the corporation buy, own, and pay the premiums for the insurance. Premiums are not deductible, but neither are they reportable as income to the shareholders. If the corporation cannot buy its own stock, the cross-purchase plan can be used.

Credit and collateral uses

Business life and health insurance can strengthen company credit, provide collateral for loans, and bolster the confidence of customers, suppliers, and employees. Adequate insurance to absorb the shock of loss of a key employee, or to guarantee business continuation at an owner's disability or death often affect the credit rating of the firm. If creditors know that death or disability of an owner or other key employee will not disrupt the firm, credit may be granted more readily.

Group insurance for employees

Group insurance is discussed in Chapter 20.

---

[4] This discussion is a cavalier treatment of a highly technical subject: the ownership of the insurance designed to protect the partnership. However, this text seeks only to demonstrate the problem and its general solution. Ownership technicalities, their tax implications, and other important technical matters are left to a life and health insurance text, or, even better, to a text on business life and health insurance and estate planning. This note applies also to the discussion of close corporation insurance in the following section.

Personal Insurance Needs

Ideally, the prospective insurance buyer determines the applicable loss exposures and then instructs the insurer to "cover this property, income, and expense against whatever perils might cause loss." But in the present state of the art, such perfection in obtaining coverage is impossible.

The life and health insurance programming process

Programming life and health insurance is a complex process. For this text an introduction and treatment of each need separately is sufficient, leaving to specialized life insurance textbooks the development of an illustrative program.[5] Six basic steps should be considered in the programming process.

Determine the purposes for which postloss resources are needed. No set of postloss needs is applicable to everyone; programming must be tailored to the individual. But most individuals have in common several basic needs for which resources may be required: executor fund, mortgage or rent fund, adjustment income, family period income, lifetime income for surviving spouse, education fund, emergency fund, and retirement income.

Determine the amount of resources needed to satisfy each purpose. In the absence of constraints, the preloss arrangement normally sought would provide exactly the postloss resources required to balance those available with those needed. However, because of constraints, primarily involving limited preloss resources, the decision normally includes trade-offs between the utility derived by spending resources currently and the utility of committing resources to provide financial security following disability, death, or retirement. The trade-off varies among individuals and is a function of factors such as living styles, income levels, asset accumulation, attitudes toward risk, and sense of family responsibility.

Even if one is willing and financially able to purchase sufficient disability or death benefits, another constraint may exist: insurers' underwriting standards. The applicant must be insurable, and the insurer must be willing to write the amount necessary for the required resources. For example, sufficient coverage is difficult to obtain to provide the required disability income if the amount exceeds $3,500 a month. Programming demands realism in establishing resource amounts needed following death, disability, or retirement.

Determine the current resources available to meet the needs. Available resources generally include: social security benefits, payments under

---

[5] See Robert I. Mehr and Sandra G. Gustavson, *Life Insurance: Theory and Practice,* 3d ed. (Plano, Tex.: Business Publications, 1984), chap. 20.

employee benefit plans, individual insurance policy benefits, annuities, real and personal property (including savings and investments), assets to be inherited, credit lines available to survivors, and the survivors' earning power.

Determine the amount of additional resources required. Resources that will be available must be subtracted from resources needed. This amount can be accumulated through savings and investments or by insurance. The problem with the accumulation method for nonretirement loss exposures is that the loss may occur before necessary resources are accumulated. So in most circumstances, the safest method of providing post-loss resources is through appropriate insurance policies. Establishing the amount of insurance needed is a process of determining the portion of the total potential loss exposure to be covered. Planning the purchase of life and health insurance is a process of classifying needs and covering first needs first.

Coordinate the postloss resources into a plan. Determining resources needed usually requires a decision as to the minimum income level at which a family can operate effectively and involves trade-offs. When considering trade-offs among coverages for different needs, two action rules are helpful.

1. Keep first needs first. Some policies have greater appeal than others and "unthinking" insurance buyers often purchase the wrong policy. Those with high appeal are college endowment education policies and limited payment whole life forms. High sales commissions paid on these policies compound the problem, as some selfish agents push high-premium plans. What has been accomplished for a child if a parent inappropriately purchases a $10,000 endowment on the child's life at age 18 at the expense of $30,000 of continuous premium whole life insurance on the parent's own life if the parent dies before that child completes elementary school? Instead of $30,000 of life insurance proceeds, the surviving family has a policy on the child requiring an annual premium of about $450. Insurance buyers should realize that using high-premium, high-cash value policies reduces the insurance available for the premium spent. Additional life insurance is needed in nearly every program.

2. Look to the future. A sound financial program must provide flexibility for the future. Thus, young unmarried persons usually should not contract for high-premium retirement income policies. Even though their current status may permit payments for high-premium policies, their future status as parents may rule out high-premium commitments if they want sufficient life and health insurance to protect their families. To change from high- to low-premium policies, they must retain their insurability.

Insurance programming also must consider the forces likely to change the balance between needed and available postloss resources. Changes in income, financial responsibilities, investment values, price levels, and social security benefits can affect that balance. A way to maintain the desired balance is to assume probable changes in needed and available resources and arrange a program that adjusts automatically to these changes.

Arrange safeguards to protect the plan.   When the final program is formulated, the insurance must be arranged to pay the proceeds to the appropriate persons, and to protect these funds from dissipation before they satisfy their planned objectives. Dividend and settlement options also must be chosen properly. (See Chapter 17.)

Executor fund

The need for an executor fund to pay final expenses is continuous. Therefore, the appropriate policy to use is whole life. Whether a limited or continuous premium whole life policy is needed depends on the amount of money the buyer has for premiums and on the alternative financial opportunities for the funds. At earlier ages, premiums vary only slightly for continuous premium whole life and whole life paid up at age 65, so an appropriate policy at young ages might be whole life paid up at age 65, as the insured can pay all premiums before retirement. However, at younger ages, the insured is likely to need as much life insurance as possible. The premium required at age 25 to purchase a $10,000 whole life policy paid up at age 65 would purchase $11,700 of continuous premium whole life insurance. If this amount of continuous premium whole life is purchased, the insured can take its paid-up value at age 65 to avoid paying premiums after retirement. An $11,700 continuous premium whole life policy taken at age 25 can be converted at age 65 into a $9,758 paid-up whole life policy using the appropriate nonforfeiture option—an exchange of $1,700 of protection when needed most for $242 when needed less.

Because medical expenses are unpredictable, they are best provided for by major medical insurance offering virtually blanket coverage for medical, hospital, nursing, surgical, and similar expenses. Major medical is discussed in Chapter 18. Various deductibles and maximums are available.[6] As all expenses are not covered under the major medical policy, other resources must be used to pay the deductible, the insured's participation, amounts in excess of the policy limits, and specified expenses excluded from coverage. Medicare provides coverage of major hospitalization expenses for those over 65.[7] Some excess coverage com-

---

[6] A substantial increase in the maximum payable under the policy would not cause as large a premium increase as would a small reduction in the size of the deductible. The higher claims frequency resulting from a reduction of the deductible (e.g., $1,000 to $250) will produce aggregate losses that will exceed those produced by an increase in the maximum policy limit from $10,000 to $15,000, as only a small minority would collect the higher amounts.

[7] See Chapter 20.

plementing Medicare also is desirable. The same medical insurance which covers last-illness expenses also covers nonterminal illnesses. Medical expense insurance should cover dependents as well as the breadwinner.

Mortgage or rent fund

In providing disability income insurance for mortgage protection, a waiting period is proper. The next payment is not due immediately following the disability,[8] and the insured's employer may continue the insured's salary for a period following the disability.[9] The policy to use depends upon the number of unpaid loan installments. If the installments have 10 years to run, a policy paying disability income for 10 years is adequate. Insurance to pay rent, or "taxes and upkeep," must provide coverage for life or to age 65.[10] With some effort, a special disability income policy can be found that provides a benefit period decreasing with the number of unexpired mortgage payments.

For life insurance coverage, several plans discussed in Chapter 16 are available. A decreasing term policy that matches the decreasing amount of unpaid principal is the least expensive. The decreasing term policy, however, provides nothing for taxes and upkeep when the mortgage expires. Some special mortgage policies combine decreasing term with whole life insurance. The decreasing term pays the balance of the mortgage, and the whole life provides a fund to pay taxes and upkeep.

Adjustment income

Recognizing the probability of a decrease in standard of living following loss of the breadwinner's income, insurance should be purchased to provide an adjustment income. An appropriate disability income policy, if affordable, is a noncancellable or guaranteed renewable contract; otherwise an optionally renewable form may have to be purchased. These forms are discussed in Chapter 18. For life insurance protection, the need is a continuing one. A middle-aged person whose family is grown still needs an adjustment income. Frequently an executor fund, mortgage insurance, and an adjustment income are all the family can afford. If so, an effort should be made to extend the adjustment income, reducing it progressively in the second and following years. This approach will give the survivors more time to adjust their budget, take job training courses, and find a job (or a working spouse) by the time the insurance proceeds are exhausted.

---

[8] Someone undoubtedly will point out that a person might become disabled on the 30th of the month with the next mortgage payment due the 1st, a day or two later. However, *that* payment would be made from income already earned.

[9] Elimination periods usually are 7, 14, 30, 60, 90, or 180 days.

[10] If a waiver of premium rider is attached to a life policy as it should be, retirement income paid from cash values or endowment proceeds can replace disability income at age 65.

Family period income

The Family Income policy provides a stated monthly income from the time of the insured's death until a given date. The period should be selected to provide the required income until the youngest child is expected to become self-supporting. Family income is available in three types of plans discussed in Chapter 16:

1. Decreasing monthly term insurance for an initial amount necessary to pay the guaranteed income to the end of the income period.
2. Family income rider usually attached to an endowment or whole life policy.
3. The traditional family income policy.

The premium for the decreasing term form is the lowest, as no cash value is involved, but death protection for a growing family usually is considered a more basic need than the accumulation of cash values. Building a retirement income can be deferred until the children are financially independent. In many families, 15 to 20 years still will remain to build a retirement fund.

If the insured wishes to use premium money for what might be termed a savings fund,[11] either a permanent policy with the family income rider or the traditional family income form would be appropriate. If no budget problem exists and the insured is attracted to life insurance as a savings medium, then either universal life, continuous premium whole life, whole life paid up at age 65, or endowment at age 65 will provide the family income and also build even larger cash values. As these latter forms include no decreasing term, the family income per month can be increased if death comes later, when the remaining family income period is shorter. An increased income would be needed if the cost of living has increased and the standard of living has advanced, both of which are highly likely.

No special policy is available for the family period disability income need. The ideal policy would decrease the benefit period by a month for each month the insured remains healthy, so that the period reduces to zero if the insured reaches the end of the family period while still able to work. Disability income insurance programming specialists have urged development of such a policy.

In arranging the family disability income, the insured may buy a separate income disability policy. Although an optionally renewable form has the lowest premium, provides higher benefit limits, and has more liberal underwriting requirements, forms with more liberal continuation provisions generally are preferable. A rider on a life insurance policy covering total disability also may be used. These riders provide for premium waivers in the event of total disability and also pay a monthly income for the duration of the disability. If the insured remains

---

[11] Cash values in permanent policy forms commonly are called a "savings fund." This term is not strictly correct; many states have laws which forbid calling cash values "savings" in advertising, sales promotion, or proposals.

disabled until age 65, the policy face amount is paid. Riders are written on a noncancellable basis and require a six-month waiting period before benefits begin. If this waiting period is too long, the gap can be filled by a short-term disability income policy. A limitation of using disability income riders on life insurance policies is that it may require the purchase of more cash value insurance than the insured can afford, because the insured usually must buy $1,000 of cash value insurance per $10 of monthly disability income. The common practice is to buy disability income coverage independently of life insurance.

Lifetime income for the spouse

A lifetime income guarantee requires large amounts of life insurance, as indicated in Table 21–1. The figures in the table are based on one insurer's contract (guaranteed) rates, which are computed using a set of mortality assumptions and a 3 percent interest rate. If the combination of mortality experienced and interest rates earned proves more favorable, the insurer pays the beneficiary more than $500 monthly. With interest rates currently earned far in excess of 3 percent, the foregoing amounts of insurance will pay more than $500 a month. However, even when insurers make payments in excess of the guaranteed amounts, the payments are generally low enough to preclude the recommendation of a life income option for a beneficiary under age 65. The $100,000 needed to pay a minimum life income of $500 a month to a woman age 55, if invested at 6 percent, would provide $500 monthly from interest alone.

In the typical program, the lifetime income need must be filled with the least expensive insurance. Even then, a compromise usually will have to be made between the income a person would like to guarantee the spouse and what can be afforded. Term insurance requires the lowest premium. Each year the insured lives, less insurance is required to provide the needed income. Thus, a form of decreasing term may be needed.

TABLE 21–1
Amount of life insurance needed to guarantee a woman a minimum lifetime monthly income of $500 from the starting ages shown

Age income starts	Face amount needed*
45	$140,000
50	131,000
55	121,000
60	100,000
65	87,500

* Less for a male.

If the lowest premium form of permanent insurance (continuous premium whole life) is used for this need, the premium at age 45 will be more than twice that of decreasing term. Limited payment whole life can be purchased if higher cash values are desired. Aside from the higher premium required, using whole life insurance means filling a decreasing need with a level amount of insurance.

Education insurance

Insuring an income for the college period in case of the breadwinner's disability is awkward because no policy is available for that purpose. A delayed benefit policy is needed that pays only during the college years, so that no benefits are paid until the child is 18 if the parent is totally disabled before that time. The best current arrangement is to buy enough disability income protection to support the family so that the child can borrow funds and supplement them with employment income while attending college. Cash values on life insurance arranged for education can be used. If premium waiver is included with the policy, the contract remains in force during the insured's total disability without requiring premium payments. When the child enrolls in college, the cash value can be borrowed and the funds used to help pay college expenses. The loan need never be repaid, as cash values increase faster than accrued interest charges when premiums are paid (either by the individual or under the waiver of premium benefit).

A simple arrangement for a college income is the juvenile endowment at age 18 with a waiver of premium rider in event of the parent's death or disability. Such policies commonly are too expensive for the typical family. Even though juvenile endowments are uneconomical, some families use them. The sales argument goes, "The money will be ready for your children when they are ready for college, whether you live, die, or are disabled." Juvenile endowments with the payor benefit will do just that: if the head of the family lives, the college money will have accumulated through the endowment portion of the policy. If the breadwinner dies or becomes disabled, premiums will be waived, and the policy will endow as planned. The educational endowment usually is impractical because it consumes premium dollars generally needed for insurance on the parents' lives.

The best education insurance plan for most families would be a policy on the parent's life that will pay a sufficient income to the children during their college years if the parent dies. The assumption is that a living parent will contribute toward the child's college expenses from current income. If term insurance is bought, the education insurance fund would be available only in event of the parent's death. But if cash value life insurance is bought and the parent survives, the policy's cash value may supplement other available resources to finance the child's college education. Funds maturing from college education policies should be left with the insurer at interest subject to withdrawal, so they can be used, if necessary, to guarantee a grade school or high school education or to offset inflation or a family financial setback.[12]

Emergency fund

An emergency fund can be established by setting aside a few thousand dollars of life insurance proceeds to be held by the insurer at interest, subject to withdrawal in whole or in part.[13] This fund covers emergency needs of a surviving spouse only. For the family of the disabled bread-winner, the best way to meet the need is to include disability waiver of premium coverage for all life insurance policies so that cash values continue to grow while the insured is disabled. The cash values can serve as emergency funds. Disability waiver of premium coverage with medical expense insurance is recommended, but rarely written. To cover insurable emergencies, life and disability income insurance should be adequate to provide an annual income sufficient to pay premiums for medical expense coverage.

Retirement insurance needs

Jonathan Lyon has programmed the income needs of his family and—should he die—has provided for them adequately with cash value life insurance. In contemplating his retirement, Jonathan expects that much of his income need will be arranged automatically. He can convert his cash value policies into retirement income at age 65. At retirement all available capital may be used to provide periodic retirement payments with or without liquidating the principal. Insurers offer many types of annuities to liquidate principal systematically. But if sufficient capital is available to provide an attractive income without liquidating principal, the annuity may not be an efficient financial instrument unless the annuitant is willing to sacrifice capital for additional income benefits. Illness often is more frequent and severe after retirement. Retirees should continue their medical coverage, as regular retirement income and social security medical benefits often are inadequate to pay medical expenses. Private plans that integrate with Medicare are written covering the gaps but eliminating the overlaps. Care must be taken to avoid restrictive Medicare supplement policies often sold by unscrupulous agents.

---

[12] Some persons insist the withdrawal privilege could be abused and money intended for college used for unnecessary purposes. However, if the beneficiary is that irresponsible, a trust rather than policy options should be used.

[13] If fear that the beneficiary may withdraw the fund for unnecessary uses persists, the amount subject to withdrawal during one year can be limited. However, this limitation will unduly restrict the survivors if an emergency requires more than the amount allowable; and if beneficiaries are so irresponsible they waste money on nonessentials even though they know the precarious income situation, a trust is recommended.

The surviving spouse. If Jonathan arranges retirement income during his lifetime only, a problem will arise if he predeceases his wife. Three solutions are:

1. Sufficient paid-up life insurance can be retained to give his widow a lifetime income which, combined with social security, will be adequate.
2. Jonathan can have his retirement income paid under a joint-and-last-survivorship annuity option, so the income will continue while either he or his wife are alive.
3. Jonathan can insure the life of his wife with permanent insurance. The cash values can be used for her retirement income.

Inflation and life insurance. A principal drawback in using life insurance cash values or conventional annuities in retirement planning is the corrosive effect of inflation. To help plan for retirement in an inflationary economy, the variable annuity discussed in Chapter 16 has been devised. By combining the variable annuity with a conventional annuity (or life insurance cash values), some inflation protection is expected without requiring the annuitant to sacrifice completely the security of the guarantees of the conventional annuity. The variable annuity also is expected to give the annuitant a stake in an expanding economy. However, in recent years, the variable annuity has been a severe disappointment, as discussed in Chapter 16. It may not be a solution for financial planning in an inflationary economy. Perhaps a "managed annuity" with shifts back and forth from stocks, short-term notes, and bonds with sophisticated money management could help, but the timing of the change has to be successful—a task that is not easy in the emotional stock markets of recent years. The patience of all involved in the variable annuity is being severely tested, and for those already retired, hope has turned into despair.

Some insurers write a cost-of-living annuity under which income increases each year by the percentage increase in the consumer price index (CPI), subject to a maximum annual increase. If prices decrease, the income payable also decreases, but never below the initial amount. These annuities offer some inflation protection without the financial risk inherent in the variable annuity. Many life insurers also write cost-of-living riders which automatically increase life insurance coverage with changes in the CPI. These riders are discussed in Chapter 17. Insurers have permission from many states to write a variable life policy discussed in Chapter 16 under which equity-based variable cash values may accumulate through level premium whole life or endowment policies. Both the policy reserve and cash value would be expressed in terms of units of a separate account invested primarily in common stocks. Death benefits would adjust for changes in the reserve value, with a minimum benefit arranged through a flexible term insurance rider. The value of the separate account units would be computed using a method similar to that used to compute the value of the variable annuity units. The cash values may be distributed under a variable annuity option upon retirement.

Estate planning. People who can provide enough income insurance for the minimum needs of their families and enough cash value insurance to place an adequate floor on retirement income may consider various investments in their financial planning. Real estate and selected common stock can be purchased as possible inflation hedges and, at the same time, the investor may *possibly* share in an expanding economy even after retirement or disability. Tax-exempt bonds also offer those in high-income tax brackets yields to offset partially the effects of inflation.

An estate including large amounts of investments may create an estate-planning problem. Death can result in a substantial loss to estate property because of estate and inheritance taxes and estate administration expenses. Life insurance is an important instrument in protecting estates from these shrinkage factors.[14] Arranging life insurance for estate protection is a difficult and highly technical task. The combined efforts of lawyers, tax experts, and highly skilled insurance agents may be necessary for adequate planning. In many cases, arrangements can be made for the reduction and payment of the remaining tax.

All estate settlement costs must be paid before any property passes to the heirs. These costs must be paid in cash; if there is insufficient cash in the estate, then estate assets must be converted into cash. Liquidation might mean forced sales and often losses. The solution is a periodic review of the estate to estimate the cash needed for administration, taxes, and outstanding liabilities at death. Arrangements should be made to have the necessary cash available. Life insurance is particularly qualified as an instrument for paying estate settlement costs as it furnishes the funds exactly when needed—at the insured's death. Life insurance provides the funds at minimum cost.

Family insurance needs

Income insurance planning tends to stress insurance needs of the breadwinner while overlooking the needs for other family members. These needs include: an estate clearance fund, insurance for the nonworking spouse, and insurance for children.

Estate clearance fund. The death of any family member costs money. Therefore, a clearance fund for each member should be considered. Medical coverage should be included to insure the cost of illness.

Insurance for the spouse. The death of a mother of young children may cause financial loss. First, income taxes will increase because the

---

[14] See Mehr and Gustavson, *Life Insurance,* chap. 21.

husband cannot take advantage of the split-income feature of the tax law. Second, someone must be paid to care for the children. This cost is deductible in part from taxable income, but the deduction is only a small part of the cost. Third, many wives earn income and contribute to the family's living standard, so income insurance should be arranged to offset the loss arising from the wife's death. Disability income insurance should be purchased on the spouse to cover the extra expenses that will arise if the mother is disabled. Adequate medical expense insurance also should be purchased to cover the wife's expenses in excess of the family's budgeted amount.

Insurance for children.   Life insurance on children has several legitimate uses. However, because these uses have high sentimental appeal, they often attract buyers who ignore more basic insurance needs. Children are better protected by insurance on their parents' lives than on their own lives. Insurance on children should not be bought until higher priority needs have been filled. Although the expenses of a child's death can adversely affect family finances, a greater hardship for the family would occur if a parent died without adequate insurance. Funeral and other final expenses following the death of a child can usually be handled with borrowed funds. Although the family's financial condition may be strained, surviving breadwinners are still available to pay off any such debts. In addition, living expenses will decline. However, if a sole breadwinner dies, the use of credit as a postdeath source of funds is generally severely restricted. The breadwinner's income that was available to repay loans covering final expenses for a child is not there to repay similar loans upon the death of a breadwinner.

If the more important needs have been covered, then insurance on a child's life can offer several benefits. The early purchase of cash value life insurance means a low annual premium is set for the life of the policy. (The insured will not pay less for the insurance. In fact, more is paid, as protection is purchased for more years.) The early purchase also will protect the child's insurability. If the primary purpose of insurance on children is to establish a low-premium, then continuous premium whole life should be used. If the purpose is to build cash values, a higher premium form would be more desirable. If the parent wants to provide early paid-up values, a limited pay policy should be purchased. But if the policy will be turned over to the child at maturity, higher premium forms should be avoided unless the policy will be paid up at that time. A young person beginning a career should not be burdened with high-premium policies. For protecting insurability, the jumping juvenile policy discussed in Chapter 16 might be considered. Under this form when the child's insurance needs jump sharply, increased protection is provided automatically. However, because the premium does not increase when the insurance increases, jumping juvenile is expensive. Insurance to cover children's medical expenses in excess of a budgeted amount also should be provided.

The family plan. A policy often appropriate for family life insurance needs is the family plan discussed in Chapter 16. The children's insurability is guaranteed, as each $1,000 of term on the children may be converted into a maximum of $5,000 of whole life when the term expires. Adequate insurance is provided for most children, but more insurance often will be needed for the spouse. In that case, a separate policy must be purchased.

Dwelling coverage

In selecting dwelling coverage, the buyer must weigh the expense of broader forms against the additional perils covered. Several of the added perils cover losses which would not have a disastrous economic effect. Glass is an example. The broader forms tend to exclude perils which can cause major losses; for example, earthquake and flood. In favor of the broader forms are their coverages against landslide, building collapse, water damage, and vandalism.

In addition to coverage against loss to the dwelling, families should protect themselves against the loss of use of their homes while being rebuilt. This loss may be insured through rental value insurance, a limited amount of which is included on fire dwelling forms. Often after loss to a dwelling, living expenses are incurred until the dwelling is restored. Additional living expense insurance reimburses the insured for this extra burden. As rental value insurance usually is insufficient to cover all additional living expenses, additional living expense insurance offers better protection. The broader dwelling forms often include broad "loss of use" and additional living expense coverage as part of the physical damage form. Some of the broader forms also pay full replacement cost for losses without deduction for depreciation, a form of extra-expense protection—the expense incurred because "old" must be replaced with "new."

Another coverage relating to the dwelling is liability insurance. Property ownership obligates its owner to maintain the property in repair and order so no one suffers bodily injury or property damage from it. Residence liability covers the homeowner's legal liability for damages arising from the maintenance and use of the residence. The comprehensive personal liability policy covers not only residence liability but also additional liability hazards. Broad liability coverage is included in Homeowners forms and usually offers the appropriate coverage for nearly all families.

Nonautomobile personal property coverage

For most insureds, personal property will be covered by one of the Homeowners forms. The extent of coverage available under the forms ranges from coverage for 10 specified perils to "all-risk" protection. For articles of high value, a personal property floater providing world-wide "all-risk" protection is recommended. The insured must be aware of the special limits of liability applying to personal property and modify the basic coverage if warranted.

For example, an insured who has a safety deposit box might consider the purchase of a safe-deposit box coverage to offset losses of securities and other property held in the box because the bank is not liable for the loss if it is not negligent.

Property excluded from Homeowners coverage must be insured under other policies, if such coverage is deemed necessary.

For one example, if a person owns a recreational vehicle, coverage for that vehicle should be considered. A reading of the Homeowners and auto policies will reveal other areas in which additional coverages might be needed.

Personal activities

A negligent act causing bodily injury or property damage to others can be costly, draining accumulated wealth and placing a lien on future earnings.

Persons engaged in sports are exposed to liability hazards. The destination of a golf ball hit by the typical player is not assured. An injured party may claim the golfer failed to give adequate warning and thus is guilty of negligence and liable for damages. The defendant would need liability insurance to pay the defense costs and any awarded damages. Other people also are exposed to liability claims. For example, to enter a building via a revolving door could cost thousands of dollars if the entering party pushed the door at such speed as to injure an exiting person.

The family's best liability coverage is comprehensive personal liability protection. Special business and personal activity endorsements generally are available. High limits are recommended. Homeowners policies incorporate a comprehensive personal liability section. The standard amounts are $25,000 for each occurrence, $500 per person for medical payments, and $250 for physical damage to property of others in cases where no liability exists.

Homeowners package versus separate policies

For the eligible insured, the Homeowner forms provide more coverage per dollar than do separate property and liability policies. In a typical situation, it would cost 20 percent more to buy the same coverage with many policies than with a Homeowners form. But some insureds are ineligible for the Homeowners. In most territories, an apartment house owner occupying an apartment in the building cannot buy Homeowners on the property if more than four apartments are in the building. Also homeowners with more than two boarders living in the house are ineligible for Homeowners. Nor can a Homeowners be purchased if the home is a trailer or is owned by an individual but rented entirely to others.

If the insured is eligible for a Homeowners, which policy should be selected? HO–2 covers 17 perils to home and contents and also provides personal liability protection. HO–1 costs less but limits coverage to fire, lightning, the extended coverage perils, theft, and vandalism. HO–1 provides "all-risk" coverage for both home and contents but costs much more than HO–2; yet many insureds believe it is worth the additional cost. HO–3 provides "all-risk" coverage for the home and covers contents against 17 perils. As a middle ground between HO–2 and the HO–5, the HO–3 has become the most widely sold Homeowners form. An apartment dweller would buy HO–4 covering contents and liability only. Insureds may apply up to 10 percent of the contents coverage to cover their interest in building improvements within their own apartment only if they do not own the premises. HO–6 is designed for condominium owners. It is essentially the same as HO–4, except that up to $1,000 of coverage is provided for fixtures, installations, or additions comprising the part of the building within individual condominium units. Condominium insurance is discussed in Chapter 15.

If the insured buys an HO–5, is any other property or liability insurance needed? Some kind of specific insurance for motor vehicles may be needed. The insured may wish to cover some of the excluded perils—earthquake, for example. The insured also may want larger limits on property away from the premises or on particularly valuable pieces of personal property.

Motor vehicle coverage

An auto owner is exposed to two fundamental losses: loss to the auto and loss arising from liability for bodily injury or property damage to others resulting from ownership, operation, or use of an auto. These exposures, the available insurance policies, and their proper uses are discussed in Chapter 14.

Summary

1. The basic insurance principle is the substitution of small certain costs for large uncertain ones. Persons should protect themselves first against losses which could be financially disastrous. If premium money is still available, coverages which are desirable but not essential may be purchased.
2. Loss exposures should be viewed in terms of the loss unit concept, considering all losses that can arise from a single event.
3. Wide price variations exist among life insurers for essentially identical coverage. Many attempts have been made to develop meaningful cost comparisons among policies. The surrender cost index and the premium payment index are more accurate than the traditional method, as they recognize the time value of money. Other methods which consider mortality and lapse probabilities and cash value accumulation patterns also have been devised.

4. Key employee insurance indemnifies a business for losses resulting from the death or disability of a key employee and as a fringe benefit to help retain key personnel sought by competing firms.

5. Insurance can be used in sole proprietorships, partnerships, and closely held corporations to facilitate ownership transfer following the death or disability of a proprietor, partner, or shareholder.

6. Life and health insurance can strengthen company credit, provide collateral for loans, and bolster the confidence of customers, suppliers, and employees in the firm's well-being.

7. Business property and liability exposures must be surveyed and where insurance is needed, the forms discussed in Chapters 11–15 should be reviewed and the appropriate ones selected.

8. In programming life and health insurance, the purposes for and amounts of postloss resources needed must be determined. Available resources should be compared to those needed, then life and health insurance may be used to fill the gaps. All resources must be coordinated into a plan and appropriately protected.

9. Life and health insurance can provide resources for final expenses, mortgage funds, rent funds, adjustment income, family period income, lifetime income for a surviving spouse, education funds, emergency funds, and retirement income.

10. Insurance on the life of a wife and/or mother should not be overlooked. Adequate disability income insurance should be purchased on the spouse to cover the extra expenses that will arise if the wife and/or mother becomes disabled.

11. If the more important needs have been covered, the early purchase of cash value life insurance on the lives of children can establish a low annual premium and protect their insurability. Adequate medical expense insurance for children usually should be purchased.

12. In selecting dwelling coverage, the buyer must weigh the expense of the broader forms against the importance of the additional perils covered.

13. For most insureds, personal property will be covered by one of the Homeowners forms. For articles of high value, a personal property floater providing worldwide "all-risk" protection is recommended. Special coverage also may be needed for fine arts and for property in bank safety deposit boxes.

14. The best liability protection is comprehensive personal liability coverage which is incorporated into the Homeowners policies.

Questions for Review

1. What is a cross-purchase plan in business life and health insurance? What other plan is available to accomplish a similar purpose?

2. Explain how life and health insurance can be used to strengthen a firm's credit standing.

3. What types of final expenses are not properly covered by life insurance?

4. Under what circumstances should insurance be bought on the lives of the wife and children?

5. When would insurance be purchased to cover losses regular enough to be considered current expenses?

6. Explain the loss unit concept.

7. Compare and contrast the six different methods mentioned in the text for life insurance cost comparisons. Is any method more useful than the other for particular purposes?

8. How does a split-dollar plan work? What is its purpose?

9. What types of plans are available to meet the family period income needs?

10. What is variable life insurance?

11. Compare the HO-2 to the HO-5. Compare the HO-4 to the HO-6.

12. What are the major steps in the life insurance programming process?

Questions for Discussion

1. Why do people often substitute the small certain cost of premiums for the small uncertain costs of losses?

2. How should buyers compare policy costs if they do not intend to surrender their life insurance before their deaths?

3. Prepare a program that will satisfy your life and health insurance needs.

4. Which of the life and health insurance needs do you consider essential? Which are merely desirable? Explain.

5. Prepare a program that will satisfy your property and liability insurance needs.

6. Which of the property and liability insurance needs do you consider essential? Which are merely desirable? Explain.

7. Should disability income insurance be purchased as a rider to a life insurance policy or should it be purchased separately, i.e. independently of life insurance? Explain.

22

Types of insurers

An industry is composed of many business units, and their ownership is organized under several different legal forms. In the retail food industry grocery stores are formed as sole proprietorships, partnerships, and corporations. Others are consumers' cooperatives owned by the customers. In some mining communities the grocery store is owned and operated by the corporation. On military posts the government owns and operates grocery stores. The pattern in the insurance industry is similar: many separate insurers (nearly 5,600 U.S. insurers at the beginning of 1984) organized under a variety of ownership forms.

A Preview

Insurers operating in the United States are owned either privately or by a government unit. Privately owned insurers are organized either as proprietary or cooperative. Government insurers are operated by either state or federal governments. The dominant type of proprietary insurer is the capital stock company; the dominant type of cooperative insurer is the mutual insurance company. The principal type of state insurer is the workers' compensation fund; the principal type of federal insurer is the old-age, survivors, disability, and health insurance program operated by the Social Security Administration under the U.S. Department of Health and Human Services.

Motives for formation

Several motives may lead to the formation of a private insurer: (1) to earn profits for its owners, (2) to extract gains for its promoters, (3) to earn fees and commissions by forming a separate company to manage the insurer or to market its product, (4) to lower insurance costs for its owners, (5) to provide its owners with a type of insurance protection not otherwise available to them in the market, and (6) to sell services only (medical, legal, or administrative) on a prepaid basis.

A simplistic statement of the difference between the *raison d'être* of a proprietary insurer and a cooperative insurer is that proprietary insurers are organized and operated for profit and cooperative insurers are formed and operated to furnish insurance at cost to members. Because the opposite also may be true, such oversimplification is misleading. Proprietary insurers have been formed and operated by other businesses to obtain their insurance at cost. (These subsidiary insurance companies are called "captive insurers" and sometimes are formed as an alternative to self-insurance.) Cooperative insurers have been organized and operated for the profit of separate insurance management companies.

Similarities and differences

Whether the insurer is a proprietary or a cooperative usually is unimportant to the buyer because the similarities are significant, whereas the differences usually are not. More important are *distinctions* among *types* of proprietary insurers, *types* of cooperative insurers, and insurers of the *same type*. The similarities between proprietary insurers and cooperative insurers are many. They write the same kinds of insurance and may use similar marketing systems. In life insurance both proprietary and cooperative insurers frequently use an agency system in which the agent serves only one life insurer. A similar marketing arrangement is used widely in property and liability insurance by cooperative insurers. The dominant marketing method used by proprietary property and liability insurers is an agency system in which the agent usually represents more than one insurer.

Proprietary and cooperative insurers may have the same pricing policy: a fixed premium with no return of an "excess charge," called a "dividend," and no additional charge, called an "assessment." However, some cooperative insurers operate on an assessment basis, and among both proprietary and cooperative insurers are those that pay regular refunds (called dividends) to policyowners. Insurance contracts under which dividends are paid regularly are called "participating policies." In life insurance all cooperative insurers and many proprietary insurers write participating policies. In property and liability insurance proprietary, insurers rarely write participating policies, and only some cooperative insurers issue "dividend-paying contracts."

A principal difference between proprietary and cooperative insurers is that policyowners of cooperatives must become owners of the insurer or be insurers themselves. They cannot enter into a simple buyer-seller relationship as customers purchasing insurance from proprietary insurers. It will become apparent as the discussion progresses that this distinction often is unimportant. Currently, cooperative insurers have the dominant position in life insurance and proprietary insurers dominate property and liability insurance based on the amount of business transacted.

Unincorporated Proprietary Insurers

Proprietary insurers may be unincorporated business units or incorporated business entities. The underwriters at Lloyd's of London are the principal unincorporated proprietary insurers operating in the United States. A few American-type Lloyds' organizations also write insurance in this country.

Lloyd's of London

In 17th-century England, the coffeehouse was the center of the insurance world. Shipowners seeking insurance for a voyage would write a proposal stating the name of the ship, its ownership, captain, cargo, destination, the amount of insurance desired, and so on. The would-be insured would place the proposal on a sideboard in the coffeehouse, then go about his coffee drinking and wait for would-be insurers to act. Merchants wanting to "take a flyer" in the insurance business, as well as established underwriters, would study the proposal. An underwriter might note that a proposal asked for £10,000 of insurance. Available resources would permit assumption of only one tenth of that amount, so the underwriter would write £1,000, indicate the rate (for example, 5 percent), then sign the proposal. The custom of the insurer signing under the proposal is the origin of the word "underwriter." Eventually, the entire £10,000 would be contracted. It was no coincidence that England became the largest exporter of marine insurance and also the greatest trading nation the world had ever seen. The merchant, adequately insured, would undertake ventures undreamed of in the absence of insurance.

The "live wire" among the coffeehouse proprietors was Edward Lloyd, who operated a house on Tower Street. Lloyd perceived that information about the condition of ships, tides, size, and types of cargoes, weather conditions, and anything remotely connected with seagoing commerce was of interest to the coffeehouse patrons. These men would wander from coffeehouse to coffeehouse, picking up the latest gossip. Lloyd reasoned that if he could gather the news and relay it to those in his coffee-house, his patrons would stay in his shop instead of roaming among competitors in their quest for news.

Edward Lloyd's coffeehouse soon became known as the place to hear all the news first, and his business prospered. In 1696 he began publication of *Lloyd's News,* a flyer that appeared three times a week. By this time, Lloyd's was in undisputed first place as an insurance center, and underwriters who frequented Lloyd's coffeehouse became the most prominent in the business. Eventually Lloyd's stopped serving coffee and moved to London's financial district. The underwriters at Lloyd's constitute one of the richest, most powerful, and important insurance groups in the world.

Nature of Lloyd's.   Contrary to the belief of the lay public, Lloyd's is not an insurer and does not issue policies. It is an association of individuals who write insurance for their own account. The New York Stock Exchange, which began as an open-air mart under a buttonwood tree at Broad and Wall streets, bears the same relationship to stock purchases and sales "on the exchange" as Lloyd's bears to insurance purchases from its members. The New York Stock Exchange, like Lloyd's, provides a hall, as well as procedures, for the transaction of business. Neither organization engages in any trade. The direct facilities of Lloyd's are open to three groups: members, subscribers, and associates.

Members are of two classes: underwriting and nonunderwriting. Underwriting members, or "names," as they often are called, are entitled to accept risks on their own account. Currently there are more than 21,000 underwriting members conducting their business through underwriting agents in their "underwriting boxes" accepting (or rejecting) proposals put before them by Lloyd's brokers. Nonunderwriting members have all the facilities of Lloyd's except the privilege of acting as insurers. They can act as brokers, placing business with underwriting members.

In 1968 in an effort to secure additional capital, non-British members were elected. Of the 240 new members elected 16 were non-British. In 1969 new ground again was broken when 46 women were elected to membership. Soon thereafter Lloyd's membership included more than 700 foreigners and more than 1,300 women.

Annual *subscribers* are those persons, in addition to members, who have been given the privilege of operating as Lloyd's brokers. More than 200 insurance brokerage firms have this privilege.

Associates are technicians, such as lawyers, claim adjusters, and actuaries who perform services for members and subscribers.

Members, subscribers, and associates must be approved by the governing body of Lloyd's called the Committee of Lloyd's—an elected body of 12 members who serve a four-year term.

Functions of Lloyd's.   Lloyd's obtains worldwide underwriting information on marine and aviation risks, maintains a complete record of losses, aids in loss settlements, and supervises salvage and repairs throughout the world. Lloyd's provides underwriting quarters for its members and a place for the transaction of insurance by member underwriters. It promulgates regulations for business transaction, arbitrates disputes, develops policy forms, and issues policies for members. Members of Lloyd's resist rules and regulations they believe are unnecessary to protect the public. While freedom is highly valued, members recognize that independence does not excuse them from observing a number of unwritten rules. The Committee of Lloyd's does not have the authority to establish underwriting rules, to make rates, or to prescribe policy conditions. An underwriter is free to write any kind of insurance and to set the premium. Committee regulations are designed chiefly to assure the solvency of underwriting members.

In the early 1980s, heavy underwriting losses (including a number of questionable losses) caused financial embarrassment to some members of Lloyd's. A subsequent suit against Lloyd's for malfeasance (settled out of court for $28 million) and the threat to the impeccable reputation of Lloyd's helped bring about the establishment of the Council of Lloyd's. The Council, made up of members of Lloyd's, was charged with the responsibility of investigating allegations of wrongdoing on the part of members. In addition, the Council was empowered to determine and carry out appropriate disciplinary action where reprehensible behavior on the part of a member is found. Formation of the Council was largely the result of pressure from the British government on Lloyd's to tighten its control over members or face governmental intervention into the regulation of Lloyd's operations.

Operations of Lloyd's. Proposals for insurance are placed before Lloyd's underwriting members or their agents by duly authorized brokers. The broker prepares the policy and submits it to the Policy Signing Office at Lloyd's. There the policy is examined, and, if it conforms to agreed-upon rules, a stamp is placed upon it. The policy then is submitted to underwriters, and those who participate in the policy will affix their signatures. Today the underwriting usually is by syndicates, each managed by an agent. Often the managing agent organizes the syndicate. The syndicate members furnish the capital; the syndicate agent manages the business. The stamp of a syndicate usually lists the participating members (referred to as "names"), showing the proportion of the total risk assumed by each member, and the affixing of the stamp is attested by the signature of the agent in charge. Any number of members may be in a syndicate, and any number of syndicates may be involved in one policy. More than 430 syndicates are currently in operation.

The underwriting agent (usually the syndicate manager) must have "underwriting instinct"—the ability to quote a rate, establish terms and conditions, and make quick decisions as to how much of the risk is acceptable. When the replica of the Mayflower was preparing for its trip to the United States several years ago, a broker entered "The Room" at Lloyd's to obtain insurance for the voyage. It is reported that one old underwriter looked at the proposal for several seconds, then said, "Mayflower II, let's see—what did I quote on the other one?" Experience is the principal ingredient in "underwriting instinct."

A number of specialists for given lines of insurance have evolved and are known as leaders for that line. A broker seeking to place a risk will try to get a leader in that line to be the first to accept a share. If the broker is successful, the job of covering the remaining shares usually is simple; other underwriters are willing to follow suit.

Members of a syndicate are responsible only for their own share of the risk. In the absence of a contrary policy provision, enforcement of the contract in court can be obtained only by proceeding against each underwriter separately. However, it is the practice for all underwriters to pay their share if one of them is judged liable. This practice, of course, facilitates the procedure for the insured in case of litigation.

The underwriters at Lloyd's never have written much life insurance, and that issued is limited to short-term policies. The Committee of Lloyd's sponsors a limited liability corporation, Lloyd's Life Assurance Ltd., to write long-term life insurance. Shares may be purchased only by Lloyd's members.

Financial strength of Lloyd's. The strength of Lloyd's lies not only in its extensive resources but also in the integrity of the underwriting members. Lloyd's has endeavored to admit only underwriters of substantial resources who place no limit on their liability. Applicants for membership in Lloyd's are investigated thoroughly to determine their willingness and ability to meet their financial obligations.

Once a person is admitted as an underwriting member, efforts are made to assure continuing financial responsibility. Accounts are examined periodically, and the association sees that insurance contracts are fulfilled. Although no legal compulsion exists, solvent underwriting members have assumed the liability of defaulting members. As a further safeguard, members of Lloyd's reinsure with one another in order to reduce their individual exposure.

Specific guarantees of financial security to Lloyd's policyowners are as follows:

1. Underwriting deposits. Deposits with the Committee of Lloyd's must be made by underwriting members. The amount required is a function of the type and volume of business the underwriter intends to handle. These deposits are held for security of the policies underwritten by the individual member and are held in the name of the corporation of Lloyd's as trustee.

2. Premium trust fund. Under the provisions of the Insurance Companies Act of 1958, each underwriter must pay into a trust fund under an approved trust deed all premiums received for insurance business transacted. Withdrawals are allowed only for payment of underwriting expenses and claims under the contract. Each member must at all times maintain a minimum deposit in the premium trust fund, and as long as this deposit remains intact, underwriting profits are distributed to the members when earned.

An American trust fund was voluntarily set up in 1939 on behalf of the individual underwriters. The trust provides that all premiums collected in dollars be placed in the American trust fund on behalf of the underwriters, to be used to pay the claims on all policies written in dollars. The trust fund is held in New York and assures prompt payment of losses, even those of catastrophic proportions.[1]

3. Central guarantee fund.   A fund of several million pounds arising from an annual levy on the premium income of all underwriting members is held by the Committee of Lloyd's, to be used to pay the insurance obligations of insolvent members.

4. Reserves held by underwriting agents.   Underwriting agents generally do not distribute the full net profits earned by the members. Instead they hold funds in reserve to pay future claims. As these funds are held in trust, they are protected from the general creditors of the underwriter.

Kinds of policies written by Lloyd's.   Although the chief business of the underwriting members of Lloyd's is to provide property and liability covers for the usual everyday exposures, all members do not confine themselves to these risks. At the beginning of the 1980s, the underwriters at Lloyd's were writing about $3 billion in annual premiums. It is virtually folklore that members of Lloyd's will underwrite any type of risk. Yet statements that Lloyd's is issuing odds and taking bets on such developments as the outcome of an election or the chance of war are erroneous newspaper phraseology. Lloyd's accepts no bets. It is true that some underwriters at Lloyd's often will issue "insurance" against the election of a particular candidate; but the person seeking the "insurance" must have an insurable interest; that is, the person must stand to lose by the event insured against before the risk will be underwritten. Thus a political employee who would be without a job if another party won the election could obtain "insurance" against the election of the opposition, but such "insurance" would not be available to someone wishing to bet on the election outcome. The underwriters at Lloyd's once refused to write a $2.4 million policy on the capture of the Loch Ness monster. A whiskey firm wanted to offer this amount as a prize in a contest. The United Press International quoted a Lloyd's spokesman as saying: "The risk is too great."

The underwriters of Lloyd's of London are licensed insurers only in Illinois and Kentucky. In other states they must operate as nonadmitted

---

[1] Lloyd's underwriters are licensed to do business in Illinois and Kentucky. In Illinois, Lloyd's underwriters have $2.5 million in trust and more than $80 million of nontrust funds for the protection of policyowners in that state. For the protection of policyowners in Kentucky they have $1 million on deposit in that state. This protection is in addition to that afforded through the American trust fund.

insurers meaning that only an agent or broker who has a "surplus lines" or "excess lines" license can place business with them and then only if the coverage sought is not available from admitted insurers. American insurance buyers, nevertheless, by initiating the contact with a Lloyd's broker and making all arrangements outside the state, can purchase insurance from underwriters at Lloyd's without the services of a licensed "surplus line" agent or broker and without the restrictions put on nonadmitted insurers.

Special contributions of Lloyd's.   An important service performed by the underwriters at Lloyd's is to provide types and amounts of coverage unavailable elsewhere. As mentioned, American insurers, because of surplus limitations, may be unable to write all the insurance for which a legitimate demand exists. Lloyd's has been particularly helpful in providing additional underwriting capacity. The underwriters at Lloyd's also especially contribute by pioneering and developing new covers such as rain insurance and comprehensive coverage for banks. Their progressive efforts have a salutary effect on the industry because other insurers often follow their lead.

American Lloyds

The success of Lloyd's of London has led to formation of associations of private underwriters in the United States, some calling themselves "Lloyds Associations."[2] American Lloyds organizations have no connection with Lloyd's of London. They have neither the same name (note the lack of an apostrophe) nor the same reputation. American Lloyds organizations are unincorporated associations of individuals who assume a specified portion of liability under each policy issued. For example, Lloyds, New York, the oldest American Lloyds (1892), currently has 11 individual underwriters who have agreed to assume the potential liability for losses under each policy written in accordance with the following percentages: 20.75, 18.75, 13.5, 12, 10.25, 8, 7.75, 3, 2.2, 2, and 1.8. These associations of individual underwriters operate through an attorney-in-fact who selects risks, develops rates, and adjusts losses using a staff of technical specialists. The financial risk is borne by the individual underwriting members. Liability is separate and not joint. Much of the risk is reinsured by other insurers.

Insurance buyers in an American Lloyds association need to check both the financial arrangements and the probable continuity of the individual insurers. American Lloyds operate under a variety of different plans. In some associations, deposits with the attorney-in-fact are made by the underwriters to guarantee payment of their policy obligations with no further liability assumed. In other associations in addition to the deposit, the underwriter assumes liability for further payments if

---

[2] Because of the doubtful value of this kind of organization, the New York Insurance Code prohibits the organization of new associations of this type.

needed to pay claims. This additional liability is unlimited in some organizations but limited in others. An American Lloyds association may operate under a plan which permits an underwriter to withdraw from acceptance of new business and eventually from the association. Withdrawal of an underwriter from the association may create a problem because some states require a continuing minimum amount of deposits from the underwriters before new business can be written. If these deposits fall below the required minimum because underwriters withdraw from the association, the association is liquidated even though financially able to handle all obligations.

Best's Insurance Reports lists 48 active American Lloyds organizations, and 46 of these operate in Texas, plus one each in New York and New Mexico. Rating laws in Texas do not apply to American Lloyds, thus accounting for their large numbers.

Beginning in 1978, legislation was passed in New York, Florida, and Illinois that allowed the establishment of Insurance Exchanges modeled after Lloyd's of London. The three exchanges include more than 60 underwriting syndicates. The New York and Florida exchanges underwrite reinsurance and non-U.S. direct business. The Illinois exchange writes direct and reinsurance business regardless of the geographic origin, but limits transactions by requiring a minimum premium of $50,000. The New York legislation established a "free trade zone" which allows underwriters to issue insurance without obtaining the insurance commissioner's approval of rates and policy forms.

Incorporated Proprietary Insurers

The typical capital stock insurer is like any business corporation in that its objective is to earn a profit for its owners—in this case by the sale of insurance and investment of funds from capital and paid-in surplus, premium income, and earned surplus. Its capital and paid-in surplus are subscribed by stockholders. Underwriting is on a corporate basis as distinguished from an individual basis, meaning that shareholders do not directly underwrite the risk as do underwriters in a Lloyds association. Both underwriting gains and losses and investment gains and losses are reflected in the surplus position of the corporation. Unlike members of Lloyds associations, stockholders cannot withdraw their funds directly from the organization, but they can dispose of their interest by selling their shares of stock at whatever prices the shares will bring in the market. These prices depend on how the market appraises the profit potential of the company and upon the market psychology at the time.

Management control of the company ultimately rests with the stockholders who elect members of the board of directors who in turn delegate administration and many managerial decisions to company officers appointed by the board. Policyowners are customers of the company, and, generally, are charged a fixed premium. These insurers usually acquire their business through independent agents and brokers, although the second largest "direct writer" (nonagency company) is a capital stock company. However, that company (Allstate) is experimenting in some localities with the use of independent agents.

Capital stock insurers write about 74 percent of the total property and liability insurance premiums written by privately owned U.S. insurers, and underwrite about 43 percent of the total life insurance in force in U.S. companies.

Special contributions of capital stock companies

The name "stock company" always has been equated with "service through agents." The capital stock property and liability insurers fostered and nourished what is known as "the American agency system." Under this system an insurance agent, serving as an intermediary between the insurer and the insured, is paid a commission in return for services to be performed for both insureds and insurers. (The nature of these services will be discussed presently.) Agency activity is not confined to a single insurer. Also, independent agents no longer are necessarily confined to representing only stock insurers. The independent agent is an independent businessperson, owning the renewals on policies written by the agency.

Independent agents must not be confused with direct writing agents (also called "exclusive agents," "captive agents," and "dependent agents") used by most life insurers and by some of the well-known, large property and liability insurers. The dependent agent performs many of the services offered by independent agents, but is limited because all insurance must be placed with one insurer, or at least that insurer must be given first chance.

In general, the agent functions as buyer for the client and seller for the insurers and, consequently, has a responsibility to each. Unless the agent performs as a conscientious professional, a conflict of interest could arise. For the insurer, the agent must help in selecting insureds, handle the forms necessary for writing the insurance, sometimes write the policy, collect the premiums, and, in some lines of insurance, pay small claims. The agent has many obligations to the insured. The client may need help in determining loss exposures and which ones to insure. The agent must prescribe the correct policy forms and place them with sound, competent, and reliable insurers on the best terms available for cost, coverage, loss prevention, and claims.

As many people are now aware, insurance is not always easy to obtain. Insurers do not want to write a policy unless they believe a profit can be earned. Insurance against certain perils and against losses of some kinds of property involving hazardous business occupancy is unprofitable at affordable rates and therefore difficult to place. Agents who supply their insurers with profitable business in some instances can persuade their insurers to accept an unprofitable class of business ordinarily rejected. Dealing with influential agents operating under the independent agency system is an advantage because of their ability to place accommodation business (as it is called) with agency companies. If clients expect agents to place undesirable business, they should also give them desirable business. Auto insurance for youthful drivers is an example of an accommodation line. If agents have placed the coverage on family business exposures with an insurer, they may be able to persuade that insurer to write coverage on the car belonging to the family's pride and joy who is attending college—provided there are no other major underwriting danger signals, such as "participation in a mobile pot party." Accommodation business is not as easy to place as it once was, and to do so the agent must have exceptionally good relations with insurers. Many insurers, regardless of their relationship with agents, would refuse certain coverages and some prospective insureds. For them, it would make no difference if the agent were the mother of the president of the insurance company.

Consumer-Type Cooperative Insurers

Cooperative business organizations in the United States are of two types: consumers and producers. Consumers' cooperatives usually are formed by those wanting lower prices. Sometimes the purpose is to control the quality of goods or services offered members. Producers' cooperatives are formed by those who wish to provide members with efficient marketing facilities. An example of a consumers' cooperative is a campus bookstore organized to furnish student members textbooks at cost. An example of a producers' cooperative is the organization of citrus fruit growers in California that sells the fruit crops of members.

Both types of cooperatives appear in the insurance industry. Consumers' cooperatives, which are more prevalent than producers' cooperatives, include reciprocal insurance exchanges and mutual insurers. Producers' cooperatives include Blue Cross and Blue Shield organizations sponsored by hospitals and doctors, and cooperative underwriting organizations such as the AFIA, which manages the foreign business of its members.

As with proprietary insurers, cooperative insurers may be unincorporated or incorporated. Unincorporated ones are called reciprocal insurance exchanges; incorporated ones are called mutual companies.

Reciprocal insurance exchanges

The reciprocal insurance exchange originated in 1881 in New York when a group of cost-conscious dry goods merchants reacted to the lack of sophistication in fire insurance ratemaking. Excessively broad rate classifications were used, charging hazardous and nonhazardous exposures the same rate. The dry goods merchants thought they were getting the short end of the bolt and decided to insure one another by exchanging insurance contracts.

A reciprocal exchange in its basic form operates as follows. Each of 1,000 dwellers in suburbia owns a house worth $80,000. The 1,000 houseowners form an interinsurance exchange. Each subscribes for $80,000 of insurance coverage, and in turn accepts (underwrites) $80,000 of risk on each of the 1,000 houses. If a subscriber's house is totally destroyed by fire, the interinsurance exchange will reimburse the loss through contributions of $80 from each of the 1,000 subscribers. The effect of the reciprocal arrangement is that subscribers instead of having an $80,000 loss exposure on their own property, have an $80,000 loss exposure spread among 1,000 properties. With this large number of exposure units, the losses become predictable within a manageable range. Consequently, a subscriber's share of the predicted loss can be calculated, and that amount coupled with a portion of expenses is the premium charged.

A separate account is held in the name of each subscriber. To this account are credited premiums paid plus interest earned. The account is debited with the subscriber's share of losses and expenses. A credit balance may be retained in the account or refunded to the subscriber in part or in full. A subscriber who terminates participation may withdraw any credit balance remaining.

A subscriber is held liable only for the agreed upon share of losses and expenses, and the maximum amount of this liability may be specified as a multiple of the annual premium. This type of liability arrangement is described as both individual (as distinguished from joint) and limited (as distinguished from unlimited).

A reciprocal exchange usually operates under a trade name and is managed by an attorney-in-fact. The insurance operation (as distinguished from that of management) is nonprofit, as members pay only their share of losses and expenses. Some reciprocals use agents to acquire business; others write business directly or through a trade association of which they may be an adjunct.

In one respect, reciprocals are like Lloyd's of London because the exchange issues no policies, merely furnishing a mechanism for members to insure one another. An important difference is that membership in the exchange is required for insurance. No one can buy insurance unless offering insurance in return. Members of Lloyd's, however, insure outsiders and, aside from reinsurance operations, do not insure one another. This distinguishing feature marks reciprocals as cooperative insurers and Lloyd's underwriters as proprietary insurers.

The reciprocal is not a corporation or a partnership. Corporations or partnerships may be members of a reciprocal, and the attorney-in-fact usually incorporates; but still the organization is individual. The foregoing describes a reciprocal exchange in its pristine form. Operational and legislative changes have modified the form to some extent, as will soon become apparent.

Operation of a reciprocal. The operation of a reciprocal exchange usually follows a general pattern. The attorney-in-fact's authority comes from an agreement (called the "subscriber's agreement") inserted in each application blank and signed by the subscriber. The attorney-in-fact, the principal administrative officer, must be qualified to direct the managerial functions of underwriting and rating risks, sales promotion, claims administration, and handling of finances. The attorney-in-fact often is controlled by an advisory committee selected by the members.

The attorney-in-fact may be paid a salary, but usually receives a percentage of the premiums collected. In some exchanges the percentage may be as low as 5 percent, but in these plans the exchange pays the operation expenses. In others the percentage often is about 35 percent from which the attorney-in-fact pays all costs except losses, loss adjustment, taxes, and fees, which are absorbed by the remaining 65 percent. What happens when the entire 65 percent is not needed for claims and expenses or when it is inadequate to cover these expenses? At this point variations appear among reciprocals that distinguish them from their original form. In the simplest form, surpluses are divided among the individual members accounts because no group surplus is retained. If the funds are insufficient, the subscribers are assessed for their separate liability up to an agreed upon amount. But as some surplus funds are necessary to absorb investment losses, to level irregular claims experience, and to finance expansion, reciprocals generally retain some of the surplus contributed by every subscriber. Reciprocal exchanges domiciled in New York are required to accumulate and maintain a special contingent surplus by retaining annually at least 1 percent of net premium income. This surplus cannot be depleted by dividend payments. New York reciprocals also must make all their assets, including those to offset subscribers' reserves, available to meet claims.

Some exchanges, particularly those writing only auto insurance, do not maintain surplus accounts for each subscriber. Instead, all surplus funds are held undivided as property of the exchange. Terminating subscribers receive nothing. These exchanges function virtually as mutual insurers, and the subscriber's relationship to the exchange is similar to that of a mutual policyowner's relationship to the insurer. Reciprocals writing fire insurance, however, usually maintain individual accounts and return to the subscribers nearly all contributed surplus upon withdrawal. The subscriber's agreement sets forth the rights of a withdrawing subscriber, but withdrawal of surplus is not permitted if it impairs the minimum surplus required. New York state requires that the exchange receive 60 days' notice of withdrawal.

Reciprocals generally can issue nonassessable policies when they have an undivided surplus (called "free surplus") equal to the minimum capital and surplus required for stock insurers transacting similar business. Under the basic reciprocal form, subscribers participate in savings and assume limited liability for assessments needed to pay their share of unpaid claims. Most fire reciprocals operate in this manner. Some reciprocals, mostly auto, charge fixed premiums, return no savings, and include no assessment provision, while others include an assessment provision yet return no savings.

Some 50 reciprocal exchanges operate in the United States. About

20 percent are California domiciled and 16 percent are domiciled in Missouri. The reciprocal exchanges write about 7 percent of the property and liability premiums in the United States, more than 75 percent of which is for auto insurance. The Farmers Insurance Exchange, Los Angeles, one of the largest insurers in the world, writes about 30 percent of the reciprocal insurance premiums.

Mutual companies

A mutual insurer is a cooperative corporation organized and owned by its insureds. An accounting student reviewing a mutual insurer's balance sheet will be surprised to find the net worth account includes no capital stock but only surplus. Policyowners of mutual insurers in many ways occupy a position similar to stockholders of stock insurers. Voting control is in their hands. When the insurer earns a profit, some may be divided among the insureds as "policy dividends." The remainder is used to strengthen the insurer by building surplus.[3] Losses are sustained by policyowners through lower dividends, assessments (if permitted by policy provisions), or by the insurer who will absorb the loss through a reduction in surplus.

A distinction between principle and practice is necessary. In a stock insurer the stockholders technically control the company through their votes for the board of directors, which in turn elects or appoints the managing officers. In practice, however, stockholders usually are so widely scattered that the control rests with those who hold a "working majority"—an amount of stock sufficient to provide the majority of votes ordinarily cast at stockholders' meetings. Often the working control is held by the active management of the corporation.

In a mutual company, theoretically, control is held by the policyowners through election of the board of directors. In practice, aside from the small farm mutuals, control is in the hands of a few officers and directors who have a working majority of votes by virtue of holding proxies—authority to vote on behalf of policyowners. Just as few stockholders ever attend a stockholders' meeting, few policyowners ever attend policyowners' meetings. Therefore, the organization usually is controlled by a few policyowners, who generally are the active managers.

Mutual insurers may be arrayed according to the method used in pricing arrangements. At one extreme is the pure assessment mutual; at the other is the perpetual mutual issuing a policy without a termination date and for a single premium. In between are varying arrangements of premium prepayment plans.

---

[3] In a mutual company the concept of surplus as an ownership interest is clouded. A policyowner upon withdrawal is not entitled to a pro rata interest in the surplus. In fact, if the insurer is dissolved, the surplus may revert to the state under the law of escheat. Withdrawing policyowners in some mutual life insurers are given a surrender dividend, but this dividend represents only part of their contribution to the surplus and is not a full return of their "theoretical" interest in the company. The surplus, therefore, represents the ownership interest only of those who remain policyowners.

Pure assessment mutuals. Pure assessment mutuals primarily write fire insurance on farm property. They often are called "county mutuals," "farm mutuals," "local mutuals," or "town mutuals." Hundreds of such mutuals exist (Illinois alone has about 200), but the premium volume is small. In Illinois, an important farm state, farm mutuals write only about one half of 1 percent of all property and liability premiums in that state. Assessment mutual insurers also are found in life insurance but usually write only burial insurance.

Assessment mutuals are the purest form of cooperative activity for handling risk. Their organization and operation plan are simple. The policyowners are its owners, each has a vote, and they elect the board of directors and officers. Usually, no more than one or two officers receive a salary. Some farm mutuals are too small to have full-time paid officers. The employed officer or officers supervise the functions necessary to the operation. One of several plans of operation may be used:

1. The insurer may issue the policy, charging a small fee, and assess each member for funds necessary to pay expenses and claims.

2. The insurer may issue the policy, charging a premium large enough to pay expenses and small losses. To provide for large losses, members sign premium notes payable if losses and expenses exceed advance premiums. Their liability is limited to the amount of these notes.

3. The insurer may issue the policy, charging a cash premium sufficient to pay expenses and small losses. If additional funds are necessary for claims and expenses, the assessment of members is unlimited. Most assessment insurers operate on this principle.

Considerations for insurance buyers. Insureds usually cannot buy from pure assessment mutuals. Their insureds are members of a local community banded together to furnish each other mutual aid. That type of operation works for a group of neighbors but would prove difficult to administer if extended over wide areas and nonhomogeneous groups. For those with the opportunity to buy from a pure assessment mutual, some question may arise whether they should. The caliber of their managements varies widely. Particularly important is the investigation of the insurers reinsurance facilities, as insurers writing properties in only one community are subject to catastrophic loss. Furthermore, even well-managed pure assessment mutuals might levy large assessments in high claim years, a factor which could deter purchase of insurance from these insurers. Well-managed assessment mutuals are plentiful, and those eligible insurance buyers who do not object to the assessment principle will find such insurers satisfactory.

Advance premium mutuals. Full advance premium mutuals charge annual premiums computed to provide sufficient funds to pay all claims and expenses and to strengthen surplus. Many of the larger mutuals charge an advance premium comparable to that charged by most stock companies and anticipate returning the policyowner at the end of the policy period a refund called a "policy dividend." A few advance premium mutuals charge amounts equal to those of stock companies without returning dividends to policyowners. Many, however, charge an initial premium considerably lower than that charged by "dividend-paying mutuals" but return no "policy dividends."

When an advance premium mutual incurs claims in excess of those assumed in the premiums, some will assess policyowners for the funds. However, the large advance premium mutuals have accumulated sufficient surpluses so they are permitted by state regulatory authorities to write nonassessable policies. Losses are then absorbed by the insurers through reduced surpluses.

Some advance premium mutuals conduct their business on the same basis as most stock insurers. They use independent agents, write a variety of coverages, and operate over a wide geographical area. Others write business on a national scale through salaried representatives or through "exclusive" agents. Distribution systems are discussed in Chapter 23. Some limit their writings to a specialty line—auto insurance, for example. The largest mutual insurers are advance premium mutuals issuing only nonassessable policies.

Perpetual mutuals.   The name "perpetual" describes the duration of the coverage written. Their policies are written without a termination date, and the insured pays a large initial premium. The premium is calculated to provide a capital fund sufficient to yield investment income each year to cover expenses, claims, and a contribution to surplus. After the policy has been in force a certain number of years, the insured is paid an annual dividend. The policy may be canceled either by the insurer or the insured; if canceled, the initial single-premium deposit is returned.

The first mutual insurance company, the Philadelphia Contributionship for the Insurance of Houses from Loss by Fire, was founded by Benjamin Franklin in 1752. This company, still operating, was formed to insure brick or stone buildings of nonhazardous occupancy in and about Philadelphia. It operates as a perpetual mutual. Since 1895, it has paid an annual dividend of at least 10 percent on deposit premiums on fire insurance policies in force at least 10 years. Currently it pays 20 percent. The dividends are 5 and 10 percent, respectively, for policies in force from one through four years and five through nine years.

The Philadelphia Contributionship was known popularly as the Hand-in-Hand, as four clasped hands appeared on the company's fire mark. This emblem was attached to the front of houses belonging to Contributionship members to show that they were insured. The Hand-in-Hand regularly made donations to the city's volunteer fire-fighting companies. These fire fighters answered calls to any dwelling, but the Hand-in-Hand officers believed that firemen would be more diligent if the fire mark of a contributor was on the burning building.

Because of unfavorable loss experience, at a general meeting of the Contributionship in 1781, it was resolved "That no houses having a tree or trees planted before them shall be insured or reinsured. That if any person in the future having a house insured shall plant a tree or trees before it in the street, if not removed in three months from the time of planting he shall forfeit the benefit of the insurance." As many householders preferred shade to insurance, they withdrew. In 1847 the dissenters formed their own company, the Mutual Assurance Company for Insuring Houses from Loss by Fire in and near Philadelphia. They chose as their fire mark a tree, and from that symbol the company became popularly known as the Green Tree Mutual.

The issuance of perpetual policies is not restricted to mutual insurers. For example, the Stock Insurance Company of the Green Tree was formed in 1949 to write nonassessable perpetual single-premium deposit policies to cover losses from the extended coverage perils (windstorm, hail, explosion, riot and civil commotion, damage by aircraft or by vehicle, and smoke damage) for policyowners with fire insurance coverage.

Perpetual policies are not available for most insurance buyers. The geographical area covered is small, and the eligible insureds are restricted. Types and amounts of coverage written also are limited. For those who qualify, a perpetual policy can be an attractive investment offering income tax savings as well as high dividends on deposit premiums. The cost of the insurance is paid from the investment income earned by the company on the policyowner's single-premium deposit. The investment earnings the company uses to pay losses and expenses are not treated as taxable income to the policyowner. The insured, therefore, pays for insurance with tax-free dollars.

Factory mutuals.   In 1822 in North Providence, Rhode Island, Zachariah Allen built a textile mill. Allen, whose hobby was fire prevention, vowed to build a factory of near-zero probability of fire even at a substantially high cost, but Allen consoled himself with rough calculations of the reduction he expected to receive on fire insurance premiums. Imagine his shock when told that he would pay the same as the owner of the ramshackle factory across the millpond. The fire underwriters advised Allen they were in the business of paying losses, not of preventing them. Allen then pledged to revise insurance company operations as he had revised mill-building practices.

After making a thorough study of insurance, in 1835 Allen became one of the moving forces in the organization of the Manufacturers Mutual Fire Insurance Company of Rhode Island. Its chief function was to investigate loss prevention and protection techniques and to establish strict conditions to be met by factories before selling them insurance. Sales were limited to owners of high moral standing who would use the best type of construction and housekeeping. If losses occurred the owner would be indemnified, but the number one objective was loss prevention.

Four factory mutuals prevail. The youngest, the Protection Mutual Insurance Company, was formed in 1887. Operations of the four are managed by the Associated Factory Mutual Fire Insurance Companies. Because the basic philosophy of the factory mutual is the prevention of loss, applicants for insurance are rigidly inspected before approval. Periodic inspections also are made after policies are issued. Only high-grade sprinklered premises are acceptable, and because inspection cost is so high, only large insureds can qualify economically. The factory mutuals own and operate a stock insurance company, the Affiliated FM Insurance Company, which issues participating policies on certain properties that fail to meet the standards of the factory mutuals, and writes Homeowners policies for employees of those insured by factory mutuals.

Prior to 1984 factory mutuals charged an advance premium many times larger than the estimated amount needed for claims and expenses. At the end of the policy period, a large "dividend" was returned, usually by deducting it from the premium for the subsequent policy period. This pricing method resulted in added safety to the insurers, increased underwriting capacity, and a substantial permanent investment account for the insurers. The same premium was charged for one-year as for three-year contracts. Typically, the dividends amounted to about 81 percent on one-year contracts and from 40 to 45 percent on three-year policies.

After 140 years of dependence on the advance premium system, the four factory mutuals have decided to go to one-year contracts exclusively, marking the end of the high-premium deposit program. Beginning in 1984, new and renewing policyholders were charged a single year's premium, with annual dividends expected to amount to about 15 percent. Competition for the factory mutuals' highly protected clientele (and, no doubt, the insureds' emphasis on cash flow and the current relatively high interest rates) appears to have brought about the installation of the new system.

The factory mutuals, though small in number, are an important factor in the insurance market. They now insure over 100,000 properties for over $500 billion. Insurance by factory mutuals is unavailable to the typical buyer. For those who qualify, however, factory mutuals provide an attractive source for insurance protection because of low costs and excellent service facilities.

Fraternal insurers. A "fraternal" is an insurer organized under the section of a state's insurance code relating particularly to social organizations that provide, among other services, insurance benefits for members. To qualify as a fraternal, the insurer must have some type of social organization—usually a lodge system. Fraternals sell only life and health insurance and usually operate on an advance premium basis, although a few operate as assessment insurers. In some instances the fraternal's insurance activity has become more important than the lodge and some insurers seeking to take advantage of less rigid regulations applicable to fraternals have only a perfunctory lodge system.

The second half of the 19th century saw the rise of fraternal life insurance. The first fraternal insurance organization, The Ancient Order of United Workmen, was formed by John Jordan Upchurch in 1869.

Upchurch's objective was a social organization which offered financial protection to dependents of deceased members. The Ancient Order's method of financing the benefits was a contribution of $1 by each member. When a member died, the dependents received $2,000 and each surviving member paid another dollar.

The Ancient Order of United Workmen had immediate popularity, and a multitude of similar societies was formed. Some of them tried to improve the plan by requiring periodic assessments unrelated to a member's death. They used the same rate regardless of age; the 60-year-old and the 20-year-old paid the same amount. Other societies varied assessment rates with the age at which a person became a member.

After two decades of drifting and experimentation, it became apparent the fraternals had to be coordinated. So, in 1886, the National Fraternal Congress was organized. An early action was a request for state legislation which many states passed to define the status of fraternals. Later amendments were offered to require fraternals to use a scientific formula for ratemaking and to operate on a sound financial basis. The volume of fraternal insurance has dropped to less than 2 percent of the life insurance in force in the United States, but today the business is on a sound basis. A wide variation is found among fraternal insurers. For many the insurance is a minor element in the operation of a lodge, and they are likely to offer policies restricted in coverage and face amount. Others offer a range of covers comparable to that offered by life and health insurers.

Savings bank life insurance.   Elizur Wright, called the "father of modern life insurance" because of his activities on behalf of life insurance policyowners, suggested as early as 1874 that low-cost life insurance should be made available by savings banks. Not until after the Armstrong investigation of 1905 in New York did his proposal receive serious consideration. Two findings of the Armstrong committee seemed to disturb Louis D. Brandeis, then a justice of the Massachusetts Supreme Court: many life insurers seemed to put policyowners' interests last; and weekly premium life insurance (called "industrial life insurance") seemed so expensive. Brandeis, later a justice of the U.S. Supreme Court, reasoned that a life insurer operates two businesses: the indemnification of beneficiaries of those who die prematurely, and the investment of funds in relatively safe outlets. The mutual savings banks of Massachusetts, Brandeis noted, already were making safe investments for depositors; so all that remained was for these banks to be given authority to open life insurance departments.

In 1907 Massachusetts passed legislation necessary to permit mutual savings banks to establish insurance departments. The law required that insurance department funds be separate from banking funds. The insurance funds are not liable for difficulties in the banking department, nor are the banking funds liable for the insurance departments' obligations. Originally, policies were limited to $500 each. The amount was raised by steps to the present limit of $62,000. This limit does not apply to group insurance. Annuities are limited to $200 annual income per bank.

In order to offer low-cost insurance, the use of selling agents is forbidden, although the savings bank system does advertise extensively and maintains a publicity program through a cooperatively supported Savings Bank Life Insurance Council. Applications are taken by banks, employers, credit unions, and other authorized outlets, and any of these, except employers, may retain a small collection fee. Insurance may be written for residents only or those regularly employed in Massachusetts.

Rate computation, medical examination, and underwriting are removed from control of participating banks and are performed by the Division of Savings Bank Life Insurance, a department of the state government. The banks pay for the services. The General Insurance Guaranty Fund, a special fund to which each bank with a life insurance department must contribute, is used to apportion death claims among the banks, thus giving them a wider spread of risk than any individual bank could achieve.

In 1938 savings bank life insurance was authorized in New York, and, in 1941, in Connecticut. In New York, all insurance must be purchased from one bank and the limit is $30,000 a person. In Connecticut, the maximum amount of life insurance that can be purchased from an individual bank or from all savings banks is $25,000. Savings bank life insurance in other states has been proposed from time to time, but no other state has passed the necessary legislation. Savings bank life insurance accounts for 3.3 percent, 2.5 percent, and 1.9 percent of all life insurance in force in Massachusetts, New York, and Connecticut, respectively.

Special contributions of mutuals

Major contribution of the mutual property and liability insurer is its ability to offer insurance usually at a lower price than the same coverage offered by a proprietary insurer. This lower price is possible principally because of lower company operation expenses. Mutuals (property and liability) using agents often pay lower commissions than do stock companies. Agents, reasoning that lower premiums facilitate sales, will accept a lower commission hoping their total earnings will be higher because of increased sales volume.

Many mutual property insurers operate through salaried representatives rather than agents. Cost savings for the direct selling insurers arise principally when the policy is renewed. One insurer using salaried representatives reports that its renewals cost is about 90 percent less than those of agency insurers who usually pay the full commission rate each time the policy is renewed. When business is sold by salaried representatives, renewals often are acquired by mail at minimum cost. No useful statistics are available that compare acquisition expenses of stock insurers with those of mutuals, but overall studies indicate that overall expenses generally are lower for mutuals.

Another consideration occasionally offered to explain the cost advantage for mutual property insurers is that they are not pressured to take accommodation lines. As explained, capital stock insurers sometimes accept unprofitable business in order to retain the favor of independent agents. Only advance premium mutuals using independent agents would be subject to this pressure.

The payment of stockholders' dividends has been offered as an explanation of higher prices for insurance in stock insurers. Mutuals have no stockholders, but an examination of the financial operation of stock insurers indicates that stockholders' dividends place little burden on the stock insurer policyowner.

Just as with stock property insurers, dividends paid to stockholders of life insurers place little burden on their policyowners. Much more important are the results achieved by both stock and mutual life insurers in maintaining low operating expenses, high investment yields, and favorable mortality experience. The success in these areas, not whether the insurer is a stock company or a mutual, determines the ability of an insurer to offer low-cost participating life insurance. In life insurance, commission rates do not vary between stock and mutual insurers, although stock insurers may pay a higher commission on nonparticipating than on participating policies.

Producers' Cooperatives

Several types of producers' cooperatives are found in the insurance business. Illustrative of one type are the dozens of organizations operating under the trade names Blue Cross and Blue Shield. Hospitals and doctors in these organizations provide the insurance and, in that sense, are the producers. Health maintenance organizations (HMOs), composed of physicians who provide medical care to the public, are another type of medical care producers' cooperative although they may be organized also as consumers' cooperatives. Another type of producers' cooperative is the underwriting organization made up of individual insurers who have banded together to improve their effectiveness in the market. Still another type of producers' cooperative is the reinsurance association composed of individual insurers joined together to become more efficient in relations with other insurers.

Medical and hospital service plans

Many nonprofit hospital and medical-care plans have been organized under special state statutes. These organizations are an interesting hybrid of mutual and proprietary forms. The best known hospital plans are those members of the American Hospital Association which call themselves Blue Cross. The most familiar medical-care plans are those sponsored by physicians' groups which are members of Blue Shield Medical-Care Plans Association. A number of Blue Shield and Blue Cross plans are coordinated to offer a medical and hospital care package. These plans are governed by boards of directors or trustees that include representation from hospitals, the medical profession, and the public. In most plans, the directors are appointed by hospitals and the medical profession. In others, governing boards are elected by the plan's subscribers and, therefore, tend to become self-perpetuating, as the persons nominated by the board usually are elected. The plans are not mutual insurance corporations in that the controlling "members" are the hospitals and physicians who furnish the protection, rather than the persons who "subscribe" to the insurance. The controlling members bear the financial risks (and determine the allocation of any surpluses). Most jurisdictions consider Blue Cross and Blue Shield organizations charitable and benevolent institutions. As such they are entitled to certain tax exemptions. Also, a growing number of dental societies offer dental care on a prepaid basis, usually under group plans.

These hospital, dental, and medical-care plans differ from insurance in that they sell services (medical and hospital care) not insurance. The cost and coverage associated with medical and hospital service plans are so varied the insurance buyer must study each plan before making a decision. Often, coverage under these plans is offered at lower cost than similar coverage offered by other insurers.

Health maintenance organizations

The growth of health maintenance organizations (HMOs) are viewed by some observers as a key to the solution of the health care delivery problem in the United States. HMOs, formerly called prepaid group practice plans, are formal organizations of physicians who provide medical service to subscribers and divide earnings according to a predetermined agreement. The largest HMO is the Kaiser Foundation Health Plan, which was originally formed to provide medical care for the employees of the Kaiser Corporation. The foundation now operates its own network of hospitals and outpatient clinics in California, Hawaii, Oregon, Colorado, and Ohio.

Each subscriber to a group practice plan pays a premium in exchange for the right to medical care when desired. HMO plans may be organized tightly (prepaid group practice) or loosely (medical foundation or individual practice). Furthermore, prepaid group practice plans may be civic sponsored and operated as consumers' cooperatives in which physicians are under salary contracts, or they may be sponsored and owned by doctors and operated as profit-making producers' cooperatives.

The emphasis of HMOs is on prevention, as the benefits offered are broader than those included by insurers in group medical expense insurance plans or by Blue Cross and Blue Shield organizations. HMO benefits are not limited to treatment resulting from accident and illnesses, but extend to preventive medicine by including physical examinations. Because the physicians receive the same total compensation regardless of the amount of service rendered, they have an incentive to keep members well in order to reduce future services required.

By 1984, 290 HMOs were operating in the United States serving approximately 13.6 million people, an increase of 48 percent in the number of plans and of 80 percent in the number of people covered since the end of 1978. This increase is expected to accelerate due largely to the Health Maintenance Organization Act of 1973 which authorized $375 million of federal funds to be spent over the ensuing five-year period for evaluation and organization of HMOs. The act provides for a comprehensive range of health care including physician services, dental care for children, short-term physical therapy services, treatment for alcoholism and drug abuse, home treatment health service, preventive medicine, outpatient and inpatient hospital care, mental health care, and emergency health service. The HMO Act of 1973 further stipulates that employers of more than 25 employees must offer enrollment in a HMO as an option to their health insurance plan if a qualified HMO is located near the employer's business. However, the employer is not required to pay more on behalf of employees for HMO services than they pay under the existing employee health care benefit plan.

The cost savings of HMOs as compared to other plans has stimulated the rapid growth in the use of this approach to the provision of health care services. The average monthly premium paid for individual coverage under a traditional program rose 46 percent from 1980 to 1982, while HMO premiums for the period increased less than 30 percent. (During this same period, consumer prices increased 17 percent.) Two large manufacturing firms that have switched to HMOs for their employee coverage, estimated their costs for 1983 to have been $1.2 and $3.5 million less than expected under their former traditional plans. Cost-conscious employers and patients are expected to cause continued growth in both the number of HMOs and the number of patients they serve.

Underwriters' and reinsurance associations

Several underwriters' associations operate in the insurance market. Two associations well known to the managers of large businesses and institutions are the Associated Factory Mutual Fire Insurance Companies and the Industrial Risk Insurers.

Operations of the four separate factory mutual companies described in this chapter are facilitated by a cooperative organization known as the Associated Factory Mutual Fire Insurance Companies. Factory mutual have separate underwriting, accounting, engineering, and sales departments, but in some functions they operate cooperatively to improve their services. Principal areas of cooperation are loss prevention research and service, policy development, provision of insurance facilities, construction of rating schedules, loss adjustment, and furnishing a complete appraisal service to policyowners.

To compete with factory mutuals, 12 large stock fire insurers formed the Factory Insurance Association (FIA) in 1890. Today 45 of the leading stock fire insurers are members. In December 1975 the FIA merged with the Oil Insurance Association to form the Industrial Risk Insurers (IRI) to improve its financial ability to write more insurance. The IRI, like the factory mutuals, insures large, high-grade, sprinklered buildings and emphasizes loss prevention. Inspection, underwriting, and loss adjusting are performed through regional and field offices. Insured properties are inspected quarterly.

Whereas each factory mutual has its own salaried salespersons, the IRI uses independent agents. The factory mutual originating the business issues its own policy, retains part of the insurance, and reinsures the rest with the other three factory mutuals. The originating insurer usually retains twice its pro rata share. In the IRI, policies are issued by the association and the liability is uniformly apportioned with members jointly liable so each policy has the backing of the combined strength of all insurers.

Some other underwriters' associations are the AFIA, which handles the foreign operations of its 10 stock property and liability insurer members; two aviation underwriters' groups, the Associated Aviation Underwriters and the United States Aircraft Insurance Group; the Improved Risk Mutuals, an underwriters' group designed to increase market capacity and to improve engineering services of several general mutual fire insurers; the underwriting syndicates of members of Lloyd's of London and the Florida, Illinois and New York Insurance Exchanges; and many others involving specific kinds of property, special hazards, special perils, or specific industries.

A third type of producers' cooperative is the reinsurance association; some of these reinsure nonmember insurers but usually restrict their operations to members. Examples of these reinsurance associations are the Workers' Compensation Reinsurance Bureau, the Excess and Casualty Reinsurance Association, and the Mutual Reinsurance Bureau.

Governmental Insurers

Government insurance, for the purpose of this discussion, includes insurers established, maintained, and administered by a branch of the government—federal or state—and organized primarily to insure other than government employees or government property.

Federal insurers

The federal government offers insurance of several types: (1) *The Federal Crop Insurance Corporation* (FCIC) offers insurance against crop failures resulting from perils of nature; (2) *the Veterans Administration* (VA) offers life insurance to members (and veterans) of the armed forces; (3) *the Department of Health and Human Services* (HHS) offers coverage for death, disability, medical care, and old age through the old-age, survivors, disability, and health insurance program operated by the Social Security Administration. Similar coverages are provided for federal civil service employees and railroad employees through other federal organizations; (4) *the Federal Deposit Insurance Corporation* (FDIC) provides bank deposit insurance; (5) *the Federal Savings and Loan Insurance Corporation* (FSLIC) protects savings accounts in federal savings and loan associations and in state-chartered thrift and home-financing institutions; (6) *mortgage and property improvement loan insurance* programs provide mortgage insurance to aid home buyers and mortgage lenders, both urban and rural; (7) *the Securities Investor Protection Corporation* (SIPC) protects customers' securities held by registered broker-dealers up to $100,000; and (8) *the National Credit Union Administration* insures credit union accounts.

Other federal agencies participate in the insuring of properties against crime, flood, riot, and risks abroad. For instance, the *Overseas Investment Group,* composed of a group of private insurers and the U.S. government's *Overseas Private Investment Corporation* (OPIC), provide coverage for private American investments against foreign political risks of expropriation and currency inconvertibility.

State insurers

State insurers offer hail insurance, life insurance, workers' compensation, unemployment, nonoccupational temporary disability income insurance, Torrens title insurance, medical malpractice insurance, and auto insurance. Not every state has all these funds. Only Wisconsin has a life insurance fund and Maryland an auto fund. Just a few states have hail insurance, title insurance, or disability income funds.

Special contributions of governmental insurers

Government insurers' principal contribution is to provide coverages that other insurers are unwilling or unable to offer. They can offer insurance without operating under the rigid actuarial principles that private insurers must follow. A frequent argument, however, is that unless actuarial principles are adhered to, the protection is not insurance, and the government agencies offering it are not operating as insurers. The beneficiaries under these programs, however, are not concerned with semantics when they collect their "social insurance" benefits (and, for that matter, neither are the tax collectors when they gather in the "social insurance" taxes), nor are the legislators thinking about semantics when they cast their "aye" votes for social insurance programs.

Selecting the Insurer

Few insurance buyers begin by choosing the type of insurer. They are following sound insurance-buying instinct in this regard. Considerations in choosing an insurer are broadly summarized in a paraphrase of Pope's *Essay on Man:*

> For forms of companies let fools contest Whate'er is best administer'd is best. . . .

General considerations

The management's quality and philosophy are the most important criteria in selecting an insurer. Unfortunately, these are intangibles not entirely revealed in statistical or financial reports. Published figures can be used principally to determine the management's ability to assure both liquidity and solvency, but they tell little about its claims policy or service. Then, where is this information to be found? Unbiased[4] and informed observers often cannot offer advice other than generalities, because their position may depend on the goodwill of the industry. Although well informed, they consider it wiser to keep personal opinions private. The best course with this group is to seek their views on a personal basis.

If one can depend on the agent to put the client's interests first and not be tied too closely to particular insurers, that agent probably is the best readily available source of information about insurers as well as about contracts. Of the two items—the clients' best interests and lack of close ties to particular insurers—the former is the more important. If the agent considers the clients' interests first, the presumption is that the agent uses a particular insurer or insurers, because of the belief they are good for clients. If unusual policies which suit the client's need are unavailable from the agent's insurers, the good agent helps the client obtain that special protection from other insurers. Financial condition, underwriting philosophy, claims policy, service, and price are more important in selecting an insurer than whether it is a reciprocal, stock, or mutual. The quality of insurers differs, and discriminating among them is not easy for the layman.

Alfred M. Best, Inc., publishes two insurance yearbooks: one for property and liability and another for life and health insurance. *Best's Insurance Reports* includes details on company history, personnel, investments, operating results, underwriting results, and other financial data. This information is reported for all types of insurers. In the property liability edition, ratings assigned to insurers usually are based on an analysis of their financial statements. In explaining its ratings, Best writes: "Our analytical tests recognize that the stability of a company or association and the desirability of its policies hinge upon the following principal factors: (1) good underwriting, (2) economy of management, (3) adequate reserves for undischarged liabilities of all kinds, (4) net

---

[4] It seems unlikely that an insurer exists that will not have some dissatisfied claimants; and these usually are the most vociferous in their opinions and most likely to give the unwary buyer "help" in reaching a conclusion. On the other hand, those who have more complete information often will have taken the trouble to acquire it because of some special interest— and that special interest may make them something less than unbiased reporters.

resources adequate to absorb unusual shocks, and (5) sound investments." These five criteria are examined by Best to arrive at its "general policyholders' rating," intended to measure the financial stability and general reliability of the insurer from the buyer viewpoint. The assigned ratings range downward from excellent (A+ or A), very good (B+), good (B), fairly good (C+), to fair (C). If adequate information is not available (either because the insurer does not cooperate or does not have a five-year operating history), the rating is omitted.

Best also supplies a financial rating intended to evaluate the insurer's net safety factor. This rating is based on policyowners' surplus, plus equities in unearned premiums and loss reserves or minus any indicated shortages in reserves. These ratings begin with class I, representing a net safety factor of less than $250,000, to class XV, representing a net safety factor in excess of $100 million. Some observers consider these "canned" ratings are of value only in excluding low-rated insurers from consideration. They place more reliance on a low rate as an eliminator than on a high rate as a selector. However, many corporate insurance buyers give serious attention to these published ratings. Best, after suspending the practice for a number of years, now assigns ratings to life insurers. (For further discussion of the ratings in *Best's Insurance Reports,* see the latest editions of these reports.)

Once people have decided to buy any item, they become interested in: how much (quantity and quality) they can get, what it will cost, and how quickly they can get it. The insurance buyer's "how much" is determined by the amount of protection and auxiliary services. Sometimes the buyer may be more concerned with the quality of the service offered such as the engineering inspection service offered with boiler and machinery coverage rather than the quality of the insurance; but generally the insurance is paramount.

A quality product in insurance demands a financially sound insurer. Insurance protection and services are sold in the present for indefinite future delivery. Whether buyers want protection or service, they will receive neither unless the insurer is financially able to deliver. In choosing insurers, estimation of future liquidity and solvency should be a principal factor.

Factors in insurers' finances

Most insureds are poor judges of insurance finance. The reliable insurer is both solvent and liquid. Solvency means owning more than one owes: total assets exceed total liabilities. Liquidity means the ability to pay off liabilities as they become due—current assets exceed current liabilities. Insureds want their insurers to be liquid and solvent at the time of loss. But that time is in the indefinite future. Therefore, wise buyers must consider the insurers loss and expense ratios, net income earned on investments, and the size and growth of surplus. In evaluating the insurer's surplus, buyers should consider the soundness, liquidity, and diversification of the insurer's assets.

Surplus should be studied in relationship to obligations. The measure used is the ratio of surplus to liabilities. Small insurers should have a higher surplus-to-liabilities ratio than large ones because unfavorable variations in experience in small insurers will be more significant: the loss of one good agency, the loss of one or two big accounts or a catastrophic loss would have greater financial impact on small insurers than on large ones. Regarding the relative size of surplus, some insurance commissioners have used the rule that the policyowners' surplus[5] should be equal to at least one year's premiums for property insurance, and not less than one half of one year's premiums for liability insurance. Other commissioners, however, have disputed the necessity of such rigid unsupportable rules. The policyowners' surplus is a measure of safety that policyowners have before the insurer is declared technically insolvent. However, because legally required procedures in insurance accounting result in a decline in statutory surplus if the insurer is growing, assuming other pertinent factors are stable, a declining surplus might not represent an unhealthy condition.[6]

Forecasting insurers' finances. Future financial results for an insurer depend on the success of management in underwriting, investing, and controlling expenses. As no management is perfect, the ability of an insurer to prosper partially is a function of the magnitude and number of managerial errors made and the surplus available to absorb them. The difficulties of prognostication often are insurmountable. One year the leading professional insurance financial-rating service gave the following policyowners' ratings to three insurers: A+, A, and B+. When the next year's edition was published, the B+ insurer was subjected to receivership proceedings by its state commissioner; and the A+ and A insurers had been forced to change management and continued to survive only with outside financial aid. These three insurers were not of the same type—stock or mutual—but all three experienced difficulties for the same reason: heavy commitments in auto insurance, a coverage frequently unprofitable.

Services to the insured

One question regarding an insurer's service can be settled quickly: Does the insurer offer buyers the policy they want? Many special coverages are available only from certain insurers. Furthermore, valid differences in underwriting philosophy allow one insurer but not another to underwrite a particular exposure. Thus, some insurers automatically are eliminated from consideration. Most life insurers, for example, do not write disability income riders; some do not insure medically im-

---

[5] Capital stock or guaranty fund, net or "free" surplus, and voluntary reserves.

[6] A part of the surplus is transferred to the unearned premium reserve account to meet state requirements. Basic concepts involved in the structure of insurance finance are explained in Chapter 26 where, hopefully, these concepts are clarified. The subject is complex and requires intensive study.

paired lives. Insurance protection for lumberyards is a specialty line for some property insurers, whereas others cater to flour mills or coal mines. Insurers lacking necessary specialized facilities or experience often will accept neither of these exposures.

Many times, underwriters will "take the bitter only with the sweet," meaning that undesirable (unprofitable) coverages are written only if the profitable ones also are purchased. Workers' compensation might be considered an undesirable line and will be offered only along with the generally more profitable fidelity and property lines (or, for some underwriters, vice versa!).

The speed and fairness of an insurer's claim service are a consideration. Ascertaining this information is difficult, for prejudiced and limited observation obscures many observers' opinions. Human nature being what it is, not all claimants receive what they think is due. Considering how few policyowners read, let alone understand, their policies, and the room for honest differences of opinion about values of lost property, it is surprising that not more difficulty exists. As one insurance teacher remarks: "To hear that an insurer has had a dissatisfied claimant is to hear no more than that it is in the insurance business."

Yet, if the buyer is to form judgment of the speed and amicability of an insurer's claim service, the buyer has at best only three sources other than trustworthy agents: its customers, competitors and *Consumer Reports*. Customers and competitors must be used cautiously with considerable weight given the experience, knowledge, and character of each informant. *Consumer Reports* publishes the results of consumer surveys of insurance company claims practices. A report on auto insurers ranked one large auto underwriter near the bottom of a list of some 60 companies. Yet a subsequent report, based on a survey made four years after the first article appeared, ranked the same insurer near the top of a group of 45 insurers. Obviously, either the new respondents viewed the company's claims services differently, or the company had actually improved. (Or maybe they were simply more liberal in the amounts paid.) As for liberality in claims payments, both extremes are undesirable. No insured wants coverage with an insurer that regularly pinches claims pennies. On the other hand, overliberal payments can damage an insurer's financial structure if not offset by higher premiums.

In some insurance lines, an additional service is important: engineering and loss prevention. The quality of engineering service varies among insurers. A qualified corps of inspectors might tip the balance in favor of an insurer for boiler and machinery coverage; an imaginative engineering department might be the deciding factor in selecting a workers' compensation insurer.

Choosing the Agent

Too many writers on the subject of "how to buy insurance" primarily emphasize selecting the insurer. Frequently, they have little or nothing to say about choosing the agent.[7] What are the characteristics of a good agent? In addition to feeling responsible for clients' welfare, the good agent must have the following qualities: knowledge of the insurance business; time and facilities for providing necessary services; good contacts with the insurance market so that prompt and favorable action for clients can be obtained; knowledge of insurers to use for special situations; an effective claims follow-up service; and, finally, the respect and cooperation of clients, competitors, insurers, and claim adjusters.

What readily visible earmarks enable the buyer to select agents wisely? The answer is: none. Two sources of information not readily visible are available: insurance buyers and insurance agents. The validity of the opinions of insurance buyers varies with the extent of their insurance knowledge and their experience with insurance representatives. An informed banker should be knowledgeable about insurance agents, provided recommendations are not limited to the bank's customers. The insurance buyer for a local factory may be informed on the comparative abilities of agents as they apply to that business, which may or may not be the same as the comparative ability of agents in dealing with retail or other trades or with homeowners. Although insurance problems of one's neighbor may be the same as one's own, so that one judges agents for the same purposes, the neighbor's judgment may be inexperienced and faulty. For these reasons, one must build a composite opinion from several sources.

In general, an agent's competitors are a valuable source of information, but here an important point must be noted: certain agents' comments about their competitors will reveal more about the commenting agent than about the "commentee." The practice of good business is to be wary of making critical remarks about competitors. Thus, a freely critical person may be telling the listener of one's own weakness. Still, the ethical agent usually cannot condone clearly unethical practices and so in such cases, will make specific comments but refrain from drawing general conclusions.

The buyer needs the answers to pertinent questions: What is an agent's experience in years and breadth of practice? Is the agent a specialist in any coverage? Does the agent deal mostly with personal lines, small or large firms, or across-the-board? What is the reputation of the insurer or insurers the agent represents? Are the agents and their staff regular attendants at schools, forums, and professional educational conferences? Do they present a unified risk management program based on a detailed analysis of loss exposures and the noninsurance as well as the insurance methods of handling them? The answers offer some measure of the quality of an agency if the source of answers is informed and honest.

---

[7] In this section the word "agent" is used in its broadest, nontechnical sense to include all types of insurance representatives—not only agents but also brokers, direct salespersons, traveling representatives from home offices, or anyone else who performs all or part of the marketing services.

The ultimate source of information about agents are the agents. They must be persons with whom the buyer is willing to discuss business and family financial details. One way to judge the competency of agents is to discuss insurance matters with them directly, but the usefulness of this method is conditioned by the extent of the buyer's knowledge. What should the buyer expect of the agent in addition to knowledge? How should the agent show a sense of responsibility for clients' welfare? How should agents use their time and facilities for providing service? To what end should they organize their market contacts? The agent has the responsibility (in addition to acquiring and keeping up with product and market knowledge) to become thoroughly acquainted with the client's problems. They should help the buyer identify loss exposures, as described in Chapters 3 and 4. The amount of agency time and energy spent should vary with the complexity of the insured's problems and, to an important extent, with the insured's contribution to agency expenses, whether through the usual commission method or through a direct fee charged for professional risk management advice.

Applying knowledge of insurance and risk management to the client's loss exposures, professional agents will help their clients reach intelligent risk management decisions. However, wise agents seldom make decisions for their clients. Regarding the insurance portion of the program, professional agents will keep up to date on their clients' loss exposures and will inform them of relevant changes in insurance rules, forms, and rates. They will seek to provide insurance at the lowest cost consistent with quality. These tasks require regular contact and cooperation between the agent and the insured.

Finally, agents may play a role in claims settlements although they have little or no official position in such settlements other than for small losses. Claims are settled by adjustment bureaus, independent adjusters, company adjusters, and public adjusters. In large agencies and sometimes in moderate-sized ones most claims may be handled by the agency, but this arrangement is uncommon. When agents have no official standing regarding claims settlement, their services may consist mainly of interpreting the positions of the insurer and the insured and in seeking a rapid and smooth settlement. The wise agent tends to be more active in behalf of the insured than the insurer and often proves better able to "sell" the insurer on the validity of the insured's position. The insured, however, should not expect an agent's support in other than a valid position. Some agents have tried to do otherwise, but those who persist sooner or later find themselves without reputable insurers to represent.

Agents' services cost money—money from premiums paid by insureds. Differences in premium levels often are explained by differences in agency services. As students of marketing put it, "distribution costs" are reduced by shifting part of the servicing burden to customers. How much service insureds wish to buy, and how much they wish to supply themselves, are personal determinations. However, the importance of the services of a *good* agent should not be underestimated.

Collecting policies versus buying insurance

The story of Poor Herman emphasizes the importance of *buying insurance* rather than *collecting policies.*[8]

> Once upon a time, in the rich land of America, in the village of Sunnyside, there dwelt a citizen known as Herman. He was a righteous and respected businessman who, since early manhood, had applied himself diligently to his trade. And not without success. Somewhat abundant was his store of worldly goods and bright indeed his prospects. Now Herman was not alike unto all of his fellowmen, for he was a believer in insurance. And he let this be known since his belief was founded upon the conviction that only insurance can remove the risk of loss. And the people to whom he spoke, spoke of it among themselves, and the word spread, and the agents of insurance did one after another seek him out. To each of these did he renew his faith saying: "Yea, I am a believer in insurance and I feel it is a good thing. For has not insurance the power to lift the crown of care from the brows of the worried?"
>
> And to him they displayed their policies, and from them did he take insurance. Even the property floater which is personal and the personal liability which is comprehensive. From one he sought security against loss by automobile and to yet another did he entrust the fire insurance on his dwelling. And thus at last was his mind at rest, and to himself he said: "Secure must I be against misfortune, for have I not of policies a full bushel and of agents a round half dozen? Surely ease and prosperity shall follow me all the days of my life."
>
> But it came to pass that on a day when Herman and his family visited in a neighboring village, a sudden and accidental rupture of the steamheating boiler did rend asunder the house of Herman. . . . Yea, from gable to foundation. And Herman upon his return did summon unto himself all of his agents of insurance, and they together examined his bushel of policies. And then at last as the truth broke upon them did they all fall back aghast; for of all the policies of Herman, none there was which would make good the destruction, and all of his good intentions availed him naught. Then truly did Herman tear his hair, and beat his breast, and cry out: "Oh Lord, what is the use?"

This story shows the importance of the services of professional agents who can and will tailor insurance to their clients' needs.

Self-Insurance versus Commercial Insurance

For most insurance buyers, the question of whether to self-insure never will arise. Self-insurance requires a large number of noncatastrophic and homogeneous exposure units so that losses can be predicted with manageable accuracy. Exposures that meet these requisites may be self-insured if the insured has the financial strength to fund a self-insurance plan and to absorb unpredicted losses. Also necessary is sufficient understanding of insurance to administer the plan.

---

[8] By an agent, as printed in the *American Agency Bulletin.*

When a self-insurance plan is used, a regular deposit (based on estimated losses averaged over a period of years) is put into a self-insurance fund. In low-loss years, the fund will grow, only to be depleted in high-loss years. Because adversity could be experienced early before adequate funds are accumulated, self-insurance should be installed gradually. Thus, a decreasing amount of commercial insurance can be purchased each year as the self-insurance fund increases, thereby protecting the self-insurer until the self-insurance fund matures. When using self-insurance, reinsurance or excess coverage[9] with commercial insurers usually is desirable to cover losses exceeding some basic figure, the size of which is an inverse function of the degree of risk involved and the amount of risk the insured can assume comfortably.

Self-insurers must provide efficient loss inspection and loss prevention activities which for some coverages are as important as indemnity. If a firm is not in a position to provide these services, it may purchase them from an insurer under an administrative services only (ASO) contract. Those few firms that can qualify might find self-insurance more economical than commercial insurance because of no selling costs, no premium taxes, and possible lower administrative costs. Lower administrative cost may not materialize if the self-insured is not equipped to perform the engineering and claims functions as efficiently as commercial insurers. A firm with favorable loss experience might find savings in a self-insurance program, as insurance merit-rating plans do not reflect individual experience fully. Through self-insurance, the insured retains the benefits of successful loss prevention efforts.

One disadvantage of self-insurance in third-party coverages, principally workers' compensation, is the lack of an impersonal claim service. A delicate relationship is created between employer and employee when an employer denies a claim as a self-insurer. If commercially insured, the employer can "pass the buck" to the insurer. Self-insurance also might create an income tax burden. Contributions to a self-insurance fund are not a deductible expense; only losses incurred are deductible. The result is that several high profit years might pass with small tax deductions, whereas high deductions may be realized in low profit years. Because of graduated tax rates, the net tax burden over several years might be less if an average annual tax deduction could be taken. Premiums paid to commercial insurers are deductible in the year paid. Therefore, the annual tax deduction for losses is spread over high and low profit years with its incidence a function of earnings and loss patterns.

Summary

1. The insurance industry may be classified into two broad categories: private and governmental. Furthermore, private insurers may be

---

[9] An excess insurance plan is one in which an insurer will reimburse the insured for losses exceeding a given figure. The insurer is not obligated to provide claims, engineering, or other services.

divided into two groups: proprietary (unincorporated or incorporated) and cooperative (unincorporated and incorporated). Cooperatives may be either consumers' cooperatives or producers' cooperatives.

2. The unincorporated proprietary insurer is illustrated by individual underwriters, the most important of which are members of Lloyd's of London.

3. Incorporated proprietary insurers, known as stock insurers, dominate the property and liability insurance field but underwrite a much smaller percentage of the life insurance in force.

4. Consumers' cooperatives are reciprocals (interinsurance exchanges) which are associations for the exchange of insurance and mutual insurers that are incorporated cooperatives and consist of several types: assessment, advance premium, and perpetual. Factory mutuals, fraternals, and savings bank life insurance are other cooperative forms.

5. Mutual property and liability insurers usually offer insurance at prices lower than comparable coverage purchased from proprietary insurers.

6. Producers' cooperatives may involve sellers of services such as hospital (e.g., Blue Cross) and medical-care (Blue Shield) plans. Additionally, producers' cooperatives may consist of other insurers organized as underwriters' associations to enhance efficiency in production and marketing of services, to provide reinsurance facilities for each other, or to market reinsurance to other insurers.

7. Health Maintenance Organizations (HMOs) may be operated either as consumers' cooperatives or producers' cooperatives. HMOs are designed to provide medical services for a fixed cost with emphasis on preventive medicine.

8. U.S. government insurers may be classified into federal (e.g., the social security fund and the Federal Crop Insurance Fund) or state (e.g., hail insurance and workers' compensation insurance).

9. Factors to consider in selecting an insurer generally are financial strength, coverages offered, cost, engineering and loss prevention activities, and claims service. Usually the insurer's type of business organization (stock, mutual) is not an important consideration.

10. Selecting the "agent" (in this discussion referring to all types of insurance distributors: local agents, brokers, and direct insurer representatives) could be more important than selecting the insurer. The qualities sought in choosing an agent include competence in insurance, knowledge of the buyer's business and personal insurance needs, the ability and facilities to service the insured adequately in event of loss, and the provision of competent continuing risk management advice.

11. Self-insurance should be used only by organizations possessing many independent and homogeneous loss exposure units, knowledge of self-insurance administration, and the opportunity and ability to operate the plan without interference from top management.

Questions for Review

1. What are the principal differences between proprietary insurers and cooperative insurers?

2. Who owns Lloyd's of London? Who owns the cooperative insurers? How does Lloyd's differ from a reciprocal exchange? How are they similar? Explain.

3. What is an American Lloyds insurer? Can they be organized in your state? Are any operating there?

4. How does a stock company differ from an American Lloyds? From Lloyd's of London?

5. Lloyd's of London has an excellent reputation for the integrity of its underwriting members. How does Lloyd's screen new members to maintain the integrity of members?

6. How do medical-care and hospital service plans (Blue Cross and Blue Shield) differ from mutual insurers? How do HMOs differ from Blue Cross and Blue Shield plans?

7. What advantages are offered by each of the following types of insurers: factory mutuals, perpetual mutuals, fraternals, savings bank life insurance, and insurance underwritten by the federal government? What limitations exist in each of these types of insurers?

8. The federal government now is participating in flood insurance. Why has it elected to offer flood insurance and not, for example, yacht insurance?

9. What services should a risk manager consider in choosing an insurer and an agent? What factors are important in a decision to continue a relationship with an insurer and an agent?

10. When a decision is made to insure a loss exposure, the question may arise as to whether to insure it commercially or to self-insure it. When will this question arise and what factors must be considered in reaching a decision?

Questions for Discussion

1. What services are offered by an independent agent but not by a "dependent" agent? Does this mean one should not patronize "dependent" agents?

2. In question (1) under Questions for Review you stated the differences between proprietary insurers and cooperative insurers. Which differences do you believe are important to the buyer?

3. Lloyd's of London had its beginnings in a bright idea: insuring oceangoing ships. Later underwriters at Lloyd's began to introduce new types of coverage. Recently some of these underwriters insured the fast-growing U.S. computer-leasing industry, but soon found themselves faced with staggering losses. What do you believe was the problem associated with writing the latter form of insurance?

4. Why are life insurance contracts usually not written by individuals?

5. Is it possible for an insurer to be sold out of insurance? Can an arrangement with Lloyd's help in this event? How has Lloyd's increased its underwriting capacity?

6. Are the benefits offered under social security really insurance or are they a federal "give away?"

7. The text states many view HMOs as a key to the solution of the health care delivery problem. What is the health care delivery problem? Do you believe HMOs offer *the* key to the solution? What criteria and standards have you used in reaching your decision? Are there any other keys to the solution? If so, what are they? Explain.

8. Why do you suppose some states offer insurance for a variety of covers whereas others offer no coverages? Cite some examples. Restrict your discussion to coverages that are also written by private insurers.

9. "The risk manager will want to buy insurance contracts at prices as low as possible." Do you agree? If you were the insurance manager of a corporation, would you self-insure all eligible risks? Discuss.

10. Do you agree with the statement that it makes no difference to the buyer whether an insurer is a stock, mutual, or reciprocal? Discuss. Consider the case of Poor Herman. How could Herman have protected himself?

11. The text states that choosing an agent may be more important than the selection of an insurer. Do you agree? Why do you think many buyers would differ with your opinion?

23

Management organization and functions: Marketing, claims, and loss prevention

The insurance industry provides employment possibilities for a wide range of interests and academic backgrounds. In addition to employing specialists in all phases of business administration, insurers employ engineering, law, medicine, agriculture, library science, and journalism graduates. From liberal arts colleges, they employ mathematicians, economists, sociologists, and psychologists. An insurer is organized by function into divisions, departments, and sections to assure maximum efficiency in every essential operation. As in any other company, four organizational patterns exist: line, line and staff, functional, and committee. Usually the structure has evolved into a hybrid combining several of the types. No standardized organization chart is adaptable to all, but a few basic departments are common to most insurers.

Every insurer must be efficient in marketing products and administering claims. Marketing is important because insurers must write as much profitable business as possible in order to accomplish their objectives as business entities. An effective marketing mechanism is necessary to assure that company products will be available to prospective insurance buyers. After policies have been sold, insurers must handle claims efficiently. Inefficient claims administration can be costly both by increasing expenses and alienating customers. Insurers also are concerned with loss prevention, important to insurers not only to reduce their expenses, but also to benefit society. Insurers often are members of cooperative organizations in order to increase the credibility of their individual statistics, to avoid unnecessary duplication of technical and administrative efforts, and to engage in public relations, education, and lobbying activities.

Management Organization

The management organization of insurers is similar to that of other businesses: authority moves downward, while responsibility moves upward.[1] The primary source of authority is the stockholders in a stock company and the policyowners in a mutual company. Theoretically, they have the final say on company administration, but this authority generally is delegated to the board of directors, who in turn delegate some authority to several executive officers who run everyday company operations. They also delegate authority, with levels of authority varying, depending on the size and scope of company operations.

The board of directors

The board usually is organized into committees to formulate policies on certain phases of operations. The board meets periodically to hear committee reports. The most common committees are the *executive committee,* which is occupied with general questions concerning insurance lines to be written, pricing, territories, marketing systems, relations with state insurance departments, public relations, employee relations, and societal problems, and which has full powers of the board between meetings; the *finance committee,* which determines the insurer's investment policy; the *auditing committee,* which audits the insurer's accounts (the actual auditing is done by public accountants who report to the committee); and the *underwriting committee,* which studies risk selection questions and determines the insurer's underwriting policy.

The company president

Although occasionally the chairman of the board exercises operating control of an insurer, this function usually is the president's. The president has general administrative supervision over all departments and may have active control of one or more departments in small companies. The president is subordinate to the board of directors, but for the directors to be controlled by the president is not unusual. Insurers often are organized and built by one or two people who assume control. One might

---

[1] This pattern is unlikely in a true university where apparently authority moves upward from the faculty (and in some cases, students), and the responsibility moves downward from the administrators.

become president and exercise control, even though technically subordinate to the board.

The job of president chiefly is one of efficient staff coordination. The president, much like a football coach, must organize his or her personnel into a smoothly functioning operation, making the best use of available talents by dividing employees into specialties, delineating lines of authority, and overseeing the total operation. The president also is involved with intercompany relations and public relations and usually is a member of the board of directors.

The vice presidents

Most insurers' vice presidents exercise active departmental supervision. A small company may use a vice president as head of more than one department. In line of authority, one of the vice presidents acts in the absence of the president. In larger insurers, functions of vice presidents usually are coordinated by an executive vice president, the "vice president in charge of vice presidents"! A few insurers will have the executive vice president perform the functions of president when the position of president is honorary rather than active.[2]

The company secretary

The responsibilities delegated to the secretary in the bylaws of an insurer usually are: (1) recording correspondence (in the sense of the directing authority and the responsibility for official correspondence), (2) issuing policies, and (3) maintaining records of board and committee meetings. Nearly all these duties are supervisory, if not theoretical. In practice, policies are issued by a policy issue department with the secretary's signature printed on the form. The transcript of the board of directors' meeting or of a committee usually is made by a professional stenographer. A company secretary's functional duties vary from department head (completely apart from bylaw duties) to general manager or even executive vice president. Moreover, many assistant secretaries are found in large insurers, and their duties vary as widely.

Other officers

The executive officers named are common to most insurers. An insurer's charter or bylaws may add more executive officers, such as treasurer, general counsel, actuary, or controller. In addition, "functional officers" perform management functions in insurer operations. They are not executive officers and consequently do not have legal power to bind the insurer to contracts. Usually, functional officers are department heads.

---

[2] However, such an appointment sometimes is made to capitalize on the celebrity's organizational ability, which can be utilized effectively even without knowledge of insurance technicalities.

Departmentalization

A small insurer as in any small business, may have flexible departmentalization with employees performing in several departments and executives in charge of several departments. Regional departments of large insurers may virtually act as individual insurers with staffs to perform all necessary functions. At least five bases of departmentalization are defined: functional, product, territorial, customer, and executive interest.

Functional departmentalization is based upon functions performed. A legal department, an investment department, an agency department, a purchasing department, a claims department, a loss control (engineering) department, and so on are needed. *Product* departmentalization determines the department's scope by the product handled. A life insurer may have ordinary, weekly premium, group, and health departments. A property and liability insurer may contain inland and ocean marine, fire, liability, auto, health, and crime departments. In *territorial* departmentalization departments are determined by the territory under their jurisdiction. A large insurer may have an eastern department, a western department, and others. *Customer* departmentalization establishes departments by the class of customers with whom they deal. Customer departmentalization often is difficult to distinguish from product departmentalization. In insurance home-office operations, customer departmentalization might consist of a reinsurance department managing sales to other insurers, a special-risks department controlling large self-rated accounts, and a group department selling only to employers and in mass rather than individual markets. Finally, *executive interest* is a practical and frequent basis of departmentalization. Departments may be organized according to interests of executives, even though those interests may be diverse.

The agency department

The agency department's function is to recruit, train, supervise, and direct special agents, general agents, branch managers, and local agents. The agency department of an insurer is its sales department. This department holds and handles sales meetings, advertising, and publicity.

The underwriting department

The underwriting department sets selection standards and chooses among insurance applicants. Underwriters review not only new business but also business already accepted. They may cancel policyowners with poor loss experience or unfavorable characteristics.[3] Underwriters review rates and policy forms on all business submitted and also develop

---

[3] Underwriting has been defined humorously as canceling business for small agents. Right or wrong, underwriters do underwrite the agent as well as the policyowner. The underwriting function is the subject of Chapter 24.

new policy forms. Problems concerning line limits and reinsurance are managed by the underwriting department.

The legal department

Insurance contracts are subject to the general law of contract as well as to laws and judicial opinions that apply to insurance. Therefore, a legal department is essential to an insurer's operation. The legal department defends the insurer against complaints from insurance commissioners and litigates the case whenever the insurer is the plaintiff. It assists the investment department by reviewing real estate titles, bond indentures, and corporate charters, and helps in foreclosure proceedings. It aids the underwriting department in preparing policies. The claim department uses the help of the legal department in investigation and defense of claims, as does the agency department in preparing agency contracts. Finally, it advises the executives on conformity with state insurance codes and helps with lobbying activities in state and federal legislatures, insurance departments, and government committees. Some insurers decentralize legal work, with various departments having their own legal staffs.

The investment department

Insurers are financial intermediaries investing huge sums of money constantly with an investment department to manage the funds. This department selects and services the insurer's investment portfolio. The investments of insurers are subject to regulatory constraints which are discussed in Chapter 28.

The claim department

Property and liability insurance claims usually are settled in branch offices or by independent adjusters. Home-office claim departments are responsible for claims administration. They operate as a personnel and records office responsible for selection and supervision of adjusters and for maintenance of adequate claims records. Claim departments, by reporting the causes of each loss, help underwriting and loss control departments develop loss prevention measures. Claim departments work with police forces, detective agencies, special investigators, lawyers, and physicians to recover losses or reduce their severity.

Life and disability insurance claims usually are handled in the home office. Life insurance claims are easy to handle, as contract exclusions and conditions are few. Double indemnity, sickness, accident, and medical claims present problems, and claim departments must be staffed with technicians especially trained to cope with these problems. Claims must be settled fairly and promptly. Unjust claims administration can do more harm to the insurance business than can be repaired with massive advertising and publicity campaigns.

The actuarial and statistical department

The actuarial department is responsible for the calculation of insurance rates, dividends, loss and loss adjustment expense reserves, unearned premium reserves, commission scales, the preparation of annual reports, and the development of operating forecasts. Actuaries establish settlement options, develop formulas for nonforfeiture values, and perform other functions concerned primarily with mathematics.[4] Property and liability insurers in the past have used statisticians rather than actuaries, primarily as a result of a scarcity of casualty actuaries. With the increasing emphasis placed on scientific rating methods and regulations requiring certification of annual statements by qualified actuaries, the statistician is giving way to the professional casualty actuary.

The loss control department

Another active insurer department (excluding life insurance) is the loss control department. In some insurance coverages, the insured is as interested in loss control services as in indemnification of loss. Boiler and machinery insurance is an example. To improve loss ratios, insurers inspect property and operations to develop recommendations to reduce loss. They also engage in safety research and loss prevention education. Loss control departments cooperate with underwriting departments and also help with rating problems. In fact, fire insurance engineers, as distinguished from other property and liability loss control experts, principally are engaged in ratemaking and only indirectly in loss prevention.

Auditing department

Where a variable such as payroll is used as the rate base, an insurer needs a staff of traveling auditors to determine the correct payroll to use in calculating the final premium. The auditor's job is not only that of checking the total payroll but also of classifying the payroll into the applicable rate classifications.

Other departments

Several departments are self-explanatory and not peculiar to insurers. They include the accounting, stenographic, filing, purchasing, supply, mail, research, personnel, publication, communication, electronic data processing, and education departments. They may operate separately or as subdivisions of other departments.

Marketing Insurance Company Products

Marketing consists of making insurance products available and desirable to prospective buyers, along with developing new products to suit

---

[4] "Actuary" has been defined as "a mathematician with a kind of insanity so rare as to be valuable."

prospective buyers' changing needs. Marketing is one of the most important insurer functions. Unless an insurer's products are easily obtainable
by a large number of prospective buyers, an insurer cannot accomplish
its objective of writing a sufficient amount of business to make its operation profitable.

Sales organizations

Most people are not aware of their insurance needs, and must be
told of their exposures. Even those who recognize the need often have
to be motivated or persuaded to cover them, particularly in health, personal liability, and life insurance. As the buyer lacks knowledge and
is prone to procrastinate, insurance must be sold. The insurance principle cannot operate effectively without a large number of widely spread
exposure units. If the volume of business is too small, loss experience
might be unstable. In order to build a large volume of business, insurers
develop strong sales organizations. Most businesses have production departments and sales departments. The sales department's function is
to sell products manufactured by the production department. An insurer's sales department must not only sell the product, but produce it.
Selling a $100,000 life insurance policy automatically produces an addi-
tional $100,000 of insurance in force.

In Chapter 26 the question of tight insurance markets is discussed—
markets where insurance is hard to obtain because of the nature of
the hazards involved, the inadequacy of the premium allowed, or insurers' lack of adequate finances to expand their underwriting. In these
situations, persons wanting insurance are the sellers and the insurers
are the buyers, a point discussed later.

Agency systems.   Although insurance is written directly between the
insurer and the buyer, the large majority of it is placed through agents
and brokers.

The American agency system.   Most capital stock and many mutual
property and liability insurers operate under a marketing system known
as the American agency system. Agents are independent, usually representing several insurers. They issue policies, collect premiums and, as
far as the insurers are concerned, retain exclusive rights to solicit renewals from customers. Insurers operating under this system are called independent agency companies. To compete on a price basis with exclusive
agency insurers (see below), some independent agency insurers have
reduced agents' commissions. In return, the insurers handle some administrative work traditionally performed by the agents, such as policy
writing and billing.

The exclusive agency system.   Some property and liability insurers use
the exclusive agency system under which agents represent only one
insurer or group of insurers under common management. The agents

do not have ownership rights, as the insurer reserves the rights to ownership, use, and control of policy records.

The exclusive agency insurers have made substantial inroads on the independent agency business. Five exclusive agency insurers now write over one third of the private passenger auto insurance premium volume. The rising cost of auto collision and liability coverage has led many customers to be price conscious, and the exclusive agency insurers are writing auto insurance at premiums below those of many other insurers. Some premium reduction is explained by savings in selling costs, and the rest by stricter underwriting. Independent agency insurers occasionally relax underwriting standards to accommodate the most productive agents. Since exclusive agents represent only one insurer, the incentive to meet the insurer's production goals and training requirements is much greater than for agents representing many insurers. This factor is claimed to encourage improved sales performance of exclusive agents.

Life insurers use the exclusive agency system. An independent agency system would not fit the operational pattern of life insurers. The principal distinguishing feature of the independent agency system is that the agents own the renewal rights on the insurance they sell. In life insurance, no renewal rights as such exist. Property liability agents usually are paid the first-year commission rate each time the policy is renewed. The life insurance agent usually is paid a high commission the first year, a much smaller commission for several years, and then a token commission for the remaining life of the policy.

Agency forces. Insurer agency forces may be organized under one or more of three systems: general agency, branch office, and direct reporting. Some insurers use at least two systems in their production operations.

The general agency system. A contract with the insurer authorizes the general agent to represent it in a given area. The territory may be a group of states, a state, or several counties. The general agent's function is to appoint subagents, hire salaried sales representatives, solicit business, develop brokerage accounts, or use any combination of methods. General agents must produce business or they will lose their contracts. General agents earn commissions on all business sold through their offices. From these commissions, operating costs, salaries, and the commissions of those who produce business are paid. Sometimes, general agents share in profits earned on business submitted by their offices, or receive a bonus for attaining a given goal. Some general agents, especially in life insurance, receive service fees and expense allowances, and in any line may be paid a small salary in addition to commission income.

A general agent's specific duties vary among agencies. In life insurance, the principal task is to develop and service business and involves recruiting, selecting, training, supervising, and motivating agents. In property and liability insurance, the agent may have duties beyond that of a sales manager, such as the responsibility for underwriting and claims administration. Large general agencies employ their own special agents, loss control experts, adjusters, and auditors. Although large property and liability general agencies commonly represent more than one insurer, life insurance general agents represent only one insurer. The general agency is the oldest form of field organization and still is used in life insurance, although decreasing in importance. It is not widely used in property and liability insurance.

The branch office system. A later development in field organization is the branch office system in which the insurer establishes its own office in a territory. The branch office performs the functions discharged by general agencies. The manager is paid a salary and usually an incentive bonus. The insurer pays all office expenses. Unlike the general agent, the branch manager is not independent but is supervised by the insurer. The manager's employees are employees of the insurer. The branch office is increasingly popular, because the insurer gains more direct control over product marketing and servicing.

Direct reporting system. Under the direct reporting or home-office system the agent deals directly with the home office rather than a branch office or general agency. The home office maintains many contacts with the field and provides numerous services. Local agents receive exclusive rights to their territories. They obtain brokerage business for the insurer as well as originate business themselves, and also may employ solicitors. In life insurance, except for the smallest insurers, the direct reporting system is rare. Property and liability insurers, however, frequently use it.

Direct selling systems. Many insurers write business directly, thereby eliminating agents from the transaction. They solicit business through vending machines, direct mail campaigns, newspaper advertisements, desks in airports and other strategic places, and salaried sales representatives. Insurers using the direct selling system are known as direct writers to distinguish them from agency insurers. The exclusive agency system insurers often are incorrectly called direct writers. The latter term should be reserved for insurers using salaried sales personnel or direct mail. Direct selling insurers often operate through well-placed branch offices, each staffed with salespersons who solicit and service business in its territory. Insurers do not always adhere to one marketing system. They may sell directly in some areas and use independent agents elsewhere.

Mass merchandising. The concept of mass merchandising in insurance is not new. Life insurance group policies have been written on a mass merchandising basis for about 75 years. However, mass merchandising in property and liability insurance is a relatively new concept anticipated to become increasingly important. It consists of selling and underwriting insurance on a group or collective rather than an individual basis. Mass merchandising is expected to increase faster in commercial lines than in personal lines in the near future. The increase in commercial line mass merchandising is expected because it allows both insurers and insureds to reduce costs. Members of trade and business associations, or franchises, will purchase insurance as a group enabling the insurer to eliminate many underwriting and processing costs, as individual selection is eliminated. In addition commissions will be lower as less agent solicitation is required. These cost reductions allow the insurer to charge a lower rate. During periods of economic hardship, businesses are especially cost conscious and thus demand for low-cost insurance mounts, increasing the probability of successful collective selling.

Many agents fear that mass merchandising will reduce the need for their services. However, others view it as a useful sales tool to increase production rather than one that will eliminate the need for competent agents to solicit and service customers.

Company selling versus buying. Insurers generally are considered to sell insurance products to prospective buyers. However, the reverse is often true; the applicant is selling the risk. Consider a 21-year-old male driver with a history of two accidents and three traffic citations. He may experience substantial difficulty in obtaining insurance. He must sell his risk to an insurer rather than be sold insurance by agents, except those representing insurers specializing in substandard (extra-risk) business. These insurers have less restrictive underwriting standards than most other insurers and consequently charge higher rates. A large business with numerous and varied exposures offers another example. Numerous insurers may have to be approached in order to find one willing to accept the risk at a price considered fair by the risk manager. In this process, the business is engaged in selling its risk to an insurer.

Producers

The insurance market contains many kinds of producers: general agents, local agents, brokers, surplus or excess-line brokers or agents, and solicitors.

The general agent. Because the true or supervising general agents assume many responsibilities and have many expenses, they are paid the highest commissions. In property and liability insurance many with general agents' contracts do not function as general agents but are important enough to their insurers to receive general agents' commissions. General agency contracts sometimes are used as a competitive device to obtain (or retain) some particularly outstanding agents.

Local agents. The local agent represents an insurer in one city. Except in life insurance, the local agent ordinarily will represent more than one insurer. The commission paid is less than general agents receive.

The local agent usually does not perform technical insurance services. Such services are offered by the true general agent or by branch or home offices. The local agent is principally a salesperson who acquires business and counsels clients.

Brokers. Not all insurance producers are tied to insurers by agency contracts or by employer-employee relationships. Some are free-lance operators, called "brokers," who seek the best coverage possible for clients. Theoretically, brokers are agents of insurance buyers and not of insurers. Nevertheless, they are paid commissions by insurers, not fees by buyers. Premiums charged buyers are "loaded" to include commissions, so, indirectly, the client pays the commissions of both agents and brokers. The broker usually receives a lower commission than the agent, allowing the agent to accept business from a broker and still retain a profit margin. Brokers, however, on occasion place business directly with the insurer, rather than through an agent.

Some brokers operate solely as salespersons, providing no technical insurance service. They depend on the insurers to provide these services. Other brokers maintain a loss control staff to help clients obtain the best rate possible. The engineers check clients' exposures, rating procedures of insurers, and advise on loss prevention activities. They also have underwriting staffs who prepare policy forms to fit their clients' needs.

Brokers are more prominent in metropolitan areas, operating extensively among businesses with large exposures. In a sense they operate as insurance or even risk managers for some corporations. While most brokers are local, some are national and others are international. Brokers are not as important in life insurance as in property and liability; they are most important in ocean marine.

Surplus or excess-line brokers or agents. Sometimes an insured will seek a highly specialized coverage not written by an insurer licensed in the home state. The market is limited for many coverages. A partial list includes auto plan excess liability, auto racing liability, strike insurance, oil pollution liability, dramshop liability, nonappearance insurance for paid lectures or their sponsors, and tuition refund insurance for colleges returning fees to withdrawing or dismissed students. To handle business with nonadmitted insurers, states license surplus or excess-line agents and brokers (see Chapter 28).

Solicitors. A final type of producer is the solicitor who usually cannot bind the insurer or issue policies. The solicitor seeks insurance prospects then handles the business through a local agent, broker, company branch, or service office.

Special agents. Salaried representatives known as special agents maintain contact between property and liability insurers and their agents. The special agent is responsible for the insurer's business in an assigned territory and may work directly for an insurer or general agency. The special agent's duties involve appointing agents, assisting them in approaching prospects when requested, helping them to plan a sales program, keeping agents informed of new coverages and forms, helping them with technical problems involving coverages and procedures, and in general maintaining the goodwill and confidence of the agents. Some local agents regard the special agent simply as the nice fellow who picks up the luncheon check on each visit. The special agent's job also is to monitor the quality of business written to assure the development of profitable business. If an agent persists in placing poor business, the special agent must investigate the cause. If the condition continues, the special agent must terminate the agent and appoint a new one.

Insurance buyers and consultants. Large industrial concerns with complex insurance problems often employ full-time insurance managers. These buyers study their companies' loss exposures and select agents and insurers with whom to do business. They may deal with agents, brokers, or direct-writing home offices. Some large firms own their own insurance agencies and trade directly with agency insurers as well as with direct writers, thus, in effect, saving the agent's commission. Other large firms organize their own insurers and buy reinsurance rather than direct insurance. Insured-owned companies are called captive insurers.

The insurance manager's job includes keeping up with developments in the insurance business. Aside from buying insurance, managers must study loss prevention techniques and attempt to minimize losses. Some insurance managers have broadened their operations to become risk managers. Insurance buyers sometimes rely on insurance consulting firms acting as advisers and charging a fee. The consultants study the coverages owned by the client, survey exposures, and, where necessary, recommend changes. The client buys insurance from any insurer or agency, although the consultant's advice also may be sought here.

Product development

In addition to sales, marketing insurance includes product development to facilitate achievement of the marketing objective of writing as much profitable insurance as possible.

Necessity of product development. As times change so do the needs of prospective insurance buyers. Insurers attempt to develop new coverages and policies to meet changing needs. If insurance products remained static, insurers would be subject to an opportunity cost consisting of premiums lost because of the failure to develop innovative products. In addition, because insurance is a social device for reducing risk, as new risks develop, insurers attempt to furnish products to meet these risks benefiting not only the individual, but also society.

Examples of product development. In property and liability insurance, examples of product development abound. In the past, homeowners had to buy separate fire and liability policies. Now complete homeowners protection is offered under one of several package policies. As the popularity of condominiums has increased, insurers have expanded condominium coverage especially designed to meet the particular needs of owners and operators. In recent years insurers have been attacked by consumers for issuing "unreadable" insurance policies. As of 1985 in response to this criticism, insurers were writing "readable" policies in major personal and business lines. Readable policies are found in auto, Homeowners, life and health insurance, and coverage designed for small businesses. This response should not be considered a display of magnanimity by these insurers, but rather a natural response of competitive firms in a capitalistic system to the demands of the marketplace. If sufficient demand exists for a new product, suppliers will invest time and funds to fill it, even insurers which until recently have long been considered steeped in tradition and highly conservative with a motto of "give me that old time religion. What was good enough for granddad is good enough for me." Fortunately that perspective is undergoing change in some enlightened segments of the property liability insurance industry, which is no longer tradition bound but still subject to an outmoded regulatory climate (Chapters 27 and 28).

Product innovation and development is found in the marketing of life insurance and annuities. Nearly every life insurer sells numerous variations of standard whole life, term, and endowment policies in an attempt to satisfy individuals' particular needs. In the 1950s it became apparent that fixed dollar annuities would subject annuitants to a purchasing power risk in an inflationary economy and to a relative standard-of-living risk in a growth economy. In response, variable annuities (Chapter 16) were introduced in an effort to solve the problem and market a product to meet a pressing need, although the stock market action of the 1970s temporarily, at least, made the product appear abortive. Variable life insurance was introduced in the United States, with the first policy written in 1976. "Managed annuities" and universal life insurance are examples of the continued growth. In fact, a growth in product innovation in life insurance is expected to reflect social, demographic, economic, and life cycle changes.

Criticism of insurer innovation. Despite numerous examples of product innovation, the industry often is criticized for failure to innovate and develop new products quickly, and insurers still are accused of excessive conservatism. Needs exist, which are not being satisfied, for various insurance products (e.g., fully flexible life insurance in which the face amount is adjusted to maintain its initial purchasing power, variable health insurance, and interest rate risk protection for mortgagors). However, in defense of the insurance industry several arguments are made, the most important of which is that if sufficient demand exists for a new product insurers will attempt to meet it. The issue may not be one of prompting insurers to innovate new products, but of making buyers aware of their needs so they will demand new products; not an easy issue because of lack of insurance consumer awareness.

A major drawback to the writing of new and innovative policies exists. Until court cases establish the legal definitions of policy terminology, there is a degree of uncertainty for both the insurer and the insured about the exact extent of insurance coverage. Therefore, policy writing is not altered capriciously but only after a proven need has developed.

Claims Administration

The basis of insurance is risk pooling coupled with the obligation of paying losses. Claims must be paid promptly and fairly. Valid claims must not be underpaid. Claims "chiseling" will result in an unfavorable reputation, and an insurer that continually underpays legitimate claims soon will be without customers. Equally dangerous is consistently over-paying claims, as it eventually leads to financial difficulty. An insurer cannot remain profitable if it continually pays higher claims than provided by competitive rates.

The mechanics of loss adjustment

The loss adjustment process begins upon prompt notification of loss to the insurer or agent. If reported to the agent, notice will be forwarded to the insurer unless the agent has authority to initiate loss adjustment. In addition to agents, four types of loss adjusters are used: company adjusters, adjustment bureaus, independent adjusters, and public adjusters. Independent adjusters and public adjusters differ in that the former represent insurers and the latter, insureds. Regardless of the adjuster used, the procedure is the same and involves checking the coverage, investigating the claim, and filing necessary reports. If the claimant and adjuster do not agree on the amount of settlement, arbitration is required. The greater amount of time and energy used by the insurer in loss adjustment, the greater the chance of a fair settlement. However, insurers must seek an optimum trade-off between loss adjustment expense and equitable claims settlement. Payment of a few invalid or exaggerated claims may be more economical than spending large sums for claims investigation.

Checking the coverage. Once notice of loss is received, preliminary inspection is made to learn if the insurer needs to continue the adjustment process. Several questions arise which must be answered yes if loss adjustment is to proceed.

1. Has a policy been issued, and is it *still in force?* This question is not always academic. Years ago a huge bridge collapsed, and the owners filed a claim with their insurer. The insurer could find no record of

the policy. When the owners produced their copy of the contract, a check of the insurer's files showed the home-office records, based on false information furnished by the agent, indicated incorrectly that the policy was issued by the agent in another name for a dwelling instead of a bridge. Because the owners held a policy issued by an agent with power to bind the insurer, the bridge owners were paid for their loss. The agent went to jail.

2. Is the loss the result of an insured peril? Insureds often do not know the perils covered and sometimes assume their coverage includes many more perils than it does. Conversely, some insureds fail to report covered losses because they are unaware their policies offer that coverage.

3. Is the property covered by the policy? A Homeowners' policyowner files a claim for the value of a stolen canary only to find that birds (as well as animals and fish) are excluded from coverage.

4. Is the loss covered? A store owner has a fire in the building. The fire is extinguished prior to damage to the building. The smoke lingers however, and the shopkeeper must air the building for two days so the shop may again be inviting to customers. Two days' business are lost because of the fire. The indirect loss of two days' profit is not covered by the usual fire policy.

5. Is the claimant entitled to the payment? If the claimant is the policyowner and has an insurable interest in the loss, the answer is clear. However, in life insurance the claimant often will not be the owner, but a beneficiary named in the policy. A determination must be made that the claimant is the legal beneficiary.

6. Did the loss occur in a place covered by the contract? A loss that produces a collectible claim in one place may not be collectible in another. An example is the auto liability policy, which covers accidents occurring within the United States, its territories or possessions, or Canada, but excludes those occurring elsewhere. If the claim is for an accident in Mexico, adjustment need proceed no further.

The foregoing questions are answered on the basis of facts submitted by the claimant. If the insurer determines that a basis exists for a claim, the claimant will be sent proof of loss forms. If the insurer finds the claim fails to meet any of the requisites, settlement proceedings will not continue.

Investigation of the claim.[5] Sending proof of loss blanks to a claimant does not mean that the insurer admits liability but only that, after study of facts submitted, the insurer has found nothing which obviously disqualifies the claimant. A more complete investigation is necessary before the insurer can determine its liability. Claim investigation involves ascertaining the existence of a loss, determining whether actions by the insured have invalidated the claim, and establishing the amount of loss.

---

[5] Part of the discussion has only limited application to liability policies, as payment under these policies is not made to the insured. Special problems of these adjustments are discussed later.

The investigation includes validating facts submitted in the proof of loss statement.

If a loss has occurred usually it is simple to ascertain, but occasionally the investigator finds no evidence of a loss. Persons with substantial amounts of life insurance have disappeared only to reappear later in remote places. The annals of marine insurance are filled with cases in which the loss claimed was later shown not to have occurred.

The second object of claim investigation is to determine whether the insured has fulfilled the obligations under the insurance contract. Has the insured with a Homeowners policy, for example, "protected the property from further damage, forthwith separated the damaged and the undamaged personal property, and put it in the best possible order?" Has the insured done everything reasonably possible to prevent the spread of the fire? Did the insured report the loss promptly? The investigation may disclose factors that nullify prima facie evidence contained in the notice of loss.

The third function of investigation is to determine the amount of loss. When the amount of loss is reported, the adjuster examines the claim and estimates the amount owed the insured. If the adjuster's estimate is not in agreement with the insured's, the adjuster explains the reasoning behind the estimate and listens to the insured's point of view. Most often they can work out a satisfactory solution. If not, the policy specifies what must be done.

Preparation of proof of loss.   Once the investigation is complete and coverage established, final papers are prepared. The papers, called the proof of loss, usually are prepared for the insured by the adjuster and filed with the insurer. The adjuster usually files a separate report summarizing conditions found and recommendations concerning loss settlement. When the insured signs the proof of loss or cashes the check, further rights to pursue the claim are waived.

Salvage and subrogation.   The adjustment process may require the adjuster to determine if the insurer can recover some of the money paid in claims. Salvage occurs when damaged property can be sold by the insurer's representative on behalf of the insured or the insurer. Sometimes, the insurer settles the claim as a total loss then seeks to salvage damaged goods in an effort to obtain funds from their sale. More often, however, the adjuster helps the insured protect the damaged property and realize the best possible disposition of it. To its dismay, one of the largest U.S. insurers found that for two years one of its claim adjusters was taking kickbacks on salvage in some cases and in others retaining the salvage and selling it for his own profit. He would replace a damaged new car with a brand new one, report a total loss to the insurer, and sell the partially damaged car to a salvage rebuilder for a profit. Upon confrontation of the evidence, the *former* adjuster explained "I don't want it to sound like I am passing the buck, but it's the system. . . . A man is told to get his piece of candy from the salvage. . . . You got to the point where you figure anything I can get by with, that's what the company is expecting out of me." He felt that stealing was expected, as the company did not have an unequivocal policy against it, a sad state of morality indeed which seems to prevail in present-day society.

When the insurer pays a claim, that payment becomes subrogated to the insured's claim against wrongdoers responsible for the loss. Thus, if a neighbor carelessly sets fire to dry grass and the fire spreads to the insured's house, the insured is entitled to damages from the neighbor. The fire insurer acquires right of action against the neighbor for the amount of the loss paid. The adjuster of any loss with the exception of life and most health insurance claims, must be aware of subrogation rights. Sometimes, these are important enough to reimburse the insurer completely for a claim payment.[6]

Arbitration. Although in nearly all cases the adjuster and the insured can reach an agreement concerning settlement, every policy provides terms for settling claims when disagreement exists as to the amount of loss. Arbitration is provided in such cases. Typically, the insured and the adjuster each appoint a disinterested party to act as arbitrator. The two arbitrators select a third disinterested party. An agreement meeting the approval of any two will be binding on both the insured and the insurer. In liability lines the court replaces the arbitrator, and no arbitration clause appears in the policy.

Difficulties encountered by the adjuster

The adjuster must be as effective at selling as the person who sells the policy. In many ways, the adjuster's selling job is greater than that of the agent; for the adjuster often must satisfy the claimant, without making all the concessions. The adjuster's work is made more difficult by attitudes many insureds have toward the fundamental purpose of insurance in general and their relation with the insurer in particular. These claimants may be classified as: mistaken claimant, misled claimant, and dishonest claimant. The adjuster must use sales ability with the first two. If the insurer's position can be made clear to the insured, the adjustment problems will be solved successfully. With the third group, little selling is needed. Insureds who try to cheat are in reality stealing from their neighbors, for their dishonesty increases the cost of insurance to everyone.

Mistaken claimants. Many claim adjuster's troubles arise from honest mistakes made by insureds in overestimating the loss amount. The first appearance of damaged property leads the insured to believe the damage is greater than that actually incurred. When the damaged and undamaged goods have been separated and the latter put in the best possible condition, the insured often finds that damage is not as much as origi-

---

[6] Subrogation is discussed in Chapter 6.

nally estimated. Another source of conflict is that many insureds place a higher than market value on their property.

Misled claimants. The adjuster faces more problems from misled insureds than mistaken claimants. Most people refuse to take the time to read their policies and thus obtain only a general grasp of the provisions. Nevertheless, they have definite ideas concerning their provisions and coverage. The adjuster has studied the policy in detail and usually knows if coverage exists. If the claimant is mistaken, the adjuster must use sales ability. Insureds who remain unconvinced certainly will change insurers. In many cases, the adjuster must say "no," but attempt to say it in such a way that the claimant will remain a client.

Claimants also are misled by lack of knowledge of adjustment procedure. In the early days these procedures were not standardized. Some insurers advised adjusters to delay settlement, so that claimants would tire of pressing their claims. Policies often were constructed to be misleading, if not prevaricating. This experience has built up in insureds a feeling they must engage in a war of wits with adjusters. They believe they must file excessive claims to be in a better bargaining position. Good public relations work by insurers and adjusters is necessary to overcome these feelings.

Some claimants, noting that insurers have impressive home-office buildings and extensive investments, consider them fair game. Many Americans regard all corporations in this light. This idea has wielded its influence in the field of insurance jurisprudence. Jurors' hearts seldom bleed for an insurer. Somewhat similar is the attitude of some claimants that as a loss finally has occurred to them, it is their big chance to get even with the insurer for all the premiums paid.

Dishonest claimants. Far different than the misled claimant who pads a claim report for strategic reasons is the claimant who seeks to defraud the insurer with faked claims or self-inflicted losses. To claimants of this sort the adjuster should be, and usually is, merciless. The adjuster need use no selling powers, as the insurer has no interest in them as clients. Insurers would like to have these persons off their books and preferably in jail.

The insurance business attracts many schemes to defraud. No branch of insurance is immune, but the fire insurance branch furnishes the most notorious examples.[7] The danger of the arsonist has plagued the

---

[7] A friend closely associated with a large auto insurer commented on reading this sentence: "I doubt this statement about fire insurance on the basis of what I've heard about auto insurance." Perhaps he heard about the claims adjuster who hired a relative to run a detective agency, then found that many auto insurance claims required outside investigation. Or maybe he heard about the adjuster who telephoned a claimant whose car had just sustained $300 damage after being hit by an insured. The adjuster posed as a lawyer and advised that the claimant could get $3,000 if the claimant returned half as a legal fee. The claimant agreed. So, a $300 loss was settled for $3,000 with the claimant getting $1,500 and the adjuster getting $1,500 (and all of us chipping in!).

fire insurance business from Nero to the present day. In recent years the problem of arson has assumed catastrophic dimensions. It was estimated that over $2 billion of fire insurance claims in 1978 were the result of arson. Professional arsonists can be hired to burn any property the client wishes to "sell" to an insurer. One professional arsonist, a leader in the field, once testified that the first job of the arsonist often is to "convince a merchant that a fire was better than a crooked bankruptcy, where the firm's books always remained a source of embarrassment, and better than a fake burglary, because the police always persisted in looking for the stolen goods." As fire so often destroys the evidence of incendiarism along with the property, detection often is difficult; and identification of the firebug often impossible. A prospective client of a professional arsonist, on asking that functionary how he proposed to make sure it would be a "complete job," was told: "Do you think I'm going to tell you how to do it and let you take the bread and butter out of my mouth?"

The high rate of incendiary and suspicious fires prompted fire insurers to begin lobbying efforts to enact and upgrade the enforcement of anti-arson laws. These efforts culminated with the passage of the Anti-Arson Law of 1982 which classifies arson as a major crime requiring FBI investigation. This step, along with the insurance industry's activities at the community level to fight arson and other property loss crimes (i.e., auto theft, vandalism, and so on) is expected to reduce the number and cost of incendiary and suspicious fires. By 1983 reports from the National Fire Protection Association estimated the cost of such losses had declined to $1.6 billion in 1982 based on 129,000 fires, 16.5 percent fewer than in the preceding year.

Unfortunately, the insurance aspect of these losses does not reflect the whole problem. Dollar losses cannot begin to show the extent of human suffering; death, disfigurement, disability, displacement from homes and jobs can all result from arson. In 1982 over 900 people died in incendiary and suspicious fires.

The positive side of the story is that 49 states have passed laws which allow insurers immunity from defamation suits when they cooperate with law enforcement agencies by sharing information about suspicious fire claims.

Life insurance also has dishonest claimants. Some years ago a woman applied for a life insurance policy and passed the company's medical examination without difficulty. Within a matter of months the insurer received a claim by the beneficiary. The insured had died of tuberculosis. The medical examiner's report was inspected by the medical director who found no trace of the disease during the examination a few months earlier. The doctor had heard of galloping consumption, but had never experienced it in so speedy a form. The claim investigation, however, revealed that the loss had not occurred. The dead woman had a twin sister who had taken the medical examination for her. It would be incorrect to emphasize this phase of the insurance business. Insurers have found that, for the most part, claimants report their losses honestly.

Examples of loss adjustment problems

Although basic principles of loss adjustment are similar in all fields of insurance, each branch has its own problems.

Property and liability losses. One of the most complicated parts of fire loss adjusting occurs when two or more policies are issued on the property and the policies are not written alike; that is, they are not concurrent. Many basic fire forms have a notice printed in boldface type that if the property is covered by more than one policy, the insured should be sure the insuring agreements are worded identically. In spite of this warning, many claims appear involving nonconcurrent policies. In simple nonconcurrency, the claimant may have one policy covering the property generally; for example, stock and machinery, and another that specifically covers stock. The question is how to apportion the payment between the two insurers in case of loss. Resolution of this question could cause confusion, delay of payments, and, in some cases, recovery for less than the full amount of the loss. The advice printed on the policy is excellent. Be sure that all policies are worded identically. Also all policies on a piece of property should be bought from the same insurer where possible. Then if a question arises as to which policy covers, the argument can continue ad infinitum among department heads *after* the insured is paid instead of among claim adjusters *before* a settlement is made.

In marine insurance the basic problem is determining the amount of indemnity. Settlement is complicated because the remains of the ship or shipment may be at the bottom of the ocean. The ship manifest is a document that is supposed to give a complete cargo inventory. Occasionally insurers doubt that all goods listed were actually on board when a ship went down; if, indeed, the ship did sink and was not just spirited away. Fortunately, attempts at deception are rare. The chief problem simply is determining the values actually lost. In valued policies the problem of settling the values will not be present, because in a valued policy the insurer pays the agreed amount without question if the loss is considered to be total.

A second problem in ocean marine insurance is adjusting general average losses. A loss voluntarily undertaken to save (and succeeds in saving) the venture is borne by all interests and not solely by the owner of the destroyed goods. If cotton is thrown overboard during a storm to lighten the load to save the ship, it would be unfair for the entire loss to fall on the cotton owner. Under the rule of general average, all other cargo owners, the ship's owner, and persons who profit from the freight charge for hauling the cargo must share in the loss. As each interest must be evaluated to decide the extent of participation in the general average settlement, this rule introduces many complications into ocean marine loss adjustment.

In settling liability claims *speed* is essential. Nearly every fire could have been extinguished by a glass of water if it had been thrown on the fire soon enough. Many liability claims could be settled quickly with a few kind words and assurance of complete payment of medical expenses, if offered early enough. After the injured has thought things over, often it is too late for such an amicable settlement. Second is the problem of *obtaining relevant facts*. Each witness may have a different version of the accident. Many views will come from unbiased and honest witnesses, not to mention the fabricated ones by those with an interest in the case. A third problem is to *preserve the facts*. Obtaining the facts is not enough, for they are more ephemeral than this week's top 20 college basketball teams. The adjuster must preserve the facts by signed depositions, photographs, medical reports, and so on.

A fourth problem is to decide the *cash settlement,* if any, to be offered. The facts, pieced together from statements of witnesses, must be analyzed by trying to view them as would a judge and jury. From this study, it may be decided to offer a settlement or to fight the claim in court. If the decision is to go to court, another problem arises. Assume that the insured has a policy with $20,000 limits and the claimant will settle for $20,000 but the insurer refuses. Suppose that the court awards an amount in excess of $20,000 to the claimant. Numerous court decisions have held the insurer liable for the full amount awarded, on grounds that the insurer acted negligently by refusing to settle for an amount within the policy limits.

Insurers, particularly those writing auto insurance, have experienced much criticism arising from the consumerism movement. One complaint is the method of claims adjustment and the long delay that often occurs. To counteract the complaints, some insurers have developed other techniques. The traditional method has been tendering settlement for an absolute release. Today, the loss adjuster may make partial payments without a release. Payments to the claimant represent advances credited toward the final settlement when agreed to which may be no more than the advance payment.

One of the insuring agreements under a liability policy is the promise to defend any suit against the insured with respect to the insurance afforded by the policy, even if the suit is groundless, false, or fraudulent. Under this agreement, the insurer must defend any suits against the insured, if the insurer must pay the claim in a successful suit. For example, if an insured restaurant owner is sued for bodily injury, alleging assault and battery on the part of the owner, what should the adjuster do? In many business liability insurance policies, coverage exists only when there is an occurrence "that is neither expected nor intended by the insured." Assault and battery performed by the insured would be neither unexpected nor unintended by the insured. If the court rules the restaurant owner is guilty, the insurer is liable neither for the defense nor damages awarded by the court. But if the insured wins the case (it proves to be self-defense, not assault and battery), the insurer will be liable for the cost of defense. This is true because the insured had not committed assault and battery. The adjuster must investigate the facts before denying defense on grounds of a contract exclusion.

Life insurance. Adjustment of life insurance policy claims is the simplest of all insurance. If the policy matures during the life of the subject, as in an endowment policy, the insurer need only check its records on the person's age, then pay the claim. When policies are matured by the subject's death, that death must be verified and so must the beneficiary's claim to receive the proceeds. The problem of loss evaluation does not exist for there can be no partial losses. True, one may act half dead, but the life insurer is not liable for payment.

The beneficiary usually is found by consulting the insurer's records. If doubt exists as to the proper beneficiary, as it might should a person name "my spouse" then marry three times, the insurer has an efficient procedure. It pays the proceeds to a court and designates that body to pay whomever it decides has the proper claim. One widow entangled in legal proceedings is quoted as saying, "This settlement is so much trouble I almost wish my husband hadn't died."

One difficulty that may arise in a life insurance settlement is that the insured has given misinformation in applying for the policy or that fraud has been perpetrated against the insurer. Because the incontestable clause found in every life policy gives the insurer only two years to uncover such chicanery, these problems seldom appear. However, one such case was given wide publicity because of the bizarre circumstances involved and because it concerned $15 million of life insurance. This is believed to be the largest single claim in life insurance history. The characters in the case would (and probably will) fit nicely into a made-for-TV movie. The cast includes: the fun-loving, hell-raising, extravagant insured who was heavily in debt; his attractive wife (the daughter of a wealthy Texas oilman) who had left him the week before his death; a bevy of frightened servants most of whom had quit their jobs shortly before the insured's death; the insured's handsome "bodyguard" once convicted of cattle rustling and fired by the insured shortly before his death; a self-styled financial expert (three times in prison) who was arranging for the insured to meet a big-time politician, reportedly to get the insured a desperately needed loan from a questionable source; and two loan brokers, one a 300-pound itinerant who always carried a bucket of fried chicken around with him and another who had attempted to arrange a loan for two holders of stolen securities; the owner of an NFL football team; the owners of the insurance agency writing the policy, one a convicted rapist and swindler, the other a swindler and later a victim of a hired gunman; a prominent Texas businessman who shared in the commissions "earned" on many of the policies sold by the agency writing the policy, including the one in question; a group of lawyers involved in the case, some of whom were powerful political figures; two doctors who signed the insured's health reports without examining him, one of whom was the cousin of the agent writing the policy, and the other, an army doctor, who filled out the forms as a favor to the agent; a representative of a credit investigation company who submitted an exaggerated report of the insured's financial condition obtained in part from an erroneous newspaper clipping after the insured had told him that his financial holdings were none of the investigator's business; and a Methodist minister who dealt in unlisted securities and once served time for federal mail fraud.

The $15 million of insurance was distributed through reinsurance to more than 100 insurers. Only one year's premium ($253,300) was paid, and the agent's commission was 95 percent. The insured apparently was murdered one year later near the end of the policy's grace period. The insurers contested the claim on the grounds, among others, that the insurance agency was not selling insurance but was selling collateral for loans. The insurers obviously believed they had been defrauded, but the question appears to be by whom? If the insured acted in good faith, the insurers could have been out $18 million ($3 million for late payment). The claim was finally settled for $8 million. The originating insurer had retained only $40,000 of the insurance.

One clause, double indemnity, often attached to life policies may cause headaches. In borderline cases, the claims adjuster investigates the facts to determine whether the beneficiary is entitled to double payment. A fascinating record of such an investigation is found in James M. Cain's modern classic, *Double Indemnity*. The fearless claims investigator tracked his suspect and eventually got his man. To prevent glorification of the insurance business, Cain chose for his villain an insurance salesman who shared the office with the claims man!

Loss Prevention

Loss prevention is as important as prompt settlement. Historically insurers were not concerned with loss prevention and considered their business as paying losses, not preventing them. Rates were based on loss experience, and insurers were content to let the law of averages produce their usual profits without worrying about loss prevention. The report of the Merritt Committee to the New York legislature in 1911 said:

> The old type of underwriter is passing. He did not believe in preventing fires; fires were what made business for the underwriters; it was the function of insurance simply to distribute the fire loss and if the people preferred to burn their property it was not his business to interfere; it was his business to see that plenty of premiums were collected to pay the losses—it was not important who paid them so long as they came in; incidentally, however, he had a shrewd eye for the business in which there was a good profit and he let his less keen brother take the rest.

Zachariah Allen, a New England textile manufacturer instrumental in founding the factory mutuals pioneered in loss prevention activity. Unless a textile mill met the factory mutual's high standards it would be refused insurance. As factory mutual rates were most favorable, millowners often made extensive changes to be eligible for the insurance.

Cooperative efforts of insurers in loss prevention

Insurance executives today have an attitude different from that found by the Merritt Committee. Insurers of all types are concerned with loss prevention. Fire insurers just after the Civil War formed the National Board of Fire Underwriters. This organization, through the use of engineers, research, investigation, and education was instrumental in reducing life and property loss from fires, windstorms, explosions, and other perils. In the mid-1960s the board merged into the American Insurance Association, which continued the work for several years. In 1970 the American Insurance Association discontinued the Fraud and Arson Service which began with the National Board of Fire Underwriters over 100 years before. The arson and inland marine theft portions of their surveillance have been discontinued, and their casualty investigation and statistical work merged into the Casualty Insurance Fraud Association.

In 1970, 12 major insurers formed the Casualty Insurance Fraud Association (CIFA). This organization, now known as The Insurance Crime Prevention Institute (ICPI), was formed to conduct investigations into losses, in an effort to break up organized accident rings. James F. Ahern, who achieved favorable nationwide publicity for handling the troubles on the Yale University campus when he was police chief of New Haven, was selected to direct the association. Mr. Ahern has estimated that 10 percent of all casualty claims contain some element of fraud. The assistant to the director of ICPI stated that special emphasis would be placed on rooting out dishonest lawyers, police officers, and doctors that damage the nation's bar, law enforcement agencies, and medical profession. (Good luck!) Other fire insurance organizations engaged in loss prevention are the Associated Factory Mutual Fire Insurance Companies' engineering division and laboratories, and the engineering and inspection services of the Factory Insurance Association (now merged with the Oil Insurance Association).

Marine insurance offers another example of early interest in loss prevention. The information center operated by Lloyd's had as one of its chief purposes supervising ship construction to attain greater safety. Marine insurers are active in the Yacht Safety Bureau, the American Bureau of Shipping, National Cargo Bureau, the Power Squadron, and the American Hull Insurance Syndicate, all of which are active in loss prevention. In 1971 the major insurers writing motorcycle coverage formed the Association of Motorcycle Insurers to advance motorcycling safety and theft prevention through education. (Those of us on college campuses who have to dodge motorcyclists are thankful for this mission but wonder about its success.)

The American Insurance Association has an accident prevention department which concentrates on industrial safety codes and standards, traffic safety, and safety education. The National Association of Mutual Insurance Companies engages in accident prevention and rehabilitation. The National Council on Compensation Insurance cooperates in loss prevention activity. Property and liability insurers support the National Safety Council. This organization provides leadership in safety of all kinds. Auto insurers support the Insurance Institute for Highway Safety, an industrywide traffic safety organization.

The Alliance of American Insurers, the American Insurance Association, the National Association of Independent Insurers, and the National Association of Mutual Insurance Companies all support mandatory installation of passive restraint devices (air bags and automatic seat belt harnesses) in automobiles. These associations believe that the devices will substantially reduce serious injuries and deaths resulting from auto collisions. A reduction of the severity of injuries would reduce auto insurers' losses and eventually result in lower auto insurance premiums (or at least mitigate premium increases). Current federal legislation requires the installation of passive restraint systems starting in 1987, but continued congressional delay of this implementation date is possible.

Life insurers were among the last to recognize the importance of loss prevention. Who can blame life insurance executives for failing to discover methods to prevent the loss of life? Several large insurers, notably the Metropolitan Life Insurance Company, inaugurated a health information service many years ago. In 1945 nearly 150 of the nation's leading life insurers formed the Life Insurance Medical Research Fund. The organization's purpose is to provide research funds for the discovery of treatments and cures for various illnesses and diseases.

Individual efforts of insurers in loss prevention

The Hartford Steam Boiler Inspection and Insurance Company, organized in 1866, has as its purpose boiler accident prevention. It employs a large staff of engineers and other experts to aid in loss prevention. With the coming of workers' compensation laws in the 20th century, insurers have conducted extensive research programs in prevention of industrial accidents. Loss prevention and control services also are offered to insureds for general liability exposures, elevator hazards, crime exposures, glass breakage, and fire exposures. In addition to direct services, insurers contribute indirectly to the insured's loss prevention program by distributing general loss prevention information and encouraging the insured to practice loss prevention by using a merit-rating system (Chapter 26).

Some observers believe that insurers are not doing nearly enough in the loss prevention field—that many losses occur which could be prevented through more research by insurers on unsafe physical conditions and practices.

Insurance and loss prevention complement each other. Both the insured and the insurer must be aware of loss prevention economics. Preventing loss is as important to risk management as is insuring losses. Frequently to obtain insurance, prospective insureds must institute loss prevention programs.

Loss prevention and the firm

Modern-day businesses are becoming increasingly aware of the importance of methods for loss prevention. Businesses installing loss prevention devices have for many years been entitled to lower fire insurance rates. Businesses are currently investigating other possible measures of loss prevention especially in the workers' compensation area, prompted by the Federal Occupational Safety and Health Act of 1970 (OSHA) and in the products safety field, motivated by the Federal Consumer Products Safety Act of 1972.

However, loss prevention techniques cannot be instituted indiscriminately by profit-maximizing enterprises. If the cost of installing loss prevention equipment or procedures exceeds the expected saving in losses, the measure should not be implemented. The question of whether the benefits of a particular loss prevention method exceed the costs usually is a difficult one. Many variables must be considered, including the cost of implementation, expected reduction in losses, duration of the loss reductions, social welfare considerations, productivity reductions caused by losses, and many other factors. The firm may also have to choose between alternative loss prevention measures.

Once all these factors are considered, the risk manager must decide as to the profitability of the proposal. Even if the risk manager believes the proposal will reduce losses at a profitable cost, the most difficult job may yet remain, that of convincing top executive officers and production line managers of the utility and profitability of the proposed loss prevention measures, and of inducing the enforcement of these measures.

Cooperative Organizations

Sometimes it is said that insurers "compete in a great spirit of cooperation." The existence of many different types of associations in the insurance business is partly responsible for this statement. A complete directory of cooperative insurance organizations would include associations for company executives, technicians, loss prevention, insurance agents, intercompany claims settlement, educational groups, public relations, buyers' groups, and so many others the reader would be drowned in a complete list.

Why cooperate?

Traditionally in America competition in insurance is controlled either by governmental regulation or cooperative action among insurers. Many insurers prefer the latter method. Therefore, they make efforts to discourage destructive competition, in spite of strong opposition from two groups: those believing in state control and those believing in free competition.

The more difficult obstacles to cooperative action involving **trade practices** come from within the industry. Some insurers refuse to cooperate—among them the rugged individualist, the new insurer seeking growth, and the insurer that does not believe that either the public interest or their own interest is best served by cooperative action among insurers. These insurers tend to believe that government regulation (discussed in Chapters 27 and 28) best protects the public from "undesirable" competition *and* from "restrictive" trade practices resulting from intercompany cooperative actions.

Competition in insurance may be classified into four categories: prices (rates), products (policy terms), service, and representation in sales outlets (agencies).

Controlling competition is not the only reason for cooperative organizations. Most industries maintain one or more trade associations for activities handled best on an industrywide rather than individual company basis. These associations lobby in behalf of legislation favorable to the industry, oppose unfavorable legislation, engage in cooperative advertising and publicity to improve public relations, establish codes of ethics for the business, gather industrywide statistics, sponsor periodic meetings for the discussion of industry problems, and engage in cooperative educational and research activities. Cooperative organizations also aid in loss adjustment activities and in providing underwriting facilities.

Ratemaking organizations

Insurers find that cooperative ratemaking is essential for many coverages. Cooperation is maintained through ratemaking organizations or through subterfuge when such organizations have been ruled illegal. The ratemaking organizations may be independent bodies offering advisory rates to insurers at a contract price, or organizations owned, financed, and managed by member insurers.[8] In those states requiring membership in rating bureaus and adherence to rates and rules promulgated by them, the organizations are closely regulated to assure fair and nondiscriminatory practices. Even if membership is not mandatory, many insurers find it desirable to join a rating bureau in order to eliminate the expense of independent rate filings in various states.[9] In addition, by combining loss statistics from many insurers, the credibility, or reliability, of the calculated rates is increased. Some insurers, nevertheless, prefer to remain outside the rating bureau and file rates independently. These are called nonbureau insurers and sometimes, by using rate-cutting practices, they become an irritant to bureau insurers.

In 1971 the Insurance Services Office (ISO), formed through consolidation of six national insurance rating or service organizations, began operation. Since its beginning, the ISO has expanded its scope of operations to include, among other activities, product development and re-

---

[8] The state of Texas owns and operates its own rating bureau.

[9] See Chapter 27 for a discussion of rate regulation.

search. In early 1975 the ISO introduced its first "readable" Homeowners policy which is now marketed in 40 states. ISO has also adopted a new, simplified dwelling fire rating program in all states.

Rating bureaus collect statistics to develop rates and rate schedules for approved policy forms. Rating bureaus often standardize insurance policies. Rate development and administration are difficult if contracts to which rates apply are not standardized. The bureaus also aid insurers in preparing merit rates for individual exposures. Rating bureaus usually administer rates by auditing each policy for the proper rate assignment and the proper forms and endorsements. Sometimes, the audit bureau is independent of the rating bureau. Life insurance rating bureaus do not exist as these rates are not cooperatively set.

Other association functions

Cooperative organizations are formed to engage in numerous other functions. National, state, and local insurance agents' associations are organized to promote agent welfare. These associations engage in lobbying activities, promote educational programs for members, and in general protect the agents' interests in relations with insurers.

The Insurance Federation, on state and national levels, is another lobbying organization designed to protect private insurers from undesired governmental interference and competition. The American Insurance Association provides a forum for the capital stock insurers to study their common problems. The industry also has social organizations, such as the Order of the Blue Goose, a fire insurance society. College teachers of insurance have organized the American Risk and Insurance Association.

Underwriting associations

Associations also are formed to provide underwriting facilities for a particular industry or for a special class of property. Through these organizations, greater insurance capacity for large or perilous exposures is available than could be offered by individual insurers. The associations, sometimes called pools, associates, syndicates, or federations, perform rating, loss adjustment, and engineering services for certain exposures more economically and efficiently than could each insurer operating alone. Specialists employed by the group carry on its functions, and profits and losses are shared by member insurers. Underwriting associations established under state and federal auspices include those designed to make insurance available in central city areas against riot, theft, and fire for most property owners and to provide flood insurance in selected areas. The insurance business is probably the most organization happy of all industries. Just name the type of organization and the insurance business probably has it.

Public relations

Many organizations in all branches of insurance have been formed to improve public relations through collecting and publishing insurance information and other efforts to educate the public. The oldest major public relations organization is the Alliance of American Insurers, sponsored and supported by the mutual property and liability insurers of America. Capital stock property and liability insurers in 1960 founded the Insurance Information Institute to coordinate public relations and education work carried on for many years by several regional organizations. It publishes *Insurance Facts,* containing some statistical series pertaining to property and liability insurance. The American Council of Life Insurance is the prime source of life insurance information for the public. It conducts invaluable studies on public opinion and collects massive statistics. Its publication, *Life Insurance Fact Book,* is an important information source. The Health Insurance Institute performs similar services and publishes the *Source Book of Health Insurance Data,* a valuable source of health insurance statistics.

Company fleets

Insurers often operate in interrelated groups. A few examples are the Aetna group, the State Farm group, the Hartford group, the Kemper group, the Sentry group, and the Nationwide group. A group or fleet is composed of more than one insurer owned or managed by the same interests. Many groups include a life insurer.

Insurance executives form groups for several reasons. One is to develop size to take advantage of economies of scale. Another is to be able to write many insurance coverages. Before multiple line underwriting powers were granted to insurers, fire insurers could write marine but not casualty lines; and casualty insurers could not write fire or marine lines. However, several insurers could be grouped to give one management organization underwriting outlets in all coverages. A third reason that insurers form fleets is to provide a means whereby different companies within the group may specialize in different markets. For example, fleets might consist of three companies with one catering to preferred risk drivers, another handling standard risk drivers, and the third accepting high risk drivers, at proportionately higher premiums. A final reason for group formation is to increase the agency representation of a management interest. If there were six insurers in a group, there could be six agents in a territory, each with "exclusive rights" for one of the group's insurers. Just as multiple line underwriting powers have reduced the need for two or more insurers, the contemporary decline in sole-representation agency contracts has reduced the need for several insurers of the same kind. As a result, consolidations have taken place. For example, one such consolidation took place in 1982 when the Connecticut General Insurance Company (CG) and the Insurance

Company of North America (INA) decided to pool their efforts and formed CIGNA. Other new combinations have been formed with companies outside the insurance industry. The primary aim of these consolidations has been to increase the firm's market share (and profit) by providing consumers with a wide range of financial services, including insurance, from a single source. Two such combinations resulted from the joining of the American Express Company with Fireman's Fund Insurance Company and the Prudential Insurance Company of America with the Bache Group, Inc., a New York brokerage firm.

Summary

1. In insurer organizations, authority moves downward, responsibility upward. Theoretically the primary source of authority is the stockholders in a stock company and the policyowners in a mutual company. This authority, however, usually is delegated to a board of directors, which, in turn, delegates authority to executive officers who run everyday company operations.

2. Insurers are composed of various departments. The major ones unique to insurers are agency, underwriting, claims, loss control, auditing, and actuarial and statistical departments.

3. Insurers' products are generally marketed through the agency system. Under the American agency system, used by the majority of property and liability insurers, the agent is independent, representing several insurers. All life insurers and many property and liability insurers use the exclusive agency system under which agents work exclusively for one insurer.

4. Insurer product merchandising consists of two functions, selling products and product development. Company sales organizations seek to make products available to all eligible prospective insurance buyers. Insurers also must be concerned with product development, in an attempt to introduce innovative products to satisfy changing needs.

5. Insurers must adjust claims promptly and fairly to remain profitable. In arriving at a "fair" settlement, the investigation cost must be balanced against the investigation benefits. For profitability it may be better for an insurer to pay a few exaggerated claims than spend hundreds of dollars in determining the claim's true value.

6. Insurers use several types of claims adjusters. Loss adjustment procedure involves checking the coverage, investigating the claim, and filing necessary reports and papers.

7. Salvage and subrogation rights may allow insurers to recover some of the money paid in claims. An efficient use of salvage and subrogation rights may determine the difference between profit and loss for a property and liability insurer.

8. Adjusters must convince claimants that payments are equitable.

This duty is difficult because of mistaken, misled, and dishonest claimants.

9. Special problems of loss adjustment vary among lines of insurance. In fire insurance, a major problem arises concerning valuation of a claim especially in the case of nonconcurrent policies. In life insurance, however, claim valuation is inherently simple, although the problem of fraud is not unknown.

10. Loss prevention activities are undertaken by insurers as a group, individual insurers, and individual insureds. Successful loss prevention benefits insureds, insurers, and society.

11. Insurers join cooperative organizations to control competition and engage in industry-related functions. Members of cooperative organizations believe that unlimited competition would be destructive to the insurance industry and have joined organizations to control competition rather than submit to more government regulation. Other insurers refuse to join cooperative organizations, believing that neither their own nor the public's best interest is served by them.

Questions for Review

1. Someone has commented that the aim of the sales department of an insurer is to sell every American an insurance policy and that the aim of the underwriting department is to see that they don't do it. Do you think there is any truth to this statement?

2. In what ways do the commission schedules in life insurance differ from those used in the property and liability insurance business?

3. Why might an insurer employ an independent claims adjuster? Would such action be an argument against such an insurer? Explain.

4. What is a major drawback to the writing of new and innovative policies? Explain.

5. How might the slowness of the development of loss prevention consciousness among insurance executives be explained?

6. In what respect must the claims adjuster be a salesperson for the insurer?

7. Explain the concept of general average loss. Could it ever be of importance to a typical insured person?

8. Explain how a business manager might approach the problem of loss prevention.

9. Why do insurers join cooperative organizations? Do these organizations promote or restrain competition?

10. What factors should an insurer consider when deciding upon the amount of investigation to undertake on an individual claim?

11. What are some typical problems that an insurance adjuster must face? Do these problems result from inadequate insurer public relations? Explain.

12. Explain how insurers, insureds, and society might benefit from loss prevention activities.

13. Explain the differences between the American agency system and the exclusive agency system. Do all life insurers prefer the exclusive agency system? Explain.

14. Would property-liability insurers prefer the exclusive agency system? Explain.

Questions for Discussion

1. What differences would you expect to find between the investment department of a large life insurer and that of a large property insurer? Explain.

2. What is a "captive" insurer? The IRS recently has been viewing captive insurers with a somewhat jaundiced eye. What might account for this attitude?

3. What do you consider to be the most important department of an insurer? Explain.

4. Should insurance agents fear the expansion of mass merchandising of insurance products? Why or why not?

5. "Insurers will market new and innovative products as soon as sufficient demand for these products exists." Can you discern any fault with the foregoing statement? Does demand for innovation in any area necessarily precede the supply? If the demand for new products does not need to precede their development, what might account for the slowness of insurer product innovation?

6. Life policies are sold at substantially lower prices in Great Britain than in the United States because the agency system is not used extensively in Great Britain. Policies are purchased directly from company offices. What are some possible advantages and disadvantages of such a system to insurers and prospective insurance buyers? Discuss.

7. The most important consideration of a firm purchasing liability protection may be the prospective insurer's reputation as a claims defender rather than for prompt and equitable claim settlement. Why might this be the case?

8. Which three of the many cooperative organizations of insurers do you believe are the most important to (a) insurers, (b) insureds, (c) the public, and (d) insurance students?

The underwriting function

Underwriting is the process of accepting or rejecting risks (prospective insureds).[1] If a risk is accepted, underwriting is further concerned with the terms under which the particular risk is insured. The purpose of underwriting is to maximize earnings by accepting a profitable distribution of risk. The underwriting profession was well established in 16th-century coffeehouses in London where persons willing to accept risk signed their names under marine insurance proposals (thus the term underwriters) indicating how much loss they would accept (Chapter 22).

The Necessity for Underwriting

A student, after having made a cursory inquiry into the theory of insurance, might be compelled to comment: "As insurance is based on

---

[1] The use of the term "risk" is expanded in this chapter to include the many dimensions of loss exposure to conform with its use by underwriters. Underwriting is a complex subject, as are most of the functional areas of insurance. The purpose of including the subject and other functional subjects in a basic text is to examine fundamental principles and practices important to an understanding of these insurance functions. For a detailed analysis of the underwriting function, see Robert B. Hutton, *Underwriting* (Cincinnati, Ohio: The National Underwriter Co., 1973).

the law of averages, why not accept all applicants and trust the laws of probability?" Such a comment is deceptively simplistic. To rely on the law of averages would be inefficient and unprofitable. In a competitive market, selection always will prevail in insurance either by the insurer or the insured.

Select or be selected against

All insurance applicants do not have the same loss expectancies. When statistical analysis of loss experience indicates a correlation between a certain characteristic and loss expectancy, insurers, if it is socially acceptable to differentiate on the basis of that characteristic, will establish a classification system with different rates for each class. An example is the use of age as a classification basis for issuing life insurance. However, even within classes, variation in loss expectancies are common. If an insurer can determine a method of eliminate the higher than average loss expectancy within each class, the insurer will earn a higher underwriting profit on its business than the insurer that accepts all risks indiscriminately. The selective insurer then can lower its rate, attract more business, and increase overall profits. Meanwhile, the nonselective insurer will lose its better risks to the insurer whose selective practices have made the lower rates possible. As the nonselective insurer now has a greater proportion of higher risks, its rate must be increased, which widens the gap between the premiums charged by selective and nonselective insurers. This wider gap encourages even more preferred risks to move to the selective insurer, placing the nonselective insurer in a vicious cycle. This illustration explains why all insurers must underwrite risks.

Some government officials and consumer advocates claim insurers are overly selective in underwriting and give too much attention to statistical analysis of insurance data, neglecting social equity. The term "actuarial equity" often is used to denote the condition under which each risk is charged a premium commensurate with its chance of loss. Given the necessity of insurance coverage for many activities (obtaining a mortgage on a home, driving a car), and the fact that some individuals cannot afford insurance at actuarially fair rates, these consumer advocates often force insurers to provide subsidies to the high-risk insureds in the form of premiums below actuarial indications. These people have argued vigorously that losses should be spread over larger numbers of people; insureds in suburbia should subsidize insureds in central cities and those outside the insurance system should subsidize the system through their tax dollars, as in social insurance plans.

If an insurer without a government subsidy were forced to insure any prospective buyer, rates eventually would move so high that self-insurance and risk assumption would be widespread. Among the less hazardous exposures only the most security minded or those who must furnish insurance to creditors would buy protection. Others would wait until loss was imminent before insuring. As shown in Chapter 16, the longer a person waits to buy *life insurance,* the smaller is the total cost of protection. Thus many buyers might wait until they were on their deathbeds to apply for life insurance. In the absence of a selection procedure the insurer would have to write the policy. The higher mortality rate experienced on converted group life policies undoubtedly arises because those who cannot meet the medical requirements of new policies convert their group insurance. The young and vigorous are unlikely to convert. If an insurer accepts all applicants, selection occurs, but by insureds, especially if competing insurers practice selective underwriting. Selection by buyers is called "adverse selection" because the insurer is left the short end of the stick.

The loss experience in dental insurance provides an excellent example of adverse selection. The first dental insurance was offered as additional coverage for a surcharge to those employees who wanted to buy dental insurance. Shortly after the plan became available and additional experience was accumulated, the insurer found it possible to classify all employees covered by the group health policy into three categories; those with good teeth, those with bad teeth, and those with no teeth. Guess which category chose to pay extra to get the dental coverage?

Profitable distribution of exposures

The primary purpose of risk selection by an insurer is to obtain a profitable distribution of policyholders. Both mutual and stock insurers seek this objective, as policyholders are as interested in dividends as are stockholders. The goal of a profitable exposure distribution does not mean that insurers try to avoid claims. They expect claims, for without them the insurance business could not exist. But an insurer does not want an excess of claims over those provided for in the rate. Sometimes houses burn the same day they are insured, but insurers probably would refuse to insure a person whose houses consistently burn immediately after the insurance attaches. The story is told of a client who, on buying a fire policy one morning, asked the agent: "Now that I've bought this policy, what would I get if my house burned this afternoon?" The agent, a born underwriter, replied, "About 10 years!"

For underwriting to produce a profitable distribution of insurance contracts, a safe distribution is essential especially in the long run. In the short run an insurer can enter into questionable contracts without proper underwriting and can prosper with luck. Eventually, it will collapse as loss reports begin pouring in. Safe distribution of exposures requires diversification among many types of properties, geographical areas and perils. Overconcentration is dangerous.

Who Is the Underwriter?

Although the agent selling the policy should make a preliminary appraisal of the exposure, the bulk of underwriting is done by full-time underwriters in home and branch offices. Groups outside the insurer, such as engineering, auditing, and credit rating firms, furnish information and recommendations to aid in the underwriting decision.

The agent as underwriter

Many insurance agents refer to themselves and their colleagues as "underwriters." Note the designations of Chartered Life Underwriter (CLU) and Chartered Property-Casualty Underwriter (CPCU) (which are awarded to persons passing a series of examinations) regardless of the functions they perform in the business. The vast majority are agents, and only a small percentage of these designations are earned by true underwriters. Agents, however, perform only limited underwriting functions, and of interest is that the most prevalent use of this euphemism is in life insurance, for which the agent's underwriting responsibilities are the least. To paraphrase a remark that Fowler, the noted English lexicographer, made concerning the use of the term "lady," "the term 'underwriter' is used largely by those who are not."

In property and liability insurance and, to a much lesser extent, in life insurance, the agent can perform an important underwriting function. If an agent knows an insurance applicant will not make a good insured, the risk should be rejected. Agents who sell persistently to persons with high loss frequencies may find their agency contracts terminated. Insurers keep records of the loss experience of their agents. They cannot afford to retain agents who fail to make even a rudimentary selection. Some agents hold profit-sharing agreements with insurers and are paid bonuses for consistently good loss experience records. However, few agents are qualified to perform effectively the complex task of selective underwriting especially when their earnings are dependent on acceptance of the application. Agents can and do refuse applicants who are in prohibited classes, but the doubtful ones are sent to a company underwriter for a decision. Doubtful applicants may be found insurable by home-office underwriters under policies with different terms or premiums. In this way, the insurer can accomplish its objective of writing as much profitable insurance as possible.

Insurer underwriting departments

No matter how good agents are in selecting suitable insureds, the ultimate responsibility of efficient underwriting falls on the insurers' underwriting departments. The specialized underwriters in these departments can view underwriting with a perspective that even the most highly qualified local agent cannot have. For instance, 50 local agents in 50 midwestern cities might write 50 individual fire policies on frame dwellings all located at a Wisconsin summer resort. Each applicant has a good reputation and financial standing and is accepted by each agent. A company underwriter, however, will reject most of these applicants unless suitable reinsurance facilities are available.[2] Because of the catastrophe hazard, the concentration of frame dwellings with no fire protection may be greater than the insurer can be reasonably expected to underwrite.

Insurer underwriting departments are divided into two sections, staff and line, according to function. Staff underwriters are concerned only with the insurer's overall underwriting policy. They make recommendations pertaining to underwriting policy, product development, and rate structures. Another function is to analyze operating statistics to determine if desirable results are achieved. Because of the supervisory nature of staff underwriters, they usually operate from the home office.

Line underwriters are responsible for the acceptance and rejection of individual risks. Line underwriters may work either at home or branch offices and are closely involved with producers (sellers) of insurance. Line underwriters are properly referred to as "underwriters," as their responsibility is to make specific underwriting decisions and establish a profitable business foundation. Expert line underwriters are invaluable to an insurer, as they are the backbone of a profitable operation.

The computer as underwriter

In recent years, the question has been raised whether computers can successfully perform the underwriting function. At first glance computers seem ideal, especially for underwriting mass lines, such as auto and Homeowners insurance. Computers are fast, efficient, and unbiased. Relevant information could be programmed, and the computer could accept or reject applicants with fewer errors and lower costs than could a human being. However, many insurance executives believe that computers cannot replace individuals as underwriters. They reason that (1) the myriad variables and subtleties involved in each decision would be beyond their current capacity of their computers; (2) the computer could not be programmed to exercise the judgment which years of experience have given company underwriters; and (3) in underwriting, no precise analytical formula method can be used to arrive at a decision as each one is partly subjective. (Computers cannot be subjective.) A few people in the insurance business believe differently. They see the computer as the sole instrument for making the final underwriting decision after all the necessary underwriting data are fed into programs designed to weigh and evaluate these data.

Although computers may or may not replace individuals as underwriters in the foreseeable future, they are important as a tool in modern underwriting. Computers are used by all major insurers in reducing paper work, providing faster access to precise information, and improving the accuracy of rating information and classification. An important use of computers in underwriting is to reduce much of the underwriters'

---

[2] See subsequent discussion of reinsurance in this chapter.

monotonous work load in mass insurance lines. All applications can be programmed into the computer. The computer will accept those clearly meeting the standards and reject the questionable ones. Company underwriters then evaluate and make decisions regarding the computer rejects. This procedure is especially valuable in processing renewal applications and freeing company underwriters from reviewing unchanged exposures, thus increasing underwriting efficiency.

The Underwriting Process

Underwriting includes both preselection and postselection of risks. Preselection involves gathering relevant information concerning the risk and arriving at a decision whether to accept or reject the risk. Once a risk is accepted, the insurer then must practice postselection, the process of reviewing persons already insured and terminating those no longer desirable.

Selection of new insureds

Rules governing selection of new insureds begin with the instructions to agents to refuse certain types of applicants. For example, agents of life insurers may be told to refuse steeplejacks, stunt flyers, professional football players, professional hockey players, those who work with explosives, persons who have had cancer, stomach ulcers, ileitis, or tuberculosis, and so on. Property insurance agents may be told to refuse burglary insurance to persons living alone who are employed outside the house. They may be warned to be particularly careful when considering applications by bachelors (men or women) for Homeowners insurance. Agents may be told to decline auto insurance, if possible, on male drivers under age 25, or persons with criminal convictions in connection with the use of autos, or those that drive high-powered sport cars. Some insurers restrict business to the most profitable exposures. For example, a property insurer may write personal as opposed to commercial business because it finds personal lines to be more profitable. Agents also are told the amount of insurance they can write for one insured. This restriction is closely connected with line limits, discussed later.

Obtaining information. Once the agent has submitted an application to the underwriter, the underwriter must obtain adequate information for making equitable and profitable underwriting decisions. Some applicants are exposed to greater chances of loss than others because of the nature of the hazards to which they are exposed. Information can help identify possible hazards and often provide insights on controlling these hazards. It also may help identify possible adverse selection.

Type of information needed. The amount and type of information needed depends on the kind of insurance offered and the applicant involved. While all possible information is needed to maximize the efficiency of underwriting decisions, the underwriter must be content with an optimum decision based on limited information, because the amount obtainable is restricted by the cost and difficulty of gathering facts.

The most important types of information are (1) the applicant's past loss experience, (2) the financial qualifications of the applicant, (3) the applicant's living habits, (4) the physical condition of the applicant or property, and (5) the character of the person requesting insurance.

Sources of information. Many sources of information are available to the underwriter. The sources chosen are a function of the particular risk, practicality, and cost.

1. Information from agents. Agents provide underwriters with valuable information, beginning with the application containing basic information regarding the risk. Agents also usually submit a report with the application answering questions regarding the risk and giving their recommendation as to its acceptability. In a number of cases the underwriter accepts or rejects a risk solely on the basis of the agent's report.

2. Inspection reports. An important type of organization in underwriting is the inspection company. These organizations provide insurers with a nationwide investigating service. The largest, Equifax (formerly the Retail Credit Company), has representatives in all major cities in North America, covering their city and nearby areas. In many types of insurance, underwriters want more information about prospective insureds than provided by the agent or applicant or may want to confirm that information. Inspection companies submit reports concerning a prospective insured. They can tell a life insurer how much liquor the neighbors (and other informers) think the applicant drinks, or they can tell a liability insurer whether a prospective insured is considered a careful driver or has had serious accidents. A typical insurance applicant would be amazed at the amount of information (and sometimes misinformation) these investigating organizations can uncover.

Insurance buyers and consumers in general have complained that credit organizations accumulate faulty information concerning investigated persons. Numerous states have passed laws to permit consumers to examine information collected by credit rating bureaus. A federal statute, the Fair Credit Reporting Act, allows the consumer access to information on file and the sources of the information. If the consumer questions some data in the file, the credit bureau must reinvestigate. In any case, the bureau must include the consumer's side of the story in the file. Furthermore, if the consumer believes inaccurate information has been given to an insurer or other organization within the past six months, the credit bureau must forward the consumer's story to such organizations. The law also requires insurers to notify applicants on whom reports have been requested, and if the insurer uses the report as a basis for denying coverage or charging a higher premium, it must notify the applicant of this development and provide the applicant with the name and address of the reporting company.

Few persons have taken advantage of the law. Equifax reports that an average of only 0.2 percent of consumers on whom reports are completed demand disclosure, and that most of them are satisfied with the explanation received. In 1977 The Privacy Protection Study Commission completed a two-year analysis of the effect of record-keeping on individuals, and recommended changes in The Fair Credit Reporting Act. President Carter submitted legislation to Congress to adopt recommended changes. However, the political winds and not the laws were changed. The National Association of Insurance Commissioners (NAIC) was left with the task of developing a model law. The NAIC Insurance Information and Privacy Protection Model Act was written in 1980. According to the act, prospective insureds must be given written notice about the kind of information sought, the type of investigation to be conducted, the persons or firms from and for whom the data will be gathered, and the procedures the insured should follow in case incorrect information is reported. More than ten states have enacted some form of this model law. Many underwriters no longer put much emphasis on these investigative reports because they contain little helpful information (and almost no negative information). Useful investigation reports may soon go the way of the 25 cent cup of coffee.

3. Underwriters Laboratories, Inc. The Underwriters Laboratories, Inc. of Chicago is one of the most important agencies performing useful underwriting services. This company began as a cooperative organization of western fire insurers at the time of the Columbian Exposition of 1893. This world's fair was noted not only for its Midway—featuring the electric dancer, Little Egypt—but also for the first large-scale use of the then new electric lighting. Insurance underwriters who were asked to insure the flimsy, combustible buildings of the Exposition organized a group to investigate the best ways to wire buildings to prevent fire. The affair of the Cow O'Leary still burned in their memories. The organization tested methods of wiring and the electrical equipment. Insurers, perceiving the value of such work, expanded the lab so that now 92 years later, Underwriters Laboratories, Inc., has become a mammoth testing organization. Virtually no fabricated device or material exists that it has not tested. Everything from corn poppers to locomotives is scrutinized. Items meeting its high standards are permitted to bear the UL label. Others are returned to manufacturers for changes if they want their product to bear the Underwriters label. The use of items approved by Underwriters Laboratories often is required by insurer underwriting rules and by building codes. The UL label has become the hallmark of safety. In underwriting certain exposures, insurers may request Underwriters Laboratories tests of specific products. Fire and burglary protection equipment is tested. Although an independent organization no longer operated by insurers, Underwriters Laboratories is important to the underwriting departments of property and liability insurers.

4. Other sources. Many other sources of underwriting information exist. Insurers often consult loss control engineers who may provide safety information to help identify liability hazards. They may offer suggestions for improvements that will reduce the chance of loss, which the underwriter can pass on to the applicant. Commercial underwriters may seek information from companies publishing financial ratings and data useful for evaluating the moral hazard and the applicant's ability to pay. Underwriters of commercial lines may consult the applicant's banker, creditors, and employer. Auto underwriters can obtain motor vehicle records (MVR) on prospective insureds from state departments of motor vehicles. Many other sources of information are available; but the value of additional information may not be worth the cost and problems involved in obtaining it.

Making the decision.   After the relevant facts are gathered, underwriters must analyze the information to make a decision. The reliability of the information and whether it is subjective or objective are important factors affecting the underwriting decision. Underwriters rely on their experience and knowledge in deciding whether to accept the application, offer modified coverage, or reject the application.

Acceptance.   If the underwriter decides the particular risk is "standard," the applicant is accepted. The applicant will be issued the standard coverage for the standard premium.

Modified coverage.   In some cases, the information may establish that the applicant has a lower than average loss experience which along with other factors allows the applicant to be classified as a "preferred risk." Preferred risks usually receive standard coverage at a lower premium. However, in most nonstandard cases information may indicate the applicant has a higher than average loss expectancy. Underwriters recognize that some of these risks can be made profitable. So, in selected cases, they may offer alternatives to rejection. In this event, the applicant is classified "substandard" and when accepted, is offered modified coverage which usually is more restrictive than standard coverage and/or may include a larger deductible. Instead of modified coverage, standard coverage might be tendered at a higher premium.

Rejection.   Some risks are "ineligible." Insurers do not believe that these applicants can be profitable at any *feasible* premium or at any reasonable coverage modification, and, therefore, reject them.

Postselection

Underwriters review renewal applications using techniques similar to those employed in considering new applicants in deciding to renew or decline the coverage. Postselection, however, has several unique aspects. Except for public criticism by those insisting that insurers have a social obligation to provide insurance to anyone at "affordable" prices, underwriters may easily refuse an application. A refusal, however, creates difficulties for the agent who lives in the community with the rejected applicant. More difficult is the problem of dealing with a current insured, now considered undesirable. The insurer has several choices.

One method is for the insurer to refrain from cancellation until the policy expires then notify the agent that the contract will not be renewed. The agent may place the client's business with another insurer who abides by less strict underwriting rules.

Circumstances may require the insurer to terminate the policy as soon as possible. If, for example, a follow-up inspection of the insured premises reveals undesirable physical conditions or unsound practices, the underwriter will recommend immediate cancellation. In one case, in which a policy inadvertently was written on property belonging to a convicted arsonist, a 24-hour-a-day vigil was kept near the premises to notify the fire department should fire occur before the cancellation notice became effective.

A person who buys an auto liability policy and then injures a girl riding a bicycle is unlikely to have trouble with the auto insurer unless the claim investigation reveals some undesirable fact not discovered when the original underwriting was conducted. If, however, this insured persists in hitting girls on bicycles, the policy probably will be canceled, if the contract permits, or not renewed when it expires. In some cases, the policy might be renewed but only at higher premiums.

Postselection is available only if the policy is cancellable or not guaranteed renewable. The life insurance policy, for example, is noncancelable. The insurer must gather and weigh all underwriting data before issuing the policy. Once the contract is delivered to the insured, the insurer has only a two-year period in which to discover and act upon misrepresentations and concealments in the application. Upon discovery of certain types of misrepresentations and concealments the insurer can rescind the contract.[3]

In health insurance, many noncancellable and guaranteed renewable policies are issued. Many auto insurers write liability contracts that give the insurer only limited cancellation rights. In most instances, however, the policies are not guaranteed renewable, but in most states, if renewal is denied, the insurer must give the insured a written explanation for nonrenewal, or notify the insured that on written request such information will be provided. In most of these states the insurer and those supplying the information leading to nonrenewal are immune from liability for libel that might otherwise arise.

Retention

After the underwriters have accepted an application, decided on the type of policy to be issued, and determined the rate to be charged, a

---

[3] This right does not apply with respect to the misstatement of the insured's age or sex; see Chapter 17. For an explanation of rescission, misrepresentation, and concealment, see Chapter 5.

question still to be answered is the amount of risk the insurer wants to retain. Underwriters must determine the amount of retention and, if necessary, the amount to reinsure. Insurers maximize profits by retaining as much of the exposure as possible subject to the constraint imposed by the possibility of an unaffordable loss to the insurer.

Even if underwriters are able to select the best risks, limitations exist on the amounts of insurance that can be sold by one insurer. Underwriters seek a safe distribution of exposure units. The financial condition and size of the insurer are important determinants of how much it can underwrite safely. A basic question is: What is the largest single amount the insurer can afford to lose on one exposure? This question must be answered by the insurer's financial officers and approved by the board. Its answer helps to establish "line limits"—the maximum amount of insurance an insurer will write on one exposure. The line limits for particular exposures are compiled into a line book to be used by underwriting departments.

Line limits in life insurance

In life insurance, ascertaining the line limit is simple. The board of directors decides the maximum amount of insurance the insurer will write on one life and the maximum amount of coverage under a policy the insurer will retain without seeking reinsurance. This latter amount is known as the *net retention.* The largest insurers will write several million dollars on a life and will retain the entire amount. Many smaller insurers will write large amounts, but will reinsure (place with another insurer) all but some amount, such as the first $50,000 or $100,000. A new insurer might reinsure nearly all its business during its first several years of operation.

Line limits in property and liability insurance

Establishing line limits in property insurance is more complicated. The line book will show net lines. These lines vary among coverages, insureds, geographical areas, and other factors. For example, assume the line book shows brick buildings in Champaign, Illinois are subject to a $200,000 limit. However, these line limits do not represent the size of the policy the insurer can write on brick buildings, but the largest amount it is willing to lose on one brick building. Two factors permit the size of the policy to exceed the line limit: Reinsurance (to be discussed subsequently) and the "probable maximum loss" (PML) that can occur to the property.

Assume that the owner of a $400,000 brick building in Champaign applies for fire insurance. The underwriters, on the basis of an engineering report, decide that if the building burns the PML would be half the value of the building ($200,000). Thus, since the insurer is "willing" to accept the risk of loss of $200,000 on a brick building, the underwriters can approve a $400,000 policy for this building, because the PML is only the $200,000 shown in the line book. If the owner wants more than $400,000 of insurance, the insurer can write higher limits if reinsurance is available.

Line limits are subject to further considerations. Assume that the value of a building in a certain town is within the line limits of the underwriting department. Also, assume other buildings in close geographical proximity already are covered by the insurer. If the underwriters insure this new applicant, its exposure to catastrophic loss is increased. A fire that begins in one building might spread to envelop the entire neighborhood. In enforcing line limits in property coverages, underwriters must note the volume of insurance written in an area subject to conflagration. Block or area limits or reinsurance must be used to protect the insurer from catastrophic losses.

Generally, in setting line limits for liability insurance, the line limits are, in effect, gross rather than net limits. An insurer, for example may decide to write auto liability insurance for limits of only $150,000/$300,000. Line limits in property and liability insurance are not absolute. While for most exposures insurers generally do not write full coverage if the PML exceeds the line limit, experienced underwriters often are given the authority to exceed these limits.

Reinsurance

Reinsurance is the insurance of insurance. When an underwriter receives an application for insurance on property exceeding its retention limit, the excess amount may be reinsured. Furthermore, if business from all agents exceeds the amount supportable by the insurer's surplus position (see Chapter 26), part of the business can be reinsured. Reinsurance prevents the strain that might result on insurer-agency relations if the insurer had to return the application to the agent with a notation that the business could not be accepted because line limits had been exceeded or surplus is inadequate to support it. The amount of business placed with the reinsurer is called the "ceded" amount. A "cession" is the document used by a direct insurer to request reinsurance coverage for each risk.

Types of reinsurance. Reinsurance may be classified broadly as treaty, facultative, or a combination of the two. Under treaty (sometimes called automatic) reinsurance the insurer must cede any amount of insurance falling under the contract agreement, and the reinsurer must accept the offered amount of reinsurance. Treaties cover a whole class of risks (e.g., windstorm) and avoid the time-consuming negotiation procedures found in facultative reinsurance. When an insurer writes a policy covered by the treaty, the reinsurance is activated and applies to that policy. Under facultative reinsurance the insurer determines for each case if reinsurance is desired and, if offered for reinsurance, the reinsurer maintains the right to accept or reject each risk on its merits. Facultative reinsurance deals predominately with one loss unit (in reinsurance ter-minology, this unit is called a "risk"). A new contract must be negotiated for each risk. To avoid the time lag associated with facultative rein-surance, two hybrids have been developed: (1) the facultative obligatory treaty,[4] wherein the insurer has the option to cede risks but the reinsurer must accept all reinsurance offered, subject to the treaty; and (2) the facultative treaty wherein the insurer has the option to cede or retain and the reinsurer has the option to accept or decline on each risk. The method for handling reinsurance, however, is determined by contract.

Reinsurance, whether facultative or treaty, is a negotiated contract between the ceding insurer and the reinsurer. All terms, rates, claims procedures, and conditions of these contracts are negotiated. There are general formats that are followed but there is no standard contract like the Standard Fire Policy.

Facultative reinsurance and reinsurance treaties are written in two forms: proportional and nonproportional.

Proportional (or pro rata) reinsurance. Under proportional (or pro rata) reinsurance an insurer shares with a reinsurer on a proportional basis both premiums and losses. The originating (ceding) insurer writes the full amount of the policy for an insured, but has an agreement with the reinsurer to share in the premiums and losses. The reinsurer might receive 30 percent of the premiums in exchange for an agreement to pay 30 percent of all losses. The reinsurer also will pay a commission to the ceding insurer to cover operating expenses. Pro rata reinsurance is used, for example, by new insurers that lack underwriting talent.

Two types of proportional or pro rata reinsurance are *quota share* and *surplus share.* For quota share reinsurance the same proportion of every policy, large or small, is shared with the reinsurer. This form of reinsurance is the simplest to manage, as the same percentage of every premium is paid to the reinsurer and the same percentage of every loss is collected from the reinsurer.

For surplus share reinsurance the percentage of reinsurance partici-pation is calculated separately for each policy. No one standard percent-age is used as in quota share reinsurance. The percentage for surplus share reinsurance is determined by the amount that the policy limits exceed the originating insurer's retention. If an insurer seeks to maintain a $50,000 retention but writes a $75,000 policy, under surplus share rein-surance the insurer will cede one third ($25,000/$75,000) of the insurance to the reinsurer. The reinsurer would receive one third of the premium (less any commissions) and would be responsible for paying one third of the losses on that policy. For another policy with $50,000 limits, no reinsurance would be involved, as the policy limits do not exceed the desired retention.

---

[4] Reinsurance contracts are referred to as "reinsurance treaties" because the first of these contracts was international in scope, and many current reinsurance contracts still are be-tween alien insurers.

Nonproportional. Nonproportional reinsurance can be classified into two major categories: excess loss and stop loss.

Excess loss reinsurance. Under excess loss reinsurance, the reinsurer is required to bear only those losses in excess of the ceding insurer's retention limit, leaving the ceding insurer to bear losses in full up to the retention amount. One type of excess reinsurance (per risk) applies to individual exposures only. Another type deals only with multiple exposures (catastrophic risks).

1. Per risk. Under individual per risk reinsurance the reinsurer agrees to pay losses on a single risk in excess of the ceding insurer's net retention limit.

The ceding insurer, as in all reinsurance arrangements, is responsible for paying the claimant the full amount of the covered loss.[5] However, it bears only those losses that do not exceed its retention. The ceding insurer is reimbursed by the reinsurer for the amount of loss in excess of this retention. In this way, the originating insurer is protected against individual losses above the limit of retention.

2. Catastrophic excess reinsurance. Catastrophic excess reinsurance always is written as a treaty. The reinsurer has no interest in individual exposures, only classes of exposures. Under a *catastrophe reinsurance treaty,* the reinsurer agrees to reimburse the reinsured, up to a stated maximum, for catastrophe losses in excess of a given amount. Population concentration subjects life and health insurers to the possibility of multiple losses in a single event, such as fire, earthquake, or hurricane. Property concentration in one area subjects property insurers to multiple-property losses from the same event, especially when the insurer is exposed to losses on several coverages. The cost of catastrophe reinsurance depends on the retention per disaster, reinsurance limit per disaster, volume of business written subject to the reinsurance, and maximum and average amounts of coverage per exposure. Catastrophic excess reinsurance coverage generally is the only type used for liability insurance, and is popular also for property insurance coverage.

Stop-loss reinsurance. Stop-loss reinsurance is used by a ceding insurer to control its loss ratio. Under the stop-loss plan, the reinsurer pays up to a predetermined percentage of the insurer's net premium income or a fixed-dollar amount whichever is *less* if the insurer's aggregate losses exceed the agreed-upon stop-loss limit. The stop-loss limit is a predetermined percentage of the ceding insurer's net premium income or a fixed-dollar amount whichever is *greater.* Both the stop-loss limit and the basis for determining the payments by the reinsurer to the insurer in the event of a loss are negotiated.

The following example illustrates the operation of a stop loss rein-

---

[5] In the settlement of claims, the insurer cannot jeopardize the reinsurer's right to refuse payment or appoint counsel.

surance program. An insurer negotiates a stop-loss reinsurance agreement under which the reinsurer agrees to pay up to 50 percent of the ceding insurer's net premium income or $300,000 whichever is less for losses incurred in excess of the stop-loss limit. The stop-loss limit in this case was negotiated at 70 percent of the ceding insurer's net premium income or $300,000 whichever is greater. Thus, for a net premium income of $500,000, the ceding insurer must incur losses of $350,000 (70 percent of $500,000) before the reinsurer incurs any obligations. Beyond the $350,000 of losses, the reinsurer will pay the next $250,000. Therefore, the ceding insurer is protected against a loss ratio greater than 70 percent provided the losses incurred do not exceed $600,000, the $350,000 insurer's retention plus the $250,000 maximum liability of the reinsurer. Remember that the reinsurer's maximum liability in this example is 50 percent of the insurer's net premium or $300,000, whichever is less. In this case, 50 percent of the insurer's net premium of $500,000 governs because it is less than $300,000.

Graphic illustration.   Figure 24–1 illustrates graphically the types of reinsurance used in the property and liability insurance business. For example, an insurer can have treaty, proportional, quota share reinsurance; facultative, nonproportional, excess of loss, per risk reinsurance; or any other combination moving from the top to the bottom of the figure.

Arrangements unique to life insurance.   Life insurance reinsurance is of two types: the *yearly renewable term (YRT) plan* and the *coinsurance plan.* Under the YRT plan (sometimes called risk premium reinsurance) the insurer reinsures only the difference between the net amount at risk and the net retention of the insurer. The net amount at risk is the policy face amount less its terminal reserve. As the terminal reserve increases throughout the life of the policy, the amount of the policy reinsured continually decreases. For example, assume that the Philo Life Insurance Company has a net retention limit of $10,000. It writes a $25,000 policy on Donna Jessee. The insurer reinsures $15,000 at the time the policy is issued. Years later, however, the terminal reserve is $13,000. That year, the amount of reinsurance will be only $2,000. The YRT plan is preferred by most small life insurers as it permits them to retain more risk on each reinsured contract and thus retain more premium receipts for investment.

The *coinsurance plan* provides for reinsuring the amount by which the original face exceeds the net retention limit. This amount continues throughout the life of the contract.[6] In the foregoing example, $15,000 of Donna's policy would be reinsured for its duration. The advantage of the plan is that the reinsurer establishes the first-year (and subsequent) reserves on its portion, thus saving the ceding insurer from some of the drain on surplus occurring the first policy year. The drain on

---

[6] Most reinsurance treaties allow the ceding company to take back, or "recapture" reinsured risks, but usually not before a substantial time has elapsed, such as 20 years. Even then, a penalty for early recapture may be involved.

FIGURE 24–1

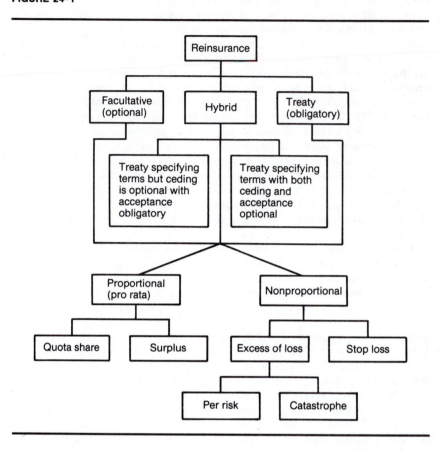

surplus resulting from writing new insurance is discussed in Chapter 26. Equity Funding created and coinsured thousands of fictitious life insurance policies in order to enhance its image as a growth company. The financial mechanism of coinsurance provided a short-term benefit from this action, but in the longer run an increasing number of fake policies had to be created in order to continue the scheme. The fraud was discovered in 1973 when the pyramiding system became too extensive to conceal.

Reasons for reinsurance

Reinsurance is purchased for several reasons. Most importantly, by eliminating the possibility of excessive losses in one occurrence, operating results of ceding insurers are stabilized. Additionally, insurers can accept individual risks larger than their own underwriting capacity otherwise would warrant, and can increase their writings on a more substantial scale than their own financial limits would support. Finally, reinsurers can provide underwriting advice to new insurers or insurers expanding into new territories and coverages. Because of its vested interest in the success of the ceding insurer, the reinsurer offers its clients assistance on many technical matters and helps in the operation of the ceding insurer.

Reinsurance principles

The reader may wonder why an insurer could not accept contracts of questionable soundness and pass most of the risk to a reinsurer. But a ceding insurer which continually cedes poor business to its reinsurer would be in the same unfortunate position as an agent who continually submits auto insurance from reckless drivers. Temporary profits might be high, but in the long run insolvency will occur. In addition reinsurance underwriters practice selection procedures in facultative arrangements as do direct underwriters, and they withdraw from continuously unprofitable automatic pools and treaties.

Reinsurance markets are jealously guarded. For this reason, underwriting departments of insurers are likely to have low gross line limits as well as low net line limits on insureds prone to have poor loss experience. A questionable contract will be written for a customer who gives the insurer a large volume of preferred business. These questionable contracts are written as an accommodation to the agent as well as the insured. Auto insurance on teenage drivers, for example, may be written because the parent buys a large volume of other insurance from the agent. Underwriters frequently authorize writing only the net retention limit on accommodations, accepting the full risk themselves thus preventing the passing of questionable exposures to a reinsurer. Reinsurance, together with appropriate net and gross line limits, helps assure the insurer a safe distribution of risks.

Reinsurers frequently reinsure part of their exposure. This process is called "retrocession." Several insurers engage only in reinsurance business. Some government reinsurance plans are made available to private insurers to help them serve the residual market (insureds and coverages which private insurers seek to avoid) in critical lines.

Special Problems of Underwriting

Besides the aspects of underwriting outlined in the preceding section, underwriters are faced with special problems concerning applicants, agents, and public pressures. These problems are those of moral hazard, conflicts between production and underwriting departments, and governmental pressures to insure applicants who would be rejected under traditional underwriting rules.

Moral and morale hazard

While the classification of moral hazard usually includes morale hazard, a separation of the terms is useful to simplify the concepts. Moral hazard is the possibility an insured will deliberately cause a loss insured against; for example, the fire policyowner who sets fire to the insured property, or the life insured who commits suicide. Moral hazard usually arises from a combination of moral weakness and financial difficulty. Fire by friction has been defined as a $100,000 inventory rubbing against a $200,000 fire policy. Professional arsonists always are looking for new clients with a large policy and a small conscience. Moral hazard exists not only if the applicant has the intention to destroy property, but also when factors exist which may encourage the applicant to do so. Factors suggesting the existence of moral hazard include in addition to moral weakness and financial difficulty, a history of questionable acts, evasion of responsibility, and a poor business reputation.

If evidence shows that an applicant intends to defraud the insurer, no underwriting is possible. When a person is suspected of intent to burn an insured building to profit from insurance, no premium less than the full value of the property plus an allowance for expenses is sufficient to cover the loss, unless some probability can be assigned to this suspicion. Where a significant moral hazard is suspected, the underwriter rejects the application. Other types of less drastic moral hazard may not prohibit acceptance of a risk. Coverages and rates often are altered in an attempt to control these hazards. For example, coverage of jewelry could be excluded from a theft policy covering personal property if the applicant is known to be in financial difficulty. Certain factors should alert the underwriter to the presence of moral hazards. Most danger signals are found in credit reports. Excessive inventories, large unpaid bills, working capital deficiencies, and an expensive custom made foreign sports car owned by a secretary—all require careful evaluation.

Although moral hazard most often is found in property and health insurance, it also appears in life insurance. The suicide clause in life insurance policies is intended to eliminate life insurance as a source of funds for liquidating debts by the voluntary liquidation of the insured. However, the number of persons willing to burn their businesses to feed their families greatly exceeds those willing to take their lives to feed their survivors. Moral hazard in health insurance produces malingering and padded medical expenses as well.

Morale hazard arises from indifference concerning loss, often brought about by the security of the insurance, which leads to carelessness. This form of hazard is difficult to underwrite. Many insureds are guilty in varying degrees of morale hazard. People leave cars unlocked with the keys in the ignition, an unsound practice and unlawful in many states. An insured with an unprofitable business may not set a match to the structure, but may do little to prevent a fire. Poor housekeeping becomes the rule; trash accumulates and causes a fire hazard.

Conflict between underwriting and production

Conflict is inevitable between underwriting and production. The production department's function is to sell as much insurance as possible. The underwriting department must obtain a safe and profitable distribution of exposure units. To the production department, underwriters often appear overly conservative. Agents want borderline applicants accepted but underwriters may have a different perception. To minimize ill will and improve relations with agents, underwriters should explain the reasoning behind decisions adverse to agents.

When a new potential type of loss arises, such as liability for polluting the air or water or fiduciary liability under the pension reform law, the underwriting department may eliminate this loss potential by rewriting the policy to exclude such claims. If rewriting the policy is impossible, rates may increase. The addition of restrictions or higher rates may reduce the policy's salability, adversely affecting agents. Underwriting and production departments must work together. New clauses are not always added when new types of losses occur, nor do good agents take applications indiscriminately, without regard to good underwriting procedure. However, each group sometimes believes the business would be much better, or at least more pleasant, without the other.

Governmental pressures on underwriting

Underwriters are subject to pressure from various governmental units, particularly to write auto and property insurance in inner-city areas and to write various types of liability coverages. The strong consumer movement has led to public examination of nearly every aspect of auto insurance. Allegations are made that people living in the inner-cities pay inordinately high insurance rates. During the 1970s governmental pressures arose against liability insurers to provide products liability and medical malpractice insurance protection even if unprofitable. Underwriters defend their practices by insisting that insurers are not meant to be charitable institutions and that the levels of loss experience in these lines support higher rates and in some cases prohibit coverage.

Chapters 11 and 15 discuss various measures undertaken by the industry and government to make insurance available to nearly everyone at reasonable rates when all factors involved are considered. Often, these programs require subsidies by some governmental units.

Examples of Underwriting

Examples of underwriting property and life insurance are given to illustrate this function in operation.

Underwriting property and liability insurance

The methods used by underwriting departments of fire insurers are typical of those followed in underwriting most property and liability coverages. For this reason fire insurance is used to illustrate the underwriting of property and liability coverage.

Underwriting a dwelling. Applications are submitted by agents who usually already have issued the policies. The local agent generally can issue a Homeowners policy knowing it will be approved by the underwriting department of the insurer at the rate quoted to the customer. The policy report usually moves through the audit department of the state's inspection bureau, where rates and policy information are checked, before reaching the insurer. The fire insurance rate for dwellings depends on the dwelling class. Dwellings are classified according to construction, type of roof, number of dwelling units, occupancy, and degree of fire protection. The degree of fire protection is a significant factor in determining the class and thus the rate.

Factors which affect the dwelling underwriting decision include the dwelling's age, neighborhood, construction, value, size, occupancy, and moral hazard. Underwriters will weigh these factors and others to arrive at a decision.

Underwriting a business structure. If the property covered is a business structure of high value, underwriters consider the risk more carefully. However, the factors involved in the decision process are essentially the same as those in underwriting a dwelling. The principal considerations in classifying and rating are construction, occupancy, exposure, and protection.

Construction. Construction refers to building materials used. For fire insurance, buildings are classified as frame, brick, or fire-resistant. Construction alone has little effect on the building's acceptability for insurance. All three types of construction are insurable. But construction of the building, when considered in its geographical location or with its occupancy, may have an important bearing on the underwriter's decision.

Occupancy. The occupancy of a building is the purpose for which it is used. To the underwriter a frame structure may be acceptable for office work, but unacceptable as a dry-cleaning plant. The effects of occupancy may be divided into three parts: ignitability, combustibility, and damageability.

Ignitability measures the chance of a fire occurring because of a given occupancy. The ignitability of a dry-cleaning plant will be high, whereas that of a church will be low. Buildings in which chemicals, paints, gasoline, and similar articles are produced or used in large quantity present a considerable ignition hazard.

Combustibility measures the burning capability of a given occupancy once a fire has started. A dry-cleaning plant and a lumberyard would have high combustibility. It is unlikely that lumber would cause ignition, as anyone who has tried to produce flame by rubbing two sticks together will testify. Once a fire has started, however, lumber burns quickly.

Damageability measures the susceptibility of contents to the amount of fire loss. The damageability of items is closely related to their values. A fire would have to destroy a great quantity of rice puffs to produce a loss approaching closely that of a small fire in a clothing store, not because clothing burns to a greater extent than do rice puffs, but because the values involved are concentrated in a small area. A characteristic of damageability also is susceptibility to water or heat damage in addition to combustion.

Exposure.   Exposure is the likelihood of damage occurring to the insured object caused by an outside source. If a building otherwise insurable is located next to a powder plant, that exposure may be sufficient to warrant rejection even though the rate for the coverage supposedly reflects the adverse exposure.

Protection.   Protection may consist of private or internal protection, such as fire alarm systems, fire doors, fire blocks in the walls, automatic sprinkler systems, and so on. Protection also includes public protection furnished by city fire departments.

Underwriting procedure.   Although underwriting procedure has been discussed, the present purpose is to illustrate the underwriting process as it is applied to fire insurance. An important underwriting information source is the application which is informal, unsigned, and not made a part of the policy. Applications for fire insurance, though not standard, contain three types of information: personal, descriptive, and coverage. Personal information includes pertinent data about the applicant or business. Descriptive information contains facts concerning the property classified under the four headings previously discussed: construction, occupancy, exposure, and protection. The descriptive information is used by the rating bureau to classify and rate the risk. The coverage information includes the types of coverages sought, coinsurance clauses, and deductibles. The underwriter may consult other sources of information except for routine residential coverages. In many cases involving business properties, however, the insurer will request a report from its engineering department or from engineering consulting firms. The inspection reports are detailed analyses similar to those used by rating bureaus in determining the building rate. If the agent questions the accuracy of the rate or believes that improvements (entitling the property owner to a lower rate) were made in the property since the most recent rating survey, a request may be made for a new survey. For some coverages, reports concerning the applicant will be obtained from Equifax or a similar organization. These reports provide details concerning the applicant's personal and business life, which enable underwriters to evaluate the human element. Underwriters then might check the applicant's financial rating in Dun & Bradstreet's guide or in a similar manual. Maps published by many cities offer information as to the type of construction and protection in particular areas.

After weighing the basic underwriting data against the rate permitted, the underwriter decides whether the risk is one the insurer wants to underwrite or, in some cases, is willing to underwrite. As mentioned earlier, a large part of the underwriter's judgment may be subjective. The business will be accepted if the underwriter perceives it to be potentially profitable.

Underwriting life insurance

The underwriting procedure in life insurance is similar, in many respects, to that in fire insurance. A major difference is that in life insurance a formal written application for a policy is submitted by the applicant through the agent to the insurer. Approval by the underwriting department is required before the policy is issued. In contrast, many fire policies are issued before the underwriting department sees and approves the application. This dichotomy is reasonable in that fire policies are cancellable whereas life policies are not.

The application. The life insurance application is a detailed document in two parts. Part 1 consists of data supplied by the applicant including birth date, address, former addresses, occupation, negotiations pending for other policies, membership in the armed forces or in organized military reserves, contemplated changes in occupation or residence, type of policy applied for, the premium to be paid, when premiums are payable, special riders or benefits to be included, disposition of dividends (if the policy is participating), the beneficiary designation, and so on. Part 2 contains the report of the medical examiner and is divided into two sections. The first section contains the physician's answers to questions, as well as the recording of the applicant's answers to the physician's questions. These questions concern medical treatment received, physical examinations taken in recent years, and diseases suffered by the applicant. A series of questions is asked concerning the applicant's family: age of parents, brothers and sisters; if parents, brothers, or sisters are dead, at what ages they died and the causes of deaths. The second section is the physician's report of the medical examination.

Many policies are written without requiring a physical examination. The maximum amount that can be written without medical examination usually varies with the applicant's age—the young applicant can buy more nonmedical insurance than can an older applicant. The maximum also varies with the kind of policy applied for. The maximum age limit usually is 40, and the maximum amount, depending on the insurer, can be as high as $300,000. In these "nonmedical" cases, the underwriter makes a decision based on answers the applicant has given to questions in a special nonmedical section of the application. The underwriter can request a medical examination if answers to the nonmedical section are unsatisfactory.

The agent's certificate.   The agent's certificate (included in Part 1 of the application) contains information about how the agent met the applicant; how long and how well the agent has known the applicant; the agent's knowledge of factors concerning the applicant's employment, marital status, financial standing, and so on. The agent is asked whether or not the applicant is recommended for insurance. This document is a minor detail in underwriting life insurance as agents are not likely to forward applications for clients they are not willing to endorse.

The inspection report.   The insurer may obtain an inspection report of personal matters concerning applicants. From the inspection report the underwriters learn if any reason exists to doubt information contained in the application. The inspection report supplies information about the applicant's finances, occupation, participation in hazardous sports, health, habits, character, appearance, and home environment.

Medical Information Bureau.   The underwriters will refer to the files prepared by the Medical Information Bureau (MIB), a cooperative organization of life insurers formed to centralize information of special interest to members about the physical condition of previous applicants for life insurance in a member company. The files of the MIB, however, do not record the action taken by the insurer on the application. The information is made available to member companies for use in making their own underwriting decision. Underwriting philosophy and practices differ among insurers. Because an applicant has been refused insurance by one insurer does not necessarily mean refusal by another.

Factors affecting underwriting.   In many respects, life insurance underwriting is much simpler than property and liability underwriting. The basic underwriting factors are age, occupation, and physical condition. In addition, residence, financial status, and family and personal history are considered.

Age.   All insurers have maximum age limits, and a few have minimum limits at which they will accept applicants. The maximum age limits are 65 in some insurers and 70 in others. Few insurers will write policies on those over 70 years old. At this age, the cost may be prohibitive and the probability of having sufficient applicants for the law of large numbers to operate is low. Where minimum age limits are set they usually are one day, one week, one month, or one year. Age is important in consideration with other underwriting factors. Overweight, for example, in those under 25 is not so serious, but beyond that age this factor is given more importance.

Occupation. The occupation of the insured is considered because some jobs present greater-than-average hazards. Those in some occupations are not eligible for life insurance under any circumstances. With most insurers these include steeplejacks, motorcycle racers, and deep-sea divers.

Physical condition. Physical condition is of great importance in life insurance underwriting. If the applicant's health is impaired, a policy may be offered at a higher premium or under one of the other plans discussed later, unless the application is flatly rejected.

Minor factors. The factors of residence, financial status, and family and personal history are secondary in importance. The residence of the applicant is of no interest to the underwriter if the applicant lives in the United States. A person may live or travel anywhere in the United States including New York City, without having to pay a higher premium.

The financial status of the applicant interests underwriters for two reasons. The insurer does not want to insure a person for amounts exceeding reasonable relationships to the potential loss caused by death and to the applicant's ability to pay premiums. If a person seeks an unreasonably high amount of life insurance, the indication may be either a moral hazard or a hidden physical hazard soon to end in a death claim. Even if the overindulgent applicant is healthy, the insurer still will want to limit the life insurance to a reasonable amount. To issue an insurance policy is costly. An oversold buyer is apt to lapse the policy within a short time making it impossible to recoup the funds spent in selling a policy. Underwriters often refuse to insure those who have records of nonpayment of bills and who appear to be buying more insurance than they can afford.

A favorable family and personal history is of little effect if the underwriters have found unfavorable information among the other factors. On the other hand, an unfavorable family and personal history may be cause for rejection. All factors are weighed in arriving at a composite judgment.

Treatment of extra-hazard applicants. Applicants for life insurance fall into one of two broad classes: insurable and uninsurable. The insurable group may be divided further into those insurable at standard premiums and those who must be charged premiums higher than standard. Those in the latter category do not meet the insurer's underwriting standards, but are sufficiently better than the uninsurables to warrant policies under some conditions. Usually, the extra-hazard applicant is issued a policy at a higher-than-standard premium, with a flat additional amount charged for each $1,000 of insurance, or, more often, the standard premium may be increased by a given percentage to reflect the expected percentage mortality increase.

Another often-used method of handling the extra-hazard applicant is to issue a policy other than the one for which the application is made. A policy requiring a higher premium (such as limited payment or endowment) will be issued instead of term or continuous premium whole life. These higher premium policies build higher reserves; hence, the amount the insurer has at risk is smaller than in either the continuous-premium whole life or term policy. In some instances the insurer might issue the extra-hazard applicant the policy applied for, but only for a smaller amount. In other cases, an insurer will write life insurance at standard rates but refuse to write double indemnity or disability insurance. For example, one company insures professional football players (outside of the major college teams) at standard rates for life insurance, but they must pay twice the standard rate for double indemnity and disability income insurance riders.

Underwriting in health insurance is much like that in life insurance, with one important difference: applicants who have suffered certain injuries, or who have had certain diseases, are accepted but riders are attached to their policies to exclude similar losses from coverage. Some insurers, however, are now writing special substandard health insurance policies that do not fully exclude future losses from preexisting conditions.

Summary

1. Insurers must practice selective underwriting to maintain profitability. Underwriting also allows insurers to charge equitable rates, each insured paying a rate that is roughly commensurate with loss expectancy.
2. The purpose of underwriting is to obtain a profitable distribution of exposures. Without efficient underwriting, an insurer would be subject to adverse selection and be unable to compete with insurers practicing selective underwriting.
3. Although agents may perform some underwriting functions, the bulk of underwriting decisions are made by full-time experienced underwriters at the insurer's home office. Computers can aid the underwriter in decision making, but computers are unlikely to replace the subjective reasoning and expertise of an underwriter at affordable costs.
4. The underwriting process consists of obtaining and analyzing information to arrive at a decision. Sources of information include applications, inspection reports, Underwriters Laboratories, Inc., engineering reports, and numerous others. The amount of information collected is subject to the constraint of the cost of the investigation process.
5. After having analyzed appropriate information, underwriters may accept the risk at standard rates and issue standard policies or they may offer the applicant restricted coverage or higher premiums (or both) in an effort to accept the risk. Some risks cannot be made

acceptable so they must be rejected. The underwriter, however, will attempt to develop alternatives in order to accept *profitable* business, if at all possible.

6. Once the risk is accepted, underwriters must decide how much of the risk to retain. The maximum amount of risk that can be retained on any one exposure is established by "line limits," the maximum amount the insurer is willing to lose on any one risk. Line limits are determined by the financial officers of the insurer, not by the underwriters.

7. If an insurer does not want to retain the entire amount of a particular risk, the amount it does not wish to retain can be shifted to another insurer in a process called *reinsurance*. The primary insurer is known as the "ceding" company.

8. Reinsurance may be facultative (optional), treaty (obligatory), or a hybrid of the two. Either of these forms may be written as proportional (pro rata) or nonproportional. Proportional may be written on a quota share or a surplus basis. Nonproportional is written either as excess of loss on a per risk or catastrophe basis, or as stop-loss coverage.

9. Reinsurance arrangements peculiar to life insurers are the *yearly renewable term* method and the *coinsurance* method. Under the yearly renewable term plan, the ceding company reinsures only the difference between the net amount at risk and the net retention of the insurer with the reinsured amount continually decreasing. Under the coinsurance plan the original reinsurance amount continues throughout the life of the contract in that the ceding company reinsures the amount by which the policy face amount exceeds its net retention limit.

10. Life insurers practice underwriting also to avoid adverse selection and obtain a profitable distribution of exposures. The selection of new insureds by life insurers, however, is in a sense more critical than in other types of insurance because life policies are noncancellable. Life insurers cannot afford to accept questionable risks and then rely on postselection to weed out the poor ones.

11. Special problems of underwriting include the problems of moral hazard, conflicts between underwriting and production, and governmental pressures on underwriting. Although insurance company officers may develop adequate methods to deal with the first three problems the threat of governmental interference subjects insurers to constant uncertainty.

Questions for Review

1. "A classification system often is required to maintain equity among policyowners and to provide insurers with an operating profit." Explain why you agree or disagree with this statement. In your answer, explain the concept of equity you are using.

2. What is the difference between preselection and postselection? What problems are peculiar to each?

3. What sources of information are available to the underwriter? Explain the functions of each source.

4. What is meant by equity among rates? Is complete equity ever possible? What problems would the insistence on complete equity present?

5. Discuss the types of proportional (pro rata) and excess loss reinsurance. Which type of insurer is most likely to use proportional (pro rata) reinsurance? Excess loss reinsurance? Explain.

6. In what respect is the underwriting of life insurance similar to that of property insurance? How does it differ?

7. "There can be no underwriting for moral hazard." Explain the logic behind this statement.

8. Discuss the various ways in which reinsurance facilitates the successful operation of the insurance industry.

9. How are extra-hazard applicants treated in life insurance? In property insurance?

10. How does fire insurance underwriting differ in its application to an individual dwelling and a large business?

Questions for Discussion

1. What are the objectives of underwriting? Are these objectives in the public interest? Discuss.

2. "The private insurance industry should be forced to provide protection at reasonable rates to all persons needing insurance." Evaluate this statement.

3. What is the difference between individual and social rate equity? Present arguments in favor of both types of equity. Which set of arguments has more appeal to you?

4. Why doesn't the government practice selection for social security? Would selection by the Social Security Administration be advantageous to society? Explain.

5. Develop a set of procedures an insurer could use to guard against moral hazard.

6. Why might some types of moral hazard (sometimes referred to as morale hazard) present more of a problem to underwriters than other forms of moral hazard?

Pricing insurance

Insurance pricing, or ratemaking, involves the calculation of each policyowner's fair share of losses and expenses. The price paid for insurance, called the premium,[1] is the rate per unit of coverage multiplied by the number of units purchased. Units of insurance are measured differently according to the type of coverage. For example, a unit can be an auto, 100 square feet of area in a building, $100 of gross receipts, $100 of payroll, $100 or $1,000 of insurance, or some other *easily measured* value for the coverage that corresponds to the exposure. (As will be seen, an *easily measured* value is not always the one that *best* corresponds to the exposure but the one that is the most practical to administer.)

The rates are established before the exposure period to which they

---

[1] The use of the word "premium" to denote the charge for insurance protection may be traced back to the bottomry and respondentia contracts of the Middle Ages. Under a bottomry contract, a shipowner would pledge his ship as collateral for a loan with the understanding that the loan would not have to be repaid if the ship were lost or destroyed at sea. For this type of loan, that is, one forgiving the debt upon loss of the collateral, the borrower had to pay a premium over the going rate of interest. The premium was to compensate the lender for accepting the risk. When the collateral for these loans was the cargo, the agreements were called respondentia contracts. Bottomry and respondentia contracts are said to be the earliest forms of risk-shifting devices regularly used in the commercial world and the forerunners of modern insurance contracts.

apply so that a forecast of the future must be made. The probable number and value of claims are forecast from historical loss experience with consideration given to trends and new developments. Insurers cannot set rates arbitrarily; rates are subject to state control.

Rates once were made individually. Underwriters judged each insurance application separately. As business volume increased and deficiencies in crude rating procedures became apparent, new and more nearly equitable ratemaking methods were demanded. Insurers found it expensive to inspect all individual properties for which insurance was sought. Cooperative ratemaking evolved as both an equitable and economical solution. Cooperative ratemaking organizations developed in most insurance lines. They published rates which were used by most insurers. Subscribers to bureau rates sometimes deviate from bureau published rates, but the published rates are a basing point for these deviations. Life, health, and ocean marine insurers set their own rates, and some "nonbureau" insurers writing other types of insurance develop premiums independently. Today's trend is toward independent ratemaking for all types of insurance.

Principles of Ratemaking

Scientific ratemaking involves adherence to fundamental principles. Rates should be adequate, not unfairly discriminatory, and not excessive. Also they should be economically feasible and encourage loss prevention. The first three principles are required by state law. The others represent more an ideal than a requirement.

Adequacy

Rates must be sufficient to pay losses and reasonable expenses of the insurer's operation. State laws require rate adequacy, as inadequate rates could result in the insolvency of an insurer and losses to policyowners. Rate adequacy also is necessary for a workable system of price competition.

The adequacy of a rate is determined by comparing the actual loss ratio with the one expected in computing the rate. The "expected loss ratio" is the estimated percentage of the total *earned premium* needed to pay *incurred losses,* including loss adjustment expenses. The remainder is available for operating expenses, taxes, and profit.

Earned premiums are distinguished from *written premiums,* and *incurred losses* are distinguished from *paid losses.* Written premiums include all premiums collected during the period under analysis (commonly one calendar year). Earned premium is the proportional share of each policy's written premium for which the term of coverage has elapsed. Whereas the entire premium is considered written on the day that the policy is issued, the earned premium is spread evenly over the exposure period of the policy. Paid losses include all losses disbursed during the accounting period. Incurred losses are all losses that occurred during the accounting period regardless of whether or not they have been paid when the financial statement is prepared.

Because most expenses associated with a policy are incurred when it is written and losses are incurred over the period in which premiums are earned, loss ratios are expressed as a percentage of earned premiums, and expense ratios are expressed as a percentage of written premiums. (Remember that losses include loss adjustment expenses.)

If inflation and other trends are ignored, a simple example of a rate level calculation can be shown as follows: Assume that the expected loss ratio for burglary insurance is 60 percent. If industrywide experience over a five-year period produces a 65 percent loss ratio at current rate levels ($600 million in premiums, $390 million in losses), these rate levels are inadequate for the industry as a whole (but not necessarily for an individual insurer) and must be increased. An 8⅓ percent increase (65–60)/60 will produce a rate level yielding the permissible 60 percent loss ratio. In practice, determining rate adequacy is not so simple, as a variety of rate classifications exists for a given coverage. On some burglary rate classifications, an insurer may have satisfactory loss ratios and, on others, unsatisfactory ones with a net adequate or inadequate overall result. Because bureau rates should be adequate for a range of these insurers, rates reflect expected losses for the mythical average bureau insurer. At these levels, the most efficient insurers earn extra profits and the least efficient ones experience underwriting losses. The latter ones have to tighten underwriting rules, claim practices, and expense budgets, unless underwriting losses are offset by investment income.

Equity

That rates are not unfairly discriminatory is important to both insured and insurer. Rates must be equitable, which means that all insureds pay their fair share of projected claims and expenses. But in practice equity is impossible. Its achievement would require each insured to be placed in an individual class, as no two insureds have the same loss probability, risk, or expenses. If each insured were in a class by itself, the principle of insurance—prediction of total loss values through large numbers of homogeneous units—would be unworkable. Thus complete equity in insurance is a contradiction.

The necessity for a uniform and practical rate base also makes perfect rate equity unattainable. For example, in workers' compensation insurance, the rate base is $100 of payroll. Company A, with a $90,000 annual payroll, pays 150 percent as much for compensation coverage as Company B, the same type of firm with a $60,000 payroll. Yet B may be using as many labor-hours as A, with the difference due to B's lower wage scale. In addition, with its lower pay scale, B probably is hiring less skillful workers and thus may have a higher accident rate. Nevertheless it pays a lower premium. Using labor-hours as the rate base is more equitable but less practical.

A practical degree of equity is obtained by pooling similar exposure units into classes. The degree of similarity among units in a class may vary widely. In Homeowners insurance, the same rate is charged for most one-family residences of frame construction with fire-resistant roofs in a given town. Although the houses vary as to the likelihood of burning, further classification to seek more equity is too expensive, with the additional expense creating a rate increase for homeowners. More classifications also might produce classes with so few members that the basic principle of risk pooling would be violated. The number of exposure units would be too small to allow loss prediction.

Not excessive

Rates can be too adequate (excessive). For example, continuing the previous burglary insurance illustration, suppose that industrywide experience produced a loss ratio of 55 percent at current levels ($600 million in premiums, $330 million in losses). State regulatory authorities and insurers sometimes do not agree that some specific rates are excessive. The commissioner, in observing loss statistics, wonders if the insurers are making excessive profits from a particular type of insurance. Insurers may be asked to justify their rates or reduce them. Regulatory authorities supposedly are as concerned with inadequate rates as with excessive ones, but for political reasons, they seek more vigorously to correct excessive ones. As the profit level is greater than was anticipated when the rates were set, some insurers, in order to capture a larger share of this profitable market, may lower rates. Or the insurance commissioner may encourage, or in some cases require, the industry to reduce rates by 8⅓ percent (60–65)/60.

Economic feasibility

Adequate, equitable, and not excessive rates are sufficient to meet state regulatory requirements, but insurers also must consider other rate-making principles. An economically feasible rate is one that makes coverage salable. Thus, the contingency insured against should have a low frequency rate, and losses that do occur should have a high severity rate. For example, full coverage for auto collision damage would require a premium so high that few insureds could afford it. However, deductible clauses have made collision insurance economically feasible for the typical auto owner by reducing its claims frequency and increasing its reported loss severity.

Inducement of loss prevention activities

Ideally rates should be constructed to encourage loss prevention activities. If a rate structure gives recognition to loss prevention activities, it is reasonable to assume that fewer losses will occur than when prevention is ignored. Rate credits can be allowed for protective devices and safe practices. As economic gains from loss prevention activities accrue to both insurer and insured, rate credits are a good insurance practice. However, encouraging loss prevention through ratemaking often is lost in practice. Rate credits are abused. Insurers, especially on large exposures, use these credits as competitive weapons to discriminate unfairly on behalf of their more favored customers, and such actions are not easily detected by insurance commissioners who seek to eliminate unfair discrimination in rate practices.

Types of Ratemaking

Ratemaking may be divided into three broad categories: judgment rating, manual rating, and merit rating. These classes are not mutually exclusive, as instances prevail in which all three are combined.

Judgment rating

Judgment rating is complete individuality in rating. Each exposure is rated on its own merits, independent of any established class, schedule, or formula. Although it is the least scientific rating method, judgment rating still is used in some coverages, especially in marine insurance, and in other coverages when credible statistics are unavailable. Judgment rating is not wholly unscientific, as ratemakers often use some other crude statistics in judging each exposure. In fact no rating system can be developed and applied without some judgment (good or bad) entering into the final rate.

Manual rating

Manual rating, defined as class or blanket rating, represents the combination of large groups of similar exposures into classes. All exposures in the classification are charged the same rate. The ability to establish similar classes and identify factors governing class boundaries is assumed. Manual rates reflect the average loss experience of the group, and are the most widely used in ratemaking. Class rates in Homeowners insurance, for example, apply to most residential property. In a specific town, all one- or two-family frame dwellings with standard roofs are assigned the same rate per $100 of insurance; all one- or two-family brick dwellings in the same community are given another rate. The important consideration in determining each class is that the units are alike in structure, exposed to similar hazards, and thus likely to have comparable loss experience over time.

The manual rate must include funds to pay (1) expected losses and loss adjustment expenses and (2) expenses, contingencies, and a contribution to surplus. That part intended to pay expected losses and loss adjustment expenses is the *pure premium*. The part intended to pay expenses, contingencies, and a contribution to surplus is the *loading*. As noted, the ratio of *incurred* losses including loss adjustment expenses to *earned* premiums, is called the *loss ratio*.

The two primary methods of determining the rate level used in manual rating are the pure premium method and the loss ratio method. The pure premium method is utilized to determine rate level changes and to obtain rate classification relativities. The loss ratio method generally is used for determining changes in the level of manual rates.

The pure premium method. The pure premium method of manual rate classification is a subtle and involved technique concerned with rate adequacy and equity among various classes. Losses are expressed in terms of exposure units for each classification as follows:

$$\text{Pure premium} = \frac{\text{Incurred losses}}{\text{Number of exposure units}}$$

Assume that for a specified auto liability rate classification, the incurred losses divided by the number of insured autos in that class is $75. This figure is the pure premium, or average loss per insured car in the class. If the current rate is based on a pure premium of $60, the rate must be increased, but with this upward adjustment no need exists to increase the expense loading unless expenses also have increased. Furthermore, to increase the expense loading by the same percentage as the loss portion of the premium may produce an excessive amount for expense. Yet the expense proportion of the rate, called the expected expense ratio, is fixed. The remainder, called the permissible loss ratio, is expected to cover losses. In the foregoing example, if the permissible loss ratio is 55 percent, an increase in the pure premium from $60 to $75 will result in a gross premium increase of from $109 ($60 ÷ 0.55) to $136 ($75 ÷ 0.55). Expense allowances are automatically increased by the same percentage. The example assumes 100 percent statistical credibility on which the change is based.

Credibility refers to the statistical significance given to the class loss exposure. The longer the experience period and the wider the rate classification, the greater is the credibility of rate statistics because of the broader spread of experience. If the data are sparse, ratemakers place less than 100 percent credence on the statistics. In the second example used earlier, statistics indicated an upward rate revision of 25 percent. Actuaries have determined that nearly 1,100 claims are necessary for an auto liability classification to have 100 percent credibility. If the pure premium of $75 is developed on the basis of only 400 claims, a credibility of 60 percent is assigned (according to the credibility table), resulting in a rate increase of only 15 percent computed as follows:

$$RM = \left(\frac{A}{E} - 1.00\right) \times C$$

where

> RM is the rate modification percentage.
> A is the actual loss ratio (in this case 75 ÷ 109, or .688).
> E is the expected loss ratio (in this case given as .55).
> C is the credibility factor (in this case .60).

Solving for RM:

$$\left(\frac{.688}{.55} - 1.00\right) \times .60 = .15$$

The loss ratio method. The loss ratio method of manual rate calculation is concerned primarily with rate adequacy and is used in rating broad groups. In the burglary insurance example the expected loss ratio (incurred losses divided by earned premiums) was 60 percent. Thus, 40 percent of the premium is available for general expenses and profits. Because the industrywide loss ratio averaged 65 percent over five years, the rate was adjusted upward by 8⅓ percent. Although general expenses probably will not increase by the same percentage as losses, this adjustment also increases the money available for expenses by 8⅓ percent. Once the general level of burglary rates is determined, the actuary must distribute the premium increase among the various manual classifications.

Judgment is an important factor in manual rating. The number of classifications, the nature of classifications, and the apportionment of general rate changes over the established classes are based to a large extent on judgment.

Merit rating

Merit rating or modification rating varies the rate charged insureds in the same classification, based on the insured's past experience, actual or anticipated experience for the policy term, or both. The purpose is to help achieve equity by providing a rating system that will reduce premiums charged large insureds whose experience is consistently better than average, and increase premiums charged large insureds with poorer than average experience. The three types of merit rating are schedule rating, experience rating, and retrospective rating.

Schedule rating. Schedule rating requires objective standards characteristic of exposures in manual classifications. An applicant's exposure is measured by this standard, and the manual classification rate is adjusted upward or downward accordingly. Schedule rating implies the possibility of making an accurate physical evaluation of an exposure and is possible only if a schedule of relevant factors can be determined and prospective hazards can be compared against them. This requirement usually eliminates those insurance fields in which nonphysical matters are important.

Schedule rating can encourage loss prevention. The fullest exploitation of this characteristic requires the assumption of an average standard exposure. Most insureds would find their rate increased due to unfavorable deviations from this assumed standard. The possibility of reducing charges by eliminating hazards is an incentive for loss prevention. Schedule rating is applicable to exposures of any size. Other types of merit rating apply only to large insureds.

In spite of its advantages, schedule rating is important only in fire insurance on commercial properties. It is used to a limited extent in liability, burglary, and glass insurance to modify experience rates. In

workers' compensation insurance, schedule rating once was used extensively, but its disadvantages now are believed to outweigh its advantages.
High administrative cost is incurred when schedule rating is applied
to changeable exposures such as workers' compensation. A second disadvantage is that schedule rating easily can be misapplied. It has been
used for competitive reasons to grant rate reductions not justified by
underwriting facts. The use of an ill-defined flexible schedule borders
on judgment rating. Finally, some loss prevention engineers contend
that too much attention is given to mechanical safety aspects and too
little to overall managerial concerns. Human factors, they contend, are
as important to industrial safety as physical factors. Examples of schedule rating are presented later in this chapter.

Experience rating.   Under an experience rating system, a modification
is made in the manual rate to reflect the insured's past experience. The
premium for the period covered will not be affected by the experience
for that year but is averaged with the experience of past years in computing rates for future years. Because past experience modifies future rates,
this experience rating plan is known as *prospective experience rating*
to distinguish it from *retrospective experience rating.* The degree to
which the manual rate is modified depends on the amount of data available to reflect the insured's experience. A credibility factor is assigned
which varies directly with the volume of experience. Rarely is the insured's experience assigned 100 percent credibility.

Retrospective rating.   Retrospective rating further modifies the manual
rate to reflect the experience during the policy period. The insured is
charged a *basic premium,* which is a percentage of the *standard premium.* The standard premium is the full experience modified manual
premium. The basic premium includes an amount to cover expenses
not associated with losses and an insurance charge to cover those losses
that are in excess of a maximum overall limit. To reflect economies
of size and the amount required for the insurance charge, the percentage
of the standard premium charged varies inversely with its size and the
relative levels of the established maximum and minimum premiums.
The losses incurred and loss adjustment cost during the period and the
state premium tax are added to the basic premium. The total is the
retrospective premium, subject to a maximum and a minimum. Within
the maximum and minimum, the premium paid is determined by the
experience of the particular insured for that period. The final computation is made after the coverage period; hence the name "retrospective."
    Rates developed by retrospective experience rating fluctuate more
than those developed by prospective experience rating because of the
weight placed on one year's experience, that is the insured's experience
in the coverage year. The insured probably will appreciate the flexibility
only in years of good experience. Whatever theoretical advantages retrospective rating may have, relatively few insureds produce sufficient premium volume to be eligible. If the insured qualifies, retrospective rating
will be used upon mutual agreement between insured and insurer. Some

large insureds consider retrospective rating an acceptable substitute for self-insurance.

Quantity discounts

Class rates also are modified to reflect decreasing costs per insurance unit with increasing quantities purchased. In life and workers' compensation insurance, the quantity discount is based solely on reduced expenses per unit; in liability and crime coverages, the discount is based both on reduced expenses and reduced loss costs per unit. The second $25,000 of liability insurance will not produce as much loss as the first $25,000. Graded commission scales that reduce unit cost with the policy size are used in some types of insurance.

Application of Ratemaking

To explore ratemaking more fully, the rating methods used in several types of insurance are discussed.

Fire insurance

Fire insurance rating offers examples of both manual and schedule rating. Dwellings are manually rated. In one small midwestern town, for example, all frame dwellings (without an unusual exposure) built for one-family occupancy may be charged $0.18 per $100. As no fire insurance quantity discount is offered, the rate for each $100 is constant. The rate is not the same in every town because the chance of loss by fire differs among localities.

In 1916 a "Standard Schedule for Grading Cities and Towns with Reference to Their Fire Defenses and Physical Conditions" was adopted and is the starting point of fire insurance rating. Each town is rated according to factors affecting the frequency and severity of fire losses. A system of deficiency points is used in grading the towns. After an inspection, they are assigned a classification ranging from 1 to 10, according to the number of deficiency points assessed. The importance of various factors is shown by the relative weights given the 5,000 deficiency points that can be assessed against a town:

Factor	Deficiency points
Water supply	1,700
Fire department	1,500
Fire alarm	550
Police protection	50
Building laws	300
General hazards	300
Structural conditions which might lead to a general conflagration	700
Total	5,000 points

A town with 500 or less deficiency points assessed against it would be in class 1, but no such town exists.[2] Class 2 runs from 501 to 1,000 deficiency points, and so on down to class 10, with over 4,500 points. The grades along with recommended improvements are explained to town authorities.

Class rates are used for large groups of insured units of similar hazard. The rates are subdivided according to the grade of the town, building construction, and number of families occupying the structure. Averages based on the loss experience for each class are published in rate manuals.

Commercial properties are individually rated according to a comprehensive rating schedule. The fundamental factors affecting the hazard are occupancy, location (or exposure), construction, and protection. *Occupancy* is the purpose for which the building is used. An explosives factory is in a different category than a church and would require a higher rate, other things remaining the same. The *location* of the property is important in measuring the likelihood that a fire will spread to the insured building from surrounding structures. Relative location is the external equivalent of occupancy. What takes place inside the building is the building's occupancy hazard; what occurs in the immediate neighborhood is the location (or exposure) hazard. *Construction* refers to the type of building—physical dimensions, materials used in the structure, and so on. Size and architectural style affect the probability of a fire loss. The *protection* of a building consists of the availability of fire-fighting equipment and personnel. This factor includes automatic sprinkler systems and other fire extinguishers.

The universal mercantile system.   The universal mercantile system, the oldest system of fire insurance schedule rating, was introduced in 1893 and still is in use, chiefly in eastern and southern states. The guide applied to measure chance of loss is a standard building in a standard town. The assumed building is so high-grade that few structures can meet it. The city assumed also is high-grade. The *basis rate* for this high-grade building in the high-grade city is the schedule's starting point.

The *key rate,* or the rate the standard building would require in the city in which the structure to be rated is located, is determined next. The city is compared with the standard city as to the building code, fire department adequacy, water supply, and the efficiency of the police department. Credits are given for items in which the city is better than the standard city, and deductions are made for items in which the city is poorer than standard. Once the key rate is determined, the actual building is compared with the standard building. Additions are made to the key rate for building features (including occupancy, neighbors, and construction) poorer than the standard. Deductions are made for features which exceed the standard. The additions to the rate are flat

---

[2] There is a rumor that one once existed—but it has burned.

amounts, but the deductions are percentages of the rate per $100 of insurance.

For example, a five-story frame mercantile building in a medium-sized eastern town might be rated as follows under one of several schedules available under the universal mercantile system. The basis rate would be 25 cents per $100 of valuation. Using the grading system for cities and towns, a charge of 50 cents per $100 is added to produce a $0.75 key rate. Then additional charges are made for various characteristics of the building. These charges are as follows: because the structure is frame rather than brick, 50 cents; because the total floor area is 10,000 square feet as compared with the standard 5,000, 5 cents; because the building is a five-story one rather than a four-story one, 15 cents; because it is occupied by three tenants instead of two, 5 cents. The final rate increases to $1.50 per $100 of coverage ($0.25 + 0.50 + 0.50 + 0.05 + 0.15 + 0.05 = $1.50). Other factors for which charges often are made include stairways, heating systems, lighting systems, roof construction, elevators, interior finish, electrical defects, and exposure. As the schedule requires a nearly perfect building as its starting point, few credits are given. The structure could have received small percentage credits for guards, fire extinguishers, and other "exceptionally good features."

The analytic system. The "analytic system for the measurement of relative fire hazard" was introduced in Illinois in 1901 and often is called "Dean's analytic system." Although this type of schedule rating resembles the universal mercantile system, significant differences are apparent. The systems are similar in that property is compared to a standard and the rate is adjusted for differences. Under the analytic system, no standard city is used; instead, a separate schedule applies to each of 10 classifications. No single standard building is used; rather three basic classifications are employed: A is fire-resistant construction; B is brick or stone, and D is frame construction. (No mistake here! Class C is nonexistent.)

The standard building for the Dean system is a one-story brick building of ordinary construction, located in a town with no fire protection. Thus, the initial basis rate is higher than that under the universal mercantile system, and more buildings will be nearer the standard. As in the universal mercantile system, the building is compared with the standard building. But here a significant difference appears. Credits and debits to the standard rate under the Dean system are in percentages of the basis rate, because Dean believed variations from the standard building cause changes in the fire hazard which are represented not by flat amounts, but by charges proportionate to the basis rate. Each rating territory has a set of basis rates per $100 of insurance that reflects the loss experience in that territory. They are subject to debits and credits for conditions relating to occupancy, exposure, protection, and structure. Flat amount aftercharges are made for such items as defective wiring and poor housekeeping (no waste cans, for example).

As an example, consider a two-story brick store building with a basement, located in a small Illinois town. The basis rate for this building in this town is $0.6038 per $100 of coverage. The following percentage charges are added to reflect various characteristics of the building and its occupancy: frame wall materials, 73 percent; type of roof, 20 percent; type and number of stairwells, 5 percent; exposure, 13 percent; and occupancy by three retail shops, 95 percent. The total charges added are 206 percent, or $1.2438, making the rate $1.8476 per $100. A 5 percent credit is allowed for fire extinguishers, which lowers the rate by $0.0924 to $1.7552.

The experience grading and rating schedule. The universal and analytic systems are elaborate and formalized methods of judgment rating and are an improvement over the days when local agents would look at a building and decide what the rate should be. These systems remain judgment systems, as rates and rate credits and debits are not based on statistical experience. E. G. Richards in 1915 devised a scheme to place fire insurance rating on a firm scientific basis. The plan would use statistical data concerning every property insured against fire. Rates for all properties could be determined scientifically.

Statistical justification for rates is inherent in the system, but the plan has serious administrative disadvantages. The cost of assembling the data and keeping them current would be enormous, and the data always would be outdated as the tabulated information would be constantly changing. In spite of these objections many people would like to try the method and are confident that modern electronic data processing techniques can overcome the objections. The experience grading and rating plan would lead to the most detailed rate manual ever compiled.

New experimental system. In 1975 the ISO tested a new commercial fire rating schedule in Indiana and by 1985 it was in use nationwide. ISO claims the new system is more efficient than either the universal mercantile or the analytic system, particularly for firms operating in many states. Much of the efficiency is the result of a computer program designed for the system, thus enabling insurers to obtain rating information instantly with the use of remote computer tie-ins. A common hazard analysis is used for all states with conversion factors that recognize and reflect differences among states. On the basis of its construction, occupancy, protection, and exposure, the building is assigned a grade of so many points. This grade then is converted to a rate requiring 80 percent coinsurance and is adjusted for class experience. A major advantage claimed for the new schedule is that it is far less complex than those previously in use. The fact that it is uniform nationwide also makes it easier to use. The new system is expected to have a significant impact on the commercial fire insurance business over the long term.

Rate level adjustment. Fire insurance rate level adjustments generally are made using the loss ratio method. Adjustments usually are based

or six-year experience moving average to improve its statistical
These adjustments are concerned with rate levels only and not
appropriateness of the classes or the components of the sched-
ate adequacy rather than equity is the adjustment goal.

insurance

Inland marine insurers use ratemaking practices similar to those for
fire insurance. Various floater policies covering personal property are
manual rated. The jewelers' block policy and coverage on instrumentalities of transportation usually are schedule rated. Most other inland marine coverages are judgment rated. Ratemaking in ocean marine insurance is judgment rating in its purest form. The rate is negotiated between
a broker, representing the shipowner or shipper, and the marine insurance agent, representing the insurer. Associations publish advisory rates
for ocean marine coverages.

Many factors must be considered in setting the rate. The ship's *physical characteristics* are among the most important ones. Most ocean vessels are built under the supervision of classification societies supervising
ship construction. They publish data about the ships, and surveys are
made frequently to determine if the ship's present condition varies
widely from its original condition. The societies' reports are given much
weight in ratemaking. A second factor is the *area* in which the vessel
is operated. Some ocean routes are comparatively free from natural hazards, and others are prone to disturbances. A third factor is the *time
period* the policy will be in force if it is a short-term contract. The
rate for a North Atlantic voyage will be higher in the winter than in
the summer. A final rating factor is the *ownership* of the vessel, which
includes the record and reputation of the captain.

If the policy applies to cargoes, the *susceptibility* of the cargo to damage is an important factor. The probability of loss to fine china is far
greater than the likelihood of damage to pig iron. In rating cargo insurance, consideration is given to the suitability of the *type of vessel* for
transporting the particular type of cargo.

Other property and liability insurance

Other property and liability coverages generally are class rated, with
larger exposures subject to experience modifications. Classification in
most liability lines is based on the insured's business. In auto insurance,
the classification is based on the type of car and the territory involved.
Auto insurance rate classifications are discussed in Chapter 14. In boiler
and machinery insurance, the classification is based on the type and
size of the object covered. Class rates are computed either by the loss
ratio or pure premium method, depending on the coverage.

The rate base varies with the coverage. In products liability, the rate
base may be $1,000 of sales; in workers' compensation, $100 of payroll.

Most general liability coverages use 100 square feet of area; in auto insurance, the exposure is measured on a per car basis. These exposure measures are not always accurate or equitable guides to the relative hazards involved, but they are the most expedient and practical. In workers' compensation insurance, for example, employee-hours worked in specific occupations might be a superior rate base than $100 of payroll, yet insurers find that the problems involved in collecting these data create an inefficient solution.

A composite rating plan often is used for large insureds with many exposures, each taking a different rate base. Under this plan, all exposures are rated on one basis—payroll or sales, for example. The plan is optional and may be applied to some or all exposures. An attempt is made to compute a rate that adequately reflects the hazards when applied to the rate base. The initial composite rate is subject to experience adjustments, just as are manual rates.

Schedule rating. Schedule rating sometimes is used in liability and miscellaneous property coverage. The manual rates may be modified in accordance with a schedule rating table, subject to a maximum modification of 25 percent to reflect characteristics not considered in the insured's experience. One schedule for workers' compensation insurance could be as follows:

	Range of modifications		
	Credit		Debit
A. Location:			
i. Exposure inside premises	5%	to	5%
ii. Exposure outside premises	5	to	5
B. Premises—condition, care	10	to	10
C. Equipment—type, condition, care	10	to	10
D. Classification peculiarities	10	to	10
E. Employees—selection, training, supervision, experience	6	to	6
F. Cooperation:			
i. Medical facilities	2	to	2
ii. Safety program	2	to	2

These debits and credits, determined by judgment methods, are applied in addition to experience modifications. They are used most often as a competitive device to obtain desirable accounts or discourage unwanted business.

Experience rating. Qualified insureds are eligible for experience rating in auto and general liability insurance, crime coverages, group life and health insurance, group annuities, and workers' compensation insurance. The experience rating method applies a modification factor to the basic manual rate based on the insured's experience. The formula used is:[3]

$$M = \frac{A - E}{E} \times C$$

M is the percentage by which the pure premium portion of the manual premium is altered; A is the insured's actual loss experience; E is the expected loss assumed in the manual rate calculation and C is the credibility factor, which measures the statistical significance or believability of the insured's loss experience. The larger the insured's scale of operations, the more likely is the loss record to present a true picture of the exposure.

Assume a manufacturer's workers' compensation exposure is experience rated. The gross premium at manual rates is $10,000, of which (assuming a 60 percent loss ratio) $6,000 represents the pure premium. If the actual losses for the experience rating period (customarily three years) averaged $8,000 per year, the experience rating modification factor is calculated as follows (assume a credibility factor of 0.54 taken from tables prepared by ratemakers is used):

$$\frac{\$8,000 - \$6,000}{\$6,000} \times 0.54 = 18\% \quad \text{(amount by which manual premium is increased)}$$

In this case, an upward adjustment will be made of 18 percent of the premium, or $1,800. The experience rated premium would be $11,800. Experience rating is not optional. If provided in the manual for insureds of this size and type, the rate must be calculated on an experience basis.

Retrospective rating. Retrospective rating may be used if the insured meets the eligibility requirements. The calculation of liability and compensation premiums for large exposures is virtually the only example of retrospective rating other than in group insurance. Retrospectively rated policies include schedule and experience rating plans where applicable. The ultimate premium is determined after expiration of the policy period. The final premium (subject to maximum and minimum limits) equals the insured's actual losses plus claims expenses plus an allowance to the insurer for the risk of assuming losses in excess of the maximum

---

[3] This formula is a *simple* experience rating formula. The one used might be complicated by the introduction of other factors, such as a W value. In determining the loss experience for the insured over the experience rating period, large losses are discounted—that is, not considered in full—in order to minimize the impact of one or more unusually large losses. The W factor is the percentage applied to the amount of the excess losses not otherwise appearing in the rating formula, and is used to give some weight to these losses. A typical formula including a W factor would be: M = (Actual primary losses + B value + [W value × actual excess losses] + [(1 − W value) × expected excess losses]) ÷ (expected primary losses + B value + [W value × expected excess losses] + [(1 − W value) × expected excess losses] where the B value is a stabilizing element or ballast serving as the credibility factor. The lower the B factor, the greater the credibility given to the insured's own experience. The W value is the percentage applicable to the excess losses, to bring these excess losses gradually back into the rating formula. The (1 − W value) times expected excess losses is an additional ballast.

premium, for administrative and related expenses, and for the premium tax charged.

Five basic retrospective plans are available in workers' compensation insurance: A, B, C, D, and J. Maximum premiums are set for all plans. Under plans A, B and C a minimum is set below which the insured's premium cannot fall. Plan C's minimum is the basic premium plus the state premium tax. Plan D combines workers' compensation insurance with other coverages. Eligibility for retrospective rating is determined by the size of the premium at experience modified manual rates. The use of retrospective rating is a matter of agreement between the insurer and insured.

Assume that an experience rated manufacturer uses retrospective rating plan B. How would the $11,800 premium charged under the experience rated plan be affected? The applicable formula is:

Retrospective premium
= [Basic premium + (Incurred losses × Loss conversion factor)]
× Tax multiplier.

The basic premium, a percentage of the standard premium, is given in the applicable table of rating values. These percentages vary with territory, size of exposure, and plan selected. The basic premium includes general administrative and acquisition charges and an insurance charge. The standard premium is developed by applying the experience rate to the payroll. Incurred losses are the actual losses paid, plus estimated losses incurred but not yet paid. The loss conversion factor converts incurred losses into a figure including claims administration costs. The tax multiplier allows for taxes.

The standard premium is $11,800. In the applicable table of rating values for plan B, the basic premium is 23 percent of the standard premium, or $2,714. Assume that the loss conversion factor and tax multiplier, which vary by territory, are 1.14 and 1.026, respectively. What would the manufacturer's premium be if losses were $2,000 for the year? $10,000? $20,000? The retrospective rating formula would produce premiums of $5,123.84, $14,480.96, and $26,177.36, respectively. However, the table of rating values prescribes minimum and maximum premiums. The applicable percentages for an insured of this size under plan B are 52.5 percent of the standard premium as a minimum, and 162 percent as a maximum. So the minimum premium is $6,195, and the maximum is $19,116. If losses are only $2,000, the insured must pay the minimum premium of $6,195; if losses are $10,000, the computed retrospective premium of $14,480.96 is charged; if losses are $20,000, the maximum of $19,116 applies. If the insured does not want to include catastrophic losses in the retrospective premium, a limit on the amount of individual losses to be considered in applying the formula can be set. For this privilege the insured is charged an excess loss premium which is added to incurred losses and multiplied by the loss conversion factor and tax multiplier in computing the final premium. The formula is:

Retrospective premium
= [Basic premium + (Standard premium × Excess loss premium
factor × Loss conversion factor) + (Ratable losses × Loss conversion
factor)] × Tax multiplier, subject to minimum and maximum
premium. Ratable losses are those single losses up to a given maximum.

The minimum and maximum premiums are unaffected by including
the excess-loss premium factor.

Guaranteed cost plan. If the eligible insured and the insurer decide
against retrospective rating, the guaranteed cost plan, known as the
premium discount plan, is used. As selling costs, payroll audits, and
administration do not increase proportionately with a premium increase, nonretrospectively rated insureds with premiums in excess of
$1,000 per year receive premium discounts. The discounts vary among
states and are determined largely by the expense loading permitted
where the exposure is located. The larger the permitted loading, the
greater the expense savings and the larger the discount. Mutual insurers
give lower discounts than stock insurers to allow for probable policyholder dividends. The discounts are applied to the experience rated standard premium.

Life insurance

Life insurance premiums are computed using assumed mortality
rates, interest, and expenses. Mortality rates are assumed death rates
at each age, usually expressed on per 1,000 basis. The Commissioners
1958 Standard Ordinary Mortality Table (1950–54), commonly known
as the 1958 CSO Mortality Table, relates the probable number dying
and living at each age from 0 to 100, assuming a radix of 10 million
lives. The radix is the number of lives selected to exist at the initial
age used in the construction of the mortality table. The basic data underlying the table are drawn from the combined mortality experience of
15 large U.S. insurers between 1950 and 1954. A section of the table is
reproduced as Table 25–1 and is used here for illustrative purposes.
The table considers only male lives but can be used for women by an
age adjustment of from four to six years. Thus, the mortality rate for
women aged 40 is approximated by that listed in the table for men
aged 35. Although a person's sex does affect mortality rates, other factors
such as race, place of residence, work habits, travel, and health also
affect mortality rates. As sex is the only factor singled out for consideration in insurance mortality tables, charges of discrimination are raised
particularly with annuities for which the life expectancy of women is
longer and thus annuity rates are higher. Recent court decisions favored
those fighting alleged discrimination against females in employee benefit plan retirement formulas, and the use of unisex mortality tables developed to treat men and women equally is increasing. But antidiscrimination advocates do not appear disturbed about *lower* life insurance

TABLE 25–1
Commissioners 1958 Standard Ordinary Mortality Table

(1) Age	(2) Number living	(3) Number dying	(4) Deaths per 1,000	(5) Expectation of life-years
0	10,000,000	70,800	7.08	68.30
1	9,929,200	17,475	1.76	67.78
2	9,911,725	15,066	1.52	66.90
3	9,896,659	14,449	1.46	66.00
4	9,882,210	13,835	1.40	65.10
5	9,868,375	13,322	1.35	64.19
6	9,855,053	12,812	1.30	63.27
7	9,842,241	12,401	1.26	62.35
8	9,829,840	12,091	1.23	61.43
9	9,817,749	11,879	1.21	60.51
10	9,805,870	11,865	1.21	59.58
11	9,794,005	12,047	1.23	58.65
12	9,781,958	12,325	1.26	57.72
13	9,769,633	12,896	1.32	56.80
14	9,756,737	13,562	1.39	55.87
15	9,743,175	14,225	1.46	54.95
16	9,728,950	14,983	1.54	54.03
17	9,713,967	15,737	1.62	53.11
18	9,698,230	16,390	1.69	52.19
19	9,681,840	16,846	1.74	51.28
20	9,664,994	17,300	1.79	50.37
21	9,647,694	17,655	1.83	49.46
22	9,630,039	17,912	1.86	48.55
23	9,612,127	18,167	1.89	47.64
24	9,593,960	18,324	1.91	46.73
35	9,373,807	23,528	2.51	36.69
36	9,350,279	24,685	2.64	35.78
37	9,325,594	26,112	2.80	34.88
38	9,299,482	27,991	3.01	33.97
39	9,271,491	30,132	3.25	33.07
95	97,165	34,128	351.24	1.80
96	63,037	25,250	400.56	1.51
97	37,787	18,456	488.42	1.18
98	19,331	12,916	668.15	.83
99	6,415	6,415	1,000.00	.50

premiums for women. (Men, assert your alleged rights and fight for equality in life insurance rates!)

Insurers may use the mortality table of their choice or develop their own for computing life insurance premiums, but they are subject to minimum reserve liabilities. These liabilities have been based on the

1958 CSO Mortality Table at 4 to 4½ percent interest in nearly all states including New York on newly issued annual premium life insurance policies (3 to 3½ percent on older blocks of policies). The statutory interest rate in a number of states, again including New York, for single premium life insurance has been 5½ percent.

In 1980, the National Association of Insurance Commissioners (NAIC) amended their standard valuation law. These long overdue changes have been enacted in all states. Under the new amendments, life insurers will begin to establish their reserves using the 1980 CSO table. In addition, the interest rates used are allowed to fluctuate with the rates on monthly averages of a Moody's corporate bond index. The rates vary according to the year of policy issue and the duration of the interest guarantee. In 1982, rates ranged from 5.50 percent for guarantee periods longer than 20 years to 6.75 percent for periods of 10 years or less. For 1983, the rates increased to 6.0 percent and 7.25 percent, respectively, and remained at this level for 1984 and 1985. By 1989, all life insurers will be required to use the 1980 CSO tables with the annually determined interest rates. (See Chapter 28.)

The reproduced table presents the 1958 CSO mortality rates as a function of age only. Mortality rates are also a function of occupation and physical condition. Most jobs do not require special attention in ratemaking, but a few hazardous ones sufficiently influence the death rate to justify an extra premium. Bartenders, professional wrestlers, and jockeys (other than the disc variety) are charged higher premiums. Most insurers will underwrite applicants in some extra hazardous occupations, and a few write insurance for nearly any occupation if the applicant pays a premium high enough to reflect the expected loss. Some applicants are charged extra because of an adverse physical condition. A physical examination is required of many life insurance applicants, whereas for others answers to a detailed medical questionnaire are sufficient. This information determines if the applicant's physical condition is standard or substandard. Insurer practices differ regarding whether the applicant will be insured and, if so, whether the premium will be standard—an amount in excess of standard or an amount below standard. Some insurers offer "preferred risk" policies to applicants with higher than average probabilities for a longer life. These applicants are given discounts of up to 40 percent if they are (like the authors of this book) slim and do not smoke. An associative factor appears to exist between smoking and longevity: a person who gives up smoking and controls eating habits is likely to be concerned about health and therefore act accordingly, and this, on the average, leads to a longer life. Discounts also are given to physical fitness freaks (not like the authors of this book).

Each insurer computes its own premiums. The actuary, a life insurance mathematician, assumes an interest rate in premium calculations. As the policy is a long-term contract, the assumed interest rate has an important effect on the premium. Today insurers use rates from 2½ to more than 8 percent. The following example assumes 4½ percent, admit-

TABLE 25–2
Present value of 1 at compound interest

Year	4½%	Year	4½%	Year	4½%
1	.95694	15	.51672	28	.29157
2	.91573	16	.49447	29	.27902
3	.87630	17	.47318	30	.26700
4	.83856	18	.45280	31	.25550
5	.80245	19	.43330	32	.24450
6	.76790	20	.41464	33	.23397
7	.73483	21	.39679	34	.22390
8	.70319	22	.37970	35	.21425
9	.67290	23	.36335	36	.20503
10	.64393	24	.34770	37	.19620
11	.61620	25	.33273	38	.18775
12	.58966	26	.31840	39	.17967
13	.56427	27	.30469	40	.17193
14	.53997				

tedly a low rate but one still currently used by several prominent insurers for participating policies. Table 25–2 lists the present value of 1 at 4½ percent compounded for 1 through 40 years. Present value tables show how much must be invested now at the designated rate to accumulate to 1 at the specified time. The present value of 1 (dollars, apples, or units of any kind) due at the end of 40 years is 0.17193. Thus, if $0.17193 were invested today at 4½ percent compounded annually, it would amount to $1 in 40 years.

Table 25–3 shows the calculation of the net single premium for a $1,000 whole life policy for a man aged 98. Of course, no one buys a whole life policy at 98, but a late age is best to use for a simple illustration. According to the mortality figures in Table 25–1, 12,916 of the 19,331 people alive on their 98th birthdays will die within that year; of the 6,415 who reach 99, none will reach age 100. Of course, a few may reach 100, but this fact does not matter to oblivious actuaries. The face amount of the policy is paid to those reaching age 100 as though they had cooperated with the actuaries by dying in accordance with the mortality rate

TABLE 25–3
Net single premium, $1,000 of life insurance at age 98*

Age	Number dying	Amount of insurance	Total claims	Present value of 1 at 4½%	Present value of claims
98	12,916	$1,000	$12,916,000	0.95694	$12,359,837
99	6,415	1,000	6,415,000	0.91573	5,874,408
					$18,234,245

* Note number living at age 98 = 19,331. $18,234,245 ÷ 19,331 = $943, the net single premium.

of 1.00 (1,000 deaths out of 1,000 alive) shown for age 99 (Table 25–1).

If 12,916 people will die at age 98, the insurer must have on hand $12,916,000 to pay $1,000 to each beneficiary by the end of the year. The insurer, of course, does not wait until the end of the year to pay the claims; they are paid when incurred. (Many insurers pay interest on the proceeds from time of death until the settlement is made.) The assumption that claims are paid at the end of the year is to simplify the calculation.

As premiums are paid at the beginning of the year, the insurer has the funds for the full year. If these funds are invested at the assumed 4½ percent, a deposit of about $0.95694 is required to equal $1 in one year. Thus, $12,916,000 multiplied by the present value factor of 0.95694 (Table 25–2) is needed to provide $12,916,000 at the end of the year. This product, $12,359,837, is the amount necessary to assure enough funds to meet estimated claims for the year. At this point the assumed interest rate makes a significant difference in computing premiums. If the rate were 10 percent, only $0.9091 would be needed at the beginning of each year to equal $1 at the end of the year, and only $11,741,936 would be needed by the insurer to pay its claims for that year.

For the second year, $6,415,000 will be paid in claims. Again, the insurer has the funds, in this case for two years. About 0.91573 at 4½ percent interest for two years, will accumulate to $1. Therefore, only $5,874,408 ($6,415,000 × .91573) will be needed now to pay claims of $6,415,000 two years hence. If interest were 10 percent, only $5,301,677 would be needed.

The total present value of future claims is the amount the insurer must have on hand today to guarantee $1,000 to the beneficiaries of each of the 19,331 people now aged 98, each assumed to buy a $1,000 whole life policy. As these payments are undertaken on behalf of 19,331 insured persons, the cost is divided among them. By dividing the total cost of $18,234,245 ($12,359,837 + $5,874,408) by 19,331, the net single premium to be charged each insured is computed to be about $943. Were the interest assumption 10 percent, the net single premium would be about $882.

The premium is very close to the policy face amount because, in this example, each insured is very close to death. This premium, the net single premium, is the amount that will be sufficient to pay the face amount upon death. It does not allow for the insurer's expenses. Expenses are provided by adding a loading charge to the net premium. Various loading methods are used for different types of policies.

Thus far, the assumption has been that a single-premium policy is written. But most premiums are paid on a level annual basis. To convert the single premium to a level annual premium, the insurer must find the amount that, if paid by all policyowners each year, as long as they live, will provide exactly enough to pay all claims as they mature. The computation is a division of the net single premium by the present value of a life annuity due of one per annum. A life annuity due is a series of annual payments made at the beginning of the year, contingent upon the annuitant's life. Premiums are paid at the beginning of the year by all surviving policyowners. Table 25–4 shows how the present value of a life annuity due of one per annum is computed at age 98, using the 1958 CSO Mortality Table and 4½ percent interest.

Note that the first payments of 19,331 are not discounted (a factor of 1.000 is used) because these payments are made immediately. The 6,415 payments are discounted for one year because they are made at the beginning of the second year. The total present value is $25,470. By dividing this figure by the number living at the beginning of the period—19,331—the present value of an annuity due of one is computed to be about 1.32. Thus, a single payment of 1.32 is equivalent to a level annual payment of one for life beginning at age 98. The level annual payment equivalent to a single payment of $943 can be determined using proportions where x equals the level annual payment:

$$x : 943 = 1 : 1.32.$$
$$1.32x = 943.$$
$$x = 943 \div 1.32.$$
$$x = \$714, \text{ the net level annual premium}$$
$$\text{for a \$1,000 policy issued at age 98.}$$

If 10 percent interest is assumed, the present value of the life annuity due would be 1.27, and the net level annual premium would be the net single premium ($882) divided by 1.27, or about $694.

The annual level premium is greater than the net single premium divided by the maximum number of years over which the premiums are scheduled to be paid because (1) most insureds die before reaching 99 and hence can no longer pay the annual premium, and (2) the insurer loses interest earnings because the total premium is not collected in advance. Changes in the interest assumption produce a greater differential in premiums at lower than at higher ages because of the longer period over which interest is earned. A change, for example, from 2½ to 3 percent will reduce the net level annual premium by nearly 9 percent at age 25. The same increase in interest assumptions at age 65 would reduce the net level annual premium by less than 2 percent.

In life insurance, the policy size is a factor in rating. The rate per

TABLE 25–4
Present value of a life annuity due 1958 CSO at 4½ percent*

Age	Number living	Promised payments of one per year	Present value of one at 4½%	Present value of promised payments of one per year
98	19,331	19,331	1.00000	$19,331
99	6,415	6,415	.95694	6,139
				25,470

* 25,470 ÷ 19,331 = 1.32.

$1,000 generally is lower on policies for large amounts than on policies for small amounts. In calculating life insurance rates, actuaries use electronic computers with the necessary assumptions to perform the computations in the program.

Health insurance

Computing health insurance premiums is similar to computing life insurance premiums: a net premium is computed, to which is added an amount to cover expenses, contingencies, taxes, and profit. The net premium is the claim rate multiplied by the average claim value. The claim rate, or claim frequency rate, is the percentage of claims arising during a year from the exposures. It is the probability that a claim will occur. The average claim value, or claim severity rate, measures the average claim amount.

In accidental death and dismemberment coverage, the proceeds payable always are those scheduled in the policy. So the claim frequency rate is all that is needed to compute the net premium. If the claim frequency for accidental death coverage is 0.55 per 1,000, then the net premium for $1,000 of coverage would be $0.55. For coverages such as disability income and hospital insurance, where both claim severity and frequency are important, actuaries have tables combining claim frequency and severity rates. These tables are called continuance tables. Table 25–5 is an excerpt from a continuance table for disability income insurance for a male age 40, based on an exposure of 100,000 lives. The values in column (2) are the number disabled per 100,000 exposures, distributed according to the length of disability. Column 3 values on a given line are obtained by subtracting the immediate previous values in column 2 from the immediate previous values in column 3. The values in column 4 are the values in column 3 added to the immediate previous values in column 4. Column 4 values are used to compute the net premium for a disability income policy.

TABLE 25–5
Continuance table for disability income insurance

(1) Days X	(2) Number disabled for exactly X days	(3) Number disabled for X or more days	(4) Total number of disability days accumulated through day X
1	1,410	32,810	32,810
2	1,810	31,400	64,210
3	2,010	29,590	93,800
71	36	1,762	574,429
72	34	1,726	576,155
73	32	1,692	577,847

Assume that a disability income policy issued at age 40 pays $20 a day after 3 days for a 70-day benefit period. Of 100,000 exposed lives at age 40, 93,800 days of disability will be accumulated through the third day. Through the 73rd day, 577,847 days of disability will be accumulated. As the policy has a 3-day waiting period and a 70-day benefit period, the total days of disability for which $20 income payments must be made, assuming 100,000 active lives insured, can be computed from Table 25–5 column 4 to be 577,847 less 93,800 or 484,047 days. The net premium would be $96.81 calculated as follows:

$$(484,047 \div 100,000) \times \$20 = \$96.81$$

Rating classes for health insurance consider such factors as age, occupation, sex, and geographical area. Their importance depends on the type of coverage. Geographical area is significant in rating major medical coverage but not disability income insurance. Broad age classes are used in rating optionally renewable disability income insurance, but narrow age groups are used for guaranteed renewable disability income coverage and major medical insurance. For most types of health insurance women usually are charged rates higher than those charged men because women experience a higher rate of disability. A 1976 study by the New York Insurance Department showed that for women in their 20s, disability income insurance should cost 40 percent more than disability income insurance for men. The differential for women in their 30s was 120 percent. Statistics reported for 1981 show women ages 17 to 44 had 30 percent more lost work days (per employed person) than men. The difference was 35 percent for ages 45 and over. An effort to require insurers to eliminate all sex discrimination in insurance rating is gaining support. Insurers are reacting with attempts to inform state legislators, insurance regulators, and the press of the reasons (where justified) for sex discrimination in insurance rates.

Summary

1. The states require insurers to charge rates that are adequate, not unfairly discriminatory, and not excessive. Rates also should be economically feasible, and encourage loss prevention.
2. One way to determine rate adequacy is to compare the actual loss ratio to the expected loss ratio. The loss ratio is the incurred losses (both paid and estimated for the period) divided by earned premiums.
3. In judgment rating, each exposure is rated on its merits; no established schedule or formula is used.
4. In manual rating all exposures in the same classification are charged the same rate. Ratemakers still must use judgment in setting class boundaries.
5. In merit rating all exposures in the same classification are charged the same base rate, but this rate is subsequently modified according

to the insured's loss experience (past, future, or both). The three types of merit rating are schedule rating, experience rating, and retrospective rating. Usually only large-sized insureds are eligible for most merit rating plans.

6. Objective standards characteristic of exposures in different manual classifications are set up in schedule rating. The insured exposure is compared to the standard, and the manual rate is adjusted accordingly.

7. In prospective experience rating, the manual rate is adjusted to reflect the insured's past experience. The losses experienced in the past several years are averaged and used to determine future rates, subject to a credibility factor.

8. The manual rate is altered to reflect the insured's experience during the policy period, under a retrospective rating system. The insured is charged a basic premium plus incurred losses, loss adjustment expenses, and premium taxes. This resultant premium is subject to both a maximum and a minimum charge.

9. Two old established fire insurance rating schedules are the universal mercantile system and the analytic system. Both, as well as a new system now in use, consider a building's occupancy, location, construction, and protection as fundamental factors affecting the rate.

10. Ratemaking for inland marine insurance is similar to that for fire insurance. Ocean marine insurance rates usually are negotiated. Ocean marine insurers consider the following factors in ratemaking: the ship's physical characteristics, the area of operation, the time period involved, and the vessel's ownership. Rates for cargo also depend on the cargo's susceptibility to damage.

11. Life insurance premiums depend upon the mortality, interest rates, and expenses assumed by the actuaries. The higher the assumed mortality rate, the higher is the premium; the higher the interest rate, the lower is the premium.

12. Health insurance rates depend on such factors as morbidity rate and expenses.

Questions for Review

1. The rate for insurance is expressed in terms of units. The units are expressed differently among various types of coverages. Explain by use of an example how and why the unit of measurement differs among coverages.

2. Distinguish earned premiums from written premiums and incurred losses from paid losses.

3. Why are loss ratios expressed as a percentage of earned premiums while expense ratios are a percentage of written premiums?

4. How can insurance premium rates encourage loss prevention activities?

5. What charges are included in the manual rate? Explain.

6. What is the pure premium method of manual rate calculation? When is it used? When would an insurer be more likely to use the loss ratio method?

7. In what lines of insurance is the schedule rating technique used?

8. Distinguish prospective experience rating from retrospective experience rating.

9. Why does the cost per unit of insurance decrease in some lines with the increase in the number of units purchased?

10. Compare and contrast the universal mercantile system with Dean's analytic system.

11. In general terms, explain the concepts involved in setting life insurance premiums.

Questions for Discussion

1. Do you agree with the statement that perfect rate equity is possible to achieve in practice? Why or why not? How can rates be made to be more equitable?

2. Part of the premium paid under retrospective rating is the amount of incurred losses for the policy period. Who might be interested in purchasing insurance under such a premium determination arrangement? Explain.

3. If an insured elects a retrospective rating plan, what might be the motivation to elect plan C rather than plan B or plan A? Explain. What would be the motivation to elect plan A or B rather than plan C? Explain.

4. What interest rate do you feel insurers should now assume when issuing a whole life policy for a person 25 years old? Why? Do you advocate a unisex mortality table for computing life insurance premiums? Annuity premiums? Explain the logic supporting your views.

5. Explain the use of a W value and a B value in a retrospective rating formula. Explain why the lower the B factor, the greater the credibility given to the insured's experience.

6. Explain why you would or would not favor the experience grading and rating schedule.

7. Explain how the concept of credibility is used in the process of (a) manual rating, (b) prospective experience rating, and (c) schedule rating.

8. Does the ratemaking process in health insurance have a greater resemblance to that in life insurance or to that in property insurance? Explain.

9. How do you explain that rates for some coverages decrease as the amount of insurance bought increases, whereas in others the rate is the same regardless of the amount of coverage purchased? Should there be this difference?

10. Auto insurance pricing tends to be full cost pricing in that rates are based on expected future costs. However, insurers have been unable to exercise control over auto accident costs. How could insurers do more to reduce the frequency and severity of auto losses? Would loss prevention activities of other property liability insurers (e.g., boilers and machinery) be appropriate for auto insurers? Explain.

Financial structure

Up to this point, attention has focused on the insurers' function of reducing risk in the economy. But, inevitably, in collecting premiums and holding the money to pay losses, insurers become investment intermediaries. Their contribution in the field of capital formation is significant. The Armstrong Investigation in New York, 1905–6, led by Charles Evans Hughes, publicly recognized for the first time the power of life insurers in investment markets. The investment potential of life insurers is much larger than that of property and liability insurers.

Two Skeleton Balance Sheets

This chapter can be simplified by first inspecting skeleton balance sheets of a property liability insurer and a life insurer. A balance sheet is a statement of assets, liabilities, and net worth. Assets are what the firm owns, liabilities are what it owes, and net worth is the difference between the two. Liabilities and net worth represent an accounting valuation of the debt and ownership interests in the assets. Thus in the balance sheets shown in Figures 26–1 and 26–2 the debt interest *reported* in the property insurer's assets is $40,085,000, represented by liabilities, and the *reported* ownership interest is $14,840,000, represented by net worth. The debt interest *reported* in the life insurers' assets is $137,-426,000, and the ownership interest *reported* is $19,155,000. An insurer's principal liabilities are reserves, which represent for a property insurer an obligation on behalf of its policyholders for premiums received but not earned and for losses incurred but not paid, including loss adjustment expenses. For life insurers, the reserve is computed actuarially to measure the insurer's net obligation under outstanding policies. Note the use of the word *reported*. True liabilities and net worth usually are different from that reported. While assets also may be misstated, the main problem in determining an insurer's true net worth is in the valuation of its reserves.

It is common to speak of reserves as if they were assets and not liabilities. When the statement is made that the chief source of an insurer's investible funds is its reserve, the statement refers to the assets that offset the reserve liability. A statement that money goes into the reserve means that the reserve liability valuation is increased by that amount. Finally, a statement that the insurer pays the claim partly from its reserve refers to a decrease in the reserve liability valuation and not to the assets used to pay the claim. Obviously, one existing liability cannot

FIGURE 26–1

THE GANDALF MULTILINE INSURANCE COMPANY
Balance Sheet
December 31, 1985

Assets

Bonds	$29,920,000
Common stocks	13,735,000
Preferred stocks	1,880,000
Real estate	460,000
Cash	570,000
Premium balances receivable	4,270,000
Investment income accrued	110,000
Other assets	3,980,000
Total assets	$54,925,000

Liabilities

Unearned premium reserve	$10,740,000
Loss and loss expense reserve	24,150,000
Reserve for taxes and expenses	1,280,000
Reserve for all other liabilities	3,915,000
Total liabilities	$40,085,000

Net Worth

Capital	$ 1,265,000
Surplus (including retained earnings)	13,575,000
Total net worth	14,840,000
Total liabilities and net worth	$54,925,000

FIGURE 26-2

THE ETERNAL LIFE INSURANCE COMPANY
Balance Sheet
December 31, 1985

Assets

Cash	$ 225,000
Bonds	58,965,000
Stocks	7,125,000
Real estate	3,280,000
Mortgage loans	70,860,000
Policy loans	11,095,000
Premiums receivable	3,795,000
Investment income accrued	1,015,000
Other assets	221,000
Total assets	$156,581,000

Liabilities

Net policy reserves	$118,980,000
Policy claims	1,005,000
Dividend accumulations	10,987,000
Reserves for dividends	2,190,000
Reserve for taxes and expenses	795,000
Securities valuation reserve	1,345,000
Premium deposit funds	1,160,000
Other liabilities	964,000
Total liabilities	$137,426,000
Capital	2,000,000
Surplus (including paid-in surplus and unassigned surplus)	17,155,000
Total net worth	19,155,000
Total liabilities and net worth	$156,581,000

be used to pay off another liability. In discussing an insurer's financial structure, the meaning of such loose statements is apparent from the context.

The principal net worth item is "surplus." Capital stock insurers also have an account called "capital," although the amount usually is less than surplus. These accounts together represent the ownership interest. The term surplus, like reserve, also is often used as if it were assets. The statement that losses are paid out of surplus means that assets decrease more than liabilities so that surplus, a residual item, also decreases. The statement that reserves are replenished from surplus means that the reserve liability increases more than assets so that surplus decreases. Again, the meaning of such statements will be apparent from the context.

Reserves of Property and Liability Insurers

Property and liability insurers maintain three principal types of reserves: unearned premium reserves, loss reserves, and voluntary reserves.[1]

Unearned premium reserves

All states require property and liability insurers to maintain unearned premium reserves, which equal the unearned portion of the gross premiums of all outstanding policies at the time of valuation. On a per policy basis, the unearned premium for a one-year fire policy written on the first day of the month with an annual premium of $120 would be $110 at the end of the first month, $90 after three months, $60 after six months, $30 after nine months, and zero at the end of the year.

If an insurer's premium writings are stable, the reserve will remain constant. A small insurer selling fire insurance policies producing a monthly gross premium income of $24,000 would always have insurance in force on which the unearned premium would be $144,000: one half of the $288,000 annual premium income, because only one half of it will be earned at any time. As long as premiums are written at the rate of $24,000 monthly, the reserve remains unchanged. If premium volume is expanding, additions must be made to the unearned premium reserve. If it is declining, the reserve will be reduced.

The unearned premium reserve is computed either by formula or on each individual policy. Three popular formula methods are in use. Under the *annual pro rata method,* the assumption is that policies are issued at an even rate throughout the year. A December 31 valuation assumes that all policies were issued July 1, the average issue date. The unearned premium reserve for one-year policies is one half of the net written premium for the policies. Net written premiums means retained premium income.[2] This formula method is used principally by insurers whose net written premiums are relatively even throughout the year.

Insurers with a nonuniform premium volume throughout the year may use the *monthly pro rata method* of computing the unearned premium reserve. It assumes that policies are issued at an even rate throughout the month and that all policies are issued on the 15th of the month in which they are written. For a December 31 valuation date, all one-year policies issued the previous January would require an unearned premium reserve of 1/24 of the net written premium. One-year

---

[1] Readers desiring more information on reserves and other financial topics should refer to Robert W. Strain, ed., *Property-Liability Insurance Accounting* (Kansas City, Mo.: Insurance Accounting and Statistical Association, 1974). Also see reference cited in footnote 8 of this chapter.

[2] Retained premium income consists of premiums not ceded to another insurer through reinsurance.

policies written in April, July, and October would require an unearned premium reserve of 7/24, 13/24, and 19/24, respectively.

The use of computers enables an insurer to calculate the unearned premium reserve *to the day* on each policy. The computer records include the effective date of the policy, the expiration date of the policy, and the policy premium. The unearned premium is the number of days remaining in the policy period divided by the total number of days in the policy period, times the premium in force. For example, if an annual policy was effective on August 2, 1983, it would expire August 1, 1984. If the premium were $400, the unearned premium calculation for December 31, 1983, would be:

$$\frac{214}{366} \times \$400 = \$233.88[3]$$

Redundancy of the reserve. Because the reserve is based on gross premiums, it contains considerable redundancy, or excess valuation, assuming competent performance by the underwriting department and an adequate rate structure. The agent retains a portion of the gross premium as a commission. The remainder is sent to the home office to be allocated for expenses (most of which are incurred and disbursed in the first month) and for payment of claims. The redundancy in the unearned premium reserve is the excess of the unearned gross premium over the expected claims and expenses for the unexpired term of the policy.

The unearned premium reserve is sometimes called the reinsurance reserve. But even if the insurer should withdraw from the business, the reserve would be redundant, as the cost of reinsuring its business should be less than the insurer charged its policyowners. Suppose an insurer with an unearned premium reserve of $1 million terminates its business. How much must it pay another insurer to assume its policy obligations? If the other insurer acquired $1 million in gross premiums through its own agents, it would have to pay commissions and other expenses associated with writing policies. So, less than $1 million would have to be paid to the acquiring insurer, leaving the original insurer assets equal to the redundant portion of its unearned premium reserve.

Even should an insurer have to refund to its policyholders their pro rata share of premiums for unexpired protection, the full unearned premium reserve would not be required. When a refund is made the agent contributes that part representing the commission. Thus, the unearned premium reserve is higher than required to meet all refund claims of policyholders. (Of course, it is conceivable that when the time comes for the agents to refund their commissions it may be impossible to find them, or they may not have the money for the refund.) This redundancy results in an overstatement of liabilities and an understatement of sur-

---

[3] The total number of days in this policy period is 366 as this term includes February 29, 1984, a leap year. If the term did not include leap year, the denominator would be 365. Although this point is a minor one, it is a persistent problem as computer programmers consistently overlook leap years in unearned premium calculations.

plus. As an insurer's ability to write insurance is a function of the amount of its surplus, the understatement of surplus can contribute to an insurer capacity problem, which is manifested by the inability of insurers to write sufficient insurance to meet the public's needs.

The unearned premium reserve is one of the larger liabilities of insurers writing property liability insurance. The insurer whose balance sheet is shown in Figure 26–1 is a multiline insurer. Its unearned premium reserve is 27 percent of its liabilities, a typical percentage for a multiline insurer.

Loss reserves

The loss reserve measures the insurer's estimated liability for unpaid claims and settlement expenses as of the valuation date. It includes the amount of liability for claims (1) reported and adjusted but not yet paid, (2) filed but not yet adjusted, and (3) incurred but not yet reported. For each category, it includes the value of the claims themselves and expenses of adjusting them.

The relative size of the loss reserve to total liabilities varies among coverages. For workers' compensation and health insurance, benefit payments scheduled to be paid during the disability period are discounted for interest and mortality. Discounting is not used in computing loss reserves for other coverages. The loss reserve for liability and workers' compensation includes estimates of the probable disposition of claims upon which litigation is pending or in process. The loss reserve for health, workers' compensation, liability, and crime insurance includes an estimate for claims under expired policies for yet-to-be discovered losses occurring before the policies expired. Fire insurance loss reserves primarily include claims in the process of being settled. Unreported fire insurance claims usually consist of losses that have occurred so recently that notice has not reached the insurer. If the policy expires and the property has not burned, no liability can arise. Also, fire insurance claims are paid in single sums rather than installments. The percentage of loss reserve to total liabilities for the multiline insurer in Figure 26–1 is 60 percent.

Calculating the loss reserve. How does the insurer determine the level of its loss reserve? Most large insurers employ an actuarial staff which is assigned the task of determining the appropriate level of the loss reserve. Actuaries utilize a variety of methods to calculate the loss reserves. In general these methods rely on historical experience to determine trends that can be applied to the present and the future.

One method that can be used if many claims are outstanding with the same relative size distribution is the average value method. This method determines the average value of claims of various types and projects trends from the insurer's prior experience. Multiplying the present number of unsettled claims by the applicable average figure approximates the value of outstanding claims.

Another method is the individual case estimate method. This method utilizes claim department personnel's estimates of the value of each outstanding loss. A correction factor then is applied to the aggregate total to cover claims not yet reported and to reflect any consistent bias inherent in past claim reserving procedures. The advantages of the average value method over the individual case estimate method are greater efficiency (especially when many claims are involved) and freedom from dependence on individual judgment. Insurers prefer the average value method for coverages where the average claim value is moderate (e.g., auto physical damage).

A third method extrapolates the needed reserve from the value of losses paid to date in light of historical rates of loss payments. This payment development approach relies on an assumption of a consistent development of loss payments. Another method, known as the loss ratio method, required by statute for auto liability, other liability, medical malpractice, and workers' compensation, is discussed in Chapter 28.

Sufficiency of the loss reserve. Is there inherent redundancy in the loss reserve as in the unearned premium reserve? The answer is no; the loss reserve does not *automatically* understate surplus. However, an insurer can be overly conservative in establishing its loss reserve, thus understating underwriting profit (excess of earned premium over incurred losses and expenses). An insurer cannot set values for loss reserves so low that they might be viewed as inadequate. To do so could create problems with state insurance regulators who are concerned with the solvency of insurers. On the other hand, insurers cannot set values for loss reserves so high that the IRS will question their legitimacy and view them as excessive. Excessive loss reserving causes profits to be understated and thus reduces the insurer's tax liability for the period.

Another advantage of overstating loss reserves is that such practice makes profits appear inadequate, thus facilitating efforts to justify rate increases (in states that require a review of rate levels). A disadvantage of excessive reserves, for stock insurers, is that the underestimation of profit that results from the overstated reserves disappoints shareholders, thus causing the price of the insurer's stock to become depressed. The final determination of the loss reserve calls for a balancing of many different interests and objectives.

Voluntary reserves

The unearned premium and loss reserves are required by law. Insurers also set up many reserves that resemble those of other businesses. Reserves for taxes and dividends are among the voluntary reserves frequently encountered. Reserves for catastrophic underwriting losses once were set up, but the Financial Accounting Standards Board has outlawed this practice.

Reserve of Life Insurers

The principal reserve of life insurers is the policy reserve. It measures the amount which together with future net valuation premiums and interest will produce the exact amount needed to pay all policy obligations as they become due *if* the mortality experienced and interest earned are precisely as assumed. The premium charged the policyholder and the *net valuation premium* are not the same because the net valuation premium (1) does not include the expense allowance, (2) is not necessarily based on the same interest and mortality assumptions, and (3) may be adjusted to reflect other than the full reserve standard for measuring policy reserve. Policy reserve valuation standards are discussed in Chapter 28.

The nature of the reserve

Although the reserve is an aggregate accounting concept, it is helpful to think of it as divided and apportioned among blocks of business. A block of business is defined as a number of policies of the same type and face amount issued to a homogeneous group of the same age in the same year. The reserve can be computed for each block of business and aggregated to equal the total policy reserve.

The policy reserve exists because most life policies require installment premiums in excess of the amount needed to pay projected mortality claims during all but the later years of the policy's duration. Based on the 1958 CSO Mortality Table at 3½ percent, the net level annual premium (without expense allowance) for a $1,000 continuous-premium whole life policy issued at age 35 is $15.03. But the projected mortality cost for the first year is $2.15, rising each year thereafter but remaining under $15.03 until age 57, when it reaches $15.54. The difference between the net level annual premium paid and the amount needed to pay projected claims for the first 22 years produces an unearned premium. In that sense the policy reserve is an unearned premium reserve, even though the law refers to it as a policy reserve. When the reserve is viewed as applying to a block of business, the concept of an unearned premium reserve becomes clear, because eventually the policy reserve will decline as mortality costs for the block exceed both the premium income and the investment income generated by the assets supporting the "unearned premium reserve." The decline continues until the reserve reaches zero when the final projected claims are paid.

Assume that the number insured is equal to the 9,373,807 living at age 35 shown on the CSO Mortality Table reproduced in Chapter 25. If these people each pay $15.03 for a $1,000 continuous-premium whole life policy the insurer will collect $140,888,319. This amount, when invested at the assumed interest rate of 3½ percent, grows to $145,819,410 in one year. According to the mortality table, 23,528 insureds will die before reaching age 36. Each beneficiary receives $1,000 for a total of

$23,528,000 paid in death benefits. The claim payments reduce the fund to $122,291,410. This amount is the liability the insurer has to the remaining 9,350,279 policyowners. The reserve is $13.08 (rounded to even cents) for each $1,000 of coverage. Note the two reserve figures: $122,291,410 and $13.08. The first is the reserve for the block of business; the second is the reserve for each policyowner in the block.

These reserves behave differently with the passage of time. The reserve on the block of business increases each year as long as the amount by which the net level annual premiums collected plus the assumed interest earned exceeds the projected amount needed to pay claims. The reserve for the block increases to $1,309,495,065 at the end of the 10th policy year and to $2,273,575,920 at the end of the 30th policy year. At the end of the 40th policy year, it is $2,520,927,953 and has passed its peak. By the end of the 63rd policy year, the reserve is $5,997,778. While the insurer's reserve shown on the balance sheet is the combined figure for all blocks of business, as it should be, many people view the reserve as allocated to each policy. But although the block reserve starts to decline, the reserve allocated to an individual policy continues to increase. The reason is that the policy reserve is divided each year among the surviving insureds. Because the yearly decline in the number of insureds is larger than the decline in the block reserve, the reserve per policy (block reserve divided by the number of insureds) increases. For example, the individual reserve at the end of the 10th policy year is $145.49. Thereafter, increases continue and the reserve reaches $497.16 at the end of the 30th year, $658.74 at the end of the 40th year, and $934.96 at the end of the 63rd year, two years before the policy matures.

Computation of the reserve

In computing the policy reserve, two assumptions are made: premiums are paid at the beginning of the policy year and death claims due are paid at the close of the policy year. The reserve may be calculated retrospectively or prospectively. Measured retrospectively, it is computed on the basis of what has happened to net valuation premiums collected since the policy was issued. Assumptions as to mortality claims paid and interest income earned are required. Although retrospectively the insurer knows the mortality claims incurred and the interest earned, the reserve is based solely on assumptions. Deviations from assumed experience are reflected in the surplus account. Measured prospectively, the reserve is based on projections regarding future mortality claims, interest earnings, and net valuation premiums collected. Because the assumptions are identical, either approach yields the same result.

Assume that the insurer issues 9,373,807 continuous level premium whole life policies of $1,000 each to persons age 35. What is the third-year policy reserve? The reserve computed retrospectively is shown in Table 26–1. Table 26–2 calculates the reserve prospectively. The net valuation premium, $15.034902, is based on the 1958 CSO mortality table with 3½ percent interest using the full valuation premium reserve

TABLE 26–1

Third-year reserve, retrospectively calculated, for a $1,000 continuous premium whole life policy issued at age 35 to 9,373,807 insureds (1958 CSO, 3.5 percent, full reserve); net valuation premium $15.034902*

(1) Year	(2) Number living	(3) Net valuation premium	(4) Total fund	(5) Total fund accumulated at 3.5 percent for one year	(6) Death claims assumed to have been paid for the year	(7) Total reserve for year	(8) Reserve per policy
1.......	9,373,807	$15.034902	$140,934,270	$145,866,969	$23,528,000	$122,338,969	$13.05
2.......	9,350,279	15.034902	262,919,497	272,121,680	24,685,000	247,436,680	26.46
3.......	9,325,594	15.034902	387,646,072	401,213,684	26,112,000	375,101,684	40.22

* Differences in this table and Table 26–2 are a result of rounding the figures. For example, column 7 in this table should be the same as column 4 in Table 26–2.

method. The reserve for the third year is $375,101,684 for the block of business and $40.22 per $1,000 as shown in columns 7 and 8 of Table 26-1. The total fund (column 4) is the reserve at the end of the previous year (column 7), plus the product of the net valuation premium ($15.034902) times the number living at the beginning of the year (column 2). The fund is accumulated at 3½ percent (column 5), and assumed death claims (column 6) are subtracted to arrive at the total reserve (column 7). The "reserve per policy" (column 8) is the total reserve divided by the number surviving the year (column 2 divided by column 3).

The reserve for the block of policies calculated in Table 26-2 is $375,102,047 (column 4), which is the present value of future claims (column 2) less the present value of future net valuation premiums (column 3). The $40.22 reserve per $1,000 (column 5) is the total reserve (column 4) divided by the number surviving the year (column 1).

The prospective method is the most common and the one described in statutes regulating reserve liabilities. But if benefits are expressed in terms of the market value of an investment portfolio (variable annuities, for example), the present value of future claims in dollar amounts is unknown. In these cases, the retrospective method is more appropriate.

Redundancy of the reserve

The life insurance policy reserve, like the property liability unearned premium reserve, is considerably overvalued. While using the gross premium to compute the unearned premium reserve for property liability insurers overstates the reserve, using a premium *less than* the gross premium for computing the life insurance policy reserve overstates this reserve. If the present value of the gross premium (rather than the lower net valuation premium) were subtracted from the present value of future claims, the reserve would be lower. As the net valuation premium usually is less than the gross premium charged policyholders minus continuing expenses, the reserve is overstated. The 1958 CSO table has built-

TABLE 26-2

Third-year reserve, prospectively calculated, for a $1,000 continuous premium whole life policy issued at age 35 to 9,373,807 insureds (1958 CSO, 3.5 percent, full reserve); net valuation premium $15.034902

(1)	(2)	(3)	(4)	(5)
Number surviving third year	Present value of future claims	Present value of future net valuation premiums	Total reserve (col. 2 − col. 3)	Reserve per policy
9,325,594	$3,121,745,504	$2,746,643,457	$375,102,047	$40.22

in safety margins, and 4½ percent interest is low. While the use of the 1980 CSO mortality table and the indexed interest rates that accompany it will reduce the amount of mandatory reserves, they will remain somewhat overstated. The new table also has built-in safety margins, and the required rate of interest earnings are not burdensome to the companies. (See Chapters 25 and 28.) Life insurers on the average now earn nearly 9 percent after investment expenses. They have earned more than 3½ percent net for 56 of the past 71 years and more than 4½ percent net for the past 22 consecutive years. Thus life insurers have an equity in their policy reserves.

Other reserve accounts

Other reserve accounts of life insurers are of secondary importance. The reserve for policy claims includes claims reported but not yet paid, plus those incurred but not yet reported. Life insurance claims are reported and settled promptly, so this reserve usually is small. Life insurers provide settlement options and sell annuities which require payments to beneficiaries over long periods. Liability for these items appears in the Reserve for Annuities and the Reserve for Supplementary Contracts. They are a part of the net policy reserve shown in Figure 26–2. Also shown is a liability for policy dividends left with the insurer to accumulate at interest, for dividends declared but not yet paid, for funds deposited with the insurer in advance to pay premiums when due and for taxes, commissions, and other expenses incurred but not yet paid. If the insurer uses interest, mortality, and expense assumptions that produce premiums lower than the minimum valuation premium, many states require the insurer to create an immediate *deficiency reserve* liability equal to the present value of the amount by which future annual net valuation premiums exceed future annual gross premiums charged policyowners.

Earned Surplus of Property Liability Insurers

An insurer's capital and surplus represent the excess of assets over liabilities. Stock insurers have net worth items, consisting of the capital stock plus surplus accounts. Mutual insurers have no capital stock account; net worth is represented by surplus accounts only. Total net worth always is referred to as the policyowners' surplus, because the excess of assets over liabilities is available to pay policyowner claims. Property and liability insurers have two sources of earned surplus: underwriting profit and investment profit.

Underwriting profit

Underwriting profit arises from insuring operations but is not the amount reported in official statements, because a peculiarity exists in accounting for income in relation to expenses. When income is deferred, the normal practice is to defer directly associated expenses. But property and liability insurers are not allowed to defer expenses. To illustrate insurance accounting procedures, Table 26–3 (p. 701) shows the monthly accounting activity that occurs for an auto insurance policy, written on January 1, 1985, and effective for one year.

Column 1 indicates that the entire written premium is credited in January. Column 2 shows that earned premium is credited evenly throughout the 12-month policy period.[4] Only 1/12th of the total premium is earned in the first month. Column 3 illustrates the expected pattern of incurred losses and loss adjustment expenses for each month. Although each individual policy will not produce losses of small values every month, the ratio of incurred losses and loss adjustment expenses to earned premium tends to be nearly constant for the insurer. The figures in column 3 represent the average incurred losses and loss adjustment expenses in relation to the policy's earned premium.

Column 4 reflects the distribution of the insurer's expense relating to this policy. The commissions paid to the agent for writing the policy are credited at the inception of the policy. State premium taxes are accrued at the inception of the policy. A majority of the costs of processing the policy also are incurred at the beginning of the policy term. The accounting department processes the premium, the underwriting department reviews the underwriting file, and the data processing department inputs and updates the computer files. Although some expenses are incurred throughout the term of the policy, a substantial proportion of the total expenses of the insurer occurs within the first month. For simplicity, the assumption is made in Table 26–3 that all expenses are incurred in the first month.

Column 5 illustrates the statutory underwriting gain each month. Underwriting gain is calculated by subtracting the incurred losses and loss adjustment expenses and the operating expenses from the *earned* premium. In January an underwriting loss of $27 is reported because of the expenses incurred in the initial month of the policy. Each subsequent month yields an underwriting gain of $3 because the incurred losses and loss adjustment expenses are less than the earned premium. Column 6 shows the underwriting gain on a cumulative basis. Throughout the first nine months of the policy, the insurer is in an underwriting loss position. Not until the policy term has expired does the cumulative underwriting gain reflect the true profitability of this policy to the insurer.

As an insurer has thousands of policies with different effective and expiration dates, it is not practical for management to wait until all policies have expired in order to determine the profitability of the company. The method used to measure profitability involves calculation

---

[4] The exact calculation of earned premium would fluctuate about $10 depending upon the number of days in each month, as explained on pages 691 and 692. For simplicity, the assumption is made here that $10 is earned in each month.

TABLE 26–3
Illustration of statutory accounting procedures applicable to an individual auto insurance policy

	(1) Written premium	(2) Earned premium	(3) Incurred losses and loss adjust- ment expenses	(4) Operating expenses	(5) Monthly under- writing gain	(6) Cumulative underwriting gain
January.	$120	$ 10	$ 7	$30	$–27	$–27
February.	0	10	7	0	27	–24
March.	0	10	7	0	3	–21
April.	0	10	7	0	3	–18
May.	0	10	7	0	3	–15
June.	0	10	7	0	3	–12
July.	0	10	7	0	3	– 9
August.	0	10	7	0	3	– 6
September.	0	10	7	0	3	– 3
October.	0	10	7	0	3	0
November.	0	10	7	0	3	3
December.	0	10	7	0	3	6
Total.	$120	$120	$84	$30	$6	(not applicable)

of the combined ratio. This ratio is the sum of the insured loss and loss adjustment expense ratio and the operating expense ratio. The incurred loss and loss adjustment expense ratio is the ratio of the incurred losses and loss adjustment expenses to *earned* premium. The operating expense ratio is the ratio of operating expenses to *written* premium. Although these two ratios have different bases, they are added together to determine the combined ratio.

In the example shown in Table 26–3, the incurred loss and loss adjustment expense ratio for January is 70 percent, column 3 divided by column 2. The operating expense ratio is 25 percent, column 4 divided by column 1. The combined ratio is 95 percent, the sum of these two ratios. The combined ratio indicates that the insurer is paying out 95 percent of the premium for losses and expenses. Therefore, the underwriting profit is 5 percent of the premium (100 − 95). As the insurer in the example shown in Table 26–3 earned an underwriting gain of $6 on $120 of premium, or 5 percent, this method provides an accurate procedure for determining underwriting profits without waiting for the expiration of each policy.[5]

Because the statutory underwriting profit from a policy is understated in the first accounting period and overstated in later periods, financial analysts adjust the reported figures. A percentage of the increase (or decrease) in the total unearned premium reserve for the period is added to (or subtracted from) the reported statutory underwriting results to introduce some realism into financial reporting. Although the percentages vary among analysts, 35 percent is an intermediate figure. For example, an insurer in 1983 reported a statutory underwriting loss of $1,030,000, but 35 percent of the *increase* in the unearned premium reserve for the year was $2,456,000. The adjustment (−$1,030,000 + $2,456,000) converted the $1,030,000 statutory loss into a trade underwriting gain of $1,426,300 before taxes. Using the combined loss and expense ratio to measure underwriting performance, a profit of $884,000 is shown, as this ratio is 99.8 percent before taxes. (The net earned premium was $442 million.) In this example, the combined ratio method of measuring underwriting results produces a profit 38 percent less than that produced using an adjustment made on the basis of 35 percent of the change in the total unearned premium reserve for the period.

Underwriting results are affected by the precision used in determining loss reserves. Unlike the unearned premium reserve, no neat formulas are available to adjust the loss reserve. Losses reflected in underwriting results are determined by subtracting the beginning loss reserve

---

[5] The formula for the adjusted underwriting result is:

$$\text{Earned premiums} \left[1 - \left(\frac{\text{Incurred losses} + \text{Loss adjustment expenses}}{\text{Earned premiums}} + \frac{\text{Operating expenses}}{\text{Net premiums written}} \right) \right] = \text{Adjusted underwriting profit or loss.}$$

In the foregoing example, the adjusted underwriting profit is $6:

$$120 \left[1 - \left(\frac{84}{120} + \frac{30}{120} \right) \right] = \$6, \text{ the adjusted underwriting result.}$$

from the sum of losses paid during the year and the loss reserve at year end. The incurred loss reserves for the period will be overstated if the beginning loss reserve is too low or the ending reserve is too high. If so, the underwriting profit will be understated. Because the loss reserve must be estimated, underwriting profits may be randomly understated in some years and overstated in other years unless the insurer tries to control its reported results by manipulating its loss reserve.

Investment profit

An insurer's investment profits may be divided into: (1) net investment income earned (rent, interest, and dividends accrued), (2) net capital gains realized from sale or maturity of investments, and (3) net unrealized capital gains resulting from changes in the market or amortized values of investments.

Property and liability insurers often incur adjusted underwriting losses. Often they not only are able to offset these losses but also to pay dividends to stockholders because of investment income. Some industry analysts point out that this phenomenon successfully obscured underwriting losses in the early 1970s. But when inflation increased rapidly in the mid-1970s and contributed to heavy investment losses, insurers were unable to appear as financially healthy as in the past. Some well-known and respected insurers were close to technical insolvency in 1974 because of large underwriting losses and huge losses in their investment portfolios caused by the massive decline in the stock market. Underwriting losses continued in 1975. When the 1975 *Best's Ratings* were published a number of reputable insurers found their financial ratings lowered. Experience steadily improved following 1975, with the results of 1978 showing both record underwriting gains and record investment income. But a 1979 underwriting loss nearly as large as the 1978 gain turned out to be a gloomy but accurate predictor of things to come.

Property and liability insurer profitability

Much discussion is focused on the rates charged by property and liability insurers. Some sources maintain that premiums are too high and profits are excessive. Others argue that premiums are too low and profits are inadequate. If profits are too low, a reallocation of resources currently used in the industry will occur along with a decrease in new resources attracted to the business. If profits are too high, the industry is guilty of a consumer ripoff and the regulators of a failure to perform their duty to maintain rates that are not excessive (Chapter 25).

Although many studies have been undertaken, most notably the Plotkin–Arthur D. Little study, to determine whether profits are excessive, nothing is available that gives conclusive guidance to regulators in evaluating rate levels and thus profit levels. Table 26–4 reports the findings of econometrician Irving Plotkin in his landmark studies comparing

TABLE 26–4
Average annual rates of return on net worth, 1955–1967

	Percent
Stock property and liability insurers	7.0
Standard & Poor's industrials	11.8
Standard & Poor's utilities	9.1

the profitability of the property liability insurance industry with the average profitability of all industrial and utility companies reported by Standard and Poor's for 1955–67. Insurance industry earnings include statutory underwriting profits and losses, plus 35 percent of the change in the unearned premium reserve, net investment income (interest, rents, and dividends), realized capital gains and losses, and unrealized capital gains and losses. The net worth also is adjusted by adding 35 percent of the change in the unearned premium reserve to the statutory policyowners' surplus. Because property liability insurers' earnings include unrealized capital gains and losses, the variability of these earnings far exceeds that of industrial companies.[6] No other major industry had profits lower than the property liability insurance industry. During the four-year period covering 1975 through 1978, the underwriting results have varied from the worst experience ever recorded (losses of $4.3 billion in 1975) to the best experience on record (a gain of $1.4 billion in 1978).

The early 1980s again brought underwriting losses, and the combined ratio for the industry moved above 110 percent. However, high interest rates and improved stock market performance kept investment income ahead of losses. Thus, despite underwriting losses in the property and casualty insurance industry of $6.3 billion in 1981 and $10.3 billion in 1982, investment income of $13.2 billion and $14.9 billion, respectively, more than offset the poor underwriting experience. But the gap between

---

[6] See *Prices and Profits in the Property and Liability Insurance Industry,* Statements of Boodman and Plotkin of Arthur D. Little, Inc., before the Subcommittee on Antitrust and Monopoly Legislation of the Committee on the Judiciary, U.S. Senate, November 25, 1969 (Cambridge, Mass.: Arthur D. Little, Inc.), pp. 42–54. Dr. Plotkin's work on the profitability of the property and liability insurance industry generally has successfully withstood the attacks made upon it by some academicians who have questioned its validity and by others who have questioned its objectivity. After reviewing the Plotkin studies and those of his critics, the National Association of Insurance Commissioners has accepted in principle the Plotkin conclusion that the property liability insurance business as currently conducted is a low-profit business, and the flight of some capital from this business supports such a conclusion. It is not denied, however, that the property liability insurance business can be made more profitable by improving its operating efficiency. Dr. Plotkin, in his November 25, 1969, statement before the Subcommittee and in a communication to that committee on March 5, 1970, examines the criticism made of his initial work (Arthur D. Little, Inc., *Prices and Profits in the Property and Liability Insurance Industry,* Report to the American Insurance Association, November, 1967) and fights back by offering what he considers to be documentation that questions the scholarship, understanding, and objectivity of several researchers who have produced results significantly contrary to his own.

investment gains and underwriting losses continues to shrink. The 1983 results showed an underwriting loss of $13.3 billion and an investment gain of $16.0 billion. The combined ratio was 112 percent. The first six months of 1984 produced a whopping combined ratio of 117 percent. During this period, although investment income was $10.4 billion, underwriting losses were up to $9.87 billion, leaving a gap substantially smaller than experienced in previous years.

Unlike the problems of the 1970s, the current situation appears to be the result of heavy price competition among insurers. Many property liability companies decided not to raise rates despite the poor underwriting results. They felt this would help them generate greater amounts of written premium, thus giving them more funds to invest at interest rates of 13 percent and higher (and, in some cases, much higher). However, in spite of the lower inflation rate of the early to mid-1980s, it was nonetheless enough to push the underwriting losses of these insurers ever closer to their investment gains.

Earned Surplus of Life Insurers

In computing premiums, life insurers assume conservative mortality, investment, and expense experience. Surplus is increased when investment earnings (including net realized and unrealized capital gains) are more than anticipated, and claims and expenses are less than anticipated. Two financial statements show the degree and direction of the change in surplus: the summary of operations and the surplus account.

Summary of operations

The summary of operations shows the source of net gain (or loss) from the insurer's operations. Table 26–5 shows the source of gains flowing from operations of a large stock life insurer. The item *increase* in reserves could be a *decrease,* if, for example, reserves released from terminating policies exceed the increase generated from the advancing duration of old policies and the issuance of new ones. As policy reserves are conservative, profit is understated when reserves increase, and loss is overstated when reserves decrease.

Surplus account

Through the surplus account, surplus at year end is reconciled with that at the beginning of the year. An illustrative account is shown in Table 26–6. The increase in surplus for the year is $8,062 which is the ending surplus of $121,332 less the beginning surplus of $113,270.

Several items need explanation. The mandatory securities valuation reserve (MSVR) is designed to reduce the impact on surplus of rising and falling securities markets. The size of annual increments is determined by a complex formula under which percentages varying from

TABLE 26–5
Summary of operations ($000)

Column 1		Column 2	
Gross premiums accrued (including all considerations received for life and health insurance, annuities, policy proceeds left with the insurer under settlement options, but excluding reinsurance premiums paid to other insurers)	$290,433	Claims paid (including death, endowment, annuity health, surrender, settlement options, dividend accumulations, and interest on policy funds)	$191,055
Net investment income (including interest, dividends, and rents less investment expenses such as investment management expenses, investment taxes, depreciation, and depletion)	57,365	General insurance expenses (including administrative expenses, taxes other than federal income taxes, licenses, and fees)	55,952
Sundry receipts and adjustments (including fees for handling deposit administration pension plans, reserve adjustments with reinsurers, uncashed checks cancelled after a reasonable period, and so on)	635	Increase in reserves (including those for life, health, and annuity insurance contracts and for settlement options and dividend accumulations)	63,417
Total	$348,433	Total	$310,424

Gains from operations before dividends to policyowners and federal income taxes	$ 38,009
Dividends to policyowners .... $ 17,019	
Federal income taxes incurred 6,150	−23,169
Net gain from operations	$ 14,840

TABLE 26–6
Surplus account ($000)

Beginning surplus	$113,270	Dividends to stockholders	$ 5,239
Net operating gain	14,840	Net capital loss (realized and unrealized)	12,248
Decrease in mandatory securities valuation reserve	10,745	Net loss from nonadmitted assets	34
		Increase in liability for unauthorized reinsurance	2
		Ending surplus	121,332
Total	$138,855	Total	$138,855

0.1 to 1.0 are applied to the statement values of specified securities. The maximum value of the MSVR also is subject to a complex formula under which percentages vary to 33⅓ of the statement values of particular securities. Net realized and unrealized capital losses are allowable as a deduction against the MSVR, again subject to a complex formula.[7] Note that the illustrative insurer reported a net capital loss of $12,248, of which $10,745 was absorbed by a decrease in the MSVR rather than by surplus. (Because of the severe adverse stock market experience in the mid-1970s, some authorities have urged a MSVR for property liability insurers.)

The net loss from nonadmitted assets is the net amount of admitted assets converted into nonadmitted assets during the year. Reinsurance due from insurers not authorized to operate in the state must be shown as a liability.

Policy dividends

Life insurance surplus management is closely related to policy dividend practices. Two decisions are: how much surplus should be allocated for dividends and how the allocated funds should be apportioned among policyowners.

How much?   To be competitive, insurers seek to maintain a liberal dividend policy while still building surplus as a cushion against adverse investment and mortality experience. How much of the annual operating gain should be retained rather than paid in policy dividends is a matter of judgment, particularly considering that conservative actuarial assumptions and valuation methods generally overstate reserves and understate surplus. But the surplus that can be accumulated by an insurer writing participating policies is limited in some states to 10 percent of the policy reserve. (Limitations of surplus to a percentage of the policy reserve appears to be a questionable practice. Insurers that are already conservative in their reserving practices have an additional safety margin when their surplus is maintained at a specific percentage of those reserves. But insurers that aren't so conservative in their reserving methods, and thus presumably need a greater safety margin in their surplus account, are allowed to operate with surplus based on the same percentage of reserves as their more conservative competitors.) As reserves increase, insurers try to increase surplus. Thus, dividends paid usually will be less than gains from operation. Insurers seek to maintain stability in dividend scales, so no fixed relationship exists between operating gains and dividends. But flexibility demands that dividend scales change when a clear and lasting trend in gains becomes apparent.

---

[7] See Joseph C. Noback, *Life Insurance Accounting: A Study of the Financial Statements of Life Insurance Companies in the United States and Canada* (Homewood, Ill.: Richard D. Irwin, 1969), pp. 105–9, for an in-depth study of the MSVR, and other life insurance financial structure subjects discussed in this chapter.

Apportionment. Most states require policy dividends to be apportioned and paid annually. Dividends are payable from surplus arising from savings in mortality costs, expense loadings, and interest earned in excess of the rate assumed in computing the premium. Savings in mortality costs arise because assumed death rates exceed those experienced by most insurers. This phenomenon is particularly true of persons recently insured. The mortality table used most often is one from which newly selected lives have been excluded. As newly insured persons have just passed selection tests, fewer deaths than predicted by mortality tables should occur. The more important reason for mortality savings is the general overstatement of mortality in the tables. The overstatement arises from the deliberate safety margin included and the general improvement in mortality experience that tends to make the table obsolete at some time during the policyowner's life. The saving in expense loading arises when the cost of acquiring and servicing the business is less than that assumed. Insurers issuing participating policies believe in collecting too much rather than too little. Any excess may be returned as policy dividends. Conservative practice dictates that the assumed interest rate be below the average rate the insurer believes it will earn on its assets. While dividends are not influenced often by capital gains on investments, they can be influenced by extended capital losses.

The objective of dividend apportionment is to achieve an equitable distribution based on each policy's contribution to the savings in mortality costs, expenses, and excess interest earned. The highest contributors to mortality cost savings are made by those policies with the highest amount at risk per $1,000 of insurance (the difference between the face amount and the policy reserve). The greatest contributors to savings in expense loading are those policies with the highest face amounts, and the largest contributors to excess investment income are policies with the highest policy reserve per $1,000 of insurance. Thus apportion dividends on only one factor would be inequitable.

In 1863, the pro rata or contribution plan of dividend apportionment was introduced and is the basis of nearly every insurer's formula for apportioning dividends, subject to modifications by individual insurers based primarily on actuarial philosophy rather than on principle. This method attempts to apportion dividends based on the contribution of each block of policies to the year's total divisible surplus. Each block of policies is credited with contributions and debited with charges made to surplus by the block. The balance is the basis for the dividend. The plan is called the three-factor system of dividend apportionment. The three factors are mortality savings, loading savings, and excess interest earned.

The three-factor system operates as follows for a given block of policies (policies of a given type issued in the same year to insureds of the same age, sex, and insurability classification).

Credit the block of policies with:

1. The aggregate reserve at the beginning of the year.
2. The excess of aggregate expense loadings over incurred expenses.

3. Interest earned for the year on items 1 and 2.

   Debit the block of policies with:

1. The aggregate reserve at the end of the year.
2. The aggregate mortality cost experienced.

The credit balance is the amount contributed by the block to surplus and is the basis upon which policies in that block will share in the surplus allocated for dividends.

Investments of Insurers

Distinct differences appear in the aggregate investment portfolios of property liability insurers and life insurers. Differences also are found in portfolios of individual insurers within classifications. Table 26–7 shows the aggregate portfolio distributions of these two types of insurers as a percentage of assets. Life insurers invest less in corporate stocks than do property liability insurers and are significant investors in mortgage loans. What accounts for these differences? Legal restrictions and expedient financial practices are important considerations. Legal restrictions are discussed in Chapter 28.

Expedient financial practices

Property liability insurers usually find that conservative financial practices dictate investing only a small percentage of assets in common stocks. The ratio of premiums written to policyowners' surplus for property liability insurers is about 2.0 to 1. If these insurers invested heavily in common stocks, a steep market decline would significantly lower sur-

TABLE 26–7
Assets held by property liability insurers and life insurers as a percentage of total assets

Type of investment	Percentage of total assets held by	
	Property liability insurers	Legal reserve life insurers
Corporate bonds	13.1	36.2
Stocks	24.9	9.5
Mortgages	.9	24.1
Real estate	†	3.5
Policy loans	NA	9.0
Government securities*	60.2	9.4
Miscellaneous	.9	8.3
Total	100.0	100.0

* Special revenue bonds are included with government securities.
† Included in miscellaneous category

plus, severely limiting capacity and threatening solvency. Aside from separate accounts, life insurers writing participating policies do not invest as much in common stocks as the law allows. Some people argue that life insurers have the capacity to increase their aggressiveness as investors.

Life insurers have accepted the thesis that good business policy dictates an interest in the environment. They have responded through their urban investment programs to improve housing, service, and job opportunities in the urban core. Management's objective in the investment of assets is the highest yield possible consistent with policyholder security and the fulfillment of social responsibility.

Financial Reporting

Much concern has been shown over the accounting practices used by life insurers. The earnings of life insurers are reported on a statutory basis and are appropriate for the purpose of revealing insolvencies. However, for the investor this method fails to reveal the present or future earning capacity of a life insurer. Under statutory reporting, an insurer that is expanding significantly may report little or no profits, whereas a moribund insurer may show large profits. To correct this condition, the American Institute of Certified Public Accountants has issued accounting guidelines utilizing generally acceptable accounting principles (GAAP) to adjust life insurance company statutory earnings to make them more meaningful to security analysts and potential investors.

Life insurers would still report their conservative statutory earnings to regulatory agencies but also would compute earnings according to the requirements of GAAP. Under these guidelines, the figures reported to investors would use the "natural reserve" rather than the statutory reserve. The natural reserve is a calculation using the same mortality and interest assumptions used in the calculation of the natural premium. The natural premium is computed to be sufficient to pay both expenses and death claims. The costs of acquiring new business would not be expensed immediately, as under statutory reporting, but would be spread over the expected premium-paying period. Although the concept of two different financial reports, one to investors and one to regulators, does not appeal to some insurance experts, many believe it to be a step forward.

For property liability insurers the NAIC has developed a standard form for measuring insurance company profits, and several members are urging that insurers be required to use it to report profits. They perceive a need for a uniform and authoritative standard to facilitate public discussion of insurer profits. A recent New York superintendent of insurance has pointed out that, without a standard profitability formula, anyone with an ax to grind can make claims or denials about the level of insurer profits. The result is not only public confusion, but also public mistrust. Even so, the industry opposes what it calls an imposition of "artificial formulas" to control profitability. It claims that diverse risks, investments, operations, and other factors including the diverse administrative, legislative, and judicial standards applied by states to the inclusion of investment income in insurance pricing, preclude using a uniform formula system to determine a profit division in insurance rates.

Summary

1. The unearned premium reserve of property liability insurers equals the unearned portion of the gross premiums of all outstanding policies at the time of valuation. As it is based on *gross* premiums, the reserve has some redundancy because many expenses occur when the policy is first issued. The requirement that insurers reserve for expenses which have already been paid results in an overstatement of liabilities and an understatement of surplus.

2. The loss reserve of property liability insurers estimates claims and settlement expenses as of the valuation date. Although this reserve contains no inherent redundancy the possibility is present for an insurer to overstate consistently the reserve to influence operating results. Regulators because of their concern for insurer solvency are concerned that insurers do not understate their reserve, whereas the IRS is concerned that insurers do not overstate their reserve.

3. The life insurer's principal reserve is the policy reserve, which measures that amount which together with future net valuation premiums and assumed interest will be sufficient to pay assumed policy obligations when due. This reserve is significantly overvalued as it is based on valuation premiums rather than gross premiums, and on low interest and overstated mortality assumptions.

4. Total net worth is called policyowners' surplus, as the excess of assets over liabilities is available to pay policyowners' claims. Property liability insurers obtain earned surplus from underwriting profit and investment profit.

5. True underwriting profits differ from that reported in statutory financial statements, as property liability insurers cannot defer expenses. Thus, formulas have been developed to convert statutory underwriting results into estimates of true underwriting results.

6. Property liability insurers sometimes are able to conceal bad underwriting results with investment profits. This practice was not possible during the mid-1970s, due to the recession and the resultant negative action of stock prices. Experience of the mid-1980s appears to reaffirm the difficulties of trying to offset underwriting losses with investment gains.

7. The surplus of life insurers is increased when (*a*) mortality costs are less than assumed, (*b*) expenses are lower than charged, or (*c*) interest earned exceeds the rate assumed in premium calculations. Many life insurers pay out excess surplus as dividends to

policyowners. The three-factor system attempts to apportion dividends to policyowners equitably on the basis of each policy's contribution to surplus.

8. Insurers differ significantly in their investment practices. Legal restrictions account for some deviations, but fundamental differences between the investment practices of mutual property liability insurers and stock property liability insurers, and between property liability insurers in general and life insurers based on expedient financial practices also are important.

9. The question of the profitability of the property liability insurance industry has received much attention over the past years. A landmark study showed that for the period 1955–67 the average annual rates of return on net worth of the property liability insurance industry was the lowest among major industries. The study has been both attacked and defended by the academic community.

10. Efforts have been made to achieve a standard of financial reporting that serves the investment community to accompany the standards that serve the needs of regulators. The American Institute of Certified Public Accountants and the NAIC have participated in the movement toward more meaningful financial reporting to the public.

Questions for Review

1. The unearned premium reserve is usually computed by formula. What type of insurer would use the annual pro rata formula? Monthly pro rata formula?

2. What does it mean to say that a reserve is redundant? What type of reserves are considered to be redundant? Why?

3. The text points out several methods that may be used to calculate the appropriate level of the loss reserve. Discuss the major assumptions needed in the use of each method, and explain how these assumptions can be useful in helping the actuary decide on the loss reserving method to use.

4. Explain how an insurer can overstate its underwriting profits by manipulation of the loss reserve. Why would an insurer want to overstate or understate its profits? How does an overstatement of loss reserves affect insurer capacity?

5. In *general* terms, explain how the policy reserve for life insurers is calculated.

6. Differentiate between the premium charged policyowners and the net valuation premium. Why do these differ? Explain.

7. Given the following information about a fire policy:

Net written premium	= $1,200
Earned premium	= 100
Loss + loss adjustment expenses	= 60
Allocated overhead	= 10
Commissions	= 300
Premium taxes	= 50
Underwriting expenses	= 120

Calculate the statutory underwriting result associated with this policy. Also compute the adjusted underwriting result. Why do these two figures differ?

8. Explain the purpose of the mandatory securities valuation reserve for life insurers.

9. Why was it necessary to devise a system similar to the three-factor method for apportioning dividends among policyowners? Which block of policies accounts for the most savings in mortality costs? Expenses? Most excess interest?

10. What basic differences are there between the investments made by life insurers and those made by property liability insurers? Explain the reasons for the differences.

Questions for Discussion

1. Discuss the problems associated with adjusting the loss reserve. Have you suggestions that would eliminate the need to adjust the unearned premium reserve or the loss reserve?

2. The emphasis in insurance accounting is on financial conservatism. Discuss three insurance accounting procedures that you consider to be conservative and show their impact on financial measurements.

3. Do you think life insurers should be required to use more realistic interest and mortality assumptions? Why or why not?

4. What has been the effect of the lack of profitability of the property liability insurance industry?

5. Does it seem strange that the use of the gross premium in computing the unearned premium creates redundancy in the fire insurance unearned premium but that the lack of use of the gross premium in computing the life insurance reserve contributes to its redundancy? Explain.

6. Explain four separate and distinct factors that can cause a drain on the surplus of property liability insurers and why such drains can lead to mounting capacity problems for these insurers. What suggestions can you offer to clog each of these drains? Evaluate your suggestions according to a set of criteria and standards you have developed for that purpose.

7. Do you believe it should be necessary for insurers to provide two different financial reports—one for regulatory authorities and another for the public? Discuss.

8. Do you believe that it is in the public interest to allow the property liability insurance industry to earn a fair profit? Explain.

Regulation of the insurance business: Objectives, methods, and history

Government control over economic activity has several objectives: (1) eliminate unreasonable monopolies, (2) regulate natural monopolies, (3) assure fair competition, (4) conserve and allocate natural resources, (5) make industry bear its full costs of production, including social costs, (6) promote an expanding economy, (7) protect the people's safety, health, and welfare, (8) eliminate invidious discrimination based on such factors as age, sex, marital status, race, and religion, (9) protect consumers and investors, and (10) regulate those businesses affected with the public interest. Regulation of insurance fits into this pattern.

Objectives of Regulation

The underlying reason for insurance regulation is to protect the public from incompetent and fraudulent insurers. Insurance requires public confidence. Incompetency and dishonesty caused many insurer failures in early American history. Failures reached a peak during the expansion period following the Civil War when policyowners lost money, and the entire industry was under suspicion. As the public had no indication the insurance business ever would conduct itself in the public interest without government supervision, public regulation was inevitable.

Why is there public concern over the continued solvency of insurers but not over continued solvency of most industrial and mercantile companies? The reason is that insurers promise to pay if and when the event insured against occurs, but payments from buyers are required in advance. Industrial and mercantile companies sell goods usually delivered to the buyers before payment. If an insurer becomes insolvent and is unable to honor its promises, its customers lose not only the purchase price but also resources relied on to replace damaged property, meet liability claims, provide income during periods of disability, pay medical expenses, or support surviving dependents. Furthermore, persons winning judgments against insureds may be unable to collect damages, creating a social injustice.

A business affected with a public interest

Insurance long has been a regulated business but not until 1914 was it held by the U.S. Supreme Court to be a business "affected with a public interest." In *German Alliance Insurance Company* v. *Lewis,*[1] the insurer contended insurance was a private business and public regulation of its rates violated the 14th Amendment declaring "No state shall . . . deprive any person of . . . property without due process of law."[2] The court ruled insurance was affected with a public interest because of its important role in other businesses. Therefore, it was in the public interest for most insurer activity including its rates to be regulated by the government.

The concept of a business affected with a public interest originated in 1676 by the British jurist, Lord Chief Justice Matthew Hale. (An interesting sidelight is that the U.S. Supreme Court apparently misunderstood Lord Hale's use of the concept of a business "affected with a public interest." In Lord Hale's writings, the concept related to items such as dedicated streets rather than commercial enterprises. In discussing the former type of commerce before the British Supreme Court, Lord Hale said it always had been subject to price regulation by Parliament. Thus, it seems that the phrase "affected with the public interest" as used in its pristine form was later misapplied, and that the concept as now used was born out of error. Nevertheless, the concept in its abortive form has been used by many courts since that early decision, and attributed to Lord Hale.) However, not until 200 years later in *Munn* v. *Illinois*[3] did the court establish *first* that a business was affected with the public interest and *then* apply "due process." In this case, the U.S. Supreme Court affirmed the state's right to regulate "properties . . . with a public interest." The Court reasoned "when [people devote their] property to a use in which the public has an interest, [they] in effect [grant]

---

[1] 233 U.S. 380 (1914).

[2] It had been decided in *Santa Clara County* v. *Southern Pacific Railway,* 118 U.S. 394 (1886), that a corporation is considered a "person" and has protection under the "due process" clause.

[3] 94 U.S. 113 (1876). This case involved state regulation of public grain elevators.

to the public an interest in that use and must submit to be controlled by the public for the common good to the extent of the interest [they have] thus created." Such control was held to be a legislative question and not a judicial one involving "due process." Thus, the courts cannot substitute their judgment for that of the legislature on a regulatory policy under the disguise of "due process." The Court said "for protection against abuses by legislatures, the people must resort to the polls, not to the courts." Until this landmark case, the right of states to regulate prices had been opposed on the ground that property owners are entitled to a reasonable return even though the property's use was "clothed with a public interest." Furthermore, the contention was that determining reasonableness is a question for the court, not the legislature. Confiscatory prices, however, may be set aside by the court.

All business is subject to governmental regulation. A business affected with a public interest means that it is forced to operate in an environment more restrictive than business in general. What is the logic of subjecting insurer management to more restraints than those imposed upon a local manufacturer? If the local company fails, some people suffer hardships: owners and employees of businesses dependent on the company's payroll for a healthy local economy. Could it be said that this business also is affected with a public interest?

What determines whether a business is affected with a public interest? Are there any criteria that can be applied to support the conclusion that an insurer but not a manufacturer is a public interest business? In *Munn* v. *Illinois,* the Court said that property becomes "clothed with a public interest when used in a manner to make it of public consequence and affects the community at large." But the court offered no set of criteria that could be applied in resolving questions of degree of "public consequence" and degree to which "the community at large" must be affected before the property becomes clothed with a public interest.

The concept of a public interest is not a fixed one. It is dynamic and varies with court opinion, which changes from time to time to reflect current social and economic conditions, along with shifts in public opinion. The concept is shaped "by the prevailing morality or the strong and preponderant opinion" relating to what is "greatly and immediately necessary to the public welfare."[4] At one time, the Court held a narrow concept, that of protecting public utility consumers from excessive charges and inadequate service. Public regulation was deemed to be more effective than competition as a regulator of public utilities because they could operate more efficiently as monopolies. The public interest concept later was enlarged to include other situations in which an inequality of bargaining power existed among participants. For states to protect the weaker party "where the parties do not stand upon an equality, or where the public health demands that one party to the contract

---

[4] *Noble State Bank* v. *Haskell,* 219 U.S. 104, 31 Sup. Ct. 186 (1911).

shall be protected against him [or her] self"[5] was held to be in the public interest.

In 1934 the public interest concept was broadened further in *Nebbia* v. *New York*[6] involving a New York statute fixing milk prices. Because milk had not been considered a public interest business, public control over its prices was challenged as a violation of "due process." The Court held that the concept "affected with a public interest" is not limited to public utilities but extends to any industry which "for adequate reasons is subject to control for the public good." The Court said "if public policy demands regulation in the public welfare, no constitutional principle bars the state from correcting existing maladjustments by legislation touching prices."

Regulation and competition

Two studies in the early 1900s reported on the effect of regulation and competition in the insurance industry. The Armstrong investigation of 1905, a New York legislative committee study of the life insurance industry, disclosed serious financial reporting abuses resulting from ineffective regulation. The Merritt Committee investigation of 1910, a New York legislative investigation of the practices of nonlife insurers, concluded that price competition led to destructive rate wars and insurer insolvencies. The premise of this report was that marginal insurers would attempt to gain fire insurance business by lowering rates. The better managed insurers would be forced to match these rate reductions, whether the new rate level was adequate or not. This action and reaction would lead to increasingly inadequate rates eventually resulting in widespread insurer insolvencies when major fires occurred. Whether this scenario developed anywhere outside the imaginations of the committee members is unclear, but the effect of the report was to support cartel insurance pricing.

The major current studies of the insurance industry refute the findings of the Merritt Committee. Former New York Superintendent of Insurance Stewart observed that

> . . . the property and liability insurance business has refined its pricing and underwriting methods, has grown and become more sophisticated, is exhibiting more diversity in price and distribution and manifests a real willingness to compete in prices. While much is still to be learned about insurance market structure and conduct, the structure is propitious for real competition—entry to the industry is easy, concentration is low, sellers are numerous, the product is largely undifferentiated, and total sales are expanding rapidly.[7]

---

[5] *Holden* v. *Hardy,* 169 U.S. 366, 18 Sup. Ct. 383 (1898). This was a case involving labor legislation.

[6] 291 U.S. 502 (1934).

[7] Richard E. Stewart, "Ritual and Reality in Insurance Regulation," in *Insurance, Government, and Social Policy,* ed. Spencer L. Kimball and Herbert S. Denenberg (Homewood, Ill.: Richard D. Irwin, 1969), pp. 29–30.

Effectively regulated price competition should increase the availability of quality insurance and reduce insurer insolvencies by discouraging the formation of marginal insurers to supply the market avoided by established insurers because of inadequate rates. Regulation and competition should reinforce each other in the interest of the consumer, with price competition the prime factor for allocating resources to and within the industry and regulation the main factor for assuring fair competition. The U.S. Department of Justice concluded that

> . . . a predominant segment of the property liability insurance industry is favorably structured for competition, with a large number of competitors, relatively moderate concentration, ease of entry, a standardized service, a relatively simple and short-term contract, and an increasingly price-sensitive consumer market.[8]

State regulatory authorities must recognize that price competition adversely affecting profit levels of less efficient insurers could lead many to offer inferior products and economize on service. These insurers might (1) introduce excessive policy exclusions, (2) engage in undesirable claims practices, (3) be tempted toward unfairly discriminatory competitive practices by servicing "low-risk" clientele and avoiding or overcharging "high-risk" clientele, (4) institute excessive nonprice competition which might mask the true nature of the product, adding to potential consumer grievances, and (5) seek to obtain business by offering established agents unusually high commissions which might lead to excessive premiums to maintain solvency. These practices could seriously damage public confidence in insurance.

In summary, the prevailing regulatory sentiment is that competition in insurance should be fostered if it remains healthy and that regulation is necessary for healthy competition. A wide range of opinion is found regarding what constitutes healthy competition and how to promote it. The various state rating laws and their administration reflect these differences of opinion. However, there appears to be no opposition to the regulatory objectives that premiums be adequate, not excessive, and not unfairly discriminatory.

The fundamental question is how to achieve these objectives? How freely should insurers be allowed to price their product? How much inconvenience and expense is reasonable to impose on those seeking to price products competitively? How much authority and responsibility should regulators have in setting standards for measuring rates against the criteria of adequacy, reasonableness, and unfair discrimination? What is an adequate rate? What is an excessive rate? Can a single rate be inadequate for one insurer, excessive for another, and proper for still another? What constitutes unfair rate discrimination? What degree of price competition or price control is in the public interest?

The answers to the many questions about the correct role of public

---

[8] *The Pricing and Marketing of Insurance,* a report of the U.S. Department of Justice to the Task Group on Antitrust Immunities, January 1977, p. xi.

regulation in pricing insurance are by no means clear, as indicated by the debate generated by the issues. Variation among state laws, in the administration of similar laws, and in the regulations applicable to different types of insurance is found.

Diverse hypotheses. The various attitudes toward rate regulation and the role of competition can be summarized in the following diverse hypotheses:

1. Open competition is the most effective means of assuring insurance availability at adequate rates.
2. Fair rates can be assured only by requiring the insurance commissioner to review and pass judgment on every rate change.
3. State made rates, to which all insurers adhere, is the optimal form of ratemaking.

These hypotheses are mutually exclusive and illustrate the conflicting viewpoints toward insurance regulation. Resolution of these conflicts is necessary in order to achieve the most effective form of insurance pricing for the public.

Other reasons for regulation

Insurance is *technical* and in some ways mysterious to the public. The buyer usually is at a disadvantage because the seller generally knows more about the product. Policies contain terms unfamiliar to the buyer. Public control is necessary to prevent some insurers from including unreasonable restrictions and exclusions in their contracts.

Another reason for government regulation of insurers is its *fiduciary nature.* Public control is appropriate in an attempt to prevent insolvencies and to protect the public following an insolvency. Professor Mayerson distinguished between solvency and rate regulation:

> Many persons tried to justify rate regulation in property insurance on grounds of solvency . . . [F]ew insurance departments are equipped to second-guess company actuaries in matters of rate adequacy. . . . [T]he only time a . . . rate is rejected as inadequate . . . the true motivation . . . has been its effect on the competitive struggle, and adequacy or the lack of it has been only an excuse . . . [C]ertain states . . . which require all companies to conform to [a] state-set rate pattern, have had more insolvencies than states which allow free competition in rates . . . [T]he branches where rates are completely unregulated—primarily life insurance and health insurance—have done much better from the viewpoint of rate adequacy than has property insurance.[9]

State regulatory authorities are concerned about insurer insolvencies and believe that research on that subject is badly needed.

The Subcommittee on Antitrust and Monopoly, Judiciary Committee,

---

[9] Allen L. Mayerson, "An Inside Look at Insurance Regulation," *The Journal of Risk and Insurance,* 32, no. 1 (March 1965), p. 52.

U.S. Senate, and Senate Commerce Committee studied the insolvency problem that occurred principally among marginal insurers writing "high-risk automobile insurance" for people who have been "indiscriminately cancelled en masse" by established insurers. Following these studies, the U.S. Senate Commerce Committee proposed a federal insurance guaranty agency to provide for a nationwide indemnification plan for victims of insolvent property-liability insurers. By 1981, insolvency laws have been enacted in all states, most of them after the federal bill was introduced in 1970. These laws provide for assessment of solvent insurers to satisfy claims against insolvent ones.

Regulatory authorities are concerned with the *availability of insurance* to all applicants who should be reasonably expected to have coverage. Insurers in general are free to accept or reject any applicant. The underwriting standards of insurers presently are not subject to public regulation. However, insurers writing automobile liability insurance (in some states also automobile physical damage insurance) and workers' compensation insurance are required to accept their "fair share" of rejected business through assigned-risk plans.[10] The court denied regulatory authorities the right to prohibit insurers from "phasing out" medical malpractice insurance. A government industry program was introduced in 1968 to make fire and extended coverage insurance available to persons unable to obtain this insurance in the traditional market, particularly persons with property in central city areas. A program known as FAIR (Fair Access to Insurance Requirements) was established under the omnibus housing act of 1968 to provide reinsurance by the federal government for those insurers writing this coverage under a FAIR plan facility. FAIR plan facilities are established in some but not all states. The FAIR plan is discussed in Chapter 11.

While insurers generally are free to establish their own underwriting rules, they cannot engage in racial or sexual discrimination. In many states insurers are subject to anticancellation laws—particularly for automobile liability insurance—prohibiting indiscriminate cancellation of policies.

Equity is another purpose of regulation. One former commissioner asserts that the objective of maintaining equity "accounts for more than half the work done by insurance departments."[11] He divides his concept of equity into reasonableness, impartiality, and fairness, and defines these subdivisions as follows:

> Reasonableness means equity to policyholders as a group, impartiality implies equity between one policyholder and another, and fairness refers to the treatment of the individual insured. Under reasonableness, for example, comes regulation designed to assure holders of participating life insurance policies a fair share of the companies earnings. Under impartiality comes regulation requiring that these earnings be distributed equitably

[10] In *California State Automobile Association* v. *Maloney,* 341 U.S. 105 (1951), the U.S. Supreme Court held that the California compulsory assigned risk law was not in violation of "due process."

[11] Mayerson, "An Inside Look at Insurance Regulation," p. 53.

among the participating policyholders. And under fairness, for example, comes the effort of regulatory authorities to hear policyholders' complaints (usually regarding claim payments) and to take whatever action deemed necessary to correct any abuses.

Regulatory goals

Kimball raises the fundamental question "why regulate at all, or why regulate with the peculiar intensity and comprehensiveness with which the business is now regulated?"[12] After reviewing the various reasons given for insurance regulation, he concludes that taken alone none of them "would seem to justify the comprehensive regulation that now exists." Although he observes that "together they may come somewhat closer to justifying it," he believes in the abandonment of "the notion that insurance deserves comprehensive and general regulation" in favor of a determination of what "particular branches of the insurance business, or what particular aspects of it, need for special reasons to be regulated."[13]

Kimball reduces the purpose of insurance regulation to two objectives: (1) to assure that the industry is sufficiently solid financially to meet the expanding demand for coverage and (2) to assure that the industry operates with a sense of fairness, equity, and reasonableness in the market. He calls the first of these objectives *solidity* and the second, *aequum et bonum*.

In summary, the objectives of insurance regulation are to assure fair competition (whatever that means), monitor the solvency of insurers, help make insurance available to those who need and are entitled to coverage, and to assure equitable treatment of the insuring public. Regulation also protects innocent parties outside the insurance transactions, such as injured parties in liability claims and life insurance beneficiaries. Public regulation is welcomed by most people in the business (the concept of regulation generally but not necessarily any one specific type) because they believe it is necessary to control the brigands of the business. Those in the business favor controls which provide the best regulatory climate in which to operate and are adept in developing public interest arguments to support their positions.

Methods of Regulation

The American form of government operates through three divisions: legislative, judicial, and executive. All are involved in the regulation of insurance. Self-regulation is a fourth regulatory system.

---

[12] Spencer L. Kimball, "The Regulation of Insurance," in Kimball and Denenberg, *Insurance, Government, and Social Policy,* p. 4.

[13] Ibid., p. 5.

Legislative control

To govern the operations of insurers, all 50 states, the District of Columbia, and Puerto Rico have their own insurance laws and rules. They legislate on many matters, such as the licensing of agents and brokers, business methods, insurance rates, insurance availability, insurer solvency, types of policies and provisions, licensing of insurers, liquidation of insurers, and taxation. The police power gives the states the right to legislate in the interest of the safety, health, and welfare of its citizens. This power is one not delegated by the states to Congress but reserved for themselves. States are free to legislate as long as such legislation is not in conflict with federal law, even though such regulation may incidentally affect interstate commerce.

Drafting of legislation in the various states has not been left solely to legislators. Individuals and groups (generally associations of insurers, agents, or consumers) submit model bills to be sponsored by friendly legislators. Sometimes insurers may sponsor legislation which agents oppose, e.g., more lenient rules for writing group insurance. Agents may sponsor legislation which insurers oppose, such as stricter licensing requirements for agents. Various legislators lack objectivity primarily because of conflicts of interest. Consequently laws in the public interest often are impossible to pass. State legislatures rely on the insurance department to sponsor legislation and appraise proposed bills. The state's attorney general assists in drafting proposed laws. The National Association of Insurance Commissioners drafts "model" legislation. Also, the New York insurance code has influenced the codes of other states. Continuing growth in regulatory activity is anticipated as insurance remains a target of public concern.

Judicial control

Insurance also is regulated through judicial procedure. The courts interpret legislation when its meaning is challenged and also settle disputes among contracting parties. A court ruling on the constitutionality of insurance legislation or actions of the insurance commissioner becomes part of the body of insurance regulation.

Administrative control

Because insurance requires specialized knowledge, its regulation cannot be left to untrained lawmakers. State insurance departments are responsible for administering insurance regulation, and the official in charge is known as the commissioner, superintendent, or director. Regardless of the official title, the person occupying the position generally is referred to as the commissioner.

Insurance departments operate under legislative authority. They make and enforce rules within that authority. Decisions and rulings of the commissioners are subject to judicial review if any affected parties wish to challenge them. In making decisions, the commissioners create rules known as "administrative law." Administrative law, which has become identified with a multiplicity of agencies concerned with the regulation of economic activity, grew from the necessity for both flexibility and technical understanding, inherently impossible either in the normal legislative or judicial processes.

Qualifications of the insurance commissioner. Kimball writes that insurance "regulation could profit much by having officials far more cognizant than they are now, not only of the technical problems with which they deal but also of their obligation constantly to ask the fundamental questions. . . ."[14] He believes regulators "do not ask . . . persistently enough, what is it we are trying to seek . . . , and how we can best achieve what we want without unfortunate side effects." He thinks habit controls regulators who often mistake means for ends and continue to operate traditionally rather than consider a more effective and efficient approach. The financial and mental resources available to state insurance departments limit the quantity and quality of regulatory authority. The necessity for political considerations to take precedence, in some cases, over rational approaches also hinders appropriate regulatory action. A gain in regulatory effectiveness apparently can be achieved by reducing its quantity and increasing its quality.

After extensive hearings and study, the Senate Judiciary Antitrust Subcommittee charged that many insurance departments have inadequate administration and are lax and ineffective in controlling many insurance operations. The subcommittee found state insurance departments' budgets inadequate to meet their responsibilities. The subcommittee concluded that many departments were lax in dealing with monopoly, restraint of trade, unfair trade practices, and mergers, ineffective in the handling of insurer examinations, and inefficient in the admission and licensing of foreign insurers.[15] (A foreign insurer is one domiciled in another state; an alien insurer is one domiciled in another country.) The quality of insurance departments varies among states with the strong tending to upgrade the weak.

The National Association of Insurance Commissioners. George W. Miller, New York's second superintendent of insurance, sought uniformity in annual statements, examination practices, and laws, and therefore invited the insurance commissioners of all states to a meeting in 1871 at which the National Association of Insurance Commissions (NAIC), a voluntary organization, was formed. Some uniformity in insurance laws has been achieved by the NAIC. Over the years, the NAIC has grown into a constructive force. Although the full organization meets only twice a year, regional meetings are held, and its various committees hold hearings and conferences with industry representatives and super-

---

[14] Ibid., p. 16.

[15] *The Insurance Industry*, "Aviation, Ocean Marine, and State Regulation," pp. 240 ff.

visory authorities. A subject for legislation is studied, with industry representatives encouraged to state their positions, either individually or through committees. Model bills are prepared, which the commissioners often present to their respective legislatures. Some of the important committees and subcommittees of the NAIC as of the early 1980s indicate the range of interest of the association. They include:

Accident and health problems	Computer applications
All lines and financial services	Consumer participation
Annual reports (blanks) of insurers	Credit insurance problems
Automobile insurance problems	Employee pension and welfare revision
Availability of essential insurance	sion
Insurance advertising problems	Property and liability insurance problems
Insurance guaranty funds	lems
Laws, legislation, and regulation	Rates and rating organizations
Life insurance problems	Regulatory information
Prepaid legal expenses	Unfair trade practices
Professional liability insurance	Uniform agents and brokers licensing
Profitability and investment income in	Valuation of securities
property and liability insurance	Variable life insurance and annuities

As of early 1980, the NAIC paid primary attention to the use of sex and marital status as classification factors in automobile ratings, comprehensive health coverage, the question of state versus federal insurance regulation, the early detection of insurer insolvencies, the certification of loss reserves by qualified professionals, and life insurance cost comparisons. To study specific problems within the broad range of its interests, the NAIC has a number of task forces composed of its members. These task forces utilize advisory committees made up of industry and public members.

Duties of the insurance commissioner. In his classic work, *The Insurance Commissioner in the United States,* Patterson says: ". . . sometimes the insurance commissioner is an official clerk, sometimes he [or she] is a judge, sometimes he [or she] is a law-giver, and sometimes he [or she] is both prosecuting attorney and [executor]. He [or she] is partly executive, partly judicial and partly legislative; and yet is not confined within any of these categories."[16]

Some of the more specific duties of the commissioner can be outlined. For example, in *regulating the financial solvency* of insurers, the commissioner has the power to (1) license insurers that meet the state's financial requirements, (2) revoke licenses of insurers with impaired finances, (3) examine insurers periodically and make spot examinations whenever expedient, (4) require adequate valuation of reserve liabilities, (5) require reasonable valuation of assets, (6) approve classes of investments, (7) require adequate rates, (8) require filing of annual statements, (9) limit insurer expenditures, (10) act as a depository of securities in

---

[16] Edwin W. Patterson, *The Insurance Commissioner in the United States* (Cambridge, Mass.: Harvard University Press, 1927), p. 6.

those states with depository laws, and (11) liquidate insolvent insurers.

In *regulating trade practices,* the commissioner has the power to
(1) approve policy contracts, (2) require that rates be neither unfairly
discriminatory, inadequate, nor excessive, (3) investigate complaints of
policyowners and others as to rates, claims, underwriting, policy cancellations, commission payments, premium notices and refunds, premium
misappropriations, an agent or broker acting without a license, and other
grievances, and (4) serve, under the Unauthorized Insurers Process Act,
as the agent accepting service of process from domiciled insureds on
unlicensed insurers operating a mail-order business in the state.

In *regulating the marketing of insurance,* the commissioner has the
power to license insurance agents, brokers, adjusters and, in some cases,
counselors.

Self-regulation

In Chapter 23 several cooperative organizations of insurers and agents
are discussed. These associations exert some control over the business
through "codes of ethics" and various cooperative agreements. For example, standards for policy forms, advertising, education, and so on have
been adopted to protect the public. The fear of more public regulation
has instilled a "conscience" into some individual insurers forcing them
to act in the public interest. Self-regulation was the first type of regulation in the United States, and in England it remains the predominant
form.

The History of Regulation in the United States

Although insurance regulation can be traced long before the discovery
of America, the concern here is with its development in the United
States. The objective is to bring into focus the problem of state versus
federal control of the business.

Regulation by charter

The first type of public control over insurance was through restrictive
provisions in charters issued to insurers under special state statutes.
These charters contained many regulatory measures now in insurance
codes, such as investment restrictions, reserve requirements, and limitations on insurance offerings. A few chartered insurers exist today operating outside the authority of their state's insurance code. Under some
charters, insurers were required to reveal facts regarding their financial
condition to the legislature and the public. Publication of annual reports
was required of domestic insurers in Massachusetts as early as 1818.
Other states soon followed and passed laws that required agents of foreign insurers to file financial statements of their insurers with the state.

State insurance departments

Much of the early legislation was not enforced. Direct control of the business by the legislature proved inadequate. When the legislatures realized that supervisory power had to be delegated to an administrative officer, they appointed some state official to serve in that capacity. In New York it was the comptroller. In Massachusetts it was the state treasurer until 1836, when the task was transferred to the secretary of state. To these officials the regulation of insurers was a sideline and was performed in a perfunctory manner. To remedy this ineffectiveness, the next move was to create an administrative department, solely for insurance regulation.

New Hampshire was the first state to have a separate insurance commission when it created a three-man board in 1851. Eighteen years later the board was replaced by a single commissioner. Other states followed. Massachusetts, after three years with a three-man board, reduced it to two and, eight years later, to a single commissioner, the prevailing pattern today. Elizur Wright, the first of the dedicated insurance consumerists, was a member of the Massachusetts two-man commission. He is responsible for long-lasting reform in life insurance. Insurance commissioners generally are appointed by the governor, but in a few states they are elected. Regardless of whether the office is a major coordinate office as in most states, or a subordinate one attached to another division, the insurance commissioner wields substantial power over the industry.

Early attempts at federal regulation

In Canada a dual system of regulation has long been in force. The federal department supervises insurer solvency, and the provincial governments regulate contract provisions, agent licensing, and general insurer operations. In 1866 a bill was introduced in the U.S. House of Representatives to create a national Bureau of Insurance in the Treasury Department. In 1868, the Senate had a similar proposal. Both proposals were defeated. The country was not ready for a system of federal or dual control of insurance.[17] Then came the important decision in *Paul v. Virginia.*

Paul v. Virginia

During early U.S. history insurance was considered a proper subject for state regulation. No one questioned the constitutionality of such regulation until after Samuel Paul of Virginia became an agent for a group of New York insurers. Virginia law provided that nonresident insurers and their agents be licensed before doing business in the state. A security

---

[17] Many bills have been introduced into Congress proposing federal regulation of insurance. To this date none has been passed. See *Report of the Subcommittee on Federal Legislation to the Executive Committee of the National Association of Insurance Commissioners,* August 29, 1944, for a recital of early attempts to bring about federal control.

deposit was required to obtain the license. Paul was unwilling to make the deposit; therefore, the license was denied.

Paul continued to sell fire insurance but not for long. He was arrested, convicted, and fined $50. The case reached the U.S. Supreme Court. Paul's defense was based on two grounds: (1) the Virginia license law violated that portion of the Constitution granting citizens of each state all the privileges and immunities of citizens in the other states, and (2) insurance written by nonresident insurers was interstate commerce, and the Virginia license law was illegal interference by a state in interstate commerce. The decision was that (1) corporations are not considered citizens within the meaning of the equal rights clause and (2) insurance is not commerce within the meaning of the interstate commerce clause. With respect to the latter argument the Court said:

> Issuing a policy of insurance is not a transaction of commerce. The policies are simple contracts of indemnity against loss by fire, entered into between the corporations and the insured, for a consideration paid by the latter. These contracts are not articles of commerce in any proper meaning of the word. They are not subjects of trade or barter offered in the market as something having an existence and value independent of the parties to them. They are not commodities to be shipped or forwarded from one State to another and then put up for sale. They are like other personal contracts between parties which are completed by their signature and the transfer of consideration. Such contracts are not interstate transactions, though the parties may be domiciled in different States. The policies do not take effect—are not executed contracts—until delivered by the agent in Virginia. They are, then, local transactions, and are governed by the local law. They do not constitute a part of the commerce between the States any more than a contract for the purchase and sale of goods in Virginia by a citizen of New York whilst in Virginia would constitute a portion of such commerce.[18]

This position was upheld for 75 years in many cases,[19] the majority of which involved efforts of insurers to obtain a ruling that insurance was commerce and therefore not subject to state regulation.

In the early 1900s proposals were made for federal regulation of certain aspects of insurance. Upon advice of its judiciary committees, Congress refrained from enacting such legislation. The committees advised that *Paul* v. *Virginia* and similar cases had established that the federal government had no regulatory authority over the insurance business.

The South-Eastern Underwriters Association case

In 1942 the Missouri attorney general was stymied in his fight against an insurance ratemaking conspiracy and turned the headache over to

---

[18] 8 Wall 183 (1869).

[19] See for example, *Hooper* v. *California,* 155 U.S. 648 (1895); *Noble* v. *Mitchell,* 164 U.S. 367 (1896); *Hopkins* v. *United States,* 171 U.S. 578 (1898); *New York Life* v. *Cravens,* 178 U.S. 389 (1900); *New York Life* v. *Deer Lodge County,* 231 U.S. 495 (1913); *Northwestern Mutual Life Insurance Co.* v. *Wisconsin,* 247 U.S. 132 (1918); *Bothwell* v. *Buckbee Mears Co.,* 275 U.S. 274, 276–77 (1927); *Colgate* v. *Harvey,* 296 U.S. 404, 432 (1935).

the Antitrust Division of the U.S. Department of Justice. After a comprehensive federal investigation, the South-Eastern Underwriters Association (SEUA), which controlled 90 percent of the fire insurance and related lines in its area, was accused by the U.S. attorney general of violations of the Sherman Antitrust Act. It was indicted by the federal grand jury in 1942 for (1) restraining interstate commerce by fixing and maintaining arbitrary and noncompetitive premium rates on fire and related lines in the Southeast and (2) monopolizing commerce in insurance. The SEUA also was charged with fixing agents' commissions, using boycotts, and compelling prospective insureds to buy only from SEUA members on SEUA terms. Nonmembers of the SEUA were refused reinsurance opportunities, and their services and facilities were disparaged. Agents who represented nonmember insurers were denied the right to represent members, and customers who purchased insurance from nonmember insurers were threatened with boycotts and withdrawal of patronage. Local boards and bureaus were maintained to police the agencies and insurers.

The SEUA did not defend itself against these charges, although it claimed that, because of the nature of insurance, many of these practices were in the public interest. Instead, it relied on the defense that as insurance is not commerce, the Sherman Antitrust Act did not apply. Therefore, regardless of their actions, they could not be guilty of violating federal law. The federal district court upheld this view and dismissed the case, citing *Paul* v. *Virginia*.[20] The attorney general appealed to the U.S. Supreme Court contending that insurance was commerce and thereby subject to the federal antitrust laws. He claimed nothing in the Sherman Antitrust Act exempted insurance from its provisions. The Supreme Court reached a decision in June 1944, surprising many in the legal profession and the insurance industry, with a four to three decision (two justices excused themselves from the case) that insurance is commerce and, when it traverses state lines, it is interstate commerce.

The dissenting justices, Frankfurter, Jackson, and Chief Justice Stone, wrote strong dissenting opinions,[21] and the Court was criticized for deciding a constitutional question without a majority vote of all members. Nevertheless, as of June 1944, insurance officially became subject to federal regulation. The majority opinion stated:

> Our basic responsibility in interpreting the Commerce Clause is to make certain that the power to govern intercourse among the states remains where the Constitution placed it. That power, as held by this Court from the beginning, is vested in the Congress, available to be exercised for the national welfare as Congress shall deem necessary. No commercial enterprise of any kind which conducts its activities across state lines has been held to be wholly beyond the regulatory power of Congress under the Commerce Clause. We cannot make an exception of the business of insurance.[22]

---

[20] *United States* v. *South-Eastern Underwriters Association et al.,* 51 F. Supp. 712 (1943).
[21] *United States* v. *South-Eastern Underwriters Association et al.,* 322 U.S. 533 (1944).
[22] Ibid., p. 552.

The dissenting justices also agreed that insurance is subject to control by Congress. Justice Jackson stated: "I am unable to make any satisfactory distinction between insurance businesses and other transactions that are held to constitute interstate commerce."[23] Justice Frankfurter wrote: "The relations of the insurance business to national commerce and finance, I have no doubt, afford constitutional authority for appropriate regulation by Congress of the business of insurance. . . ."[24] Chief Justice Stone wrote: "Nor do I doubt that the business of insurance as presently conducted has in many aspects such interstate manifestations and such effects of interstate commerce as may subject it to the appropriate exercise of federal powers."[25]

The dissenting justices, however, did not accept the majority view that Congress intended the Sherman Act to apply to insurance. They would concede only that Congress had the power to regulate insurance under the commerce clause but that, as yet, Congress had not exercised that power. The majority opinion nevertheless was that the Sherman Act applied because it did not specifically exclude insurance.

The SEUA decision led to confusion and a belief that "if you disobey the State laws requiring rate-making organizations, for example, you will be punished, and if you obey them, you will suffer the eternal damnation of the Sherman Antitrust Act."[26] The matter, however, was not that serious, so only state laws not contrary to federal legislation applied. The rest were nullified by the SEUA decision. The power of the states to regulate insurance was not challenged by the SEUA decision. Justice Black pointed out in the majority opinion:

> Another reason advanced to support the result of the cases which follow *Paul* v. *Virginia* has been that, if any aspects of the business of insurance be treated as interstate commerce "then all control over it is taken from the States and the legislative regulations which this Court has heretofore sustained must be declared invalid." Accepted without qualification, that broad statement is inconsistent with many decisions of this Court. It is settled that, for constitutional purposes, certain activities of a business may be intrastate and therefore subject to state control, while other activities of the same business may be interstate and therefore subject to federal regulation. And there is a wide range of business and other activities which, though subject to federal regulation, are so intimately related to local welfare that, in the absence of Congressional action, they may be regulated or taxed by the states.[27]

If the Supreme Court in 1869 had upheld the right of the state of Virginia to regulate insurance on the grounds "that states may regulate interstate affairs so long as they do not improperly burden interstate

---

[23] Ibid., p. 585.

[24] Ibid., p. 583.

[25] Ibid., p. 563.

[26] J. B. Gontrum, *"Paul* v. *Virginia*—A Review of the Past and Look into the Future,"* American Bar Association, *Report of the Proceedings at the Chicago Meeting 1943–1944*, section on Insurance Law, p. 15.

[27] *United States* v. *South-Eastern Underwriters Association et al.*, 322 U.S. 533 (1944).

commerce, and so long as Congress is silent," it could have been spared the embarrassment of a reversal of an awkward decision held for 75 years.

Public Law 15

The continued authority for state regulation of insurance was clear. While the SEUA decision was pending, the Bailey-Van Nuys bill was introduced to establish congressional intent that the states continue to regulate insurance and that insurance should be exempt from the Sherman and Clayton Antitrust Acts. The "bureau" stock insurers (members of the rating bureaus) supported the bill because they did not want the antitrust laws to apply to their activities. The NAIC withheld its support because of its desire to curb the monopolistic practices which had led to the SEUA decision. The "independents" (those not members of the rating bureaus) also opposed the bill because of their interest in a freer competitive climate. This bill passed the House but failed in the Senate. The NAIC supported proposals that eventually were incorporated in the McCarran-Ferguson Act passed by Congress in 1945, as Public Law 15. This law ultimately was supported by all segments of the industry.

Public Law 15 stated that continued regulation and taxation of insurance by the states is in the public interest and that congressional silence is not to be construed as a barrier to state regulation. The law specifically exempted insurers from the Sherman, Clayton, and the Federal Trade Commission Acts until January 1948, later extended to July, when the fair-trade and antitrust acts became applicable to insurance if not regulated by state law. Section 3 (b) of Public Law 15, however, states that "nothing contained in this Act should render the said Sherman Act inapplicable to any agreement to boycott, coerce, or intimidate, or act of boycott, coercion, or intimidation."

The House Judiciary Committee report accompanying the McCarran-Ferguson bill stated:

> Nothing in this bill is to be so construed as indicating it to be the intent or desire of Congress to require or encourage the several States to enact legislation that would make it compulsory for any insurance company to become a member of rating bureaus or charge uniform rates. It is the opinion of Congress that competitive rates on a sound financial basis are in the public interest.[28]

Some interested parties interpreted this statement to mean that under the McCarran Act "only *voluntary* action in concert is to be sanctioned, and then only when regulated by States."[29] However in *Allstate et al.* v. *Lanier et al.* it was ruled that North Carolina's law requiring all insurers writing automobile liability insurance in the state to be members of the North Carolina Automobile Rating Office, with no rate devia-

---

[28] House Report No. 143, 79th Congress, 1st session.

[29] Arthur C. Mertz, *The First Twenty Years* (Chicago: National Association of Independent Insurers, 1965), p. 6.

tions permitted, is not in conflict with the McCarran Act or the Sherman Act. A U.S. district court said that the state is "authorized and has the power to go into complete regulation of the insurance business if the state legislature should so desire. If this is so, then the state can also limit the methods of competition."[30] This decision was upheld by the Court of Appeals for the Fourth Circuit, and the Supreme Court declined to accept the case for review.[31]

Developments after the McCarran Act

Congressional deference to state regulation of interstate commerce can be justified so long as this regulation remains in the public interest. If it becomes apparent that state regulation is deficient in serving the public, Congress is apt to assume the primary regulatory role. It is expected to review state insurance regulation periodically. During the first decade following the passage of the McCarran Act, states, under the leadership of the NAIC, passed laws to strengthen the supervision of insurance.

Model rating laws.   At a meeting of the NAIC Subcommittee on Federal Legislation in 1945, an all-industry committee was formed to study the effects of federal antitrust acts on insurance. The all-industry committee was composed of representatives from 19 national insurance trade organizations representing all segments of the industry. NAIC committees developed model fire and casualty insurance rating bills. After the bills were drafted and adopted by the NAIC, its subcommittee worked with the all-industry committee to reconcile disagreements. An important area of disagreement was whether filing of rates with the commissioner for review was necessary except where rates were made in concert. Independents believed that insurers making their own rates were free from antitrust action and needed no protection. Bureau insurers would not agree to a rating law requiring the filing of bureau rates only. However, independents and bureau insurers agreed to guarantees that would foster competition and not require the reporting of loss experience on classification systems inconsistent with filed rating systems.

Another disagreement focused on when rates were to be effective. Should rates have prior approval of the commissioner before they could be used, or should they be effective immediately after filing? Bureau insurers wanted "prior approval," and independents wanted "file-and-use." The compromise provided that filed rates could be used after a specified time unless specifically disapproved by the commissioner. However, the commissioner would retain the power to disapprove rates at any time even though they had been tacitly approved by failure to act during the initial period. A few states with model rating laws have adopted the file-and-use provision rather than the compromise recom-

---

[30] 242 F. Supp. 73 (E.D.N.C., 1965).
[31] 361 F. 2d 870 (4th Cir., 1966), Certiorari denied 385 U.S. 930 (1966).

mendation. The final rate regulatory bills, known as the All-Industry Commissioners Bills, were adopted unanimously by the NAIC in 1946.

During 1947 more than two thirds of the states passed new rate laws or amended old ones. By 1951, the other states had passed rate regulatory laws. Most of them generally followed the All-Industry Commissioners Bills, which neither require nor prohibit membership in rating organizations. Under these laws, if an insurer has its rates filed by a rating organization, it must use those rates unless it has the commissioner's permission to deviate. The rating organization may oppose the deviation at a commissioner's hearing. Any aggrieved insurer or rating organization can demand a hearing on any order of the commissioner, and following the hearing, it has the right to a judicial review of the commissioner's order.

The bureau insurers have taken advantage of the opportunity to resist deviations considered to be a major threat to their competitive position. While commissioners decide most cases, some are taken to court. The cost involved in fighting opposition to a proposed deviation generally outweighs the benefits expected, because in many jurisdictions the approval is for one year only. Independent filings, therefore, seemed less of a problem and more of an opportunity for aggressive insurers to compete favorably in products and prices. Opposition was met here, too, when an insurer wanted to subscribe to bureaus for some rates and file others separately. The New York Fire Insurance Rating Organization asked the New York Insurance Department to withdraw approval of the independent rate filings of the Insurance Company of North America. The INA, along with other insurers, had dropped their subscription in NYFIRO for most dwelling classes but retained their subscription for commercial fire lines and some dwelling classes. NYFIRO argued that INA could not subscribe to NYFIRO's rates for some classes and file independent rates for others. The commissioner upheld the right of partial subscribership pointing out that the All-Industry Commissioners laws do not give a rating organization a monopoly in rating services and that independent filings contribute to the type of competition sought by Congress and the New York Legislature. The commissioner's ruling was unanimously confirmed by the New York courts. The U.S. Supreme Court dismissed an appeal.[32]

NYFIRO also requested a hearing on independent rate filings of Allstate Insurance Company for fire and extended coverage on dwellings. NYFIRO claimed these rates (about 20 percent below those of NYFIRO) were inadequate because they could not be supported by Allstate's loss experience and that they would be confiscatory for NYFIRO companies. Allstate was then new in the fire insurance business and had based its rates on expected savings in expenses. Allstate contended that NYFIRO had no right to a hearing as an aggrieved person. The commissioner agreed with Allstate, but when his successor took office he granted

[32] *Cullen* v. *Bohlinger,* 284 App. Div. 963 (1954), app. dism. 308 N.Y. 866, app. dism. 350 U.S. 863.

NYFIRO the hearing, then ordered Allstate to increase its rates by about 6 percent. Neither party was satisfied so both appealed. Four years later the New York appellate division upheld the ruling.[33] The legal counsel for Allstate said that for the five-year litigation period Allstate showed substantial underwriting profits on the $3 million of premiums written at rates claimed inadequate by NYFIRO. The litigation had cost Allstate nearly $100,000.[34]

Other rating laws. Model laws are not in force in every state. Other types of laws are classified broadly as mandatory and permissive.

Mandatory laws either require membership in a specified rating bureau or vest ratemaking responsibility in a state agency. Mandatory rating bureaus are required for workers' compensation insurance in some states, fire insurance in others, and for both casualty and fire insurance in still other states. In one or more states, rates are state-made for workers' compensation insurance, automobile liability insurance, fire insurance, and general casualty insurance. The Senate Judiciary Committee observed that the "requirements of several state statutes for mandatory bureau membership substantially lessens competition and appears to be in conflict with the McCarran Act . . . in compelling all insurers to be members of rating bureaus or requiring that all rates be uniform by legislative fiat."[35] However, as mentioned, the Supreme Court refused to review a case in which the North Carolina compulsory uniform automobile rating law was upheld.

Under the *permissive laws,* if filing is required, insurers must file rates for information only. Rating bureaus are authorized, but the use of bureau or rating systems cannot be required. Members are free to use whatever bureau's rates and policy forms they wish. An agreement among members and subscribers or with the bureau to charge uniform rates is illegal. Insurers are free to charge bureau rates with the limitation that these rates not be excessive, inadequate, or unfairly discriminatory.

In several states with the *permissive-type laws,* the terms excessive and inadequate *are defined.* A rate is excessive only if unreasonably high *and* no reasonable degree of competition prevails. A rate is inadequate only if unreasonably low *and* its continued use would either endanger the insurer's solvency or create a monopoly. The terms excessive and inadequate, though appearing in *All-Industry Commissioners laws,* are *not defined.*

Permissive-type laws, known as no-filing and open-rating laws, have been enacted in more than half the rating jurisdictions. In some, these laws apply both to fire and casualty insurance, whereas in others they apply only to casualty insurance. One state with model rating laws ap-

[33] *Cullen* v. *Holz and Allstate* (1959), 181 NYS Ib 163, aff'd. by Court of Appeals, 161 N.E. Ib 392.

[34] *The Insurance Industry,* pp. 1251–55.

[35] *The Insurance Industry,* "Insurance: Rates, Rating Organizations and State Regulation," pp. 77–78.

plies them only to those insurance lines for which the commissioner determines that competition is lacking. In another state with model rating laws, independent casualty insurers are excused from filing rates. An argument against open rating is that competition does not prevent unfair price discrimination. Open rating has led to a variety of policies and rating systems which sometimes produce unfair price discrimination. Insurance departments, in administering open-rating laws, must be aware of possible abuses and attempt to prevent them.

Fair trade laws.   A Model Unfair Trade Practices Bill was approved by the NAIC, and all states have enacted the bill or a similar one. A number of practices are defined in the bill as either unfair methods of competition or unfair or deceptive acts. They include misrepresentation, false advertising, defamation, boycott, coercion, intimidation, false financial statements, questionable stock operations, suspicious advisory board contracts, unfair price discrimination in life and health insurance,[36] and commission rebates to buyers. The list of practices was not exhaustive, nor was it "intended to limit the powers of the Commissioner or any court review. . . ." In general, the unfair trade practices model bill grants the commissioner broad power to regulate, within the area of his or her jurisdiction, unfair competition and unfair trade practices.

Many states have passed antitrust laws applying to insurance under which interlocking directorates and capital stock acquisition of other insurers are permitted if the result does not "substantially lessen competition generally or tend to create a monopoly." In many states, control over mergers, acquisitions, and directorships is provided in insurance codes or by general business legislation.

Federal Trade Commission's challenge.   The general belief was that passage of state regulatory laws similar to the Sherman, Clayton, and Federal Trade Commission Acts would satisfy the McCarran Act provisions and therefore would eliminate any contingent applicability of these statutes. This belief was directly challenged by the Federal Trade Commission when it issued complaints against 41 insurers stating their health insurance advertising violated the Federal Trade Commission Act. The commission sought general jurisdiction over interstate advertising, in spite of state laws covering the subject.

The commission's theory was: (1) the state laws could not, by reason of constitutional limitations against extraterritorial regulation, effectively regulate advertising beyond its borders, thus leaving a vacuum in interstate advertising regulation that could be filled only by the Commission; and (2) the states and the Federal Trade Commission have concurrent jurisdiction, and the first one to regulate, by issuing a cease-and-desist order, has ultimate authority. These arguments were unanimously rejected by the U.S. Supreme Court.[37] Two insurers involved

---

[36] Unfair price discrimination in nonlife insurance is prohibited in the rating laws.

[37] *FTC* v. *National Casualty Co.,* and *FTC* v. *American Hospital and Life Ins. Co.,* 357 U.S. 560 (1958).

in the litigation were licensed by states in which they operated. They wrote no mail-order business and confined advertising to point-of-sale literature. The court reasoned "there is no question but that the states possess ample means to regulate this advertising within their respective boundaries." The Supreme Court, in denying the commission jurisdiction, developed two criteria for determining if the commission has jurisdiction.

1. The commission's jurisdiction is limited to advertising distributed within those states, other than an insurer's domiciliary state, having no regulatory law of the type contemplated by the McCarran Act. The Model Unfair Trade Practices Bill or its equivalent was judged to be such a law. The court found that all states had enacted the requisite laws so no jurisdictional gaps remained. Thus, the commission had no jurisdiction.

2. Even though a state has such a law, the commission has jurisdiction over advertising distributed in the state if constitutional (due process) limitations on the state's authority to regulate such advertising exist.

After losing the foregoing cases, the FTC withdrew its accident and health insurance advertising rules[38] and dismissed all other cases except those involving insurers using direct-mail advertising. It continued to assert jurisdiction over these insurers because mail-order insurers are not subject to the jurisdiction of states in which they solicit business. Therefore, those state laws could not protect their citizens against misrepresentations through the mail. Due process limitations on the states' authority made their laws ineffective, thus activating the standby authority of the commission.

The commission's assertion of jurisdiction over mail-order insurers was challenged. The Eighth Circuit Court ruled that the FTC had no jurisdiction, but the U.S. Supreme Court reversed the circuit court and remanded the case for further proceedings.[39] The basis of the circuit court's holding was that statutes of the insurer's domiciliary state (Nebraska) provided sufficient regulation to relieve the FTC of jurisdiction. A Nebraska statute prohibits a domestic insurer from engaging "there or elsewhere" in unfair or deceptive acts or practices in the conduct of the insurance business. The key to the 6 to 3 majority opinion of the Supreme Court is:

> We are asked to hold that the McCarran-Ferguson Act operates to oust the Commission of jurisdiction by reason of a single state's attempted regulation of its domiciliary's extra territorial activities. But we cannot believe that this kind of law of a single state takes from the residents of every other state the protection of the Federal Trade Commission Act. In our opinion the state regulation which Congress provided should operate to displace this federal law means regulation by the State in which the deception is practiced and has its impact.[40]

---

[38] These rules closely resembled those adopted by the NAIC one year earlier.

[39] *Travelers Health Assn.* v. *FTC,* 362 U.S. 293 (1960), reversing 262 F. 2d 241 (1959). The Travelers, a Nebraska mail-order health insurer, solicits in all states. It is licensed only in its home state of Nebraska and in Virginia.

[40] Ibid., pp. 298–99.

Thus, simply because an insurer's domiciliary state statute is worded to apply to an insurer's out-of-state operations, the protection available under the Federal Trade Commission Act is not denied to citizens in other states.

The Supreme Court did not consider the effect of regulation by states other than Nebraska because the circuit court had ignored the question. However, the question was considered by the circuit court when it received the case on remand. Its opinion was "the ultimate compulsiveness which would be necessary to enable the state to achieve control" would be absent even though the commissioner could issue a cease-and-desist order or an injunction.[41] The FTC has jurisdiction over unauthorized mail-order insurers for unfair trade practices by its power to initiate cease-and-desist or investigative actions. The FTC issued a "Guide for the Mail Order Insurance Industry" to apply to insurers selling through the mail in states where they are not licensed or if licensed do not sell through local agents.

U.S. Justice Department's challenge. The U.S. Department of Justice questioned the acquisition of the Kansas City Title Insurance Company (KCTIC) by the Chicago Title and Trust Company (CTTC), claiming it would result in the control by CTTC of over 70 percent of the title insurance business in Missouri and Wisconsin thus violating Section 7 of the Clayton Act.[42] It already controlled more than 95 percent of the business in Illinois. A court order was sought to require CTTC to divest itself of KCTIC. The defense was that the McCarran Act exempted the acquisition from the Clayton Act. The Justice Department argued that, as the acquisition cannot be regulated adequately by any one state, the McCarran Act exemption does not apply, and if it is to apply, the state must have a statute similar to Section 7 of the Clayton Act. The U.S. district court held for the Justice Department and noted that Illinois antitrust laws do not apply to insurance or to combinations with parties outside the state and, as CTTC is not licensed in Missouri, Missouri could deal only with the acquired insurer.

Although many insurers have merged without challenge, the Justice Department challenged the merger of the International Telephone and Telegraph Corporation and the Hartford Fire Insurance Company, a merger first rejected by Connecticut's insurance commissioner and later approved on revised terms. The Justice Department claimed the merger violated Section 7 of the Clayton Act by encouraging illegal reciprocity, by discouraging actual and potential competition, and by tending to trigger mergers by other companies seeking to protect themselves from the impact of this one. ITT and the Justice Department reached an agreement under which ITT was given the option of divesting itself within three years either of Hartford Fire or of three other specified holdings.

---

[41] *Travelers Health Association* v. *FTC,* 298 F. 2d 820 (8th Cir., 1962).

[42] *U.S.* v. *Chicago Title and Trust Co. et al.,* 242 F. Supp. 56 (N.D. Ill., 1965).

ITT chose to keep Hartford. The Justice Department said the settlement would help curtail the trend toward undue concentration by merger, but regretted not having a Supreme Court ruling on the applicability of existing antitrust law to big conglomerate mergers.[43]

Boycott, coercion, and intimidation are forbidden under the Sherman Act, and the McCarran Act offers no relief regardless of state regulation. Before the SEUA decision many insurance practices would have violated the Sherman Act had this act applied to insurance. After the SEUA decision, the Justice Department had to force discontinuation of these practices. For example, the Investors Diversified Services was held in violation of the Sherman Act by requiring its borrowers to place all their insurance on mortgaged property through a specified agent, broker, or insurer named by IDS. IDS was required by a consent decree to notify all loan applicants of their right to insure through any agent.[44] The lender, however, can require the borrower to use approved insurers, but the lender's standards must be reasonable.

In pre-SEUA days, local stock agents' associations introduced and enforced several rules involving boycott, coercion, and intimidation that would have been illegal under the Sherman Act. Restrictions were placed on both insurers and agents to curb competition. For example, a member agent was not allowed to represent (1) nonstock insurers, (2) insurers that bypassed agents by writing policies directly, (3) insurers that sold below bureau rates, or (4) insurers using local agents who were not association members. Insurers were restricted to a specific number of agents in an area and to reinsurance of member insurers only. Six years after the SEUA decision, the National Association of Insurance Agents informed state associations of its decision to refrain from helping to enforce these restrictive rules, but some local associations retained the rules anyway. The Justice Department had to attack these rules in court.

In *U.S.* v. *Insurance Board of Cleveland,*[45] the Justice Department questioned the legality of rules of the Cleveland Board. The court held that prohibiting member agents from representing insurers writing policies without agents and prohibiting agents from representing nonstock insurers were a group refusal "to deal which relies upon coercion to effectuate its purposes; and . . . it must be held to impose an unreasonable restraint of competition in interstate commerce." Similar action was taken against the New Orleans Insurance Exchange[46] with an identical decision affirmed by the U.S. Supreme Court. The defendants argued that the McCarran Act made the antitrust laws inapplicable, but the courts set aside this argument in view of Section 3(b) of the McCarran Act that "nothing contained in this chapter shall render the said Sher-

---

[43] The ITT merger also was challenged by consumer advocate Ralph Nader, who attempted to stall it through a series of legal moves.

[44] *U.S.* v. *Investors Diversified Services,* 297 CCH Trade Cases 116, Section 69, 574 (1954).

[45] 144 Supp. 684 (1955); 188 F Supp. 949 (1960).

[46] *U.S.* v. *New Orleans Insurance Exchange,* 148 F. Supp. 915, aff'd., per curiam, 355 U.S. 22 (1957).

man Act inapplicable to any agreement to boycott, coerce, or intimidate or act of boycott, coercion or intimidation."

U.S. Securities and Exchange Commission's challenge. Because the McCarran Act is limited to insurance, an important issue is the meaning of the "business of insurance." A significant question was whether variable annuities are insurance contracts and therefore entitled to the specific insurance exemption granted under the Securities Act of 1933 and the Investment Company Act of 1940. In a 5 to 4 decision, the U.S. Supreme Court overruled the U.S. district court and the U.S. court of appeals and held that the Securities Act of 1933 and the Investment Company Act of 1940 applied to insurers selling variable annuity contracts.[47] The court reasoned that variable annuities are not insurance because the issuing insurer "assumes no true risks in the insurance sense." The dissenting justices, however, considered the assumption of the mortality risk sufficient to make the variable annuity an insurance contract.[48]

Thus, life insurers writing variable annuities are subject to both state and federal regulation. The annuity is regulated as a security, the separate common stock account as an open-end investment company, and the salespersons as security broker-dealers.[49] However, exemption from the Securities Act of 1933 and the Investment Company Act of 1940 is granted by the SEC to equity-funded noncontributory group annuities written to fund qualified pension plans covering initially a minimum of 25 employees.[50] Also exempt from the Investment Company Act of 1940 are separate accounts to fund special retirement plans for the self-employed. However, variable annuities issued under these plans are subject to the Securities Act of 1933.

In October 1975 the SEC, by granting certain exemptions to the Variable Life Insurance subsidiary of the Equitable Life Assurance Society of New York, opened the way for that insurer to market VLI in nine states beginning in 1976. In November 1976, the SEC adopted a rule that would exempt VLI from some requirements of the Investment Company Act of 1940. Among other features, the rule granted certain exemptions applying to the limitations on sales loads. Also VLI separate accounts are exempt from a regulation which prohibits an unregistered investment company from operating and are exempt from the minimum capital requirements during the early years of the account. The premiums charged for variable life insurance are allowed to be determined on the basis of such considerations as age, sex, medical underwriting standards, and premium mode. A nonforfeiture option under VLI (including an automatic loan if required) may not comply with the requirement of the act. Thus legal problems are mostly eliminated, so that VLI is expected to expand in the near future. (However, the major draw-

---

[47] *S.E.C.* v. *Variable Annuity Life Insurance Co. of America et al.,* 359 U.S. 65 (1959).
[48] Variable annuities are discussed in Chapter 16.
[49] *Prudential Insurance Company of America* v. *SEC,* 326 F. 2d 383 (1964).
[50] See Chapter 19 for a discussion of qualified pension plans.

back of VLI lies not in legal complications, but in the major tenet of the insurance. VLI assumes that common stock price is positively correlated with the consumer price index in the long run. In the short run, this assumption does not always hold true, thus does not provide the originally intended advantages of VLI.)

State versus federal regulation

The issue of state versus federal regulation of the insurance industry is not new, having been a subject of debate for nearly two centuries. At certain times the controversy surrounding this issue has intensified, such as during the *Paul* v. *Virginia* case and the SEUA case. Currently, the intensity of the controversy again is increasing. President Carter appointed a National Commission for the review of Antitrust Laws and Procedures. One area of concern for this commission was the antitrust immunity that the McCarran Act provides for the insurance industry. In 1979, the commission produced its final report with the following recommendations:

1. The current antitrust immunity should be repealed and replaced with narrowly drawn legislation allowing cooperative activities only for limited, essential endeavors.
2. Competition should be relied upon as the most effective regulatory method.
3. The federal government should undertake additional analysis of insurance regulation.

Preferred regulation: state or federal?   A question frequently discussed is whether federal or state insurance regulation is preferable. Kimball comments: "To put the question . . . as if it were . . . one simple system against another is impossible to answer in so naive a form." He says "[T]he question should be refined to consider not only the kinds of federal regulation contemplated but also the changes that may occur in state regulation." The issue is not if federal "regulation is to be preferred to state regulation but rather what combination . . . of the two, in what variations of each, would best serve the interests of the public." Acknowledging it is a complex problem, he believes summarizing the advantages claimed for federal regulation and for state regulation is useful "even though it is . . . clear that neither will ever exist to the complete exclusion of the other, that they can be combined in different proportions and that each system is almost infinitely flexible and alterable."[51]

Advantages claimed for federal regulation.   Until F. D. Roosevelt's New Deal, many insurers favored federal regulation. Starting with *Paul* v. *Virginia* and continuing until the *SEUA* case, insurers presented brief after brief against state regulation insisting insurance was commerce.

---

[51] Spencer L. Kimball, "The Case for State Regulation of Insurance," in Kimball and Denenberg, *Insurance, Government, and Social Policy,* p. 414.

They favored federal supervision, because they believed it less burdensome. For many years, the states were more active than the federal government in controlling business. In recent years many insurers have shown increased interest in the alleged advantages of federal regulation because of disillusionment with state regulation, particularly rate regulation.

The following arguments in favor of federal control have been advanced:

1. The lack of uniformity in state codes and rulings complicate the problem of insurers operating in more than one state.

2. State regulation is expensive. Insurers are required to file reports in each state in which they operate. Maintenance of 51 regulatory bodies also is required.

3. Federal control would be more competent. Under a system of state regulation, insurers must guard against "bad" legislation in 51 jurisdictions, whereas, under federal control, lobbying activities could be limited to Washington. Because they are full-time representatives, members of Congress should be better equipped as legislators than are state lawmakers. They have more time to study legislation and are less subject to local pressures. Federal regulation advocates argue that a federal insurance commissioner appointed on merit would be better qualified than many state commissioners.

4. Exclusive, rather than partial, federal control of insurance would eliminate confusion created by conflicting and overlapping regulation.[52]

5. A final contention is that the national scope of insurance supports the logic for federal control. States find it difficult, if not impossible, to deal with some foreign and alien insurers.

Many of these arguments are illusory. First, a federal regulatory system probably would have regional offices issuing rulings inconsistent among districts. Second, other federal regulatory agencies are likely to increase their involvement in insurance regulation, resulting in confusion, conflict, feuds, and overlapping of jurisdiction. Third, bright young people attracted to Washington (if indeed they are) are not always attuned to reality and may lack the wisdom to recognize their limitations.[53] They are nevertheless eager to manipulate institutions regardless of a lack of knowledge or understanding of the issues and problems.

Advantages claimed for state regulation. Several arguments in favor of state control have been advanced.

1. State regulation, by considering local conditions which Washington authorities may not understand, helps assure equity.

2. Federal regulation might be arbitrary and bound in red tape. Insur-

---

[52] Dineen, Procter, and Gardner, "The Economics and Principles of Insurance Supervision," p. 53. One major life insurer reports that it is dealing with 65 federal agencies and departments (Institute of Life Insurance, *With an Eye on Tomorrow* [1967], p. 133).

[53] Kimball, "The Case for State Regulation of Insurance," in Kimball and Denenberg, *Insurance, Government, and Social Policy*, pp. 417–21.

ers can communicate more effectively with state lawmakers and regulators.

3. Some disadvantages of state regulation, such as nonuniformity, multiple examination of insurers, and ill-advised legislation, tend to be eliminated by the NAIC.

4. An error made in regulation is restricted to one jurisdiction, making experiments possible in limited areas without adversely affecting the entire country if the experiment fails.

5. Federal control could become a leveling factor weakening regulation in those states where both the code and its administration are strong.

6. Decentralization of political power is a desired objective. Problems which can be handled effectively by states should not be shifted to the federal government.

7. State regulation is a known entity. To cure the ills and build on the strengths of the present system is better than creating a new one.

Which is better?   The importance of the foregoing arguments depends on one's biases and perception. At the present time, politics suggests that states' rights are to be protected, but not at all costs. If the public interest can be served efficiently by state regulation, then states should be encouraged to meet the challenge. Federal control should be exercised only to fill a void in state laws. If this answer appears to be equivocal, its appearance is not deceiving. Those who fear federal regulation are aware that state regulation is now on probation and that federal regulation is "warming up in the bullpen." One observer interprets the regulatory scene as follows:

> If one wanted to plan for a Federal intervention, one could hardly conceive of a better approach than to foster such conditions which would make it impossible for state regulation to survive. . . . Those of us who have had experience with this problem in other fields know that the inroads made by the Federal Government are made a step at a time.[54]

The question of regulation of insurers is in a state of flux, and most parties do not want to abandon state regulation without giving it a chance to survive or providing it enough rope to hang itself. As of this writing, it is too early to know the probable outcome of the controversy.

Summary

1. Insurance is a business "affected with a public interest" and thus subject to regulation.
2. Regulation assures that the industry continues to be financially sound to meet the expanding demand for insurance and fulfill its fiduciary responsibility. Regulation also attempts to assure that the

---

[54] Paul S. Wise, "Discussion on Rate Regulation Revisited," in *Insurance and Government*, ed. Charles C. Center and Richard M. Heins (New York: McGraw-Hill, 1962), p. 433.

industry operates with a sense of fairness and equity and that it makes insurance facilities available to all persons who reasonably should be expected to have these facilities. It strives to provide insureds protection from unreasonable restrictions and exclusions in their policies.

3. Insurers are regulated by legislative, judicial, and executive authority. The executive authority is exercised through the state insurance commissioner. To some extent insurance also regulates itself.

4. The U.S. Supreme Court in the 1944 SEUA decision ruled that insurance is commerce, *reversing* the 75-year-old *Paul* v. *Virginia*. Nevertheless, regulation is predominately exercised by the states, although the FTC, the U.S. Justice Department, and the SEC have exerted control over some aspects. The debate continues as to whether state regulation should be replaced by federal regulation.

See Questions at the end of Chapter 28.

Regulation of the insurance business:
Regulated functions and taxation

Many functions are performed by the insurance business, and public regulation affects virtually all of them. Insurance also is subject to many taxes. The purpose of this chapter is to examine what is regulated and to discuss briefly how insurers are taxed.

What Is Regulated?

In analyzing the nature of regulation the discussion can be divided into financial, product, and business methods. To the extent permitted by financial resources, quality of personnel, and the commissioner's philosophy, a state insurance department will attempt to discharge its regulatory functions. Many observers claim that some state insurance regulatory agencies do not go far enough in meeting their mandate, whereas others go too far. One former commissioner, extremely vocal about his goals, said that the office motto which he would have translated into Latin and hung on his door was "The consumer has been screwed long enough!" He insists that the consumer of insurance services needs as a representative someone who cares.

Financial regulation

To control insurer solvency, the law regulates many aspects of the business such as rates, expenses, reserves, valuation of assets, investments, surplus, policyowners' dividends, organization and licensing of insurers, annual reports, and liquidation of insurers.

Rate regulation. Rate *levels* for individual life and most health and ocean marine insurance are not regulated. The minimum rates for group life are regulated in several states.[1] Property and liability rates in most states are regulated in accordance with the model rating laws. These laws provide that rates reflect past and prospective loss and expense experience, conflagration, and catastrophe hazards, reasonable margins for underwriting profits and contingencies, and for participating insurers, dividends, savings, or unabsorbed premium deposits allowed or returned by insurers. In these states insurers must file premium rates, rating plans, coverage, and rules for the commissioner's approval. Supporting data, consisting principally of statistics on losses and expenses, are required. An insurer may satisfy this obligation through a licensed rating organization that files for members and subscribers. The commissioner has the power to disapprove a filing but must specify the reasons. The commissioner also may withdraw approval after a hearing is granted. Also, any person or organization aggrieved by the commissioner's action on a filing is entitled to a hearing. The burden of proof that filings comply with the law is on the insurer or bureau.

Rating organizations must be licensed by the commissioner. Every rating organization must permit any qualified nonmember insurer to subscribe to its services. Furthermore, each rating organization must furnish its services to members and subscribers without discrimination. Rating bureaus are subject to supervision and examination by the commissioner. Members and subscribers of rating bureaus are required to adhere to bureaus' rates, unless the commissioner approves an application for a deviation. The commissioner will not approve a rate modification that produces inadequate, excessive, or unfairly discriminatory premiums. These standards are general, so the commissioner needs guidelines to determine if a rate qualifies. To help commissioners with rate supervision, rating laws include technical requirements concerning methods of recording and reporting loss and expense experience, exchange of rating plan data, and consultation with other states. The commissioner may designate one or more rating or other organizations as statistical agencies to assist in collecting and compiling the required data.[2]

---

[1] Renewal premiums are not subject to established minimums and are allowed to reflect the group's experience. These regulations apply only to the minimum premium charged new group life insurance policyowners.

[2] For a discussion of these agencies, see Leroy J. Simons, "Statistical Agencies," in *Insurance, Government, and Social Policy,* ed. Spencer L. Kimball and Herbert S. Denenberg (Homewood, Ill.: Richard D. Irwin, Inc., 1969), pp 260–78.

Some observers believe that auto insurance rate regulation has become too political. To them commissioners seem more concerned with the "excessive" standard than with the "adequacy" standard. Political fortunes of the regulators, they believe, take precedence over insurer financial solvency. One commissioner wrote:

> Though most departments try courageously to tackle such problems on their merits and to base their action on the statistics supporting such rate requests, it is difficult to ignore the public clamor for a lower rate at all costs, and some insurance departments have yielded to such demands. There is at least one case on record of an insurance commissioner who approved an automobile rate increase shortly before an election and was promptly fired by his governor; the governor then appointed another commissioner whose first act was to rescind the rate increase.[3]

Many states have withdrawn their support of direct regulation of property liability insurance rates. This retreat is based on two contentions. First, the property liability insurance industry has enough sophistication in assimilation and statistical analysis of data to determine reasonably profitable rates, and insurance is sufficiently competitive to eliminate excessive rates. Second, even if some insurers are overoptimistic in measuring loss potential and unknowingly charge inadequate rates, a growing number of commissioners are confident of their ability and facilities to detect insurers bordering on insolvency before the public is hurt. (Even so, the National Committee on Insurance Guaranty Funds reports that property and liability insurers were assessed about $200 million to settle claims against 57 insolvent insurers during the nine-year period ending January 1, 1979. All states now have property liability insolvency associations.) The thought is that supervision of various financial accounts is sufficient to protect the public without specific attention to the price at which insurance is sold. The foregoing beliefs have resulted in proposals for the removal of insurance regulators from the pricing decision.

Such proposals have resulted in file-and-use and no-file rating laws. Generally, under a file-and-use law an insurer will file a requested rate change and statistical support for it. The insurer then can use the new rate until the commissioner disapproves it. Under a no-file law, statistical support for a rate change does not have to be filed, and rate changes can be initiated without notifying the commissioner. However, most no-file laws require that the commissioner be notified of rate changes within a specified period.

While the nonprior approval laws remove the state insurance departments from the initial pricing decision, the laws still require that rates be adequate, not excessive, and not unfairly discriminatory. Even under no-file laws commissioners may (and usually do) make periodic examinations of rates to determine if these criteria are met.

Rating laws generally do not apply to ocean marine insurance in

---

[3] Allen L. Mayerson, "An Inside Look at Insurance Regulation," *The Journal of Risk and Insurance* 32, no. 1 (March 1965), pp. 57–58.

order to give American insurers flexibility to compete in world markets. Furthermore, as buyers generally are represented by knowledgeable brokers; bargaining power between parties in ocean marine insurance transactions seems to be equal.

Life and health insurance. Life insurance rates are regulated indirectly by rules applying to the valuation of the insurer's reserve liability. The legal reserve requirements for life insurers are not directly related to the premium charged. If the insurer's premium structure is inadequate, its assets will be insufficient to offset the required reserve. In life insurance, as in property liability insurance, unfair price discrimination among buyers of the same policy from the same insurer is prohibited. However, unit prices may vary inversely with the policy size and the applicant's insurability.

The theory has been that competition would assure nonexcessive rates. However, because buyers generally are unaware of both the price they pay and the prices charged for alternative policies, the effectiveness of competition as a regulator of life insurance prices is questionable.[4] The typical buyer has neither the technical competence nor the data needed to analyze the prices of cash value life insurance. The life insurance industry has offered formulas for preparing indexes for price comparisons. These price indexes are widely published for a large number of life insurers.[5] Various states have published buyers' guides showing comparative life insurance prices. In 1979 the Federal Trade Commission completed a study of the effectiveness of state price disclosure legislation. Life insurance price comparisons and price disclosure laws are discussed in Chapter 21.

Because of abuses in credit life and health insurance (abuses known as "reverse competition"),[6] rates for these coverages are subject to control in nearly all states.

Many states require that rates and occupational classifications for health policies be filed with the commissioner. In many states, the commissioner may disapprove health insurance forms if benefits are unreasonable in relation to the premium. A few states require estimates of expected loss ratios with health insurance filings. All states require filing of annual statements of loss ratios in health insurance by policy forms. Although public interest requires supervision of health insurance rates, they often escape regulation because of conviction that they cannot be regulated effectively. So many different health policies are issued that understaffed insurance departments are unable to check rates against benefits. Blue Cross and Blue Shield rates, however, are controlled.

---

[4] See Joseph M. Belth, *The Retail Price Structure in American Life Insurance* (Bloomington: Bureau of Business Research, Graduate School of Business, Indiana University), pp. 236–39. Also see Joseph M. Belth, *Life Insurance: A Consumer's Handbook* (Bloomington: Indiana University Press, 1973), *passim.*

[5] *Life Rates and Data* (Cincinnati: National Underwriter Co.).

[6] In many cases the rate is negotiated between the insurer and the lending agency and is set at the level that will provide the highest profit to the lender in commissions and policy dividends.

Expenses. Insurer expenses must be controlled for effective financial regulation. No specific regulation of expenses exists in property and liability insurance. Expense regulation is tied directly to rate regulation. An important expense is the cost of acquiring business. Since the SEUA decision, the activity of organizations that once controlled commission rates became illegal. If commission wars jeopardize public interest, the commissioner has the power to restore order.

The expenses of life insurers are regulated by several states. The New York law is the most complex, and as it applies to all insurers doing business in New York, it affects nearly 70 percent of the life insurance written in the United States. New York law limits total expenses and acquisition costs. Commission and fees on individual policies are restricted, and practices such as awarding prizes or bonuses based on the volume of business written are controlled. Complicated aggregate limits are set on first-year and total field expenses. Renewal commissions and policy service fees also are subject to maximum limitations. In addition to compensation allowances the insurer may pay a reasonable training allowance for new agents under a plan approved by the commissioner, subject to a set of statutory limitations.

Admitted assets. Statutory policyowners' surplus is the amount by which assets exceed liabilities, as measured by state regulators. It measures insurer solvency. Except for the regulatory restrictions applying to valuations, the concept of policyowners' surplus is the same as the concept of equity in ordinary business finance.

Only "admitted assets" are considered in measuring solvency. In general, admitted assets include most legal portfolio investments of the insurer but no investments in operational assets such as supplies, furniture, office equipment, and autos. Two exceptions are noted: home and branch office buildings and, in some states, the fully depreciated value of electronic data processing equipment. Advances to agents, unsecured loans, and loans secured by collateral that does not qualify as an insurer's legal investments, prepaid expenses, and deferred charges are nonadmitted. Nonadmitted assets are not included in statutory policyowners' surplus.

Some admitted assets are more easily valued than others. *Cash and bank deposits* are valued at face amount. *Real estate* may be valued at book value (cost less depreciation) or market value (estimated value based on a fair appraisal). *Mortgage and collateral loans* are valued at the amount of the outstanding debt, if the security behind them meets legal standards. If not properly secured, these loans must be valued at less than the loan amount. *Bonds* amply secured by earning power and not in default are valued at amortized value. Bonds in default or inadequately secured according to standards of the Committee on Valuation of Securities of the NAIC are valued at the market value indicated by this committee. This committee also prepares "convention values" for *stocks*. These values are actual market values on December 31. Where no market values are available, the committee uses various forms to prepare make-believe values. Insurance commissioners generally accept the valuations of the committee but are not required to do so. Other items, such as *open accounts and premiums in course of collection,* are valued at book value. Estimated bad debts must be deducted.

Two conflicting goals are involved in determining asset valuation: the need for a minimum cash liquidating value in the event of a forced sale and the desire for stable year-to-year valuations. Although most insurers continue normal operations over the years, minimum values are necessary to determine the worth of insurers that are forced into liquidation. For this reason, furniture, office equipment, and similar assets are not included as admitted assets, and common and preferred stocks are valued at their market value. On the other hand, to allow dramatic shifts each year in the value of assets, and consequently in the amount of surplus, would generate difficulties both for management and regulators. Therefore, bonds are valued at their amortized values rather than their market values. As interest rates rise, as they have over the past two decades, market values of bonds are less than their amortized values, thus violating the liquidation-value goal. The current compromise between liquidating values and stability in values is not a satisfactory solution and is likely to be changed in the future. Current thinking appears to be in the direction of eventually requiring that bonds be valued at their market price. A solvent insurer is one whose admitted assets equal or exceed its statutory liabilities. Any insurer able to pay claims when due may make itself appear to be solvent if it were free to value its liabilities below asset values. But insurers do not have such unlimited freedom. Reserves are the major liabilities of insurers, and the valuation of reserves are subject to state regulation.

Reserves. Property and liability insurers are required to maintain unearned premium reserves and loss reserves. The unearned premium reserve equals the unearned portion of gross premiums of all outstanding policies at the time of valuation. The loss reserve is the insurer's estimated liability for claims and settlement expenses as of the valuation date. States require that the minimum auto liability, other liability, medical malpractice, and workers' compensation loss reserves be computed in accordance with the *formula* or *loss ratio method.* The minimum loss reserve required under this method for each of the three most recent accident years is based on the expected loss ratio. The expected loss ratio is 60 percent for auto liability, other liability, and medical malpractice and 65 percent for workers' compensation, if fewer than three of the five years immediately preceding the most recent three years (that is, the fourth through the eighth preceding years) have a premium volume of at least $1 million. If three or more of these five years have a premium volume of at least $1 million, the expected loss ratio is the lowest reported accident year loss and loss adjustment expense ratio incurred for any one of these specified five years. However, the expected loss ratio may not be less than 60 percent (65 percent for workers' compensation) nor more than 75 percent. The expected loss ratio is multiplied by each accident year's earned premium to determine the minimum allowable loss evaluation. The loss and loss expense payments made are subtracted from the minimum loss evaluation to obtain the minimum loss reserve. The minimum loss reserve applies whenever it exceeds the loss and loss adjustment expense reserve established by the insurer.

Regulators primarily are concerned that insurers do not set loss reserves that are too low, because an understatement of liabilities can lead to insolvencies when loss payments become due. On the other hand, to allow insurers to overreserve can result in excessive rates. Insurance departments usually do not have the qualified personnel necessary to determine the adequacy of loss reserves on a company-by-company basis, and must rely on rough formulas that approximate the needed reserves. Thus, on occasion, insurers have been able to conceal financial weaknesses that in some cases have led to insolvencies. Experts who have studied the problem of the loss reserve and its regulation insist that the approach to the adequacy of this reserve is in need of reform.[7]

The principal reserve of life insurers is the policy reserve, which measures that amount which, together with future net valuation premiums and assumed interest, will exactly meet all policy obligations as they become due. The net valuation premium differs from the premium charged policyowners, as it includes no allowance for expenses and may be based on different interest and mortality assumptions. The amount of the policy reserve is a function of the mortality and interest rates assumed and the system used in its computation. The 1980 NAIC amendments to the standard valuation law require all insurers to use the 1980 CSO mortality table with interest rates specified by an index of corporate bond interest averages. (See Chapter 25.) The law does allow insurers to use a modified reserve system; that is, one based on other than the full net valuation premium. Life insurers frequently value their policy reserve in excess of the statutory minimum.

Modified reserve standards.   Life insurers incur most of their total expense per policy during the initial policy year. The first-year expenses include the agent's commission, which frequently equals half or more of the first-year gross premium. Each policy also must make its contribution to the insurer's general expenses. A premium tax must be paid, and the policy must bear its share of mortality costs. Once these payments are made, little of the first year's premium remains for the insurer. It is certainly not enough to offset the policy reserve for the end of the first year if this reserve must be computed on a full reserve basis. Because the reserve liability, when computed on a full reserve basis, is increased by an amount in excess of the assets retained from the first-year pre-

---

[7] See Allen L. Mayerson, "Ensuring the Solvency of Property and Liability Insurance Companies," in *Insurance, Government, and Social Policy,* ed. Spencer L. Kimball and Herbert S. Denenberg (Homewood, Ill.: Richard D. Irwin, 1969), pp. 172–81; and Stephen W. Forbes, "Loss Reserving Performance within the Regulatory Framework," *Journal of Risk and Insurance* 37, no. 4 (December 1970), pp. 527–38.

mium, surplus is decreased. Younger and smaller insurers using a full reserve system soon would find themselves sold out of business if they grew rapidly. Their surpluses would be depleted before the expiration of a year.[8]

To meet the needs of these insurers, alternative methods allow postponement of the full policy reserve. One plan, the *full preliminary term reserve plan,* requires no policy reserve at the end of the policy year. For every year thereafter, the reserve is the amount that would be required under the full reserve basis for a policy issued one year later, for a period one year shorter. For example, a 30-pay life policy issued at age 20 is treated, for reserving purposes, as a one-year term policy issued at age 30 plus a 29-pay life policy issued at age 21. As the reserve upon expiration of any term contract is zero, this policy has no reserve liability after one year. At the end of the second year, the reserve is the full reserve of a one-year-old 29-pay contract issued at age 21. This method allows the insurer to use the entire first-year premium for initial expenses and first-year claims, without depleting its surplus account, as no first-year reserve liability is required.

The *Commissioners Reserve Valuation Method* (CRVM), the minimum legal reserve standard permitted, requires modification of the full preliminary term reserve system. Under the CRVM, policies are divided into two classes. Class 1 includes policies for which the modified net level valuation premium (net valuation premium increased by the level amount necessary to develop the full reserve when all premiums are paid) does not exceed that for a 20-pay whole life policy issued at the same age for the same amount. For class 1 policies, the CRVM permits the use of the full preliminary term reserve system.

Class 2 policies are those for which the modified net level valuation premium exceeds that for a 20-pay whole life policy issued at the same age for the same amount. To use the full preliminary reserve standard for these policies would produce an excessive first-year expense allowance and could encourage insurers to incur inordinately high expenses. For example, under the CRVM method a 20-year endowment issued at age 35 would, as a class 2 policy, require a first-year reserve of less than the full reserve of $39.04 per $1,000, but more than zero as under the full preliminary reserve system. The amount required under the CRVM for the first year is $25.01, which is the level amount that must be added each year to the full preliminary term reserve computed for a 20-payment whole life policy of $1,000 issued at age 35 to bring the reserve for a 20-year endowment policy steadily to its full reserve of $1,000 after 20 years.[9]

---

[8] A similar problem of heavy expenses in the first few weeks also plagues property and liability insurers.

[9] For an explanation of how the figure of $25.01 is calculated, see Robert I. Mehr and Sandra G. Gustavson, *Life Insurance: Theory and Practice,* 3d ed. (Plano, Texas: Business Publications, 1984), pp. 674–75.

Capital stock and surplus accounts.   An insurer's surplus consists of paid-in surplus and earned surplus. A capital stock insurer also will have paid-in capital.

Capital stock accounts.   An insurer's capital stock account represents the dollar value nominally assigned to shares issued to stockholders. Most states require that stock initially be issued at a premium (the value assigned to the stock must be less than the money paid in by stockholders), thus creating a paid-in surplus. For example, New York stock life insurers must have a minimum paid-in fund of $3 million—$1 million is assigned to the capital account and $2 million to paid-in surplus.

Paid-in-surplus account.   A minimum paid-in fund is required for mutual insurers, but as mutuals have no capital stock, this fund is assigned entirely to paid-in surplus. The minimum paid-in fund is $150,000 for a New York domestic mutual life insurer and $500,000 for a domestic multiple line insurer. These initial funds usually are supplied by lenders but are treated as guarantee funds and not liabilities. Interest may be paid on these funds, and the principal may be repaid from earnings.

Capacity for new business.   If a Homeowners policy with a $120 premium is sold, the agent retains, say, $20.40 as commission and remits $99.60 to the insurer. Premium taxes are about $2.40, and home office overhead amounts to several more dollars. The insurer must show $120 as the unearned premium reserve at the beginning of the period, $110 after one month, and $100 after two months. More than two months will elapse before even the $20.40 paid in commissions is earned. Conceivably new business could increase at a pace fast enough to cause the insurer to become insolvent because of the exhaustion of surplus and the resultant impairment of its capital or reserve account. However, before allowing such impairment, the insurer would stop writing additional business. This point was reached in the United States immediately following World War II. Many insurers legally were "sold out" of insurance: they had written as much new business as possible without reducing their surplus accounts to dangerously low levels. Unless able to attract new capital (generally not a viable solution), they were forced to discontinue writing new insurance or became overly selective in underwriting. Only the most profitable business was accepted, and the less profitable was left uninsured. This feature of the postwar insurance scene, the "capacity problem," has been one of the most widely discussed issues in property and liability insurance.

The amount of premiums an insurer may write is limited by its policyowners' surplus. Sufficient surplus is needed to guarantee the insurer's continued solvency for a period long enough to detect and correct adverse underwriting and investment experience. The amount of policyowners' surplus needed is a function of the degree of loss predictability for the coverages written, stability of the value of the insurer's investment portfolio, ability to estimate loss reserves, and the insurer's anticipated growth rate. But measurement problems in quantifying these variables make specifying exactly how much surplus is necessary difficult. Until practical solutions are developed, state regulatory authorities and insurance managements will continue to use simple rules of thumb.

One rule of thumb expounded for years is Roger Kenney's unsupported hypothesis that net written premiums should not exceed twice the policyowners' surplus.[10] This rule (or a modification) is widely used in regulatory circles. Usually a ratio of 3 to 1 is allowed, and some commissioners might permit a ratio as high as 4 to 1. One major purpose of an insurer's surplus is to help offset operating losses. An insurer writing at a 4 to 1 premium to surplus ratio, would have the inverse of that ratio, or 25 percent of its premium, as a contingency fund for operating losses. If operating losses for a given insurer were to exceed 25 percent of its premium, a fate experienced in 1977 by 3 percent of the property liability insurers, that insurer would exhaust its surplus completely if its premium to surplus ratio were 4 to 1.

Another purpose of surplus is to fund any deficiency in the loss and loss adjustment expense reserve that may exist. For insurers that write slow closing lines such as workers' compensation, medical malpractice, and auto liability, loss and loss adjustment expense reserves often equal or exceed annual written premiums. If an insurer's loss and loss adjustment expense reserve equals its written premium, a 25 percent reserve deficiency would consume all the surplus of an insurer operating at a 4 to 1 premium to surplus ratio. Premium to surplus ratio rules of thumb are to be applied only after an analysis of all pertinent facts regarding the insurer's underwriting, investment accounts, and balance sheet. If more than the required surplus exists, the excess sometimes is referred to as "surplus surplus."

In the early 1970s, capital stock insurers with "surplus surplus" became attractive takeover targets for other companies (especially cash-poor noninsurance firms). The object was to buy the insurance company, then turn insurance company assets into cash and declare a large corporate dividend. This action put large amounts of cash into the pocket of the new owner. Certainly the most celebrated case of this type was the purchase of the Hartford Fire Insurance Company by International Telephone and Telegraph. Shortly after the purchase was completed, Hartford Fire declared a $175 million dividend, most of which went to ITT.

In life insurance, there appears to be no threat of a capacity problem because no need exists for large surpluses. The concept of "surplus surplus" is less important in life insurance because of statutory limits

---

[10] Roger Kenney, *Fundamentals of Fire and Casualty Insurance Strength*, 4th ed. (Dedham, Mass.: The Kenney Insurance Studies, 1967), pp. 97–102. Kenney's rule of thumb seems to have no theoretical base. It comes as an edict. Kenney seems to offer only the statement on page 97 that he made "a thorough study of the difficulties into which certain casualty companies had fallen in the early 1930s" and had come "to the conclusion that in the great majority of cases the venturesome area was entered when a company's premium volume began to exceed $2 for every dollar of policyholders' surplus."

placed in many states on surplus accumulation by those insurers issuing participating policies. The purpose of surplus is to protect against operational losses and declines in investment values and to finance the insurer's growth. In life insurance, sufficient safety margins are included in premiums to guard against adverse experience in mortality costs and investment income. The statement values of life insurer investments usually are stable because of the valuation methods used. A mandatory securities valuation reserve is used to reduce the impact of fluctuating common stock values.

Dividends.   The amount of the annual gain from operations that should properly be paid to policyowners as dividends is a matter of judgment. Some states seek to regulate this decision by limiting the amount of surplus that may be accumulated by an insurer writing participating policies to 10 percent of the policy reserve. Such limits are imposed to prevent the building of a large surplus at the expense of current dividends, to protect the equity among policyowners at different stages of the insurer's development, and to prevent insurers from accumulating a surplus large enough to be a temptation for the inefficient use of assets.

Investments.   When financial trouble besets life insurers it is usually a result of investment problems; when it besets property liability insurers, it is usually a result of underwriting problems. To protect policyowner interests in insurer solvency, discourage concentration of economic power, and encourage the commitment of funds for socially desirable purposes, state laws regulate the investment of insurer assets. Laws vary widely among states, although the NAIC seeks to reduce the variations. The extraterritorial application of the New York Code also contributes to uniformity of investment practice. New York law requires foreign insurers to comply substantially with the investment laws applicable to domestic insurers.

Laws are concerned with both qualitative and quantitative restrictions and deal with types of investment media, portfolio distribution among approved media, amount of security required for authorized media to qualify, percentage of a firm's outstanding common stock that may be held, percentage of admitted assets that may be invested in a single corporation, percentage of admitted assets in a single investment issue of a corporation, and the source of investment funds.

Life insurers.   Because they deal primarily in long-term, fixed-dollar contracts with premiums and reserves computed on the basis of specific interest rates, life insurers are largely restricted to investing in high-grade bonds and mortgages with a fixed rate of return. Limited funds may be invested in preferred stocks, common stocks, and real estate. New York permits life insurers to invest in *qualified* common stocks up to 5 percent of their admitted assets but not more than an amount equal to half of their surplus. Not more than 2 percent of the outstanding common shares of any one corporation may be held, nor can more than

0.2 percent of the insurer's admitted assets be invested in any one corporation. Qualified common stocks are defined loosely as dividend-paying, marketable issues of adequate-size corporations with a record of reasonable earnings for an extended period. No overall limit is placed on the amount that can be invested in qualified preferred stocks.

Most states are more liberal than New York, allowing 10 to 15 percent of admitted assets to be invested in stocks. They may include preferred stocks in the limitation. Other states allow investment in common stocks of assets exceeding the required minimum capital and surplus. Some states have no limit on the amount of common stock investments.

Life insurers can establish separate accounts subject to less stringent limitations than those for general funds. Separate accounts allow life insurers to compete with other financial institutions for equity funded retirement plans. New York does not restrict investment for separate accounts, except that the account may not hold more than 2 percent of any one corporation's stock and the insurance commissioner may reject any proposed investment program.

Some states authorize the investment of life insurance assets in multiple housing projects and commercial rental properties, under strict limitations as to proportion of total assets so invested. Life insurers' real estate holdings include apartment complexes, multipurpose skyscrapers, neighborhood shopping centers, and downtown centers. Life insurers have purchased commercial properties and then leased them back to their former owners or developers. These transactions provide the insurer a profitable outlet for large volumes of funds and relieve the original owners of the necessity of tying up capital in fixed assets, thereby releasing more funds for working capital.[11]

Life insurers may invest in real estate to the extent necessary for transacting business—primarily home office and regional office buildings. Real estate acquired by foreclosure must be disposed of within a limited time, usually five years. The commissioner can extend this period if the insurer would suffer from a forced sale. Mortgage loan investments usually are limited to first mortgages and restricted to a stated percentage of the property's appraised value. The aggregate amount of home and regional office real estate permitted by New York is 10 percent of admitted assets. The limit on mortgage loans is 50 percent of admitted assets with a limit of 2 percent of admitted assets applicable to any one property. Restrictions in other states may be less severe. Life insurers are authorized to commit a small percentage of admitted assets (3½ percent in New York) to investments not otherwise qualified.

---

[11] The IRS is not pleased about one advantage when the transaction involves old property. Some properties owned by businesses have been depreciated to a book value of zero. Therefore, their owners cannot charge further depreciation as an expense. If the property is sold subject to a leasing arrangement, the seller reports a capital gain then reports its payments on the lease as expenses. Meanwhile, the buyer can charge depreciation against the purchase price paid for the property. Thus, depreciation charges can be taken again against the property as an income tax deduction. It is all quite legal.

Property liability insurers.   Some states require property liability insurers to invest assets equal to their minimum required capital and surplus in the media available to life insurers. They may invest assets exceeding their required capital and surplus in stocks of solvent corporations. Other states are more realistic and apply the stricter standards to assets equal to required unearned premium and loss reserves rather than minimum required capital and surplus. The following regulations illustrate the nature of the restrictions placed on property liability insurers:

1. The investment of assets representing the required minimum net worth is limited to U.S. bonds, bonds of the individual states and civil subdivision, mortgage loans, and, in some cases, restricted classes of railroad and public utility bonds.
2. The investment of assets representing required reserves is limited to the above classes of investments plus certain bonds and preferred stocks of corporations that satisfy requirements as to solvency and earning power.
3. The investment of assets representing that amount in excess of the required minimum capital and surplus is allowed in common stocks of solvent corporations.

New York law restricts the investment of assets equal to the minimum capital requirements to obligations of the U.S. government, New York state, its subdivisions, those of other states, and mortgage loans on property located in New York. (Given the 1975–80 financial problems of New York City and the speculative quality of its bonds and those of many New York state agencies, one questions the propriety of continuing to allow investments in such issues.) Assets equal to 50 percent of the unearned premium and loss reserves are restricted generally to investments for which life insurers are eligible.

Exact restrictions vary among states. Certain other limitations may be prescribed as to the quality of securities and percentage of assets that may be invested in foreign government bonds, real estate, and the securities of a single private corporation. This latter restriction is designed to achieve diversification in portfolios; it also applies to life insurers. While insurance commissioners have no power to dictate the investments an insurer must make, they can disapprove investments they consider not in the best interests of insureds.

Requirements for organizing and licensing insurers.   Insurance codes prescribe conditions for the formation of new insurers. They deal with the insurer's name, publication of notice of intention to form an insurer, incorporation, and organization, and seek to protect the public from misleading company names, from insurers organized by people of questionable reputation, and from promoters whose sole purpose is to profit from sale of the insurer's stock. The laws seek to protect policyowners and investors from the birth of inadequately conceived insurers, but evidence suggests that state regulatory birth control policy regarding life insurers has not been successful.[12] Some states are making an effort to reduce both the birth and death rate among new life insurers through administrative regulations and by increasing minimum capital and initial paid-in surplus requirements for insurers. Commenting on the capital and surplus requirements for organizing or licensing of insurers, one insurance commissioner wrote:

> The problem confronting a new company is . . . that of not obtaining enough business initially to cover overhead expenses. The problem is independent of the type of business. . . . I would prefer . . . an up-to-date minimum capital and surplus requirement, . . . one . . . many times the standard now in use by most states, and apply such standard uniformly to any company wishing to transact one or more branches of life or property insurance business.[13]

The organizational laws relating to insurers vary over time and among states, types of insurers, and types of coverage to be written.

States also have authority for licensing insurers and control insurance chiefly through this licensing power. A license is a document stating that the insurer has complied with the state laws and is authorized to engage in the business for which it has applied. Insurers, however, may operate in a state without a license by conducting their business through the mails.

A license to write insurance may be issued to a domestic, foreign, or alien insurer. The state can establish stricter licensing requirements for alien and foreign insurers than for domestic ones. This practice is justified because domestic insurers' assets are generally in the state and more easily subject to the commissioner's control through court procedure.[14]

Licenses usually are permanent for domestic insurers but subject to yearly renewal for foreign or alien insurers. The commissioner may revoke a license, forcing the insurer to discontinue business in the state. The insurer may seek a court reversal of the commissioner's decision, but the insurer must prove that the license should not have been revoked. The licensing power is an effective weapon of control for it is nearly impossible to have the commissioner's action set aside. The commissioner will license insurers meeting minimum statutory standards of financial strength, if no incorporator or proposed director has a record of fraud or dishonesty, and if the licensing does not seem to jeopardize the public interest.

Unauthorized insurers. The regulation of unlicensed insurers (called nonadmitted or unauthorized insurers) creates special problems, partic-

---

[12] See J. S. Hanson and D. R. Farney, "New Life Insurance Companies: Their Promotion and Regulation," *Marquette Law Review,* Fall 1965, p. 176 ff.

[13] Mayerson, "An Inside Look at Insurance Regulation," p. 63.

[14] The legal grounds for allowing such discrimination was established when the U.S. Supreme Court held that corporations are not citizens within the meaning of the 4th and 14th amendments to the federal Constitution. These amendments gave persons the right of privacy (4th) and the right of equal protection of the law (14th).

ularly with mail-order insurers. Wisconsin was the first of many states to pass an unauthorized insurance law prohibiting unauthorized insurers from doing business in the state except in accordance with the surplus lines statute discussed later. "Doing business" is broadly defined to include soliciting, writing, rating, administering, and servicing an insurance contract, whether by mail or otherwise. Excluded from the definition are reinsurers, insurance owned by residents before moving into the state, and insurance independently procured outside the state without the aid of a licensed agent in the state. Also excluded is insurance issued by Teachers Insurance and Annuity Association (TIAA). The law makes unauthorized insurers subject to jurisdiction of state courts in actions brought by the state to enforce its laws (and in suits brought by resident policyholders against the insurer). Unauthorized insurers are subject to fines and state premium taxes.[15]

Two uniform acts deal with unauthorized insurers: (1) the Unauthorized Insurers Service of Process Act (enacted in 48 jurisdictions) under which the commissioner is made the agent of foreign insurers for service of process (summons by which a defendant is brought to court for litigation), and (2) the Uniform Reciprocal Licensing Act (passed in more than one third of the jurisdictions) under which a domestic insurer's license may be revoked if it operates without a license in another state with a reciprocal licensing statute. States also control unauthorized insurers by limiting them to business placed by licensed surplus lines agents or brokers. Insurance may be purchased from unauthorized insurers only under specified conditions discussed later.

Annual reports.   Insurers must file annual reports with the states in which they do business. These reports are in accordance with a form (called the "convention blank") developed by the NAIC and are detailed as to premium income, expenses, investments, reserves, and other financial information. State insurance departments verify the information by direct examination of the insurer (but not more than once every three years) under a zone system with no more than one examiner from each of the five zones outside the home zone participating. The zone system was designed by the NAIC to improve the efficiency of insurer examinations. Individual states need not examine every licensed insurer within its borders. The country is divided into six zones with each zone

---

[15] The constitutionality of the Wisconsin unauthorized insurer statute was upheld by the Wisconsin Supreme Court (*Ministers Life and Casualty Union* v. *Haase*, 30 Wis. 2d 339, 141 N.W. 2d 287, 1966). The U.S. Supreme Court dismissed the appeal for want of a substantial federal question (December 5, 1966–No. 634). In 1975 the U.S. Supreme Court declined to review a Wisconsin Supreme Court decision. That decision held the Wisconsin premium tax on unauthorized mail-order insurers in violation of the due process clause of the U.S. Constitution because the tax was not apportioned to activities within Wisconsin (*Wisconsin* v. *National Liberty Life Insurance Co.*, April 28, 1975, No. 74–193). However, the Wisconsin state court decision that a *proper* premium tax, if *appropriately applied*, may be imposed upon premiums received by an unauthorized mail-order insurer from its policyowners in Wisconsin was not reviewed and therefore remains the law of that state until the issue of jurisdiction to tax an unauthorized mail-order insurer is decided to the contrary.

including several states. An individual state is represented in the examination process by an examiner from its zone. The insurance department of the insurer's domiciliary state chairs the examination, and the insurer pays the cost. At least one state now requires annual audits of domestic insurers by independent CPAs as a part of its surveillance system.

Liquidation of insurers. When an insurer is found to be technically insolvent, the commissioner takes over the insurer for liquidation, rehabilitation, or conservation. The commissioner may act any time evidence shows that continued operation of the insurer is not in the policyowners' interest. Many grounds for liquidation usually are outlined in the insurance code, such as insolvency, failure to cooperate fully with examiners, impaired capital, refusal to remove a dishonest officer or director, or willful violation of state laws. The suspected insurer is entitled to a court hearing, but the insurer's assets become vested in the commissioner when the liquidation order is entered. If the takeover proves to be insupportable, the assets of the insurer must be restored to its former management.

Several states have adopted the Uniform Insurers Liquidation Act, designed to obtain uniformity in handling claims and distributing assets when liquidation involves insurers doing business in more than one state. The act puts creditors in each state on an equal footing. Creditors in the domiciliary state receive no preferential treatment.

Product regulation

Insurance policies are so complicated that even lawyers do not always know what they mean, as shown by the number of cases that reach court for interpretation. It is understandable that lay persons may be unable to comprehend them. This inability to interpret a policy presents an opportunity for unscrupulous insurers to draft contracts containing exclusions and provisions unfavorable to the insured. Even the scrupulous insurers may, without intent to defraud, use clauses and policy provisions which are misleading. A former commissioner known for his sweeping statements said that a scientific scale of readability found the auto policy more difficult to understand than Einstein's celebrated theory. Some insurers agree that policyowners are entitled to forms they can understand and are issuing simplified contracts stripped of most legalese and fine print. Some states encourage insurers to simplify policy language. As a result, the Insurance Services Office has filed readable Homeowners policies in most states, reducing the words by about 40 percent and increasing type size by 25 percent, with more space between lines. (See Chapter 7.) Readable policies have been developed for other insurance coverages, both personal and business as well as life and health insurance.

Approval of policy forms. To protect both the public and reputable insurers against irresponsible insurers, insurance departments are empowered to approve policy forms. The objective is to disapprove policies that are ambiguous, deceptive, or misleading. In some states, special "gimmick" type policies in life and health insurance are outlawed. In certain coverages, e.g., fire and workers' compensation, standard policy forms are required. In others, e.g., life and health, certain provisions must be included in all contracts and others are prohibited. Generally, the commissioner may disapprove a policy if it contains provisions that are unjust, inequitable, deceptive, or encourage misrepresentation. Unfortunately, most insurance departments do not have funds for their personnel to give policy forms more than a cursory examination.

In states where model rate laws are in effect, supervision of policy forms and rates is interrelated. When an insurer or bureau files a rate, it must include a description of the coverage offered. A policy issued subject to that rate must contain the coverage contemplated when the rate was filed.

Regulation of business methods

Insurance regulation also seeks to protect the public from incompetent and dishonest agents and to maintain fair competition. The states regulate methods used by insurers to acquire new policyowners. Such regulation is concerned with ethical standards of activity for insurers and their agents. Insurance departments maintain bureaus to investigate numerous real as well as ungrounded complaints of insureds.

Licensing of agents and brokers.   Agents and brokers must be licensed by any state in which they do business. Qualifications for a license vary widely among states. In an increasing number, applicants for an agent's license must pass a written examination in certain insurance subjects. A few states require formal courses in insurance before the examination. As a result of a political scandal in the grading of agents' examinations, one state now uses the reputable Educational Testing Service (Princeton, N.J.) to prepare, administer, and grade the examinations to eliminate political influence. In some states where no written examinations are required, the law assumes, quite naïvely, that as the agent has broad powers to commit the principal, the insurer would select its agents with care. The law may require from the insurer only certification of completion of an approved training course. This requirement is highly questionable as protection for the public against poorly trained agents. The NAIC is studying state licensing laws with the goal of proposing a model uniform agents' and brokers' licensing bill.

Agents' licenses usually are issued for one year and renewed automatically. The commissioner may refuse or revoke licenses, but this action cannot be arbitrary. Dishonesty usually is grounds for rejection of a license application or revocation of one issued. Misrepresentation, rebating, unfair discrimination, or other law violation usually is sufficient cause for revocation. A few states regard incompetence or ignorance as grounds for revocation. In some states, to protect the "locals" from outside competition, licenses are issued only to residents. A few states license counselors. If licensing of agents is to be more than a source of state revenue, increased attention must be given to professional qualifications.

Most states have a countersignature law requiring that property and liability insurance contracts written in the state be signed by a resident agent. These laws vary widely among the states, and neither logic nor consistency appears to determine how the laws treat the subject. Many states require a mandatory division of commissions between the producer and resident agents, with the resident agent usually receiving 25 to 50 percent. Because resident agents usually do nothing but sign their names, many observers regard the mandatory division of commission as featherbedding and therefore contrary to the interests of buyers, as well as inconsistent with professional conduct. In 1963 the NAIC unanimously adopted the following resolution: "Resolved, that it is the sense of this subcommittee that countersignature laws in the various states requiring a mandatory division of commissions between the producer and the countersigning agent be abolished." This resolution has suffered the fate of many New Year's resolutions.

Surplus line agent or broker. In all states except Iowa, an agent or broker who wishes to place business with an acceptable nonadmitted insurer must have a surplus line license. The surplus line laws vary among states, but they generally include the same types of restrictions: (1) the insurance must be unavailable in the admitted market in spite of diligent effort by the agent or broker to find it; (2) the surplus line agent or broker must pay a premium tax which in many states is higher than the premium tax on admitted insurers; (3) only nonadmitted insurers meeting specific requirements are acceptable (requirements include filing an acceptable financial statement, appointing the commissioner as attorney for service of process, obtaining a certificate of compliance from the state or country of the insurer's domicile, and maintenance of a trust fund in the United States by alien nonadmitted insurers); and (4) the surplus line agent or broker must pay a special license fee, post a bond, and usually be a resident of the state.[16]

Surplus line laws have been attacked for restricting the freedom of buyers. If coverage is available in the admitted market, buyers are not allowed to place insurance with an unauthorized insurer, even though it is financially stronger, offers lower prices, and will write a contract more suitable than that found in the admitted market. One insurance commissioner observed:

> Although justified as an attempt to protect citizens of the state against buying coverage in an unsound company, this goal can be achieved much more simply, for example, by requiring an affidavit from the insured that

---

[16] For a summary sketch of surplus line laws in the jurisdictions that have them, see Keith Brown, "Nonadmitted Alien Insurers and Insurance Regulation," in Kimball and Denenberg, *Insurance, Government, and Social Policy*, pp. 293–306.

[he or she] understands that the insurer is unlicensed and that, under certain circumstances, [. . . he or she] may not have the protection of the courts or [the state] insurance department. . . . It is difficult to argue that a citizen, fully cognizant of what . . . [he or she] is doing and warned of the possible consequences, should be forbidden to buy insurance from a not-admitted insurer if [. . . he or she] wishes."[17]

Misrepresentation and twisting.   State statutes usually prohibit a misrepresentation of facts about a policy and its coverage, or the relationship between the insured and the insurer. "Twisting" refers to misrepresentation by an agent in order to induce a policyowner to substitute one contract for another. The definition of twisting must include failure to disclose all facts. An agent's recommendation to an insured to replace one policy with another is not necessarily twisting. Unfortunately, fear of accusation of twisting discourages some agents from making sound recommendations involving dropping one policy in favor of another. Furthermore, misrepresentation and twisting are not easy to prove and often go undetected or unpunished.

Twisting, found principally in life insurance, is referred to as the replacement problem. The NAIC has developed model replacement solicitation and marketing bills requiring that complete and accurate written information on a proposed replacement including a comparison between the existing and proposed policies be supplied to policyowners. The bills require that each insurance company with a policy in force likely to be affected by a replacement be given the opportunity to evaluate and comment on the comparative information given the policyowner.

Rebating.   Agents who refund part of the commission to the applicant are violating antirebating laws found in all states. These laws are designed to maintain fair competition among agents and to protect career from avocational agents.[18] State laws usually provide that a rebate may consist not only of a return of part of the premium, but also of any inducement, favor, or advantage not specified in the policy. Few rebating cases reach court because they are difficult to prove. Both the buyer and seller are guilty and will not want to testify against each other. For certain coverages, however, it is not uncommon for the agent's commission to be subject to legal negotiation.

Unfair discrimination.   Unfair discrimination gives one insured a lower rate than others under the same conditions and specifications and usually is prohibited by state insurance codes. The word "unfair" should be stressed, for in one sense the practice of insurance by nature is dis-

---

[17] Mayerson, "An Inside Look at Insurance Regulation," p. 57.

[18] Antirebating laws have been justified as protecting the public interest. The argument is that the public interest is damaged if, by rebating, big agencies drive out small agents and thus lessen competition. Some argue, however, that knowledgeable, sophisticated buyers should not be prevented, under the guise of protecting the public interest, from driving a hard bargain in purchasing insurance any more than when they purchase other goods and services.

criminatory, as good underwriting calls for discrimination among exposures.

With government encouragement and sometimes insurer acquiescence, a growing number of people appear to support the concept that private insurance is a method of spreading losses without regard to equitable distribution of cost in the actuarial sense. As a result, "unfair" discrimination is sanctioned in the private insurance system, often as a means for forestalling government takeover of various coverages. For example, insurers yielded to heavy political pressure when they agreed to organize automobile insurance plans (formerly called assigned risk plans) at the expense of a departure from what they believed to be sound principles for private insurance. In an unsuccessful effort to keep the Federal Insurance Administration out of the crime insurance business, the National Association of Independent Insurers urged the states to place a surcharge on property insurance premiums and to use the funds to subsidize private crime insurance. Another example of actuarially inequitable loss spreading is the assessment of solvent insurers to satisfy claims against insurers that have been declared insolvent. However, if the private sector is to operate profitably and provide the public with the quantity and quality of insurance it needs at "affordable rates," these practices may be necessary, unless a government subsidy is made available for coverages in problem areas.

Taxation of Insurance Companies

Insurers, like all business, must pay taxes and fees[19] including income taxes, license fees, filing fees, real estate and personal property taxes, assessments for insurance department examinations, franchise taxes, ocean marine underwriting profit taxes, special fire insurance taxes, special workers' compensation insurance taxes, and a premium tax. The foregoing taxes and fees, except federal income taxes, are paid primarily to state governments with some paid to local communities.

Insurers pay federal income taxes according to *special* and, in some cases, complicated *formulas* set forth in the Internal Revenue Code. Several states impose an income tax on insurers often as an alternate to premium taxes. In some states, a tax is levied on the net investment income of domestic insurers. License fees include those for licensing insurers and agents. Filing fees are charged for filing the annual statement and supporting documents. The cost of examination is paid by the examined insurer. To examine the Prudential Insurance Company of America or some other giant-sized insurers requires three years. Real and personal property is taxed on the same basis as for any taxpaying owner. Some states impose on insurers a franchise tax which varies widely among these states. Many states tax the underwriting profits from

---

[19] For an extensive discussion of state taxation of insurers, see Robert I. Mehr, "Taxation of Insurance Companies," chap. 22 in *Report of the Commission on Revenue of the State of Illinois* (Springfield, 1963), pp. 760–94.

ocean marine insurance in lieu of a tax on ocean marine insurance premiums. Most states levy a special tax on fire insurance premiums for support of the state fire marshal's office or to support local fire departments. A special tax is levied on insurers writing workers' compensation insurance to pay the cost of administering the system, build security funds, and finance second injury funds (designed to facilitate employing physically handicapped workers by eliminating a possible additional cost).

The premium tax

The most criticized of all insurer taxes is the premium tax. Premium taxes originally were imposed "partly in the guise of defraying . . . expenses of regulation."[20] State insurance departments now receive only a small part of the revenue derived from the premium tax. The remainder is used to finance other state services. Insurers object to this tax on the grounds that it is inequitable to single them out for special treatment. However, the revenue from premium taxes is easy to collect and valuable to the states, and policyowners who ultimately pay these taxes have shown no organized resistance to them. Although a number of states now have or are considering an income tax in addition to or in lieu of the premium tax, they recognize the problem of measuring an insurer's true income. States vary widely in how they measure income.

Insurers also object to premium taxes because they are not uniform as to rate, rate base, offsets, and "in lieu of other tax" provisions. The tax rate varies from a high of 4 percent to a low of 1.7 percent with 2 percent the most common. Some states either do not tax domestic insurers or charge them lower rates than out-of-state insurers. The NAIC is seeking elimination of premium tax discrimination between foreign and domestic insurers.

Most states (46) levy a retaliatory tax in excess of the tax normally charged out-of-state insurers to equalize the tax rate that their domestic insurers must pay in another state. If a domestic insurer in state A is required to pay a 3 percent premium tax in state B, then state B's domestic insurers must pay 3 percent in state A even though A's tax rate is 2 percent. The purpose of the retaliatory tax is to control the urge to raise taxes on out-of-state insurers; it is especially effective in those states that have a politically powerful domestic insurance industry. The NAIC is seeking the elimination of retaliatory taxes. The federal government has called for an investigation of the economic and competitive effects of retaliatory taxes.

The premium tax rates in some states vary by lines of insurance. A reduction in the premium tax is allowed in some states if a given percentage of the insurer's assets is invested in the state. Some states allow a deduction for reinsurance paid, whereas others allow a reduction for

---

[20] Bruce E. Shepherd, "Taxation of Life Insurance Companies in the United States," *Transactions of the Thirteenth International Congress of Actuaries,* Scheveningen, Netherlands, 1951 (Amsterdam: North Holland, 1951), p. 63.

reinsurance premiums received. In most states the insurer may deduct policy dividends from the tax base, but in a significant minority of states, dividends may not be deducted. The majority of states specify that the premium tax is in lieu of some other tax or taxes, while in some states other taxes offset premium taxes. The lack of uniformity is burdensome to insurers with multistate operations and creates inequities when policyowners in low premium tax states are charged premiums equal to those charged policyowners in high premium tax states, as is usual for individual life and health policies. One is led to raise this question: Should the premium tax be treated as a sales tax rather than loaded into the premium?[21] Insurers also may be subject to premium taxes levied by municipalities.

Summary

1. The financial solvency of insurers is overseen by regulation of (*a*) rates, (*b*) expenses, (*c*) valuation of reserves and assets, investments, surplus limitations, and dividends, (*d*) organization and licensing of insurers, (*e*) annual reports, and (*f*) insurer liquidations.
2. An insurer's statutory policyowners' surplus is the excess of admitted assets over liabilities. Admitted assets include most portfolio investments but no operational assets with the exception of home and branch office buildings and electronic data processing equipment.
3. Insurers' major liabilities are their reserves. Property liability insurers must maintain an unearned premium reserve equal to the unearned portion of the gross premiums on outstanding policies. They must also have a loss reserve, which estimates the insurer's liability for claims and loss adjustment expenses. The main reserve for life insurers is the policy reserve, which measures the amount necessary (along with future premiums and assumed interest) to meet policy obligations when due. Insurers are permitted to have a reserve for first-year policies less than normally required to allow for the many expenses occurring only once when the contract is written.
4. A capacity problem sometimes is encountered in property liability insurance. When insurers write many new contracts, their surplus tends to be depleted, and their ability to write more policies is restricted. Capacity problems are rare for life insurers.
5. Some states regulate dividend payments to prevent the building of large surpluses, to protect the equity among policyowners at different

---

[21] One argument against considering the premium tax, as currently levied, a sales tax is that premium taxes are paid throughout the premium paying period and not levied on the full cost of the insurance at the point of sale. Also insurers are allowed to absorb the premium tax without identifying it to the policyholder, whereas the sales tax must be paid directly by the buyer on the full price rather than on a limited base. See Robert C. Goshay, "Net Income as a Base for Life Insurance Company Taxation in California: Implications," *The Journal of Risk and Insurance* 43, no. 1 (March 1976). However, the law could be changed to make the analogy appropriate.

stages of the insurer's development, and to prevent insurers from consciously operating inefficiently.

6. The laws regulating investment practices of life insurers are usually more strict than those for property liability insurers. As a general rule life insurers invest less in common stocks than do property liability insurers, and mutuals invest less in common stocks than do capital stock property liability insurers.

7. Product regulation is sought by empowering state insurance departments to approve policy forms prior to public offering.

8. Business methods are regulated by licensing of agents and brokers and by prohibiting misrepresentation, twisting, rebating, and unfair discrimination.

9. Some taxes insurers pay are identical to those paid by other business concerns, but some are basically different. Variations exist among states both as to the nature of insurer regulation and the taxes levied on insurers.

Questions for Review

1. What is meant by the concept of a "business affected with a public interest"? How does this concept relate to insurance regulation?

2. Name the primary goals of insurance regulation. Are any of these goals in conflict with each other? If so, how may the conflicts be resolved?

3. What was the effect of the 1944 SEUA decision on *Paul* v. *Virginia?* What was its effect on insurance regulation?

4. How does the regulator attempt to determine if an insurer is approaching insolvency? What tools may the regulator use to prevent an impending insolvency? How may the regulator improve the ability to foresee and forestall insolvencies?

5. How are common stock investments valued for statutory financial reporting purposes?

6. What is the full preliminary term reserve plan? Why was it introduced? How does it work? Should it be allowed for all policies? Explain.

7. How can an insurer be "sold out" of insurance?

8. Why are insurance commissioners concerned about insurer investment practices? Why are they more concerned with investments of life insurers than those of property liability insurers?

9. How do state insurance departments achieve product regulation and the regulation of business methods? Why do some of these measures fail?

10. What is the relationship between the requirements for insurer reserves and the regulation of the valuation of assets?

11. What are the purposes of an insurer's policyowners' surplus? Explain how the policyowners' surplus is computed.

12. What are the two conflicting goals involved in determining asset valuation? Is the current compromise between the goals satisfactory? Explain.

Questions for Discussion

1. If you were a member of Congress, how would you vote on a bill designed to establish federal regulation of the insurance business? Explain your vote, pointing out the criteria and standards used to reach a decision.

2. If you were free to alter specific regulatory measures presently in effect, what changes would you make? Which regulations would you eliminate (if any) and what would you add (if any)? Explain.

3. A basic tenet of the free enterprise system is that the best long-range test of the propriety of a price is the marketplace. Do you believe this tenet is applicable to insurance? Does your answer differ as between life and property liability insurance?

4. If your constituents did not railroad you out of office for your answer to question 1, how would you propose a compromise between rate regulation and the role of competition, keeping in mind the conflicting views of various insurers as well as conflicting views of state insurance commissioners?

5. Regulatory authorities are concerned with making insurance facilities available to all people who should reasonably be expected to have these facilities. How are regulators trying to achieve this goal? Do you have any suggestions that would aid regulators in optimizing insurance availability? Do you agree with the basic premise that insurance facilities should be made available to all who should reasonably be expected to have the facilities? Explain. What concept of "reasonably be expected" are you using in your answer to this question?

6. The terms *excessive* and *inadequate* appear in All-Industry Commissioner laws but are not defined in them. At the risk of insulting Webster, define these adjectives with respect to their meaning implied in the laws and point out your interpretation of what the boundaries should be.

7. To what extent do federal laws now apply to insurers? Would the answer to this question have been the same 50 years ago? Will it be the same five years hence? Explain.

8. In order for consumers to make a rational comparison of available insurance products, they must be able to determine the benefits and costs of each policy. Few consumers, however, can comprehend an insurance contract or calculate the true cost of the policy. Does the regulatory process help to assure the consumer of comprehensible and valid product information? Do you believe that the regulator could or should provide the consumer with price and product information? Explain briefly.

9. Why should operating assets not be considered as "admitted" for statutory reporting purposes? Explain. Do you agree with the logic you just used in answering this question? Discuss.

10. Do you think the N.Y. extraterritorial rule (called the Appleton rule) is constitutional? What good does it accomplish? Is it at all harmful?

11. What is meant by the concept of "surplus surplus"? Can it cause any problems? Is it a concept restricted to property liability insurance or life insurance, or may it apply to both? Explain.

12. Do you believe it is logical to limit a participating life insurer's surplus to a percentage of its policy reserve? If so, why? If not, why not?

Current issues in insurance

This chapter deals with some important issues whose resolution is likely to produce change in the insurance industry now or in the foreseeable future. A complete survey of current insurance issues is unnecessary to fulfill the objectives of this chapter. Therefore only a few have been selected for discussion. They are products liability, insurance marketing, regulation, sex discrimination, and auto safety. The objectives of this chapter are (1) to illustrate that the field of insurance is constantly evolving (or as some cynics would claim, revolving), and (2) to present the background and various sides of these issues so the reader can have a better understanding of any media coverage that develops in the months and years ahead.

Customarily, discussions of current insurance issues are presented either (1) in the form of a conflict of divergent views with consumers, insurance regulators, and insurers pulling against each other to win acceptance for the position favorable to their side, or (2) as issues that primarily affect only one section of the triad. Using either approach, the recommended solution to issues depends on who is making the recommendation, and that in turn is influenced by whose ox is being gored.

In this text, the issues are viewed neither parochially nor as of primary importance to one class only. Instead the concerns of all sides are recognized as fundamental to any lasting acceptable solution. A solution always is more difficult to reach when all sides of the issue are considered. Only when full consideration is given to all views, followed by practical trade-offs, can an intelligent compromise be reached.

Products Liability

Beginning with the first chapter of this text, the reader has encountered numerous examples of cases where consumers have sued a manufacturer seeking compensation for injuries sustained while using the manufacturer's product. The number of these suits as well as the average size of awards has increased dramatically during the past decade (including a 50 percent increase in number during the period 1979 to 1984). In 1982, the average product liability award was more than $530,000, a 51 percent increase over the previous year. During the fiscal year ending in June 1983, more than 9,200 product liability cases were commenced in federal district courts.

Consumers

Injured consumers appear to be getting the best of the manufacturers in these suits. If out-of-court settlements were included, obviously the number of cases mentioned in the preceding paragraph would be higher (probably substantially higher). In the current legal environment, nearly any injury that results while a product is in use merits consideration as a potential product liability claim. For example, a housewife left the cover off a vacuum sweeper she had cleaned. The next day her son was injured when the unguarded machine started while he sat on it. A suit was filed, and the claimant was awarded nearly $100,000 in damages for the 11-year-old's unplanned circumcision.

A worker was injured while using a machine produced over 30 years before the accident. The machine had been bought and sold three times before the injury took place. In addition, it had been modified from the manufacturer's specifications, and safety equipment had been removed. Nonetheless, the worker not only received workers' compensation benefits, but also won a product liability suit against the machine's maker. (See Chapter 13 for a more detailed discussion of cases of this type.)

The survivors of a woman who died in a head-on collision sued the manufacturer of the auto she was driving. This case was settled before going to trial reportedly because the manufacturer was concerned about losing and about the precedent the case would set if it was lost. Sources close to this case indicated that the victim's claim was to be based on the fact that in 1976 the auto company had the technology to install air bags but did not make them available to its customers. Thus, the company agreed to a high six-figure settlement rather than assume the juridical risks and the possibility of a precedent that might engender many similar suits.

These cases help illustrate the powerful position of injured consumers in current products liability actions. Obviously the consumers involved won their claims and received compensation awards (sometimes very large awards). But consumers share—at least indirectly—in these costs. The manufacturer's cost of defending against and paying claims is normally shared with insurance companies. The latter are generally profit-making organizations (or at least intended to be that way) and raise their premiums when expenses exceed receipts. These increases averaged over 200 percent per year from 1971 to 1977. If manufacturing companies are required to pay higher premiums, the increase can cause them to raise the price of their products—prices paid by consumers.

Manufacturers

As a result of the Consumer Products Safety Act of 1972 and a number of precedent-setting court cases, product manufacturers are attempting to meet more rigorous standards for consumer safety than were applied some 15 years ago. New standards required greater attention to (1) product design, (2) the expanded use of warning labels, (3) tamper-proof safety equipment, and (4) quality control. Yet manufacturers who appeared to be operating in accordance with the new standards have lost products liability suits where the danger or defect was not known at the time of production. In some cases it has been found that the producer should have known of the danger, or the danger was knowable if sufficient research had been conducted. Manufacturers have also lost cases where the product was modified before the injury took place (i.e., the removal of warning labels, safety shields, or protective devices) and where the product was misused. If, following the products' manufacture, new research reveals a potential danger or hazard to consumers, even a nationwide effort to recall and rework the products in question may not be sufficient to avoid a successful product liability suit.

A few well-known cases have revealed that business decisions were made during a product's design stage based on the projected cost of safety equipment versus the projected cost of consumers' suits for loss of life and limb. Such an approach to product design may appear, at first glance, to be an unfeeling, uncaring, and even greedy approach to the production of a consumer good. But the solution lies somewhere between the following extremes: production of a fail-safe product (probably an impossible task), which will likely be unaffordable for customers, or production of a highly marketable but inferior (from a safety standpoint) product, which can generate extra profits to be used to combat expected products liability suits. This continuum between extremes has dollar amounts all along its length. Apparently it is preferable for management to describe the point at which it intends to operate without referring to specific dollar amounts.

A few manufacturers (notably some suppliers to the automotive industry) simply chose to go out of business rather than continue production without the benefit of insurance protection or pay what they considered to be unaffordable insurance premiums. Although factors other than insurance costs were likely considered before the businesses were terminated, insurance costs and the adverse products liability environment were seen as primary reasons.

Legal factors

In addition to consumers and manufacturers, courts, juries, and attorneys also have their respective parts to play in the legal environment of products liability. Statutes and precedence of the jurisdiction in which a suit is brought have an enormous impact on the outcome. No pervasive federal products liability law exists, leaving the 50 states free to set the ground rules for products liability actions brought within their own jurisdictions. A manufacturer that sells its product in many states is subjected to different standards of responsibility depending on where a suit is pressed. (No pun intended!) For example, if Rodney Hale lives in Virginia, buys a Widget International Skweezer in Georgia, and is injured in Florida when the defective Skweezer squeezes back, he may decide to bring suit in any of the states mentioned. Further, headquarters of the Widget International Skweezer Company, Inc. (WISCI), are in California, so Hale, upon hearing that California courts are a happy hunting ground for claimants in products liability suits, may decide to initiate action in that state. Certainly Hale and his attorneys will investigate the advantages and disadvantages of bringing suit in the various states. WISCI's attorneys will be engaged in the same research. Hale will likely be looking for a state that allows a claimant to collect punitive damages. WISCI will search for a state that prohibits punitive actions. Patently the first legal battle may be to determine the situs of the case.

Some observers believe that sympathetic courts and juries have gone along with claimants in the search for the "deep pockets." Claimants who follow this approach try to extend liability to some person or entity that appears to have the ability to pay large awards or settlements, with lesser emphasis placed on the extent of the well-heeled defendant's contribution to the loss. For example, Jake takes his broken television set to El Cheapo TV Repair Service to get it fixed. El Cheapo's repairman does not get the job done right and joins two wires that should not be touching. While turning the set on one evening, Jake receives a severe electrical shock that knocks him unconscious and burns his hand and arm. The suit that follows includes a products liability action against World Wide Electronics, Inc. (WWEI), the manufacturer of Jake's TV set. Jake and his attorney realize that a negligence claim against El Cheapo probably will not produce a large award because El Cheapo is a small sole proprietorship of modest means. But WWEI is a large corporation with millions of dollars worth of assets. Thus the decision is made to go after the "deep pockets" in the case and to try to show that WWEI should have designed the set so as to make it impossible to connect the wires in question. In spite of the fact that WWEI neither licensed, authorized, nor had any connection with El Cheapo, the court allows the suit against WWEI to proceed. WWEI now stands to lose at least the cost of defending against the suit and could lose much more if the jury believes that Jake, a watch repairman, may never again be able to use his hand in his chosen profession. The extent of Jake's lost income cannot be replaced by an award from El Cheapo, but WWEI (the deep pockets) does have the resources to cover a large award to Jake.

Attorneys also are criticized for their role in products liability suits. According to the October 14, 1984, broadcast of CBS's popular "60 Minutes," over $1 billion in asbestos-related claims have been paid, and over $700 million in attorneys' fees have been incurred for handling the cases. One of the program's criticisms was based on the repeated use of depositions (sworn statements) and the fees associated with taking them. For example, the deposition of an expert witness was taken concerning the harmful effects of breathing asbestos fibers. The proceedings, according to a participant, were attended by at least 20 attorneys. Only one or two questioned the witness; the rest listened. Afterward, a copy of the deposition was obtained by those in attendance, each of whom presumably charged a client for the time.

Proposed legislation

The much publicized problems of products liability as well as substantial lobbying efforts from various groups prompted the introduction of bills in both houses of Congress in early 1984. The Senate Commerce Committee held hearings and cleared its bill by an 11 to 5 vote. The following are major parts of the Senate bill:

1. The bill would preempt all state products liability laws, thereby providing a single nationwide statute.
2. Courts would be required to decide whether the benefits and uses of a product outweigh its potential for serious harm.
3. The plaintiff would be required to prove that the manufacturer was negligent in addition to proving the product defective.
4. Only the first consumer to bring suit would be allowed to sue for punitive damages.
5. A system of time limitations would be established after which a manufacturer would no longer be liable.
6. The consumer would have to show that an alternative product design was available, better, and economically feasible.
7. The court would judge the conduct of the manufacturer, thereby ending the use of strict liability in products liability cases.

Two strong supporters of the proposed legislation are the Reagan administration and the National Association of Manufacturers. The major opposition comes from a number of consumer groups and the Association of Trial Lawyers of America.

Neither the House nor the Senate version of the bill came to a vote during the 98th Congress. It appears likely, however, that some form of products liability law will be enacted in the near future. Hopefully, a law will be passed that protects a socially responsible manufacturer against unreasonable claims. At the same time it should allow consumers sufficient freedom of action to discourage and severely punish those manufacturers who act irresponsibly and without due regard for the health and safety of consumers. Consumers should be adequately and reasonably compensated when injured by an unsafe product. But many observers of the products liability scene believe that a substantial number of recent awards are so far above adequate as to be unreasonable. Balance and sensible reform are needed.

Insurance Marketing

Over the past two decades, notable changes in the insurance marketplace have occurred. Generally the thrust of these changes has been to offer insurance products in combination with other financial services. The formulation and development of the concept "buy term and invest the difference" prompted life insurers to seek combination sales of mutual funds and life insurance. (See Chapter 16.) Mutual fund companies, induced in part by falling stock prices and fund sales in the late 1960s, began to sell life insurance with their investment programs. In order to make the investment products available to life agents, life insurers either purchased or merged with existing investment companies, or formed their own mutual funds. The mutual fund firms moved in a similar fashion to buy or merge with insurers, or to start their own life companies. The intent of these ventures was to increase profits and market share by selling the two products—investments and death protection—as a combined package.

As the combination approach to marketing gained popularity, other firms became interested, and the idea of "one-stop shopping" for financial services began to take form. Although the mutual fund companies and life insurers were in the forefront of this movement, property-liability insurers, banks, securities firms, and some major credit institutions also began to move into the life insurance and investment areas. Part of the reason for this progression of nonlife companies into the life insurance business appears to have been based on the theory (as expressed by a number of knowledgeable observers of the life insurance industry at the time) that "you can make money in life insurance in spite of bad management."

While this characterization of the life insurance business may have contained some truth for the period before the mid-1970s, it certainly has been shown not to be true since that time. Price competition, particularly in the market for term insurance (the death protection portion of the combination sales package), has become keen and occasionally even cut-throat. As consumers became more educated about their personal financial needs, agents began to lose business to other insurers when their clients found better prices and products.

Early success in the combination of protection and investment sales by some mutual fund companies encouraged other investment firms to make life insurance products available to their sales forces. One of the early successful ventures into the life insurance business by a mutual fund firm took place in 1957 when IDS Life Insurance Company was formed by Investors Diversified Services, Inc. This action made IDS Life products available to clients of this old and reputable investment firm. The approach proved to be so successful that, by the time the new insurer was 25 years old, it had become one of the country's 15 largest life insurers as measured by admitted assets.

While the early emphasis of the one-stop shopping concept centered on the combination of investments and death protection, a few companies began to sell life insurance through property-liability agents. Both Allstate and State Farm had large, well-established sales forces which were highly successful in the sale of personal auto and homeowners coverages. Although State Farm's life insurance affiliate was incorporated in 1929, its major growth did not occur until the 1960s. The marketing efforts of State Farm agents produced spectacular results, and by the late 1960s State Farm Life was the fastest growing company among the 30 largest companies in the country. Allstate Life's performance was equally impressive. Within six years of its formation in 1957, the life insurance in force for Allstate Life topped the $1 billion level. The phenomenal growth of these two companies brought them both into the group of 15 largest life insurers, as measured by total life insurance in force.

The entry of growth-conscious firms

The potential for combination sales of financial services caught the imagination of many growth-conscious firms. While some interested firms had produced and sold financial services in the past, many had no previous connection with the insurance industry. The lack of managerial expertise in insurance, however, did not deter them from plunging headlong into the insurance arena. The number of companies involved in insurance sales grew rapidly during the late 1960s and early 1970s. During this same period experienced insurance executives (financial as well as marketing) were trying to learn to cope with new economic and market conditions. Factors such as inflation, high interest rates, and new tax laws, particularly those laws which allowed some income taxes to be deferred until retirement, all served to encourage new strategies for the production and marketing of financial services. Unfortunately not all of the new entrants enjoyed the kind of advantages possessed by IDS, State Farm, and Allstate. These three firms were able to use an approach which, even if it failed, was unlikely to threaten the continued viability of the parent organization or the loss of customers' investments. Further, each had a large sales force already in place staffed by people who were at least marginally familiar with the new financial service before the marketing effort began.

The importance of these advantages may be seen in an account of a firm that entered the insurance market without such backing. Baldwin-United Corporation (BU) was a holding company made up (originally) of shares of the successful Ohio-based manufacturer of pianos and other musical instruments. BU's move into the financial services area was achieved by the purchase of existing financial service companies including banks, insurance firms (both life and nonlife), and savings and loan organizations. Due to favorable interest rates and tax law changes enacted during the 1970s, BU's life affiliates (primarily National Investors Life Insurance Company, National Investors Pension Insurance Company, and National Equity Life Insurance Company), along with other life insurers, found the single-premium deferred annuity (SPDA) to be a promising retirement savings vehicle. When the BU companies began selling their SPDAs, they had neither a large agency force nor the name recognition and image of a large, financially secure institution.

They did, however (at least with stockbrokers), have the Baldwin-United image of a rapidly growing holding company entering the financial services market. In order to compete effectively for an agency force, BU companies paid high sales commissions relative to other SPDA writers. Also, to take advantage of their growth image, BU offered customers high initial interest rates on their SPDAs. The combination of high commissions and high interest rates attracted salesmen and customers.

The marketing effort proved to be successful as word spread that BU had a product that was lucrative for agents as well as easy to sell based on the promise of interest rates higher than those available with most competing SPDAs. When representatives of firms such as Prudential-Bache and Merrill, Lynch, Pierce, Fenner & Smith, Inc., began to sell the new BU product, sales grew so quickly that they outstripped the ability of BUs life operations to set up adequate reserves and pay sales costs. Such circumstances called for a drastic slowdown in sales or an infusion of funds from an outside source—usually the parent company.

The need for funds was handled (unwisely) by moving stock of other BU subsidiaries into the life companies. (Unfortunately, the more valuable assets of the holding company were needed to consummate BU's $1.17 billion purchase of the MGIC Indemnity Corporation, a large mortgage, surety and liability insurer.) The effects of the stock transactions were questioned by the insurance commissioner of Arkansas, who ordered a securities valuation of the assets of BU's three life insurers domiciled in that state. As a result, the shares of BU affiliates held by the life companies were found to have been overvalued by more than $160 million.

These financial problems eventually forced the Arkansas and Indiana insurance commissioners to take over the management of the six BU life insurers domiciled in the two states. Two months later, the BU holding company filed for bankruptcy. At this writing, the final disposition of the SPDAs written by BU insurers has not been set. However, Merrill Lynch and Prudential-Bache have moved to offset losses of their clients who purchased the BU product.

Certainly not all ventures into the insurance market by noninsurance firms end in bankruptcy. But it is important that top executives who instigate the addition of insurance subsidiaries to their holding companies understand the differences in managing an insurance operation as opposed to a noninsurance operation.

Banks in insurance

The most recent financial services group to show interest in the insurance business has been the banking community. Prior to 1980, the expansion of financial services offered by insurance companies, thrift institutions, and securities firms tended to take the form of depository services previously available only from banks. Savings accounts and, in some cases, limited check-writing privileges were provided by nonbank financial institutions.

When a modicum of deregulation in the banking area took place in the late 1970s and early 1980s, the banks jumped at the opportunity to regain some of their lost business and customers, and to move into the new financial services field. Nationwide banking firms, particularly banks with major credit card operations, have pushed hard to enter the insurance business. In 1983, South Dakota enacted legislation that allowed out-of-state banks to buy state-chartered banks and further allowed state banks to sell insurance. Citicorp, First Interstate Bancorp, Security Pacific Corporation, and Bank America Corporation all tried to take advantage of the new law until the move was vetoed by the Federal Reserve Board. The boards reaction had the effect of maintaining the prohibition on federally chartered banks from engaging in nonbanking operations such as selling insurance.

Despite these restrictions, banks are beginning to get around the rules by renting or leasing lobby space to financial service organizations including insurance operations, real estate companies, and tax shelter firms. These actions are strongly opposed by insurance agents' associations, and lobbying efforts to restrict banks from the market have begun. Although the agents' unstated objective is to retain the insurance market for themselves, they do have a meritorious argument regarding the credit tie-in sale. When a bank with an interest in an in-house insurance operation (i.e., a lease or rental agreement based on a percentage of sales) makes a loan, the borrower may find himself or herself ushered to the insurance desk by the loan officer. While the customer might prefer an agent or insurance company not represented in the bank, the involvement of the loan officer (even if he only mentions the bank's insurance capability) may be sufficient coercion to prevent the customer from leaving without buying insurance. Although this approach has long been used in the sale of credit life, health, and property-liability insurance, ordinary individual life insurance and personal lines of property-liability (i.e., personal auto and homeowners) policies have not been generally available through banks. Moreover, due to abuses in credit insurance sales by banks and other lenders, all 50 states now prohibit premium charges above a stated maximum.

Yet while various insurance organizations complain of the entry of banks and securities companies into the insurance market, insurance firms have been in the securities business for more than 25 years and are currently establishing "nonbank banks." For purposes of the Bank Holding Company Act, a bank is a financial institution that accepts demand deposits and makes commercial loans. In order for an insurance holding company to own a bank and yet avoid regulation as a bank holding company (the subsidiaries of which are prohibited from engaging in nonbanking activities such as selling insurance), the insurance operation needs only to have its newly purchased bank divest itself of its commercial loan portfolio. The result is an unregulated nonbank that can offer customers financial services, excluding commercial loans, like a regulated bank plus whatever tie-in services may be available from sister subsidiaries of the holding company. For example, at least one insurance-dominated holding company is considering providing customers of its nonbank with an additional $900,000 of deposit insurance in excess of the $100,000 available to its depositors from the Federal Deposit Insurance Corporation (FDIC). The coverage will be written with the holding company's reinsurance subsidiary.

The 98th Congress failed to act on legislation that would have more closely defined the boundaries between banks and nonbanks and the powers of states to regulate state banks (thus closing some state-enacted loopholes). However such legislation will likely appear on the agenda for the 99th Congress.

Regulation

In the wake of the failure of Baldwin United, as well as other less famous reversals, insurance regulators have been criticized for their inability to control the financial solvency of insurance companies and thereby protect consumers.

Control of financial solvency involves both sides of the balance sheet; assets are evaluated by regulators to determine the correctness of values assigned by the insurance company, and liabilities are scrutinized to establish the accuracy of reserve calculations. Because the formulas for life and annuity reserve calculations are mandated by state law, control of the financial solvency of life insurance companies depends to a great degree on asset valuation.

Examinations of the financial condition of insurance companies are conducted at regular intervals unless unusual circumstances indicate the need for a special audit. The valuation of assets is a primary function of the examination and may be the only reason for a special audit, as was the case when the Arkansas commissioner conducted a special audit of Baldwin United insurers, described earlier in this chapter. One of the problems in the BU case was that the state's investment law allowed life companies to hold an amount not to exceed 25 percent of their assets in the form of securities of affiliated companies. Investment laws that govern insurance company assets differ widely among the states, and at least 10 states impose no restriction on investment in affiliated firms. Thus, the BU insurer transactions (if not the valuations) were legal in Arkansas. Yet even a correct valuation would not have protected the insurers' balance sheets because, within three months of the transactions, the parent organization was unable to make scheduled payments on its borrowings and the value of its subsidiaries fell sharply.

Imprudent behavior on the part of insurance company management, including actions carried out at the direction of holding company management, must be recognized and acted on by state insurance regulators. Regulators need the legal backing to support their actions (e.g., statutes and regulations that limit investment in affiliates), up-to-date financial information, and the computers and manpower to analyze and control financial solvency. Few regulators, however, have all of these required capabilities.

The need for legal support is evident from the Baldwin United situation. Transactions within a holding company can be complex (occasionally by design), making them difficult for a regulator to follow and analyze. If insurers are prohibited or severely limited with regard to investment within the holding company, the adverse effect of such transactions can be eliminated or at least minimized.

Insurers are required to submit financial statements to all jurisdictions in which they operate. But the ability to evaluate information is hampered by the lack of manpower and money available to most state insurance regulators. In 1983, although states collected more than $3.8 billion in premium taxes, it was estimated that they spent less than 6 percent of that amount to finance regulatory activities. This shortage of funds has kept many insurance departments from installing computer facilities, the one action that could help make up for lack of manpower.

In an effort to lessen the burden on state regulators, the National Association of Insurance Commissioners (NAIC) has developed the Insurance Regulatory Information Service (IRIS). This service is a computerized analysis of the annual statements of more than 4,700 insurance companies which account for 96 percent of the property-liability companies and 90 percent of the life insurers operating in the United States. The system compiles annual data and computes financial ratios. The service lists companies with ratios outside an established range (based on studies of companies that have had financial problems or became insolvent) so regulators can more closely scrutinize their activities. IRIS is available to all 50 states. In addition, a state computer network has been developed enabling an insurance regulator to order information on a single company and receive a response within 24 hours. During a study in 1977, the IRIS identified, at least one year in advance, 95 percent of property and casualty companies that became insolvent.

Sex Discrimination

Discrimination based on sex has become a topic of much discussion and some fear among insurance executives and regulators. The first signs of trouble appeared in 1978 when the United States Supreme Court decided for a female employee in the case of *Los Angeles Department of Water and Power* v. *Manhart*.[1] The department was found to be in violation of Title VII of the Civil Rights Act of 1964 because it required higher pension contributions from women than from men for the same monthly retirement benefits.

A second employment-related sex discrimination case (*Arizona Governing Committee for Tax-Deferred Annuity and Deferred-Compensation Plans* v. *Nathalie Norris*[2]) again resulted in a finding of discrimination against a female employee. Norris' voluntary payments into the plan purchased a lower monthly benefit than equal payments made by a male employee of the same age. In each of these landmark cases, the court stated that the rulings were to apply only to future contributions, and thus retroactive plan adjustments were not required.

As *Manhart* and *Norris* addressed sex discrimination in employee plans, life insurers quickly adjusted the pension plans they insured to meet the new requirements. Unisex annuity rates were added to plans to take effect for contributions made after July 1983, the date of the *Norris* decision. In addition, some insurers established unisex tables for annuities and, to a lesser extent, for life insurance sold to nonemployer groups and individuals.

The traditional practice of insurers and pension plan administrators had been to require higher contributions from women for retirement benefits equal to those of men or to maintain equal contributions but provide lower benefits to women. The practice was based on the fact that women, as a *class,* live longer than men. But Title VII prohibits discrimination in employment based on an individual's race, color, religion, sex, or national origin. Thus, equal treatment, in the Court's view, requires equal treatment of individuals, not classes.

Problems of past sins

Perhaps the greatest fear of the life insurance industry and other pension providers is of a court decision or congressional action requiring retroactive payments. The cost of complete retroactive adjustment for employee-related pensions has been variously estimated to range from $1.2 to $2.5 billion per year. Of course these additional amounts have not been funded, and pension experts believe the financial burden of adjustments would cause the insolvency of some life insurers and pension plans.

In late 1984, the Supreme Court refused to hear *Spirt* v. *TIAA–CREF*

---

[1] 435 U.S. 705 (1978).
[2] 103 S.Ct. 3492 (1983).

and Long Island University after previously remanding the case to the lower court for reconsideration in view of the *Norris* decision. The U.S. Court of Appeals for the Second Circuit stood firm with its original decision that called for retroactive adjustments. However, the retroactive portion of the decision is limited to retirees who began receiving benefits after May 1, 1980. Upon refusal by the high court to rehear the case, TIAA–CREF announced that it would adjust annuity payments to 35,000 annuity owners who began receiving payments after May 1, 1980. Further, future payments to 760,000 annuity holders still in the accumulation stage will be adjusted to a unisex basis for premiums paid before August 1983. TIAA–CREF had already begun the use of unisex tables for contributions after August 1, 1983, based on the discrimination finding in the *Norris* case. Although no dollar figure was indicated for the cost of benefit adjustments, changes for annuity owners who made contributions before the 1983 cutoff date will range from 1 to 8 percent.

In 1984, committees in both houses of Congress considered bills designed to prohibit the use of gender as a basis for insurance benefits and rates. Heavy lobbying efforts to influence the content of the legislation were used by business and the insurance industry on one side and women's groups on the other. These proposals and one from the Reagan administration placed major emphasis on equal treatment for women employees in pension plans and how this pension equity would be reached. Further, the question of the interests of wives and widows in their husbands' plans was discussed and will likely receive more attention. Under current law, a married male retiree can choose a pension with no survivor benefits for his spouse and receive a greater income during his lifetime at the expense of an income to his spouse if he dies first.

No legislation of this type was enacted by the 98th Congress, but continued pressure from women's groups will keep sex discrimination on the agenda. Another feature of future legislation will deal with the problem of whether to make retroactive adjustments in pension plans or to allow prospective adjustments only. State insurance regulators will find more insurers with financial solvency problems if retroactive adjustments are mandated in a new law.

Sex discrimination in auto insurance rating has already prompted three states to adopt new rating schemes to eliminate gender. Based on the equal rights amendment to the Pennsylvania state constitution, the state Supreme Court rendered its decision abolishing gender as a characteristic of a rating class. Ironically, the case began with a complaint to the state insurance commissioner from a young male driver. The commissioner agreed with the complaint and ordered gender to be eliminated from auto insurance rating. The Hartford Accident and Indemnity Insurance Company appealed the order, claiming the commissioner lacked the authority to abolish gender-based rates. The court sided with the commissioner, thus forcing compliance with the order by all auto insurers operating in Pennsylvania.

Michigan auto insurers are also using unisex rates and have found substantial differences in premiums from the previous gender-based classifications. After the first year on the new system, single males under 25 found their premiums averaged 15.1 percent less than the previous year. Premiums for single females in this age group increased an average 20.9 percent. The unisex average for single drivers under 25 was $508.84, compared to previous rates of $599.34 for men and $420.33 for women.

Auto Safety

For nearly three decades the controversy over safety equipment for automobiles has ebbed and flowed between those who would make it mandatory for all vehicles and those who decry its cost and inconvenience. Some of the early safety efforts by U.S. manufacturers (not including the installation of brakes and, 20 years later, rearview mirrors) appeared in the early 1950s in the form of collapsible steering wheels and padded dashboards. Seatbelts, despite their well-known application in auto racing, were available only in the aftermarket for auto accessories and had to be installed privately.

Attempts to persuade manufacturers to build safer automobiles were largely unsuccessful. Carmakers contended (correctly) that safety equipment would add to the cost of cars and, in the case of seatbelts, would not be used by many drivers. But a heightened public awareness of safety began to have its effects on politicians in Washington, if not on auto producers in Detroit. In 1966, the Department of Transportation (DOT) ordered seatbelts installed in all new cars beginning in 1968. A great hue and cry went out from Detroit over the cost of the new devices, but the order stood. And American drivers and passengers sat for the most part on their seatbelts.

The need for passive or automatic restraint systems soon became evident. One such system, inflatable air bags, appeared to have substantial potential for protecting occupants in front-end collisions. First patented in the early 1950s, the apparatus consists of a nylon bag attached to a pressurized container of sodium azide set to release its contents at the instant of impact. Inflation of the nylon bags in front of each occupant is fast enough to keep them from being thrown against interior parts of the vehicle, such as the dashboard, windshield, or steering wheel. Deflation occurs nearly as quickly, allowing passengers to escape. The elapsed time for the entire process is about 0.04 seconds. Tests of the new devices were conducted in the early 1970s by study groups of the auto industry, the federal government, and the insurance industry. The results of the studies were similar and showed that approximately 9,000 auto accident deaths would be avoided annually with the use of air bags; severe injuries would also be reduced. The insurance industry tests also found that the safest approach was to use both seatbelts and air bags. In addition, while seatbelts alone were shown to be effective to some degree in all accidents, they were most effective in crashes involving speeds not in excess of 35 miles per hour. The effectiveness of air bags, on the other hand, was found to be substantially better than that of seatbelts in accidents where speeds exceeded 35 miles per hour.

In the period from 1969 to 1971, the DOT ordered that air bags be installed in all new cars by 1974 and then pushed the deadline back twice, each time calling for a year delay. From 1974 to 1984, new deadlines were established and then delayed for various reasons including fear of a consumer backlash and testing deficiencies. Finally in July of 1984, Transportation Secretary Elizabeth Hanford Dole promulgated a new order for mandatory passive restraint systems.

The new rule requires air bags or automatic safety harnesses to be installed in at least 10 percent of all 1987 models, thereafter increasing annually to 25 percent, 40 percent, and 100 percent by the 1990 model year. The order also established two alternatives that would allow the auto manufacturers to avoid installation of any passive restraints. First, the restraint ruling will be dropped if states with two thirds of the nation's population pass mandatory seatbelt legislation—a requirement that can be met if the 16 largest states enact laws acceptable to the department. Second, if automakers design crash-resistant interiors that protect unrestrained occupants in crashes up to 30 miles per hour, the requirement for installation of air bags will be vacated.

The result of this ruling has prompted the auto industry to begin lobbying in state legislatures calling the effort their "number one priority." Consumer safety advocates and the insurance industry believe strongly in the use of both seatbelts and air bags. Because Secretary Dole's order pits seatbelts against air bags (and the safety advocates do not want to be accused of fighting mandatory seatbelt laws), their lobbying efforts may be directed toward passage of laws which will not fully meet necessary safety requirements. Three primary approaches are currently being discussed by legislators who favor air bags. First, a fine of less than the $25 prescribed by the DOT could be set for drivers caught not wearing their belts. This tactic was used in the New Jersey law, which only levies a fine of $20. Illinois considered a second approach which would allow unrestrained drivers and passengers, injured in an accident, to recover damages. Recovery by unbelted persons is restricted under DOT requirements. Finally some safety-minded legislators are considering the passage of a law acceptable to DOT but with an added "sunset provision" which would cause the law to expire in 1989.

Both Ford and General Motors have indicated they intend to meet the DOT order by installing automatic seatbelts instead of air bags. Automakers predict that even then only about 20 percent of auto occupants will use them (compared to about 15 percent where manual buckling is required) since the harnesses will be detachable. The auto makers' fear is that if the new system is not detachable, buyers will go elsewhere and buy cars that have detachable belts. Of course, if nondetachable belts were required for all new cars, the consumer would not have that option.

Whatever the next few years bring in the way of new auto safety standards, it appears likely that safer cars and fewer deaths and injuries will be the result. By early 1985, three states had enacted mandatory seatbelt laws, and 42 others are expected to address the issue before 1986. These changes, along with increased efforts to remove drunk drivers from the road, represent significant progress toward the goal of eliminating the cost and suffering of auto accidents.

Summary

1. The insurance industry is faced with a number of issues whose resolutions are likely to bring about change in the next decade.
2. This chapter reviews several of these issues to point out the evolving nature of insurance and the need to look at all sides of an issue in reaching intelligent and lasting solutions.
3. The products liability problem has reached the point where manufacturers are being forced to pay enormous sums for injuries to consumers. Courts apply different and sometimes new standards in the various states making it difficult for producers (and consumers) to know what to expect. As insurance premiums for products liability insurance rise, consumers will pay higher prices for products. The legal profession, on the other hand, appears to be in good shape by pressing consumer claims or defending manufacturers. Federal legislation, nearly certain to be enacted within the next few years, is unlikely to please all parties involved but could help bring balance and reason to a situation in which little of either currently exists.
4. New players in insurance marketing are producing increased competition and anxieties. Banks, securities companies, property-liability insurers, and others have entered the life insurance business, while life companies try to return the favor by entering the banking area, selling mutual funds and property-liability insurance. The concept of "one-stop shopping" for financial services has produced some spectacular successes as well as some equally spectacular failures. Boundaries between the various institutions currently operating in the insurance market have been blurred by the extent of crossover activity. New legislation may redefine the boundaries but certainly will not stop the change in this highly dynamic arena.
5. Although the new look of the insurance marketplace appears to require a more timely and sophisticated approach to regulation, few regulators are in a position to handle the job adequately. As competition increases the need for closer scrutiny of insurers has placed a 20th-century burden on regulators, who are still using 19th-century tools. The bright spot for regulators may prove to be the computer network set up by the National Association of Insurance Commissioners.
6. The *Manhart* and *Norris* decisions represent landmark cases to insurance and pension managers for their impact on the long-honored practice of treating males and females differently for insurance. No longer will women receive smaller employee pension benefits than

men simply because women, as a class, live longer than men. Some states have passed laws to require the use of unisex rates for auto insurance, thus providing lower premiums for men and higher premiums for women than were charged under the gender-based rating system.

7. The dispute over how to save lives and reduce injuries from auto accidents was brought to the front pages when the Department of Transportation issued its new ruling in July 1984. Automakers were ordered to install passive restraint systems in new cars beginning in 1986. Alternatives to the order will pit air bag advocates against seatbelt advocates in state legislatures throughout the country. Safety advocates, the insurance industry, and auto manufacturers have all pledged to lobby vigorously. The resulting changes are likely to produce safer cars and lower fatality and injury rates.

Questions for Review

1. How should issues in insurance be approached in order to reach a lasting and intelligent solution? Explain.

2. Discuss the role of each of the major groups involved in the products liability problem.

3. What are the strengths and weaknesses of the proposed products liability legislation?

4. Discuss the strategies used to enter the life insurance marketing area. What problems are noninsurance firms likely to face?

5. What is meant by the term "one-stop shopping" in the financial services industry?

6. What problems do insurance regulators encounter when noninsurance holding companies enter the insurance business?

7. Discuss the major advantage attributed to banks in the sale of insurance.

8. Discuss some of the major problems regulators face in their efforts to control financial solvency.

9. What effect did the *Manhart* and *Norris* cases have on pension planning and funding?

10. Do wives have an interest in their husbands' pension plans? Explain.

11. Why do proposals for mandatory seatbelt laws disturb the insurance industry and safety advocates?

12. What strategies are available to legislators who favor air bag installation as opposed to the alternatives specified in the Department of Transportation's July 1984 order?

Questions for Discussion

1. Who will be the winners and losers if the proposed products liability legislation described in this text is enacted?

2. What criteria and standards would you set for the evaluation of products liability bills to be considered by Congress?

3. Discuss the role and required expertise of a financial planner selling insurance and other finance services. Is there any single type of financial institution better equipped than others to offer "one-stop shopping" of financial services? Explain.

4. The entry of noninsurance firms into the insurance business presents problems for the insurance industry and its management. Identify these problems. Explain and discuss.

5. How should insurance regulators control the financial solvency of new entrants into the insurance business?

6. The insurance industry and safety advocates say they were "mouse trapped" by the DOT order issued in July of 1984. Explain.

7. What strategies would you suggest to legislatures that want to support seatbelt bills but also want air bags to be installed in all new cars?

Index

*This book has been set Videocomp, in 9 and 8 point
Primer, leaded 2 points. Chapter numbers are 36 point
Spectra Extra Bold and chapter titles are 16 point Spectra Bold. The size of the type page is 27 picas by 45½
picas.*